A Ko

PRINCETON THEOLOGICAL MONOGRAPH SERIES

en signe

Dikran Y. Hadidian

General Editor

d'amitié

— François

Nov. 98

12

LUKE THE THEOLOGIAN

Thirty-Three Years of Research (1950-1983)

LUKE THE THEOLOGIAN

Thirty-Three Years of Research (1950-1983)

By

François Bovon

Translated by

Ken McKinney

PICKWICK PUBLICATIONS
Allison Park, Pennsylvania

Originally published as
Luc le théologien. Vingt-cinq ans de recherches (1950-1975)

Printed in the United States of America

Library of Congress Cataloging-in-Publication Data

Festugière, A.-J. (André Jean), 1898-1982
Freedom and civilization among the Greeks.

(Princeton theological monograph series ; 12)
Translation of: Luc le théologien
1. Bible. N.T. Luke--Criticism, interpretation, etc.--History--20 century. 2. Bible. N.T. Acts--Criticism, interpretation, etc.--History--20 century. 3. Bible. N.T. Luke--Theology. 4. Bible. N.T. Acts--Theology. I. Title. II. Series.
BS2589.B6813 1987 226'.406' 0904 87-7969
ISBN 0-915138-93-X

CONTENTS

ABOUT THE AUTHOR AND CONCERNING THE ORGANIZATION OF THE BOOK

Born in Lausanne in 1938, François Bovon studied theology in several European universities. After a brief pastoral ministry, he was named professor of theology at the Université de Genève. He teaches New Testament and the origins of New Testatment at the faculty of theology, where he also served as dean. He was the president of the Société suisse de théologie from 1973-1977. His name figures among the collaborators of the **Traduction oecuménique de la Bible** (TOB). Among his publications are: **De vocationes gentium. Histoire de l'Interpretation d'Actes 10. 1-11, 18 dans les six premiers siècles** (Tübingen, Mohr, 1967); **Les derniers jours de Jésus. Textes et événement** (Neuchâtel, Dela - chaux et Niestlé, 1974). He also collaborated in **Exegesis. Problems of Method and Exercises in Reading (Genesis 22 and Luke 15). Studies Published under the direction of François Bovon and Grégoire Rouiller** (Pittsburgh, The Pickwick Press, 1978) (FT. **Exegesis, Problème de methode et exercise de lecture**. (Neuchâtel, Delachaux et Niestlé, 1975).

The book which you are holding in your hands presents the theological research consecrated to the Gospel of Luke and the Acts of the Apostles which has appeared from 1950-1983.

The bibliographies of the different chapters mention hundreds of articles and books. The most important are summarized and appreciated in the text and notes. The first chapter deals with the most burning question of the 1950's, the relations between history and eschatology, whereas the last examines the Lucan doctrine of the Church, a subject which holds our attention today.

At the center of the book we find Christology according to a logic which the Evangelist has taught us to respect, i.e. between pages concerning the Old Testament and those treating the Holy Spirit and salvation. From objective salvation, we pass to its subjective side, i.e. to conversion and faith.

Thus the organization of this book is explained, a book which is not content simply to present the actual research but also offers a coherent and sometimes original interpretation of the theological project of Luke.

FOREWORD

This book presents the principle theological research consecrated to the Gospel of Luke and the Acts of the Apostles, which has appeared in the last quarter of the century (1950-1975). Our starting point is 1950 for this date represents a turning point in Lucan studies [**1**].

When we began the task, we envisaged a state of the question for the Acts of the Apostles. Afterward, we opted for the theological problems alone, abandoning the literary, historical and textual problems. It was then necessary to integrate the studies of the Gospel, which we did as we were able. This change in direction may explain the lacunas concerning the first book to Theophilus.

To accord one's preference to theological problems does not signify a renouncement of exegesis nor the scorning of history. The theological positions which we mention are most often the result of an interpretation of the Biblical text. They take into consideration the place Luke occupies in the development of primitive Christianity. However, by an understandable reaction, the study of theology allows us to specify the historical insertion of the Evangelist, who, we must admit, remains imprecise at the junction of influences from Mark, the source of the logia (Q), the Jerusalem Church (Peter and James) and Paul: in a Greek environment, attached to Biblical traditions and around 80-90 A.D.

As our work gradually progressed, an outline imposed itself upon us: beginning with the most burning problem in 1950, the relations between history and eschatology, and ending with the Church, a theme, which today, holds our attention. At the center Christology is placed, according to a necessity which the Evangelist himself was held to respect. The logic of the Lucan faith incited us to insert the chapter concerning Christology between the pages dedicated to the OT and those dealing with salvation. From objective salvation, it was fitting to pass on to subjective salvation, i.e. the reception of redemption by conversion and faith. This explains the organization of our book, which begins with God and his plan to come to men and women living in the Church.

Concerned by the desire to be complete, we have sometimes had difficulty to disengage the main tendencies to Lucan studies and to perceive the theological implications. Finally, we decided to present in the text, the most representative and most original studies and to place in the notes the other books and articles.

If time had permitted, we would have dealt with other topics: the Lucan discourse on nature (God creator), the place of culture in Luke's theology (these two would be centered on Act 14 and 17) [2], and finally the pre-Lucan traditions concerning the apos - tles [3]. With regard to this last subject, we would have affirmed, against a strong theological current, that the first Christians were interested in the life of the apostles and communities, bringing forth facts and gests in a liturgical and parenetic perspective. Thus a rooting would have appeared, a Sitz im Leben of the divers accounts brought by Luke, thus taking away from the book of the Acts its radically new character and its author a theological originality which many are pleased to reproach him for.

At the head of each chapter, there is a bibliography in chronological order (within each year the order is alphabetical). The arrow followed by a date refers normally to this biblio - graphy. In other cases, we have placed a chapter number before the arrow. The asterisk indicates that we did not read the book or article in question.

Let us mention that the different conclusions were written at one time, at the end, when the body of the seven chapters was composed.

In consulting the table of contents, the reader encounters the grand themes of Lucan theology and the main stages of recent interpretation. Thanks to the indexes, he can discover several interpretations of the same Lucan text, divers analyses of such and such Greek term or the general position of an exegete.

Several works arrived too late for us to study as they merit. Here is a list: E. Franklin, **Christ the Lord. A Study in the Purpose and Theology of Luke-Acts** (London, 1975); R. Glöckner, **Die Verkündigung des Heils beim Evan - gelisten Lukas** (Mainz, n.d. (1975?)); G. Hayas-Prats, **L'Esprit, force de l'Eglise. Sa nature et son activité d'après les Actes des apôtres** (Paris, 1975); G. Lohfink, **Die Sammlung Israels. Eine Untersuchung zur lukan - ischen Ekklesiologie** (Munich, 1975); P. S. Minear, **To Heal or to Reveal. The Prophetic Vocation According to Luke** (New York, 1976); L. Monloubou, **La prière selon saint Luc. Recherche d'une structure** (Paris, 1976); as well as the last unpublished dissertations summarized in **DissAbstr**.

The work we are presenting today would not have been possible without the following instruments of work: **Elenchus Bibliographicus Biblicus** of **Biblica** (Rome), **Internationale Zeitschriftenshau für Bibelwissenschaft und Grenzgebiete** (Düsseldorf), **New Testament Abstracts** (Cambridge, Mass.), **Dissertation Abstracts International**, A (Ann Arbor, Mich.); and A. J. and Mary Mattill's **A Classified Bibliography of Literature on the Acts of the Apostles** (Leiden, 1966).

Furthermore we have mentioned other states of the question of Lucan studies [**4**], the most important being those of W. Gasque, E. Rasco and E. Grässer [**5**]. We have added several in the notes [**6**].

We are following the abbreviation system of **Elenchus Bibliographicus Biblicus** 55 (1974) pp. V-XXX, edited by Father P. Nober. For the signs which do not appear in this volume of **Elenchus**, we are conforming to the indications found in volume 49 (1969) pp. III-XII and as a last resort, the list of abbreviations in A. J. and Mary Mattill's **A Classified Bibliography of Literature on the Acts of the Apostles** (Leiden, 1966) pp. XIII. XVIII.

It is agreeable for us to note that the most important part of the bibliographyical pursuit, tracking down and reading was taken over successively by Marcel Fallet, Jean-Marc Prieur, Daniel Roquefort and Joël Dhauteville during their passage at the Faculté de théologie of Geneva. Without them, we have would no doubt been unable to swim through the waves of the innumerous publications. We thank them with all our heart. The Société Acadamique de Genève merits our thanks as well, as they granted us an important subsidy to remunerate one collaborator. Our thanks also goes out to the Comité genevois pour le protestantisme français, who through several subsidies, permitted the work of other collaborators. We address our hearty feelings of thankfulness to the Conseil national du Fonds national suisse de la Recherche scientifique which accorded us a large subsidy for the publication. Finally, we would like to express our gratitude to Mrs. Janine Chérix who typed with great care our manuscript, Mrs. Marie Molina who read without letting up the proofs of this book, Mr. Frédy Schoch who established the indexes with precision [in the French, the translator] and Miss Michèle Rosset and the Editions Delachaux & Niestlé, who facilitated the publication, to the printers and typographers of the Imprimerie des Remparts in Yverdon, to the librarians at the

Bibliothèque Publique et Universitatire de Genève and the library of the Pontifical Biblical Institute in Rome [7].

Christmas, 1976. François Bovon

FOREWORD TO THE ENGLISH EDITION

The French language has lost the privileged position, it held in the eighteenth century. It has ceased to be a universal-international language between the divers civilizations. As we all know, it has been supplanted in this function by English.

This declaration explains the joy of an author of French expression, from the French part of Switzerland, before the English translation of one of his works. This joy is accompanied with gratitude: to Dr. Dikran Y. Hadidian who after having en - couraged this translation welcomes it now into the collection which he is responsible for, to Mr. Ken McKinney who had the idea and realized it with energy, devotion, perseverence and competence; to the Société auxiliaire de la Faculté de Théologie de l'Université de Genève as well as the Fondation Ernst and Lucie Schmidheiny both of which provided important subsidies thanks to which this translation was made possible. I express my warmest gratitude to each one.

The original work appeared in 1978 and quickly sold out. The English edition has the advantage of making accessible this state of research which covers the years 1950 to 1975 again. It also has the supplementary advantage of offering the translation of an article which was written later. It brings up to date - in a form a bit different from the book - the studies published concerning Luke between the years 1975 and 1983.

Geneva, November, 1986. François Bovon

Translator's Note

There should be no difficulty understanding our abbreviations. As for the Biblical references, I have followed no one system, but they should be understandable. The italics in the French version have been underlined, and the book titles and journal abbreviations are in bold. References to German titles have usually been kept and not translated (eg. **TWNT** is the German abbreviation for the **Theological Dictionary of the New Testament** or popularly called "Kittel". The same is the case for Conzelmann's **Die Mitte der Zeit**, ET **The Theology of Luke**). I have kept the same abbreviations to journals as in the French, which uses **Elenchus Bibliographicus Biblicus** 55 (1974) pp. V-XXX (cf. Foreword). The index is based on a simple system of division (eg. 2, I, a = chapter 2, main section I and subsection a). I have included the authors mentioned in the notes of the Appendix in the index.

Ken McKinney

CHAPTER 1

THE PLAN OF GOD, SALVATION HISTORY AND ESCHATOLOGY

Chronological Bibilography

[An asterisk signals a book or article which we did not read.]

1948

E. FUCHS , "Christus das Ende der Geschichte", **EvT** 8 (1948-1949) 447-461; taken up in E. Fuchs, **Zur Frage nach dem historischen Jesus. Gesammelte Aufsätze**, II (Tübingen, 1965^{2}), pp. 79-99.

B. NOACK*, **Das Gottesreich bei Lukas. Eine Studie zu Lk 17, 20-24** (Upsalla, 1948).

1949

R. MORGENTHALER, **Die lukanische Geschichtsschreibung als Zeugnis. Gestalt und Gehalt der Kunst des Lukas**, I-II (Zurich, 1949).

1950

P. H. MENOUD, "La mort d'Ananias et de Saphira (Ac 5, 1-11)", in **Aux Sources de la tradition chrétienne. Mélanges M. Goguel** (= **Sources, Goguel**) (Neuchâtel - Paris, 1950), pp. 146-154.

G. HARBSMEIER, "Unsere Predigt im Spiegel der Apostelgeschichte", **EvT** 10 (1950-1951) 352-368.

P. VIELHAUER, "Zum Paulinismus der Apostelgeschichte", **EvT** 10 (1950-1951) 1-15; included in P. Vielhauer, **Aufsätze zum Neuen Testament** (Munich, 1965), pp. 9-27.

1952

H. CONZELMANN, "Zur Lukas-Analyse", **ZTK** 49 (1952) 16-33; included in G. Braumann (ed), **Das Lukas-Evangelium. Die redaktions- und kompositionsgeschichtliche Forschung** (= **Lukas Forschung**, Braumann) (Darmstadt, 1974), pp. 43-63.

1953

O. BAUERNFEIND, "Vom historischen zum lukanischen Paulus. Eine Auseinandersetzung mit Götz Harbsmeier", **EvT** 13 (1953) 347-353.

J. SCHMITT, "L'Eglise de Jérusalem ou la 'restauration' d'Israël d'après les cinq premiers chapitres des Actes", **RevScRel** 27 (1953) 209-218.

1954

O. BAUERNFEIND, "Zur Frage nach der Entscheidung zwischen Paulus und Lukas", **ZSTh** 23 (1954) 59-88.

H. CONZELMANN, **Die Mitte der Zeit. Studien zur Theologie des Lukas** (Tübingen, 1954, 1962^{4}). We are referring to the 3rd ed. of 1960.

E. KÄSEMANN, "Das Problem des historischen Jesus", **ZTK** 51 (1954) 125-153; included in E. Käsemann, **Exegetische Versuche und Besinnungen** (= **Exeg. Versuche**, Käsemann), I (Göttingen, 1970^{6}), pp. 187-214 (esp. pp. 189-199); (French translation [= FT], **Essais exégétiques** (Neuchâtel, 1972), pp. 145-173, esp. pp. 157-158).

J. KÖRNER, "Endgeschichtliche Parusieerwartung und Heilsgegenwart im Neuen Testament in ihrer Bedeutung für eine christliche Eschatologie", **EvT** 14 (1954) 177-192.

E. LOHSE, "Lukas als Theologe der Heilsgeschichte", **EvT** 14 (1954) 256-275; taken up in E. Lohse, **Die Einheit des Neuen Testaments. Exegetische Studien zur Theologie des Neuen Testaments** (= **Einheit**, Lohse) (Göttingen, 1973), pp. 145-164; and in **Lukas Forschung**, Braumann, pp. 64-90.

J. MUNCK, **Paulus und die Heilsgeschichte** (Aarhus, 1954).

H. P. OWEN, "Stephen's Vision in Acts 7, 55-56", **NTS** I (1954-1955) 224-226.

1955

E. DINKLER, "The Idea of History in Earliest Christianity", in **The Idea of History in the Ancient Near East** (New Haven, 1955), pp. 169-214; also included in E. Dinkler, **Signum Crucis. Aufsätze sum Neuen Testament und zur christlichen Archäologie** (Tübingen, 1967), pp. 313-350.

1956

P. BORGEN*, **Eschatology and 'Heilsgeschichte' in Luke-Acts**, unpublished dissertation, Drew University (Madison, N. J., 1956).

H. J. CADBURY, "Acts and Eschatology", in W. D. Davies and D. Daube (eds),**The Background of the New Testament and its Eschatology. Mélanges C. H. Dodd** (Cambridge, 1956, 1964²), pp. 300-321.

E. HAENCHEN, **Die Apostelgeschichte neu übersetzt und erklärt** (Göttingen, 1956, 1968⁶) (the 3rd ed. of 1959 modifies certain positions of the 1st: with regard to the sources; the 6th contains a bibliographical supplement and presents several recent studies), 1977⁷).

E. SCHWEIZER, "Gegenwart des Geistes und eschatologische Hoffnung bei Zarathustra, spätjüdischen Gruppen, Gnostikern, und den Zeugen des Neuen Testaments", in in W. D. Davies and D. Daube (eds),**The Background of the New Testament and its Eschatology. Mélanges C. H. Dodd** (Cambridge, 1956, 1964²), pp. 482-508.

1957

R. BULTMANN, **History and Eschatology** (Edinburgh, 1957) (FT Neuchâtel-Paris, 1959).

J. DANIÉLOU, "Eschatologie sadocite et eschatologie chrétienne", in **Les manuscrits de la mer Morte, Colloque de Strasbourg, 25-27 mai 1955** (Paris, 1957), pp. 111-125.

F. P. FORWOOD*, **The Eschatology of the Church of Jerusalem as Seen in the Book of Acts**, unpublished dissertation, Southern Baptist Theological Seminary (Louisville, Ky., 1957).

E. GRÄSSER, **Das Problem der Parusieverzögerung in den synoptischen Evangelien und in der Apostelgeschichte** (Berlin, 1957, 1960²).

E. KÄSEMANN, "Neutestamentliche Fragen von heute", **ZKT** 54 (1957) 1-21; taken up in **Exeg. Versuche**, Käsemann II (Göttingen, 1970³) pp. 11-31, esp. pp. 28-30 (FT **Essais exégètiques** (Neuchâtel, 1972), pp. 123-144, esp. pp. 140-143).

J. KÖRNER, **Eschatologie und Geschichte. Untersuchung des Begriffes des Eschatologischen in der Theologie R. Bultmanns** (Hamburg-Bergstedt, 1957).

M. SMITH, "Pauline Problems, Apropos of J. Munck, 'Paulus und die Heilsgeschichte'", **HarvTR** 10 (1957) 107-131.

É. TROCMÉ, **Le 'Livre des Actes' et l'histoire** (Paris, 1957).

1958

A. EHRHARDT, "The Construction and Purpose of the Acts of the Apostles", **ST** 12 (1958-1959) 45-79.

W. G. KÜMMEL, "Futurische und präsentische Eschatologie im ältesten Urchrist - entum", **NTS** 5 (1958-1959) 113-126.

R. H. SMITH, "The Eschatology of Acts and Contemporary Exegesis", **ConTM** 29 (1958) 641-663.

R. H. SMITH, "History and Eschatology in Luke-Acts", **ConTM** 29 (1958) 881-901.

1959

H. W. BARTSCH, "Zum Problem der Parusieverzögerung bei den Synoptikern", **EvT** 19 (1959) 116-131.

H. CHADWICK, **The Circle and the Ellipse. Rival Concepts of Autho - rity in the Early Church. An Inaugural Lecture Delivered before the University of Oxford** (Oxford, 1959).

A. C. WINN, "Elusive Mystery. The Purpose of Acts", **Interpr** 13 (1959) 144-156.

1960

H. CONZELMANN, "Geschichte, Geschichtsbild und Geschichtsdarstellung bei Lukas", **TLZ** 85 (1960) 241-250 (cf. review of E. Haenchen's commentary -> 1956).

E. LERLE, "Die Predigt in Lystra, Act 14, 15-18", **NTS** 7 (1960-1961) 46-55.

U. LUCK, "Kerygma, Tradition und Geschichte bei Lukas", **ZTK** 57 (1960) 51-66; included in **Lukas Forschung**, Braumann, pp. 95-114.

W. C. ROBINSON, "The Theological Context for Interpreting Luke's Travel Narra - tive (9, 51ss)", **JBL** 79 (1960) 20-31, taken up in German in **Lukas For - schung**, Braumann, pp. 115-134.

W. C. VAN UNNIK, "The 'Book of Acts' the confirmation of the Gospel", **NT** 4 (1960) 26-59; taken up in W. C. van Unnik, **Sparsa Collecta. The Col - lected Essays of W. C. van Unnik** I (= **Sparsa**, van Unnik) (Leiden 1973), pp. 340-373.

1961

C. K. BARRETT, **Luke the Historian in Recent Study. A. S. Peake Memorial Lecture** (London, 1961).

W. ELTESTER, "Lukas und Paulus", in J. Kroymann and E. Zinn (eds), **Eranion. Mélanges H. Hommel** (Tübingen, 1961), pp. 1-17.

G. KLEIN, **Die Zwölf Apostel. Ursprung und Gehalt einer Idee** (Göt - tingen, 1961).

F. MUSSNER*, "Die Idee der Apokatastasis in der Apostelgeschichte", in H. Gross and F. Mussner (eds), **Lex tua veritas. Mélanges H. Junker** (Trier, 1961), pp. 293-296.

F. MUSSNER, "'In den letzten Tagen' (Apg 2, 17a)", **BZ**, N. F., 5 (1961) 263-265.

J. C. O'NEILL, **The Theology of Acts in its Historical Setting** (London, 1961, 1970^{2}).

U. WILCKENS, **Die Missionsreden der Apostelgeschichte. Form- und traditionsgeschichtliche Untersuchungen** (Neukirchen, 1961, 1974^{3}), pp. 193-218 of the 1st ed.

1962

J. DUPONT, "Les discours missionnaires des Actes des apôtres d'après un ouvrage récent", **RB** 69 (1962) 37-60; included in J. Dupont, **Etudes sur les Actes des apôtres** (= **Etudes**, Dupont) (Paris, 1967), pp. 133-155.

F. MUSSNER, "Wann kommt das Reich Gottes. Die Antwort Jesu nach Lk 17, 20b-21", **BZ**, N. F., 6 (1962) 107-111.

W. C. ROBINSON, **The Way of the Lord. A Study of History and Eschatology in the Gospel of Luke** (Basel, 1962) The German title is **Der Weg des Herrn. Studien zur Eschatologie im Lukas-Evangelium. Ein Gespräch mit H. Conzelmann** (Hamburg-Bergstedt, 1964).

H. SCHÜRMANN, "Evangelienschrift und kirchliche Unterweisung. Die repräsentative Funktion der Schrift nach Lk 1, 1-4", in **Miscellanea Erfordiana** (Erfurter Theol. Studien, 12) (Leipzig, 1962), pp. 48-73; taken up in H. Schürmann, **Traditionsgeschichtliche Untersuchungen zu den synoptischen Evangelien, Beiträge**, (Düsseldorf, 1968), p. 251-271; and in **Lukas Forschung**, Braumann, pp. 135-169.

1963

H W. BARTSCH, **"Wachet aber zu jeder Zeit!" Entwurf einer Auslegung des Lukasevangeliums** (Hamburg, 1963), esp. pp. 106-123.

O. BAUERNFIEND, "Tradition und Komposition in dem Apokatastasisspruch, Act 3, 20 s", in O. Betz, M. Hengel and P. Schmidt (eds), **Abraham unser Vater. Juden und Christen im Gespräch über die Bibel. Mélanges O. Michel** (Leiden-Köln, 1963), pp. 13-23.

G. BRAUMANN, "Das Mittel der Zeit. Erwägungen zur Theologie des Lukas", **ZNW** 54 (1963) 117-145.

G. BRAUMANN, "Die lukanische Interpretation der Zerstörung Jerusalems", **NT** 6 (1963) 120-127.

C. E. B. CRANFIELD, "The Parabole of the Unjust Judge and the Eschatology of Luke-Acts", **ScotJT** 16 (1963) 300-325.

F. V. FILSON, **Three Crucial Decades, Studies in the Book of Acts** (Richmond, 1963).

S. SCHULZ, "Gottes Vorsehung bei Lukas", **ZNW** 54 (1963) 104-116.

H. D. F. SPARKS, recension of H. Conzelmann, **Die Mitte der Zeit**, and J. C. O'Neill, **The Theology of Acts**, **JTS**, N. S., 14 (1963) 454-466.

1964

C. K. BARRETT, "Stephen and the Son of Man", in W. Eltester and F. H. Kettler (eds), **Apophoreta. Mélanges E. Haenchen** (Berlin, 1964), pp. 32-38.

D. P. FULLER, **Easter Faith and History** (Grand Rapids, 1964), pp. 188-223.

A. GARCIA DEL MORAL*, "Un possible aspecto de la tesis y unidad del libro de los Hechos", **EstBib** 23 (1964) 41-92.

H. HEGERMANN, "Zur Theologie des Lukas", in U. Meckert, G. Ott and B. Satlow (eds), **"...und fragten nach Jesus". Mélanges E. Barnikol** (Berlin, 1964), pp. 27-34.

G. KLEIN, "Lukas, 1, 1-4 als theologisches Programm", in E. Dinkler (ed), **Zeit und Geschichte, Mélanges R. Bultmann** (Tübingen, 1964,) pp. 183-216; included in G. Klein, **Rekonstruktion und Interpretation. Gesammelte Aufsätze zum Neuen Testament** (Munich, 1969), pp. 237-261.

G. KLEIN, "Die Prüfung der Zeit (Lukas 12, 54-56)", **ZTK** 61 (1964) 373-390.

X. LÉON-DUFOUR, **Les Evangiles et l'histoire de Jèsus** (Paris, 1964).

1965

O. CULLMANN, **Heil als Geschichte. Heilsgeschichtliche Existenz im Neuen Testament** (Tübingen, 1965), pp. 214-225 (FT Neuchâtel, 1966).

E. E. ELLIS, "Present und Future Eschatology in Luke", **NTS** 12 (1965-1966) 27-41.

H. FLENDER, **Heil und Geschichte in der Theologie des Lukas,** (Munich, 1965, 1968^2) (we are citing from the 2nd ed.).

E. RASCO, "Hans Conzelmann y la 'Historia Salutis',. A propósito de 'Die Mitte der Zeit' y 'Die Apostelgeschichte'", **Greg** 46 (1965) 286-319.

J. C. LEBRAM, "Zwei Bemerkungen zu katechetischen Traditionen in der Apostelgeschichte", **ZNW** 56 (1965) 202-213.

A. Q. MORTON and G. H. C. MACGREGOR*, **The Structure of Luke and Acts** (New York, 1965).

1966

P. BORGEN, "Von Paulus zu Lukas. Beobachtungen zur Erhellung der Theologie der Lukasschriften", **ST** 20 (1966) 140-157.

H. CONZELMANN, "Luke's Place in the Development of Early Christianity", in L. E. Keck and J. L. Martyn (eds), **Studies in Luke-Acts. Mélanges P. Schubert** (=**Studies,** Keck) (Nashville-New York, 1966), pp. 298-316; taken up in German in **Lukas Forschung**, Braumann, pp. 236-260.

A. L. MOORE, **The Parousia in the New Testament** (Leiden, 1966).

J. REUMANN, "Oikonomia-Terms in Paul in Comparison with Lucan Heilsgeschichte", **NTS** 13 (1966-1967) 147-167.

C. H. TALBERT, **Luke and the Gnostics** (Nashville, 1966).

W. C. VAN UNNIK, "Luke-Acts, A Storm Center in Contemporary Scholarship", in **Studies,** Keck, pp. 15-32.

U. WILCKENS, "Interpreting Luke-Acts in a Period of Existentialist Theology", in **Studies**, Keck, pp. 60-83; taken up in German, in U. Wilckens, **Rechtfertigung als Freiheit. Paulusstudien** (Neukirchen, 1974), pp. 171-202.

1967

J. DUPONT, **Etudes sur les Actes des apôtres,** (Paris, 1967).

A. GEORGE, "Tradition et rédaction chez Luc. La construction du troisième Evangile", in I. de la Potterie (ed), **De Jésus aux Evangiles. Tradition et rédaction dans les Evangiles synoptiques** (Gembloux-Paris, 1967), pp. 100-129.

L. KECK*, "Jesus' Entrance Upon His Mission", **RExp** 64 (1967) 465-483.

G. KLEIN, "Der Synkretismus als theologisches Problem in der ältesten christlichen Apologetik", **ZTK** 64 (1967) 40-82; taken up in G. Klein, **Rekonstruktion und Interpretation. Gesammelte Aufsätze zum Neuen Testament** (Munich, 1969), pp. 262-30l.

A. SALAS, **Discurso Escatológico Prelucano. Estudio de Lc. 21, 20-36** (El Escorial, 1967).

S. SCHULZ, **Die Stunde der Botschaft. Einführung in die Theologie der vier Evangelisten** (Hamburg, 1967), pp. 239-296.

W. C. VAN UNNIK, "Die Apostelgeschichte und die Häresien", **ZNW** 58 (1967) 240-246; taken up in **Sparsa**, van Unnik, pp. 402-409.

1968

O. BETZ, "The Kerygma of Luke", **Interpr** 22 (1968) 131-146.

J. LINDBLOM*, **Geschichte und Offenbarungen. Vorstellungen von göttlichen Weisungen und übernatürlichen Erscheinungen im ältesten Christentum** (Lund, 1968).

F. D. LINDSEY*, "Lucan Theology in Contemporary Perspective", **BS** 125 (1968) 346-351.

J. REUMANN, "Heilsgeschichte in Luke, Some Remarks on its Background and Comparison with Paul", in F. L. Cross (ed), **Studia Evangelica**, IV (Berlin, 1968), pp. 86-115.

1969

H. D. BETZ, "Ursprung und Wesen christlichen Glaubens nach der Emmaus - legende (Luk 24, 13-32)", **ZTK** 66 (1969) 7-21.

M. CARREZ, "L'herméneutique paulinienne peut-elle aider à apprécier la con - ception lucanienne de l'histoire?" **RTPhil**, 3rd series, 19 (1969) 247-258.

R. A. EDWARDS, "The Redaction of Luke", **JRel** 49 (1969) 392-405.

A. EHRHARDT, **The Acts of the Apostles. Ten Lectures** (Manchester, 1969).

E. E. ELLIS, "Die Funktion der Eschatologie im Lukasevangelium", **ZTK** 66 (1969) 387-402; appeared in English in the collection Facet FB Books, Biblical Series, 30 Philadelphia, 1972; in French in F. Neirynck (ed), **L'Evangile de Luc, Problèmes littéraires et théologiques. Mémorial L. Cerfaux** (= **Evangile**, Neirynck) (Gembloux, 1973), pp. 141-155; taken up in German in **Lukas Forschung**, Braumann, pp. 378-397.

F. O. FRANCIS, "Eschatology und History in Luke-Acts", **JAmAcRel** 37 (1969) 49-63.

J. D. KAESTLI, **L'eschatologie dans l'oeuvre de Luc, ses caractéris - tiques et sa place dans le développement du christianisme primitif**, (Geneva, 1969).

K. LÖNING, "Lukas-Theologie der von Gott geführten Heilsgeschichte (Lk, Apg)", in J. Schreiner (ed), **Gestalt und Anspruch des Neuen Testaments** (Würzburg, 1969), pp. 200-228.

G. LOHFINK, "Christologie und Geschichtsbild in Apg 3, 19-21", **BZ**, N. F., 13 (1969) 223-241.

J. PANAGOPOULOS, ' *Ὁ Θέος καὶ ἡ Ἐκκλησία. Ἡ Θεολογικὴ μαρ- τυρία τῶν Πράξεων Ἀποστόλων*, (Athens, 1969).

F. SCHÜTZ, **Der Leidende Christus. Die angefochtene Gemeinde und das Christuskerygma der lukanischen Schriften** (Stuttgart-Berlin-Köln-Mainz, 1969), pp. 91-92.

S. G. WILSON, "Lukan Eschatology", **NTS** 16 (1969-1970) 330-347.

1970

C. BURCHARD, **Der dreizehnte Zeuge. Traditions- und komposi - tionsgeschichtliche Untersuchungen zu Lukas' Darstellung der Frühzeit des Paulus**, (Göttingen, 1970).

E. FRANKLIN, "The Ascension and the Eschatology of Luke-Acts", **ScotJT** 23 (1970) 191-200.

A. J. B. HIGGINS, "The Preface to Luke and the Kerygma in Acts", in W. W. Gasque and R. P. Martin (eds), **Apostolic History and the Gospel. Biblical and Historical Essays. Mélanges F. F. Bruce** (= **Apostolic History, Bruce**) (Exeter, 1970), pp. 78-91.

W. G. KÜMMEL, "'Das Gesetz und die Propheten gehen bis Johannes'. Lukas 16, 16 im Zusammenhang der heilsgeschichtlichen Theologie der Lukas - schriften", in O. Böcher and K. Haacker (eds), **Verborum Veritas. Mé - langes G. Stählin** (Wuppertal, 1970), pp. 89-102; included in **Lukas Forschung**, Braumann, pp. 398-415.

W. G. KÜMMEL, "Luc en accusation dans la théologie contemporaine", **ETL** 46 (1970) 265-281; included in **Evangile**, Neirynck, pp. 93-109; in German **ZNW** 63 (1972) 149-165, and in **Lukas Forschung**, Braumann pp. 416-436.

I. H. MARSHALL, **Luke: Historian and Theologian** (Exeter, 1970).
A. J. MATTILL, "The Purpose of Acts: Schneckenburger Re-considered", in **Apostolic History, Bruce** (Exeter, 1970), pp. 108-122.
P. H. MENOUD, "Le salut par la foi selon le livre des Actes", in M. Barth, et al., **Foi et Salut selon saint Paul (épître aux Romains, 1-16) - Colloque oecuménique à l'Abbaye de S. Paul hors les murs, 16-21 avril 1968** (Rome, 1970), pp. 255-276 (pp. 272-276; discussion); included in P. H. Menoud, **Jésus-Christ et la foi. Recherches néotestamentaires** (= **Jésus-Christ**, Menoud) (Neuchâtel, 1975), pp. 130-149 (cf. discussion on pp. 146-149).
B. RIGAUX, "La petite apocalypse de Luc (17, 22-37)", in **Ecclesia a Spiritu Sancto edocta (Lumen Gentium, 53), Mélanges G. Philips** (Gem - bloux, 1970), pp. 407-438.
R. SCHNACKENBURG, "Der eschatologische Abschnitt Lk 17, 20-37", in A. Deschamps and A. de Halleux (eds), A. Descamps and A. de Halleux (eds), **Mélanges Bibliques. Mélanges B. Rigaux** (= **Mélanges, Rigaux** (Gembloux, 1970), pp. 213-234.
C. H. TALBERT, "The Redaction Critical Quest for Luke the Theologian", in **Jesus and Man's Hope, Pittsburgh Theological Seminary**, I (Pittsburgh 1970), pp. 171-222.

1971

M. P. BURNIER, "Une vision prophétique es eschatologique de l'histoire: le livre des Actes", **Cahiers bibliques, Numéro hors série, Mélanges Suzanne de Dietrich**, of **FoiVie** 70 (1971) 138-145.
J. KODELL, "La théologie de Luc et la recherche récente", **Bulletin de Théo - logie biblique** I (1971) 119-149.
G. LOHFINK, **Die Himmelfahrt Jesu. Untersuchungen zu den Him - melfahrts- und Erhöhungstexten bei Lukas** (Munich, 1971).
R. PESCH, "Der Anfang der Apostelgeschichte: Apg I, I-II, Kommentarstudie", **EKK**, Vorarbeiten Heft 3 (Zurich-Neukirchen, 1971), pp. 7-35.
E. SAMAIN, "L'évangile de Luc et le livre des Actes: éléments de composition et de structure", **Cahiers bibliques,** 10, of **FoiVie** 70 (1971) 3-24.
E. SAMAIN, "Le discours-programme de Jésus à la synagogue de Nazareth (Luc 4, 16-30)", **Cahiers bibliques**, 10, of **FoiVie** 70 (1971) 25-43.
R. H. SMITH, "The Theology of Acts", **ConcTM** 42 (1971) 527-535.

1972

J. DUPONT, "L'après-mort dans l'oeuvre de Luc", **RTLouv** 3 (1972) 3-21; German abridged version in P. Hoffmann, N. Brox and W. Pesch (eds), **Orientierung an Jesus. Zur Theologie der Synoptiker. Mélanges J. Schmid** (Freiburg-Basel-Vienna, 1973), pp. 37-47.
W. ELTESTER, "Israel im lukanischen Werk und die Nazarethperikope", in E. Grässer, et al., **Jesus in Nazareth** (Berlin-New York, 1972), pp. 76-147.
H. K. FARRELL*, **The Eschatological Perspective of Luke-Acts,** un - published dissertation (Boston, 1972).
J. DE KESEL*, **Le salut et l'histoire dans l'oeuvre de Luc** (typed thesis), Pont. Greg. Univ. (Rome, 1972)
A. J. MATTILL*, "Naherwartung, Fernerwartung, and the Purpose of Luke-Acts: Weymouth Reconsidered", **CBQ** 34 (1972) 276-293.
A. J. MATTILL*, "The Good Samaritan and the Purpose of Luke-Acts: Halévy Reconsidered" **Encounter** 33 (1972) 359-376.
J. PANAGOPOULOS, "Zur Theologie der Apostelgeschichte", **NT** 14 (1972), 137-159; Spanish abridged version **SelT** 49 (1974) 50-65.

S. ZEDDA, **L'eschatologia biblica, I, Antico Testamento e Vangeli Sinnottici** (Brescia, 1972), pp. 273ff. et passim.

J. ZMIJEWSKI, **Die Eschatologiereden des Lukas-Evangeliums. Eine traditions- und redaktionsgeschichtliche Untersuchung zu Lk 21, 5-36 und Lk 17, 20-37** (Bonn, 1972).

1973

R(UTHILD) GEIGER, **Die Lukanischen Endzeitreden. Studien zur Eschatologie des Lukas-Evangeliums** (Bern-Frankfurt, 1973).

H. R. HIERS, "The Problem of the Delay of the Parousia in Luke-Acts", **NTS** 20 (1973-1974) 145-155.

P. S. MINEAR, "Dear Theo. The Kerygmatic Intention and Claim of the Book of Acts", **Interp** 27 (1973) 131-150.

B. PRETE, **Storia e Teologia nel Vangelo di Luca**, (Bologna, 1973) (collection of articles: 1) Lk 1:34; 2) Lk 1:26-38; 3) Messianic perspectives of the Lucan *σήμερον*; 4) Lk 10:42; 5) Lk 24:5-7; 6) Lk 24:13-35; 7) Act 1:13-14).

J. SCHLOSSER, "Les jours de Noé et de Lot; A propos de Lc 17, 26-30", **RB** 80 (1973) 13-36.

A. STÖGER*, "Die Theologie des Lukasevangeliums", **BiLit** 46 (1973) 227-236.

W. C. VAN UNNIK, "Once More St. Luke's Prologue", **Neotestamentica** 7 (1973) 7-26.

1974

F. BOVON, "L'importance des médiations dans le projet théologique de Luc", **NTS** 21 (1974-1975) 23-39.

W. G. KÜMMEL, "Heilsgeschichte im Neuen Testament?" in J. Gnilka (ed), **Neues Testament und Kirche. Mélanges R. Schnackenburg** (Freiburg-Basel-Vienna, 1974), pp. 434-457.

P. S. MINEAR, "Jesus' Audiences, According to Luke", **NT** 16 (1974) 81-109.

C. H. TALBERT, **Literary Patterns, Theological Themes, and the Genre of Luke-Acts** (Missoula, 1974).

M. VÖLKEL, "Zur Deutung des 'Reiches Gottes' bei Lukas", **ZNW** 65 (1974) 57-70.

1975

G. FERRARO, "Kairoi anapsyxeos. Annotazioni su Atti 3,20", **RBiblt** 23 (1975) 67-78.

E. FRANKLIN, **Christ the Lord. A Study in the Purpose and Theology of Luke-Acts** (London, 1975), pp. 9-47 et passim.

R. GLÖCKNER, **Die Verkündigung des Heils beim Evangelisten Lukas** (Mainz, n.d. (1975?)). Cf. the review by E. Schweizer, **TR** 72 (1976) 373.

A. J. MATTILL, "The Jesus-Paul Parallels and the Purpose of Luke-Acts: H. H. Evans Reconsidered", **NT** 17 (1975) 15-46.

O. MERK, "Das Reich Gottes in den lukanischen Schriften", in E. E. Ellis and E. Grässer (eds), **Jesus und Paulus. Mélanges W. G. Kümmel** (Göttingen, 1975), pp. 201-220.

E. RASCO, "Jesús y el Espíritu, Iglesia e 'Historia': Elementos para una lectura de Lucas", **Greg** 56 (1975) 321-368 (English summary on p. 368). This article represents a chapter in the book mentioned in 1976, pp. 126-172.

G. SCHNEIDER, **Parusiegleichnisse im Lukas-Evangelium** (Stuttgart, 1975).

1976

A. J. HULTGREN, "Interpreting the Gospel of Luke", **Interpr** 30 (1976) 353-365.

E. RASCO, **La Teología de Lucas: Origen, Desarollo, Orientaciones** (Rome, 1976).

1977
J. ERNST, **Das Evangelium nach Lukas übersetzt und erklärt** (Regensburg, 1977).
G. SCHNEIDER, **Das Evangelium nach Lukas**, 2 vols. (Gütersloh-Würzburg, 1977).
G. SCHNEIDER, "Der Zweck des lukanischen Doppelwerks", **BZ**, N.F., 21 (1977) 45-66.
1978
J. ERNST, **Herr der Geschichte. Perspektiven der lukanischen Eschatologie** (Stuttgart, 1978).
I. H. MARSHALL*, **The Gospel of Luke: A Commentary on the Greek Text** (Exeter,1978).

Chapter 1

GOD'S PURPOSE, SALVATION HISTORY AND ESCHATOLOGY

Introduction

Everything began with history and eschatology. Luke was caught between the anvil of redaktionsgeschichtlich exegesis and the hammer of Bultmannian theology. For many the objectification of faith into creed or history was a temptation which early Christianity could not have been able to resist. From the beginning, eschatology or rather eschatological conscience had to seek for temporary and contingent forms of expression. These forms were found in the apocalyptic sphere. R. Bultmann, P. Vielhauer, H. Conzelmann, E. Haenchen, S. Schulz, E. Dinkler, E. Grässer and G. Klein [1] think that the Evangelist modified this mode of expression and by choosing historical narrative instead of the apocalyptic urgency, he betrayed the cause and revealed a loss of the eschatological sap. Settled in the Roman Empire, which for some was peaceful and for others,dangerous, Luke would have lived according a gospel, which had become a holy and ideal evangelical story and as well as a hope in a distant resurrection from the dead. Associated with a certain but as yet remote return of the Son of Man, absent because of the Ascension, this hope could no longer nurture, except in an ethical manner, an existence whose origin was more ecclesiastical than Christological. For the present, this memory and hope would leave an uncomfortable situation in which the presence of the Spirit was unable to institute eschatological fullness, but only an Ersatz (= substitute). Considered from a Bultmannian theological point of view and read in a redactional manner, Luke seems to be quite distinct from Paul, perhaps even opposed to him. With the existentialist Paul serving as the norm, the canon within the canon, Luke emerges from the investigation perhaps admired, but with the admiration one has for a gifted culprit and the verdict is in any case guilty. He is guilty of having historicized and - this is the same as - having de-eschatologized the Kerygma. Furthermore, by doing so he is also guilty of having given a false solution to a real problem, a solution which only touches the apocalyptic framework of the delay of the Parousia and not the existential and eschatological reality of the Gospel. The stages of salvation history necessarily project backward into the past the eternal present of the Word, which still rings out. Moreover, the idea of a Church history contradicts the conviction of the first Christians for whom Jesus Christ was the end of history. An over optimistic consideration is given to the Old Testament (= OT), whose promises are highlighted, and this in turn provokes the ignoring of the failures [2]. The manifestation of Jesus, itself, culminates in a powerful proclamation and a privileged resurrection. The cross, the paradoxical center of a still actual message becomes a failure which, for Luke, is quickly effaced. It is merely a human obstacle overcome in three days by a God whose power is a little too visible. Moreover, who tells us that the image of this God remained Biblical? What if the God of Luke was an avatar of a Greco-Roman fatum of inescapable decisions? Concerning this, unity was not to be found within the Bultmannian school. Some pointed out that in Luke's thought the role of the freewill, which expressed in an unconcern, should have hindered him from having a solid doctrine of grace. Does Luke give too much to man by limiting God to his heaven? Is secularization the final word of historization? If this is so, we should underline the word history in the expression "salvation history". Or does Luke give too much place to God by making men into puppets? The helping strokes of God in history would be intolerably imperialistic: history would advance in miraculous bounds, and Luke would be wrong in ob-serving the famous Heilstatsachen with the aid of his binoculars of an experienced historian. The positivism of revelation could be the ultimate consequence of a salvation history conceived only from the angle of salvation. Whether too human or too 'theophile', Luke is condemned either way. Certain Protestants wonder what an author who is so Catholic is doing inside the canon.

Today, the sculptors of image of Luke have grown older. Their blows have weakened and they are becoming rarer. Others have come to give yet another banal or eccentric form to the abused evangelist. And yet others have been happy to wrest this view from the hands, declared unworthy on the occasion. Quite numerous are the others, impressed by the intelligence and exegetical talent of Conzelmann and friends, accept his general schema and limit their ambitions to the correction of certain details. Finally, still others understanding that Luke, less original concerning eschatology than first thought, judge that his interests lie in the Church and the moral life of the communities. This is why Lucan studies have taken a new direction. The dissertations concerning the Eucharist, the ministries, the Church, etc. are multiplying. Salvation history, so vigorously defended by O. Cullmann in the peak of the storm, frightens less now. Many German Catholic exegetes wonder if it (salvation history) cannot get along with eschatology, an eschatology whose definition remains still unclear or even ambigous? The existentialist Paul was not the historical Paul and Luke lives a generation after him. Could not a Lucan rereading of the Gospel be one of the legitimate actualizations of the message of which we speak of so often today? Formally, Luke inserts the Gospel into his time differently than Paul. But did he do so responding to the same requirements of faith? The certainty which he wishes his readers to share (against Bultmann and company) could not be the assurance of the modern intellectual who has verified the facts and accepted the proof. This is an anachronistic view of reality. The aporia mentioned above, between a tyrant God and a God who is absent, between a human robot and a Promethean man, can be surpassed by a new conception of history, of the real action, but this conception is mediated by God, in a world where men are taken seriously. This not only in their abstract existential existence but also in their corporality, their finiteness, which is also the true mark of the image of God. Luke is the theologian of social realities, of the popular incarnation, of collective hope, of conflicts for bread. The space of man, henceforth, takes on an autonomous theological dimension, coexisting and not subugated to salvation history. It is a cultivated space.

Twenty-five years of Lucan studies have passed: the preceeding lines have summarized what seems to us to be the essential ideas of the discussions concerning history and eschatology. It is now the moment to discover in detail, the position of each and how the exegetes and theologians have advanced - not always making progress - the debate.

I. FROM ESCHATOLOGY TO SALVATION HISTORY

The setting in motion: P. Vielhauer and H. Conzelmann

a. Under the intellectual guidance of R. Bultmann **[3]**, P. Vielhauer (-> 1950) examines the theology of Luke by opposing the figure of Paul, painted in the Acts, and the one discovered in the Epistles. Being a bearer of pre-Pauline Christological traditions, Luke shows himself posterior to Paul in his understanding of natural theology, the role of the Law and eschatology. This, according to the eyes of the late professor of Bonn, has become secondary. Locus de novissimis, eschatology only serves, here and there (Act 17:30), to incite repentance. Having been marginalized, it has been trans - formed: unfaithful to what Vielhauer thinks is the essence of primitive Christian eschatology (the paradoxical contempora - neity of the present and the future of salvation), Lucan eschatology combines chronologically and quantitatively the ties which bind the 'already' and the 'not yet'. The existence itself of the Book of the Acts suggests a Christianity which is turning its back on the primitive eschatology and settling into the world. Thus the little interest that Luke has for eschatology is confirmed. By assembling historical documentation, as Luke writes in his intention in the Prologue (Lk 1:1-4), he is anticipating with an "enormous prolepsis" the second century Apologetics and the Christian historiography of the fourth century. By doing this, he offers his readers human security (*ἀσφάλεια* of Lk 1:4), which is incompatible to the risk of faith.

b. If Luke defines his Gospel as a first book (Act 1:1), he must intend to write a second. The history of Jesus, which is still the last for Mark, becomes Luke's next-to-last. The end of history is transformed into the middle of history. To express this conviction, Conzelmann gave his book the title, **Die Mitte der Zeit** (= 'The Middle of Time'; ET. **The Theology of St. Luke**)..

The first part of this book (-> 1954) presents a continous reading of Luke's Gospel. The continuity of the text, understood in its redactional nature, witnesses, for Conzelmann, to a deliberate linking of the places (Galilee, the journey, Jerusalem). The exegete does not doubt the theological virtue of this geography: Galilee is the place where Jesus becomes con - scious of his Messiahship and gathers witnesses whose ulterior mission will be decisive. The journey attests that this Mes - siahship will be in suffering, whereas Jerusalem, the city where the miracles cease and teaching rings forth, loses its eschatological function: in entering the capital, Jesus hastens the coming of the cross and not the Kingdom of God (moreover, Luke disconnects the announcement of the fall of Jerusalem, henceforth secular, from the coming of the end times). From these geographical stages Conzelmann formulates his very distinct chronological steps, marked by the epiphanies of Jesus and followed by the scenes of rejection: the baptism and lack of success in Nazareth; the transfiguration and Samaritan inhospitality; and the entry into Jerusalem and his Passion. The reality of this historical schematization appears each time at the term of an analysis of the materials, especially those of Mark, which the Evangelist has reinterpreted. For example, John the Baptist is no longer the forerunner. Luke places him with the OT prophets. His message, as his sermon to the guilds attests, ceases to be eschatological and becomes moral. Satan leaves the scene to return later at the eve of the Passion, thus offering Jesus an unperturbed salvific period. The disciples' equipment will have to vary according to the circumstances: stripped materially (Lk 10) during the time when Jesus protects them, they must arm themselves for the period when they will be deprived of the Master's comforting presence (Lk 22:35-36).

This dissection of the periods of Jesus' life is but one aspect of a more abundant theological effort: to grasp the total historical reality from the viewpoint of the divine will, which adapting itself to history, molds latter according to its purposes. The life of Jesus was preceded by a preparatory period of the prophets and the time of the Church, which can be subdivided itself into a first period of the happy beginnings and the contemporary era, is called to endure. The three last parts of the book take up again the study of the three large sections of redemptive history, from an analysis of the vocabulary related to the project of God and his providence. It is a salvation history, not a philosophy of history.

Between the first part, consecrated to geography and chronology and the last three, Conzelmann inserts an investigation of the Lucan texts which are strictly eschatological. He comes to the following results: the Lucan rereading of the apocalyptic vocabulary (the notions of tribulation, of conversion and of kingdom) and the composition of the two eschatological discourses (Lk 17 and 21) confirm the geographical indications and the heilsgeschichtlich schema: everything which concerns the believers and the world loses its eschatological coloring and everything which touches on the last days is thrown back to the end of history, in the distant future. Jesus announces the Kingdom but not the proximity of the Kingdom. This kingdom exists in heaven; its image can be seen in anticipation in the life of Jesus. But today only the message of the Kingdom rings out, the kingdom is absent .

It remains to be seen why Luke carried out this huge project. The answer is simple: as the Parousia was delaying, Christians could not continue to maintain the imminence ("Verharren im Trotzdem" [4]). A radical solution commanded attention if Christianity wanted to develop and expand itself; it was to renounce the imminence and replace it with a full salvation history. Luke's theological merit lies in having given this answer. Alas, it is an answer which betrays the existential perception that should have been given to the eschatological message of Jesus and the first apostles. Just as he specified the bodily appearance of the dove at Jesus' baptism, Luke materialized the eschatological vocabulary of Jesus and of primitive Christianity. Jesus and Paul announced eschatology and it was salvation history which came.

We would like to indicate several of the criticisms which have appeared since the arrival of this book, impressive because of its distant stringency. If the three great periods of salvation history are confirmed by the existence of the three books: the Septuagint, the Gospel of Luke and the Acts, the exact partitioning of these periods are not nearly as clear as Conzelmann thinks: does the time of Jesus begin only <u>after</u> John the Baptist? Do not the infancy narratives, which his inquiry curiously neglects, serve as an overture to the account of salvation in Jesus Christ (in an opera, the overture is an integral part of the work)? As a theologian of salvation history, does not Luke insist more on continuity, on the dynamic movement of history, than on the periods (W. C. Robinson)? Does not he seek to designate this continuity with characters or events which we might call "hooks" ("crochets"): thus John the Baptist would serve as the link between the OT and Jesus' time. He belonged to both, just as the double narrative of the Ascension would unify the time of Jesus with the time of the Church [5]. This movement, which the periods are content to scan, would explain why the passage from the second to the third period is so difficult to fix. Conzelmann, himself, hesitated to date it: was it at the new irruption of Satan just before the Passion? If so, would the death and resurrection no longer be a part of Jesus' time? Is it at the Cross, at Easter or at the Ascension? Luke would no doubt prefer the Ascension, even if he refuses to fix the passage from one time to the other on one certain day.

Finally, there is the theological criticism. Yet we must admit that Conzelmann does not become vehement and refuses to speak of <u>Frühkatholizismus</u>.

The Momentum Continues

c. Even if the article of G. Harbsmeier (-> 1950) is more theological than exegetical, it merits mention for it claims to draw dogmatic conclusions from the positions presented above and demonstrates well the hostile state of mind which reigned among the German Protestant theologians. The author openly admits that he accepts the conclusions of Vielhauer and compares them with Christian life and thought in order to deduce that Luke's influence on the churches was and remains stronger than Paul's. Even if this influence is rather secretive with regard to natural theology, the law (baptism considered as circumcision) and Christology (Jesus as an example), it is acknowledged with respect to salvation history. This is how the author diagnoses the churches coming from the Reformation (it is evident for the author that in this case Catholicism can also claim to be conformed to the Bible, at least with one part, Luke). While for Paul, the history of the world is identified with the history of the salvation of this world (through Jesus Christ alone), for Luke, salvation history is a history separate from universal history. It is this conception, so widespread in the churches, which is to be criticized in the name of Paul and with the help of Christ, present by his Spirit. However, it is not suitable to exclude Luke from the canon, for the Bible is and must remain a human collection where the tares and the good grain have grown together.

Three criticisms are in order: 1) since he himself accepts the risk, the attack brought against Luke - our critical distance taken - comes more from the theologus praesens than from the Christus praesens! 2) The essential of the Lucan message, centered on the manifestation of Jesus the savior, is totally neglected to the benefit of the theological themes which Luke considers secondary or he could not yet treat them as such. 3) By refusing to ban Luke from the canon, the author remains simply at the level of words; i.e. he refuses to place a coherent act with his thought. Thus he finds refuge in ideological dis - course. This theological position corresponds to acrimony against Luke, who is reproached precisely for having inserted the Gospel into the historical structures of this world: "So ist das Reich Gottes im Siegeszug in dieser Welt begriffen..." (p. 357). Is it incorrect to see in this reaction the influence of Kierkegaard and the refusal of a Hegelian interpretation of the Gospel?

d. E. Grässer's monograph (-> 1957) interests us for it completes Conzelmann's study on two points: 1) it places the

Lucan effort within the history of doctrines of early Christianity and 2) it pursues the analysis of Luke into the Acts (curiously neglected by Conzelmann). Let us begin by the second point. As the exegesis of the first chapter of the Acts shows, Luke was conscious of the problem caused by the delay of the Parousia and gave a definite solution, in itself satisfying. There is indeed an intermediate time between the resurrection and the Parousia. Whether this acknowledgment worries, saddens or rejoices, we can but verify it here. This period can and must be qualified theologically: it is the time of the universal mission, which is provoked and sustained by the Holy Spirit. Such is the purpose of God which appears in the last resolutions of the Resurrected One, in the declarations of the angel at the Ascension or in the activities of the first Christians. Moreover, the Parousia, that Luke never denies as a future reality, is eclipsed by the death of the individual, because of the time which endures. Future salvation seems to be bound as much, if not more, to this after-death - in concert with J. Dupont (-> 1972) - than to the Parousia. Grässer thinks that the remainder of Acts confirms his exegesis of the first chapter: Pentecost brings the Holy Spirit, a welcome response to the delay of the Parousia of the Son of Man. The speeches of Acts do not associate the resurrection of Christ to eschatology but to the past events of the cross, and in a non-eschatological manner. The Acts places Christianity, considered as a religion, within world history. If Luke continues to speak of the Kingdom of God in Acts, he can carefully avoid mentioning its arrival. Finally, a text like Acts 28:28 reveals that Luke anticipates a history which will endure.

In his analysis of the Gospel of Luke (pp. 178-198) and in the few pages (pp. 199-204) consecrated to the Word and the Church as an Ersatz (an unfortunate term in our opinion) of eschatological existence, Grässer relies heavily on Conzelmann. He is more personal in the pages where he inserts Luke's thought into the history of early Christian doctrines, for Conzelmann did not attempt this approach (in the introduction of third edition of **Die Mitte der Zeit**, p. VI, he explains the methodological reasons which motivated him to isolate Luke. Since then, H. Conzelmann (-> 1966) has proposed an insertion of this type). Nonetheless, Grässer's originality remains formal for he arrives at a conclusion close to Conzelmann's premises: the Lucan solution is an isolated case in the New Testament (=NT).

In evaluating this solution, Grässer thinks, we must admit that this elaboration of a salvation history, which emphasizes the durable intervention of the Word and the Spirit in a Church which participates in the world, is a regrettable peculiarity. O. Cullmann justly condemns this deduction, along with the theory common to both German theologians according to which the delay of the Parousia was the major instigator - eminently negative - of this construction.

As for us, we accept the movement described by Grässer: divers solutions have been offered for the problem of the delay: He will come anyway. He is coming, so let us remain vigilant. He is absent but the Holy Spirit is present. He desires to delay to give everyone a chance. Yet it seems to us that Luke is less original than has been said. Several NT authors, particularly Mark and Paul, on whom Luke relies, considered that the time between Easter and the Parousia was designated for the evangelization of the world and should not be seen as the absence of God, but rather characterized by the presence of the Spirit. Luke simply develops a conception common to several movements within primitive Christianity.

Moreover, in doing this, Luke does not betray his kerygmatic heritage, whether it is Synoptic or Pauline, for a salvation history does not contradict ipso facto an eschatological perspective. J. Panagopoulos has described it well: the Church and the activity of the Spirit guarantees a presence of salvation, indeed the last salvation and Luke's contemporaries are called to be associated to it. Furthermore, it is not certain that Luke elaborated his salvation history because of the delay. Certainly, the delay favorized this view, but the OT tradition of a salvation embedded in history, as well as the concrete proclamation of Jesus facilitated and, we would say, legitimated this theological perspective as well. Others like, C. K. Barrett, G. Klein and C. H. Talbert, will add that the antignostic polemic also played a role in Luke's refusal to move into the disincarnate world of spirituality.

e. In the debate which holds our attention, E. Käsemann's interventions are limited to a few pages (-> 1954 and -> 1957), which prove to be incisive. Leaning on P. Vielhauer, the German exegete affirms that the existence of the book of the Acts attests to the weakening of the apocalyptic hope, in Luke. A broad salvation history, well demarcated and organized, replaces the primitive eschatology. Historian, psychologist, pastor and theologian, Luke sees his Gospel as a life of Jesus where the effects correspond to the causes and the materials are grouped as in a secular historical work of antiquity. The exterior order, i.e. the composition of the double work, reflects an interior order, the purpose of God. This Lucan position merits the qualification of theological, but it is a theology of glory which moves away from a theology of the cross, so typical of the early Christians. Indeed, Luke had to pay a high price to exchange eschatology for salvation history. Jesus became the founder of a new religion; the cross, a misunderstanding; the resurrection, a welcome correction; Jesus' teaching, notorious morals; his miracles, visible demonstrations of celestial power; in short, the story (Geschichte) of Jesus is transformed into past events (Historie). Associated with the fate of the apostles, these events are formed into an ideal and exemplary era. While in early Christianity, history is inscribed in eschatology, in Luke, eschatology forms a chapter of history. More than the time of Jesus (Conzelmann), it is the epoque of the Church which constitutes the center of history, the Mitte der Zeit. Luke, the first Christian historian, is a theologian of Frühkatholizismus which is getting settled. Henceforth, the Church controls the message, that until then had defined it. The Evangelist has earned his theological position by reason of the circumstances, particularly by opposition of the wave of enthusiasm which unfurled itself on the Church. Later we shall show that we cannot accept the positions of Käsemann as they stand.

f. S. Schulz (-> 1963), who wrote an introduction to the theology of the Gospels (-> 1967) in which he takes a critical position with regard to Luke (a proto-catholic according to this view), presented a shattering thesis, which to our knowledge has yet to receive the criticism due. The professor of Zurich starts with Conzelmann's position which he first tries to con - solidate by analysis of 1) the numerous verbs composed with the preposition πρό, that underline the will and providence of God. These are important themes in a time and an environment which can no longer content itself with authoritative arguments from Scripture [6]; 2) the subject of these verbs which is no longer God but his purpose; 3) the verbs which indicate "to fix" or "to determine" and eclipse the vocabulary of individual election to the benefit of a reflection interested in collectivity; 4) the vocabulary of "economic" necessity, a necessity that ceases to be eschatological and makes game of men and transforms them into pawns stripped of their autonomy. His conclusion goes beyond Conzelmann's views: comparatively speaking, the God of Luke and his purpose do not fit into the OT tradition of Yahweh who elects his people, but rather fit into the Greco-roman context in which he submits himself to des-tiny (ἀνάγκη - τύχη - fatum) [7]. The article ends with a list of the exegetical ways Luke uses to make known, not only destiny but, the destiny that anticipated this history of Christ and the Church: the historization of the tradition, the miracles, the visible legitimation of the divine prescience, the interventions of the Spirit and the angels which orient the action, the Scriptural testimonies as proof of the providence (especially Lk 22:22), the predications, the testimonies and apologies as instruments God uses to vigorously direct history.

At least three arguments can be brought against Schulz: 1) if Luke had accepted the Greco-roman concept of history, he would not have overlooked the opportunity to better relate the death of his hero with this divine necessity: is it not this rapport that privileged especially the belief in the Moirai?; 2) in as much as such a generalization is authorized, it is necessary to remark that the notions of εἱμαρμένη and fatum were associated with the individual in a static way. Luke has a dynamic perspective which regards history and people together; it is significant that ancient historiography hardly used the idea of destiny as a vector of the related elements (at least during the Hellenistic era); 3) finally, Luke witnesses to a God who desires the salvation of people. This perspective fits into the line of the OT historiography even if certain abstract notions such as the concept of βουλή come from Hellenism (certain Hellenistic terms had already been taken over by Jewish historiography).

g. In a difficult article (-> 1964), G. Klein attempts to complete the interpretive model of Conzelmann, based on Luke's prologue: significantly, he calls this prologue a theological pro - gram and presents a redactional type of exegesis. Up to this time it had been studied particularly from a literary point of view.

Briefly, here is this new interpretation:

1: Luke criticizes his predecessors (ἐπιχειρεῖν has a pejora - tive sense) who had already sensed the problem of tradition [8]. However, these men had contented themselves with fixing in writing the life of Jesus which circulated (the διήγησις is the account of the witnesses and not the product of the work of Luke's forerunners).

2: Between the events themselves and the predecessors, Luke assigns the decisive function to those who had been the eyewitnesses and had become the guardians of the word. The understanding of this link is new with regard to all the previous Synoptic tradition. Luke limits this formidable privilege of having transmitted the διήγησις (not the πράγματα) to the twelve apostles.

3: Luke claims for himself all the authority of the apostolic tradition: the "ἔδοξε κἀμοί reveals a pretension to inspiration, parallel to that expressed in the apostolic decree. He wants to go over the heads of his predecessors and go back to the events themselves (what happens to the poor apostles and their authority?: "Tendenziell ersetzt für ihn die eigene Warheitsfindung den Rekurs auf die apostolische Tradition." (p. 206f. / p. 250)).

4: Luke wanted to produce a secular as well as scientific work (Klein speaks of verification, yet does not say how it happens in history!). Luke extends the story of Jesus at the beginning by telling the infancy narratives (the ἄνωθεν, dictinct from ἀπ' ἀρχῆς indicates this backtracking in time) and at the end, by linking the time of Jesus with the contemporary age by means of primitive Church's history (it is καθεξῆς which has to express all of this: this is a term which indicates not the order of the narrative, but its fullness). With this complete and serious story, Luke desires to communicate a knowledge (ἵνα ἐπιγνῷς) and not faith (of course!). The ἀσφάλεια, first a certainty of knowledge, will become a conviction that assures me of my salvation (Heilsgewissheit). I am finally saved, for I have read the work of Luke who is certainly right, Theophilus will say to himself. He would also unscrupulously neglect the essays of Luke's predecessors (the λόγοι are the literary products of the πολλοί).

Having erected this beautiful construction, Klein criticizes it as incompatible with true faith.

We think that Klein merits numerous criticisms. First of all, he uses extreme language and harsh tone, and while his desire is to bring out the problems, he, in fact, often makes them anachronistic and unlikely: to cite but one example, many will not see what is for him the "unübersehbare Differenz" (p. 198/p. 242) between πράγματα and πεπληροφορήμενα. Furthermore: 1) it is not said that ἐπιχειρεῖν is pejorative; 2) διήγησις is the product of the predecessors and not the account of the apostles; 3) the fulfillment of the events is one and the same thing; 4) the object of παρέδοσαν is πράγματα rather than διήγησις; 5) no reader in antiquity could have imagined that one could find behind ἄνωθεν and καθεξῆς what Klein believes to have discovered; 6) ἔδοξε κἀμοί reflects no pretension to religious or inspired character (in the apostolic decree, the authority of the text lies in the mention of the Holy Spirit, which is precisely absent here).

In reality, we can only accept only one of Klein's points: Luke is sensitive to the time factor and feels like a man of the third generation who is concerned to maintain contact with the origins. But this contact is neither exclusively secular nor scientific. Rather this contact has to do with faith, which the historical account requires and confirms: thus the apostolic witness coincides with - as would later be the case with an Irenaeus, for example - history that can be written from the primitive events. Nothing says that here *ἀσφάλεια* is a Heilsgewissheit: the point is that the certainty of faith is based on knowledge, knowledge of what has happened.

One must read the critique of E. Haenchen [9], the commentary of H. Schürmann (-> 1962) and the exegesis of W. C. van Unnik (-> 1973) to situate the literary, historical and religious preoccupations of Luke in his time and not ours, in short, to understand him [**10**].

h. The pages of E. Dinkler (-> 1955) consecrated to Luke in his presentation of early Christian historiography, also follow the line opened by Bultmann and his disciples: Luke is the Christian author whose intentions and accomplishments come closest to the modern historian's: "...he sees connections and endeavors to explore their meanings and explains sequences through a motive and power..." (p. 333). He thinks in terms of anticipation and of a temporal future. For him, the development of mission is a historical fact which requires form and meaning: "This has to do not with stories but with history." (p. 334). The double consequence is: 1) a salvation history with a center and 2) the succession of cause and effect produces a secularization of history. This is why, in Luke, there are synchronisms between the Christian events and universal history.

As this summary shows, some obscurity remains: how can we reconcile salvation history, which according to this exegetical current, makes history sacred, and the secularization which is also acknowledged, which projects sacred events in the secular realm. Without explanation, Dinkler dissociates human history and history directed by God, which are but one for Luke.

i. The same tension appears in the appendix that E. Haenchen (-> 1956) adds to the 1968 edition of his commentary of the Acts. It comes to light in a rejoinder - one of the only that we know of from the pen of the disciples and friends of Bultmann - addressed to those, who to the surprise of the author (p. 670) are the defenders of Luke. In fact, the attack is directed against Wilckens, who we will speak of below. The reaction of the famous commentator can be summarized in three theses of which only the last interests us [**11**]. It is not because Luke is fond of a theological pertinence of history, as Wilckens would like, but rather it is because of the sine die report of the Parousia, and thus the chronological conception of eschatology, that Luke is able to write his double work and insert materials, relative to the history of the church into his work. The massive character of the Lucan presentation of the resurrection of Jesus is not to be confounded with a positive valorization of history. The presence of the Name of the Resurrected One, who is himself absent, which accompanies the manifestation of the Holy Spirit, does not suffice to give time its existential connotation. For history and salvation history, and human interventions and divine actions do not coincide. The death of Jesus belongs to the secular horizon: Luke does not succeed in giving it the soteriological importance it should have.

At the end of this section, we would like to present two monographs on the eschatological texts in Luke, one is by J.-D. Kaestli and the other, Ruthild Geiger. Both of them know the criticisms addressed to the exegetes presented above by Wilckens and Flender and finally, in the majority of the cases, they side with the author of **Die Mitte der Zeit.**

j. J.-D. Kaestli (-> 1969) knows well the bibliography concerning this subject. The first part is exegetical and confirms the de-eschatologization of the Synoptic Tradition which had struck Conzelmann [**12**]. Luke substitutes here a perspective, unconcerned with time, for an apocalyptic hope (we ask what happens to the words "to taste death" then in his explanation of Lk 9:27, as well as, the theme of judgment and the notion of kingdom in Acts?) [**13**]. Moreover, he transfers the "delay" of the Parousia, which the tradition suggested, over onto the life of the individual (Lk 12:57-59, p. 22). Furthermore, he takes the accent which lies on eschatology and places it on ethics (Lk 18:1-8, p. 37). He justifies the delay of the Parousia in the parable of the talents (Lk 19:11-27). These motifs clearly appear in the two major eschatological discourses in Lk 17:20-18:8 and 21:5-36. As can be seen, the exegesis often stays within the path outlined by Conzelmann.

The second part of the study intends to situate Luke's eschatology in the history of early Christianity. In fact, the author rather confronts the line, we would call Bultmannian, with important nuances which distinguish, for example, a Conzelmann from a Käsemann, and the critical positions which have emerged since then, especially from H. W. Bartsch, H. Flender, W. C. Robinson, O. Cullmann and U. Wilckens. At the end of all this arbitration, he decides on the following solution: 1) the schema of salvation history exists indeed; 2) the delay of the Parousia played an important role in its elaboration; 3) but it is not the principle factor; 3) Luke is less original than was said, for

Paul himself defends a salvation history and Mark, before Luke, had already sketched out the life of Jesus and interpolated the mission between Easter and the Parousia; 5) it remains that Luke does not succeed in conferring a positive meaning to the cross, which is a serious lacuna (p. 92); 6) but Luke redeems himself, if we may say so, by conferring a positive sense on de-eschatologized history, which he studies as a scholar (Lk 1:1-4); this optimistic perspective would be acceptable to thetheologian because of the Word and the Spirit, on the one hand, and the ethical responsibility of Christians, on the other. Luke's originality lies in this new historical consciousness (cf. p. 91), which expresses itself in a dialectical unity between the historical event and its kerygmatic significance (p. 90) [14].

k. In her dissertation in Würzburg, Ruthild Geiger (-> 1973) concentrated her attention on the two eschatological discourses in Lk 17 and 21.

The tradition taken over in Lk 17:20-37 comes from the source of the Logia of which it formed the conclusion (the warning with regard to the seductions of false messiahs). Its eschatology is primitive. Furthermore, Luke introduces the notions of faith and humility into literary units which henceforth frame this eschatological chapter.

In the exegesis that follows, the author stops at length on the famous verses 20-21, presenting the principle interpretations. In her opinion, Luke refuses the presages concerning the arrival, whether spatial or temporal, of the Kingdom which regularly occupied Jesus' audience. Concerning the future, Luke prefers to speak of the Son of Man rather than the Kingdom, and he associates the latter with the historical activity of Jesus. The Kingdom and the Son of Man remain related as the content of Christian preaching, but they are still separated by the present moment which is sandwiched between the manifestation of the Kingdom and the Parousia of the Son of Man (the separation is marked in Lk 17:22, by the change in audience). Sudden and inescapable, the future of the Son of Man is however not unknowable, for it is articulated in Jesus' past, marked by suffering (Lk 17:25 is redactional). In an original way, Geiger valorizes the historical abasement of the Son of Man [15].

The explanation of the parables of Noah and Lot (Lk 17:26-30) that Luke transforms into allegories, following a Jewish Hellenistic tradition, leads the author to seek for the Lucan significance of the word "day". In the singular, the term signifies the eschatological event disconnected from history. Vielhauer and Conzelmann had already thought this. On this day of the

Son of Man, rewards and punishments will be distributed to men. In the plural, the days characterize the long present period, the daily life of the community. Our German exegete rejects all qualitative relations between these days and the last day: "Bei Lukas hat die Geschichte keine über sich hinausweisende Kraft, sondern erschöpft sich in der Zeit vor der Vollendung, die dann ein ganz und gar von aussen gesetzter Akt ist." (p. 108). We find here a bit out of place the distinction between history and eschatology which the Bultmannian school believes to have discovered in Luke. Salvation is for tomorrow. Only today can the call to salvation be heard according to the Book of Acts. Different from Vielhauer and Conzelmann, she thinks that Luke, with regard to his sources, emphasizes the importance of this final day. The problem of the delay of the Parousia does not occupy the Evangelist here. In later chapters of his work (12 and 17), Luke has already found a solution by rejecting the "when" and underlining the "that". Framed by redactional passages which should orient the interpretation (Lk 17:2O-21 and 18:1-8), the discourse, taken from Q, becomes a balanced exposition on the end of time and its demands for today **[16]**.

In our opinion, the exegesis of chapter 21 is inferior to that of chapter 17. The author depends even more heavily on Con - zelmann and ignores almost all the non-German literature **[17]**. She also proposes several explanations which are difficult to support. Let us summarize a few of the conclusions: 1) three motifs are at the source of the Lucan rereading of Mark 13: the time of the Church which endures: the evangelization of the nations and the significance of the Temple and Jerusalem; 2) the "days" which will see the destruction of the Temple are historical and not eschatological (as we have seen with regard Lk 17). Later we will find again, the distinction between historical events and eschatological ones (vss. 10-11, p. 170); 3) verses 7-11 attack heretics and not the partisans of the imminent Parousia (p. 169). At this point, the author parts company with Conzelmann. 4) Reaching the final events, with the *σημεῖα* of vs. 11, Luke, as Conzelmann had seen, turns back to his present history, marked by persecutions (vss. 12-19). With regard to verses 12-19, we would like to ask several critical questions: in what way does the meaning of *μαρτύριον* (vs. 13) differ from its use in Mark? Was Luke aware or not of the Marcan saying concerning the evangelization of the pagans (Mk 13:10)? Does the presence of the name of Jesus permit us to deduce that suffering brings one near to the Lord (p. 189)? Who would accept the following explanation to the mysterious vs. 18: "...es liegt hier sicher ein Schluss a minori ad majus vor: wie viel weniger kann dann die Person existentiell gefährdet werden!" (p. 190)? 5) According to Geiger, the "time of the pagans" first of all indicates the period of the Romans' triumph, but also the era of the mission to the Gentiles; this the book of Acts so amply narrates (p. 207). 6) The rough passage from vs. 24 to vs. 25 confirms that Luke is hardly worried about an apocalyptic reading of the world but his concern is rather an eschatological one (p. 216). But what have we gained by saying this? Moreover, does not this idea seem to contradict the thesis of the dissociation of the historical and the eschatological? 7) Finally, we think we have understood the author: the long history of the Church is distinct from the last times. By separating itself from a chronological type of eschatology, the present time has lost all its apocalyptic coloring. However, even with this it does not become a secular period (here again Geiger parts from Conzelmann), because it moves toward the end (this is what the author should call the eschatological understanding of the world, p. 209, 'eschatological' in the qualitative sense introduced by Bultmann). All of this is very complex and should be clarified. We still feel a contradiction between the thesis on p. 108, which refuses any transcendental (eschatological) vector into history, and the one on p. 209, which contrariwise confers an eschatological charge to it. In our opinion, for Luke, the his - tory of the world and the Church (the "and" must be elucidated) are part of salvation history, and salvation history is marked by the promise (of the Scripture, Lk 21:22, and of Jesus) and is fed by the presence of the Spirit and the Word. For all of this, it is not eschatological in the chronological sense, since the purpose of God seems to have programmed a distant Parousia [18].

II. SEVERAL REACTIONS

Before broaching the authors, who have given personal support to the problem of Lucan eschatology in studies, consecrated to this subject, we first would like to point out several reactions of lesser import. They are grouped naturally into four themes.

History

a. O. Cullmann (-> 1965) [**19**] welcomed with approval Conzelmann's work and accepted Luke's ambitious accomplishment. Yet on two decisive points, the professor of Basel deviates from his colleague in Göttingen: 1) Luke is not the inventor of salvation history, Paul, John and even Jesus were its defenders before him. 2) It is not the delay of the Parousia alone which is at the root of Luke's elaboration: Jesus had already preached an intermediary period that Mark and Paul, to cite but two of Luke's inspirers, proclaimed without shame [**20**]. Far from being a betrayal of the kerygma, the Lucan schema is a faithful presentation of the purpose of God; the present, marked by the resurrection of Christ and the outpouring of the Holy Spirit, is already the time of salvation which is not yet come to its fulfillment. Let us mention that between **Christ et le Temps** (Neuchâtel-Paris, 1947, = **Christ and Time**, ET, 1950) and **Le Salut dans l'histoire** (= **Salvation in History**, ET, 1967), Cullmann read G. von Rad's OT theology [**21**] and understood that at the risk of falling into Offenbarungspositivismus, it was necessary, with regard to salvation history, to evoke contingency as well as continuity.

For F. Schütz (-> 1969), the Church lives in the time of persecutions (Lk 21:12-19) which is no longer identified with the end times. By adhering to an argument from **Die Mitte der Zeit**, the author is led to criticize the concept of history of Conzelmann, Käsemann and even Wilckens. These men were wrong to presuppose that history has two levels, the one, human and the other, divine, and they were also wrong to say that, inspite of the crucifixion, salvation history continued. There is but one history, and it is God's, mediated by men: God acts by allowing the rejection of the Messiah. He has foreseen this. Jesus' resurrection would not be a correction along the way; it is rather the pursuance.

Salvation

b. It is the same according to W. C. van Unnik for Luke's global project (-> 1960). For the Dutch exegete, the German exegesis, presented above, insisted too much on salvation history and not enough on salvation. For the moment it is fitting to recall the importance of this theme and its vocabulary.

The concern is to modify the normal interpretation of the book of the Acts: this second volume does not represent the history of the Church (the call to mission, the parenetic effort and the apologetic worry are secondary motives of composition).

The book of Acts, as much as Luke's Gospel, proclaims the kerygma, just as attested in the program of Heb 2:1-4, which is a parallel to the book of the Acts. The saving activity of Jesus is confirmed in the apostolic preaching, as Luke transmitted it in writing. At the center of both, the Gospel and the Acts, there is the conviction that God offers salvation to the world. The one complements the other and they reinforce one another like the two witnesses required by the Mosaic law. The redaction of Acts does not represent a fleeing into secular activity, but rather the fulfillment of an evangelizing mission which the eschatological nature of the present time imposes. Historical research and literary anxiety are but means used to this end [**22**].

I. H. Marshall, in his work (->1970) [**23**], is also centered on Luke's intention concerning salvation. History, which Luke studies by means of his time and the traditions of his Church, is the field where salvation emerges. History and eschatology are on equal footing, as the Christian revelation fits into time.

The Number of Periods

c. As we have seen, Conzelmann distinguishes three periods in salvation history with subdivisions (at least for the last two). The number and nature of the periods have provoked divers reactions. Many have criticized the break at the Ascension: for them, Lk 16:16, the cornerstone of Conzelmann's argument, indicates only two epochs: the time of Promise and that of the accomplishment. Reading the Lucan double work confirms them in their view. More important than the break, there is a unique quality which links Jesus' time with the time of the Church: the Gospel is proclaimed and salvation is present. Luke, in their view, only knows the opposition between the old and the new covenant. The period of the Church differs from an uncomfortable waiting room where we find consolation in contemplating the image of Jesus, who through his works and days, prefigures the kingdom which is slow in coming. Besides Cullmann, van Unnik and Marshall, who draw their criticisms from this reservoir, we can add S. G. Wilson (-> 1969-1970), C. Burchard (-> 1970), J. Kodell (-> 1971) [**24**], G. Lohfink (-> 1971) [**25**], J. Panagopoulos (-> 1972), W. G. Kümmel (-> 1970, both titles) [**26**] and the authors the latter indicates. Generally, it is admitted that the Ascension marks the break, not of the kerygma which continues to ring out, but of the situation of the believers with regard to Christ: being absent, the Christ finds in the person of Holy Spirit, not an Ersatz, as Conzelmann would like, but a substitute (the Spirit is henceforth present in the Church). Also to be recognized is that the history of the Church does not always remain identical to itself. If Conzelmann distinguished the first days of the Church of the Pauline period, C. Burchard (-> 1970) and C. H. Talbert (-> 1974), for example, separate the period evoked in Acts from the contemporary era. For Burchard, the present is not, strictly speaking, a period, given the imminence. Talbert, on the other hand, thinks that Luke considered the contemporary epoch as decadent. This leads him to propose a salvation history in four movements.

The Motifs

d. Conzelmann grants a primary function to the delay of the return of Christ. Divers authors, who accept generally the Lucan schema of salvation history, propose other constitutive factors, which are perhaps more important. In a book which deals with diverse problems of introduction [**27**] and presents the research of several scholars [**28**], C. K. Barrett (-> 1961) thinks that a reading of Acts is difficult because of the double image of the Church which appears: the primitive Church which Luke wants to describe and the Church of his own time, which he sometimes projects into the past. According to Barrett, the Church in Luke's time has to fight against gnosticism. Taken up in this fight, Luke accentuates the historical aspect of revelation and the corporality of the resurrection. This view is similar to G. Klein's (-> 1961), who differs in his procedure. We will describe Klein's view in a later chapter: to avoid the dispersion of revelation and authority, Luke creates the concept of the Twelve, protectors of the tradition, and ravishes Paul from the Gnostics by domesticating him. "That Luke-Acts was written for the express purpose of serving as a defense against Gnosticism" (p. 15) is also the thesis that C. H. Talbert desires to establish in his first work (-> 1966) [**29**]: the notion of authorized witnesses, the correct interpretation of the Scripture, the transmission of the tradition, the public character of the Christian proclamation, the materiality of the events, are thus indications of the polemic that Luke embraces [**30**].

e. Two other authors have proposed another motivation. For G. Braumann (-> 1963, first title), it is the persecution endured by the church, not the delay of the Parousia, which incited Luke to dissociate eschatology from the present time. Eschatology is pushed into the indefinite future of the present time. In the present painful situation, the Church comforts itself by looking into the past (we ask: is it not a meager consolation for those who suffer, to know that they are not the only ones and that John the Baptist and Jesus were martyrs before them?). By refusing to be exalted today, believers will avoid humiliation at the last punishment [**31**]. F. Schütz comes to a similar result (-> 1969). Luke's work contains various indications concerning suffering which posed a painful problem to the faith of the Church, awaiting the imminent triumph of its Lord. Lucan theology would then be the answer to this anxiety. At its heart, the encouraging figure of the suffering Christ.

III. SALVATION HISTORY AND ESCHATOLOGY

We would like to look step by step at the main authors who have addressed the central problem of salvation history in Luke, either independent of H. Conzelmann or in dialogue with him [**32**].

E. Lohse (-> 1954)

a. Contrary to varying critiques, we do not think that E. Lohse interprets Luke independently of Conzelmann's theses. If he could not have referred to **Die Mitte der Zeit** which appeared the same year as his own investigation, he knew of Conzelmann's article, "Zur Lukas Analyse" which appeared in -> 1952 as well as Vielhauer's -> 1950. The polemic had already been launched in the same review in which his article appeared (cf. the articles by G. Harbsmeier and O. Bauernfeind). We can esteem that Lohse opted for a peaceful position in this battle.

His analysis of the prologue (Lk 1:1-4) shows that Luke in introducing the Gospel and the Acts is presenting a literary text as well as an edifying work. With the conscience that explains his method, Luke differs from his predecessors, while having the same goal. His goal is to tell the story of the events that God has accomplished, with organized testimonies in historical narrative. Lohse insists on the three terms, events, God and accomplishment. In doing this, he refers to other revealing passages: Lk 9:51 and Acts 2:1. The two steps in the life of Jesus like the first days of the Church were truly the accomplishment of the plan of God, already announced in the Scriptures. "In diesem Aufriss, nach dem Heilsereignisse über das Leben des irdischen Jesus hinaus sich in der Kirche fortsetzen, hat Lukas eine Theologie der Heilsgeschichte entworfen, die von dem Evangelium des

Markus ebenso charakterisch unterschieden ist wie von der Theologie des Paulus." (pp. 264-265). The difference resides in the concentration on the Christ event, or more precisely on the cross, which is characteristic of Paul and Mark.

The Lucan work is rooted in the OT in two ways. First, the life of Jesus affirms the persevering faithfulness of God with regard to his people Israel, the first addressee of the Gospel. Then, the literary genre of the double work reminds us of the OT historiography, especially Deuteronomy.

This bridge which links the past of salvation history to the present launches a final ark. As the "today" of Deuteronomy brings the Mosaic past and present of Israel together, in similar manner, the historic recollection, which Luke offers, goes beyond the evocation of the past and becomes reality in an interpellation: the present time - here Lohse most vehemently opposes Conzelmann - must not only endure the effects of a past salvation, but receives the nourishing presence of Christ. This is why there are abundant occurances of the title *κύριος* in the Gospel of Luke. That this may happen, the intervention of the apostles is clearly necessary. Luke goes as far as to intentionally project the title into Jesus' life. Faithful to the proclamation, the disciples will also be submitted to the fate of their master. "Wie Christus starb, so enden auch seine Zeugen." (p. 273). As for the simple believers, they are edified by listening to the words of the Lord, as the Parousia ceases to be imminent. They feel that their Christian conviction, born from the hearing of the Word, is confirmed in the reading of the mighty acts of God told by the Evangelist throughout his work.

On the whole, we agree with Lohse's study, particularly with the positive value, he gives to the present period. Yet we would have liked that the notion of *ἀσφάλεια*, which plays such an important role in Bultmann and Klein, was better analyzed **[33]**. Thus, we would have known whether or not the historical presentation threatened the authenticity of faith.

H. J. Cadbury (-> 1956)

b. We found it difficult to understand all of Cadbury's argu - ments. Let us note several impressions of the whole. The author discusses more the theses of C. H. Dodd on realized eschatology than the opinions of the German theologians summarized above, and finally comes to a position close to O. Cullmann's. Cadbury considers Luke was not an original theologian, but rather a believer with firm but simple convictions.

He thinks that Acts was as much an interpretation as an exposition of the prior events and, finally, attempts to situate the Lucan texts in the evolution of early Christianity.

If primitive Christianity, especially Paul, believes in the resur - rection of Jesus, the Parousia and the actual presence of the Spirit, Luke is to be praised for having established a relation be - tween the three. The Spirit is not poured out until after the resurrection (we would say the Ascension, cf. Acts 2:33) and he is associated to the Parousia by the addition of the "last days" of the quotation from Joel (Acts 2:17). A resurrection on the earth implies an ulterior ascension, as the Parousia also demands a departure from the earth.

However, there was not only one conception of the resurrec - tion in early Christianity. Differing from, for example, the Gospel of Peter, Luke places the appearances before the Ascension . These apparitions are spread out over forty days and follow the return to life of the one who had been three days in the tomb. Another characteristic of Luke is the objective, realistic, even massive presentation of the bodily resurrection of Jesus who returns to his physical activities, for instance, eating and drinking. "Luke himself had apparently an orderly mind and a strong belief in objective reality." (p. 303). Different from Talbert, Cadbury does not conclude an antignostic polemic.

It would be wrong to understand the objective information Luke gives concerning the Resurrected One and the Parousia as poetic expressions or projections of the inconscious. It would also be an error to desire to place all the data of the Acts into the eschatological program, for certain uses of the verb ἀνιστάναι and the word ἀνάλημψις cannot be associated, with certainty, to any precise event, such as a resurrection or an ascension.

Even if Luke does not describe the Parousia after reflection and in detail, he perceives it as a historical and real event. It can be supposed that, he is waiting for a spectacular return of the Son of Man with the angels. This will be the time of the reestablishment, the judgment and the resurrection: "As far as the eschatology is concerned it is consistent enough to have been acceptable to the simple mind of the writer." (p. 312). The attention which Luke gives to Jerusalem implies, without a doubt, that just like the resurrection and Pentecost, the Parousia will happen in the holy city. Without resolving the enigma, Cadbury judges that Luke had a precise reason for minimizing the role of Galilee.

Miraculous healings, Jesus' resurrection and the outpouring of the Spirit are an anticipation of the end. But this anticipation is not to be summarized by realized eschatology, for it does not supress the objective reality of the act to come. Acts does not spiritualize hope nor does it emphasize the imminence of the end. The Church's condition in the world led Luke to correct an impatient hope into a persevering waiting.

This admirable book, which was written concerning the cultural environment of the Book of Acts [**34**], attests that Cadbury feels more at home in historical rather than doctrinal discussions and this historical rigor and fear of anachronisms can serve as hedges to the promenades of theologians.

U. Luck (-> 1960)

c. Luck's article represents an intelligent theological reaction to Conzelmann's position. He sets out with one conviction: that contemporary studies centered on salvation history do not yet reach the heart of Lucan thought. They only describe the frame - work.

From the prologue of the Gospel, and more precisely the *λόγοι* (Lk 1:4), Luck thinks that this term designates the kerygmatic schema of the Christological speeches in Acts. This is the same as to say that Luke's objective was to confirm the Christian message.

Contrary to the most widespread interpretation, this confirma - tion is not of a rigourous historical kind, as if the facts could prove the meaning. On the contrary, the Lucan discourse must attest that the facts are not profane, that they fulfil the OT or, at least, the purpose of God.

The Lucan concept of the Spirit is the major argument in favor of this thesis. In his history of the Synoptic tradition [**35**] , Bultmann already noted Luke did not unfold a continuous history, but rather, a series of interventions of the Spirit. In the Lucan texts, the Spirit has a double mission which is practical and hermeneutical: He is the instrument, God uses to act and the sign indicating the supernatural signification of the events.

God acts in history by His Spirit : this central conviction per - mits Luke to resolve the problem of the particularism of revelation. Without the presence of the *πνεῦμα*, the particular history of a Jewish messiah remains obscure for the Gentiles. Scriptural proofs change nothing, for they come from a book whose authority is not universally recognized. Nature and the unknown God, which Luke turns to in Act 17, as arguments can sway but their character is not convincing. Moreover this is seen in Athens, where Paul's presentation provokes laughter not faith.

To convince, to overcome the last obstacle of human resistance, the work of God, Himself by His Spirit is needed: the story of Cornelius shows this especially well.

Scriptural argument like the apostles' witness does not con - vince by its logic or evidence. The agreement between the pro - mises and the life of Jesus is not a mathematical equation, but rather is the explanation of "from faith to faith" given by the Resurrected One. Similarly, the witness of the apostles attests, not to the historicity of the facts, but to the pneumatic activity of God in history. This active presence of the Holy Spirit is not limited to the time of Jesus. Luke can speak about it, for he is living it. It is even what links Luke's time to the time of Christ, much better that an abstract continuity of a salvation history. Thanks to the Spirit, Jesus' time, which belongs to the past, can become present.

We share Luck's sentiment with only one reservation. Taken up by the polemic, this exegete affirms (p.64) that the Spirit, not salvation history, is the exclusive gate to the story of Jesus. Luke would not have written two books if he had been so Pentecostal! Access to Jesus through history is not barricaded. Only the access to the truth of this story is reserved to the Holy Spirit. Moreover, the author realizes this when he says that history and the kerygma go together. Neither history nor the pure call to decision can suffice in themselves.

U. Wilckens (-> 1961) **[36]**

d. This German exegete presents and evaluates the theolo - gical project of Luke **[37]** and from the speeches, he believes he is able to establish its redactional nature. He is convinced that his work confirms several of the ideas of Conzelmann and Haenchen. Widely accepted by contemporary criticism as far as they describe the Lucan realization, these theses are rightly the object of lively controversy as soon as they offer value judgments. Wilckens declares that a simple comparison of the respective doctrines of Paul and Luke, like Vielhauer does, is inadequate. It is necessary to keep in mind the historical situations of both before judging them. We would not go as far as Wilckens, who following W. Pannenberg, says that such a treatment, simply human, is demanded by the essentially historical character of God (p. 195; we will return to this thesis that exaggeratedly links the essence of God to history).

There are four indications which attest Luke's historical dis - placement with respect to Paul: 1) while Paul receives a keryg -

matic and liturgical tradition, which is still homogenous, Luke has to struggle with prolific traditions [38]. 2) Luke assimilates the Synoptic tradition, which Paul, according to Wilckens, does not yet know; 3) Paul's religious situation is completely different from Luke's. Paul fights on two fronts: against Judaism and Gnosticism. While Luke - Wilckens can only describe negatively - is no longer threatened by Judaism and while the Gnostic danger is inexistant; 4) the situation of the Christians in the world has modified: persecution,still local in Paul's time has become general (this is not evident in our opinion).

Wilckens finds a common denominator in these four differences: the space of history which was closed to Paul, has opened up wide to Luke's life and reflection: "das Problem der inzwischen überall wirksam und also aufdringlich sichtbar gewordenen geschichtlichen Zeit des Christentums, das theologische Problem der Kirchengeschichte und damit der Geschichtlichkeit der christlichen Glaubens als solcher." (p. 200).

We follow Wilckens until here. He finds the appeal to the delay of the Parousia, which Conzelmann invokes, too limited and too negative. We appreciate his emphasis on the present time which receives a "heilsgeschichtlich" dignity (p. 201). Yet we consider that this author leaves the exegetical terrain and moves toward a more contestable systematic approach, when he sees history, like Pannenberg, as the horizon enveloping Christian theology. For, to accept the historical and secular character of the manifestation of God - which becomes a past event - Wilckens saves normalcy in a queer manner: he does not invoke the present intervention of the Spirit, as Luck does, but discovers an intrinsic organization made up of announcements and fulfillments in history. In this manner, the relationship between the OT and the time of Jesus is explained, as well as the relation between Christ's period and the contemporary era. To conclude that Luke's merit was that he knew how to elevate these representative structures to the level of a reflective theology, is to make Luke a systematic theologian, which he certainly could not have wanted nor have been. To say that Luke situated Jesus' life in a salvation history is no doubt correct, but to add that he inserted this Heilsgeschichte into a universal history is again an exaggeration. This is to give too much weight to the synchronisms which situate the lives of John the Baptist and Jesus. To go from a theory of universal history to a concept of God who manifests his essence by acting in history, there is but one step that Wilckens does not hesitate to take. To add that God is not immanent in history, since he is not metahistorical, seems to be a restriction which approaches retraction. He is closer to the truth when he declares that God's intervention, in the resurrection of Christ, fits into history, and since it is historical, it has universal importance for Luke by reason of the prophecies.

When he evokes the Name of Jesus and the Word of God as dynamic elements which link the two periods, the author dilutes his wine a bit. History could not be the only necessary mediation for salvation. All the better!

For the author, three deductions emerge from these theses, which are hard to understand and summarize:

1) For Luke, faith is oriented first towards the past of Jesus and not toward the living Christ. This is indicated by the narrative schema of the Christological speeches, especially Act 10:34-43. From the Lucan prologue, we would say that the believer comes to know the life of Jesus when he meets the living Christ.

2) Primitive Christianity does not become a sphere connected to the salvific times of Jesus, that we contemplate, powerless to attain except by imitation (against Käsemann).

3) Luke insisted on Jesus as the bearer of salvation, but he did not know how to explain why Jesus was the savior nor in what salvation consisted. The cross has no redemptive import, which truncates the concepts of justification, the Law and conversion. Therefore Luke is indeed the theologian of glory that Käsemann claims he is. Here, Wilckens, in our opinion, accepts too quickly the ideas of the Bultmannian school [**39**].

W. C. Robinson (-> 1962)

e. The German version of this dissertation from Basel written and published first in English is subtitled "Dialogue with Conzelmann". This shows the influence exerted by **Die Mitte der Zeit** and the trouble the author goes to to make his own way (at the Parousia we will see if it was the Lord's way as well!). The work contains two parts but their relationship is difficult to see. The first and most original is titled "The Composition of the Lucan Material" and the second where the dependence on Conzelmann becomes more evident, "Eschatology in the Gospel of Luke". Always simple in his formulation,Robinson sometimes seems to insist exaggeratedly on the details. This is particularly true in certain criticisms of Conzelmann, where he is decidedly overcritical. This subtility and <u>acribie</u> sometimes leads him into misunderstandings which could be serious: on p. 28f , the reader may have difficulty grasping whether the present period is deprived of salvific character, like Conzelmann, or whether the period of salvation extends into the time of the Church.

The work begins with a double criticism, which is precisely done: 1) contrary to Conzelmann's reports, Luke did not intend to "de-eschatologize" John the Baptist and his message (which were already de-eschatologized in the tradition Luke took up). He simply wants - for polemic reasons - to reduce the prestige of the forerunner. This perspective forbids the exaggeration of the heilsgeschictlich break between John (which Conzelmann placed, as we know, in the old covenant) and Jesus **[40]**.

2) The impressive division of the life of Jesus into three periods, which Conzelmann proposes, is an optical illusion. These breaches are not clear: moreover, Conzelmann does not always situate them in the same place (this is especially true for the third stage). If the baptism and the transfiguration can be considered as the epiphanies inaugurating a new time, we cannot say as much for the entry into Jerusalem. The rejection, which according to Conzelmann regularly follows the divine manifestation, does not clearly appear except at Nazareth and in Samaria, in the first and second parts of the life of Jesus. Whereas Lk 13:32f. may suggest a life of Jesus in four movements, other texts such as Lk 9:51 **[41]** favor only one break within the evangelical history. In any case, Luke's gospel, despite Conzelmann, does not incite one to see a psychological development of Jesus' messianic consciousness.

With these two criticisms, Robinson does not seek to question the notion of salvation history as applied to Luke's work. He attempts to remove what was static and external from Conzelmann's presentation . What is important for Luke - and this is the thesis of the whole work **[42]** - is not the stages which divide (the author thinks he has shown that the exact chronology of the periods is of little import to Luke), but rather the movement of the salvation history, the internal dynamic. After his striving with Conzelmann, to demonstrate this continuity, this progress, Robinson puts all his strength in these pages, which finally come to life. For this, Luke 23:5 is the crucial verse which explains the sequence of the whole gospel. Jesus's entry on stage constitutes the new principal of salvation history, marked until then by the promises. Luke expresses the accomplishment of the purpose of God in its totality as a walk or a way (Act 1:21; cf. Act 1:2; Lk 9:51; 4:13; 13:35; 19:38). The movement, crossing over the thresholds and stages is more important than geography or chronology which dissect. The theme of the way appears in the quotation of Isa 40:3, which Mark transmits to Luke. The author also resorts to the use - to us , in a limited and rather conventional manner - the terms δρόμος, ὁδός, εἴσοδος and the verb πορεύεσθαι. The way is not man's, not even Jesus' but God's. God has come to visit his people (the second part contains a precious study on the Lucan theme, inspired from the LXX, of visitation). The insistant presence of the divine πνεῦμα attests that this way realizes the very plan of God.

In the second section; Robinson admits with Conzelmann, that the coming of the Kingdom - not to be identified with Christianity, against Vielhauer - is postponed indefinitely. He recognizes also that Lk 21 dissociates the fall of Jerusalem from the last events (a dissociation which Mark hasalready operated, against Conzelmann). However, the fall of Jerusalem, following Jesus' rejection by the holy city, is not a secular event (against Conzelmann), but the vindicative visitation of God, announced by the prophets and Jesus himself. Like the present life of the Church, the Jewish war is not eschatalogical but it nonetheless fits into the course of salvation history.

From this presentation, three criticisms come to mind: 1) Where does Luke get his theme of the way? It is not enough to speak of the influence of the LXX. What is this way exactly, a life, a path to follow? The texts, which speak of it, do not seem to make any allusion to the history which <u>God</u> maintains with his people. Furthermore, these passages are too fragile to support Robinson's entire thesis. How does this way of the Lord coincide with the commonplace course of events? Does it suffice to say that history has no meaning (against Conzelmann and Wilckens), but that it <u>receives</u> its signification from God? How are these divine interventions wrought about; by the absurd death of a man or by the miraculous healings of a gifted thaumaturge? Even though the author does not answer these questions, we must admit that he astutely perceives the dynamic movement of the history of Jesus, foreseen and instigated by God, and this Luke avows.

2) What about the present time period? Robinson denies that the Ascension occasions a radical rupture in the time of salvation inaugurated by Jesus. Nevertheless he admits that the life of the Church beginsin less favorable conditions than those of the master: Despite all, the passage from one book to the other, on a formal level, and the departure of Jesus, on a thematic level, indicate a solution of continuity. However,

Robinson does not clearly consider the rift and continuity between Jesus' time and the time of the Church.

3) Is it exact to say that the composition of Luke's gospel was effected from Lk 23:5? When G. von Rad explains the origin of the Pentateuch from Dt 26 [**43**], he can demonstrate the traditional and archaic side of this confession of faith. Robinson does not furnish the same demonstration concerning Lk 23:5 [**44**].

D. P. Fuller (-> 1964) [**45**]

f. This book, another dissertation from Basel, first alignes six chapters consecrated to the interpretation of the resurrection from the seventeenth to the twentieth centuries. It comes to an end with a long last chapter written in the honor of Luke or rather to a certain image of Luke.

Conservative in questions of introduction, the author paints a portrait of Luke with marked traits. The evangelist would have been a man with a square face, simple ideas and strong convic - tions, which he must believe at the risk of spiritual shipwreck because of the hardening of one's heart!

In writing Acts, Luke pursues several objectives of which the main is the account of the diffusion of the gospel among the pagans according to the project of Act 1:8, which, in fact, is only true for the first nineteen chapters. Making the passage of Paul at Ephesus a turning point, Fuller perceives of this trip of the apostle to Jerusalem as the return to mission: it was not to deliver the collection but to tell of his missionary success. This evocation considers - and this is its principle function - the activity of the grace of God.

All of the positive events, such as the conversion of Paul or his free activity at Rome where he is nonetheless prisoner, must be connected to this divine grace which Fuller makes the heart and motor of Lucan thought. The effectiveness of this heavenly favor, expressed in the conversion of several Jews and the vocation of the pagans, must originate in the resurrection of Christ. This is why one thought passes logically to the proof of the other: the success of the mission to the pagans proves the value of the apostolic witness and the reality of the resurrection of Christ proves in turn the generosity of divine love. Thus Luke's participation in the last events (Lk 1:1) and the knowledge of the eyewitness account of the apostles (Lk 1:2) offer Theophilus historical evidence which would confirm his first instruction. This is, for Fuller, the signification of the Lucan prologue.

What remains to be defined is the importance of the facts and the nature of the proofs. Fuller achieves this in the following way: the facts that Luke reports are historical, and because of their historical character, they are evidence which should convince the human intelligence: "Since the mission to the Gentiles cannot be explained apart from the granting of this teaching ministry to Paul by the risen Jesus, and since the Gentile mission is an unquestioned fact of history, Paul's divinely given teaching ministry is therefore historically verifiable. Consequently, Theophilus could not know that the teaching of the apostles and of Paul was from God, for they had been appointed by Christ to have a teaching office and to be witnesses." (p. 226f.).

In the last pages, the writer has to explain why, if the proofs are constraining and the resurrection is an "inescapable" (p. 232) empirical evidence, everyone does not believe. The first answer is: to accept the historical evidence, God's help is necessary (in this way the author thinks to distance himself from Pannenberg). "For Luke, revelation is to be found in history, but history itself is not sufficient to produce faith. Faith comes only when one is the recipient of special grace that turns one from the powers of darkness to light so that he will be willing to own up to the persuasiveness of the historical evidence." (p. 237). He concludes with two levels of history, the first, empirical, and the second, where the causes, coming from God , cease to be immanent (p. 252).

We cannot accept this positivistic conception of history and revelation for Luke has more nuanced a view of salvation and of events. Moreover, his insistence on grace hides another aspect of Luke's thought: the reminder of man's responsibility which has been sometimes taken as a synergetic tendency. Finally, forgetting the importance which the west of the Empire gave to Luke, Paul and the Roman Clement, Fuller bestows an excessive function on Paul's sojourn at Ephesus: the mission to the Gentiles is not terminated in Ephesus, not even symbolically **[46]**.

H. Flender (-> 1965)

g. A systematic mind, Flender rebukes Conzelmann for having applied modern categories, such as salvation history, to the antique thought of Luke. He also reproaches him for having conceived of the Lucan project in a simplistic manner. In reality, according to Flender, Luke did not succumb to the attraction of a positivism of revelation, for dialectic is the principle mark of his gospel: it is found as much on the formal level, where similar attracts opposite, as on the thematic level where the historical and eschatological relay and complete one another.

The title of the work is **Heil und Geschichte in der Theologie des Lukas** and it is divided into three parts. The first part sets out the schemas of Lucan thought as well as their literary expression: the correspondences, the "crescendos" and the antitheses. These literary indications are meant to demonstrate that Luke does not conceive of history as a simple chain of cause and effect. The reality is more complex than that. The "crescendos", for example, signal that on the human level , a divine reality superimposes itself.

The second part concerns preaching as Luke conceives it: centered on a Christology which dialectically considers the historical Jesus and the present Christ. The evangelical message also contains two elements, the one, kerygmatic, is related to the Easter elevation of Christ and the other, apologetic, associated with the history of Jesus. Flender wrongly calls the kerygmatic element of preaching, "heavenly", but is right to underline its existence. The other aspect, which the author, differing from Conzelmann, is pleased to note is the domain of history. Yet Luke has chosen it for a theological reason: divine revelation reaches us in our profane reality. Thus the important remonstrance against Bultmann entitled, "Die Eingehen der Christusbotschaft in die weltlichen Ordnungen." (p. 69-83). The following affirmation can be read: Luke specifies the human side of the eschatological reality (p. 77); and further: the work of Christ is neither conform to the world nor a stranger to it (p. 77). Luke also dialectically associates man's "demondisation" (Bultmann's position) and the sanctification of the world, both of which are effected thanks to the Word.

So the conclusion of the second part is that Luke does not historicize reality in a positivistic manner. The third part establishes that the evangelist does not sacralize the history of the Church in a supernaturalistic way either. Flender begins with the conviction that Luke accepts a spatial concept of time which appears, for example, in Revelation (ch 12). According to this conception, the eschatological fulfillment is not to come, rather it is above: if men have not reached the last days, it is not because the latter are to be awaited, for they are elsewhere, in the heaven. It is understood that this "spacialization" of eschatology confers decisive importance on the ascension of the Resurrected One, who, in this way, reaches his Kingdom. By regrouping the future and the celestial under the term, eschatological, Luke maintains the tension between the present and future of the eschatological reality which he inherited from the apostles' generation. However something has been modified: Luke joins the exaltation to the theological content that Mark and Matthew still associate with the Parousia.

From this, Flender thinks he is able to evaluate the continuing history of the Church and the world. He uses the notion of Israel as the frame of the existence of the Church and the world. The Jews, having rejected the Messiah, become the image of the world condemned by God. Insofar as Judaism transmits the promises, it finds its legitimate continuation in the Church, the true Israel. The continuity is assured, on a historical level, and the discontinuity or novelty, on the eschatological level (Flender tries to show this from the terms *λαός* and *ὁδός*).

Flender is able to conclude his book by affirming that the present period is not a dismal stage of transition (against Conzelmann). For the Holy Spirit is presently active, by reason of his double - not contradictory - character, eschatological and heilsgeschichtlich. The Spirit is echatological as the instrument of God: men, according to Luke, never have free disposition. The author describes the present interventions of the Name of Jesus and the Word of God, in the same manner.

Until now the presentation of this book has held to theological theses. So that the reader might realize the skill of the exegesis, we would like to indicate the meaning given to the crucifixion. With Conzelmann, Flender admits that Luke tends to historicize the Passion narrative and there is indeed, in Luke's work, a reference to the visible and historical level, yet this is only one side of the reality. For the believer, the agony and death of Jesus arouses existential perceptions. This agony and death suggest, if we may say so, a return to a cause, which is not historical, and a descent toward an effect, which is not verifiable. This signifies for faith, that the eschatological character of the cross, which emerges from the conformity to the purpose of God, induces the faithful to bear his own cross.

Our criticisms can be divided twofold: 1) Fender's exegesis is often arbitrary and represents a form of redactional analysis which discovers meaning in the compositions and the whole. His exegesis could have and should have, engaged itself more in a diachronic perspective and distinguished tradition and redaction more clearly.

2) The rebuke addressed against Conzelmann can be turned against Flender. If the modern category of salvation history is not without danger, what can be said of the constant use of the category called dialectic? No doubt, Luke perceives that history which strikes the senses, is not the last word on reality. But does he really perceive the affinity between historical and eschatological, between the visible and the heavenly, dialectically [47]? If Flender does not give the word, dialectic, a Hegelian sense, how does he mean it?

J. Reumann (-> 1968) **[48]**

h. To pass from Flender to Reumann is to pass from an exe - gesis which is engaged in the ways of systematic theology to an exegesis which limits its ambition to a dialogue with history. The American exegete first shows the cultural burden that the term salvation history has carried for the last two centuries [**49**]. Choosing from numerous approaches, he analyzes the background of the term *οἰκονομία* . For the Greek world, *οἰκονομία* meant among other things, the divine administration of the universe (in a cosmic, not historical, perspective). Following the Hebrew Bible, the Septuagint gives no importance to this term. On the other hand, Hellenistic Judaism little by little appropriated the vocabulary of the "economy" to qualify the rule of God over the universe. In this take over, we witness a certain opening up of the cosmic sense toward a historical significance. When Reumann reaches the Pauline corpus, he proposes that we not read the patristic concept of the economy of salvation too quickly [**50**].

Arriving at Luke, Reumann parts company with his project, since the term *οἰκονομία* does not occur in Luke and the nearest vocable, *διάθηκη* is exceptional. This is of little importance for Luke certainly composes his work in a salvation history perspective. The question of the origin of this perspective is thus posed. Reumann jettisons any apocalyptic or gnostic influence on Luke and - because of lack of evidence - refuses to make Jesus the father of salvation history.

Whereas two directions are evident, he will follow one and then the other. The first is the way of Greek, Roman and Jewish historiography: it seems clear that certain historians, like Polybius, Posidonius and Josephus, explained the course of events by destiny or providence [**51**]. It could be that Luke was influenced by this historiographic movement.

Yet Luke does not seem to record events in a divine plan which embraces the whole of history. Reumann hesitates to follow Conzelmann to the end. Hence he prefers to go in the other way: the Jewish liturgy recalls in summary fashion certain important acts of God in the history of his people. Inspired by the thesis of K. Baltzer on the Bundesformular [52], Reumann supposes that the synagogue maintained the custom, on certain solemn occasions, of relating one of the covenants of God which according to the formulary was preceded by a historical reminder. "I think it not unlikely that Luke's most heils - geschichtlich surveys owe something to this background." (p. 112). A difference surely exists: the primitive Church associated the last intervention of God in Jesus Christ with these historical evocations. The beginning of the latter could vary between the creation and the royalty, passing by way of Abraham and Moses. The Christian kerygma was therefore not evoked without reference to its historical precedents.

For a sociological reason, Reumann thinks this Jewish background is more likely than the other: while it is not clear which Christian audience could have been interested in a Christian history written after the canons of the Greek historiography, we understand without difficulty that the first disciples of Jesus readily accepted an account which took up Israel's liturgical tradition. Even if the explicit references to the covenant are rare in the NT, the covenant formulary, which included a historical reminder, an evocation of engagement as well as a declaration of blessings and curses, could very well be the background of several early Christian documents. His prudent conclusion is: "...the possibility that Luke's view of Heilsgeschichte roots in covenantal recital deserves consideration."

This important study suggests several remarks: 1) After a wave favorable to the covenantal formulary, presently - if we are well informed - we are witnessing a resistance to this hypothesis. The research must continue.

2) The recourse to the formulary seems to explain certain Lucan texts which are strongly influenced by the Jewish liturgy (Act 4; 7; 13), whose traditional character is generally recognized. However, it does not take into consideration the global project of Luke.

3) Reumann still does not always keep to the program he has fixed for himself (a diachronical semantic study of the term "economy"): he seeks in historiography what writers offered as a universal principle of history (in this case, they refer more to

destiny or providence than to "economy"); from the Jewish liturgy, he retains a literary structure and not the concept of covenant. The same hesitation is found concerning Luke. Without precisely defining either, Reumann debates sometimes the general intention which organizes the facts into a salvation history and sometimes certain texts or terms of which we do not see the corresponding rapport with the totality of the work.

4) Nonetheless, understood as a study of the possible background of the Lucan work, the two milieus presented surely merit consideration. As for us, we prefer the way marked out at the beginning of the article: a Greek reflective idea desirous to take into consideration the totality of the universe. This idea would then have beentaken over and adapted by Hellenistic Judaism with a religious and historic perspective [**53**].

O. Betz (-> 1968)

i. In his article entitled, "The Kerygma of Luke", Betz also challenges the excess of redactional analysis as well as the theo-logical consequences which are drawn. He prefers to grasp the major themes in Luke-Acts and then look for the background. Luke did not betray the primitive kerygma, for unlike the historians, he did not write a Christian Antiquities, but a gospel. The Lucan presentation of history remains kerygmatic.

To clarify the meaning of Jesus' preaching, as the Evangelist presents it, Betz turns to the fragment from Cave 11 of Qumran, relative to Melchizedek. Three of the characteristics of the messenger of God, which the Hebrew text announces, are to be found in the Gospel: 1) the good news concerning the heavenly defeat of Satan is proclaimed on the earth (cf. the preaching of Jesus in Nazareth, Lk 4:16-30); 2) this proclamation is destined to the entire earth (cf. Luke's universalism); 3) the messenger is anointed of the Holy Spirit (cf. the baptism of Jesus and the allusions to the anointing, Act 10:38, etc.): "The early Christian exegetes must have linked the ministry of Jesus with similar traditions, and it is Luke who points most clearly to them." (p. 136).

Against the Qumran fragment, Luke considers Jesus not only as the messenger of good news but also the agent of the eschatological reign of God. Expulsed from heaven, Satan fell to the earth where he continues to prevail. Jesus does not content himself with announcing the heavenly victory, he tears Satan's victims from him [**54**]. In a similar double activity, the apostles fall into line behind Jesus.

It is necessary to wait for the book of Acts to witness what corresponds in the Christian regime, to the heavenly enthroning of Micheal or the Savior: the exaltation of Christ. Like other scholars before him, Betz indicates the distinguished role that the divine promise made to David (2 Sam 7:12ff.) plays here. It is more the early Christian kerygma, inspired by the Davidic prophecy than the personality of Luke, which explains the relation between the speeches in Acts (for example, Act 2, given by Peter, and Act 13, by Paul).

In his third section, Betz indicates the personal note which Luke gives to the primitive kerygma: the distinction between Easter and the Ascension. This provokes other displacements: 1) pushed back to the end times, the apocatastasis hoards an eschatological character which the Ascension no longer possesses; 2) the title Son of God and the Messianic unction of the Spirit make, if we might say so, an inverted journey: Rom 1:3f. associates them with the resurrection and Luke takes them back to the human origins of Jesus. These signs of Easter become emblems of Christmas. Using Jewish material, especially taken from 2 Sam 7, Luke can respond to the expectation of the Greek world which hoped for the birth of a savior.

Against Vielhauer, Betz concludes that Luke maintained a relationship between the Son of Man and the Kingdom, between the kerygma of the apostles and Jesus' kerygma, because Jesus Christ reveals the Kingdom. Moreover, Luke cannot be reproached for being "frühkatholisch", for the historical framework of his work maintains a non-objective and eschatological connotation. Furthermore, even if Luke did not understand the theology of the cross, he shares with Paul the same conviction concerning the resurrection of Christ. Finally, even if ministry is linked to the Twelve, it preserves a dynamism which prevents its hardening into an indurated institution.

R. H. Smith (->1958 and 1971); **H. Hegermann** (->1964); **F. O. Francis** (->1969) and **A. J. Matill** (->1972)

j. We would like to regroup here the results of several articles which claim not only that Luke maintains an eschatological character of revelation, but also that he was a defender of a near, even imminent, character of the Parousia. Since each study comes to its conclusions in a different manner, it is best to summarize each of them **[55]**.

We know of three articles by R. H. Smith: the first (-> 1958, first title) is a state of the question which places Bultmann's disciples on one side and the partisans of a historical eschatology on the other. Without saying so, the author allows us to establish that before Conzelmann, Bultmann had already spoken of Luke's historicization of revelation (E. Rasco -> 1976 will also note that the author of **Die Mitte der Zeit** is less original than has been said). Curiously, elsewhere, Smith does not make it clear enough that Cullmann is in the second category of exegetes. The second article (-> 1958, second title), often paraphrasing the third gospel, insists on the universal mission of the Church which is not a substitute of eschatology, but a sign of the end. The same is true for the preaching and persecution which accompany mission (p. 891). The delay in the Parousia corresponds to the patience of God (p. 895) and despite all, Luke maintains the imminence (p. 896). In summary, he declares, "he [Luke] sees eschatology unfolding historically." (p. 882). It is Christ's intervention in Luke's person, by the power of grace, that we owe this theological concept (we would like to know how Smith succeeded in delving into the evangelist's heart!). Luke makes the resurrection the cornerstone of his theology of history and eschatology. The third article (-> 1971) investigates the theology of the book of the Acts by starting at the end of the work, Paul's stay in Rome (Act 28: 17-31). Paul's journeys, like this one, have a double function: on the one hand, it is through them that God confers on history a general cohesion and, on the other hand, they make apparent the inner trek of the believer. These two functions manifest the continuity which is established between the Scripture, Jesus and the preaching of the Church. By putting Paul's arrival at Rome and the elevation of Christ in parallel, Luke shows how to resolve the problem of the distance between the two figures. This solution is neither mystical nor institutional; it is totally Christological. It is the risen Christ, who alone assures the continuity. Generally well documented, these three articles set out with a conviction that Luke shares with them (which is that history and eschatology do not exclude one another) but the exegesis is not rigorous enough to move from impressions to certitudes.

H. Hegermann's brief article (->1964) presents three theses: 1) Luke kept the hope in an imminent end alive (the verse concerning the generation that would not pass away, Lk 21:32, cannot be understood otherwise). The expression "the time of the nations" (Lk 21:24) and the quotation of Zechariah 12:3 (LXX), both have an apocalyptic coloring which confirms the parallel in Rev 11:2. Luke integrates the fall of Jerusalem, unrelated to the Parousia, into an apocalyptic schema. This time of the pagans could cease at any moment and the end would come immediately (we do not understand how the author can say that Luke, different from Mark, eliminates all mention to the great tribulation, which would be placed before the last events. Is it not playing with words to say that this trial is integrated into the end times? Lk 21:10-19 does not deal exclusively with the past).

2) His second thesis is that it is necessary to propose another division of the periods of Jesus' life, Israel and the Church, other than Conzelmann's. Thus Luke places a time of rejection before a joyous period of success: this is the way of salvation.

3) The present time is not deprived of the benefits of salvation. It is preaching which saves today from negativity. The fulfillment of the Kingdom is still awaited, but its proclamation already rings out: cf. Lk 17:20f.; 19:11 and 16:16. From this the forgiveness of sins and the gift of the Spirit come forth for today.

Confidently, F. O. Francis (-> 1969) proposes nothing less than a new model for understanding Luke's eschatology. Indeed, he thinks that exegetical verification does not confirm the model of the Bultmannian school. For lack of understanding concerning the exact nature of the new model, we choose to present only a few of his hypotheses. Francis rightly retains the lesson "in the last days" of Act 2:17 (as F. Mussner, ->1961, second title, had already proposed) and deduces from it that Luke considers the outpouring of the Spirit on the early Church eschatological. Act 2:21 indicates that salvation is a proleptic realization of the Parousia of the Lord. Since Jesus Christ, the center of the kerygma, is resurrected, the apostolic message which it concerns can only be eschatological (cf. Act 26:22b-23, 6-8 and 4:2-10). Believers participate in the transcendence within history (a Bultmannian speaking of historicity could accept this formulation but he would doubt the phrase reflects faithfully Luke's orientation). The second and less con-vincing thesis is the following: the sequence of Lk 21:12-26 (the time of the testimony, the fall of Jerusalem and the heavenly signs) constitutes an eschatological meditation on Joel 2. Thus Luke does not dissociate the fall of Jerusalem from the last events. This manner of doing makes the eschatological question even more heated. His third thesis is that Luke maintains the imminency but refuses immediacy! He is conscious of the lively tension which characterizes the Christian life and understands this tension in a temporal (Lk 19:11-27 is to be interpreted from Lk 12) or in a spatial (Lk 10, it seems) manner. By incorporating eschatological materials, Luke hints that the kingdom is near in the ministry of Jesus (Lk 4:16ff.) and the witness of the seventy (Lk 10:1ff.). The success of Luke's theology depends on the synthesis which occurs between the historical narration and eschatological truth. The opposition which the apostles encounter in the Acts attests that the evangelical history does not convince simply by its claimed coherence and positivity. It is obvious that this article offers less than it claims, for several studies before it have claimed the eschatological character of history and this sometimes from the same texts and arguments.

A. J. Matill who has given us an indispensible bibliography on the Acts as well as divers recent articles **[56]**, follows a completely different path to defend the imminency of the Parousia. Rejoining R. F. Weymouth, whom he must have read while writing his doctoral dissertation on the history of the interpretation of Acts, the American exegete invites us, in the name of healthy philology, to give a value of immediate future to the uses of *μέλλειν* which the Acts utilize to signal (Matill would say to date!) the end times: Act 17:31; 24:15,25 (cf. Act 10:42). We were not convinced. If Luke had really wanted to underline the imminency he would have taken the effort to add *ταχύ* or *ταχέως* **[57]**, as the author of the Revelation so wisely did (Rev 22:20). He would not have composed in so a solemn manner Act 1, a chapter which imposes the mission for today and postpones the Parousia until later. Neither would he have edited the framework of the parable of the unjust judge (Lk 18:1-8) nor modified the one of the talents (Lk 19:11-27). Finally he would not have regularly put in the mouths of Jesus' adversaries or the badly formed disciples the question concerning the date of the Parousia (for example, Lk 17: 20). According to the Evangelist, this question should not preoccupy us: the exegetes of our century have hardly followed these instructions!

E. E. Ellis (-> 1969) and **S.G. Wilson** (-> 1969 and -> 1973)

k. After a methodological preamble and a state of the matter, Ellis' article proposes to begin with Lucan anthropology which is monist, like the anthropology of other Biblical books. This excludes the concept of the individual death understood as *ἔσχατον* as well as the Platonic contrast of time and eternity.

Following this, it is proper to introduce Christology, which in Luke occupies the whole of soteriology: cf. Lk 11:20. If the kingdom can be near in the preaching of the disciples (Lk 10:9), this means that the "Twelve" are Jesus' plenipotentiary agents, according to the shaliah principle, and that they are associated to their master in corporative solidarity, dear to Semites. To complete this, it is necessary to add a Christian eschatology in two phases, issued from the Jewish conception of the two aeons. At this point, the essay becomes more difficult and perhaps more clustered. If the activity of the Holy Spirit by Jesus has made salvation present, the judgment and consummation of all things are transferred to the end time. While, by his resurrection, Jesus is off the scene, his disciples have to wait. Their participation in salvation can only take place at present by "being" corporally "with Jesus" (Lk 23:43)or "in God" (Lk 20:36). What could be called the vertical dimension of eschatology is not an announcement of a heavenly accomplishment on earth, but rather the earthly realization of the resurrection of Jesus manifested in heaven. If we have understood correctly, Luke's eschatology has a spatial quality; thus it is attainable or realizable. This does not contradict the corporal character of salvation history, which continues to the end.

When Jesus Christ intervenes in the history of men, it constitutes, at one and the same time, an accomplishment, a deliverance from evil (here the insistence is on continuity) and a novelty (the accent, here, is on discontinuity).

This eschatology may have a polemic function. It dismisses, on the one hand, the "spiritualists" by insisting on the corporal resurrection and, on the other hand, the partisans of a "political messianism", by distinguishing that period from the coming Kingdom. Eschatology must calm the deceptive hopes of an anticipated accomplishment. The last section, which owes much to Cullmann, serves to demonstrate this: the delay of the Parousia is not a "problem" that would have engendered salvation history; rather, from a historical point of view, it is a weapon that Luke uses against those who were too impatiently waiting for the Parousia, and they were numerous in the first century. "Theologically, the delay motif is set in relation to the two-phase eschatology mentioned above. Since the eschatological reality is present, the length of the interval until the consummation takes on no crucial significance" (p. 154 ET of the French version). The Holy Spirit and the Resurrected One make this reality present.

Ellis' position is interesting, but in order for it to be solid, it would be necessary that it be supported in two ways. First, on a conceptual level, is it correct to arrange Luke's anthropology in the "conceptual context" of eschatology? What is a "conceptual context" of eschatology, if not an abstract reality? Yet this is not what the author wants to say. Furthermore, when he affirms that the "identification of the eschatological accomplishment with Jesus provides the explanation which permits one to understand the relation of the present age and the age to come." (p. 150 ET of the French version), he does not tell us which "Jesus" he means, (the historical Jesus or the resurrected Christ). He does not consider that the question might be asked concerning the sort of identification intended,. We could lengthen the list of terms rich in meaning, which go undefined: for example, continuity, newness, presence, anticipation and accomplishment. Finally, since the author desires to avoid Platonism in his theology, he should have stated precisely in what consists exactly this anticipated accomplishment, through the Spirit, in the form of incorporation in the Christ.

Secondly, we must turn to the exegetical level. We did not verify if Ellis' commentary on Luke (**The Gospel of Luke**, London, 1966) answers our questions, but the article, in any case, does not always provide sufficient exegetical argumentation. In particular, Ellis seems to attribute to Luke a Pauline conception of "being in Christ" which is foreign to the Evangelist. He spurns a bit too quickly the texts which favorize an eschatology of the individual type which becomes reality at the death of man.

Pages 59-87 of S. G. Wilson's thesis (cf. Ch 7 -> 1973) are consecrated to Lucan eschatology. They are the content of an article which appeared in **NTS** (-> 1969-1970) [**58**].

The author detects two series of texts and begins with two different eschatological conceptions in the Gospel of Luke. According to the one, the date of the Parousia is postponed (Lk 9:27; 19:11, 41f.; 21:20-24; 22:69; Act 1:6-8); and the problem of the death of believers is resolved by an individual resurrection and a private Parousia (Lk 14:12-14; 16:9, 31; 24:43; Act 7:56). According to the other, Luke maintains, on contrary, the imminence of the second coming (Lk 10:9, 11; 12:38-48; 12:54-13:9; 18:8, where ἐν τάχει signifies "soon" and not "suddenly"; 21:32). Wilson refuses to hand the second conception over to tradition and to reserve the first to the Evangelist. He is also opposed to a later date of composition (before 70 A.D.) which would explain both of the perspectives. He believes to have found the correct explanation in Luke's <u>pastoral</u> concern which protects his sheep from two dangers: the presumption of an apocalyptic fervor of low quality and the discouragement from the delay in the Parousia. From a theological point of view, Luke is less original than has been said. Following a movement already sketched out by Mark, Luke modified Jesus' eschatology to include the mission to the Gentiles in salvation history.

According to Wilson, Acts ignores the imminence and was written much later than the Gospel. In this second work, Luke would have substituted a schematic salvation history and a present activity of the elevated Christ for the imminence.

Wilson's explanation is not very ambitious: It could be partially valid, though the eschatology of Acts contradicts it. For if the theme of imminence has a polemic function against discouragement or spiritualism, it should appear strongly in the Acts, written after the Gospel, at a period even more menaced by these dangers. The explanation, without a doubt, does not consider enough the results of redactional exegesis, which seem to us, to situate the delay in the forefront of Luke's preoccupations. Finally, we wonder if Luke, by this claimed pastoral preoccupation, would not have complicated the problem and confounded the minds of his reader-parishoners (this is at least the opinion of G. Schneider ->1975).

J. Panagopoulos (-> 1972) **[59]**

I. The author of **God and the Church. The Theological Witness of the Acts of the Apostles** (-> 1969 written in Greek), the Orthodox J. Panagopoulos, knows German Protestant exegesis well. He condensed his ideas in an important article (-> 1972), which dialogues mainly with Käsemann. The writer analyzes successively the beginning of Acts, the Christological discourses, the historical scenes and the summaries. Different from many exegetes, he places God Himself at the center of Lucan theology. He accepts the term salvation history and even theology of glory, but, as we will see, he redefines these terms.

In what he calls the prooemium of Acts, which is in fact chapter 1, a theocratic program is presented. The time of the Church is a history, determined and realized by God, who fulfills Israel's past (continuity) and participates in the last "nouveauté". As others, Panagopoulos does not think that history and eschatology are incompatible.

The narrative of Pentecost, especially the theological dating of Act 2:1, which takes over Lk 9:51, confirms and completes this interpretation: the gift of the Spirit which is both fulfillment of the prophecy of Joel and irruption of the new reality, is an eschatological event. This Spirit incites the Church's own prophecy and the contemporary σημεῖα. This eschatological reality will conclude the Parousia (this is the meaning Luke gives to the Joel citation). The future Parousia neither takes the eschatological radicality away from Christian existence nor transforms it into a "worldly" conformity. The time of Jesus and the time of the Church have a clear relationship: they are related to the eschatological salvation already inaugurated. Here we can sense the Orthodox heritage in Panagopoulos' conception of the Church which is the place of actualization of the Christ's presence and the eschatological reality.

Against U. Wilckens (-> 1961), Panagopoulos considers the Christological schema of the speeches (Act 2; 3; 4 and 10) as anterior to Luke and he does not think they offer profit toward the Evangelist's theology [**60**]. What matters, is the orientation that Luke gives to each speech (Act 2:36; 3:13; 10:36 are considered as redactional touches) [**61**]: the manifestation of the glory of Jesus in the present activity of the Church. If Luke shares with the early Church the conviction that God directs history, he confers a particular note to this salvation history by insisting on the actual manifestation of this *δόξα* of the Resurrected One.

The speeches in Act 7 and 13 allow us to understand how Luke perceives the economy of salvation, and so salvation history: on the one hand, there is the history of Israel, made up of the promises which God will make good on later and the engagements that the people have not respected. On the other hand, there is the time of the fulfillment of salvation in Jesus Christ and in the Church. The Church must not be content to remember the historical Jesus. She can rejoice in the presence of the Risen One, who is not the middle of time but the end of history, a history of salvation which counts but two stages.

The narratives confirm this ever active presence of the Risen One, who forbids us to speak of a diminution of the intensity of eschatology (of an eschatology defined quite differently from Käsemann).

Panagopoulos continues by maintaining that the Spirit, which he had noted has an eschatological character, does not become the property of believers or institution. We would be wrong to speak of this as Frühkatholizismus. The article ends with a presentation of the eschatological character of the Church and the believer. In short, everything remains eschatological and the message of the Acts shines with an eschatology close to Jesus' as it is primitive.

Four remarks are in order concerning this article that often expresses some legitimate theses in a somewhat grandiloquent style: 1) if he is right to insist on the role of God in history, strangely overlooked in numerous works, it is our opinion that Panagopoulos exaggerates the importance of the present epi - phanies of the glory of Christ. For us, Luke senses the absence of the Resurrected One as much as his presence, which moreover remains always mediatized [62].

2) Even if he claims that the Church is not an institution of salvation, the Greek exegete nonetheless perceives the Lucan Church as a nourishing mother who generously dispenses her eschatological benefits. He goes as far as to say the Church thus becomes a sort of continuation of Christ: "Die Kirche ist als die Zeit der eschatologischen Erfüllung schlechthin verstanden." (p. 158, the underling is ours).

3) Since the Church is historical, he logically concludes that Luke sees a soteriological factor in history (p. 157). We can admit that salvation occurs in history, but this seems to be a modern perspective, foreign to Luke. The secular character of the events, that Luke is also pleased to note, are totally eclipsed.

4) Finally, we wonder, if it is still legitimate to call eschato - logical, what was formerly called transcendent or supernatural and which is not organically related to a temporal end.

K. Löning (-> 1969), **J. Zmijewski** (-> 1972) and **G. Schneider** (-> 1975)

m. "Lukas-Theologe der von Gott geführten Heilsgeschichte" is the title of Löning's brief but precious contribution. He doubts that Luke was a disciple of Paul and formulates the literary intention of the double work in the following manner: the evangelist longs to provide a reliable presentation of the known events. This presentation contains kerygmatic texts (the Gospel and the speeches in Acts) and narrative texts (in the Acts but also in the Gospel). As the latter are of a historical character and known to the readers, Luke does not seek to make them known but to make them understood. Thus the Lucan presentation holds a median position between proclamation and information. Because argumentation plays a role, we have to speak of an apologetic work. The death of Jesus is at stake in the debate with the Jews. The resurrection, the triumph of God, shows the Jews that the death of Jesus does not prove his non-messianity.

The Passion and the whole life of Jesus thus receives a soteriological character. The historical narration, for apologetic reasons, corresponds to a heilsgeschichtlich understanding of revelation. This is Löning's original thesis which explains salva - tion history not from the delay in the Parousia but from apolo - getics.

Löning devotes a second paragraph to Luke's disposition of his material. The arrangement of the related Samaria traditions (Acts 8: 5-25: one relative to Philip and the other, to Peter), for example, are explained by the following redactional reasons: 1) the mission is not repeated in the same place; 2) it developes from place to place; 3) from Jerusalem; 4) once the cities are evangelized, it is the country's turn to receive the visit of the preachers; 5) the mission is not the fruit of chance, but of the work of the ministers designated for this reason.

The notion of "way", taken over from W. C. Robinson, permits the author to explain in a third section the composition of the Gospel and the Acts. The indications of time and place attest to the dynamic character of this way, which successively crosses over two domains, the land of the Jews and then the oikoumené.

The fourth point which deals with the theology of the way, seems to us to be neither very original nor very clear. According to Löning, God wants to go right to the point and accomplishes his plan without men and women being able to oppose it effectively. This realization, in the form of the "way", is a fulfill - ment of the prophecies.

The preaching of Jesus of Nazareth, greatly reworked by Luke, contains all the themes that Luke will later develope. This fifth part can be summarized in the following manner: at Nazareth, the promise is fulfilled and the time of salvation arrives in the form of proclamation which is for all people; but Israel cuts itself off voluntary, which permits God to open it up to the Gen - tiles.

Sixthly, Löning presents the passage from Jesus to the Church, which in the first phase of its history, claims Israel's heri - tage. Jerusalem and its Temple mark this continuity. This heritage is not irremovable for what matters, more than the tie with Israel, is the relationship with Jesus and thus the apostles' role as witnesses. Since Luke is not very interested in the future of the Church, he does not elaborate a doctrine of apostolic succession.,

Finally, the author shows that the concept of the "way" issues forth with a call for individual responsibility. Invited to faithfulness, believers are guided by the ministers, installed for this reason (Acts 14: 23).

As can be seen, the most interesting part of Löning's contribution concerns the theological import of the historical narrative. We have a few reserves concerning the rejection of Israel which would be too long to enumerate. Finally, it seems that the OT is summarized in a promise. We think it erroneous not to insert the time of Israel into the unfolding of salvation history. The reader is surprised that Löning, like Conzelmann, pays so little attention to the infancy narratives (Lk 1-2). This negligence is detrimental to the study of Christology.

n. The work of J. Zmijewski on Lk 17 and 21 [**63**], a dissertation from the Catholic Faculty of Bonn, would have been better had it been half as long (it has 591 pages!), as repetitions and redundancies abound. The first part (pp. 43-325) explains Lk 21:5-36. After having placed this eschatological speech in its context (at the conclusion and height of Jesus' instructions to the people), the author enumerates more than analyzes certain formal indications (indications of time and place; parenetic and directive elements). He thinks that Luke did not benefit from any sources other than Mark and proposes a conventional division of the text into eight parts (Lk 21: 5-7; 8-11; 12-19; 20-24; 25-28; 29-31; 32-33; 34-36). At the end of this introductory section, he discovers a <u>continuous</u> description of the final phase of salvation history in this discourse (against Conzelmann).

It would be fastidious to summarize the elaborate exegesis of all the verses. Let us simply note the author's manner of working and several interpretations. Different from Mark, the double question in Lk 21:7 is aimed at the end of time. Verses 8-11 indicate that during the Jewish War, the Christian community was submitted to both external and internal dangers. The following explanation is characteristic of an exegete who, in our view, requires too much of the text; these verses indicate that the decisive moment arrives when preaching rings out and through it, Christ draws near.

Verses 12-19 manifest three Lucan tendencies: to adapt the teaching to the reality of the Roman Empire, to establish correspondences with the Acts (especially the martyrdom of Stephen) and to correct the Marcan doctrine of history. On pages 157-161, we find an excursus on the Lucan notion of the "name". Luke sets out the idea of "perseverance" not because of deferment of the Parousia (Conzelmann) but because of the engagements accepted by believers. For us, two affirmations seem to be arbitrary: 1) it is said that the persecutions are eschatological, because Jesus exercises the function of eschatological judge during this time; 2) here the Lucan Christ is concerned about the unfolding of salvation history (we would rather say, he is preoccupied rather by the diffusion of the Word).

The center of the speech is verses 20-24. Luke certainly de - taches the fall of Jerusalem from the last events but it is a chronological separation. From the content point of view, he reinforces the links between this historical event and the end times. Henceforth - and this is the main thesis of the book - this catastrophe is just as eschatological as historical and heils - geschichtlich. It correponds to the plan of God, fulfills Scriptural prophecy and fulfills one of Jesus' prediction. From the angle of Heilsgeschichte, Jerusalem is not exclusively a positive place as it is also the theater of the punishment of Jesus' adversaries. In the "time of the Pagans" which begins with this Jewish drama, Zmijewski foresees both the conversion of the Gentiles and the power of Rome. The writer succumbs to allegory when he adds that Christianity, detached from Judaism, becomes the esta - blished religion "in the villages" (p. 21). He takes up again (p.222) the habitual and contestable interpretation of the har - dening of Israel which provokes the call of the Gentiles and brings to fulfillment the universal and salvific plan of God. (How much has been written concerning the little καί joining verses 24 and 25!) Rightly, Zmijewski refuses to see a clear break be - tween the historical events and the eschatological future (Con - zelmann) but he goes to the other extreme by saying that the be - ginning of vs. 25 establishes a sachlich or thematic link between the Parousia and the fall of Jerusalem. In vss. 25-28, relative to the Parousia, Luke makes the apocalyptic color pale. The signs are no longer the forerunners, but represent the negative side of the coming of the Son of Man. Zmijewski does not accept Con - zelmann's interpretation that the proximity of the Kingdom will not appear until the end of time. Because of the "already" and the "not yet", there is henceforth, a sachlich link between history and the end times. Therefore, because of the eschatological character of history - here again we find the central thesis - there are now signs of the end that believers are invited to discern. To claim as the writer does, that vs.32 signifies that there will be men until the end of the world, seems to sidestep the meaning of the words. Verses 34-36 are clearly redactional and Conzel-mann is right to say that they encourage believers to persevere, during the time which is prolonged, while preparing for a sudden Parousia. To this negative ethical foundation, the exegete adds exegete adds another positive side: the faithful engage themselves to live with dignity, for their present is eschatological in its own manner.

The second part (pp. 326-540) explains the eschatological discourses which Jesus spoke to his disciples after a brief dia logue with the Pharisees (Lk 17: 20-37). In the Evangelist's vision, there are not two speeches but one in two parts. To a degree of variable verisimilitude, vss. 20b, 23f., 26f., 28-30, 33, 34f. and 37b are traditional, while vss. 20f., 22, 25, 32 and 37a must be redactional. Zmijewski divides the text into six units: Lk 17: 20-21; 22-25; 26-30; 31-33; 34-35 and 37.

We would retain what the author says about the famous verses 20-21. Luke adapts a traditional saying of Jesus: "The Kingdom of God is not coming visibly, but the Kingdom is among you." He introduces the Pharisees, who frequently, are observers with an interest in the Kingdom and its coming. By multiplying their efforts and asking for signs, these hearers do not understand the Kingdom as already present, hidden, of course, but accessible to faith. The eschatology in these two verses - like in the two speeches - is characterized in a fourfold manner: 1) it is <u>God's</u> affair; 2) it is tied to the person of <u>Jesus</u>; 3) the hidden presence of the Kingdom is maintained in a <u>heilsgeschichlich</u> manner in the Church; 4) the <u>human being</u> has the responsibility, not to observe but to believe. It seems to us that point 3 is badly established in the text and is full of doctrinal prejudice.

In the following verses (22-25), Luke distinguishes "the days" of the Son of Man from "the day". The days represent the period which goes from the Ascension to the Parousia. The day desig - nates the precise moment of the return of Christ.

If the parable of Noah (vss. 26-27) describes the present situation (from the Ascension to the Parousia), the parable of Lot (vss. 28-30) illustrates the day of the second coming. Logically, the first exhorts to faith, while the other contains a promise.

In his explanation of the last verses (vss. 31-36), the writer insists on the anthropological character of eschatology: at pre - sent, believers live the humiliation of Christ. They will participate in his elevation when he comes. We feel however that the theme, dear to the author, of Christ suffering <u>in</u> his Church, (for example, just as we can be hurt in our arms or legs) is exceptional in Luke. The only place, we have met it is in the Christ's answer to Saul on the ground: "I am Jesus, whom you persecute." (Acts 9:5).

The last section of the book compares the two speeches. The relation is evident: they have the same genre of rereading of the traditions, the same vocabulary and same center of interests. However, we must note several differences. The audience changes from one discourse to the other. Furthermore, Lk 17 depends on different sources, principally Q, while Lk 21 takes up Mk 13. Finally, it can be noted that the orientations, if not different, are, at least, complementary. The persecutions, the fate of Jerusalem and the mission to the pagans characterize Lk 21, whereas, the polemic against the Pharisees, the hidden presence of the Kingdom, the distinction between the days and the day of the Son of Man, the allusion to Jesus' suffering, the ideal of poverty, the night, the last judgment and the overturning of values are only found in Lk 17. "In Lk 21 kommt das eschatologische Thema mehr unter dem allgemeinheils - geschichtlichen Aspekt zur Sprache, in Lk 17 dagegen mehr unter dem besonderen Aspekt der Gemeinde bzw Jüngershaft." (p. 556).

These two speeches complete one another to present a rich eschatological teaching: centered on God, this doctrine makes manifest the accomplishment of the divine plan in the person of Christ, who belongs to the past, by his earthly history, and to the present, by his exaltation. This Christ confers on the history of the world and the Church, a perspective, both heilsgeschichtlich and eschatological. It is obvious that Zmijewski developes the theses of Löning, whom he cites on several occasions. One thing is peculiar to him, the link between eschatology and ethics indicated above.

By way of a conclusion, the author affirms there is neither contradiction nor rupture between the eschatological con - ceptions of Jesus, Paul, John and Luke. They are in harmony and complete one another (pp. 565-572).

Besides the criticisms developed along the way, we would like to end by indicating our agreement on one point and our disagreement on another. We rejoin the positive appreciation of present time and the basis of perseverence which follows. Our criticism concerns the very term, eschatology, which designates, like for Panagopoulos, all actual relations with God and all present interventions of God among men. At the same time, the writer maintains the chronological meaning of the term which thus defines any ultimate intervention of God. Moreover, if we have understood well, Zmijewski gives the adjectives "present" and "actual" a different meaning than Bultmann: eschatology does not fulfil itself in historicity but in history. How?

We are not told. In which portion of history? No more precision is given: the fall of Jerusalem? certainly, but what about the other wars? In the early Church? but how far can the gene - ralizations go (contemporary churches, sects, etc.)? To what should the eschatological impact be confined, to the Eucharist, to preaching, to practical accomplishments? Is there still a distinction between eschatological history and plain history? These are the questions which this book, despite its volume, does not answer.

o. At the beginning of the next volume, G. Schneider (-> 1975) refuses to insert Lucan eschatology into the evolution of primitive Christianity (p. 5). In our opinion, this renunciation is explained by the difficulty that is confronted presently in grasping the development of the first Christian doctrines. It is non the less regrettable, for Luke continues to float on the surface of history without obtaining a suitable anchor. The author prefers to concentrate his attention on the Lucan nature of the texts relative to the Parousia.

A suggestive introduction (pp. 9-19) sketches the present discussions concerning Lucan eschatology.

His first chapter (pp. 20-54) presents a rereading of the parables, Luke receives from the Logia source (Lk 12:39f.; 41-46; 35-38; 19:12-27; 17:26-30). Schneider attempts to illuminate the history of tradition of each text and the successive redactions. It seems the Logia source had already perceived the delay of the Parousia but maintained the imminent character . The exegesis of the parable of the steward (Lk 12:41-46) reaches results characteristic of the whole work: clearly redactional, Peter's initial question in vs. 41 and the adjective "wise" placed together with the "steward" reveal Luke's attention for the leaders of the community. This declaration is confirmed by the addition of two isolated sayings, related to the same subject, to vss. 47 and 48. Thus Luke gives an ecclesiastical slant to the texts dealing with the Parousia: in his hand, they become exhortations directed to the leaders of the community. We have noted that explanations of this type are often found among Catholic exegetes [**64**].

Further, Schneider continues that Luke does not seem to provide a new explanation to the delay of the Parousia. He inscribes his interpretation in the perspective which he inherits. Luke tells us in this parable that the Church must be conscience of the delay. This is why the servant, who understands the delay of his master (vs. 45), is not declared "bad". For the hope of an imminent return, Luke substitutes a vibrant call to be always ready.

The parable of the vigilant servants (Lk 12:35-38) confirms the interest that Luke has in the faithful work of the ministers in the Church (we are not so sure that Luke desires here to shift the spotlight from believers to their spiritual leaders). Moreover, this pericope strongly attests Luke's consciousness concerning the delay. A third Lucan characteristic appears: a tendency toward allegory, which manifests itself in the addition of the verb "to wait" to vss. 35 and 36. Verse 37b, which describes the banquet of the Kingdom, in terms which are hardly veiled, confirms this taste for allegorical constructions. Luke demonstrates a preference for a second sense in his interpretation of the parable of the talents (Lk 19:12-27). The first two verses, which describe the man of noble birth who goes abroad, undoubtedly hint at the exaltation of Christ. With this evocation, the parable indicates a fourth characteristic of Luke's redactional work; unhappy to vigourously push back all impatient expectation, the Evangelist offers, contrary to Matthew, a solid Christological foundation to the delay of the Parousia [65].

The second chapter (pp.55-70) broaches the eschatological material, taken over from Mark. These pages seem less original to us as the author relies heavily on Conzelmann. Lk 21 takes Mk 13 over (here the use of a second source is excluded). According to Mark, the parable of the fig tree, already related to the apocalyptic speech, considers the fall of Jerusalem as a sign of the end. For Luke, who establishes a relation between the Parousia and redemption (Lk 21:28), the parable (Lk 21:29-31) constitutes a promise: it will be before summer and its blessings when the Son of Man comes. In other words, the Kingdom will be near. The Evangelist perhaps rediscovers the initial sense which the parable had in Jesus' mouth. Other prophecies must still come to pass before the end (the death and resurrection of Jesus, the fall of Jerusalem, and the universal mission), but these fulfillments, announced in the Scriptures and by Jesus, will be historical not eschatological.

The absence in Luke of certain Marcan texts (Mk 1:15; 13:10 and 32) and the modifications of certain passages of the second Gospel (Lk 9:27; 19:28-40 and 22:69) do not allow us to declare that Luke sought to maintain the imminence of the Parousia.

The third and last chapter analyzes what is particular to Luke. Before Luke took it over, the parable of the unjust judge (18:1-8) proclaimed the certainty of the answer inspite of the troublesome impression of the long entreaties which remained unanswered. On the traditional level, the adjunction of vss. 7b-8a guarded the imminent character of the Parousia [66]. By concluding with a new formula (8b), Luke changes the perspective into a paranetic sense, already perceptible in the redactional introduction of the parable (vs. 1) [**67**]. The Evangelist formulates this exhortation, which is a criticism at the same time, because his community is not perseverant enough in prayer.

The study of what is particular to Luke illuminates a last mark of Lucan eschatology: a certain individualization of the expecta - tion and hope. Different texts (Lk 12:16-21, 33f.; 16:1-9; 6:20-26; 23:43 and 21:19; 16:25) give to understand that the moment of death is for man an eschatological event. Luke can thus carry over certain ideas that tradition had reserved for the Parousia onto the afterlife of the individual. This is clearly the case with the phrase "by your perseverance, you will gain your souls" (21:19) and the answer of the good thief (23:42). From this declaration, three remarks emerge: 1) if Luke individualized eschatology, we understand how he can say, without contradicting his conception of the delay, the kingdom is near to the believers (10:9, 11).

2) Luke avoids calling this place of the afterdeath the king - dom: he uses the word "paradise" (23:43) or "Abraham's bosom" (16:22).

3) Inspite of all, Luke is not thinking of an intermediate state. The book ends with an appendix reserved to the eschatology of the book of the Acts. Schneider takes up again the theories of Conzelmann and Vielhauer concerning the delay of universal eschatology as well as Barrett's concerning an individual version.

Schneider's work, by the nature of things, remains conjectural. Certain reconstructions of the relation between tradition and redaction will not convince. Neither could this study be original in each section. The weight of the heritage of Conzelmann is felt; Schneider refuses to accept that Luke maintains the assurance of the imminence beside the delay (against Kümmel and S. G. Wilson). To this must be added the influence of Dupont concerning individual eschatology (later we will present the Belgian exegete's position). Finally, Schneider has the merit of not abusing the term eschatology: it seems, he does not use it for the present time of the Church which he, nonetheless, does not reject into the profane sphere. We regret that he did not attempt to build a bridge between universal and individual eschatology. It is not enough to say that the spatial concept of the abode of the dead completes the temporal concept of the Kingdom (p. 83f.). It is neccesary to define this complementarity. Did Luke really sense the problem? Must we await death to see more clearly? Finally Schneider's position seems to float on one point: concerning Lk 12:39f. and 42-46, he says that Luke takes up partially the perspective of Q (suddenness does not exclude imminence); but he quickly adds that Luke resolutely refuses all traces of the imminence to the profit of the delay. Is not this contradictory?

J. Dupont (-> 1972)

p. Modestly, Dupont points out several authors who, opening up the way for him, have evoked the Lucan distinctness with regard to individual eschatology [**68**]. In his first edition of his **Béatitudes** (1954), he himself had already drawn attention to this point [**69**]. But the research of the last years, which has concentrated on the delay of the Parousia, eclipsed this statement. A new study became necessary.

By individual eschatology, Dupont means the destiny of the individual not only in the end times but also at the end of life. If Luke gives particular attention to these two decisive moments, the latter is going to be the dominating topic of this study.

His first section treats several texts from Lk 12. The parable of the foolish rich man (12:16-20) finds its meaning modified in the passage from tradition to redaction. In Luke's perspective, "the folly of the rich man is not so much in not having thought about death but rather having forgotten what comes after death." (p. 5). The difficult vs. 21 ("so is the man who stores things for himself and is not rich toward God") is a creation of Luke. It does not accord with the parable at all. Lk 12:33 allows us to uncover the meaning of the difficult words *καὶ μὴ εἰς θεὸν πλουτῶν*: this verse, which freely adapts the saying of Jesus about heavenly treasure (cf. Mt 6:19-21), indicates the way to constitute this treasure is by distributing one's possessions to the poor. It is precisely for not having followed this prescription that the rich man of the parable is punished. The decisive moment here, according to Luke, is not at the Parousia but at the individual's death. Beyond this parable, this perspective commands all the development from vss. 13-34.

At a traditional level, Lk 12:32 ("Do not be afraid, little flock, because it is pleasing to your father to give you the kingdom") promises Jesus' hearers that they will benefit from the Kingdom when it arrives. It could be that on the redactional level, the promise is valid for the death of the believers. In the same way, Luke has perhaps modified the traditional declaration which we read in the Acts: "it is [by passing] through tribulations that we enter the Kingdom of God" (Act 14:22). According to Lk 24:26, did not Jesus, himself, enter glory through necessary suffering? To receive the heritage among the sanctified (Act 20:32) could designate the entrance into the Kingdom at death, like the analoguous expres-sion in Act 26:18 could mean integration into the Church. Dupont concludes this section by returning to Lk 12. Comparing Lk 12:4f. with its parallel in Mt 10:28, he thinks that Luke wanted to avoid the expression "to kill the soul" and that he spontaneously places his attention on what happens after death. The reality of Gehenna becomes tangible to the guilty one at death and not only at the last judgment.

Lk 16, to which the second section of the article is consecrated, begins with the parable of the shrewd manager. Dupont concentrates first on the difficult vs. 9 ("Make friends using your dishonest wealth so that when it is gone, they will receive you into the eternel dwellings."). "The best use that one can make of money is therefore to make friends for the future life." (p. 13). This conclusion takes up again the affirmation found in Lk 12:33. The moment money fails is the individual's death, as the antithetical parallel of the foolish rich man (Lk 12:20f.) indicates. The mention of the "eternel dwellings" which describes not a temporal reality but a spatial one, is not contrary to this interpretation.

The parable of the wicked rich man and the poor Lazarus (Lk 16:19-31) serves as the counterpart to the one concerning the clever manager. After having spoken of the right use of money, Luke's Jesus presents what can be the bad use. God does not wait for the Parousia to inverse the destinies of Lazarus and the rich man. It is clear that it is the death of each one which marks the turning point. Dupont approaches the contrast of the beatitudes which Luke accentuates with the opposition of the "now" and the future, in saying, "it is difficult to escape the conclusion that the "afterward", to which this νῦν is opposed, is that of the time which, for every one, will follow the present existence." (p. 17). At the end of this section, Dupont wonders if Lk 21:19 does not testify to the same passage from cosmic to individual eschatology.

Finally, in the third section, Dupont questions Jesus' answer to the good thief (Lk 23:43). The reproaches of the onlookers of the crucifixion (Lk 23:35, 37) attest that Luke associates the power to save with Jesus' messiahship. Answering the bandit, Jesus does not speak of the coming of the Kingdom which the latter mentioned, but rather of Paradise: Dupont refuses to make an appeal to the Jewish conceptions concerning the temporary dwelling place of the righteous. He prefers to say that Luke is correcting a hope as yet still imperfect: it is "today" that everything is at stake and can be won. The unfortunate counterpart of the good thief, Judah goes toward his dwelling place (Act 1:25), which is, no doubt, Gehenna. He also must surely go there without waiting for the Parousia.

By way of a conclusion, Dupont reminds us of Luke's interest for the afterlife and notes that Luke did not establish a rapport between the two eschatological forms which are found in his writing. He supposes that Luke's individual eschatology is rooted in the Jewish apocalyptic (cf. principally the Book of Enoch). With consideration for his Greek formation, Luke corrects this heritage by refusing to bind together the individual's fate and the events of the end times.

It is hard for us to accept that Luke did not reflect on this rap - port. The evangelist certainly affirms the delay of the Parousia, but to our knowledge, he never explicitly pushes this event beyond his own generation. It is possible that he reserves individual eschatology for those who die during the interim period.

A second question arises concerning Lk 23:43. How can Luke's Jesus promise the thief a place with him today since he would be risen only on the third day and exalted forty days later? This is a question if we identify paradise with the kingdom. Yet if we separate them, how can we distinguish and identify each of them? Both the naive and learned reader remain in a quandry.

C. H. Talbert (-> 1966, -> 1970, -> 1974)

q. Talbert follows his own way despite the criticisms en-countered. In 1966, he wrote a book, mentioned above [**70**|, in which he refuses the omnipresence of the delay of the Parousia in the Lucan corpus. Conzelmann's declarations with regard to the redactional preoccupations of Luke and accentuations are to be explained, not by the motif of eschatology in transformation, but rather by reason of a polemic and apologetic motif. Luke wants to hinder his Church from succumbing to Gnosticism.

This idea of the anti-Gnostic front which the author shares with Klein (who curiously goes unmentioned) has been serious-ly shaken by several exegetes, especially W. C. van Unnik [**71**]. The latter thinks that Luke writes in a relatively calm ecclesiastic climate. We are not far from thinking he is correct.

In an ulterior article (-> 1970), the author takes up again the study of the Lucan eschatological texts and comes to the same conclusions. The Lucan adaptation of the eschatological traditions does not respond to the delay of the Parousia. The schema of salvation history is not an accommodation to the delay of the second coming of Christ. It rather expresses a polemic conviction which rejects a false interpretation of the primitive Christian hope: one which claims an actual realization of the Kingdom and the resurrection in a spiritual form. "Luke's history of salvation scheme is an expression of the Evangelist's eschatological reservation." (p. 196). Luke takes his place among the antiheretical Christian writers. The eschatological distortion, fought by Luke, is frequently found in Christian antiheretical literature. It corresponds generally to Gnosticism.

That Luke follows up the Gospel with the Acts of the Apostles and that he understood the gospel as a life of Jesus are Conzelmann's exact statements. Yet they are not explained by the delay of the Parousia, but rather, by Luke's literary intention. The book of 1974, toward which we turn now, developes this last section of the article.

This study opens with a perspective which claims to be new. Luke, the theologian, is also an artist, as the style variation and the binary architecture of the work and its sections witness. Talbert proposes to take into account the structural elements of the whole composition and possible parallels taken from contemporary literature.

The first chapters skillfully analyze one and the same procedure of the composition, banal but significant so it seems: parallelism. First it is the history of Jesus and the apostles' which respond to one other (Luke is the only Christian writer who considers that the two presentations necessarily call for one another.) Then it is the symmetry within the Acts (1-12 and 13-18) that Luke imposes without respect to his sources. Finally, there are the series of texts which balance one other in an architectural and thus esthetic alternance: Lk 9:1-48 // 22:7-23, 16; Act 1:12-4: 23 // 4:24-5:24; Lk 4:16-7:17 // 7:18-8:56; Lk 1-2 // 3-4. It may also be the antithetical parallelisms and chiasms but they must always be binary. The reader can see for himself - sometimes with surprise - the references proposed in the book . Each time, Talbert decides a balance of the literary units exists, it is always Luke's conscious will and never the product of tradition.

At this point in his investigation, the author declares that, at the same period in the Mediterranean area, the same "architectural" construction can be found: either in literary works, like The Aeneid, or in works of art like Augustus' Ara Pacis in Rome. Judaism has also resorted to this way of doing as the book of Jonah attests (but we know that Israel freely borrowed forms which it needed). The Protoevangelium of James, which it is proper to situate side by side with Luke-Acts, witnesses to the favor Christianity accorded to this literary architecture.

Several interesting remarks conclude this section of the book: 1) the pattern required a slight unbalance to avoid the monotony, the symmetry risked to cause; 2) since Aristotle, writers were advised to write a sketch of their work before writing the final edition: this intermediate stage allowed the author to care for the composition and foresee the effects of alternance. 3) With regard to their education and the almost corporal movement of the symmetries, the readers could not remain insensitive to the effects of style which were suggested to them. 4) If the ancient use of pattern corresponded perhaps to a requirement of mnemonic technique, at the epoch we are interested in, it responded to doctrinal preoccupations.

This is why Talbert directs his investigation toward the relationships which are established between architecture and the theology of Luke-Acts. If we accept that Luke appropriates for himself the popular Greek image of philosopher, followed by his disciples, to express the traditions relative to Jesus and the apostles, the use of the pattern in the symmetry is explained . Among the typical characteristics of the philosopher, we must note the journeys, the proclamation as the mode of transmission, the style of life as the acceptance of a doctrine, the presence of the disciples who learn by following their master and the theme of the authentic heritage of the master which must be preserved. The parallelism between Paul and the primitive Church allows the legitimation of the activity of Paul and his successors.

A theory of the present decadence was widespread in the Empire. To find virtue and the truth again, it was necessary to look into the past, to go back to the origins. Luke shared this conviction: the post-apostolic age, i.e. the contemporay epoque has proved to be inferior to the time of the beginnings. So Luke-Acts, constructed in a binary fashion, functions as the authority and criteria of the legitimacy of the "elders" installed in the succession of Paul. The parallels which are established between Jesus and the early Church, on the one hand, and between the early Church and Paul, on the other, have thus a semantic import.

Talbert inserts here the contents of the article which he had consecrated to the so-called anti-Gnostic Christology of Luke (cf.

see the bibliography for Chapter Three, -> 1967). He believes in this manner he can take into consideration the three parallels: Lk 9 // 22-23; Lk 9 // Act 1 and Lk 24 // Act 1. The narratives of the Ascension and the baptism, in their Lucan version, insist of the physical reality of the body of Jesus. They are opposed, we are told, to the doceticism of - let us say - Cerinthus.

The work ends with a chapter which makes a bridge between the literary genre of Luke-Acts and the presence of numerous parallels within the work (the use of the famous pattern). The author chooses Diogenes Laërtius (The Lives, Teaching and Sayings of Famous Philosophers) which he brings together with Luke-Acts: he concludes, following the hypothesis of H. von Soden, that the evangelist has reworked his sources under the influence of the literary genre, the biography of a philosopher. The relation is triple. It concerns first the contents: both, Luke and Diogenes, relate the life of their hero and supplement it with informa-tion about his doctrines and disciples. Secondly, it is also formal: the lives of the disciples correspond to the life of the founder. Neither Diogenes nor Luke consider the evolution which the doctrine has undergone in the passage from the master to his succes - sors. Finally, the relation is functional: sometimes, the narrative serves the polemic side and at other times the apologetic. The relation must allow the defense of a certain figure and a certain tradition which flows from it.

The examination of the differences leads the author into subtle distinctions. For him there was an ancient pattern of the lives of the philosophers which evolved in two directions. Firstly, Diogenes' direction enumerates several philosophers but then insists little on their successors and then, Luke's which retains but one "philosopher" but describes abundantly the authentic tradition of his legitimate successors. The general public was to represent the Sitz im Leben of the first category and the community, the second. In the latter case, the text served as a cultural legend that legitimated the pretensions of such a branch of the school or sect.

The presence of a dedication and the letters within Luke-Acts indicate an influence of ancient historiography, whereas the narrative of the shipwreck of Paul attests to a literary relationship with the Hellenistic novel. Yet these are two complementary in - fluences. It is within the literary mold of the philosophical bio - graphy, that Luke melted his work. Moreover that he also resorted to the binary pattern of the parallelisms, which was widespread universally, can be better explained in that he inscribed his work in the biographical tradition which completed the master's portrait with the story of the disciples: "The (a) + (b) structure of a biography that is composed of the life of a founder of a philosophical school plus a record of his successors and selected other disciples innately tends towards balance." (p. 135).

If we can give a brief evaluation of these works, we would begin by saying that Talbert is indubitably right to advance that salvation history is not the indispensible (and urgent!) answer to the problem of the delay of the Parousia. But he is wrong to deny the insistance Luke puts on "erasing" the imminence. We also doubt the anti-Gnostic character of the work: a work, which attacks heretics, - if we want to be sensitive to the literary genre, as Talbert desires - uses other means of expression. Polemic is much more explicit: we have only to read Ireneus, Tertullian and Epiphanius.

Let us turn now to the literary analyses: compared to those A. Vanhoye wrote concerning the letter to the Hebrews, these appear simplistic and sometimes forced. It is not enough to mark off a binary system. It is comparable to an art historian, who has not yet understood a doric temple simply because he has counted the columns or a baroque facade because he has noted the number of orders: Far from rejecting this type of analysis and thinking that Talbert went too far, we think contrariwise that he has not sufficiently pushed his structural analysis, or to take up one of his terms, "architectonic". This would have permitted him to realize a certain literary fact, that is not included in his beautiful edifice: the life of Jesus is divided in three sections, not two.

It is necessary to note another fault: it is his speculative generalizations concerning the spirit of the first century. Before accepting that everything goes in pairs, it is necessary first to prove that the "understanding" (Greek - *ἐπιστήμη*) of that time thought in this category. Can we just speak of the "spirit of Roman imperial times" (p. 100)? Talbert takes this uniformity for granted too easily. Could the intellectual preoccupations and mental categories of a Jewish zealot, a Greek rhetorician and a Roman historian be the same?

Finally, we were surprised that Talbert never mentions the literary genre of the parallel lives. Would not this be a way to pursue in understanding the literary genre of Luke-Acts which precisely puts the life of Jesus and the life of Paul in parallel? Was not Plutarch a contemporary of Luke?

Our last remark is to the credit of this exegete, who has an allergy to redaktionsgeschichtlich elaborations, too often subjec - tive. He is right to look for thought schemas and comparable forms of expression in Luke's contemporary epoch. His incursions into the domain of comparative literature and even art history merit our attention, and, of course, critical attention.

R. H. Hiers (-> 1973), **M. Völkel** (-> 1974),
O. Merk (-> 1975) and **E. Rasco** (-> 1976)

r. For exterior reasons of time and space, we are obliged to briefly summarize the more recent works.

Hiers defends two theses. The first, shared with Conzelmann, can be summarized in the following manner: Jesus, according to Luke, did not proclaim the imminency. The redactional omissions, additions and transformations which the exegete mentions are well known,and it is useless to repeat them. His second thesis goes against Conzelmann's view: Luke retains, for his generation, the perspective of an imminent Parousia, for Jesus' prophecies, relative to the fate of Jerusalem, the appearence of false prophets and the evangelization of the nations, are fulfilled at present. Unknowingly, Hiers proposes an interpretation close to H. W. Bartsch's (-> 1963). One of his arguments seems original to us: for Luke, the mission of the Twelve (Lk 9), which corresponds to the beginnings of Christianity announces the Kingdom and not its proximity. The mission of the Seventy (Lk 10), which evokes the evangelization of the nations, has as its content the imminent coming of the Kingdom. Contrary to the author,we do not think that these two theses dissolve the darkness which envelopes Lucan eschatology. To take an example cited, we would recall that the Seventy must establish (and not only announce) the proximity of the Kingdom *ἐφ' ὑμᾶς* and not the absolute imminence of the Kingdom coming in power, as the author believes.

s. M. Völkel's article (-> 1974) is subtle, with a subtility which might hinder its power to convince. Let us attempt to present without betraying it. The writer perceives of the *βασιλεία* as an organic part of the theological whole of the Lucan redaction. Not only does this notion designate a condensation of the preaching of Jesus (like in Mark and Matthew), but it also expresses, in a reflected manner, Jesus' perception vis-à-vis his being sent. Be - cause of this second Christological aspect, the preaching of the Kingdom, for Luke, is continued after Easter.

The first speech of Jesus of Nazareth (Lk 4: 6-30), which is substituted for Mk 1:14f., explains what the Kingdom of God is. Since Lk 4:43 confirms it, Luke is not content to affirm that the divine promise is accomplished, but specifies the person of the one who fulfills the prophecies. This link between the message and the messenger, between the Kingdom and Christ, will not become explicit until after the Passion. Yet it is present from the beginning. Völkel sees a supplementary indication in the Lucan rereading of the order to the demons to be quiet concerning Jesus' messianism (Luke insists (Lk 4:41) on the title, Christ, which he associates with the Passion, whereas Mark evokes the only Son of God).

To this Christological connotation of the *βασιλεία*, the author adds an ecclesiastic nuance from Lk 2:34 on and especially in Act 28:17ff. Lk 4:25-27 already establishes the link between the Jews and the Gentiles. The end of the Acts describes this relation even more clearly not as a separation of Israel, inducing a transfer to the pagans, but rather as an incorporation of the Jews and the Gentiles into the Church. The automatic access to salvation, by belonging to the Jewish community, is followed by an individual in-sertion of the Jews and the Gentiles into the people of God. For this reason, the Christian discourse passes (Act 28: 31) from the evocation of the Kingdom to the proclamation of Christ, whose title evokes the suffering, and from that, to the accomplishment of the Kingdom, in Jesus the suffering Messiah.

Luke is not content to simply receive passively the vocabulary of the *βασιλεία*. In the new expression, he forges ("to evangelize" or "to preach the Kingdom"), he integrates a Christological and ecclesiastical reflection.

This essay attempts, after many others, to explain the co - habitation of the proclamations centered sometimes on the King - dom and sometimes on Christ. However, it does so perhaps in a too doctrinal manner. This does not prevent that he perhaps illu - minates a subjacent structure of Lucan thought. Effectively, it is not without reason that the book of the Acts begins and ends with a mention of the Kingdom (Act 1:3 and 28:31). Yet we must admit that we did not understand how the personal engagement expected of each believer explained in Act 28:31 the double mention of the Kingdom and Christ.

t. O. Merk's article follows the line of study staked out by U. Luck (-> 1960) and M. Völkel (-> 1974). It is a critique of Conzel - mann which begins with methodological considerations and several statistical elements.

Lk 4, the speech of Jesus at Nazareth (particiuliarly Lk 4:43) as well as the use of βασιλεία τοῦ θεοῦ in the Acts (especially Act 28:23) permit one to imagine that the Evangelist integrates the whole life, passion and resurrection of Jesus in the notion of the Kingdom of God. This Kingdom of God does not appear in the Gospel in the typical and transient manner or according to its timeless essence (Conzelmann): when Jesus preaches at Nazareth, the Kingdom is present in all its eschatological consistency by reason of the Spirit confered on Jesus; this Conzelmann neglected in a surprising way. Lk 10:18, 23; 11:20; 16:16 and 17:20f. also attest to this conviction.

The theological problem that Luke had to overcome was not the delay of the Parousia, but the survival of the Kingdom during the time of the Church. The resurrection is a first solution, for it links the two periods while qualifying them at the same time. But it is chiefly the conception of the Kingdom of God which offers the decisive answer. According to the teaching of Jesus, the Kingdom of God which embraces the present and the future, remains important at present thanks to the present activity of the Spirit. Luke shows the time of the Church belongs to the time blessed with the presence of the Kingdom in the person of Christ, by projecting the time of the Church into Jesus' (cf. especially the travel narrative). As Völkel, Merk establishes links between the Kingdom, Christology and eschatology.

Our summary cannot be preciser, for if the declaration of his results is clear, the way taken by the author remains borrowed. It is, therefore, difficult to say if the conclusions hold. We doubt that Luke has the sense of historical continuity so much that he cannot see in the travel narrative a simple description or projection of the time of the Church. Merk does not sufficiently consider the rupture which occurs at the Ascension. This break provokes a modification of the sense of the βασιλεία which the Acts never associated with its coming. Thus, we cannot say that the allusions to the imminency in the travel narrative of Jesus portray an imminency which has become real at the time of the Church! To want to deny a certain sclerosis in the notion of βασιλεία at the end of the first century, especially in the Acts, is to prefer theology to history. In return, Merk is right to think that Luke considers the time of the Church as a blessed time, during which salvation is made present. However the Evangelist chooses other ways to express this conviction, rather than resorting to the βασιλεία : the Holy Spirit, the presence of the Word of God and the effectiveness of the Name are his main arguments.

u. At the same period, an important history of Lucan studies, the work of E. Rasco [**72**] (-> 1976) deals basically with three theological themes; Christology, pneumatology and salvation history. He does not tarry with long exegetical developments, but presents a synthesis which finds support in the most recent works.

Jesus introduces the eschatological era. Luke collects and transmits this conception which he makes his own. Leaning basically on G. Voss (cf. below 3,IV,b), Rasco refuses the term "adoptionism" in order to insist on the communion of the Son with the Father. (rightly he insists on Lk 10:21f., a text neglected by Conzelmann.) Where a servile submission had been seen, Rasco perceives a confident abandon into the hands of the Father (Lk 23:46). The union of the human and the divine in the person of Jesus, attested to in the nativity account, precludes docetism and adoptionism. To interpret the meaning of the death of Jesus according to Luke, the author refers to an article by A. George (cf. see the bibliography, Ch. 3, -> 1973). Luke certainly does not explicitly associate salvation with the cross. Yet he is not for all that a defender of a <u>theologia gloriae</u>, for he maintains a narrow link between the death and resurrection of Jesus. Going beyond A. George, Rasco thinks that the entire ministry of Jesus considered as a path, allows the believer more than an imitation, a salvific insertion into the horizon of God. Luke shows in a narrative manner what theologians, like Paul, call a death for us or an expiation for our sins. The Lucan account of the Lord's Supper confirms this conception.

Concerning πνεῦμα, Rasco opposes Conzelmann's interpre - tation which is content to see it as an <u>Ersatz</u> of the eschato - logical benefits. He is able to show without difficulty the ties that Luke establishes between Jesus and the Spirit (cf. Act 16:7) especially between the Ascension and Pentecost. The relation of Christ to the Spirit corresponds to the relationship of the Son to the Father. The Spirit, like Jesus, is not only an <u>instrument</u> in the hands of God. He establishes a Trinitarian collaboration which induces an eschatological qualification of the time of the Church. Since the Spirit, given at Pentecost, proceeds from the Son, now elevated to the right hand of God, it is incorrect to disparage his presence to a meager <u>Ersatz</u>. The πνεῦμα ἅγιον is the plenipotentiary representative of Christ during the time of the Church.

The relationship between believers and Christ is brought about thanks to the Spirit but this does not mean that simply a vague spiritual communion is established between the Lord and his disciples. Luke emphasizes sufficiently the role as witnesses which the Twelve have: the apostolic ministry has a function of direction and canalization. If Luke writes his work, it is because of the multiform presence of the Spirit in the Church.

Finally, E. Rasco deals with the highly debated question of eschatology. He, first, criticizes the separation which occurs frequently concerning the difference between Luke and Paul. It follows that distinguishing the historical problem of their personal relations and the theological question of their doctrinal positions is primordial. His attacks are directed at the critical positions of P. Vielhauer (-> 1950), H. Conzelmann (-> 1954), with his consorts, who Rasco thinks return to Bultmann. For support, he finds P. Menoud (-> 1970), M. Carrez (-> 1969) and P. Borgen (-> 1966) who demonstrate that Paul, less existentialist that has been said, is also a defender of salvation history and Luke does not conceive of history in a positivistic manner. J. Zmijewski's work (-> 1972), which we analyzed above comes to his aid here.

Jesus and his history (and not only his word) constitute the time of salvation. The time of salvation is not completely interrupted by the Ascension, for it continues within the Church. "Para introducirnos en este hecho escatológico, que es Jesús, ya en su propio ministerio (contra Bultmann), más aún, según Lucas, ya en su infancia; ministerio, que es sin duda un tiempo privilegiado de salvación (con Conzelmann), pero que no termina en Jesús (de ahí nuestra insistencia en la fusión de la época de su ministerio y de la de su señorío por medio del Espíritu), que es tiempo de salvación aún presente (en parte con Bultmann, y contra Conzelmann), no por medio de una Iglesia constituida en "institución de salvación" independiente del Espíritu sino sometida a él y al Señor Jesús, Lucas no ha tenido que renegar de la historia, ni ha tenido que hacer que escatología se la devore. Al contrario, Lucas ha iluminado la plenitud de su realidad con la iluminación escatológica que procede del Señor Jesús y del Espíritu. Historia e Historia de la Salvación conviven sin cancelarse." (p. 162).

Rasco brings forth divers arguments to buttress his thesis: for example, by transforming the historical present in Mark to the perfect, Luke shows the historical character of Jesus' life and at the same time, its still actual import.

If we have understood well, the distinction which can be read in Lk 17, between the days of the Son of Man and the day serve as indications of the two aspects of the Lucan salvation history, the existential continuity and punctuality.

The Lucan vocabulary of the way, life (in relation with Christ) and conversion respects these two aspects as well.

We can really speak of the coexistence of the historical and eschatological (p. 168) in the Lucan corpus, for Jesus is the unique and polyvalent figure who while being historical also interprets history.

We too believe that the Spirit is the work in the Church and eschatology can be present in the continuity of history. Yet we wonder, where is the Church today? Without saying explicitly, does Rasco think that it is in the Roman Catholic Church? If this is the case, the study can be read entirely in a triumphalistic per - spective: The Roman Church received the Spirit, it is the place where redemptive history continues and where eschatology is accomplished. Is not Luke's Christology which has been presented, open to later developments (p. 129) by his insistence of the union of the divine and human in Jesus? **[73]**

Conclusion

Luke thinks - and who would dream of contradicting him? - that events happen in space and time. These events can be narrated and their choice depends on the narrator's point of view: in the beginning, the Evangelist exposes the criteria which determined their selection (Lk 1:1-4).

The spatio-temporal details of these events fit into the frame - work of the powerful masters: the kings and leaders who reign at a certain moment in time. The Lucan synchronisms do not differ on this point from the dating which the OT prophets offered. No more than the Jewish historians of his time, Luke is not interested in this frame. Different from the apocalypticians, he does not dream of the destiny of the empires. This constatation prohibits us from discerning in Luke two parallel histories, for he does not elaborate a secular history. The principle of reality incites him, nonetheless, to situate concretely what he desires to narrate.

Which painting does he desire to put into this frame? Does he want to narrate a holy history or an irruption of the Word of God? To express this debated problem in other terms, does he believe in a revelation in and through the events which, when under the shock, becomes a visible manifestation of God, a holy history whose coherence would then be intelligible? Or does he prefer a punctual revelation through the Word which would snub space and time?

The analysis of the typically Lucan phrases where the verb is ἐγένετο, permits us to refuse this dilemma, though set forth in contemporary dogmatics remains foreign to the Evangelist's thought. By way of example, let us read the famous synchronism in Lk 3:1ff. which places the evangelical account on the same scale as the reigns of the world. The evangelical content, which provokes the narration, or simply what has happened (ἐγένετο), is first ῥῆμα θεοῦ. The action of God plays on the mode of speaking. It is not possible henceforth to affirm positively that God intervenes directly in history and provokes events which inherently have a salvific character. But the text continues and passes from the level of the Word to the level of facts. The verifiable facts are certainly not swollen with divine force. They are not in themselves revelatory. For God, in a certain measure, withdraws while advancing at the same time: he speaks, but to communicate his Word, he uses a relay: the man he has chosen and to whom he addresses his Word; in this case John the Baptist. The latter belongs to concrete life: he has a name, an age, a graspable reality. What distinguishes him from the others, what makes of him a link between God and men, does not belong to the visible or verifiable order. While he travels across the country (vs. 3a) he does what every man could do, he becomes an original, new, bearer of God among men, when he preaches a baptism of repentence with a view to the forgiveness of sins (vs. 3b). We can speak of salvation history, only on the condition that we not place under this banner, an installation of the Divine in history or, at the other extreme, limit God's intervention to a proclamation without effect on the events of the world. There is a salvation history because men and women, under the action of the word of God, provoke a history and live it. A voice, preserved in the book of promises, confirms this specificity of salvation history: in this case, it is the voice of the prophet Isaiah that Luke quotes in vss. 4-5 (Isa 40:3-5).

God's intervention is described here in terms of the Word. It is not always so. What has roused the grounds for grievance of the theology of glory directed against Luke, are the so-called "miraculous" acts where God seems to put his hand to the plow of history. First of all, let us say that these gests are never those of God himself, but of his messengers: angels, the Spirit, etc. Furthermore, Luke is not concerned with the risk that he runs in mentioning the celestial forces, for again such interventions are words, orders, messages of encouragements. Moreover, this Word is destined not for just anyone but for believers and this situates the reception in the order of faith. Ambiguity often characterizes these manifestations. We forget too frequently that in Act 21:4, the disciples in Tyre beg Paul "by the Spirit" not to go up to Jerusalem. At the same time, Paul, not to mention Agabus (Act 21:11), affirms that from city to city the Holy Spirit announces to him the suffering which awaits him in the capital (Act 20:22f.). Finally, let us note that Luke is constrained to speak of these divine interventions afterward. This suppresses any aspiration to a direct and autosufficient revelation. Luke, of course, can declare that the tongues of fire came down on the disciples at Pentecost or that the Holy Spirit came upon Jesus in bodily form, but he recognizes at the same time - what we forget too often - the metaphorical character of these affirmations. The miracles themselves must be read in the perspective of the first century as signs of the active presence of the Divine and not as proofs to convince unbelievers. Luke takes care regularly to associate them with faith. He does not elaborate a conception of nature where "miracles" come to perturb the natural order.

In summary, Luke integrates without hesitation the fulfillment of the purpose of God (cf. the importance of the term *βουλή τοῦ θεοῦ*) into the lives of men. It is this junction, for lack of a better term, we will call salvation history, for, if we dare say, God is coherent with his ideas: his project is accomplished by stages linked by thresholds.

Let us not forget, the main stage is the life of Jesus of Naza - reth, the center of the Lucan message. This life, which should not be subdivided, passes by way of death - Luke does not tone it down: he even cultivates its memory -, in order to arrive at the resurrection and especially the Ascension. Here again, and especially here, God called forth a human presence, a person, Jesus, Son of God through the intervention of the Spirit and the lineage of Adam (Lk 3:23-38). The Parousia, or at least the date of the end, loses its importance. Only the *ἀρχή* counts. The *τέλος*, the end, depends of it: not by reason of a historical determinism but rather by theological necessity.

Without a doubt, Luke thinks that the end of history will be marked by a divine intervention of another type: a direct sort, "in power", where God triumphs This type will manifest and openly realize his plan. If this is the case, the last divine activity will correspond to the first, creation, which was visible as well. In Luke, these two are differentiated from the more discreet and in - direct interventions which stake out salvation history, the love relationship of God and his people.

This Lucan conception of the intervention of God among men, particularly the eschatological sending of the Son and the Spirit, is less original that has been said. With the other Christians of the apostolic age and his time, Luke deems that the history of humanity, our concrete history, has a positive sense by reason of the Word which rings out and the Spirit which is distributed.

Luke's originality resides in the responsibility of believers, activated by the gest of God, attested in the kerygma and confirmed in the narrative. This human side of the eschatological reality, attested by *μετάνοια*, is expressed in the apostolic function. It also explains the presence of the Book of the Acts side by side with the Gospel. This proximity suited the Christians of later centuries, who attentively placed the epistles next to the gospels. Like them, Luke believes that, by the Word of God and the word of human beings, by the Holy Spirit and the presence of the Church, believers are placed in a double and yet unique relation with the living Christ and the historical Jesus. The gift of God and the welcome he reserves for men constitutes the totality of salvation history. Even if we need not identify the Christ and his Church, we can no longer separate them.

CHAPTER 2

THE INTERPRETATION OF THE OLD TESTAMENT

Chronological Bibliography

1922

W. K. L. CLARKE, "The Use of the Septuagint in Acts", in F. J. Foakes Jackson and K. Lake (eds), **The Beginnings of Christianity, I, The Acts of the Apostles**,2 (= **Beginnings**, Foakes Jackson) (London,1922), pp. 66-105.

1939

W. BEYSE*, **Das Alte Testament in der Apostelgeschichte** (Munich, 1939).

1950

L. CERFAUX, "Citations scripturaires et traditions textuelles dans le livre des Actes", in **Sources, Goguel**, pp. 43-51; taken up in **Recueil L. Cerfaux**, II (Gembloux, 1954), pp. 95-103.

1953

J. DUPONT, "L'utilisation apologétique de l'Ancien Testament dans les Discours des Actes", **ETL** 29 (1953) 289-327; included in **Etudes**, Dupont, pp. 245-282. We are citing **Etudes**.

1954

H. CONZELMANN, **Die Mitte der Zeit. Studien zur Theologie des Lukas** (Tübingen, 1954), pp. 128-157 of the 3rd ed.of 1960.

E. HAENCHEN, "Schriftzitate und Textüberlieferung in der Apostelgeschichte", **ZTK** 51 (1954) 153-167; included in E. Haenchen, **Gott und Mensch. Gesammelte Aufsätze** (Tübingen, 1965), pp. 157-171.

P. SCHUBERT, "The Structure and Significance of Luke 24", in W. Eltester (ed), **Neutestamentliche Studien. Mélanges R. Bultmann** (Berlin 1954), pp. 165-186.

1955

J. B. TYSON*, **Luke's Use of the Old Testament. Examples of the Use of Old Testament Quotations in Luke and Acts,** unpublished dissertation, Union Theological Seminary (New York, 1955).

1956

E. L. ALLEN, "Jesus and Moses in the New Testament", **ExpTim** 67 (1956) 104-106.

J. DUPONT, "Λαὸς ἐξ ἐθνῶν", **NTS** 3 (1956) 47-50; taken up again with an additional note in **Etudes**, Dupont, pp. 361-365.

M. WILCOX, "The Old Testament in Acts 1-15", **ABR** 4 (1956) 1-41.

1957

N. A. DAHL, " A People for His Name", **NTS** 4 (1957-1958) 319-327.

J. MÁNEK, "The New Exodus in the Books of Luke", **NT** 2 (1957-1958) 8-23.

1959

A. KERRIGAN, "The 'sensus plenior' of Joel 3, 1-5, in Acts 2, 14-36", in J. Coppens, A. Descamps and E. Massaux (eds), **Sacra Pagina. Miscellanea biblica congressus internationalis catholici de re biblica**, 2 (Gembloux-Paris, 1959), pp. 295-313.

1960

S. AMSLER, **L'Ancien Testament dans l'Eglise. Essai d'herméneutique chrétienne** (Neuchâtel, 1960), pp. 63-75.

1961

J. DUPONT, "La destinée de Judas prophétisée par David", **CBQ** 23 (1961) 41-51; taken up in **Etudes**, Dupont, pp. 309-320.

J. DUPONT, "'Τὰ ὅσια Δαυὶδ τὰ πιστά' Act 13, 34 = Is 55, 3", **RB** 68 (1961) 91-114; taken up in **Etudes**, Dupont, pp. 337-360.)

B. LINDARS, **New Testament Apologetic** (London, 1961.

E. LÖVESTAM, **Son and Saviour. A Study of Acts 13, 32-37. With and Appendix: 'Son of God' in the Synoptic Gospels** (Lund, 1961).

H. RUSCHE, "Zum Schriftverständnis der Apostelgeschichte (Dargestellt am Zeugnis von Erhöhten Herrn)", in **Fünfzig Jahre katholischer Missionswissenschaft in Münster** (Münster, 1961), pp. 187-194.

1962

J. DUPONT, "L'interprétation des Psaumes dans les Actes des apôtres", in **Le Psautier. Ses origines. Ses problèmes littéraires. Son influence. Etudes présentées aux XIIe Journées Bibliques de Louvain (29-31 août 1960)** (Leuven, 1962), pp. 357-388; included in **Etudes**, Dupont, pp. 283-307.

1963

J. BIHLER, **Die Stephanusgeschichte im Zusammenhang der Apostelgeschichte** (Munich, 1963).

1965

T. HOLTZ, "Beobachtungen zur Stephanusrede Acta 7", in **Kirche, Theologie, Frömmigkeit. Mélanges G. Holtz** (Berlin,1965), pp. 102-111.

M. WILCOX, **The Semitisms of Acts** (Oxford, 1965).

1966

L. C. CROCKETT*, **The Old Testament in the Gospel of Luke: with Emphasis on the Interpretation of Isaiah LXI, 1-2**, unpublished dissertation, Brown University (Providence, Rhode Island, 1966).

L.C. CROCKETT, "Luke 4, 6-30 and the Jewish Lectionary Cycle: A word of Caution", **JJS** 17 (1966) 13-45.

N. A. DAHL, "The Story of Abraham in Luke-Acts", in **Studies**, Keck, pp. 139-158.

J. GARRALDA - J. CASARETTO, "Uso del Antiguo Testamento en los primeros capítulos de 'Hechos'", **RBibArg** 28 (1966) 35-39.

C. GHIDELLI, "Le citazioni dell'Antico Testamento nel cap. 2 degli Atti", in **Il Messianismo. Atti della XVIII Settimana Biblica** (Associazione Biblica Italiana) (Brescia, 1966) pp. 285-305.

E. SCHWEIZER, "The Concept of the Davidic 'Son of God' in Acts and its Old Testament Background", in **Studies**, Keck, pp. 186-193.

1967

J. W. BOWKER, "Speeches in Acts: a Study in Poem and Yelammedenu Form" **NTS** 14 (1967-1968) 96-111.

W. R. HANFORD, "Deutero-Isaiah and Luke-Acts: Straight forward Universalism?" **ChQR** 168/367 (1967) 141-152.

1968

C. H. CAVE, "Lazarus and the Lukan Deuteronomy", **NTS** 15 (1968-1969) 319-325.

D. GOLDSMITH, "Acts 13, 33-37: A Pesher on 2 Sam 7", **JBL** 87 (1968) 321-324.

T. HOLTZ, **Untersuchungen über die Alttestamentlichen Zitate bei Lukas** (Berlin, 1968).

M. H. SCHARLEMANN, **Stephen: A Singular Saint** (Rome, 1968).

1969

L. C. CROCKETT, "Luke 4, 25-27, and the Jewish-Gentile Relations in Luke-Acts", **JBL** 88 (1969) 177-193.

M. RESE, **Alttestamentliche Motive in der Theologie des Lukas**, (Gütersloh, 1969).

1970

J. BLIGH*, **Christian Deuteronomy (Luke 9-18)** (Langley, 1970).

E. E. ELLIS, "Midrashic Features in the Speeches of Acts", in **Mélanges, Rigaux**, pp. 303-312.

1971

C. WESTERMANN, "Alttestamentliche Elemente in Lukas 2, 1-20", in G. Jeremias, H. W. Kuhn and H. Stegemann (eds), **Tradition und Glaube. Das frühe Christentum in seiner Umwelt. Mélanges K. G. Kuhn** (Göttingen, 1971), pp. 317-327.

1972

J. A. FITZMYER, "David, 'Being Therefore a Prophet...' (Acts 2,30)", **CBQ** 34 (1972) 332-339.

S. H. LEE*, **John the Baptist and Elijah in Lucan Theology**, unpublished dissertation, Boston Univ. School of Theology (Boston, 1972). Cf. **DissAbstr**, A, 33 (1972) 2483s-A.

1973

G. DELLING, "'...als er uns die Schrift aufschloss'. Zur Lukanischen Terminologie der Auslegung des Alten Testaments", in H. Balz and S. Schulz (eds), **Das Wort und die Wörter. Mélanges G. Friedrich** (Stuttgart, 1973), pp. 75-83.

J. D. DUBOIS, "La figure d'Elie dans la perspective lucanienne", **RHPhR** 53 (1973) 155-176.

J. DUPONT, "Les discours de Pierre dans les Actes et le chapitre 24 de l'évangile de Luc", in **Evangile**, Neirynck, pp. 329-374 (p. 352f. et passim). The article was written in 1968.

D. H. HAY*, **Glory at the Right Hand: Psalm 110 in Early Christianity** (Nashville, 1973).

A. SCHMITT, "Ps 16, 8-11 als Zeugnis der Auferstehung in der Apostelgeschichte", **BZ**, N.S., 17 (1973) 229-248.

P. S. WHITE, **Prophétie et prédication: une étude herméneutique des citations de l'Ancien Testament dans les sermons des Actes** (Lille, 1973).

1974

J. DUPONT, "'Assis à la droite de Dieu'. L'interprétation du Ps. 110, 1 dans le Nouveau Testament", in E. Dhanis (ed), **Resurrexit. Actes du Symposium international sur la résurrection de Jésus, Rome, 1970** (Rome, 1974), pp. 94-148.

R. P. GORDON, "Targumic Parallels to Acts 13, 18 and Didache 14,3", **NT** 16 (1974) 285-289.

T. C. G. THORNTON, "Stephen's Use of Isaiah 66, 1", **JTS**, N.S., 25 (1974) 432-434.

1975

K. KLIESCH, **Das heilsgeschichtliche Credo in den Reden der Apostelgeschichte** (Bonn, 1975).

1976

M. DUMAIS, **Le language de l'évangelisation. L'annonce missionnaire en milieu juif (Actes 13, 16-41)** (Tournai-Montreal, 1976).

M. GOURGUES, "Lecture christologique du Psaume 110 et fête de la Pentecôte", **RB** 83 (1976) 5-24.

Chapter 2

THE INTERPRETATION OF THE OLD TESTAMENT

Introduction

a. The OT holds a considerable place in the Lucan work, particularly in the Christological speeches of the first half of Acts. If the body of the third Gospel contains but a few citations [**1**], the extremities are deeply saturated: the vocabulary of the infancy narrative (Lk 1-2) is full of OT expressions [**2**], and the ministry of John the Baptist, like Jesus', begins under the auspices of the prophet Isaiah: Luke lengthens the quotation of Isaiah 40 that Mark already cites concerning the Baptist (cf. Lk 3:4f.) and con - structs the scene of Jesus' first predication in the synagogue of Nazareth (cf. Lk 4:18f.) around the prophecy of Isaiah 61 ("The Spirit of the Lord is upon me ..."). Without citing any one OT text, the last chapter of the third Gospel reveals, through the voice of the risen Christ, how Christians should use the OT [**3**], (Lk 24:25, 27, 44-47)..

In the first half of Acts, the quotations are numerous. Taken most frequently from Psalms and the Prophets, they appear in the speeches (ch. 1-15), and in the majority of the cases have a Christological inclination. They help to recognize the Messiah in Jesus and understand the Passion and the resurrection of Christ [**4**].

In the second half of the Acts (ch. 16-28), OT quotations are rare. Yet, in concluding his work, Luke does not overlook the opportunity of composing, with the help of the OT, a final text consecrated to the Christian mission, a counterpart to ch. 24 of his Gospel. The quotation, from Isa 6:9-10 (concerning the hardening of the Jews), justifies the misson to the Gentiles, who are called to salvation.

Besides the OT citations, it is necessary to note the numerous OT allusions, which often evoke the figures of biblical history: Abraham, Joseph, Moses, David. Jesus takes on certain of their characteristics to bring them to their fulness. Finally, on two occasions, in the speech of Stephen (ch. 7) and Paul's at

Antioch of Pisidia (ch. 13), Luke summarizes the sacred history according to a scheme which is found in certain texts of ancient Judaism [**5**].

This OT presence in the Lucan work poses three major problems: 1) from which biblical books do the quotations and the allusions come? 2) which textual form do they transmit? Does Luke cite the Septuagint, other Greek translations or does he return to the Hebrew text, to oral traditions of Targumic or Midrashic nature? 3) What theological and hermeneutical function do these, often free, OT references fill? [**6**]

It is our opinion that the solutions to these problems have theological repercussions. The origin of the quotations reveals Luke's scriptural preferences and the traditions he uses. The form of the text allows us to situate Luke and by that, his theology, in the stream of primitive Christianity. Then, the nature of the scriptural argument specifies the logic of Lucan faith.

b. One of the works, written before 1950, which merits our attention is from the pen of W. K. L. Clarke; the article appreared in the second volume of **Beginnings of Christianity** (-> 1922). The title is significant: "The Use of the Septuagint in Acts". First of all, the author examines the influence of the LXX on the vocabulary of Acts, an influence weaker than was thought before the discovery of papyri, other witnesses of Koine Greek. Afterwards, he distinguishes the citations, which agree with the LXX, completely (five examples) or substantially (seven quotes), from the 16 other cases, where Luke seems to quote the LXX quite freely. His view is that there are several factors which explain this deviation between the text quoted and the text of the LXX: deficient memory, the concern to take into account the context, etc. Finally, Clark studies the allusions to the OT in the speeches (especially in ch. 7 and 13) and the narratives of the Acts. In Luke's perspective, the God of the Christians and the resurrected Christ must express themselves in "biblical" language. Is it possible that Luke might have constructed certain narratives from OT texts rather than historical recollections (this would be a blow to Luke's claim to historian set forth in the prologue of his work Lk 1:1-4)? Like the other narratives between Act 8 and 12, the encounter between Philip and the Ethiopian could have been based on Zephaniah (cf. Zeph 2:4 LXX. 11-12; 3:10 and 3:4) This OT influence must have influenced the tradition rather than Luke. If this influence seems less evident to us than to Clark, most of the other conclusions of the author can be considered as established.

I. LUKE'S HERMENEUTICS

a. Several factors provoked a revival of interest in Lucan theology around 1950. It was natural from this moment on that the Lucan interpretation of the OT be examined in this new perspective [7].

P. Schubert (-> 1954) drew the attention of exegetes to the literary and theological conclusion of the third Gospel, ch. 24. He noted that the structure of this chapter was trine and that the account culminates in the appearance of the risen Christ explaining the Scriptures. The empty tomb, the disciples of Emmaus, the appearance and Ascension are the three periods. In the three cases, Luke seems to dispose of a tradition which he interprets according to his theology, a theology which can be described in the following manner: proof by fulfilled prophecy. The legend of the empty tomb does not interest Luke except where it can be integrated into the argument which is dear to him: not the historical proof of the resurrection, but rather the accomplishment of the promise. "Why do you seek him, who is living, among the dead? He is not here, he is risen. Remember how he spoke to you, when he was still in Galilee: he said it was necessary that the Son of Man be delivered over into the hands of sinners, be crucified and rise on the third day." (Lk 24:5-7, these verses are clearly redactional).

In the case of the disciples of Emmaus, the traditional account which vss. 13, 15b, 16 and 28-31 must have formed the core, culminated in the recognition of the Resurrected One by Cleopas and his friend. Luke modifies the perspective by adding vss. 25-27 which describe the Risen One, as yet anonymous, interpreting the OT: "Minds without intelligence, slow to believe all that was announced by the prophets! Was not it necessary for the Christ to suffer these things in order to enter into his glory? And beginning with Moses and going through the prophets, he explained to them everything that was said concerning him in all the Scriptures." (Lk 24: 25-27).

Chapter 24 terminates with the appearance of the resurrected Christ to the apostles (Lk 24:36ff.), but the account does not interest Luke except in that he can conclude it with a last instruc - tion concerning the understanding of the Scriptures; the messianic sense of which is forcefully noted: Lk 24:44-48.

We regret that Schubert affirmed more than he analyzed Luke's interest in Scriptural argument. He says simply in a note: "However, the warning should be added that the proof-from-prophecy theology of Luke-Acts is but the hard rational core of what we should more adequately call Luke's theology of history." (p. 173. note 20 which goes on to the next page). However, we must thank him for 1) drawing our attention to Lk 24; 2) showing in this chapter, like in the rest of the Gospel [8], the importance of the argument of accomplished prophecy; 3) indicating that this theology, different from Paul's, "considerably simpler, cruder, more naive, more rational and rationalistic than Paul's" (p. 185), was not Luke's alone, but was spread throughout Christendom of the end of the first century.

b. Commencing with Lk 24, Schubert goes back through the third Gospel, in order to evaluate the weight of the prophetic argument in Luke's thought. Contrariwise, in a series of articles, at the same epoch (-> 1953, -> 1956, -> 1961, -> 1961, -> 1962) [9], J. Dupont sets off from the "lesson of Christian hermeneutic" (p. 246) contained in Lk 24, in order to go down the current of the book of the Acts. This step is imperative, because, according to Dupont, if Luke defines the Christian meaning of the OT in ch. 24 of his Gospel, he does not indicate which biblical texts are most apt for this Christological demonstration. It is the citations in Acts which fulfill the program announced in ch. 24.

A series of assertions come forth from these studies which allow the definition of the Lucan hermeneutic.

1) Even if the quotations are found most frequently in the speeches, they reflect a redactional use [10]. The same use of Psa 16 ("my flesh will not see corruption") is found in speeches attributed to two different authors: to Peter in Act 2 and to Paul in Act 13. When we remember that Luke is the only writer in the NT to use this text and the resulting argument, it is easy to admit the redactional origin of this citation and most of the others. The case of Act 15 confirms this allegation: James' argumentation would crumble if it rested on the Hebrew text of Amos 9. The universalism that the brother of the Lord recommends in his speech, can only find Scriptural support in the Greek version of the OT, and it is highly unlikely that James spoke Greek at the conference of Jerusalem (p. 270 ff) [11].

2) Luke uses the Septuagint and seems to be unaware of the Hebrew text. Dupont is suspicious of exegetes [12] who attempt to detect an influence of the original text or targumim. To explain the occasional swerves between the quotations of Luke and the LXX, he invokes two arguments: a) in Palestine before the Christian era, the LXX had undergone correction from the Hebrew text, as Father J. D. Barthélemy has shown [13]; b) Luke, sometimes, permits himself to modify a certain citation in

order to adapt it to the context or to include expressions coming from another important OT text. Dupont explains the substitution of the verb *ἐξουθενέω* (to disdain) which comes from Isa 53:3 to the verb *ἀποδοκιμάζω* (to reject) in the quotation of Psa 118:22 in Act 4:11 (p. 260f.) in this manner.

3) Most of the quotations respond to a Christological preoc - cupation. As the program in Lk 24 indicates, the OT, for Luke, is above all a prophetic book, whose promises foretell the Christ: the Messiah would have to suffer and rise. All the nations are summoned to believe in Him. If certain texts of the OT cited, concern men, they do not interest Luke except in their relation to the Christ: a) the enemies of Jesus during his Passion: Herod and Pilate (the quote from Psa 2 in the prayer in Act 4:25f.) as well as Judas (the curious citations in Act 1:20 about his death) [**14**]; b) the men called to decide for or against the message of Christ, dead and risen: the Jews who harden their hearts (the quotation from Isa 6:9f. in the last speech in Acts, Paul's speech at Rome in Act 28); pagans who are called to integrate themselves into the Church (eg. Amos 9:11f. in Act 15:17). Therefore we can see that the "perfectly defined program in Lk 24:46f." (p. 278) is fulfilled in the messianic message of the Acts. Scriptural proof is generally related to the Passion and resurrection. "By the texts, we intend to show that the sufferings endured by Jesus and his subsequent resurrection were the object of prophecies relative to the Messiah; consequently, Jesus is truly the announced Messiah." (p. 278). Dupont could have underlined that the Scriptural program of Lk 24 also implied the identification of the Messiah with Jesus of Nazareth. Luke's program would then include four points and not three: a) the Messiah was to suffer; b) he was to rise from the dead; c) Jesus is this Messiah; d) the nations are called to believe in Him, whereas the majority of the elect harden their hearts.

4) Lucan exegesis is not allegorical in the modern sense of the word (p. 276). It contains certain elements of typology (the parallelism between Moses and Christ: with the two elements tribulations and salvific mission, while discrete, is still undeni - able). But it is most often literal: "the demonstration profits from the terms used, even occasionally from the amphibology of certain Greek terms." (p. 276). Thus Luke plays on the double meaning of the verb *ἀνίστημι* which signifies both "to rouse or suscitate" and "to resurrect or rise"(cf. Act 3: 22-26).

Despite his attachment to the letter, Luke's Christian exegesis does not convince the Jews. Why? Of course, it is re- lated to Jewish exegesis (the same love for the letter which the

Pharisees have and the same concern for fulfillment of the Essenes) [**15**], but it does not follow the same logic. In fact, it does not seek to convince the mind: "the point is not to prove the resurrection."(p. 278f.). Rather it is theological: "It moves totally within the interior of faith, ex fide in fidem." (p. 290). The joy of the resurrection illuminates the OT which confers a deep meaning to the Easter event (Psa 110:1 and Psa 2:7 show that the resurrection of Jesus was much more than a mere return to life: it was an elevation and an enthroning). The letter of the OT convinces only believers,who alone, for Luke, properly understand it.

5) More than a demonstration, the concern is that the Scriptural witness confirm the apostolic witness. From this a paradox surges forth, which Dupont perceives without clearly noting it: Lk 24 implies a univocal sense to the entire Scripture, while only limited texts from the Prophets (especially Deutero-Isaiah) and the Psalms are cited.

c. Few exegetes have aided the progression toward the understanding of the Lucan hermeneutic as much as Dom J. Dupont. The Belgian scholar succeeded in integrating Lucan exegesis into early Christianity, especially, so he thinks, the movement which came out of the Hellenists (p. 273f.). Nevertheless he insists on the the originality of this call upon the Scriptures. One might wonder if it is not too easy to guarantee this hermeneutic under the convenient cap of the plenary sense. How can we admit theologically that for Luke the resurrection confers to the OT its "true import" (p. 280) while the "primary sense" of the Biblical text which we attempt to reach with our historical critical methods" (p. 274) are far from Luke's preoccupations! Is it not necessary to admit that Luke sometimes solicits Biblical texts?

d. In the section of his book, entitled, "God and Redemptive History" (p. 128ff.), H. Conzelmann deals with Luke's relations with the Biblical past. These relations are established by the intermediary of Scripture and the people of Israel.

Like Schubert and Dupont, Conzelmann accords a place of honor to chapter 24 of the third Gospel. In this chapter, Luke projected the Christian Scriptural argumentation into the life of Jesus (cf. Lk 24:44) and deemed that the witness of the Scriptures received its full weight only from the resurrection (cf. Lk 24:27). Luke indicates thus both the function of the Scripture for the Church and the interpretive principle which must be applied to it.

An analysis of the introductory formulas to the quotations (ἐν βίβλῳ, γραφῇ etc.) permits to conclude in an understanding of Scripture as prophecy (cf. the transformation of the simple καθὼς γέγραπται, Mk 14:21 to κατὰ τὸ ὡρισμένον in Lk 22:22). Yet the OT is not only a selection of promises; there are also requirements . The Law and Prophets are not distinguished by their imperative nature, on the one hand, and, their prophetic nature, on the other; the entire OT is both law and prediction simultaneously. If we must accept with Conzelmann and many others,the prophetic function of the Law (Lk 24:44), we still wonder if Luke really presupposes the normative value of the teaching of the prophets. Even the Law does not play a preponderant role in the Christian ethic, as Conzelmann himself admits **[16]**. From which texts can Conzelmann affirm that the Law and the Prophets are the "Grundlage des Bussrufs"? (p. 148) **[17]** Is not this view more Lutheran than Lucan?

Conzelmann moves onto more solid ground when he ana - lyzes the import of OT prophecies. He adds at the right place an element to Dupont's list which, furthermore, the latter accepts (p. 151, n. 1) **[18]**: if Luke does not explicitly base the birth of Jesus on the Scripture, he does resort to the OT to describe the beginning of Jesus' ministry as an "Anbruch des Heils" (p. 150) **[19]**, an irruption of salvation, from which Luke underlines its universal perspective at the two extremities of his work (Lk 2:30; 3:4ff. and Act 28:28). In compensation, Luke never turns to the Scriptural argument to define the end times: "Andererseits scheinen Eschaton und Gericht nicht in den Radius der Schrift-weissagung zu fallen" (p. 150) **[20]**. The last step of salvation history, foreseenby the Scriptures, is the gift of the Spirit: cf. Lk 24:49 and Act 2. Christian teaching alone (Lk 21; or for Luke, the preaching of Jesus) allows one to imagine what the end of history will be. We wonder why the apocalyptic texts of the OT could not serve this function. Could it be that prophecy only extends to the next period in the history of redemption?

Finally, Conzelmann insists on a neglected point: the Church alone is the heir of Israel. From now on, the correct understanding of OT texts depends on her. As Act 13:27 indicates, the Jews do not understand the OT, but Luke seems to excuse them temporarily: for even the disciples were mistaken concerning the Christ and the Scriptures before the resurrection, but now, the things foreseen by the OT have been fulfilled. History has given a consistency to Scripture: the clarity of the kerygma and the strength of the Scriptural argument makes the unbeliever inexcusable. If the Jews and pagans do not enter into the movement of faith, they become unpardonable [**21**].

Reading the texts, we can accept this reasoning - as cruel as it may be - concerning the Jews: by the promises of the OT, the ministry of Jesus and their own election, they had everything to believe. Their refusal of the message makes them guilty. Luke, on the other hand, does not envisage the destiny of the pagans rebellious to the evangelical message. He only knows those, who are far off, whom the Lord will call (Act 2:39), will answer affirmatively to the evangelical message.

e. In a dozen pages his thesis, **L'Ancien Testament dans l'Eglise**, S. Amsler (-> 1960) touches on the role of the OT in the book of the Acts. The chapter is subdivided into three sections: 1) the apostles' statements in Acts concerning Scripture, 2) the OT quotations and 3) the narrative recollections. A general thesis seems contestable: since the OT quotations appear in the speeches, Luke, himself, is little interested in the OT, and the hermeneutic of the Acts reflects more the apostles' tradition than the author's. In our opinion, if Luke cites the OT in the speeches., it is because his first desire is to show the coincidence of the prophetic witness with the apostolic witness. Moreover, the speeches have, in his view, a particular function: to interpret the events in a theological perspective [**22**]. The entire movement of the book, which narrates the diffusion of the word of God, first to the Jews who harden their hearts, then to the pagans who open up to the Gospel, fulfills, according to Luke, the OT promises. The Evangelist puts them into the mouths of the apostles, but they are dear to him. It is thus wrong to speak of "an absence of personal interest [Luke's] for the Scripture." (p. 64).

Having made this reserve, it is necessary to congratulate Amsler for having clearly defined the function of the OT in the book of the Acts [**23**] and for having been the first to note certain characteristics which complete the portrait, only sketched until now. The most important concerns the relation which is established between the prophetic text of the OT and history. Certain introductory formulas to the citations "affirm the divine authority and the historical character of the Scriptural word simultaneously." (p. 66).

The historical character of the OT witness, precisely because it was a prophetic voice [**24**], does not prohibit an identification of the events of the life of the Christ or of the Church, with the object of this witness of the past. According to Amsler, this object of the OT witness is only recognizable in the light of the events themselves in which the Scripture is fulfilled. The ignorance, which Luke speaks of concerning the Jews responsable for Jesus' death, implies "that the Scriptural testimony remained veiled or ambiguous until then." (p. 67). The irruption of the events clarifies the meaning of the prophecies. History, we can say following Amsler, has a coherence and a consistency which the Scripture could not do without. Revelation is real insofar as the reality of the text meets the reality of history.

II. TYPOLOGY

a. Dupont and Conzelmann limited typology to several elements that we meet in the Lucan corpus. Since then, certain exegetes have taken up the question and estimated that the OT figures of Abraham, Joseph, Moses, David and Elijah held an important place in Lucan theology. Instead of presenting these works chronologically, we will take up the characters in the order that they appear in the flow of Biblical history.

Abraham

b. An important article of N. A. Dahl (-> 1966) **[25]** analyzes the person of Abraham in Luke-Acts and regroups the references to the patriarch in the following manner: 1) the God of Abraham, Isaac and Jacob, the God of the fathers; 2) the covenant, oath and promise of God to Abraham; 3) the children of Abraham; 4) Abraham in the hereafter; 5) divers (the geneology of Jesus, Lk 3:34; Abraham's purchase of a tomb, Act 7:16).

On two points, the Lucan image exceeds the OT witness: 1) on several occasions, Luke evokes Abraham in an eschatological context; 2) the description of the patriarch sometimes separates itself from the OT in order to draw near to certain conceptions of Hellenistic Judaism. In any case, it is necessary to note that the description of the eschatological fate of Abraham comes from the evangelical tradition. Luke himself hardly pays it attention. Elsewhere, Luke clings to the text of the OT in the most strict manner, like certain Hellenistic Jewish authors **[26]**.

On the whole, Luke does not transforms Abraham into an example or type of Christ or believers. Abraham, according to Dahl, is, above of all, a historical person. "Thus the summary stresses those themes which are fundamental to the whole outline of Israel's old history, starting with God's revelation to Abraham and leading up to the conquest of the promised land." (p. 142). It is here that Luke the theologian is interesting, for this historical personage was the first to benefit from the promises of God [**27**], promises which were gradually fulfilled, culminating in the service in the name of Jesus, celebrated by the Church. (Dahl insists of the redactional importance of the quotation of Gen 15:13f. in Act 7:6f.) [**28**]. Far from revealing a typological exegesis on the OT, the figure of Abraham in the Lucan work confirms the author's theology of history which underlines the accomplishment of the prophecies. The few typological elements, which concern Moses and Joseph, depend on a theology where the schema promise-accomplishment dominates [**29**]. Thus, Luke does not need to give a Christological interpretation to the promises made to Abraham [**30**].

The image of Abraham, which is described by Stephen (Act 7:2-8), Paul (Act 13:32f.), and Peter (Act 3:25), is coherent; it corresponds to what Luke himself tells us of the patriarch in his Gospel (Lk 3:8; 13:16; 19:9). We can conclude that we have a redactional conception [**31**], especially since the theme of fulfillment of the prophecies is one of the major themes of Lucan theology [**32**]. N. A. Dahl quotes opportunely a recent author: "To see what a writer makes of Abraham, is to understand clearly what he is trying to explain. [**33**] " [**34**]

Moses

c. In his article, **Jesus and Moses in the New Testament** (-> 1956), E. L. Allen [**35**] thinks that Luke uses the figure of Moses as a polyvalent paradigm. In the first speeches of Acts, Moses allows Luke to develop a Christology of the Prophet and, perhaps, of the Servant. Act 3:22ff. defines Jesus as the Prophet of Dt, like Moses, whose authority was unquestionable. Furthermore, Jesus shares the title *παῖς* (servant) with the Moses of the LXX. Finally, prophet and servant, Jesus, like Moses, is a mediator (concerning Moses the mediator, Allen mentions Act 7:38).

It seems erroneous to us to insist on Christ the new Moses in the Lucan work. The text of Dt 18:15-19 (annnouncing a prophet like Moses) interests Luke more by the prophecy it contains (cf. Act 3:24) than by the comparison of Moses and the coming prophet. The title *παῖς* furthermore, is not reserved for Moses in the LXX, and its application to Jesus does not imply a typological argumentation. The speech of Stephen alone, as we will see, describes Moses in such a manner that a rapport of type-antitype can be established naturally, even if Luke does not explicitly define it. What brings Moses and Jesus together, in Luke's thought, is - here Allen is right - the failure which the two messengers of God meet in their effort to convey a message of deliverance.

d. J. Mánek (-> 1957) went much further than Allen, but perhaps too far. He thinks that Luke systematically developes a typology of the new Exodus. He begins with the expression which is peculiar to Luke, "[Moses and Elijah] spoke of his *ἔξοδος* [Jesus'] which he had to accomplish (*πληροῦν*) in Jerusalem". This expression appears in the Transfiguration narrative (Lk 9:31) The Czechoslovak exegete thinks that the Passion of Christ and his exaltation correspond typologically to the Exodus from Egypt and the entry into the promise land. The earthly Jerusalem - Mánek recognizes that this does not come forth in the text - would then represent Egypt, as the place of unbelief where God intervenes to judge and save. When Jesus eats his last meal with his disciples, he reiterates the first Passover. When he leaves the city to go to Gethsemane, he repeats the exit from Egypt, His death on the cross corresponds to the crossing of the Red Sea. Like Moses, Jesus attracted people after him toward salvation. These examples show the excess of the method used by Mánek. The word *ἔξοδος* is certainly important in the Transfiguration narrative, but it is a euphemism for death rather than a reminder of Israel's Exodus. We think that Stephen's speech alone contains typological elements, as Bihler has noted.

e. For J. Bihler (-> 1963), Stephen's speech is redactional and the presentation of Moses which it contains, corresponds to Luke's theology. Following the stages of salvation history, Luke describes the time of the Exodus after that of the patriarchs (Abraham - Joseph). The story of Moses unfolds in periods of forty years (Act 7:23, 30, 36) and already partially accomplishes the promise made to Abraham (cf. Act 7:17). Moses, himself, occupied the role of leader and liberator, rejected by his own. The formulas which describe the work of Moses (*ὁ θεὸς διὰ χειρὸς αὐτοῦ δίδωσιν σωτηρίαν αὐτοῖς*, vs. 25; *τοῦτον τὸν Μωϋσῆν, ὃν ἠρνήσαντο...*; *τοῦτον ὁ θεὸς καὶ ἄρχοντα καὶ λυτρωτὴν ἀπέσταλκεν...*, vs. 35) ressemble those which Luke uses elsewhere to describe the mission and function of Jesus. Compared to the text of the OT, the narrative is centered more on Moses than on God. The Christology appears implicitly: Moses is described as the type of redeemer invested with a mission and divine authority which the elected people reject in unbelief. However, the quotation of Dt 18:15 (in vs. 37) reminds the exegete that for Luke,the typology is in keeping with the framework of a theology of promise [36].

David

f. No one to our knowledge has analyzed the figure of David in the writings of Luke [37]. Like Abraham, David is, first and foremost, a historical personage of Israel's past. In a summary of holy history (Act 13), Luke says this about David: "Having removed [Saul], he [God] brought forth David as king. He gave this testimony about him: "I found David, the son of Jesse, a man after my heart, who will accomplish all that I will. According to his promise, God has brought to Israel, Jesus as savior," from David's descendents, (Act 13:22f.). It is neither the virtue of David nor his royalty, which interests Luke. David is an important figure insofar as he is connected to the present by the accomplishment of the promises. Thus, David survives in two ways in the memory of Luke:

1) as *πατριάρχης* (Act 2:29), ancestor of the Messiah and beneficiary of the promise of 2 Sam 7, he received the assurance from God, that his descendent would rule the universe;

2) as *προφήτης* (Act 2:30), herald of the Messiah and author of the Psalms, he prophesied of the resurrection, the exaltation and the enthroning of the Messiah, his descendent [38].

Luke does not insist on the typology David-Jesus, but rather on the continuity of history and its fulfillment in Christ: more than a new David, Jesus is the <u>descendent</u> (the son) of David, he in whom the promise <u>is fulfilled</u>. The resurrection of Jesus shows that the Scripture is accomplished and the descendent surpasses the ancestor. The flesh of David saw corruption (Act 2:29), David himself did not go up to heaven (Act 2:34), while Christ has risen and attained his heavenly throne. Therefore, Luke prefers to note the ontological difference in the continuity of redemptive history rather than the identity in the contemporaneousness of the figures. As a relative of David, Jesus is not less distinguished by his universal reign and his celestial exaltation.

Certain OT texts relative to David which are applied to Jesus, especially the three quotations in Act 13:32-37 (Psa 2:7; Isa 55:3 and Psa 16:10) have been the object of countless studies [**39**]. It would be impossible to consider them all in an exhaustive manner.

g. The Swedish exegete E. Lövestam published a book on these verses (-> 1961) [**40**]. First of all, he situates the three citations in the course of the speech of Paul at Antioch of Pisidia (vss. 16-22: a historical retrospective where the author insists of the leaders who saved Israel; vs. 24ff.: the kerygma concerning Jesus; vss. 32-37: the Scriptural argument; vss. 38-41: the conclusion in the form of a call to the hearers). Finally, he ana - lyzes (pp. 8-48) the quote taken from Psa 2:7 ("you are my son, today I have begotten you") and ties the ambiguous words, *ἀναστήσας Ἰησοῦν* - "Jesus having been resuscitated (or resurrected)", to the resurrection rather than to the ministry of Jesus. He connects the divine sonship to the promise made to David (2 Sam 7) because of the messianic exegesis of Psa 2 in Judaism and early Christianity. The quotation of Psa 2 in Act 13 demonstrates the universal royalty of the one called "my son": Jesus the risen one (the resurrection and the ascension coincide) fulfills the promise made to David. The old crux interpretum "I will give you the holy and sure things of David" (Isa 55:3 LXX) are the object of the following chapter (pp. 48-81). According to Lövestam, these words are comprehensible only in the framework of the eternel covenant between David and God, the covenant that Judaism and early Christianity did not lose sight of. According to this covenant, God promised a universal reign to a descendent of David. The import of Isa 55:3 corresponds to that of Psa 2:7. The whole passage refers to 2 Sam 7. Lövestam understands the words *ὅσια* and *πιστά* in the context of the covenant in the way that Hellenistic Judaism understood it. The eternity of the Davidic reign and the firmness of the promise were on equal footing. Finally, Lövestam (pp. 81-83) analyzes the quote from Psa 16 to which Luke attributes less importance than to Isa 55:3. As in Act 2, the quotation of Psa 16 finds its prophetic strength in the fact that it is not fulfilled in the person of David. Jesus, alone, did not know *διαφθορά*.

h. With T. Holtz [**42**], we wonder if Luke had this context of the covenant in mind, when he edited Act 13. It is not so sure, for is it not surprising that Luke does not cite the words which in Isa 55:3 LXX, immediately precede *τὰ ὅσια Δαυίδ τὰ πιστά* and correspond so well with Lövestam's hypothesis: *καὶ διαθήσομαι ὑμῖν διαθήκην αἰώνιον* ("and I will establish an eternal covenant with you") ? It could be that Luke had only the promise made to David in sight. In fact, he only desires to give two citations: Psa 2:7 and Psa 16:10. Only these two are introduced with a formula: "As it is written in the second psalm" (v. 33) and "he says in another psalm [psalm not "text"(vs. 35)] [**43**]". The expression in Isa 55 was perhaps suggested to him by the presence of the hook-word *ὅσια* which is close to the *ὅσιος* of Psa 16 [**44**]. Yet, it is possible that at the traditional level of the speech [**45**], the three quotations in Act 13 were already grouped in a messianic context of covenant. E. Lövestam's impressive investigations of the Jewish and Christian exegetical background of the quotations make the hypothesis likely. Luke would have reinterpreted them in the sense of his theology of promise.

i. Without going into detail, let us mention the results of the articles of Dupont and Schweizer. According to Dupont (-> 1961, second title), the reference to Isa 55:3 is not a direct prophecy of Jesus' resurrection, but rather an announcement of the fruit that Christians can derive from this redemptive act of God. From now on, sanctification (*ὅσια*) and justification (*πιστά*) are accessible to us, for Jesus, the son of David, is immortal (he will not see corruption, vs. 34).

E. Schweizer (-> 1966) discovers two lines for the interpretation of the Davidic promises in Judaism and Christianity. In the first , the descendent of David is the Israel of the last days (corporate grandeur), whereas in the second, he is the Messiah-King. The quotations in Act 13:33, which sees the fulfillment of Psa 2:7 in the resurrection confirm the predominance of the latter conception in the NT. The Church can not benefit from the privi - leges of the Son of David, except by the mediation of the risen Jesus. Adoption passes through Christology and does not reach God directly [46].

III. THE TEXT OF THE OLD TESTAMENT

a. The precise study of the textual tradition of the OT quotations in the Lucan corpus is not without theological interest. After a detailed investigation, L. Cerfaux (-> 1950) came to some interesting conclusions. He thinks it fitting to distinguish the isolated texts which follow the LXX text from the composite citations, where the deviations from the LXX are more important. To explain this distinction, it is necessary to suppose "that a general cause intervenes which could be Luke's contact, or rather, an early apologetic with collections of Biblical citations." (p. 51). The majority of these quotations in series would come from a collection of Testimonia. "The textual tradition, has hardly modified the primitive purport of the citations. We notice, however, a tendency in **B** [the text supposedly at the base of the uncials B, A, C and 81] to take unduly certain quotations back to the text of the LXX... **D** [Western text] is certainly the cause of a good number of the cases where it has conserved the primitive reading ..." (p. 51).

b. It is mainly against this rehabilitation of the Western text [**47**] that E. Haenchen (-> 1954) rose up. Several of the readings of **D** which Cerfaux thinks primitive can be explained either by the influence of the latin (the Codex Bezae, the main representative of the Western text is bilingual) or by the theological tendencies of the Western text [**48**] (especially its idea of Christian universalism, its Heidenfreundlichkeit).

Only a detailed analysis would allow one to adopt a definite position on the matter, which is a singularly complex affair. Let us note an example where a theological difference occurs between the Egyptian text and the Western text. The passage is a composite citation found in Act 2:30. The OT quotations are from Psa 131:11 and 2 Sam 7:12.

The Egyptian text is: *ὅρκῳ ὤμοσεν αὐτῷ ὁ θεὸς ἐκ καρποῦ τῆς ὀσφύος αὐτοῦ καθίσαι ἐπὶ τὸν θρόνον αὐτοῦ.*

The Western text is: *ὅρκῳ ὤμοσεν αὐτῷ ὁ θεὸς ἐκ καρποῦ τῆς καρδίας αὐτοῦ κατὰ σάρκα ἀναστῆσαι τὸν χριστὸν καὶ καθίσαι ἐπὶ τὸν θρόνον αὐτοῦ* [**49**].

As Cerfaux notes, "in the text of **B**, it is difficult to know which connection to establish between the following three things: the quality of the prophecy attributed to David, the oath which was made to him and the prediction of the resurrection. Contrariwise, in the Western text, the three elements arrange themselves according to an ancient theological theme: because David is a prophet, he "sees" the formulation of the divine oath: God "will raise up" (*ἀναστῆσαι*) the Christ, according to the flesh, and this *ἀνάστασις* according to the flesh symbolizes the *ἀνάστασις* according to the power of the Spirit." (p. 49f.). If we have understood properly, for Cerfaux, the Pauline logic of the Western text goes back to Luke, for the author of the Western text cannot be made responsible, as he betrays Paul's thought elsewhere (Act 13:39). Luke himself must have relied on a collection of Biblical quotations. Contrary to this, for Haenchen, here the Western text improves, as is often the case, the difficulties of the text it is copying. It does so by referring more closely to 2 Sam 7:12 and by enlarging the contents of the oath. It did not feel that the resurrection and the ascension formed a unity (which we think may have been the case with Luke!) and distinguished *ἀναστῆσαι* from *καθίσαι*· p. 169 of the volume. For us, two arguments tip the scale in favor of the Egyptian text: a) it would be difficult to tolerate *ἀναστῆσαι* in the sense of "raise up" (the only sense possible aside the words *ἐκ καρποῦ τῆς ὀσφύος αὐτοῦ* and *κατὰ σάρκα*) since in the next verse, *ἀνάστασις* means resurrection; b) the accused words *κατὰ σάρκα ἀναστῆσαι τὸν χριστόν* do not correspond to the thought of Luke, who is unaware of the *κατὰ σάρκα - κατὰ πνεῦμα* pair as well as the joining of *σάρξ* and *ἀνίστημι*.

c. In his book on the semitisms in the Acts (-> 1965), M. Wilcox consecrates a chapter on the OT quotations ("The Old Testament in Acts", pp. 20-55) [**50**]. He reckons that Luke's citations do not all come from the LXX. Here is how he presents the project of his investigation: "Our present problem is to obtain a "test-group", that is to assemble a group of instances of quotation and allusion in which the OT text cited in Acts deviates from the accepted text of the Septuagint in such a way as to find support in some other authority, Greek, Hebrew, or Aramaic." (p. 20).

In the first section, the author attempts to discover traces of targumic textual tradition in the citations in Acts. The speech of Stephen (Act 7), in particular, contains a certain number of traits which can be explained by an influence of the Targumim. For example, Act 7:10b qualifies Joseph as *ἡγούμενος*, a term absent from the Masoretic text and present in Psa 105:21 of the LXX, while, the corresponding Aramaic word srkn can be read in the Targum of the Pseudo-Jonathan. We wonder if the resorting to the targum is necessary here, since we know that the title *ἡγούμενος* is frequent in the LXX to designate a leader or a minister [**51**].

Without a doubt, it is erroneous to speak of the influence of the Targumim on Luke; nevertheless, it is probable that a weighty Jewish and early Christian exegetical heritage is hidden behind certain quotations in Acts, especially those which are composite or grouped in series. This heritage can only be imagined. The citations in Acts resemble a thin layer of hardened lava, which covers the unknown depths of an active volcano [**52**].

The second section discovers only two cases where the Lucan text comes nearer to the Hebrew text than the LXX: in Act 7:16 *παρὰ τῶν υἱῶν* Εμμώρ (cf. Josh 24:32; LXX *παρὰ τῶν* 'Αμορραίων) and Act 8:32 (a quotation of Isa 53:7f. according to the LXX except for one point which recalls the Hebrew text). Here again, Wilcox' argument is not convincing: we cannot make conclusions based on a proximity to the Masoretic text. It is not said that Act 7:16 alludes to Josh 24, it even seems rather unlikely. The Lucan witness of this verse does not agree with the Biblical data. As J. Dupont notes (in the Bible de Jerusalem, fascicle Les Actes des Apôtres, Paris 1964[3], p. 78, n. b), "Stephen follows a tradition which confuses 1) the cave in Hebron bought by Abraham in Ephron (Gen 23) with the field in Shechem which Jacob bought from the sons of Hamor (written like this in Hebrew: Gen 33:19); and 2) the funeral of Jacob in Hebron (Gen 50:13), with Joseph's burial in Shechem (Josh 24:32)." Since we are talking about a tradition and not a quotation, we cannot say this passage is nearer to the Hebrew text than to the LXX. Moreover, Wilcox does not think that Luke resorted to the Hebrew: he only supposes that Luke could have known other traditions of the LXX and this is what he attempts to show in the last two sections of his chapter.

In the third section, entitled, "Evidence of an aberrant Old Testament Text", he draws attention to several curious cases where on several occasions, Luke mentions a similar text which deviates from all the known textual tradition: the text is Dt 18:15 (or 18) in Act 3:22 and 7:37; Ex 3:6 in Act 3:13 and 7:32 and Dt 21:22 in Act 5:30 and 10:39b **[53]**. In the fourth section, the author compares these strange quotations to the fifth column of the Hexapla of Origen, the LXX of Hexapla, which we know transmits two Greek translations. The one (asterisk) seems to be closer to the Masoretic text; the other (obelus) leans toward the Samaritan Pentateuch: Wilcox concludes from this: "Perhaps the most that can be said is that, while there may be here some indication of a degree at least of textual affinity between certain portions of the OT employed in Acts and their original Hebrew forms, in contradistinction to their LXX forms, the facts are nevertheless not inconsistent with the use of an alternative recension of the Greek Bible." (p. 44).

Despite our reservations, we must note Wilcox' prudence in his allegations and approve of his effort to explain the allusions which depart from the LXX. More than to another Greek translation, we would rather turn toward the use of a revised LXX (cf. J. Dupont, above 2, I, b) and toward the Jewish Hellenistic exegetical traditions.

d. T. Holtz' Habilitationsschrift, **Untersuchungen über die alttestamentlichen Zitate bei Lukas**, finished in 1964 and published in -> 1968 **[54]**, is without a doubt the most important work on this subject to appear in the last twenty years [55]. The author fixed as his first goal, to locate the books of the Septuagint that Luke cites in a selbständig manner, i.e. he knows personally [56]. His second goal is to discover the form of the OT text which the Evangelist had at his disposal. If the results of the first quest render a service to the Lucan exegete, the answers of the second question are useful for the historian of the LXX.

First, let us mention the conclusions which concern us directly. Holtz thinks that Luke only knew the LXX and, from the LXX, a text close to the A family, of which the Alexandrinus is the main witness. Thanks to Luke, the existence of this family is attested in the first century, which is three hundred years before this uncial. If this conclusion is clear for the Minor Prophets and Isaiah, it is less convincing for the Psalms, which is not surprising, for liturgical usage strongly influenced the manuscript tradition of the Psalms.

Holtz was able to demonstrate - here we pass over his other conclusions - that Luke had at his disposition the text of the Minor Prophets, Isaiah and the Psalms [57]. These are his preferred books; those he knows well, uses often and to which he refers to verify or correct a traditional citation. Luke shows a great faithfulness to the text. When he deviates clearly from the LXX, he does it inadvertently or by literary necessity [58]. Holtz plays down the idea of intentional theological transformations. This is precisely where Rese rightly criticizes him[59]. It is rather by lengthening or shortening a traditional citation that Luke manifests his doctrinal intentions: for example, in Acts 15, vs. 16 (= Am 9:11) diverges from the LXX and cannot be considered a selbständig quotation for it is a traditional citation. Luke took it up in James' speech and, after the reading of the scroll of Amos, he followed it up with vs. 17 (= Am 9:12), the next verse in the prophetic text, which is faithful to the LXX. Here, Holtz accepts a theological reason: Am 9:12, according to the LXX, proclaims the universalism of salvation, contrasted with the particularism of Am 9:11 (vs. 16). We wonder if the whole Amos citation is not redactional, for vss. 11 and 12 of Am 9 do not contradict one another, rather they reflect a schema which is dear to Luke (and Paul): the reestablishment of Israel (first phase) which leads to the opening up to the nations (second phase). More generally, we wonder if Holtz is right to say that when a quotation differs from the LXX, it must be traditional and when it is true to it, redactional [60]. In this manner, he thinks the quotation of Ps 69:26 in Act 1:20a, which diverges from the LXX, must be traditional (it was taken from the narrative of the death of Judah), while Ps 109:8 in Act 1:20b, true to the LXX, is redactional. Indeed, the account of the choice of Matthias is strongly marked by Luke's theology. In a similar manner, he can break down the quote from Ps 16 in Act 2:25-28: vs. 10 of Ps 16 ("you will not abandon my flesh to Hades") must be a traditional testimonium (we find it again not farther than vs. 31). Luke has enlarged the quotation with the help of his scroll of the Psalms.

Luke's preference for the Minor Prophets, Isaiah and the Psalms was already known, but the conclusion of the study of the citations taken from the Pentateuch, is more original and startling. Holtz notes that they are rare and almost all diverge from the LXX text [**61**]. Here the German exegete concludes that Luke had no text of the Pentateuch and had no interest in the laws of the OT or the narratives of Genesis or Exodus. The quotations of the Pentateuch which he passes on must not be from his pen. Luke took them over from the Jewish or Christian tradition which must have constituted a series of small collections of Testimonia (the Scriptural succession, in Act 3:22-25, where Dt 18:15, Lev 23:29 and Gn 22:18 follow one another, or in Act 13:33-35, where Ps 2:7, Is 55:3 and Ps 16:10 do the same, could be an indication in favor of such collections). The historical reminders in Act 7 and 13 do not affirm Holtz' idea, for they would be traditional for the most part. Luke would have Christianized, for example, the speech of Stephen, originally Jewish, with the redactional vss. 35 and 37, and the addition of a conclusion, vss. 51-53, which he would have taken from another source. If Luke did not align the narrative of the origins of Israel closer to the Bible, it is because he was unable to, for he did not have a copy of the Torah and the Historical Books on hand. Holtz, however, does not conclude that Luke rejects the Pentateuch, but he cannot help himself from bringing the Evangelist's attitude close to those of other contemporary religious movements; Qumran, for example, where the Prophets and the Psalms attracted more attention than the Pentateuch. Unfortunately, Holtz does not push ahead in the delimitation of this Jewish milieu friendly to prophecies and the Psalms [**62**].

Before ratifying Holtz' attractive thesis, the four critical questions, which follow, must be answered:

1) Is it not proper to distinguish the brief citations from the longer ones? A long citation has more chance having been verified, since in this case, the mind may falter. Since the quotes from the Pentateuch are generally short, certain could be redactional. Sure of himself, Luke may not have checked them.

2) This is our most fundamental criticism: Is Holtz right in speaking of selbständig quotations for the instances where they are conform to the LXX and reflect Lucan preoccupations? It seems that Holtz has forgotten the principle, verified on the quotations of Clement of Alexandria [63], according to which the verbatim citations often come from books which the author knew less, and to which, he must refer to the text in order to verify it, in a quite unselbständig manner. We do not want to conclude that Luke knew the Minor Prophets and the Psalms especially badly, but we draw attention to this phenomenon which, paired with the brevity of the quotations, could explain the references to the Pentateuch. Luke's most selbständig citations are found among these imprecise citations!

3) On the whole, does not Holtz neglect the theological reasons which may be at the origin of the modification of certain quotations? Is the conviction correct,which holds that fidelity to the text surpasses freedom? To take but one example (Act 2:17), is it likely that Luke wrote *μετὰ ταῦτα* (the text of the LXX) and that the manuscript tradition corrected this exact quote into "in the end of days" [64]? Did not Luke want to express an aspect of his eschatology, by these last words? [65]

4) Does not Holtz underestimate Luke's literary effort? He does not notice, unless error, that the historical recollections of Act 7 and 13 complete one another: in Act 7, the reminiscence touches on the origins of Israel, while in Act 13, it concerns the royalty. As an author who seeks to please, Luke varies the content of the speeches. We are sure that Luke depended on Hellenistic Jewish exegetical traditions, but in these speeches, the redactional impact is more important that Holtz thinks [66]. The principle of selection which Holtz uses concerning Act 7 does not convince us [67].

Despite these critical questions, the importance of Holtz' work should be recalled, both by the quality of his analysis of the quotations and the original hypotheses he proposes.

e. If Holtz underestimates Luke's editorial effort in the quota - tions, M. Rese (-> 1969), contrariwise, exaggerates perhaps in the other direction [68]. His opinion is that the differences between the LXX and the Lucan citations arise either from Luke's literary preoccupations or his theological ideas. Luke manipulates the OT text with a freedom which Holtz did not recognize.

Rese's research fits into the contemporary redactional analysis scene (redaktionsgeschichtlich). If he limits his investigation to the OT references related to Christological intention, he widens it, compared to Holtz, by inserting allusions and the Christological titles.

We would expect an author, sensitive to redactional problems, to study the Biblical quotations by following the thread of the Lucan discourse, but this is not the case. Rese begins with the Acts and goes back to the Gospel afterwards. First, he isolates the speeches in Acts and then chapters 1 and 2 in the Gospel. He maintains the same order for the quotations, allusions and Christological titles. Each time he asks the same three questions: what is cited (text), how is it cited (the form of the text) and why is it cited (the significance and function of the text). It is in the answer to the third question which he is the most original and makes the most progress [69].

This German exegete proposes to distinguish four types of citations, according to their function in the Scriptural argument: He calls the first and most numerous type (in his analysis), hermeneutical quotations. In these cases, Luke does not seek to demonstrate a truth, but to make an event or reality understood. This hermeneutical use of the Scripture is pre-Christian and is more frequent in Luke than was thought. The frequency is quite surprising from a defender of redemptive history, for in such an explanation of Scripture, the distance which separates the OT text from the present, is neglected. For Rese, the quote from Joel 3 in Act 2 is this type.

Rese calls the second type of quotation the simple Scriptural proof. The time factor still does not intervene, but the function of the citation is different; it is not to explain, but to prove. Therefore, the references to Ps 16 and 110 prove the Messiahship and lordship of Christ.

The third and forth types, less frequent in Luke than believed, fit into the promise-fulfillment schema and take into consideration the time separation. The former [70] emphasizes the present accomplishment: Such is the case with Act 13:32ff., where Luke affirms that the present kerygma fulfills the promise of old. The latter [71] insists on the past prophecy: so in Act 1:16ff the predicted death of Judah comes to pass. A successor to the traitor must be found for Scripture had already spoken of this succession [72].

Is not this division too schematic and do not the majority of the quotations fit into the promise-fulfillment schema? At the same time, that the manifestation of the Scriptural argumentation can be hermeneutic (the first type) or demonstrative (the second), which both ignore the time difference, as is sometimes the case at this period (Qumran) and as it could happen in patristic exegesis, seems a valuable acquirement to us.

To distinguish between the traditional citations and the redac - tional ones, Rese uses a different method than Holtz': he exam - ines the citation in question to see if it appears in other Christian writings and if an exegetical tradition can be discovered. If such is not the case, the mentioned quotation is probably editorial.

Rese thinks that the time of theological syntheses has not yet arrived. This is why he refuses to draw general conclusions from his research. It is, therefore, difficult to present the results of an investigation which is often microscopic. Nonetheless, we will try to discern several strong points.

1) True to the exegetical traditions **[73]**, Luke is very free with regard to the Scripture, whose text (of the LXX) is not sancrosanct. On p. 173, he remarks "dass mit L(k) 20,18 das extremste Beispiel für die Freiheit des Lk bei der Heranziehung von Schriftzitaten vorliegt." The theological criterion, with literary exigency, is the most important motif of modification.

2) This liberty is shown not only in the choice of the citations or their transformation but also in how they are delimitated. Rese insists on the fact that Luke knows perfectly well how to cut off a citation at the point which suits him (either in that the last phrase cited fits perfectly or that the following, which he does not quote, contradicts his idea). Therefore, according to his view, Luke terminates the quotation of Joel 3 at vs. 5a (Act 2:17-21), as vs. 5b has a particularistic coloring (p. 50); Ps 16 is cut off at vs.11b, for vs. 11c does not correspond to his pneumatology (Act 2:25-28) (p. 55); Isa 53 is stopped at verse 8c, for 8d brings in the expiatory value of the death of the servant (Act 8:32f.) **[74]**; Isa 55 ends with vs. 3b, because he refuses to mention the divine convenant with David, knowing the covenant with Abraham (Act 13:34) (p. 86ff.) **[75]**. Accepted by others, Rese rejects the influence of the rabbinic rule on Luke, according to which a quotation evokes the context from which it comes. Given Luke's pagan origin, this is not impossible, yet the case in Act 2 shows how much the context of Joel 3:1-5 - and not only the citation - has an influence on Peter's speech (cf. p. 39).

3) For Luke, the Bible is certainly a book of prophecies and sacred history, but it is also a divine message which permits the interpretation of the present time and the comprehension of the person of the Christ. This definition of Scripture shines through Luke's hermeneutical usage.

4) Throughout his exegetical progress, Rese gleans a series of sprouts from the same grain. Bound in sheaves,they form a

striking image of the importance of the theme of salvation in the work of Luke[76]. Is it not remarkable that several Scriptural quotations or arguments terminate with a mention of the salvation of the people or the nations?

Simeon, paraphrasing Isa 40:5, says, "my eyes have seen your salvation" (Lk 2:30); or concerning John the Baptist, Isa 40:3-5 ends with the words, "all flesh will see the salvation of God" (Lk 3:6); or again Peter, citing Joel 3, cuts off the quote with, "whoever calls on the name of the Lord will be saved" (Act 2:21); and further, after having cited Isa 6:9f. (the hardening of the Jews), Paul concludes his speech in Acts with,"therefore, know that the salvation of God has been sent to the Gentiles and they will listen" (Act 28:28).

5) Concerning Christology, Rese thinks that we cannot speak of adoptionism. The famous phrase "God made him Lord and Christ" (Act 2:36) is the conclusion of the Scriptural argument of the hermeneutical type: Ps 16 affirms the messianism of the Christ (by the resurrection) and Ps 110, his lordship (by means of his elevation). Vs. 36 summarizes the message of these two quotations. Despite an interesting analysis of the Isa 53 quote that Lk 22 makes in the Passion narrative, Rese concludes, with many others, that Luke refuses all expiatory value to the cross of Jesus [77].

We can reproach Rese for not having formulated himself these conclusions which imposed themselves in the reading his book. Furthermore, we would criticize him for overinterpreting certain textual data and discovering theological intentions where there were none. It also seems dangerous, for example, to draw arguments from Biblical passages that Luke does not cite (cf. preceding page): can we affirm [78] that Luke avoids linking the miracles of Jesus to the Holy Spirit because in Lk 4:18f. (the first sermon of Jesus in Nazareth), there is no mention of healing? This does not degrade the fact that by the emphasis on the hermeneutical type of citations and the quality of certain detailed exegesis, Rese has contributed to a better understanding of Luke's view of the Scripture [79].

Conclusion

We have already mentioned the valuable results of the works analyzed: Dupont, Schubert and Conzelmann have shown us that Luke hears the Scripture like a prophetic voice which announces the coming, death and resurrection of the Messiah.

The evangelical kerygma, based on recent history, invites the identification of the Messiah with Jesus of Nazareth. The promises of the OT aim also at the universal extension of the Church and the hardening of the first beneficiaries of revelation. The studies of the OT figures, Dahl's especially, have shown us that Luke, first, sees the great OT characters as men of the past; men who received promises which are fulfilled in the now and thus tied to the present. Rare are the occasions where Luke interprets these figure as types of Christ.

If the Scripture is a prophetic word, it is also a text, reporting the events in which the historical and profane nature cohabit with divine revelation, in a coexistence that the conclusion of our first chapter attempted to state precisely.

The textual criticism, effected by Wilcox and Holtz, revealed that if Luke depended on the LXX, he is, nonetheless, influenced by Jewish and Christian exegetical traditions, summaries of redemptive history and short collections of Testimonia. Luke's freedom with the LXX is disputed: Holtz underlines Luke's fidelity to the sacred text, and Rese, the liberty that he takes with a text which is not sacrosanct for the evangelist. In any case, the choice of citations - he prefers the Minor Prophets, Isaiah and the Psalms - allows Luke to explain the theological truths he deems essential.

In rereading the quotations and the reminiscences of the OT in the Lucan text, we have come to several convictions which we would like to present to the reader, at the end of this chapter.

Even if the Scripture is never cited in an explicit manner, the infancy narrative is bathed in a Biblical ambiance. Luke seems concerned to prolong the OT discourse and introduce the reader, who at the outset of his reading, learns that the beginning is followed up (cf. the genealogy of Jesus, Lk 3:23-38).

Compared to the first chapters of the Acts, the body of the Gospel is poor in Biblical references. Above all Luke desires to relate the novelty, tell of the salvific events and present Jesus. The beginning of the Acts fulfills a similar function with reference to the dawning Church, but he will indicate the conformity of the recent events to the ancient promises. He will provide in this way the meaning of the historical facts.

This hermeneutical mission is not absent from the Gospel, which here and there, mentions the accomplishments of the prophecies in John the Baptist and, especially, in Jesus: the voice foretold crying in the desert (Isa 40:3-5) in Lk 3:4f.; the Spirit of the Lord on Jesus (Isa 61:1f.) in Lk 4:18f.; the stone rejected by the builders (Ps 118:22) has become the cornerstone in Lk 20:17 and the Messiah counted among the wicked (Isa 53:12) in Lk 22:37.

The quotations in the first chapters of the Gospel affirm Jesus' authority, the Messiah enabled by God. The last citations, in the context of the Passion, witness to the truth which is hard to swal - low: the way of the Messiah must pass by suffering and rejection.

Situated between these two groups are several references to the OT understood as Law. Following the Christian tradition, Luke perceives the core of these, in the double commandment of love (Lk 10:27) and in the Decalogue (Lk 18:20). To make love a commandment constitutes a paradox: the gesture of love inscribed in a law, by nature constraining, becomes obligatory, while in its essence, it can be but voluntary and free. Nevertheless, the evangelical context in which Luke situates his calls to the law modifies the sense of the requirements. This flows from the initiative of God, who in sending his son Jesus has come to save what was lost. From now on, the law is placed with the promise side by side the liberty received in salvation.

This declaration explains perhaps the curious use of the term *διαθήκη* in Luke. The only convenant of old that Luke notes expli - citly is the one God offered to Abraham (Lk 1:72; Act 3:25 and 8:8). The Sinai covenant does not appear as such and Moses plays the role of a mediator, not in the establishment of the covenant, but in the transmission of the Law, or more precisely, the living oracles (Act 7:38). This fact should orient the interpretation of Pentecost where the typology of Sinai seems probable: here the narrative of Act 2 represents less the establishment of a new covenant (it has been established by the blood of Christ, Lk 22:20, if the long text is authentic) than the diffusion of the Spirit and the Word of God.

We have seen in this chapter the extent of Scriptural applica - tions: it unfolds from John the Baptist to the Christian mission, inspired by the Spirit at Pentecost. , Jesus Christ is at the core of it, especially the Easter reality of the resurrection. Except for one or two exceptions, it does not touch the Parousia, last judgment or resurrection of the dead.

The Scripture aims at the "Christic" reality. But for Luke from what type of knowledge does this Scriptural logic come? Since the force of the argument is not always constraining and Luke accords a large place to obtuseness and ignorance, that is, the willful blindness of Israel (cf. the finale of Acts), it follows that the Scriptural proof, like the Gospel narrative, belongs to the rhetoric of persuasion. It is not enough to open the book, one must open his eyes and beyond his eyes, his mind and heart.

A relation is restored between the book, that Israel is right to open each Sabbath, and the readers, who often refuse to accept this reading. Open one's self up to the Gospel is, according to Luke, to welcome a message (the kerygma centered on Jesus Christ) and to retain a text (the OT); open one's ears to the Word and one's eyes to the Scripture. From this convergence faith proceeds, faith which is not a passive reception, but rather, the adherence to a God who expresses himself in the Scripture and the Gospel. Thus, faith does not come from the intervention of the Holy Spirit. The Scriptural quotations are destined to those who accept their authority.

Conzelmann was right to remind us of another relation, the tie which binds the Scripture to the Church. Of course, Luke spontaneously entrusts the interpretation of the Scripture to the Church and her main spokesmen. Yet it does not follow that he restricts the number of interpreters, to give them an exterior authority, endowed with a juridical power or a historical anteriority. On the contrary, the Christological interpretation that the apostles give to the Scripture draws its truth from the Holy Spirit who dwells in them. It is Peter, filled with the Spirit, who correctly interprets the present situation with the help of Joel 3 (Act 2) and who applies Psa 118:22 (Act 4:8, 11) to Jesus. It is the same for Stephen when he paints the historical fresco of Israel (Act 6:8, 15 and 7:51, 55). And if the Spirit permits a proper perusal of the Scripture today, it is because, formerly Christ himself was an exegete: at Easter and even from the beginning. Since he received the Spirit himself, he can give the explanation in the form of an application of Isa 61, "the Spirit of the Lord is upon me", (Lk 4:21). More than a reading with an ecclesiastical character, Luke extols a reading illuminated by the Spirit and the Christ.

At the term of this conclusion, we would like to propose two tasks to research: the first, which we can already feel the lure, would be to specify the Hellenistic Jewish and Christian exegetical milieu in which Luke swims and determine which type of exegesis most influenced him (the recent distinctions between Targumic, Midrashic and haggadic, etc. hermeneutic have little influenced Lucan studies so far) [**80**]. The second would be to analyze meticulously the literary function of the citations. Structural analysis of the narratives is sensitive to the quotations in a text, for, after all, it is a text within a text [**81**]. This structural approach of the citations will perhaps be fruitful to the understanding of Lucan thought [82].

CHAPTER 3

CHRISTOLOGY

Chronological bibliography

1913

E. NORDEN, **Agnostos Theos. Untersuchungen zur Formengeschichte religiöser Rede** (Leipzig-Berlin, 1913, 1923[2]; reprint Darmstadt, 1956).

1920

F. J. FOAKES JACKSON and K. LAKE, "Christology", in **Beginnings**, Foakes Jackson, 1, pp. 345-418.

1933

H. J. CADBURY, "The Titles of Jesus in Acts", in **Beginnings**, Foakes Jackson, 5, pp. 354-375.

H. J. CADBURY, "The Speeches", in **Beginnings**, Foakes Jackson, 5, pp. 402-427.

1936

C. H. DODD, **The Apostolic Preaching and its Developments. Three Lectures** (London, 1936); we are referring to the 1963 ed. (FT Paris, 1964).

1939

J. GEWIESS, **Die urapostolische Heilsverkündigung nach der Apostelgeschichte** (Breslau, 1939).

1948

W. L. KNOX, **The Acts of the Apostles** (Cambridge, 1948), pp. 72-80.

1949

P. BENOIT, "L'Ascension", **RB** 56 (1949) 161-203; included in P. Benoit, **Exégèse et Théologie** I, (Paris, 1961), pp. 363-411.

M. DIBELIUS, "Die Reden der Apostelgeschichte und die antike Geschichtsschreibung", in **Sitzungsberichte der Heidelberger Akademie der Wissenschaften Phil.-hist. Klasse** (Heidelberg, 1949), I. Abhandlung; taken up in M. Dibelius, **Aufsätze zur Apostelgeschichte** (Göttingen, 1961[4]), pp. 120-162.

J. SCHMITT, **Jésus ressuscité dans la prédication apostolique. Etude de Théologie biblique** (Paris, 1949).

1950

O. CULLMANN, "Jésus Serviteur de Dieu", **DViv** 16 (1950) 17-34.

J. DUPONT, "Le problème du livre des Actes d'après les travaux récents" (Leuven, 1950); included in **Etudes**, Dupont, esp. pp. 105-124.

J. DUPONT, "Jésus, Messie et Seigneur dans la foi des premiers chrétiens", **VSp** 83 (1950) 385-416; taken up in **Etudes**, Dupont, pp. 367-390.

B. GÄRTNER*, "Missionspredikan i Apostlagärningarna", **SvExAb** 15 (1950) 34-54.

H. W. WOLF*, **Jesaja 53 im Urchristentum** (Berlin, 1950).

1951

J. R. GEISELMANN, **Jesus der Christus. Die Urform des apostolischen Kerygmas als Norm unserer Verkündigung und Theologie von Jesus Christus** (Stuttgart, 1951) and under title **Die Frage nach dem historischen Jesus** (Munich 1965^2).

A. RÉTIF, "La place du Christ dans la prédication missionnaire des Actes des Apôtres", **EglViv** 3 (1951) 158-171.

J. SCHMITT, "Le récit de la résurrection dans l'évangile de Luc", **RevSR** 25 (1951) 119-137 and 219-242.

J. STARCKY, "Obfirmavit faciem suam ut iret Jerusalem. Sens et portée de Luc 9, 51", **RecSR** 39 (1951) 197-202.

N. B. STONEHOUSE*, **The Witness of Luke to Christ** (Grand Rapids, 1951).

1952

H. BRAUN, "Zur Terminologie der Acta von der Auferstehung Jesu", **TLZ** 77 (1952) 533-536; included in H. Braun, **Gesammelte Studien zum Neuen Testament und seiner Umwelt** (Tübingen, 1962), pp. 173-177.

K. Y. CHUN*, **The Resurrection of Jesus in Luke-Acts and in the Fifteenth Chapter of First Corinthians**, unpublished dissertation (Boston, 1952).

W. G. MILLER*, **Resurrection of Christ in Peter's Speeches**, unpublished dissertation (Dallas, 1952).

C. SPICQ, "Le Nom de Jésus dans le Nouveau Testament", **VieSpir** 36 (1952) 5-18.

1953

C. CHARLIER*, "Le Manifeste d'Etienne (Actes 7). Essai de commentaire synthétique", **BiViChr** 3 (1953) 83-93.

J. DUPONT*, "Les pèlerins d'Emmaüs (Luc 24, 13-35)", in **Miscellanea Biblica B. Ubach** (Monserrat, 1953), pp. 349-374.

J. MUNCK*, "Den aeldste Kristendom i Apostlenes Gerninger", **DanTTs** 16 (1953) 129-164.

A. RÉTIF, **Foi au Christ et Mission** (Paris, 1953).

J. SCHNEIDER, "Zur Analyse des lukanischen Reiseberichtes", in J. Schmidt and A. Vögtle (eds), **Synoptische Studien für A. Wikenhauser** (Munich, n.d. (1953)) pp. 207-229.

1954

H. CONZELMANN, **Die Mitte der Zeit. Studien sur Theologie des Lukas** (Tübingen, 1954, 1957^2, 1960^3).

G. KRETSCHMAR, "Himmelfahrt und Pfingsten", **ZKG** 56 (1954) 209-253.

E. LOHSE, "Missionarisches Handeln Jesu nach dem Evangelium des Lukas", **TZBas** 10 (1954) 1-13. 158; taken up in **Einheit**, Lohse, pp. 165-177.

P.H. MENOUD, "Remarques sur les textes de l'ascension de Luc-Actes", in W. Eltester (ed), **Neutestamentliche Studien. Festschrift R. Bultmann** (Berlin, 1954), pp. 148-156; included in **Jésus-Christ**, Menoud, pp. 76-84.

H. D. OWEN, "Stephanus' Vision in Acts 7,55", **NTS** 1 (1954-1955) 224-226.

1955

E. L. ALLEN, "Jesus and Moses in the New Testamennt", **ExpTim** 67 (1955-1956) 104-106.

J. G. DAVIES, "The Prefigurement of the Ascension in the Third Gospel", **JTS**, N. S., 6 (1955) 229-233.

B. GÄRTNER, **The Aeropagus Speech and Natural Revelation** (Lund, 1955).

G. W. H. LAMPE, "The Lucan Portrait of Christ", **NTS** 2 (1955-1956) 160-175.

A. R. C. LEANEY, "The Resurrection Narratives in Luke (24, 12-53)", **NTS** 2 (1955-1956) 110-114.

E. LOHSE, **Märtyrer und Gottesknecht. Untersuchungen zur urchristlichen Verkündigung vom Sühnetod Jesu Christi** (Göttingen, 1955, 1963^{2}), pp. 187-191 of the 2nd ed.

J. C. O'NEILL, "The Use of Kyrios in the Book of Acts", **ScotJT** 8 (1955) 155-174.

E. SCHWEIZER, **Erniedrigung und Erhöhung bei Jesus und seinen Nachfolgern** (Zurich, 1955), pp. 35-44 et passim.

1956

C. F. EVANS, "The Kerygma", **JTS**, N. S., 7 (1956) 25-41.

E. HAENCHEN, **Die Apostelgeschichte neu übersetzt und erklärt** (Göttingen 1956, 1959^{3}, 1968^{6}, 1977^{7}). We are citing the 3rd ed.

J. HAROUTUNIAN, "The Doctrine of the Ascension. A Study of the New Testament Teaching", **Interpr** 10 (1956) 270-281.

J. A. T. ROBINSON, "The Most Primitive Christology of All?" **JTS**, N. S., 7 (1956) 177-189; included in Robinson, **Twelve New Testament Studies** (London, 1962, 1965^{2}), pp. 139-153.

1957

O. CULLMANN, **Die Christologie des Neuen Testaments** (Tübingen, 1957) (FT Neuchâtel, 1958, 1962^{2}, 1968^{3} and ET London, 1959, 1963^{2}, 1980).

F. GILS, **Jésus prophète d'après les Evangiles synoptiques** (Leuven, 1957).

A. F. J. KLIJN, "Stephen's Speech-Acts 7, 2-53", **NTS** 4 (1957-1958) 25-31.

R. LAURENTIN, **Structure et théologie de Luc I-II** (Paris, 1957).

C. S. MANN, "The New Testament and the Lord Ascension, **ChQR** 158 (1957) 462-465.

J. E. MÉNARD, "Pais Theou as Messianic Title in the Book of Acts", **CBQ** 19 (1957) 83-92; taken over in French in **StMontReg** I (1958) 213-224.

C. F. D. MOULE, "The Ascension. Acts 1, 9", **ExpTim** 68 (1957) 205-209.

C. F. D. MOULE, "The Post-Resurrection Appearances in the Light of Festival Pilgrimages", **NTS** 4 (1957-1958) 58-61.

E. SCHWEIZER, "Zu den Reden der Apostelgeschichte", **TZBas** 13 (1957) 1-11; taken up in Schweizer, **Neotestamentica. Deutsche und Englische Aufsätze 1951-1963** (Zurich-Stuttgart, 1963), pp. 418-428.

E. TROCMÉ **Le "Livre des Actes" et l'histoire** (Paris, 1957), pp. 207-214.

A. W. WAINWRIGHT, "The Confession 'Jesus is God' in the New Testament", **ScotJT** 10 (1957) 274-299.

C. S. C. WILLIAMS, **A Commentary on the Acts of the Apostles** (London, 1957, 1964^{2}), pp. 44-48 of the 2nd ed.

1958

R. P. CASEY, "The Earliest Christologies", **JTS**, N.S., 9 (1958) 253-277.

M. McD. COFFEY*, **A Study of the Apostolic Preaching on the Person of Christ**, unpublished dissertation, Union Theological Seminary (Richmond, Virginia, 1958).

J. G. DAVIES, **He Ascended into Heaven. A Study in the History of Doctrine** (London 1958).

O. GLOMBITZA, "Die Titel διδάσκαλος und ἐπιστάτης für Jesus bei Lukas", **ZNW** 49 (1958) 275-278.

O. GLOMBITZA, "Acta 13, 15-41. Analyse einer lukanischen Predigt vor Juden", **NTS** 5 (1958-1959) 306-317.

A. HASTINGS*, **Prophet and Witness in Jerusalem. A Study of the Teaching of St. Luke** (London, 1958).

C. M. LAYMON*, **Christ in the New Testament** (New York-Nashville, 1958).

J. MÁNEK, "The New Exodus in the Books of Luke", **NT** 2 (1957-1958) 8-23.

I. DE LA POTTERIE, "L'onction du Christ. Etude de Théologie biblique", **NRT** 80 (1958) 225-252.

R. RUSSEL, "Modern Exegesis and the Fact of the Resurrection", **DowR** 76 (1958) 251-264 and 329-343.

P. A. STEMPVOORT, "The Interpretation of the Ascension in Luke and Acts", **NTS** 5 (1958-1959) 30-42.

V. TAYLOR, **The Person of Christ in New Testament Teaching** (London-New York 1958) (FT Paris, 1969).

U. WILCKENS, "Kerygma und Evangelium bei Lukas (Beobachtungen zu Apg. 10, 34-43)", **ZNW** 49 (1958) 223-237.

1959

H. BALTENSWEILER, **Die Verklärung Jesu. Historisches Ereignis und synoptische Berichte** (Zurich, 1959), pp. 125-133.

W. BARCLAY, "Great Themes of the New Testament - 4. Acts 2, 14-40", **ExpTim** 70 (1959) 196-199 and 243-246.

R. G. BRATCHER, "Having Loosed the Pangs of Death", **BiTrans** 10 (1959) 18-20.

J. DUPONT, "Ressuscité 'le troixième jour'", **Bib** 40 (1959) 742-761; included in **Etudes,** Dupont, pp. 321-336.

A. GELIN, "L'annonce de la Pentecôte (Joël 3, 1-5)", **BiViChr** 27 (1959) 15-19.

W. GRUNDMANN, "Fragen der Komposition des lukanischen 'Reiseberichts'", **ZNW** 50 (1959) 252-270.

M(ORNA) D. HOOKER, **Jesus and the Servant. The Influence of the Servant Concept of Deutero-Isaiah in the New Testament** (London, 1959), pp. 107-116; 137-139.

J. F. JANSEN, "The Ascension, the Church, and Theology", **TTod** 16 (1959) 17-29.

J. E. MÉNARD, "Le titre *παῖς θεοῦ* dans les Actes", in J. Coppens, A. Descamps and E. Massaux (eds), **Sacra Pagina. Miscellanea biblica congressus internationalis catholici de re biblica**, 2 (Paris-Gembloux, 1959), pp. 314-321.

P. MIQUEL, "Le Mystère de l'Ascension", **QLiPar** 40 (1959) 105-126.

W. M. RAMSAY*, **The Christ of the Earliest Christians** (Richmond, Virginia, 1959).

B. REICKE, "The Risen Lord and His Church. The Theology of Acts", **Interpr** 13 (1959) 156-169.

A. C. WINN, "Elusive Mystery. The Purpose of Acts", **Interpr** 13 (1959) 144-156.

1960

G. A. GALITIS*, *'Αρχηγός - 'Αρχηγέτης* dans la littérature et la religion grecques", ΑΘΗΝΑ 64 (1960) 17-138.

G. A. GALITIS, *Ἡ χρῆσις τοῦ ὅρου "ἀρχηγός" ἐν τῇ καινῇ διαθήκῃ. Συμβολὴ εἰς τὸ πρόβλημα τῆς ἐπιδράσεως τοῦ Ἑλληνισμοῦ καὶ τοῦ Ἰουδαισμοῦ ἐπὶ τὴν καινὴν διαυθήκην* (Athens, 1960).

A. J. B. HIGGINS, "The Old Testament and Some Aspects of New Testament Christology", **CanJT** 6 (1960) 200-210.

U. LUCK, "Kerygma, Tradition und Geschichte Jesu bei Lukas", **ZTK** 57 (1960) 51-66; included in **Lukas Forschung**, Braumann, pp. 95-114.

W. C. ROBINSON, "The Theological Context for Interpreting Luke's Travel Narrative (9, 51 ff)", **JBL** 79 (1960) 20-31; taken up in German in **Lukas Forschung**, Braumann, pp. 115-134.

E. SCHWEIZER, "The Son of Man", **JBL** 79 (1960) 119-129.

1961

R. A. BARTELS*, **Kerygma or Gospel Tradition... Which came First?** (Minneapolis, 1961). Cf. W. Klassen, **JBL** 81 (1962) 96f.

J. DUPONT, "*Ἀνελήμφη*", **NTS** 8 (1961-1962) 154-157; included in **Etudes**, Dupont, pp. 477-480.

E. LÖVESTAM, **Son and Saviour. A Study of Acts 13, 32-37. With an Appendix: 'Son of God' in the Synoptic Gospels** (Lund-Copenhagen, 1961).

B. M. F. VAN IERSEL, **"Der Sohn" in den synoptischen Jesusworten. Christusbezeichnung der Gemeinde oder Selbstbezeichnung Jesu?** (Leiden, 1961, 1964^2). We are citing the 1st ed.

L. S. MUDGE*, **The Servant Christology in the New Testament**, unpub - lished dissertation, Princeton University (Princeton, N. J., 1961).

J. C. O'NEIL, **The Theology of Acts in its Historical Setting** (London, 1961, 1970^2).

H. SCHLIER, "Jesu Himmelfahrt nach den Lukanischen Schriften", **GeistLeb** 34 (1961) 91-99; included in H. Schlier **Besinnung auf das Neue Testament** (Freiburg, 1964) (FT Paris, 1968, pp. 263-278).

R. TANNEHILL, "A Study in the Theology of Luke-Acts", **AnglTR** 43 (1961) 195-203.

U. WILCKENS, **Die Missionsreden der Apostelgeschichte. Form- und traditionsgeschichtliche Untersuchungen** (Neukirchen, 1961, 1963^2, 1974^3). Our references are to the 2nd ed.

1962

J. DUPONT, "Les tentations de Jésus dans le récit de Luc (Luc 4, 1-13)" **ScE** 14 (1962) 7-29; taken up in J. Dupont, **Les tentations de Jésus au désert** (Bruges-Paris, 1968), pp. 43-72.

J. DUPONT, "L'interprétation des Psaumes dans les Actes des apôtres", in R. De Langhe (ed), **Le Psautier. Ses origines. Ses problèmes littéraires. Son influence** (Leuven, 1962), pp. 357-388; included in **Etudes**, Dupont, pp. 283-307.

J. DUPONT, **"Le discours de Milet", Testament pastoral de saint Paul** (Paris, 1962).

J. DUPONT, "Les discours missionnaires des Actes des apôtres d'après un ouvrage récent", **RB** 69 (1962) 37-60; included in **Etudes**, Dupont, pp. 133-151.

G. A. GALITIS, *Εἰσαγωγὴ εἰς τοὺς λόγους τοῦ Πέτρου ἐν ταῖς πράξεσι τῶν Ἀποστόλων* (Athens, 1962).

A. GEORGE, "La Royauté de Jésus selon l'évangile de Luc", **ScE** 14 (1962) 57-69.

P. H. MÉNOUD, "Pendant quarante jours (Act 1, 3)", in **Neotestamentica et Patristica. Mélanges O. Cullmann** (Leiden, 1962), pp. 148-156; taken up in **Jésus-Christ**, Menoud, pp. 110-118.

H. N. RIDDERBOS*, **The Speeches of Peter in the Acts of the Apostles**, London, 1962.

W. C. ROBINSON, **The Way of the Lord. A Study of History and Eschatology in the Gospel of Luke** (no place, 1962). The German translation is **Der Weg des Herrn: Studien zur Geschichte und Eschatologie im Lukas-Evangelium. Ein Gespräch mit Hans Conzelmann** (Hamburg-Bergstedt, 1964).

S. S. SMALLEY, "The Christology of Acts", **ExpTim** 73 (1962) 358-362.

K. STALDER, "Die Heilsbedeutung des Todes Jesu in den lukanischen Schriften", **IntkiZ** 52 (1962) 222-242.

1963

J. BIHLER, **Die Stephanusgeschichte im Zusammenhang der Apostelgeschichte** (Munich, 1963).

H. CONZELMANN, **Die Apostelgeschichte erklärt** (Tübingen, 1963, 1972[2]).

M. C. DUCHAINE*, Παῖς θεοῦ **in the Acts of the Apostles**, unpublished dissertation (Leuven, 1963).

G. A. GALITIS, *Χριστολογία τῶν λόγων τοῦ Πέτρου ἐν ταῖς πράξεσι τῶν 'Αποστόλων* (Athens, 1963).

F. HAHN, **Christologische Hoheitstitel. Ihre Geschichte im frühen Christentum** (Göttingen, 1963, 1966[3]).

H. H. OLIVER, "The Lucan Birth Stories and the Purpose of Luke-Acts", **NTS** 10 (1963-1964) 202-226.

L. SABOURIN, **Les nom et titres de Jésus. Thèmes de théologie** (Bruges, 1963).

B. M. F. VAN IERSEL, "Saint Paul et la prédication de l'église primitive: Quelques remarques sur les rapports entre I Cor 15, 3-8 et les formules kérygmatiques des Act 1-13", in **Studiorum paulinorum congressus internationalis catholicus, 1961...**, I (Rome, 1963), pp. 433-441.

1964

C. K. BARRETT, "Stephen and the Son of Man", in W. Eltester and F. H. Kettler (eds), **Apophoreta. Mélanges E. Haenchen** (Berlin, 1964), pp. 32-38.

M. COUNE, "Sauvés au nom de Jésus (Act 4, 8-12)", **AssSeign**, 1st series, 12 (1964) 14-27.

R. D. KAYLOR*, **The Ascension Motif in Luke-Acts, the Epistle to the Hebrews and the Fourth Gospel**, unpublished dissertation, Duke University (Durham, N. C.,1964). Cf. **DissAbstr**, 25 (1964) 6792-6793.

G. D. KILPATRICK, "The Spirit, God, and Jesus in Acts", **JTS**, N.S., 15 (1964) 63.

R. SWEALES, "Jésus, nouvel Elie, dans Saint Luc", **AssSeign**, 1st series, 69 (1964) 41-66.

1965

A. GEORGE, "Jésus Fils de Dieu dans l'évangile selon Saint Luc", **RB** 72 (1965) 185-209.

G. D. KILPATRICK, "Acts 7, 56: Son of Man", **TZBas** 21 (1965) 209.

W. OTT, **Gebet und Heil. Die Bedeutung der Gebetsparänese in der lukanischen Theologie** (Munich, 1965), pp. 94-99.

G. VOSS, **Die Christologie der lukanischen Schriften in Grundzügen** (Bruges, 1965).

1966

N. ALLDRIT, "La Kristologio de la Parolado de Sankta Petro en Agoj 10, 34-44", **BiRe** 7 (1966) 28-31.

D. L. JONES*, **The Christology of the Missionary Speeches in the Acts of the Apostles**, unpublished dissertation, Duke University (Durham, N. C., 1966). Cf. **DissAbstr**, A, 27 (1967) 3925-A.

O. J. LAFFERTY*, "Acts 2, 14-36: A Study in Christology", **DunwR** 6 (1966) 235-253.
R. LAMARCHE, **Christ vivant. Essai sur la Christologie du Nouveau Testament** (Paris, 1966), pp. 21-23 et passim.
B. M. METZGER, "The Meaning of Christ's Ascension", **ChristTod** 10 (1966) 863-864.
P. S. MINEAR, "Luke's Use of the Birth Stories", in **Studies**, Keck, pp. 111-130
C. F. D. MOULE, "The Christology of the Acts", in **Studies**, Keck, pp. 159-185.
R. C. NEVIUS, "Kyrios and Iesous in St Luke", **AnglTR** 48 (1966) 75-77.
R. PESCH, **Die Vision des Stephanus, Apg 7, 55-56 im Rahmen der Apostelgeschicht** (Stuttgart, n.d. (1966)).
J. H. ROBERTS, "Παῖς θεοῦ and ὁ υἱὸς τοῦ θεοῦ in Act 1-13", in **Biblical Essays, OTWerkSuidA**, 1966, pp. 239-263.
G. SCHILLE, "Die Himmelfahrt", **ZNW** 57 (1966) 183-199.
E. SCHWEIZER, "The concept of the Davidic 'Son of God' in Acts and its Old Testament Background", in **Studies**, Keck, pp. 186-193.
E. YARNOLD, "The Trinitarian Implication of Luke and Acts", **HeythJ** 7 (1966) 18-32.

1967

T. JACOBS, "Die Christologie van de redevoeringen der Handelingen", **Bijdr** 28 (1967) 177-196 (pp. 195-196, summary in German).
F. NORMANN, **Christos Didaskalos. Die Vorstellung von Christus als Lehrer in der christlichen Literatur des ersten und zweiten Jahrhunderts** (Münster, 1967), pp. 45-54.
C. H. TALBERT*, "The Lukan Presentation of Jesus' Ministry in Galilee. Luke 4, 31-9, 50", **RExp** 64 (1967) 485-497.
C. H. TALBERT, "An Anti-Gnostic Tendency in Lucan Christology", **NTS** 14 (1967-1968) 259-271.
A. VANHOYE, "Structure et théologie des récits de la Passion dans les Evangiles synoptiques", **NRT** 99 (1967) 135-163.
U. WILCKENS, "Tradition de Jésus et Kérygme du Christ: la double histoire de la tradition au sein du christianisme primitif", **RHPhilRel** 47 (1967) 1-20.

1968

O. BETZ, "The Kerygma of Luke", **Interpr** 22 (1968) 131-146.
G. E. LADD*, "The Christology of Acts", **Foundations** II (1968) 27-41.
J. SCHMITT, "La prédication apostolique, les formes, le contenu", in J. J. Weber and J. Schmitt (eds), **Où en sont les études bibliques. Les grands problèmes actuels de l'exégèse** (Paris, 1968), pp. 107-133.
E. SCHWEIZER, **Jesus Christus im vielfältigen Zeugnis des Neuen Testaments** (Munich-Hamburg, 1968), pp. 136-154.
W. THÜSING, "Erhöhungsvorstellung und Parusieerwartung in der ältesten nach-österlichen Christologie", **BZ**, N.F. II (1967) 95-108; 205-222 and 12 (1968) 223-240 (published in one volume under the same title, Stuttgart, 1970).
S. G. WILSON, "The Ascension: A Critique and an Interpretation", **ZNW** 59 (1968) 269-281.

1969

H. D. BETZ, "Ursprung und Wesen christlichen Glaubens nach der Emmauslegende (Lk 24, 13-32)", **ZTK** 66 (1969) 7-21.
A. GEORGE, "Les récits d'apparitions aux Onze à partir de Luc 24, 36-53", in P. de Surgy et al., **La résurrection du Christ et l'exégèse moderne** (Paris, 1969), pp. 75-104.

V. HASLER*, Jesu Selbstzeugnis und das Bekenntnis des Stephanus vor dem Hohen Rat. Beobachtungen zur Christologie des Lukas", **SchwTUm** 36 (1969) 36-47.
G. LOHFINK, "Christologie und Geschichtsbild in Apg 3, 19-21", **BZ**, N. F., 13 (1969) 223-241.
M. RESE, **Alttestamentliche Motive in der Christologie des Lukas** (Gütersloh, 1969).
L. F. RIVERA, "De Cristo a la Iglesia (Heh 1, 1-12)", **RBigArg** 31 (1969) 97-105.
G. SCHNEIDER, **Verleugnung, Verspottung und Verhör Jesu nach Lukas 22, 54-71. Studien zur lukanischen Darstellung der Passion** (Munich, 1969).
F. SCHÜTZ, **Der leidende Christus. Die angefochtene Gemeinde und das Christuskerygma der lukanischen Schriften** (Stuttgart-Berlin-Köln-Mainz, 1969).
R. ZEHNLE, "The Salvific Character of Jesus' Death in Lucan Soteriology", **TS** 30 (1969) 420-444.

1970

G. BOUWMAN, "Die Erhöhung Jesu in der lukanischen Theologie", **BZ**, N. F., 14 (1970) 257-263.
C. BURGER, **Jesus als Davidssohn. Eine traditionsgeschichtliche Untersuchung** (Göttingen, 1970), pp. 107-152.
C. F. EVANS, "Speeches in Acts", in **Mélanges, Rigaux**, pp. 287-302.
E. FRANKLIN, "The Ascension and the Eschatology of Luke-Acts", **ScotJT** 23 (1970) 191-200.
D. GILL, "Observations on the Lukan Travel Narrative and Some Related Passages", **HarvTR** 63 (1970) 199-221.
J. GNILKA, **Jesus Christus nach frühen Zeugnissen des Glaubens** (Munich, 1970), et passim.
D. L. Jones, "The Title Christos in Luke-Acts", **CBQ** 32 (1970) 69-76.
F. LENTZEN-DEIS, **Die Taufe Jesu nach den Synoptikern. Literarkritische und gattungsgeschichtliche Untersuchungen** (Frankfurt, 1970).
I. H. MARSHALL, **Luke: Historian and Theologian** (Exeter, 1970).
I. H. MARSHALL, "The Resurrection in the Acts of the Apostles", in **Apostolic History, Bruce**, pp. 92-107.
I. DE LA POTTERIE, Le titre *κύριος* appliqué à Jésus dans l'Evangile de Luc", in **Mélanges, Rigaux**, pp. 117-146.

1971

T. BALLARINI*, "Archegos (Atti 3, 15; 5, 31; Ebr 2, 10; 12,2: autore o condottiero?" **SacDoc** 16 (1971) 535-551.
J. BLINZLER et al.*, **Jésus dans les évangiles** (Paris, 1971).
E. DES PLACES, "Actes 17, 30-31", **Bib** 52 (1971) 526-534.
W. DIGNATH, **Die lukanische Vorgeschichte** (Gütersloh 1971).
J. K. ELLIOTT, "Does Luke 2, 41-52 Anticipate the Resurrection?", **ExpTim** 83 (1971-1972) 87-89.
X. LEON-DUFOUR, **Résurrection de Jésus et message pascal** (Paris, 1971), pp. 279-281.
G. LOHFINK, **Die Himmelfahrt Jesu. Untersuchungen zu den Himmelfahrts- und Erhöhungstexten bei Lukas** (Munich, 1971).
C. M. MARTINI, "Riflessioni sulla cristologia degli Atti" **SacDoc** 16 (1971) 525-534.
R. PESCH, "Der Anfang der Apostelgeschichte: Apg I, I-II. Kommentarstudie", in **EKK, Vorarbeiten Heft 3** (Zurich-Neukirchen, 1971), pp. 7-35.

G. SCHNEIDER, "Lk 1, 34-35 als redaktionelle Einheit", **BZ**, N. F., 15 (1971) 255-259.
R. F. ZEHNLE, **Peter's Pentecost Discourse. Tradition and Lukan Reinterpretation in Peter's Speeches of Acts 2 and 3** (Nashville-New York, 1971).
1972
H. BOERS, "Where Christology is Real. A Survey of Recent Research on New Testament Christology", **Interpr** 26 (1972) 300-327.
G. DELLING, "Die Jesusgeschichte in der Verkündigung nach Acta", **NTS** 19 (1972-1973) 373-389.
E. GRÄSSER et al. **Jesus in Nazareth** (Berlin, 1972).
E. F. HARRISON*, "The Resurrection of Jesus Christ in the Book of Acts and Early Christian Literature", in J. Reumann (ed), **Understanding the Sacred Text. Mélanges M. S. Enslin** (Valley Forge, Pa., 1972), pp. 217-231.
E. KRÄNKL, **Jesus der Knecht Gottes. Die heilsgeschichtliche Stellung Jesu in den Reden der Apostelgeschichte** (Regensburg, 1972)
B. PAPA, **La cristologia dei Sinottici e degli Atti degli Apostoli** (Bari-Rome, 1972).
J. ROLOFF, "Anfänge der soteriologischen Deutung des Todes Jesu (Mk 10, 45 und Lk 22, 27)", **NTS** 19 (1972-1973) 38-64.
J. SCHMITT, "Art. Prédication apostolique", in **SDB** 8, Paris, 1972, col. 246-273 (the fasicle containing this article appeared in 1967-1968).
V. TAYLOR, **The Passion Narrative of St. Luke. A Critical and Historical Investigation** (Cambridge, 1972).
1973
F. BOVON, "Le salut dans les écrits de Luc. Essai.", **RTPhil**, third series, 23 (1972) 296-307.
R. E. BROWN, **The Virginal Conception and the Bodily Resurrection of Jesus** (New York, 1973).
J. DELOBEL, "La rédaction de Lc 4, 14-16a et le 'Bericht vom Anfang'" in **Evangile**, Neirynck, pp. 203-223.
J. DUPONT, "Les discours de Pierre dans les Actes et le chapitre XXIV de l'évangile de Luc", in **Evangile**, Neirynck, pp. 328-374 (the study dates from the "Journées Bibliques" of 1968).
J. DUPONT, "Ascension du Christ et don de l'Esprit d'après Actes 2, 33", in B. Lindars and S.S. Smalley (eds), **Christ and Spirit in the New Testament. Mélanges C. F. D. Moule** (Cambridge, 1973), pp. 219-228.
G. FRIEDRICH, "Lk 9, 51 und die Entrückungschristologie des Lukas", in P. Hoff - mann, N. Brox and W. Pesch (eds), **Orientierung an Jesus. Zur Theologie der Synoptiker. Mélanges J. Schmid** (Freiburg-Basel-Vienna, 1973), pp. 48-77.
A. GEORGE, "Le sens de la mort de Jésus pour Luc", **RB** 80 (1973) 186-217.
R. G. HAMERTON-KELLY, **Pre-existence, Wisdom, and the Son of Man: a Study of the Idea of the Pre-existence in the New Testament** (Cambridge, 1973), pp. 83-87.
A. HOCKEL*, "Angelophanien und Christophanien in der Apostelgeschichte", in H. Feld and I. Nolte (eds), **Wort Gottes in der Zeit. Mélanges K. H. Schelkle** (Düsseldorf, 1973), pp. 111-113.
JAN LACH*, **Jesus syn Dawida (studium egzegetyczno-theologiczne)** (Warsaw, 1973).

G. W. MACRAE, "'Whom Heaven Must Receive Until the Time'. Reflections on the Christology of Acts", **Interpr** 27 (1973) 151-165.

P.-G. MÜLLER, Χριστὸς ἀρχηγός **Der religionsgeschichtliche und theologische Hintergrund einer neutestamentlichen Christus-prädikation** (Bern-Frankfurt, 1973), esp. pp. 249-278 and 328-333.

I. H. MARSHALL, "The Resurrection of Jesus in Luke", **Tyndale Bulletin** 24 (1973) 55-98.

P. VON DER OSTEN-SACKEN, "Zur Christologie des Lukanischen Reiseberichts", **EvT** 33 (1973), 476-496.

I. PANAGOPOULOS, Ὁ προφήτης ἀπὸ Ναζαρέτ. Ἱστορικὴ καὶ θεολογικὴ μελέτη τῆς περὶ Ἰησοῦ Χριστοῦ εἰκόνος τῶν εὐαγγελίων (Athens, 1973).

E. SAMAIN, "Le récit lucanien du voyage de Jésus vers Jérusalem. Quelques études récentes", in **Cahiers Bibliques** 12 of **FoiVie** 72 (1973), N° 3, 3-23.

E. SAMAIN, "La notion de ἀρχή dans l'oeuvre lucanienne", in **Evangile**, Neirynck, pp. 299-328.

F. SCHNIDER, **Jesus der Prophet** (Fribourg, Switzerland-Göttingen, 1973), esp. pp. 163-172.

S. S. SMALLEY, "The Christology of Acts again" in B. Lindars and S. S. Smalley (eds), **Christ and Spirit in the New Testament. Mélanges C. F. D. Moule** (Cambridge, 1973), pp. 79-93.

G. W. TROMPF, "La section médiane de l'Evangile de Luc", **RHPhilRel** 53 (1973) 141-154.

J. WANKE, **Die Emmauserzählung. Eine redaktionsgeschichtliche Untersuchung zu Lk 24, 13-35** (Leipzig, 1973).

J. B. XAVIERVILAS*, **Christos in the Gospel of St. Luke. A Redaction-Critical Study of the Christos-texts in the Third Gospel,** another unpublished dissertation, Pont. Bib. Inst. (Rome, 1973).

1974

J. DUPONT, "La portée christologique de l'évangélisation des nations d'après Luc 24, 47", in J. Gnilka (ed), **Neues Testament und Kirche. Mélanges R. Schnackenburg** (Freiburg-Basel-Vienna, 1974), pp. 125-143.

F. HAHN, "Die Himmelfahrt Jesu. Ein Gespräch mit Gerhard Lohfink", **Bib** 55 (1974) 418-426.

D. L. JONES*, "The Title 'kyrios' in Luke-Acts", in **Society of Biblical Literature, 1974 Seminar Papers,** II (Missoula, 1974), pp. 85-102.

M. MIYOSHI, **Der Anfang des Reiseberichts. Lk 9, 51-10, 24. Eine redaktionsgeschichtliche Untersuchung** (Rome, 1974).

Resurrexit. Actes du Symposium international sur la Résurrection de Jésus (Rome, 1970) E. Dhanis (ed), (Rome, 1974).

1975

R. E. BROWN, "Luke's Method in the Annunciation Narratives of Chapter One", in J. W. Flanagan and A. W. Robinson (eds), **No Famine in the Land. Mélanges J. L. McKenzie** (Missoula, 1975), pp. 179-194.

M. GOURGUES, "'Exalté à la droite de Dieu' (Actes 2, 33; 5,31)", **ScEsprit** 27 (1975) 303-327.

F. MUSSNER, "Wohnung Gottes und Menschensohn nach der Stephanusperikope (Apg 6, 8-8,2)", in R. Pesch and R. Schnackenburg (eds), **Jesus und der Menschensohn. Mélanges A. Vögtle** (Freiburg-Basel-Vienna, 1975), pp. 283-299.

R. F. O'TOOLE, **Acts 26. The Christological Climax of Paul's Defense (Ac 22, 1-26, 32)**, excerpt of a dissertation, Pont. Bib. Inst. (Rome, 1975).

G. SCHNEIDER, "'Der Menschensohn' in der lukanischen Christologie", in R. Pesch et R. Schnackenburg (eds), **Jesus und der Menschensohn. Mélanges A. Vögtle** (Freiburg-Basel-Vienna, 1975), pp. 267-282.

E. RASCO, "Jesùs y el Esprítu, Iglesia e 'Historia': Elementos para une lectura de Lucas", **Greg** 57 (1975) 321-368 (a chapter of his dissertation published in 1976; p. 368: summary in English).

M. RESE, "Einige Ueberlegungen zu Lukas XIII, 31-33", in J. Dupont (ed), **Jésus aux origines de la christologie** (Gembloux, 1975), pp. 201-226.

P. W. WALASKAY, "The Trial and Death of Jesus in the Gospel of Luke", **JBL** 94 (1975) 81-93.

1976

J(EANNE) D'ARC, **Les Pélerins d'Emmaüs** (Paris, 1976).

R. E. BROWN, "The Meaning of the Manger; The Significance of the Shepherds", **Worship** 50 (1976) 528-538.

E. FRANKLIN, **Christ the Lord. A Study in the Purpose and Theology of Luke-Acts** (London, 1976).

M. GOURGUES, "Lecture christologique du Psaume 110 et fête de la Pentecôte", **RB** 83 (1976) 5-24.

P. S. MINEAR, **To Heal and to Reveal. The Prophetic Vocation According to Luke** (New York, 1976), pp. 102-121 et passim.

J. M. NÜTZEL, "Zum Schicksal der eschatologischen Propheten", **BZ**, N.F., 20 (1976) 59-94.

E. RASCO, **La teología de Lucas. Origen, Desarrolo, Orientaciones** (Rome, 1976).

1977

R. E. BROWN, "The Presentation of Jesus (Luke 2, 22-40)", **Worship** 51 (1977) 2-11.

R. E. BROWN, **The Birth of the Messiah** (Garden City-London, 1977).

U. BUSSE*, **Die Wunder des Propheten Jesus. Die Rezeption, Komposition und Interpretation der Wundertradition im Evangelium des Lukas** (Stuttgart, 1977).

Chapter 3

CHRISTOLOGY

Introduction

Fifteen monographs and more than 150 articles, without counting several unpublished dissertations are the total sum of the works on the Christology of the Acts of the Apostles, which have appeared the last 25 years [1]. So that our account be neither too long nor too monotonous, a selection had to be made. The lack of originality or excessive of fantasy of certain contributions facilitated this choice which is necessarily partial.

When we approach Christology, the distinction between the Gospel and the Acts is hardly justifiable. The Christ of the Acts cannot be dissociated from the Jesus of the Gospel, at least if we place ourselves in the Lucan perspective. However, to take into consideration all the studies consecrated to the Jesus of the third Gospel would be beyond our strength. That is why, we opted for a compromise, which still remains unsatisfactory. Beside the works which treat the whole of Lucan Christology and those which touch the Christology of the Acts alone, we have retained for several sections of the Gospel, divers recent contributions, which elucidate particularly the redactional approach.

After a reminder of the main Christological ideas, we will address successively the studies which follow the redak - tiongeschichtlich line (I); those which react negatively to these methods or their excesses (II); those which pay attention to the traditions beyond Luke (III); those which attempt to give a global image of the Lucan Christ (IV); and finally, those studies which deal with a precise Christological text (V) or Christological title (VI).

In Luke's Gospel, chapters 1 and 2 announce the coming of the Messiah. We must ask ourselves what was Luke's role in the arrangement of these narratives and hymns. The existence of the Gospel of Mark allows us to determine the Lucan perspective of Jesus' baptism, his temptations in the desert as well as his Galilean ministry culminating with the Transfiguration (3:21-9:50). The interest of the exegete turns especially to the travel narrative (9:51-19:27) to detect the Christological import of these chapters which are Luke's alone. The comparison with Mark is taken up again in the Passion account (22:1-23:56). Luke 24 retains our attention because of the accounts of the appearances of the Risen One and the first text of the Ascension.

Let us now evoke the image of the Christ which comes forth from the Acts.

The Christ of the Acts is alive: "He presented himself to them alive after the Passion..." (Act 1:3); "and they had discussions with him (Paul), relating to their particular religion and a certain Jesus, who is dead, but who Paul affirms is alive" (Act 25:19).

He is alive for he is risen. The resurrection of Jesus is the heart of the Lucan message. As the work of God, it opposes the death of Jesus, which is the consequence of the destructive will of humanity, encouraged by Satan. We might wonder if Luke, who makes Jesus the object, not the subject of the resurrection, does not prefer *ἐγέιρω* (with God as subject) to *ἀνιστάναι* (often with Jesus as subject).

The resurrection implies (and Luke is the only NT author to explicitly say so) that Jesus did not suffer decomposition (cf. Psa 16:8-11, cited and commented in Act 2:25ff. and 13:35). Moreover, the resurrection of Jesus is accompanied with a mention of his elevation to (or "by") the right hand of God (cf. Act 2:33ff. and 5:31). After his resurrection, Jesus led a normal human life (he ate and drank with his disciples, cf. Act 10:41), before being lifted up to heaven. The two Ascension narratives, in Lk 24:50-53 and Act 1:9-12, clearly distinguish this event from the resurrection at Easter.

Luke associates the Twelve to the Resurrection and the Ascension: he prefers the mention of witnesses to the idea of appearances (*ὤφθη* in Act 13:31 and *ἐμφανῆ γενέσθαι* in Act 10:40 are exceptions).

From now on, Christ is in heaven, where he remains until the Parousia (cf. Act 3:21). Localized and individualized, the Risen One must pass by the mediation of angels, visions, light or voices to manifest himself to his Church. On the earth, his absence is sensed, but, fortunately, he left two substitutes: his name and the Holy Spirit, once called "the Spirit of Jesus" (Act 16:7). These realities maintain a link between him and the Church, his people (Act 18:10).

This glorious and individual destiny of the Christ brings salvation to humanity, inspite of all (cf. Act 15:11 and 16:31).

Luke relates conversion, forgiveness of sins and the gift of the Spirit to the resurrection (cf. Act 5:31; 2:38; 13:38; 26:18 as well as Lk 1:77 and 24:47). This is why the Lord Jesus is the giver of Life (Act 11:18): he is the *ἀρξηγὸς τῆς ζωῆς* (Act 3:15).

The Risen One is none other than Jesus of Nazareth (Luke insists on the title Ναζωραῖος which surely must be interpreted geographically). This Jesus was a man (is it necessary to see in this *ἀνήρ*, Act 2:22 and 17:31, the expression of an ancient adoptionistic Christology?). Having become a man of God, i.e. a prophet, by the spiritual unction associated to his baptism, Jesus fulfils a ministry of healing throughout Galilee (the Acts speak little of his teaching): he is, at the same time, the New Elijah, in his abasement, and the New Moses, in the role of guide and liberator.

If Luke seems to be unaware of the preexistence of Christ (only Act 2:25 could be interpreted in this sense) **[2]**, on the other hand, he knows (cf. Lk 1 and 2) of the messianity of Jesus, the spiritual son of David from birth. Yet this messianity which fulfils the OT promises, is particularly fulfilled in the Passion and the resurrection (cf. Lk 24:44-47).

I. A REDACTIONAL CHRISTOLOGY

a. What was the situation like around 1950? The study of the Christology of the Acts is at a turning point, prefigured twenty years before, for the **Beginnings of Christianity** contains two contributions relative to Christology. One of them, from the editors F. J. Foakes Jackson and K. Lake, appears in the first volume (-> 1920). It is exclusively interested in the origins of Christology of the early church (the Christology of Acts is but one way of access to this primitive doctrine); the other, found in the fifth volume (-> 1933) deals with the Christological titles in Acts. H. J. Cadbury, who is the author, guards himself from writing a prehistory and analyzes the meaning of these titles as they appear in the Lucan redaction. In this manner, he announces the turn to which we referred.

In fact, until 1950, the majority of exegetes, following Foakes Jackson and Lake, used Acts as a witness to primitive Christology. To different degrees, they all insisted on the traditional nature of the Christological statements imbedded in the missionary speeches of Acts. Whether it was G. Gewiess, in Germany, W. L. Knox, in Great Britain or J. Schmitt, in France, each considered the Christology of the apostles, the eyewitnesses, more important than Luke's [3]. They were also all convinced that the author of Acts faithfully transmits the primitive doctrine: the insistence in Acts on the humanity of Jesus, the presence of the archaic titles, servant and Son of Man, the emphasis on the Easter enthronement, the relative silence of the Lucan texts concerning the expiatory value of the death of Jesus and the absence of the themes of preexistence and of the body of Christ are all indications of its primitiveness. As a faithful historian, Luke reports the Christological doctrine, or better, the Christological proclamation of the first Christians.

b. Toward 1950, the situation changes. A series of exegetes, German for the most part, rediscover the importance of the editor of the Acts, who consequently gains the status of a writer. This change came about thanks to three discoveries: M. Dibelius (-> 1949) determined the redactional importance of the speeches in the composition of the book of the Acts. By a comparison with the practice of the historians of antiquity, he notes that speeches in ancient works are the place par excellence where the author expresses his convictions and indicates the meaning he gives to the events. Of course, Dibelius adds immediately that Luke is also an evangelist and oft hides behind the kerygmatic tradition of his Church (with Dodd, Dibelius believes he is able to elucidate a traditional Christological schema in Acts). The gates are opened and the German scholar will be overrun on his left by a young troup of disciples who consider the Christological schema itself as redactional. That this overflow might take place, a doctrinal study was also necessary and P. Vielhauer [4] was in part responsible for this work. He showed in four points, one being Christology. that far from reflecting a primitive theology, the Lucan work sets forth theses later than those of the apostle Paul. Finally, the schol-ars begin to doubt more and more the relationship that Dodd thought to establish between I Cor 15:3b-5 and the kerygma of Acts.

In his famous monograph, H. Conzelmann makes manifest the Lucan reinterpretation, not only of the early eschatology, but also of the Synoptic Jesus. E. Haenchen, followed by C. F. Evans, U. Wilckens, J. Bihler, J. C. O'Neill, G. Lohfink and E. Kränkl, thinks the speeches in Acts and their doctrinal content are the work of the editor.

The few lines which E. Haenchen (-> 1956) consecrates to the Christology of Acts in his commentary are revelatory of this new perspective: "Man hat Lukas gelegentlich gelobt, weil er die primitive Theologie der christlichen Anfangszeiten so treu darzustellen vermocht haben. Aber es ist seine eigene schlichte

Theologie (die er mit seiner Gemeinde teilte), welche er überall voraussetzt und die man aus den Predigten, Gebeten, liturgischen Wendungen und gelegentlichen Bermerkungen in der Apg entnehmen muss." (pp. 81-82).

Therefore, everything must be placed on Luke's account: the absence of preexistence, the adoptionism (Jesus, man appointed by God), the Easter exaltation of the Lord (the titles, Lord and Christ, impose themselves to the detriment of the title, Son), the preeminence of the resurrection over the Passion, the function of the eschatological judge, the present sitting at the right hand of God where the Christ sends the Spirit which he received from the Father, the necessary passage through the Church for access to the Lord, the invocation of the name of Jesus (not to be confused with the magical usage of names in antiquity) and the submission of the servant to God who glorifies him.

If we ask how so simple a Christology can appear in so recent a writing (more recent, for example, that the epistles of Paul where a cosmic Christology is already developed), these authors answer that Luke includes himself in a popular Hellenistic Jewish-Christian tradition which is little influenced by the creative genius of a John or a Paul. The simplicity of a doctrine does not necessarily imply its antiquity: it could correspond to the frankness of a mind or the popular expression of a faith, while remaining late. These authors, attentive to grasp the theological specificity of Luke, have, nonetheless, remained vague in the delimitation of Luke's sociological and ideological roots; they content themselves too frequently, to speak of a man of the third generation, of a Christian at the end of the first century (when it is not, like J. C. O'Neill, at the beginning of the second), of a Gentile Christian, etc. We would like more precision.

c. The term subordinationism, already pronounced by J. Weiss [5], had been released: H. Braun (-> 1952) attempted to show, from the vocabulary of the resurrection, that Luke preferred to speak of God who revives than Christ who raises. Certainly to make God the subject of Christ's resurrection is an ancient characteristic, but it is inserted in Luke into a late frame which modifies the sense. For, in Luke, this primitive feature corresponds to the recoil of the *ὤφθη* where Christ is the subject. The official collegium of the Twelve, which sees the Risen One and, by that, guarantees the value of the apostolic message, is substituted for the Christ, who appears resurrected, as the subject of the verbs relative to the resurrection. The point of view becomes that of a historically correct declaration of a raw fact. "Der Rahmen, in den die alte adoptianische, subordinatianische Christologie hier eingehängt ist, tendiert zur Anbringung jener Sicherungen, die den Frühkatholizismus einleiten. " (col. 535).

d. H. Conzelmann's monograph (-> 1954) better discerns Luke's concept of the role and the person of Jesus Christ. Chapter two of the first part consecrated to the geographical representations and the fourth part which treats the center of history will preoccuppy us now.

The schema of the life of Jesus in three periods, which are lived out in three distinct places, serves to show the lineaments of an evolution of the personage. M. Dibelius had already noted that the Lucan account of the Passion had turned to the genre of the acts of the martyrs; Conzelmann shows that the entire life of Jesus is perceived as that of a historical person. Even if he does not develope a psychology of Jesus, Luke is interested in the infancy and adolescence of his hero. He makes the reader think that during the Galilean period, Jesus, conscious of his Messiahship, gathers around him those to be called to be the witnesses of his life, and preaches the gospel of the Kingdom, more by miracles than by speech. Satan has left Jesus and it is the period of proleptic salvation. During the journey, the perspective of a suffering Messiahship comes to Jesus, who does not travel so much elsewhere as differently (that is, with the perspective of death which must unfold in Jerusalem for dogmatic reasons). From his entry into Jerusalem (the triumphant entry is emptied of all eschatological and political overtones), Jesus ceases to do miracles and displays a more didactic activity. Satan reappears. Jesus' Messiahship becomes more evident and can no longer be confused with an earthly political power. The guilt of the death of Jesus rests on the Jews, not on the Romans, who recognized his innocence of political activity. The disciples, who witnessed his life, are also witnesses of his death (in Mark, things are different).

Thus, Luke's Christology is elaborated under the convergent impulse of the geographical schema and the historical unfolding. His life is linked to Palestine (the Church will have the mission to announce the Gospel to the rest of the world) and follows the history of Israel and precedes the history of the Church. These geographic and historic coordinates explain Jesus' theological situation: Jesus is submitted to God who remains the master of redemptive history and the Lord of the fate of all peoples. God alone is creator (Luke is not acquainted with the preexistence of Jesus). Jesus is the instrument of God's will. There are several indications of this subordination: the Christological title κύριος has no cosmic signification; the Lucan insistence on the prayers of Jesus underlines the submission of the Son to the plans of the Father. With Jesus' resurrection and the birth of the Church, the situation of Christ is modified: from being the sole receptacle of the Spirit, the risen Jesus becomes the giver of the Spirit. Jesus passes from being active to being relatively passive: henceforth, he intervenes indirectly by his name. The union between the will of the Father and the Son, already present in the Gospel, is intensified.

Conzelmann finally notes that, according to the Lucan re - flection of Lk 22: 67-70, the Christological titles tend to become synonymous. Conzelmann's main conclusion can be sum - marized in the following manner: Luke disconnects the account that he narrates from the evangelical kerygma (with Mark, the account and the gospel still coincide). That is to say that the Lucan portrait of the Christ ceases to be kerygmatic <u>stricto sensu</u> in order to become historical. Thus, Luke is the first theologian to seek for the historical Jesus behind the Christ of faith. Jesus comes out as a character of the past - which Conzelmann regrets. Jesus is no longer the figure of the eschatological present that he was.

We will have the occasion to observe the weaknesses of Conzelmann's theological analysis, whose coherence is impres - sive . We will do this by signalling the criticisms which have been addressed to him, but for the moment let us continue with the investigations of this epoch which extol Luke's theological independence and determine his specificity **[6]**.

e. In his theology of the Acts (-> 1961), J. C. O'Neill dedicates a chapter to the Christological titles. The general perspective, not the detail, interests us here. For the writer, Luke retains a primitive use , here and there, but most of the time, the titles, the most frequent, *ὁ χριστός* and *κύριος* reflect Luke's theology or rather, the theology of the milieu in which the author of Acts bathes. ' Ὁ *χριστός*, which is a title and no longer (!) a proper name, far from revealing a primitive sense, manifests, just like *παῖς*, a post-apostolic perspective which is found in the apostolic fathers and Justin. These two titles are marked by the contemporary conflicts between the Church and the Synagogue. *κύριος* witnesses to the war of the "lords" which Christian and pagan religions fought at the same time.

f. U. Wilckens' work (-> 1961) is important for it tempers singularly the generalized optimism which reigned around the year 1950 [7]. The author attacks all who attribute a normative value to the Christology of the missionary speeches because of their kerygmatic schema which is supposedly traditional. This reprimand has born fruit for, since then, it is not possible to blindly follow the seductive theses of C. H. Dodd and M. Dibelius.

Our presentation of this book will, nonetheless, remain summary as the reader can refer to the article of J. Dupont (-> 1962, fourth title) which summarizes and criticizes Wilckens theses. The missionary speeches in chapters 2, 3, 4, 10 and 13 of the Acts have a well-known recurrent structure. They seem to reflect a logical unfolding of the apostolic preaching, but this is only an allusion. In fact - and here are the two main results of the first seventy pages - they deviate as much from the background as from the form of the ancient credo, found in 1 Co 15:3b-5. Each one has its own characteristics which are explained by the narrative context, which Wilckens thinks redactional. The discourses, most probably, originate from the pen of Luke. This redactional nature will become, for Wilckens, a certainty at the end of second part when he analyzes the main function of the kerygmatic speeches in the economy of the Lucan work and their various theological themes. Wilckens esteems that the essential function of the speeches is to promote the constitution and expansion of the Church (a movens heilsgeschichtlich, as he says). By their presence throughout the account, they must attest that it is the Word which permits the edification of the Christian communities. We admit that this is a thesis dear to Luke. Concerning the divers theological themes which the discourses develope, almost all are eminently editorial or, at least, reworked by Luke. The person of John the Baptist, the absence of a redemptive value of the cross, the resurrection of Christ as well as the titles reflect Luke's theological preoccupations which Conzelmann illustrated from the Gospel. The dominating idea is the subordination of Jesus to the will of God during all the periods of his life (Wilckens rejects the term adoptionism, despite Act 2:36; in his opinion, there is never, in Luke, a moment when Jesus is not yet the Christ or the Lord. Jesus is simply Messiah and Lord submitted to God, the almighty master of salvation history).

Our account would be incomplete if we did not say a few words about the materials Luke had at his disposal. Wilckens does not dare to claim that Luke started with nothing. For the kerygmatic part of the speeches, Wilckens believes that he has discovered several traditional kernels:

a) With a missionary goal, Hellenistic Judaism used a schema of preaching which invited the Gentiles to leave their idols and turn to the living God. The schema, slightly Christianized, is found in the two speeches of Acts in which the Gentiles are addressed (Act 14 and 17). Wilckens imagines that Luke elaborated his preaching program, directed toward the Jews, from the one originally destined for the Gentiles. We think this a shaky construction.

b) To describe the death of Jesus, Luke had brief summaries at his disposition and Mark also supposedly used these summaries to formulate his three announcements of the Passion. It seems to us that Wilckens' imagination has taken over a bit too much here.

c) To explain the criticisms of the Jews, Luke, we are told, resorted to traditional arguments of Hellenistic Christianity.

In each case, Luke altered these traditions in the direction of his own theological perspective. Wilckens knows but one example where Luke allowed a doctrinal concept, which did not correspond to his own ideas, slip through: Act 3: 19-21 (conversion which hastens the coming of the times of refreshing, etc.). Here, Luke leaned on an apocalyptic tradition relative to Elijah. Wilckens follows essentially Bauernfeld's hypothesis, on this point.

g. In the eyes of certain [**8**], Wilckens made his own task easy by discarding the speech of Stephen from his investigation. Conzelmann, in his commentary on the Acts (->1963), in fact, presupposes a source behind Act 7. A Roman Catholic exegete, J. Bihler (->1963), flew to Wilckens' aid to protect the Achilles' heel of his theory. Following an analysis of the structure of the style and contents of Act 7, Bihler concludes that this discourse, which the majority supposed to be an independent article, is redactional. "Daraus lässt sich nur der eine Schluss ziehen: **Die Rede ist eine Komposition des Lukas**." (p. 86). This speech intervenes at a crucial moment of the history as Luke constructs it: at the moment when Christianity, after having been offered to the Jews in vain, is going to be announced to the Pagans (the historical Paul [**9**] is different here. For him, the Gospel is for one group and the other, whereas, according to Bihler, Luke considers that it was to be preached to the one and then to the other). To compose this enormous fresco of the history of Israel, Luke was not deprived of materials: he was influenced by a Jewish apocalyptic, rather than a Pharisaic, stream. At the same time, he stressed the traditional reminders of the past of Israel in the rhythm of his own redemptive history. Elsewhere, he voluntarily drafts the fate of Joseph and the mission of Moses so that the reader will discover Christ prefigured. We cannot help but think, in reading this book, that Bihler underestimates the role of the Jewish exegesis of the OT. He attributes too much to the characteristics of Lucan redaction which could be indications of the Jewish Haggadah [**10**].

h. G. Lohfink recently (->1969) took up the problem of Act 3: 19-21, the only erratic block that Wilckens bequeathed to tradition. With a meticulous stylistic analysis, this scholar rejects the hypothesis of Bauernfeld, that Wilckens and J. A. T. Robinson shared. His view is the verses are completely Lucan [**11**] and the theology, they present (if understood properly), fits perfectly into the Lucan program: "the times of refreshing" do not correspond to a letting up of the eschatological ordeals but simply designate the final salvation. Luke does not desire to convert others so that the end times might arrive, but explains to the Christians of his time that the apostles offered a last occasion for salvation to the Jews. With their refusal, the hour of the Gentile mission had rung. The idea is not that the Messiah is elected or instituted, but that he is elected and instituted "for you" (i.e. for Peter's Jewish audience). If God is the subject of the verb "to send" (vs. 20), it is because Luke makes God the director of all the acts of salvation history. Here, Luke wants to make known that God is also the master of the Parousia. These verses fit into the Lucan tendency to reabsorb the imminence of the Parousia without denying its existence. In our text, the question is not of *ἀποκατάστασις πάντων* but of the redactional telescoping of two ideas: the final reestablishment (*ἀποκατάστασις*) and the thesis that "all that God has declared by the mouths of the prophets" (cf. vs. 24). Here again Luke does not begin with nothing, but at the same time, he does not simply take over a continuous text: to his own ends, he uses certain traditional elements. The expressions are sometimes from the OT (forgiveness of sins; chosen in advance), sometimes from the apocalyptic realm (until he comes...; the times of the apocatastasis) and sometimes from the Christian context (conversion, Messiah, Jesus), even liturgical (what God has said by the mouths of the prophets). This mosaic technique is also found in Act 17.

Lohfink's study is impressive, yet does he not force the meaning of the words by eliminating the idea of an intermediary time in the Lucan rereading of vs. 20a, in the name of Luke's general coherence?

i. We pursue our *Redaktionsgeschichtlicher* survey with mention of C. F. Evans (-> 1956 and -> 1970). Evans was one of the first to rejoin Cadbury [**12**] and go beyond Dodd. In 1956, he observed again that the speeches in Acts did not correspond to the kerygma which Paul knew. From a stylistic as well as doctrinal point of view, they represent the Lucan perspective. For Evans, their redactional character is even more imposing since no *Sitz im Leben* surfaces to explain their origin. The author takes up this study in 1970. In a very subtle manner, he proposes the rejection of the appellation of sermon or catechism for the speeches. The stylistic (the vocative ἄνδρες, for example) as much as the rhetorical (*captatio benevolentiae* etc.) proceedings orient us toward the literary genre of the speech, which is more precisely called apologetical discourse. Each time, Peter or Paul defend themselves from real accusations (or virtual, as in Act 13). The proclamation of Jesus' resurrection, which is central in these speeches, is inscribed in a polemic and not in a predication (the repentance desired of the Jews in Act 2 is not a general, but a precise, repentance because of the death of Jesus).

Evans is firm in his conviction that the speeches of Acts are the work of a writer who, in his work, confers a precise function on them. Speeches, not sermons, they respond to the aspiration of an author who wants to be historian and, who destines his work not to believers but to unbelievers.

Agreeing with the general argumentation of Evans' study, we, nonetheless, judge (cf. Lk 1:4) that Luke's work is also directed *ad intra* and the speeches have an edifying function as well.

j. In a brief but suggestive article, C. M. Martini (-> 1971) thinks that Luke presents not only a doctrine concerning the Christ, but also an edifying and polemic Christological message. Act 3:6; 2:22 and 10:38 grant the charismatic and thaumaturgical character of Jesus. Those who were sensitive to this feature were the Gentile listeners, who were fond of θεῖοι ἄνδρες, and, without a doubt, - here the argument becomes hypothetical - the enthusiastic and apocalyptic Christians of Galilee, which Luke combats. These aspects, however, go beyond this aspect and complement it by describing Jesus as the suffering and risen Messiah in the plan of God. The presentation in Act 7-8 (Moses, Joshua, Stephen) and the Emmaus account (Lk 24) confirm Luke's polemical tendency against enthusiasm. The polemic - it is characteristic of Luke - engulfs the charismatic aspect in order to perfect it, whereas Paul rejects it (at least concerning the miracles of the apostles).

k. Finally, a book on the totality of the speeches of Acts ap - peared more recently. Its author, E. Kränkl, is less interested by the titles than by the confessions of faith and the coherent image of Jesus. The first section (pp. 1-81) presents a thorough summary of the actual situation (to begin with, the author wanted to prepare a history of interpretation of the speeches). In reading these pages, we can see how the nineteenth century exegetes often preceded those of the twentieth century (this is true of the traditional schema, presupposed by M. Dibelius and C. H. Dodd). We also learn of the impulsion that the genetic study of the credo gave to the exegesis of sermons. At the end of this survey, Kränkl discerns in the discourses, a recurring narrative scheme, which goes from the baptism to the Ascension. In a suggestive manner, he shows that this schema is more developed and consequently, later than the earliest kerygma, but less ample than the Gospels. Yet, it is not to be concluded that there existed a confession of faith whose formu - lation was already fixed in the first century; rather it is more proper to think that, at the time of Luke, Christians were accustomed to summarize the main periods of the intervention of the God in Jesus of Nazareth for divers occasions, predication, catechism or liturgy. Kränkl compares the Lucan program (especially Lk 24:46-48) to certain texts of the apostolic fathers and Justin (Apol. I, 31). This is original compared to earlier works and his results are interesting. The summaries of the second century included the nativity which goes unmentioned in Acts. The speeches of the Acts are, therefore, characteristic of the Lucan era. In what follows, Kränkl does not doubt that they contain traditional elements **[13]**, but examines them in a redactional perspective. It is permitted to wonder why Kränkl did not study the whole of Lucan Christology. Is not limiting oneself to only the speeches, to submit again to the a priori of the antiquity of the texts, which has been rightly criticized?

In an order and zeal of a schollboy, the second part of his book analyzes what the speeches say about the various stages of the life of Jesus. In a general way, we can characterize these developments in the following manner: Kränkl yearns to make the affirmations of the Acts coincide with the facts in the third Gospel, for he desires to proclaim the redactional character of the speeches, the core of Lucan theology. This concern hinders him from recalling that the speeches do not agree with the Gospel on the question of the beginning - and Luke's interest for ἀρχή [14] is well known: the speeches begin at the earliest with the baptism of Jesus [15]. Corresponding to this tendency, we meet with an insufficient perception of the traditions: Act 13:29b, to take but one example, says that the Jews buried Jesus. This is surely an ancient tradition which the Gospel of Luke has toned down, to the profit of Joseph of Arimathea. Contrariwise, Kränkl thinks that Luke is not interested in the people who buried Jesus. He generously attributes the data of the gospel and this notice in Acts to Lucan redaction (p. 117).

Concerning the major thrusts of Lucan theology, Kränkl follows Conzelmann [16]: salvation history, delay in the Parousia and submission of the Son to the Father. Nevertheless, he developes four theses which merit presentation [17]:

1) The heilsgeschichtlich meaning of the death of Jesus.

Kränkl deems that the death of Jesus has the same sense in the speeches in Acts and in the Gospel; both of which are to be distinguished from Mark and Matthew. The Jews, not the Romans, carry the burden of the responsibility. The tone becomes polemic against the inhabitants of Jerusalem, who condemned Jesus, like their ancestors had rejected the prophets. The proclamation of the gospel offers them a last chance to come out of their ignorance (Luke projects backward into the origins of the Church the recognition that the Lucan community should be distinct from the synagogue). In contrast, Jesus who is innocent, fits into the plan of God, for the death of Jesus - Luke follows traditions here - is not a slap in the face of God's providence. It is rather conform to the plan of God, even if Luke does not emphasize its redemptive value. Without opting for one of them, Kränkl evokes three explanations for this reserve and mentions that the same silence concerning the salvific value of the cross, dominates certain late writings (James, Jude and 2 Pt). We might reply that it also appears in other tardive texts like Ignatius and I Clement.

2) The importance of the Exaltation.

In the life of Jesus, the decisive moment for salvation history, is neither Good Friday nor even Easter, but the Ascension: "Tod und Auferweckung Jesu sin darin nur Etappen, Durch - gangsstufen zu seiner Erhöhung. Erst mit ihr endet das Leben Jesu auf Erden, beginnt die neue himmlische Existenzweise." (p. 166). The ascent of the one who is the legitimate heir, to the right hand of the Father, represents his enthroning (cf. Act 2:36; 5:31; 13:33 which are redactional texts and Lk 19:11-27). It sets in motion the proclamation of the Church, releases the irruption of the Spirit, permits men to believe and hope, and - we might add - even incites Luke to write. The lordship of Christ is the central theme of Luke's theology (p. 185f.). Absent from the earth, Christ, who because he is now enthroned according to the divine plan prepared long ago, reigns and intervenes by his name and his Spirit. Salvation is not obtained only by the detour taken by the historical Jesus and faith is not uniquely faith in a past event (against Wickens -> 1961). This would be to forget the soteriological import of the Ascension (pp. 176-186 study the benefits of the Ascension which are the presence of the Name, the forgiveness of sins, the manifestation of the Spirit and justification by faith) [**18**]. We think that here Kränkl forgets that the Ascension was also a painful breach and the loss of Jesus for the community. Held back by the heavens, Christ must turn to mediation in order to act. On the whole, the man Jesus could help more effectively [**19**].

3) The role of the witnesses.

With finesse, Kränkl notes first of all, that according to Luke, it is the same for the disciples as for Jesus in primitive Christianity: "Sie werden aus Verkündigern zu Verkündigten." (p. 167) [**20**]. He follows with an analysis of the term *μάρτυς* which, despite the author's excellent information and certain timely formulations of - fers nothing very original (cf. below 7, III, 2, j concerning the recent works on this subject). One new hypothesis does merit our attention. We know that Luke reserved the title of "apostle" to the Twelve, and it is the same for "witness" with the exception of Paul and Stephen. Various explanations are set forth to explain this anomaly and Kränkl proposes a new one. Paul and Stephen are also witnesses but not on the same level as the apostles for they did not walk with Jesus in Galilee nor meet the Risen One in the same manner as the others. They are witnesses but to the elevated Lord and the appearances which follow the Ascension differ greatly from those which precede. Whereas, it was a question of the bodily presence of the risen Jesus, but henceforth, it is now a question of fleeting appear - ances of the elevated Christ.

This hypothesis seems too subtle for us. Luke does not retain two definitions for the term "witness ", a witness of the life and resurrection, on the one hand, and a witness to the Ascension, on the other. Neither does he distinguish between two types of appearances.

4) The sense of succession

At a literary level, exegetes have crossed swords to know where Luke placed the landmarks of his work. In a suggestive manner, Kränkl places his adversaries back to back: John the Baptist, for example, is neither exclusively the last prophet nor uniquely the forerunner-prophet. He is one of those figures which Luke paints to serve as conclusion and introduction, at the same time. Luke has the sense of thresholds, of links, of nexuses, for he has the sense of continuity. John the Baptist is described sometimes as he who terminates the prophetic tradition and other times as he who prepares the way for the Lord (pp. 88-97). It is the same for the risen Christ who goes up to heaven. The Ascension, which ends the life of Jesus in the Gospel, serves as a solemn beginning of the time of the Church in the Acts.

We will make two criticisms of the work of Kränkl and pose a question:

a) To say that the exalted Lord is always present in his community (p. 208 and passim) is not exactly correct. A correction needs to be made: he is present, while being absent, held back in heaven. He can manifest himself only through intermediaries. This is what makes Luke's theology not simply a theologia gloriae.

b) Does Kränkl not exaggerate the breach between Easter and the Ascension and does he not give too much weight to the exaltation? Do not the speeches say that the ἀνάστασις is the core of Christian preaching, which Kränkl admits himself (p. 146)?

c) If Luke knows how to distinguish as well as link together the periods, could we not have an explanation to the mysterious use of ἀνάλημψις in Lk 9:51? We are told that this word covers different salvific events which Luke carefully separates. In this case, the going up to Jerusalem, the Passion, the resurrection and the exaltation would be one and the same threshold, the one which intersects the time of Jesus and the time of the Church. This threshold would have a name, true to the heart of Lucan theology as Kränkl sees it, ἀνάλημψις. This exaltation, far from excluding Easter, includes it as well as the Passion.

These are, in summary, the works of the exegetes who attribute the Christological speeches to Luke himself and therefore to an author at the end of the first century, where earlier scholars discovered ancient, even apostolic **[21]**, traditions.

At the risk of simplifying, we would say that the other research went in three directions, according to the personal manner which the exegetes reacted to the theses of the Redaktiongeschichtler. An important fringe of the exegetical world, frequently British and Catholic, when not Greek or

Swedish, reacted critically to the ideas of Conzelmann and company. The theses seem to be excessive and badly supported for this group. Another series of scholars, preocuppied by the origins of Christology, accept the essential of the results mentioned above, but admit to using, inspite of all, the Acts of the Apostles, next to the Gospels and the Epistles, to study the genesis of Christian doctrines. For them, the Redaktionsgeschichte must articulate itself, on the Über - lieferungsgeschichte in order to specify not only later theology, but also the theology of the beginnings. Finally, a third group wants to submit to criticism, not the redactional nature of the Christology of the Lucan writings which is admitted, but the contents that the exegetes of the Fifties believed to have discovered.

II. A TRADITIONAL CHRISTOLOGY

The schema of the speeches takes over the schema of primitive kerygma

a. Despite the existence of the redactionsgeschichtlich works which we have just described, the influence of M. Dibelius and C. H. Dodd continues to be felt. Resorting to the formgeschichtlich method, both of them came to similar results, by way of different paths. For example, Dodd (-> 1936) succeeded in reconstituting a primitive kerygma with the help of pre-Pauline Christological fragments, which are spread through - out the letters of the apostle. Despite certain differences be - tween the Epistles and Acts, he thought that the speeches in Acts had been composed from the same kerygma. "We may with some confidence take these speeches to represent not endeed what Peter said upon this or that occasion, but the kerygma of the Church at Jerusalem at an early period." (p. 21). The convergence of the Epistles and Acts toward a unique primitive kerygma gave impressive weight to his thesis.

b. In the introduction to his thesis, Wilckens [**22**] evoked the success of the theories of Dodd and Dibelius. Among the works, which appeared during the period we are studying, we can mention the monograph of E. Trocmé (-> 1957), the introduction to the commentary of C. S. C. Williams (-> 1957) [**23**], Cullmann's Christology (-> 1958) [**24**], a brief article by S. S. Smalley (-> 1962) [**25**] and as examples, the interpretations of V. Taylor (->1958) and B. Reicke (-> 1959).

The first part of Taylor's book draws up an inventory of the Christological information of the NT: the author distinguishes - the distinction is significant - the data of the Gospel of Luke and that of the Acts. On several points (the absence of the virginal birth and the recoiling of the title of the Son of Man), the Acts has a different Christology than the Gospel [**26**]. The Christology of the Acts insists on the humanity of Jesus, the Messianic identity of Jesus (non-political), the ancient title of servant and the pascal Lordship of Jesus. Inspite of the emphasis it places of the enthronement at the resurrection, it cannot be called adoptionistic.

The second section of the book is historical and theological. It narrates the genesis of Christology in the first century. The writer believes that primitive Christology, where the conviction of the believers won over their concern for expression, remained faithful to itself, in parallel with the personal developments of the great theologians, Paul, John and the author of the letter to the Hebrews. For Taylor, it is the speeches in Acts which give us access to this original doctrine, where the accent fell on the resurrection of Jesus. Of course, the death of Jesus was not forgotten, but it is interpreted along the lines of the servant who accomplishes the plan of God. With this, this Christology desires to be conformed to the Scriptures. Firm and venerable, this Christology, nonetheless, had its limits that later elaborations would surmount: the link between Jesus Christ and his work remained implicit, like the relation between the power of the Risen One and the omnipotence of God. The divine sonship of Jesus was barely explained: the title, Son of God, was absent, like the virginal birth.

c. In his article, "The Risen Lord and His Church, The Theology of Acts" (-> 1959), B. Reicke synthesizes and completes the results of the exegesis of Act 1-7, which he had published two years before. The Christology of the Petrine speeches (Act 2, 3, 5 and 10) does not coincide with the narrative sections of Acts, thus these latter are redactional. Here we have an ancient Palestinian Christology, intended for Israel, which has for the center of its ellipsis, the titles of Servant and Messiah. Here the emphasis is on the past, in which the divine sending of Jesus and his historicity are paired up. The traditional nature of these speeches is demonstrated by the fact that Luke, a Hellenistic Christian, would have had no reason to attribute to Peter, ideas which are so Judeo-Christian (in our opinion, it must still be proved that these ideas are Judeo-Christian and do not correspond to Luke's theology). Reicke continues by saying that the Christology of Stephen's speech and Paul's sermons is somewhat different. Being more universal and ecumenical, this Christology is elaborated in an anti-Jewish polemic in Act 7 (against the concentration of the cult in Jerusalem and the Temple) and follows a hostile attitude toward idolatry in Act 17 (reflected in the Pauline sermon to the pagans, which leans on the Jewish-Hellenistic missionary schema). The accent here falls on the future of Christ. In the narratives which he composed, Luke, himself, insists on the present power of the Resurrected One and his actual interventions by the Holy Spirit. In conclusion, "This variety does not mean that there are different Christologies in Acts. It means only that Luke has given illustrations of how the kerygma was partly adapted to the audience to which it was addressed... Certainly there was also in the Christology of the church a gradual transition from particularism to universalism. This is faithfully reflected by Acts. Luke himself, however, does not think it is a question of different Christologies". (p. 162).

As he indicates himself (p. 160), Reicke remains very reserved concerning the results of certain contemporary exegetes. On the other hand, Luke, the historian, inspires confidence in him.

The speeches are authentic

d. Long ago, the works of Norden, Cadbury and Dibelius showed with what liberty the historians of antiquity worked, in the editing of speeches to punctuate their works. Neither these works, nor the studies of the Redacktionsgeschichtler, which we have analyzed, have prevented certain contemporary authors from defending the authenticity of the speeches against wind and wave. Without declaring Jesus himself as author of the kerygma, as does R. A. Bartels (-> 1961) **[27]**, they do not go beyond the point which Dodd believed he had reached with the help of Formgeschichte. We would not linger over these works if they did not include several pertinent exegetical remarks of philological and theological nature.

In an article consecrated to Act 2, W. Barclay (-> 1959) put forth four arguments in favor of the veracity of the speeches:

a) in times past, we learned by rote with ease (the memory was all the less deficient as the entire Church sought to recall);

b) a Christian does not forget the sermon by which he was converted;

c) the preaching of Peter in Act 2 is curiously Jewish ("all the house of Israel", for example, is part of the Kaddish);

d) the Aramaisms are more numerous in the speeches than in the narrative sections.

In his exegesis of Act 2, Barclay mentions the importance that vs. 22 accords to the humanity of Jesus. He concludes: "The fact is that here we have the most primitive christology and the christology is Adoptianist." (p. 244). Vs. 23 displays a double conviction concerning the death of Jesus, which is characteristic of the book of Acts: the Passion of Jesus is both the accomplishment of the plan of God and the most terrible crime of history. Verses 24-31 extend to the resurrection of Jesus which is the pivot of the argumentation and the heart of his Christology. This resurrection is perceived in a theocentric perspective: "The Resurrection is not the achievement event of Jesus Christ; it is the Divine act of the power of God." (p. 245). In summary, the kerygma of Peter is centered on the act of God. This act is aimed at Jesus Christ who then, orients all history and in particular the life of whoever adheres to the faith (cf. the reaction of the audience of Peter's speech). "Such then, was the pattern of the first preaching, and it is a pattern which is still the pattern to be copied."

For our part, we believe neither that the preacher of our time must "copy" the evangelical pattern, nor that the speech is authentic (it would too be brief and intolerably dense). Furthermore, if certain themes are traditional in origin, the composition is clearly editorial. As for adoptionism, it has to be defined.

e. It is necessary to say a few words about the two works of the Thessalonian professor, G. A. Galitis (-> 1962 and -> 1963), words which are all the more necessary, since the productions, written in Greek, have not received sufficient attention by exegetes. The first tome does the spadework on the questions of introduction concerning the Christological speeches of Peter. A first chapter presents the speeches of Act 1:16-22; 2:14-36, 38, 39, 40; 3:12-26; 4:8-12, 19f.; 5:29-32; 10:34-43; 11:5-17 and 15:7-11. The second analyzes the form of these speeches and underlines the features which are Jewish and Christian (an ecumenical opening), at the same time. The third chapter begins with a philological analysis in order to resolve the historical problem of their authenticity. The speeches are surely edited by Luke (p. 86), but Luke, as a faithful historian, reproduces the authentic oral, or rather written, sources, no doubt in Aramaic and perhaps written up by Mark, the disciple of

Peter. The author attempts to do justice to the critical research of the twentieth century, which he knows perfectly, and the traditional theory of the apostolic origin. The archaic side of the Christology is not the lesser argument used in favor of the ancient content of the discourses (p. 94). An echo of the words of Peter, these sermons summarize the kerygma of the apostles and the early Church [28].

The apostolic value of these documents merit a special theological attention. The author gives this attention in his second volume entitled, **The Christology of Peter's Speeches in the Acts of the Apostles.** He even hints that the theological interest of the sermons depends partially on the results of the philological and historical analysis that must assure the authenticity (p. 11).

The author intends to analyze the Christological motifs of the Petrine speeches and by this, to understand the deep meaning of the portrait of Jesus composed by the first community. The first chapter sets out the three elements which guarantee the theological value of the speeches: the breath of God which passes through them, the promises of the OT which proclaim the fulfillment in Christ and the apostolic testimony to the life of Jesus. The six remaining chapters deal with the Christological titles in the following order: the Christ of the Lord, the Servant of God, the Son of David, the Prophet, the Savior and the Lord. His method aims at being analytical and synthetic, and in the analysis, the author uses his philological competence well, while, in our view, he does not appeal enough to the tools of the überlieferungsgeschichtliche Methode. This evasion is intentional for, believing that he has the original before him, he cannot seize the present nuance of such titles in relation to their anterior Christian usage. The only points of comparison remain the OT and Judaism [29].

In a synthetic perspective, Galitis sees the substance of the Christological titles organize itself in two series. The first includes the titles, Messiah of the Lord, Servant of God and Son of David. God confers on Jesus the "elevated" title of Messiah by spiritual unction. The "low" term of the Son of David applies to Jesus' humanity. The title Servant of God can be understood as a link between these two extremes. The titles Prophet, Savior and Lord form a second series which anticipates the triple office of Christ of later theologies: prophet - the prophetic office, savior - the priestly office and Lord - the royal office. The two series also reflect the paleo-Christian conscience of the two natures of Christ: Prophet designates the human nature and Lord, the divine nature (savior serves as an intermediary between the two, like παῖς does in the first series).

Briefly summarized, these are the main conclusions of an in - vestigation where the procedures of the most recent science and the presuppositions of the most ancient Tradition are placed side by side in a most surprising way. This union is often favorable for analysis but mortal for synthesis. The presentation of the two series, for example, which serves as the scaffolding of the work was not convincing.

Tradition resists the Redacktionsgeschichtler

f. Three exegetes think that the role of tradition is more important than the Redacktionsgeschichtler admit. The critical account of Wilckens' book by J. Dupont (-> 1962, fourth title) is a model in this genre. The learned Benedictine is not content to summarize the work, he gives his personal opinion on each point. The schema used in the preaching to the Jews, in his view is not redactional simply because it has no real parallel in the NT. It is also unlikely that Luke constructed this schema from the one which was destined for the Gentiles. The traditional "summaries" of the Passion as Wilckens envisages them did not strike Dupont's fancy The latter reproaches Wilckens also for designating too many elements as redactional which could be traditional. Of course, he is conscious of the immensity of the editorial work but thinks that this work was more often rereading than creating (this is the case with all that concerns the ministries of John the Baptist and Jesus). Concerning the vocabulary of the resurrection, glorification and repentence, Dupont does not accept the editorial finesse which Wilckens believes to have discovered. If these speeches are silent about the expiatory virtue of the cross, this is because of their literary genre and not a weakness in the theology of Luke (as soon as the literary genre becomes ecclesiastic, missionary as it was, for example, in Act 20, the topos of the redemptive death appears). Another lacuna is that Wilckens does not dwell long enough on the Christological titles. Dupont analyzes them carefully with tradition and redaction in mind. To conclude, the Belgian exegete rises to arms against the anachronistic usage of the terms, subordinationism and adoptionism (Wilckens retains the former and rejects the latter). For him, the Christology of the speeches is a pascal Christology **[30]**. It is indeed a question of subordination of the Son to the Father, but it is situated at the level of the divine economy and not, as would be the case in the third century with the strict subordinationism, at the level of the natures. Personally, we regret Dupont's ambiguity concerning the term, subordinationism, and cannot accept the distinction which is a bit too practical, between the function and the nature, i.e. between salvation history and the Trinitarian and Christological dogmas. The Lucan distinction goes beyond the functional simply in that it is not counterbalanced with a reflection on the nature. The subordination of the Son remains the last word of Luke on the question (but Luke is not the only NT author).

g. I. H. Marshall's article (-> 1970, second title) is more conservative and less rigorous. He limits himself to the clearly important theme of the resurrection of Jesus according to the discourses in Acts (it seems he does not know the important work by J. Schmitt, 1949, on this question) [**31**].

The basics of his argumentation can be summarized in the following manner: the resurrection of Jesus, as Acts presents it, is a given which is anterior to Luke. Three arguments are laid out to support this idea:

a) the disputes, mentioned by Luke, between the Sadducees and the Pharisees, concerning the resurrection of the dead, are traditional. For Luke who, writes after 70 A.D., the date of the decline of the Sadducees, would not have invented these arguments (we hardly see the strength of this argument).

b) the speeches in Acts are more traditional than Con - zelmann, Haenchen and Wilckens admit. The theme of the resurrection of the Messiah, which is central, is traditional: indeed, I Co 15 already speaks of the resurrection of the Messiah (and not of Jesus). The theme of the Messiah who must suffer is neither as late nor as Lucan as O'Neill would like;

c) the Scriptural arguments, not only those taken from Ps 2 and 118, but also those from Ps 16 (he will not see corruption), are traditional (in agreement with Holtz and partly with Lindars).

It is necessary to reject the thesis of H. Braun, taken up again by Wilckens. They say Luke, for theological reasons (subordina - tionistic Christology), prefers ἐγείρω (Auferweckung) to ἀνίστημι (Auferstehung). Despite these authors, we do not sense the Lucan preference for the former. Moreover, ἐγείρω is well im - planted in the vocabulary of early Christianity. The idea of a Christ who raises himself is posterior to primitive and Lucan Christology (it appears in John and, we might add, Ignatius). If Luke sometimes puts ἀνιστάναι in the active with God as subject, it is not to correct a doctrine of the resurrection which displeases him by its insistance on the initiative of the Son, but uniquely to improve the style [**32**].

Luke is not hostile to the expiatory bearing of the cross, but simply identifying himself with tradition, he makes the offer of pardon and the outpouring of the Spirit, depend on the resurrection. Neither does the third evangelist innovate in underlining the importance of witnesses (the importance for the apostle to have seen the Risen Lord is already emphasized in Paul). By doing this, Luke is no more frühkatholisch than Paul.

It seems legitimate to us to show the continuity which goes from tradition to redaction. However, we resent an excessive apologetic concern in Marshall's writing. He wants to assure us (and assure himself) that Luke is, truely, a faithful witness of the apostolic age. The editorial work, so minutely analyzed by Wilckens and others (perhaps too minutely), is flattened out to the point that the stimulating theological differences between Luke and the origins are stumped. Luke's portrait is slowly blotted out even when he had gained colors which we would like more assured. Finally, we ask that terms like "primitive" not be used without specification and, especially, that arguments of authority disappear from exegetical works. Without being sure if we have understood correctly, we do not know what to do with a sentence like, "So important an event as the resurrection must rest on firm historical attestation." (p. 105) [**33**].

h. Following one of J. A .T. Robinson's intuition (-> 1956, cf. below 3, III, a), R. F. Zehnle (-> 1971) concentrates his attention on the Christological speeches in Act 2 and 3 which he distinguishes from the others. Having made this distinction, the author makes another: Act 2, rhetorically more successful, is an elaborate summary of Lucan theology and, more precisely, a program of normative theology which Luke inculcates into his epoch in the name of the apostles. Act 3, older and less artistic, is a traditional text which Luke touches up but slightly (Act 3:61 is editorial). Jewish and Judeo-Christian themes abound. For example, there is conversion which speeds up the end times and a Moses-Jesus typology, present in Act 7 and in second and third century Judeo-Christian texts, which places the two personages on the same level. The redactional discourse in Act 2, that is an adaptation for the contemporary period of the speech in Act 3, which is still very Jewish, reflects one of the first Christian sermons to a Jewish audience.

This solution of the rapport between tradition and redaction seems simplistic; it does not consider enough the traditional elements of which Act 2 is comprised (Zehnle ignores the later works of J. Schmitt, -> 1968 and 1972, cf. 3, III, c) and underestimates, inversely, the part of redaction in Act 3 (cf. G. Lohfink, -> 1969, cf. above 3, I, h, is ignored as well). The two interesting points of this thesis are the illumination of a Jewish-Christian typology, Moses-Jesus and the consideration given to the audience in understanding the speeches. Still to be verified is the existence of this typology, and the relation between the hearers and the sermons has to be specified (the excusable ignorance of Act 3 is not as unique as Zehnle thinks; and with this, it is not exclusively associated with the Jews in Jerusalem; the theme of *ἄγνοια* - certainly in a wider sense - reappears in the speeches in Antioch of Pisidia, Act 13:27 and the Areopagus, Act 17:30).

III. THE ORIGINS OF CHRISTOLOGY

a. The works of L. Cerfaux (1950, 1954^2), E. Schweizer (1955, 1962^2), O. Cullmann (-> 1957), W. Marxsen (1960), F. Hahn (-> 1963), W. Kramer (1963), Ph. Vielhauer (1965), R. H. Fuller (1965), P. Lamarche (-> 1966), J. Knox (1967) and W. Thüsing (1970) [**34**] on the origins of Christology are known. We are also aware of the efforts unfurled by the exegetes, anxious to reach the first elaborations concerning the resurrection of Jesus (a good bibliography can be found in X. Léon-Dufour's work of 1971). Although each of these authors turn to the traditions contained in the Lucan corpus, a presentation of their investigations, methods and results would go beyond the goal of our work. We shall fix our limit with certain exegetes who concentrate their attention on the archaic Christological elements, hidden in Acts and occasionally in the Gospel of Luke [**35**]. While all of these authors accept the fact of Lucan redaction, but, nonetheless, hope that an investigation, comparable to that of a detective, will allow the return to an archaic stage.

Even if it has been refuted several times (see above the article of G. Lohfink), the hypothesis of J. A. T. Robinson (-> 1956) is stimulating enough to be explored for a moment. The author perceives contradictions within the Luke-Acts corpus: the Messiahship of Jesus seems to be imposed at various moments, according to the pericope; for example, at the nativity, the baptism, the resurrection, etc. These tensions reflect perhaps Luke's difficulty and partial failure in the assimilation of ancient

Christological witnesses. Thus Act 2:36 reveals an adoptianistic concept (Messiah and Lord since the resurrection) which is anterior to Luke's personel position (Messiahship from birth). Robinson is not the first to have set forth this idea. The writer's new suggestion (notice the question mark which concludes the title of the essay) is to go beyond the Christology of Act 2 toward a rival Christology, of which Act 3:12-26 still bears the mark (vs. 18 is Lucan for Robinson). Robinson thinks he is able to analyze vss. 19-21 as an attestation of a hope (of the first Christians, who belonged to John the Baptist's movement and remained attached to the historical Jesus) according to which the Messiah would not be installed and manifested until the end of time. The resurrection of Jesus does not yet coincide with his Messianic enthroning. At Easter, Jesus, prophet and savior, recovers his rights but the Messianic function is not yet given him. He is simply designated (this is the sense of προκεχειρισμένος in 3:20) as the Messiah that God will send at the Parousia. Until then, he is detained in heaven without a specific mission. In this "most primitive christology", the Resurrected One does not yet have the titles of Christ and Lord (this is why they are rare in the speeches in Acts). Therefore, Act 3:20 does not speak of the second coming, but of the eschatological manifestation of the Messiah, still to come.

In our view, a stylistic analysis shows that the speech in Act 3 is more Lucan than Robinson thinks. Furthermore, the term προκεχειρισμένος must be understood otherwise: Jesus is not designated Messiah, but he is installed *for you*, the Messiah who must come. Verse 18, with its mention of the sufferings of the Messiah, is not more recent than vss. 19-21. It is, therefore, improbable that, for certain early Christians, the Messianic enthronement was associated with the Parousia. It is more likely that the resurrection and enthronement were paired up from the beginning.

b. Let us turn now to the second part of van Iersel's book, **"Der Sohn" in den synoptischen Jesusworten** (-> 1961) and toward an article entitled "Saint Paul et la prédication de l'Eglise primitive" (-> 1963). The title of van Iersel's work lends itself to confusion, for one of the four sections concerns the speeches in Acts. After a serious investigation, the author chooses the middle way. Edited by Luke as the style and vocabulary show, the Christological speeches contain, nonetheless, three traditional elements: a) the schema, b) the *testimonia* and c) the major Christological titles. After this, he studies the titles, Son of God and Servant of God, to arrive at the following conclusions. Concerning the Servant, he concludes: despite the absence of the theme of expiation in the kerygmatic discourses, the influence of Is 53 is felt, though weak (the theme of expiation will appear in the later phase of catechism); and it would be wrong to exclude other more important Scriptural influences. Concerning the title, Son of God, he thinks: even if Luke associates the title with the preaching of Paul (Act 9:20 and 13:33), he does not make it the exclusive prerogative of the apostle to the Gentiles. The themes which this title induce appear in other speeches of Acts (Peter's in Act 2, for example). For Luke, this title, rarely from his pen, belongs to the whole of the primitive Church. It is probable that Luke is not wrong; the title, with its thematic and Scriptural associations (2 Sm 7:12-14 and Ps 2:7), was part and parcel, with the kerygma, of the common good of the first Christian communities. It designated, like Christ and Lord, Jesus as the Messianic king, enthroned at Easter, according to the promise made to David. Is it necessary to speak of adoptianism here? The writer notes the relation between this primitive Christology, just described, and that of the Ebionites, which is adoptionistic (no salvific import given to the cross; no preexistence; enthronement of Jesus as the Messiah). Yet two noteworthy differences appear: first, the most ancient kerygma is still unaware of the virginal birth, while the Ebionites deny it; the Ebionites make the baptism the precise moment of the enthronement-adoption, while the first Christians place it at Easter, without excluding a certain anterior Messianism. "Mann kann deshalb im Adoptianismus ein Abfallprodukt der ersten christologischen Besinnung erblicken, die einerseits zur [ortho - doxen] Lehre der Präexistenz, andrerseits zum Adoptianismus führte." (p. 87). By repeating the first Christology, without adapting it, the Ebionites have falsified it even more that the orthodox Christians who elaborate it by inserting, for example, preexistence into it. This is the author's thesis [**36**].

Without saying anything about the basic question, we think it is reasonable to accept that Luke takes over, with adaptation, a Jewish-Christian "Messianology" and "pedology". While at the same time, it seems difficult to reach these conclusions without analyzing the title *ὁ χριστός* and without bringing into play texts like Lk 1-2 where the traditional-redactional problem is similar.

In his article, van Iersel takes up the comparison, which was Dodd's success, between 1 Co 15:3-8 and the scheme of the kerygma of the Acts. Even if a structural relation is evident, van Iersel is right to note the differences in literary genre and Christological content. For him, 1 Co 15:3-8 is a catechetical formula, the speeches in Acts are kerygmatic fragments. With regard to the differences of content, they are clear: the death of Jesus is the salvific work of God in 1 Co 15 and the fruit of the violence of the Jews for Acts; at the resurrection, Jesus is more active in 1 Co 15 than in Acts. The recourse to the Scripture is also different here and there. The mention of the investiture of Christ and call to repentence is lacking in the pre-Pauline formula. In short, 1 Co 15 is Christocentric, while the kerygma in Acts is theocentric.

From these differences, already verified by several exegetes, van Iersel leads us to a path which will concern more than one scholar. In his view, even if the formula in 1 Co 15 is pre-Pauline and even if the first letter to the Corinthians was written long before the Acts, the essential of the kerygma of the Acts is earlier that the credo in 1 Co 15. "No matter how primitive the formula is, it is, nevertheless, less ancient and less primitive than the kerygmatic formulas of the book of the Acts." (p. 441). We find again the distinction, which was already encountered in his book, between preaching and catechism, the one preceding the other in time.

It seems wiser to us, having distinguished the literary genres and the theological information, to remain very reserved as to the age of the traditions. Until more ample information, we consider the pre-Pauline formula of 1 Co 15 (which must be limited to vss. 3b-5) as the more solid declaration of the primitive faith. It is not that the book of Acts does not give us useful information, but Acts inserts it into a redactional rereading, which is more important than van Iersel thinks.

c. With vigor and virulence, J. Schmitt, whose thesis in 1949 concerning the Christology of Acts, reaffirmed the traditional value of divers elements, contained in the speeches. The reader will refer to his great article in the **Supplément au Dictionnaire de la Bible** (-> 1972), which followed an article of remarkable synthesis (-> 1968).

For the exegete from Strasbourg, 1 Co 15 3b-5 must not be the only to benefit from the monopoly of seniority. Certain prayers and formulas of faith contained in the epistles as well as several portions of the speeches of Acts are archaic and help us to penetrate into the faith of first Christians. Wisely, he notes that exegesis alone can orient us toward the traditional or redactional character of the texts, studied one after the other. Perhaps still too marked by source criticism, he tries to extricate the traditional fragments and renounces for the moment to resolve the age of a schema.

The writer distinguishes, for example, three original items of different age, in the speech at Pentecost: "Verses 22b to 24a are both the center and pearl of the speech: they reproduce the kerygma, and this according to an archaic declaration of which there is no example in the other vestiges of the apostolic witness cf. 1 Co 15:3b-5; Act 3:13-15; 4:10b; 5:30 and parallels)." (p. 117 of the article). The numerous hapax, the rudimentary nature of the Christology and the influence of a Palestinian Scriptural argumentation are the major arguments advanced in favor of the great age of these verses. Vs. 24b serves as the hinge and introduces vss. 25-31 which constitute an interpretation of the kerygma, originally independent. Traditional as well, these verses are, however, more recent than 22b-24a and more worked by Luke (they are the reflection of an old Jewish polemic concerning the incorruption of David). In their turn, vss. 32-35 are detached from what preceded. If the interpretation of Ps 110:1 is old, the argument which is drawn from it, corresponds to Luke's intentions.

We have chosen this example, for it demonstrates well the method applied by Schmitt, who analyzes each speech after this manner. The result is that Act 3:12-26 is one of the most ancient pages of the Acts; Act 4:9-12 is a rather secondary variation of the kerygma; Act 10:34-43 is a text amply edited, even if the information remains basically traditional and probably Palestinian. (that which must have been dispensed to the Palestinian proselytes); Act 7:2-53 is a theological message of disciples recently coming from Palestinian Judaism with special attachments in the Jewish reform milieus; Act 13:16-41, inspite of its heavy Lucan accent, is an example of the initial preaching of Saint Paul; Act 17:12-31 is an example of the new orientation which Christian preaching took, when it changed audiences and was addressed to the pagans.

J. Schmitt thinks he is able to reconstruct the main elements of the primitive Christology, which was centered on the death and resurrection of Jesus. The pre-Easter ministry served only as a backup argument. The cross and resurrection formed the moment when everything was at stake (the defeat of Satan and the victory of God). As the death of the just, the cross provoked the justification of many. The resurrection was understood as the exclusive act of God. Resurrected, Jesus received the fullness of the Christological prerogatives. He was also given to confer the Holy Spirit, henceforth. Schmitt even believes he can, already at his period, speak of Jesus, the new Man, and of a resurrected spiritual body.

The research for the origins of Christology must be done exegetically, as Schmitt wishes. However, the "construction", which M. Dibelius recommended for the formation of the evangelical tradition, must intervene as well. With the construction of the hypotheses which allows a proper consideration of the Christological needs of the primitive community we can be more precise. It is in this direction that we would go to verify, throughout all early Christian literature, the interaction, age and development of themes of the enthronement and resurrection, Messiahship and sonship, Easter elevation and abasement (either in death or in flesh). The themes of the Easter enthronement, humanity and resurrection of Jesus surely link up the Christology of Acts with an ancient Christology, but they also correspond to what Luke defends and appreciates. This is why we think that Luke, at the end of the first century, presents a Christology which remains quite embryonic and has not been contaminated by the elaborations of a Paul or a John. However, the archaic character of the formulation does not imply that the sense must stay the same.

d. It is this sort of approach which G. Bouwman (-> 1970) takes concerning the Ascension, and J. Roloff (-> 1972), concerning the death of Jesus. The first shows that Luke the theologian insisted on the exaltation (which he identifies with the Ascension) and distinguished, chronologically, the resurrection from the exaltation-Ascension. Yet these editorial traits must not hinder us from seeing an archaic theme in the elevation, all the more that it is found in other traditions collected in the epistles, and as a *pascal* elevation, it becomes competitive with the Lucan conception of salvation history. Luke the historian was, therefore, one of the witnesses of a traditional conception of the exaltation of the Messiah: "Jedenfalls ist damit nicht ausgeschlossen, dass die Auferstehung vom Anfang an *erfahren* wurde als die Rechtfertigung des Propheten, als die Erhöhung des Gerechten." (p. 263). Nonetheless, Bouwman recommends prudence, for Luke could have wanted to "archaize" (the elevation and adoptionism which is associated with it do not appear in the first chapters of Acts). As for Roloff, he indicates three attempts of early Christianity to give meaning to the Cross of Christ: a) the first appears in the speeches in Acts: it is the *Kontrastschema* (death, guilt of men; resurrection, work of God), which must be older than Luke. b) The second is anterior to Mark and governs the Passion announcements and narratives: it is *heilsgeschichtlich* - *kausal*. Corresponding to the Scriptures, the death of Jesus was necessary (δεῖ) c) Independent of the two others, the third interpretation is soteriological: dead for you, for many, etc. It is the *ὑπέρ* - Formal that we meet in Gal 1:4; Rom 4:25 etc.

Roloff's personal effort is on the third for which he seeks to discover the origin. In the search, exegetes have most frequently invoked Isa 53, but since Morna Hooker's book (-> 1959), this has become problematic. E. Schweizer, followed by E. Lohse and others, put forth the Jewish conception of the righteous one suffering for his own as a possible solution, but Roloff is reticent with regard to this possibility. He prefers to go by way of Mk 10:45 and Lk 22:27 in order to get back to the historical Jesus' very conception of his ministry. Viewed with a critical eye, this ministry was defined by Jesus as a service (*διακονεῖν*) and lived in commensalism. If Jesus saw his life as a service to others, it was easy for the first Christians to conceive of the death of their master as a service for others, too. We will have found the oldest link which permitted the first Christians to understand the death of Jesus soteriologically.

We have two remarks to make:

a) One influence must not be singled out to the detriment of the others. G. Schneider (-> 1969) has shown the impact of the suffering Righteous One, on the redaction of Luke's narrative of the Passion. This influence goes back to the origins. Jesus himself bathed in a Jewish milieu and he might well have understood his ministry in the light of the OT revelation where the prophet, servant and the righteous must pay of their person.

b) It is interesting to note that Luke kept a saying in which Jesus explains the service he renders to others in his life. Several indications (cf. Lk 22:37 among others) make us think that in imitation of the first Christians, the evangelist enlarged this service to include the death of Jesus. To speak of Luke's rejection of the soteriological import of the cross, as many do, seems erroneous to us.

IV. THE LUCAN PORTRAIT OF JESUS

a. These past years, several exegetes have reexamined the portrait of Jesus which Luke paints [**37**]. They often came to results different from those of the Redaktiongeschichtler which we have spoken of in former paragraphs. Their methods of investigation vary. They can be characterized either by a critical research of the general coherence or by a minute study of the most accepted editorial indications [**38**].

Instead of defining the particularities of Lucan Christology, by examining the modifications made by the Evangelist of his sources, G. W. H. Lampe (-> 1955-56) chose what he believed the simplest path: to analyze the major Lucan Christological themes and discover if they are sufficiently consistent and distinctive to be able to speak of a Lucan portrait of Jesus.

To investigate this coherence, Lampe studies the major Christological speeches of the Acts one after the other. Whatever the source they are integrated into the Lucan work and thus are made his. Moreover, Lampe is inclined to consider the speeches as summaries of the Lucan conception of the Gospel.

A reading of these texts reveals a doctrinal unity with artistic variety. The "saving events" are found everywhere, but each speech has its own accent. Compared to Act 2, the one in Act 3 insists on the eschatological coming of Christ the Judge. Confronted by the others, the speech in Act 13 is the only to evoke justification by faith.

On the whole, the speeches have many points in common with the remainder of the NT, especially Mark. Yet we find the personal stamp of Luke. What is it?

a) The main theme is God's sending his word to Israel, in and through the ministry of Jesus. Anointed by the Spirit, the latter accomplishes miracles and announces the kingdom, but he is rejected by Israel. The ignorance and hardening of the Jewish authorities led to his death, but the plan of God is fulfilled nonetheless: resurrection, exaltation and Pentecost.

Different from Wilckens, Lampe underlines the glorious exaltation of Jesus: "Through death to the heavenly throne. This is the picture of Christ's work which Luke is most concerned to show us." (p. 167). Here we have an OT pattern (cf. Joseph) where the restoration of Righteous one overcomes his disaster. However, the pattern is modified at one point: the Lucan Christ is also the ἀρχηγός. His fate opens a breach which allows his disciples to follow him (Voss will also note this of Jesus, who as a leader, directs his troups in his steps) [39].

b) Secondly, Lampe remarks on the Lucan insistance on the Holy Spirit. Jesus is anointed by the Spirit during his earthly ministry. Once ascended, he can transmit the Spirit. If Jesus received the Spirit, he is, then, a prophet, a prophet similar to Moses: the designation of the Twelve and the seventy (or seventy-two) (cf. Num 11) is, with the speech of Stephen, the indication of this typology between Jesus and Moses.

c) A prophet like Moses, Jesus also has the characteristics of Elijah who received the word of God on Mount Horeb, was persecuted and finally translated to heaven.

d) Afterwards, Lampe signals more briefly the accent Luke puts on Christ the savior, an accent which exists even if a Joshua-Jesus typology remains curiously absent from the Lucan writings.

e) Lampe detects in the relation between the Father and the Son, a certain tension between Acts, where Jesus, the man, is adopted as the Son, and the Gospel, where he is the Son of God from the beginning (especially the infancy narratives). Yet, according to Lampe, it would be false to discern a contradiction here. As Act 3:20 says, the plan of God predestined Jesus, from the beginning to be the Messiah (predestination rather than preexistence). If already in the Gospel, Jesus is called by the glorious titles, which are fitting only for the Risen One, it is because of an intentional prolepsis.

Inspite of all, the ties between the Father and the Son are less solid than in the Pauline or Johanine thought. We can characterize them in the following manner: God links himself to Jesus by his Spirit. Jesus is tied to the Father by prayer (on this cf. W. Ott. -> 1965) [40].

f) The relationship Christ-disciple. Lampe correctly notes that Luke specified more precisely, than the others, the relation which is established between Christ and his disciples. Jesus chooses and forms his disciples. This formation, which contrasts with the hardening of the Jewish leaders, culminates in the instructions, peculiar to Luke, that Jesus gives to his disciples at the last supper. Thus, the relationship Christ-believer corresponds to that of a master and a student. The idea of a communion in Christ is absent (Act 9:4 must not be pressed). The tie between master and disciple is not only exterior and scholarly, for the outpouring of the Spirit and the invocation of the Name, unifies Jesus and his people in a similar fate.

The Lucan portrait, according to Lampe, has a specific coherence. We accept on the whole his proposed results, but think, nonetheless, that a comparison between redaction and tradition should highlight other important traits. Some of these are: a) the Lucan Christ fulfills divers OT prophecies; b) he fits into salvation history which grows longer and hardens, at the same time; c) Luke distinguishes, more clearly than Lampe is willing to admit, between the resurrection and the Ascension; d) and finally, we are not convinced that in speaking of "prolepsis", the English exegete has resolved the tension which emerges between the two first chapters of the Gospel (Jesus is the Messiah, the Son of David, the Savior and the Lord from the nativity) and certain speeches in Acts where the Messianic enthronement takes place at Easter.

b. The mongraph of the Catholic scholar, G. Voss (-> 1965) [**41**], is less striking than Lampe's article. The author invites systematic theologians to overcome the quarrel over the two natures of Christ and do justice to the work accomplished by Jesus in his life and death. The study of Lucan Christology must facilitate this task and consequently, favorize a new interpretation of soteriology. For Luke's Jesus is the point of orientation and model, the Ursprung and Urbild of believers.

The author recommends and practices the redaktiongeschichtich method, which he completes with thematic developments, often too dogmatic. By this, he wants to avoid the pulverization of the texts and the 'system' spirit. Volontarily refusing (p. 19) to insert Luke's thought into the development of Christian theology - we would reproach him for this - , he seeks a balance between an examination of the redactional contexts and those of the Christological titles.

As his point of departure, Voss chooses the relation which Luke establishes between the ministry of Jesus and the kingdom of God. An analysis of a variety Jesus' sayings on the kingdom allows him to conclude that, for Luke, Jesus' healings express the gracious visitation of God, and efficiently prefigure, even if only provisionally, the last redemption. So in Luke's eyes, Jesus was invested and conscious of an authority that made him the lieutenant of God and initiator of the kingdom (Voss adds an "already and not yet" of Jesus, the Son of Man to the well known "already and not yet" of the kingdom).

As a good analysis of the titles of Savior and Lord shows, the mission of Jesus was doubly soteriological: it accomplished what men were incapable of doing and gave them a model to follow, at the same time. Thus, despite a formal dependence on Hellenism and material from the OT, the titles, Savior and Lord, portray a specific figure: that of an envoy of the unique God, a messenger, who differing from other saviors, does not speak in his own name, but acts in place of and for his father. "Durch die Titel *σωτήρ* und *κύριος* wird Jesus von Lukas als der von Gott bevollmächtigte König gekennzeichnet, durch dessen Auftreten sich Gottes Herrschaft geltend zu machen beginnt." (p. 60).

The second chapter, entitled "Jesus, the Messianic King", determines the relationship of Christ with his father. Based on a tight exegesis of the triumphal entry into Jerusalem (Lk 19:28-

38), the annunciation (Lk 1:28-37), the baptism of Jesus (Lk 3:21f.) and the temptations (Lk 4:1-13), the author declares that the soteriological function of Jesus is based on the unique relationship of the Son and his Father. As the Son (Voss studies this title), Jesus is also the King, the Messiah whose Davidic origins are not carnal, but spiritual. The anointing of the Spirit given to Jesus indicates that God was with him, like he had been with the great liberators of the old covenant. So, salvation history continues. The baptism of Jesus, in the Lucan perspective, is a royal enthronement and not the sending of a humble servant to a mission. However, the great temptation for the Messianic King, after the baptism, like after the entry into Jerusalem, will always be the dictatorial exercise of power: the abuse of royalty in a zealot understanding, instead of its appli - cation in the perspective of a servant.

Thus, Voss comes naturally to his third section on the passion of Jesus. In these pages, the writer extricates the Lucan perspective which does not remain insensitive or allergic to the suffering of Christ. We think he is right here. Far from escaping the plan of God, the death of Jesus is the supreme expression of the submission of the suffering Righteous One, who obeys the will of the Master of history. The narrative of the institution of the Communion where, following H. Schürmann, the author prefers the long text, shows that "die Paradosis des Menschensohnes ist somit kein rein passives Geschehen, sie ist die Tat des Gehorsams zugleich aktivisch." (p. 104). Yet, different from Mark, Luke does not conceive the death of Jesus as a sacrifice, but rather - Voss follows E. Lohse (-> 1955) - as the death of the Righteous One suffering for his own. The speeches to the disciples after the Last Supper (Lk 22:24-38) as well as the figure of Simon of Cyrene, indicate that the Christ, who offers himself for his own, is also a model for life and faith for believers. Voss insists on this double function of the Passion; it is both soteriological and mimetic, in a Catholic manner, of course, but which finds its support in Luke. Nonetheless, to deduce that Christ is thus the beginning of a new humanity and that Luke established a parallel between Christ and Adam seems exaggerated. Another exaggeration which appears here, (p. 129), but also throughout the book, is the role of Satan, who omnipresent, holds captive humanity under his power until Christ returns. Luke is, no doubt, aware of the power of the devil (J. Dupont has recently showed this concerning the temptations of Jesus) [42], but he does not develope a doctrine, comparable to Paul's, concerning the slavery of men and their liberation through Christ.

The fourth chapter treats the elevation of the Crucified One and poses, in a few pages, the delicate question of the meaning and function of the Ascension. If Jesus is enthroned king at his baptism, even at his birth, what further authority can the Ascension confer on him? Briefly, how can the nativity (Lk 2:11, "Today, is born to you, in the city of David, a Savior, who is Christ the Lord."), baptism (Lk 3:22, "You are my son, today I have begotten you.": a text that Voss retains) and Ascension after Easter (Act 2:36, "God made him Lord and Christ, this Jesus that you have crucified." Cf. Act 5:31), be reconciled? Christ's post-Easter Ascension confirms that the ministry of Jesus was itself a progressive elevation (*ἀνάλημψις*, Lk 9:51) toward God. An ecclesiological function is then added to the Christological; the baptismal enthronement conferred the Holy Spirit on the only Messiah and the Easter enthronement permits the outpouring on believers. In fact, it is necessary to wait for Easter and the Ascension in order for Christ to become truly the *ἀρχηγὸς τῆς ζωῆς*, the principle and model of salvation. One might wonder if the solution, Voss offers, is satisfying. Beside the fact that it seems dogmatic, it leaves the sonship and the Messiahship of Jesus from his nativity in the dark. Neither does it consider the possible tensions between competing traditions and redaction.

Finally, we do not see why the author adds here a final chapter, consecrated to Jesus, the eschatological prophet. He considers the first sermon of Jesus in Nazareth (Lk 4:16-30) and the Transfiguration (Lk 9:28-36, which he explains in a sophisticated manner: Moses guarantees the glorious, prophetic and royal Christological title of the servant and Elijah - why? - the title of the humiliated Son). His last analyses treat the Lucan allusions to the servant in Isaiah.

In his conclusion, Voss draws the dogmatic consequences of his study. Firstly, the Lucan Christology contains a cognitive aspect: knowledge of the periods of the life of Christ opens the eyes of the believers and teaches them what their own life should become. Secondly, this Christology affirms that the redemption offered by Jesus Christ is not only a knowledge, but also an ontological reality. Thirdly, Luke's Christology has an anthropological orientation: the kingdom set in motion by Jesus offers man a zone of liberty in which he must engage himself responsibly. Fourthly, Luke lets us know that this engagement is not the imitation of an ideal, but the following of a person. From which we gather the personal character of the Lucan writings. Finally, as a good Catholic, Voss thinks that Luke defends the two natures of Christ; the true humanity of Jesus against all docetism and his true divinity against all adoptionism.

On two points, Voss confirms and specifies certain of Con - zelmann's conclusions. From the first chapter, we retain the love which Luke has for the periods of redemptive history. Since it is only a provisional irruption of the Kingdom, the ministry of Jesus remains distinct from the definitive reign of God. From the second chapter, we note the absence of the title God as an attribute of Jesus [**43**], an absence which confirms the Son's constant submission to the Father. The fourth chapter confirms this subordination, for it is God who raises the Messiah, voluntarily abased. On two points Voss corrects the image of Christ painted by the author of **Die Mitte der Zeit**: the sub - mission of the Son does not equal a veritable subordinationism, for Luke accepts, in these certainly ambiguous terms, a glorious Messiahship of Jesus from his origins. Here, Voss, was not able to light our lantern. The other point, to which we adhere is the Passion of Jesus - theme of the third chapter - is not the wart in the work of Luke; it constitutes with the trip to Jerusalem and the resurrection, one of the heilsgeschichtlich steps of the *ἀνάλημψις* of the Son toward his Father [**44**].

c. Professor Moule's project (-> 1966) is more limited and more polemic. He divides his article into three: first of all, he compares the Christology of Luke's Gospel with that of the Acts, then, distinguishes a variety of Christologies in the book of the Acts and, finally, confrounts these Christologies with the rest of the NT.

In distinguishing the Jesus of the Gospel from the Christ of the Acts, Moule refuses to agree with the critical theologians who discover in the Gospel the doctrine of the Church and not the pre-Easter history of Jesus. Against the current of a widespread opinion, he shows that the use of the titles differs here and there. Certainly, Jesus is already called *κύριος* in the Gospel, but it is in passages where the Evangelist expresses himself and not Jesus or his contemporaries (with the exception of Lk 1:43, 76 and 19:31). The title is therefore post - resurrectional and bears a triple mark: 1) it designates the absolute power of the Risen One (Act 10:36), 2) it qualifies the Father as well as the Son and 3) it is associated with the invocation of the name of Jesus Christ, while in the OT, the name called on was Yahweh.

In the Gospel, Jesus is only a prophet; in the Acts, he is the prophet of Dt 18:15 (cf. Act 3:22f. and 7:37). There is also a difference in the sense and frequency of the title, Son of Man; while it is frequent in the Gospel and associated with suffering, it is exceptional in the Acts and related to glory. As for the titles, Savior and Son, of course, they appear in the Gospel, but heavenly beings or visionary prophets use them. In the Acts, they become common among believers.

We must not conclude from these differences, that there is a discontinuity of the persons. As the title, Nazarene, attests, Luke does not doubt that the Resurrected One is the crucified prophet from Galilee.

The second section is also polemic. It attacks another widely accepted theory, according to which the Christology of the Acts is uniform and redactional and, that the differences are to be explained by Luke's historical or literary preoccupations. Moule does not take up the conservative theory as it is, but in an original manner, he proposes that the Christological variety is due not to a diversity of the speakers but to a plurality of the literary genres and the Sitze im Leben.

His first attack is aimed at J. A. T. Robinson, whose work is summarized above in 3, III, a. The Christology of Act 3:19-21 is not anterior to that of Act 2, for "it is simpler, surely, to interpret the crucial words to mean that Jesus is already recognized as the previously predestined Christ (the term προκεχειρισμένος, so interpreted, is in line with Luke's penchant for predestination), who at the end is to be sent back again in the world." (p. 168).

On the other hand, Moule would like to dissociate the usage of the title παῖς in Act 3 and 4. The Christology of Act 3 is apologetic and παῖς designates the servant of Isa 53 whereas Act 4 is doxological and παῖς has royal overtones [45].

Finally, if the expiatory virtue of the death of Jesus does not appear in except Act 20, it is because of the literary genre of the Lucan texts and the editor's theological reticence. It was not usual, in early Christianity, to underline the salvific power of the cross in the sermon. Rather, this was done in catechism. This is why, the ὑπὲρ ἡμῶν appears in the epistles, reflecting a catechism, and in the sole speech in Acts addressed to Christians (Act 20:28).

In the third section, Moule repeats what he has already affirmed: it is not enough to distinguish the speakers, it is also necessary to consider the variety of the situations (Sitze im Leben). If the speeches in Acts resemble one another, it is not simply because of their Lucan origin, but also because of their missionary character. As soon as the situation changes, as in chapter 20 where the hearers are converts, the speech changes as well. The author comes to the same conclusion that J. Dupont (-> 1962, fourth title) came to: the speech to the elders in Ephesus (Act 20) resembles the epistles because of the same ecclesiastic situation. As for us, we would add, it resembles the Pastoral epistles, more than the authentic epistles, which situates Luke at the end of the first century, at the beginning of the postapostolic era.

Moule, however, does not neglect the speakers: thus the connections, not always convincing, between the speech of Peter and the first letter of Peter and between Paul's and the Pauline epistles (cf. Act 13:38f.) The professor from Cambridge is forced to admit that it is not always so clear: the use of *χριστός* in the Pauline speeches in Acts differs from that of Paul in his letters. In Acts, it is a title, and a proper name in Paul's writings. Here again, Moule thinks he finds the answer in the literary genres: Christ is a proper name in the liturgical texts of the Acts and the epistles; it is a title in the apologetic sections of the Acts and the epistles (e.g. Rom 1:3 and 9:5). One must consider both, the situations and the speakers. This declaration does not solve the problem in our opinion.

The article comes to an end with several comparisons with other NT writings:

a) The Pastoral epistles and Revelation develope an imperial Christology and, thus, in a period of persecution, fight against a divinized Caesar. Contrariwise, the Acts never says that Jesus is king (only the enemies of the faith claim it: Lk 23:2 and Act 17:6f.). We can conclude that the Lucan community is not oppressed by the Empire. If we admit this last observation, in agreement with S. Brown (ch 7, -> 1969) and against H. Conzelmann (-> 1954) and F. Schütz (-> 1969), it seems that Luke with A. George (-> 1965) insists on a royal Christology more than the two other Synoptics.

b) Different from John and Paul, Moule notes that the Book of the Acts is unaware of a corporate conception of the Christ. Jesus Christ is an individual personality, localized at the present in heaven (the only allusion to the ecclesiastic body of Christ is associated with the person of Paul, Act 9:5). The baptismal doctrine in the name of Jesus in Luke differs from what happens in Paul and is not transformed into a sacramental conception of the incorporation into the *σῶμα χριστοῦ*. On this point, Moule is certainly right.

He concludes that the Christology of the Acts is not uniform and that it reflects generally the beliefs of the early Church. The Christologies of Paul and John are the fruit of the reflection of the isolated geniuses.

The English exegete is right to attract our attention to the tensions within the Christological declarations of Luke and Acts (he could have noted others, e.g. the date of the Messianic anointing). He correctly explains certain particularities by the difference of the ecclesiastic deeprootedness, but he has not sufficiently evoked the traits peculiar to the Lucan Christ. This weakness is perhaps due to the too radical distinction which he makes between the Christology of the Gospel and that of the Acts, with preference to the latter.

d. Like Moule's contribution, F. Schütz' dissertation (-> 1969), which we present at the end of this section, is polemic. It attacks all those who see in Luke a partisan of the theology of glory. The thrust of the charge is Conzelmann's thesis, according to which the time of Jesus (the ministry in Galilee and the journey) was a blessed, preserved and salvific time.

For the author, there are strong indications that the Lucan community suffered much more than thought (p. 9). As a theological solution to this problem, Luke and his Church de - veloped a Christology of the cross, which by its soteriological and exemplary marks, would have comforted them.

The book opens with a chapter which deals with the Lucan community, marked by persecution and impatient to discover the meaning to the tribulation which afflict them: "Die lukanische Schriften lassen keinen Zweifel daran, dass die Lage der Gemeinde in dieser Welt de facto durch θλίψεις bestimmt ist." (p. 11). "Das Unverständnis der Jünger für das Leiden ihres Herrn wird transparent für das Unverständnis der Kirche für ihre durch θλίψεις bestimmte Lage." (p. 24).

The second chapter analyzes the vocabulary of the Passion and death of Jesus. Πάσχειν (παθεῖν) enters into the religious vocabulary of Judaism by way of the LXX. In the NT and especially in Luke, this verb comes to mean to die, a meaning which was unknown to secular Greek: "Das Sterben wird zum Inbegriff der παθήματα." (p. 30). In our opinion, Schütz does not convincingly demonstrate this thesis. The vocabulary of the cruficixion (σταυρός; σταυροῦν), in Luke, designates the death of Jesus more than the type of execution suffered. This death was perceived by Luke, sensitive to the Passion of Christ, as a violent death. The use of ἀναιρεῖν (4 times) and διαχειρίζεσθαι (Act 5: 30) should confirm this thesis but we fear that the author sometimes senses imaginary nuances. Such excess can result with the redaktionsgeschichtich method.

The following idea is more tempting: Luke associates the death of Jesus with his rejection by the elected people (this connection appears when the verbs ἀρνεῖσθαι and ἀγνοεῖν are analyzed). The Evangelist establishes this link in an edifying and heilsgeschichtlich perspective (p. 35). In this way he distinguishes himself from Paul, who ties the death with the intervention of God.

The third chapter is the most original and the most debatable: the author wants to show that for Luke the whole life of Jesus is a path of suffering. The rejection in Nazareth is typical of the whole Galileen period: Jesus expresses his claim and program, but immediately he runs head on with the incomprehension and hostility of his people. The pericopes, Lk 4:14-5:16; 5:17-6:11; 7:36-50, like the rest of the Gospel, show that at each step of his life, Jesus is a σημεῖον ἀντιλεγόμενον (Lk 2:34). The allusions to the Passion of Jesus do not keep us waiting, as Conzelmann believes: they exist already in Lk 4:13 (an indirect allusion) and 9:7ff. (the first explicit mention). With its mention of Jesus' ἔξοδυς, the transfiguration terminates the first part of the Gospel, already marked by suffering coextensive with the Messianic ministry, and, despite Conzelmann, it does not introduce the second. The result is that the second section of the Gospel, the journey, is not marked by suffering more than the two other parts. We would rather speak of the edification of the community and, with Conzelmann, the clarification of the fatal consequence which the Passion at Jerusalem will be. Unable to convince, Schütz believes that from the speeches in Acts he is able to deduce that the ministry of Jesus was accompanied by and not followed by suffering. With Conzelmann and against Schütz, we deem that Luke delineates the periods and makes the Passion of Jesus succeed a fruitful ministry.

However, Schütz must be right against Conzelmann, when he deems (p. 86f.) that the death of Jesus is positively integrated into the plan of God. The speeches of the Acts, the account of the Transfiguration, the insistence of δεῖ (6 times in Luke's Passion narrative and only once in Matthew and Mark), the Scriptural arguments, Jesus' last prayer (God is directing the Passion), the famous verse, Lk 22:53 (for Satan received his power from God!) and the announcements of the Passion point toward this signification. "So ergibt sich, dass die lkn [lukanischen] Aussagen über das Herrsein Gottes über die

Passionsereignisse in einen grösseren Zusammenhang einzuordnen sind. Dieser ist dadurch gegeben, dass Jesus von Anfang an von Gott zum Leiden bestimmt ist." (p. 90). For us, the larger framework is the plan of God and not the life of Jesus alone. Schütz rejoins our interpretation on pp. 91ff. where he attacks the Lucan concept of history as conceived by Conzelmann, Käsemann and Wilckens: this redemptive history is not uniquely a song of triumph, briefly interrupted by the failure of the cross, but the continuous intervention of God who knows how to use the destructive power of Satan and his cohorts. The death of Jesus has a positive meaning (p. 94f.) and the resurrection is not a correction of direction, but the continuation of the plan of God. Certainly, Luke insists less on the salvific value of the cross than the other writers of the NT, but he unifies it with the resurrection and Jesus' ministry, in order to integrate it into salvation history: "In den lukanischen Schriften bildet die Passion jedoch einen festen Bestandteil der Geschichte als Geschichte Gottes mit der Welt, dh [das heisst] als Offenbarungsgeschichte" (p. 96).

Without really showing it, the author thinks that Luke, by doing this, is leaning on two traditions: the one, which he, alone of the Synoptics, relates, deals with the suffering of the Messiah and is found in 1 Peter and the letter to the Hebrews. The other is that of the Servant of God (along the line of Isa 52-53).

This theology of the cross allows the Lucan community to live an existence in faith comparable to Jesus', in which mission and persecution cohabit.

The work ends with two chapters consecrated to the mis - sionary successes and Jesus' soteriological function. If the majority of the people hardened their hearts and succombed to ἀπιστία, a minority, made up of marginals, women and fishermen, responded to the call of the master in πίστις and obtained salvation. Jesus' insistence on converting his people must have particularly incited the Church to continue the evangelization of the Jews. Schütz minimizes Luke's hostility toward the Jews: certainly guilty, according to Schütz, they have a chance of conversion which is offered again by and through the Church.

Here emerges one limit of the redaktionsgeschichtliche method: what could invalidate a so-called editorial thesis (here Luke's interest for the Jews) is resolutely carried over to the account of tradition (so with Lk 23:11) or to a literary redactional intention with no doctrinal repercussion (so with the elimination of Mk 15:16-20, the insults of the Roman soldiers).

Above we said that the insertion of the Passion into the plan of God seems to be one of Luke's profound conviction [**46**]. It is F. Schütz' merit to remind us of this, even against a strong exegetical current; yet in doing this, the author no doubt pushed this discovery or rediscovery too far: the Lucan writings are covered by an excessive mortal shadow. The Galilean ministry of Jesus, especially, has clouds much too dark gathered in its sky. The pendulum has swung to the other extreme [**47**]. There is no doubt, the via media is more faithful to the witness of the texts [**48**].

V. SEVERAL CHRISTOLOGICAL TITLES

Space is lacking for a presentation of all the works which have dealt with a text or a group of particular Christological texts. Thus, we will limit ourselves to three monographs, which from a unique literary unit, elucidates the redactional work of Luke: first, R. Laurentin on the infancy narratives, then G. Schneider on the Passion account and finally, G. Lohfink on the texts of the Ascension. We will signal in the footnotes several important articles concerning these pericopes and others.

The Infancy Narratives (Lk 1:5-2:52)

a. R. Laurentin's monograph (-> 1957) renews a subject studied on numerous occasions. The study is characterized by a double concern, to analyze the formation of the traditions contained in Lk 1:5-2:52 and to clarify the theological intentions of the Evangelist, with the help of the literary structure of the two chapters. It forms a welcome bridge between the attention given to these chapters by the partisans of Mariology and the lack of interest the Redaktionsgeschichtler show them.

Lk 1:5-2:52 is organized into two diptychs consecrated to John the Baptist and Jesus as children: the diptych of the annunciations (1:5-56) and the other of the births (1:56-2:52). Each diptych closes with a complementary episode: the visitation, on the one hand (1:39-56) and the boy Jesus in the Temple, on the other (2:41-52). Several indications (the adjective "great" without a relative clause, reserved for Jesus, in 1:23; the title "Son of God" in 1:32-35; the implicit identification of Jesus with God in 1:17, 76) show that the parallelism of the two is accompanied by a contrast in favor of Jesus.

The writer reveals the fecundity of his method in chapters 2 and 3, where he confronts the history with the OT prophecies, for he thinks Luke elaborates an implicit Christology with the aid of the Scriptures, understood in a Midrashic manner.

Laurentin esteems that there is an interaction in our pericope, between the story of Jesus and the prophecies in Dan 9 and Mal 3. A directive idea results from this thought: the new times have been inaugurated and, this, in the cultic framework of the Temple in Jerusalem. If Dan 9 evokes the visit of the Messiah and Mal 3 the entry of Yahweh himself into his Temple, these two texts are not irreconciliable. For the Danielic Messiah tends toward becoming a heavenly being and the God of Malachi, an incarnate figure, by condescendence. Luke actualizes these texts with regard to Jesus the Christ, the Lord. He gives them a particular Messianic sense: the one sent by God singularly draws near to the transcendence of God. Is this not the "glory", i.e. the eschatological habitation of God, promised by the prophets?

The OT background is still far from being totally clarified: Luke identifies the promise in Zeph 3:14.17 with the virginal conception of Mary (Lk 1:26-33): Yahweh will dwell in the womb of the daughter of Zion; this is the prophetic resumption of the ancient theme of the presence of God (Ex 33:3 and 34) in the ark of the Covenant (Ex 40:35). As for Lk 1:32f., it fits into the flow of Davidic messianism which flows from 2 Sam 7:12-16, but Luke idealizes the Messianic figure (the shadow on the table, 2 Sam 7:14b, disappears and the divine sonship comes to the forefront). Lk 1:35 must be brought near to Ex 40:35, even if the manner of "overshadowing" has changed: the divine indwelling is effected mysteriously in Mary. 2 Sam 6:2-11 serves to compose Lk 1:33-44: like the ark transferred to Jerusalem by David, Jesus goes up to Jerusalem in the womb of his mother. After having suggested a new parallel between Judith 13:18f. and Lk 1:42, Laurentin arrives at the Magnificat: this hymn must resolve a theological problem. How can we explain that the coming of the Messiah, whose dimensions accede to transcendence, remained an obscure event? The answer of the Magnificat is that "God loves the humble and the poor. The coming of the Messiah is an extreme exaltation, in extreme humility." (p. 83). By doing this, the hymn goes back from Mary to Abraham, as the personification of Israel. As we know, the narrative of the nativity recalls the oracle in Micah 4:7-5:5. Finally, Lk 2:35 serves as a counterpart or rather as a realization of Isa 8:14: like Yahweh, Jesus will be a stumbling block. "Here is a group of contacts, some clear and others obliged, even disputable, which witness to a constant process, and identify , in a convergent way, Jesus with Yahweh and Mary with the daughter of Zion." (p. 90f.). Agreeing with the majority of these connections, we, nevertheless, formally refuse to speak of an identification of Jesus with God: Luke always respects a distance between the Father and the son. Lk 1-2 are far from contradicting this thesis: the Son is the manifestation of the Father, his envoy, his glory, but we cannot speak of an assimilation of Jesus to Yahweh (against p. 130).

The result of these analyses is that Luke tells "the infancy of Christ depends on the allusions to Scripture. Such a procedure belongs to Midrash." (p. 93). The Scripture is, however, not the only involved party, for there are also historical reminiscences which Laurentin ventures to take back to Mary herself (pp. 96-99) [**49**]. The literary genre (ch 4) which results from this interaction of history and interpretation is Midrash. The usage of this literary genre reveals precise theological options: the continuity of revelation, the faithfulness of God to the old covenant and the consciousness of having arrived at the eschatological times. Luke is not the only one responsible for this composition. Even if his editorial role is important, according to Laurentin, he leans on ancient Judeo-Christian traditions (p. 102). It is Luke's particular worry to reconcile Lk 1-2 with the visible manifestation of the Messiah from the baptism: Lk 1-2 become the dawn of the eschatological times (p. 107). Another of Luke's preoccupations is to fight against Jewish messianism. Against the Essenes, Luke accumulates royal and priestly messianisms for Jesus. Against John the Baptist's sect, he maintains the Baptist's prophetic function as precursor. We would have liked for Laurentin to have tried to distinguish between the tradition and the redaction and taken a position with regard to Conzelmann's book, which is so close and so far from his preoccupations [**50**].

The fifth chapter analyzes the Christological titles of Lk 1-2. Jesus is the Messiah, explicitly royal and implicilty priestly. He is, of course, the king, but Luke avoids all collusion with a political messianism. The light and glory of God now manifest, he is above all the Savior (Laurentin believes he has found traces of etymological allusions in the name of Jesus). Always present, but in an allusive manner, the transcendence of this Savior is noted by Luke. Laurentin signals an indication of this transcendence: Jesus is the Christ and the Lord (Lk 2:11) rather than the Christ of the Lord (the LXX already sketches this solution, favorable to the dignity of the Messiah, Lam 4:20).

Where is Luke situated in what Laurentin calls the develop - ment of revelation? Luke is placed at the moment when Jewish exegesis had pushed to the limit the results which could be drawn from Dan 9 (the transcendence of the Son of Man) and Mal 3 (the condescendence of God) before going in reverse, by sending God to heaven and the Messiah to the earth. In the Christian tradition, Luke seems, for Laurentin, to be closer to John than to Paul. Indeed, it is the resurrection, not the nativity, which reveals, according to the apostle to the Gentiles, the mystery of the divinity of Jesus. John, on the contrary, in his prologue, explicates the ideas, which Luke merely sketches in an allusive manner. Luke's theological effort will find its accomplishment in the fourth Gospel: Mary will pass into the background, but the divinity and the preexistence will be proclaimed without reserve. The manner which Luke connects Jesus to Yahweh is not metaphysical reflection (hypostasis), but Scriptural intuition (Son of God). Lucan Christology still begins from below, while John's opts for the descending mode.

The last chapter is consecrated to Mary. The author summarizes it in the following : "This theology of the divinity of Christ is discovered essentially through a theology of the Virgin who appears as the place of residence, the personal actualization of the Daughter of Zion and type of the ark of the convenant..." (p. 162).

Laurentin is to be congratulated for having recalled the Christological importance of Lk 1-2 (curiously neglected by Conzelmann) and for having discovered the interaction of the Scripture and eschatology in these chapters. To this must be added, the judicious interpretation of Jesus as the last manifestation of the glory of God in Jerusalem, in the Temple and among the people of Israel. Yet, we must indicate three weaknesses of this brilliant demonstration: 1) the lack of rigor with which the writer distinguishes the traditions and redaction, 2) the apologetic concern to derive certain traditions from Mary herself and 3) especially, the excessive proximity in which he places the Father and the Son **[51]**.

The Trial, Passion and Death of Jesus (Lk 22:1-23:56) **[52]**

b. There is a rich debate among exegetes concerning the meaning to give to the death of Jesus in the Lucan perspective.

All agree to recognize that Luke rarely confers a soteriological function to the cross, but the minds are divided in the explanation of this given.

At the beginning of this century, J. Weiss deemed that Luke had preserved old pre-Marcan traditions, dating from a time when the death of Jesus was not yet conceived of positively as a sacrifice [**53**]. As Weiss had discerned, this hypothesis collides with the presence of the theme "died for us" in the archaic formula in 1 Co 15:3b-5. This hypothesis has generally been abandoned today.

Others, like Ph. Vielhauer, H. Conzelmann, E. Haenchen, U. Wilckens, E. Käsemann and J. D. Kaestli [**54**], have followed another path. They feel that Luke is hostile to this theologoumenon and eliminates the traditions which use it. The long text of the institution of the Lord's Supper (if it is authentic) and Act 20:28 are the only two traditional formulations that have escaped his vigilance. The Christological speeches in Acts, redactional for these authors, are the striking proof of the disinterest which Luke has for the sacrificial death of Jesus.

E. Lohse (-> 1955) leans in this direction, but nuances his stance. He judges, for example, that Luke did not eliminate the phrase concerning the *λύτρον* (Mk 10:45) from his Gospel because of an aversion to the idea of expiation. Rather, he thinks that the title *παῖς* indeed evokes Isa 53 and following a rabbinic procedure in Act 8:32f, Luke adds salvific import to the death of the servant, even if he only cites Isa 53:7 and 8 where the idea does not yet appear [**55**]. He, nevertheless, recognizes that the Lucan corpus hardly connects the idea of redemption with the death of Jesus. Why is this connection so weak? Three explanations come to his mind: a) Luke is addressing Greeks and an apologetic concern holds him back from evoking an expiation more intelligible to the Jews than to the Gentiles; b) Luke belongs to the frühkatholisch period where curiously, the notion of sacrifice is toned down. In the Pastorals and the writings of the apostolic fathers, the situation is comparable. Traditional formulas concerning the death of Jesus are taken over, without development, but Jesus is particulary seen as the revealer of the salvific will of God [**56**]; c) the main reason is Luke's heilsgeschichtlich perspective includes the Messiahship and present activity of Jesus by the intermediary of his apostles; this hinders the Evangelist from developing a doctrine of the expiation of the cross.

Elsewhere, we noted another explanation. According to J. Dupont (-> 1962, third title) and C. F. D. Moule (-> 1966) [**57**], the variety of the literary genres accounts for the rarity of the allusions to the redemptive death of Jesus. Indeed, Acts presents sermons and the early Christian kerygma, destined for the unconverted, does not mention this mystery, which the later catechism would reveal. The two allusions to the soteriological value of the cross appear in texts where believers are addressed. Luke is not hostile to a sacrificial redemption. It is not necessary to confront the doctrine of the missionary speeches of Acts with the one concealed in the confession of faith in 1 Co 15, but it is necessary to distinguish the literary genres [58].

Two other responses exist [59]. Several exegetes maintain that the debate has not taken into consideration the Lucan Passion narrative enough. In this account, Luke does not minimize the importance of the cross and does not see it in an exclusively negative perspective: so M. Rese (-> 1969) who insists upon the citation of Isa 53 in Lk 22:37; and particularly F. Schütz (-> 1969), we noted his excess; and A. Vanhoye (-> 1967) who notes a personal and parenetic accent in the Lucan account of the Passion. Luke, in fact, seems to underline the responsibilities of the believer with regard to Jesus' death. The Evangelist magnifies the suffering Christ with accents of devotion and admires the moral grandeur as well as the innocence of Jesus. Finally, the exegete brings the death of Jesus and individual conversion together, and this rightly so: the Passion of Christ is effective and positive to the degree that it favorizes and facilitates conversion. We (-> 1973) suggested that Luke, convinced by the effectiveness of the sacrifice of Christ, forbids himself, nonetheless, to speak of it too often, in order not to transform salvation into a mechanical redemption and thus overshadow the indispensible conversion.

Finally, several scholars have followed up on the idea set forth in his time by Dibelius [60]. The German master noted that Luke gave his account of the Passion the mark of the acts of the martyrs. The value of the death of Jesus was, in his view, first of all, moral and exemplary. Several Catholic exegetes, by tradition hostile to the idea of substitution, for them stained by Lutheranism, developed this thesis. They were inspired by E. Schweizer (-> 1955) and E. Lohse (-> 1955). These two showed, indeed, that in Judaism side by side with the conception of expiatory sacrifice, a doctrine of the martyr or the suffering righteous one circulated. According to this martyrology, the death of the victim was not only exemplary, but also permitted the redemption of his own people. G. Voss (->

1965) and then, G. Schneider (-> 1969) set forth the hypothesis that Luke, influenced by this trend of thought, had understood Jesus' death in this way. The cross is no longer the expiatory sacrifice that it was in Paul and Mark. It has become the fate, equally positive, of the righeous one, suffering for his own. Let us see how G. Schneider developes this interpretation.

After two chapters of introduction (the first in the form of the state of the question and the second concerning the anterior oral tradition, parallel to Mark), the writer begins a critique of the sources (his investigation bears only on Lk 22:54-71). He comes to the following conclusions: Luke leans upon Mark and another non-Marcan source. In the episode of the denial (vss. 54-62), he basically follows Mark (the "and going out, he cried bitterly", vs. 62 is probably an addition later than Luke, taken from Matthew). Contrariwise, the mockeries (vss. 63-65) originate from the non-Marcan source (vs. 64c is perhaps taken over from Mark). The appearance before Herod (vss. 66-71) is composed with the help of the non-Marcan source (vss. 66-68, with the exception of part of vss. 66-67c, which are perhaps from Mark) and Mark (vss.69-71). This is to say that Luke, after important editorial work, followed the order of the non-Marcan source, intergrating, especially at the two extremities, elements taken from Mark (Peter's denial and the phrase about the Son of Man). The redactional elements are found in vss. 59a-b, 61a, 65a-b, 70a and 71d.

The fourth chapter widens the investigation to the whole of the Lucan Passion narrative and leads into the fifth chapter consecrated to the theological declarations in Lk 22-23. It opens with a theological analysis of vss. 54-71.

While Mark contrasts Jesus, who confesses his faith, and Peter, who denies his Master, Luke presents Jesus with the traits of a martyr, denied by his first disciple and mistreated by his adversaries. The Lucan Jesus confesses his Messiahship and sonship in a sovereign manner, inspite of all (p. 169).

He is also a prophet who knows all things in advance, and yet his message and his identity remain hidden to his enemies. "So weiss Jesus auch bei der christologischen Selbst - prädikation um die tödlichen Folgen seiner Aussage." (p. 169).

Since he thinks vs. 62 is secondary, G. Schneider is op - posed to A. Vanhoye's insistence on the parenetic perspective: for Luke, after his denial, Peter did not repent immediately. The parenetic impact, which Schneider does not entirely reject, arises here from the gaze of Christ and not Peter's attitude.

Luke softens the insults, with respect and pity for Jesus. He does not see here the fulfillment of OT prophecy, as Mark does. We have the suffering of a martyr and not the signs of the Messiah. Against this theory, which rests on Lk 23:47; 13:33; 24:7 and Act 3:13f., we must recall that Luke is the author of the NT who insists most on the necessity of the suffering of the Messiah (cf. Lk 24:44ff.). It could be that the insults, nonetheless, constitute an attestation to Jesus Messiahship. Schneider admits this himself on p. 175.

What is the editorial perspective of the trial? Jesus doubly proclaims his Messiahship and his sonship (we might add: in an indirect manner). The Sanhedrin's hostility indicates that all discussion with Judaism is from now on destined to fail. The Jewish people are without excuse. Schneider forgets here Luke's heilsgeschichtlich emphasis and passes from the past to the present with no transition. He neglects the theme of *ἄγνοια* which implies a certain innocence. In Luke's thought, it will not be until the refusal of the last offer of conversion, in the time of the Church, that the hardening of Israel will become definite and unforgivable (Act 28:26-28).

"From henceforth the Son of Man will sit at the right hand of God almighty" (Lk 22:69) opens the time of the exaltation and with it, the time of the Church. When Stephen sees the Son of Man standing next to God, the situation is identical: Jesus, the Son of Man is condemning Israel. However, this judgment is heilsgeschichtlich and not eschatological. "Damit erfahren die Juden, dass sie das heilsgeschichtliche *νῦν* (Lk 22, 69a) und seine Chance verpasst haben." (p. 173). The historical destruction of the Temple is the demonstration of this phrase.

The Sanhedrin's second question flows from Jesus' answer, as the *οὖν* of vs. 70 signals: he who is at the right hand of God can claim the dignity of the Son of God.

Verses 67-70 indeed represent a compendium of Luke's Christology, as Conzelmann noted (-> 1954). Yet Schneider thinks that Luke is more marked by tradition than the latter believed.

Moreover, not without contradicting himself later (cf. p. 177), Schneider sets forth that Christology allows Luke to develope his conception of salvation history and not the inverse. In his eyes, Conzelmann is unilateral when he sees the beginning of salvation history in the delay of the Parousia (p. 174).

On pp. 174-196, Schneider disengages the "Theologische Anliegen der gesamten lukanischen Passion." Jesus' prophetic knowledge and the numerous δεῖ and μέλλειν which punctuate the text, indicate that the suffering of Christ fits into the plan of God. It is not an accident. The importance of the Scriptural argumentation (Lk 22:37; 24:25, 44, 46f.) confirms the Passion's insertion into salvation history.

Despite the ties which bind the Passion and the resurrection and, in Luke, make them almost tip over into the time of the Church (from the ἀλλὰ νῦν, Lk 22:36 and ἀπὸ τοῦ νῦν, Lk 22:69), they are two distinct periods. The Passion is the step which leads to glory, but it has salvific value: it is the death of the martyr, the suffering of the righteous one; a fate which both Jews and Greeks could understand (p. 181).

Willed by God, the Passion of Jesus marks nonetheless the victory of Satan (cf. Lk 22:53). It is distinguished from Jesus' ministry where the devil was excluded. In this, it is close to the time of the Church where the evil one is at work (Schneider borrows from Conzelmann here).

The Passion according to Luke insists on the complicity between the Father and the Son: "Die Führung durch Gott entspricht auf Seiten Jesu, dass er sich mit dem Vater besonders verbunden weiss und sich immer wieder dem Plan und der Führung Gottes unterwirft." (p. 185). Jesus' submission reveals him as Son (cf. the last prayer of the agonizing Jesus: there is no question of being abandoning, but of communion). This relation between the Father and the Son is not prejudicial to human beings. On the contrary, it exhorts them to μετάνοια (p. 186).

Believers are to follow the exhortation and this is even easier for them as they have the Lucan Christ as model; "Jesus ist nicht als der nachzuahmende Heros geschildert, sondern als die paradigmatische heilsgeschichtliche Gestalt, mit der sich der Leser vereinigen soll und deren Weg er nachahmen muss." (p. 189).

It is obvious that Schneider takes up some of Conzelmann's theses as well as some of Voss': the insistence on the periods and their succession comes from Conzelmann, whereas the heilsgeschichtlich value of the Passion and nature of the martyr who redeems his own, while inviting them to walk in his footsteps, comes from Voss. Schneider is to be praised for having propped up these theses with solid exegesis.

At the end of the chapter, the author reminds us of the importance of the localities (Jerusalem) **[61]** and witnesses of the Passion for Luke, before integrating Jesus' end into the totality of the Vita Jesu.

Schneider's treatise constitutes a solid study and though it may not excel in originality, it recalls at an opportune moment, without falling into the excess of Schütz, that the death of Jesus, for Luke, completes an important step in the plan of God **[62]**.

The Ascension (Lk 24:50-53 and Act 1:1-12)

c. We have placed everything which deals with the Lucan resurrection narratives in the footnotes. It is not because the resurrection is secondary in Luke; on the contrary, it is even a main theme; the speeches in Acts, at least, signal it as the proof for Jesus' Messiahship. It is neither because the works relative to Lk 24 are uninteresting; it is simply that they are less numerous. With regard to the studies which deal with the whole of the Lucan work, we have considered them in the first part of this chapter **[63]**. Included in the Passion and the resurrection in Lk 9:51, with the term *ἀνάλημψις*, the Ascension is narrated in two passages peculiar to Luke, apparently isolated within the NT. It is not surprising that these texts have drawn the attention of the partisans of the redactional critical method. The most important contribution to this subject since the imposing but apologetic treatise of V. Larrañaga (1938) was for a long time the ample article of the Father P. Benoit (-> 1949) **[64]**. Since then, each year as yielded contributions of quality often unequalled **[65]**, but in 1971, Lohfink's remarkable study appeared and overtook everything which had been done to that date.

In his introduction, Lohfink presents the state of the question and limits to five the possible interpretations:

1) Lk 24 and Act 1 form two eyewitness accounts of the Ascension and can be harmonized (V. Larrañaga).

2) The (invisible) Ascension having taken place at Easter, the account of the Ascension evokes the last visible appearance. This is W. Michaelis thesis (1925) and P. Benoit (who propounds, as well, a necessary relation between the Ascension and the exaltation) shares it.

3) The Ascension account is a popular legend, the consequence of the materialization of the Easter appeareances. R. Bultmann and liberal Prostestant criticism acquiesce here.

4) It is a legend attached to the kerygma of the exaltation. This hypothesis, developed by A. Harnack (1908), L. Brun

(1925) and Ph. Menoud (1954), actually goes back to D. F. Strauss.

5) The Ascension accounts are Luke's work. A. Friedrichsen (1925), is the only one to have maintained this idea.

Until now, the distinction between tradition and redaction had not been established with enough care and perseverence. This will be the large part of Lohfink's effort, but the author will begin by offering a history of comparative religions, with interest to the form and possible parallels.

The subject of the first chapter is ascensions in the Biblical milieu. It is best, Lohfink informs, to distinguish in Greco-Roman antiquity, the heavenly journeys of the soul and the actual translations. For the translations, the Greeks used the verbs *ἀφανίζομαι*, *ἁρπάζω* and *μεθίσταμαι*. Several elements appear frequently in their accounts, especially the one of Romulus: a mountain, a fire, a bolt of lightning, a tempestuous wind, a celestial chariot or an eagle, a cloud, divers phenomena (earthquake, darkness, heavenly light, etc.), a heavenly confirmation, an ulterior veneration with the establishment of a sect and, most evidently, the translation of the hero.

In the OT and Judaism, similar stories are told but, here again it is suitable to distinguish between the various literary genres: the trip to the heavenly world to receive revelations with the return to earth (usually the body and soul go together); the definitive carrying off of the soul at death (the body remains in the grave); the translation of a living body which goes to heaven never to return to the earth: so <u>Enoch</u> (cf. 5:24: *μετέθηκεν* according to the LXX and especially the Slavic Enoch (long version) 67, which is the most important parallel to the Lucan narrative of the Ascension of Jesus), <u>Elijah</u> (2 Kgs 2:1-18); <u>Esdras</u> and <u>Baruch</u> (cf. 4 Esdras and 2 Baruch where we find the succession: reception of a revelation, an intermediary time of forty days and a translation). Without a doubt neither a translation of Moses (Josephus **Jewish Antiquities** IV 8, 47f. according to Lohfink does not favorize this hypothesis) nor of the Messiah ever existed. There is a fourth genre which is the disappearance of God or an angel after an apparition (e.g. Gen 17:22; 35:13; Jub 32:20; Paralipomenon of Jeremiah 3:17; Judg 6:21f.; Tob 12:20-22 (Sinaiticus) and Test Abr (short version) 4:4). In this case the ascension is a <u>return</u> to heaven and the technical verb is most often *ἀνέβη* (*ἀπῆλθεν* or *ἐπορεύθη* in Judg 6:21; *ἀνελήφθη* in Test Abr 4:4).

If we limit ourselves to the strict meaning, all the motifs which accompany the Jewish accounts correspond to the Greco-

Roman ones. However, peculiar to Judaism are the forty days, the last words of the one departing and the distinction between death and translation.

From a formal and thematic point of view, the narratives in Lk 24:50-53 and Act 1:9-12 are neither heavenly journeys nor translations of the soul after death, nor even the return to heaven after an apparition. What we have is translation in the strict sense, as the verb *ἀναλαμβάνομαι* indicates. This is how Justin, the first Christian interpreter of these texts, understood them. We can be thankful to Lohfink for having distinguished the literary genres and for having carefully classified the two Lucan accounts. Against several exegetes, he shows that the Lucan texts are neither more sober nor shorter than other secular texts (p. 78f.).

Chapter 2 seeks for traces of the Ascension in the non-Lucan texts of the NT and in patristic literature. The result is evident: the Pauline epistles are unaware of the Ascension and place the resurrection and the exaltation together in one event (even Col 3:1 and Eph 1:19f.; 2:5f. and 4:8-10; this could be argued, in our opinion). The *ἀνελήμφθη* of I Tim 3:16 is an invisible elevation and not an ascension in front of witnesses. In I Pet (1:20f.; 3:18f., 21f.) and Heb as well, the resurrection and elevation are detached from one another, but the latter is not transformed into an ascension controlled by witnesses (inspite of 2:20, Mark, with Matthew, does not know of the Ascension). While we might have expected the Son of Man to be carried away, the Synoptic tradition knows only the death and resurrection.

Lohfink then leads us on a long peregrination through the fathers of the Church (pp. 98-146), and the result is apparently indisputable: the patristic literature knows nothing of a visible Ascension of Jesus until influenced by the Gospel of Luke and the Acts of the Apostles. This influence has already taken place in Justin and Irenaeus. All the allusions of the apostolic fathers are to an invisible exaltation, still associated with the resurrection.

The only exceptions are: Barn 15:9 (still uncertain), Gosp Pet 9ff. (35-42) and Mk 16:3 (ms. Bobbiensis, k), where a visible ascension takes place on Easter day, and certain gnostic texts where the Ascension takes place either eighteen months or twelve years after the resurrection. Without being convincing, Lohfink thinks that the gnostic texts are influenced by the Lucan schema. Concerning the feast of the Ascension, celebrated in the fourth and fifth centuries in Syria and, in Jerusalem, on Pentecost day, Lohfink partially rejects Kretschmar's hypothesis (cf. below 4, II, c) and refuses to accept that it is an ancient tradition. If this is so, we cannot see how a celebration at the end of a great day of joy (the fifty days) could have been instituted at an epoch when Acts and their forty days had become canonical. This section of Lohfink's treatise seems less dependable to us: we can sense the author's impatience to take the introduction of a visible Ascension into the Christian system back to Luke, and Luke alone.

The study maintains all its qualities in the chapters which follow. Chapter 3 analyzes the smallest literary units in the Lucan accounts from a formal point of view. He shows that the succession of events in Lk 24:34-53, from Jesus' appearance and his recognition by the disciples (vss. 36-43), to his teaching (vss. 44-49) ending with the scene of the separation (vss. 50-53), is redactional. If there is tradition, it must be hidden isolatedly in each part. As for the tradition of the Ascension, we can disregard vss. 36-49. What remains is not very long after the clearly redactional elements have been eliminated. The same can be said of Act 1:1-12: vss.1-2 are Lucan and represent the first two points mentioned in the schema above. Vs. 3 is a Lucan summary, vss. 4-5 serve as a transition, and the narrative really begins in vs. 6, but in vss. 6-8, we have a Lucan procedure of question and answer, articulated with a hookword. In vss. 9-11, the three points of the traditional schema can be found, but a tradition of translation may be hidden underneath. Vs. 12 is editorial except perhaps for the Mount of Olives and the forty days. Summarily, Lohfink says, "Was bei Lukas in Evangelium und Apostelgeschichte jeweils als längere Himmel - fahrtserzählung erscheint, ist in Wirklichkeit eine literarische Komposition, die aus den verschiedensten Einheiten zusammengesetzt ist und die ihre Geschlossenheit und Anschaulichkeit erst der schriftstellerischen Kunst des Lukas verdankt." (p. 159).

The fourth chapter attempts to tighten the vise on this hypothetical tradition of the Ascension without succeeding, to the author's great joy. This time, the various elements of Lk 24:50-52 and Act 1:9-12 are passed through the sieve. What comes out is that Luke did not take over two traditions nor double a unique tradition, for the quasi-totality of the vocabulary and themes are specifically Lucan. As others, Lohfink simply discovers an influence of the LXX in Lk 24: Sir 50:20, where we meet an identical succession: elevation of the hands, blessing, worship and thanksgiving. A tie between elevation and worship is also found in secular texts. It is the same for connnection between the translation and joy (Romulus, Emperor): "Wie die Entrückung des Kaisers zum εὐαγγέλιον wird, so führt die Himmelfahrt Jesu, des wahren κύριος, die 'grosse Freude' herbei." (p. 176). However, these are motifs and not narratives that Luke takes up, and, furthermore, these motifs are not applied to Jesus; they were Jewish and Greco-Roman traditions.

Lohfink concludes his analysis of Act 1:9-12 in the following manner; the forty days are editorial ("Heilige Zwischenzeit", of which length is more important than the exact duration); the cloud has a double function: it is vehicle and screen (as the Lucan account of the Transfiguration confirms). Curiously, the author terminates his analysis of the Mount of Olives without noting the traditional link which united this hill with the Jewish hope of the Parousia. This lacuna surprises all the more as Lohfink insists on Luke's drawing the Ascension near to the Parousia.

In short, the vocabulary, style and thought of these two passages are Lucan on the whole; only certain motifs have been taken over and these from Jewish or Greco-Roman narratives and certainly not from a tradition relative to a translation of Jesus established by his disciples.

The fifth chapter addresses all the Lucan texts touching on the elevation and Ascension of the Christ. We can observe in it either the editorial mark which views the whole life of Jesus as an ἀνάλημψις (so Lk 9:51-52a and Act 1:1f. and 1:21f.), or the Lucan rereading of a paleo-Christian tradition of the Easter elevation (in this case, Luke carefully accentuates the difference between the resurrection and the elevation, by making the latter a distinct phenomenon either verified by witnesses, as in Act 5:30-32; or attested by another Scriptural text than the resurrection, so Act 2:32-35), or even a tradition of the elevation in which Luke emphasizes the resurrection to the detriment of the Ascension (Act 13:23f.). Concerning the texts which mention Jesus' entrance into his glory (Lk 24:26 etc.), Lohfink thinks they concern the resurrection alone and exclude the Ascension.

Lohfink tends to say systematically; a) the Christian writers, except Luke, associate the resurrection with the elevation (which is invisible); b) Luke is the only author to dissociate the resurrection and the Ascension (which is visible).

In the above, it seems to us that in the analysis of the patristic and gnostic witnesses, a certain prejudice hinders Lohfink from accepting any distinction between the resurrection and the Ascension which does not come from a Lucan influence. We think he is obsessed by a complementary concern: to make sure that Luke always dissociates the resurrection and the Ascension, whereas he must acknowledge that Luke knows how to group the various steps of the life of Jesus (the resurrection and the Ascension included) under one term (e.g. ἀνάλημψις). His thesis would have profited in not being so categorical and by using less frequently peremptory affirmations ("not the least indication", "not one case where", etc.).

The most successful chapter is 6 which attempts to establish a pathway moving from the paleo-Christian tradition of the Easter elevation to the Lucan redaction of the Ascension. The author notes that the elevation is a primitive interpretation of the fact of the resurrection, with the help of the Scripture. Afterwards, he declares that in an ulterior Hellenistic milieu, the vocabulary of the elevation and an inclination of Christology to become cosmic favorized the dissociation of the resurrection from the elevation. However, more often than not, this dissociation made the elevation into a supraterrestrial movement, the journey across the celestial spheres. Having received these themes in this milieu, Luke chose a personal path: he includes the elevation in history (p. 248). If he takes this step, it is because he likes the concrete and visible and also obeys the literary precepts of the historians of his era, who were attentive to concretize the events they narrated. He takes this step with ease as Judaism and the Greco-Roman world offered him the materials to describe a visible ascension. Finally, Lohfink wonders if this materialization of the Ascension was provoked by polemic anti-gnostic motives. He does not exclude this possibility, which, for C. H. Talbert, is evident! The Ascension is not a naive legend springing from a popular milieu, but a thematic elaboration of a theological writer.

What theological intentions preside over the editing of these two accounts? The last chapter attempts to discern them [67].

The first narrative is conceived and constructed as the last period of Jesus' life (the Lucan Jesus prepares his followers for the Ascension, not Good Friday or Easter). Lohfink aligns four indications favorable to this idea:

1) the *χαρὰ μεγάλη* is not mentioned in the Gospel except for the birth of Jesus and his Ascension;

2) a second <u>inclusio</u>: the adoration of God in the Temple (in the beginning, Zachariah and here, the disciples);

3) the adoration of Jesus: Luke, different from Matthew, excludes all worship of Jesus before the Ascension;

4) a blessing marks the end of a life (or a liturgy).

The first account of the Ascension concludes, literarily, the end of Luke's first book and, theologically, the salvific period of Jesus.

The second account is turned toward the future, toward the Parousia, in particular. In vss. 5-8 of Act 1, Luke explains that the gift of the Spirit does not signify the end of time and far from coming immediately, Jesus is going to depart. The narrative of the Ascension (vss. 9-12) illustrates this affirmation: the Ascension is a Parousia in reverse (he leaves now on a cloud which must bring him back); it constitutes a warning: the Church must avoid all false hope and use positively the delay accorded for mission. Lohfink, in agreement with Conzelmann on the role of the delay of the Parousia, deviates from him on one point: the qualificative of eschatological is convenient inspite of all for the present time.

The two accounts of the Ascension separate the time of Jesus and the time of the Church. Yet certain motifs prove that Luke also wanted to guarantee the continuity of redemptive history despite this rupture: Jerusalem, which is not far from the Mount of Olives (cf. vs. 12b); the forty days during which the Risen One prepares the apostles for their later ministry; the witnesses themselves, who, Luke repeats this five times, see the Lord go away from them; finally, the Holy Spirit assures the continuity.

Lohfink concludes that, for Luke, the elevation coincides with the Ascension, even if the accounts of Lk 24 and Act 1 do not signal the sitting at the right hand of God (the cloud hinders them from seeing the end of the trip!). The ulterior intervention of the Lucan Christ will be from heaven.

A last section deals with the question of the historicity of the Ascension. Lohfink finds an answer in the distinction, historical and real. Just like the resurrection, the Ascension-elevation is a real phenomenon, but which escapes historical investigation. Luke has historicized an event, in the style of the OT writers. This support gives warrant to and legitimizes his undertaking.

Generally we appreciate the way with which Lohfink renders manifest Luke's editorial effort [**68**]. In our opinion, Lohfink is right to insist on this endeavor. His principle thesis, according to which the narratives of the Ascension fit the traditional theme of the elevation of the Risen One into redemptive history, seems correct to us. We also agree with the results of the comparative analysis of religions: in order to materialize this elevation, Luke used elements taken from the Jewish and Greco-roman accounts of translation. Our hesitations remain on two points: 1) is it necessary, at this point, to distinguish between the Ascension (visible) and the elevation (invisible) and, consequently, isolate Luke from the rest of the NT (are not John and Hebrews, by insisting on the elevation, closer to Luke than Lohfink is willing to admit?)? 2) Was Luke really the only historian to historicize the elevation? Did not the primitive Christians (cf. Barn 15:9 and Gosp Pet 9f. (35-42)) sense the same need to integrate the Easter elevation into salvation history [69]?

VI. THE CHRISTOLOGICAL TITLES

a. We do not think that the Christological titles are the principle manner of getting at the Lucan Christ. However, they have been studied, as much by the defenders of Lucan redaction as by the supporters of ancient traditions, as the preceding pages indicated here and there. We will present the major contributions without returning to the general studies of the Christological titles, already summarized above: J. Dupont (-> 1950, first and second titles; -> 1962, fourth title; -> 1973, first title); U. Wilckens (-> 1961) and E. Kränkl (-> 1972). Concerning all of the Christological titles of the NT, we can mention the books by O. Cullmann (-> 1957), F. Hahn (-> 1963) and L. Sabourin (-> 1963).

Prophet

b. As interesting as it may be, the book of I. Panagopoulos (-> 1973) has not supplanted the treatise by F. Gils (-> 1957) **[70]**. On one essential point, he reproduces the position of the scholar from Leuven: the title of 'prophet' goes back to Jesus, himself; it met with relative success in the early time of the Church before being eclipsed by the more glorious titles of Messiah and Savior. This Greek scholar developes this thesis in the framework of a larger study of Jewish prophetism and, in particular, Jesus' prophetic consciousness. Jesus puts an end to the prophecy of the old covenant by becoming the center of the new. The work deals with the person of Jesus and his view, as a prophet, of God, the world, the Church and himself. He barely touches the redactional perspective of the Evangelists. The author hopes to follow up his research with a description of the prophetism of the ancient Church.

While concentrating his attention on the prophetic consciousness of Jesus himself, F. Gils sprinkles his work with judicious notes concerning the compositional endeavor peculiar to each evangelist [**71**].

First of all, let us set forth the principle theme of the work. Jesus' attitude, his remarks concerning the present and future, his visions make him a true prophet in the line of the nabis of the OT [**72**]. Before being understood in a royal sense, the accounts of the baptism and the transfiguration were told in a prophetic perspective with the Passion as the target. Even if he is but rarely designated as prophet, Jesus was conscious of being the Messianic prophet sent by God. An ancient Christological title, as it goes back to Jesus, himself, "prophet" suffered a rapid decline in the early Church. The apostles do not use this title, nor do the Evangelists, in their narrative sections. Luke, alone, already in the infancy narratives, remembers the young Samuel and appreciates the prophetic character of Jesus.

According to Gils, how does Luke interpret this prophetic attitude of Jesus? The Evangelist remarks that Jesus was acclaimed prophet (Lk 7:16) and suggests an Elijah-Jesus typology in this context: "as a thaumaturge, Jesus takes his place among the prophets of Israel" (p.27). Considered as a prophet (Lk 7:39), a prophet similar to Moses (Lk 24:19 and 21), Jesus expects to suffer the fate of the prophets (Lk 13:33). In Luke, the verb *λαλεῖν* [73] takes on a precise sense, already conferred by the LXX and parallely by John: to prophesy.

Characteristic of Luke without being his own, the joining of Jesus and Moses is developed from the Jewish then Christian exegesis of Dt 18:15 and the hope of a prophet similar to Moses, which originated from it (cf. Act 3:22 and 7:37).

The first Christology, from Isa, insisted on the Spirit's anointing of Jesus (cf. Act 2:22; 10:38). "For his gospel, Luke was inspired by this Christology. In the scene of the baptism, he naturally mentions the gift of the Spirit, but different from the other Synoptics, he is bent on recalling this consecration several times." (p. 70) Gils also refers to Lk 4:1, 14, 18f.; 5:17; 10:18. By the coming and presence of the Spirit, Jesus is accredited among men as a prophet for the Evangelist: "By insisting on the 'pneumatic' character of Jesus, the writer makes it clear that he recognizes in him a major trait of all prophetic portrayal." (p. 71).

Luke also underlines that Jesus sounds hearts (Lk 6:8; 9:47): this trait, which was not to displease the readers in the Hellenistic world, does not alter the portrait of Jesus for Gils (p. 88). What he wants to say clearly is that a light Hellenistic touch does not disfigure the semitic image of Jesus. Gils is probably right, but we would say, it is a Greek who depicts this prophet of Jewish origin.

In the Announcements of the Passion, Luke accentuates the prophetic character of Jesus: Jesus is able to understand the prophetic Scriptures in contrast to the ignorance of the disciples (cf. Lk 18:31, 34; 24:26f., 44-46). On this point, Luke depends on Paul rather than on an apocalyptic tradition. Inspite of Gils' reference to 2 Co 3:14-17, this last hypothesis seems quite fragile.

Gils terminates his work by summarizing the viewpoint of the three Synoptics, especially Luke's (p. 164f.), as we have developed above.

We have no trouble believing that Luke underlines Jesus' prophetic function, but how can one explain - Gils does not deal with this question which remains decisive - that this interest emerges at a time when this Christology of Christ the prophet was losing momentum? Should we imagine a "Judeophilian" Luke, sensitive to the sequence of God's interventions in history?

No doubt, J. Jervell would answer by the affirmative, and E. Kränkl would bring this prophetic aspect close to the title *παῖς* which is not the prerogative of Jesus alone. We prefer to think that it is but one aspect of Luke's Christology which elsewhere is royal, Messianic and Lordly; an accentuation related to Jesus' abasement to his mission for his people. There is nothing surprising that when Jesus, the prophet, fulfills his mission in the Gospel, he yields up his place to the exalted Lord in the Acts. All this is according to the divine plan which is harmoniously arranged.

Master

c. O. Glombitza (-> 1958, first title) made a penetrating remark. In Luke, only non-disciples use *διδάσκαλος* for Jesus; the disciples never call their master this title, which the Jews and the Gentiles used to designate respectively their rabbis and philosophers. They used *ἐπιστάτης* (Lk 5:5; 8:24; 9:33, 49; 17:13) **[74]**, a term which has the double advantage of not evoking the philosophical schools **[75]** and including the idea of authority. Therefore the Church is not one school among others, and Jesus, filled with authority, is radically distinguished from other masters.

Several years later, F. Norman (-> 1967) wrote an important study on the didactic Christ in the first centuries. Persuaded that Jesus' designation as master is a constituitive part of Christology, he shows how, in the second century, the term διδάσκαλος received a new meaning which allowed Christian apologetic to encounter the Hellenistic culture with success.

A study of the whole of early Christian literature leads the author to a balanced judgment concerning the Lucan work (pp. 45-54). Compared to Mark, who remains influenced by the memory of a Jesus, the rabbi, surrounded by his disciples, and Matthew, who portrays Jesus as the grand master who accomplishes the Torah with his teaching, Luke does not pay particular attention to the theme of Jesus, the teacher. The usage of the term διδαχή recedes (p. 49, footnote 28). The title ἐπιστάτης, more solemn and important than διδάσκαλος, is preferred by Luke: it evokes more the superiority than the teaching of the Master [76]. The Acts confirm this recoil in Act 11:16 and 20:35 (Norman could have noted Act 1:1ff. here).

Faithful to the tradition, Luke does not discard all mention to Jesus' teaching. He even accords it a special significance. Jesus' teaching is public (so Luke's preference for the teaching of Jesus in the Temple, p. 49), while Mark reserves it especially for the disciples. Consequently, the circle of the disciples is enlarged (p. 52f.). The term μαθηταί designates the followers other than the Twelve. Since women can become disciples, this conception of teaching deviates from the official Judaism. The content of the teaching is also modified. We know that Luke evokes Jesus' action before his teaching (cf. Act 1:1 and Lk 24:19). Moreover, elsewhere he suggests that Jesus is going to teach and an action actually follows (especially Lk 4:14-30 and the following narratives). According to the speeches in Acts (10:42 and 13:47), Christ gave orders rather than teaching (p. 48). To become a disciple is therefore to fit into this action of Christ.

Norman underestimates the didactic activity of Jesus according to Luke and neglects the parables, particularly the parables peculiar to the Evangelist. In the Gospel, a large part is given to the formation of the disciples. Nonetheless, the pedagogical element of the journeys (Lk 9:51-19:23) is as important as the Christological import. Furthermore, after the resurrection, according to Lk 24 and Act 1, Jesus fulfills his activity as Master, with regard to one point in particular, hardly underlined by Norman: the comprehension of the Scripture clarified by history and illuminating it. E. Fascher's formula that the author takes over is well composed: in Acts, where Jesus is above all Messiah and Savior, the disciples are going to receive, after the Greek use, a name from their Lord. Henceforth they will be Christians (Act 11:26): "Hat hier der κύριος über den διδάσκαλος gesiegt..." (E. Fascher, "Jesus der Lehrer. Ein Beitrag zur Frage nach dem 'Quellort der Kirchenidee' ", **TLZ** 79 (1954) 334.) This is clear, but of which Lord? Of the Lord, who came to inform and form his people by his teaching.

Son of Man

d. C. K. Barrett (-> 1964) explains in the following manner the unique and surprising mention of the Son of Man in Acts (spoken by someone other than Jesus, Stephen, the martyr): for the Christian, who is dying, like Stephen, there is a sort of private and individual Parousia of the Son of Man who comes to meet him [**77**]. Luke offers to his community in this way a solution to the delay of the Parousia.

E. Kränkl (-> 1972, pp. 152-156) takes up the question again. He offers a good overview of the recent studies and comes to the following solution: the martyr is the imitator of Jesus; there exists an evident parallel between the death of Jesus and Stephen's. Stephen's vision of the Son of Man is the counterpart of the word of Jesus, during his trial, concerning the Son of Man who is going to come. Luke, the writer, avoids repetition and monotony , by varying the formulation within the parallelism. One should not therefore accord too much significance to the participle "standing".

Let us mention another position: J. C. O'Neill (-> 1961, p. 139f.) notes that when James was martyred, according to Hegesippus cited by Eusebius, **Ecclesiastic History** II, 23, 13, he too used the title Son of Man. O'Neill presumes a bit too rapidly the historicity of Act 7:56 and that there was a tradition according to which the first martyrs of Jerusalem called on the Son of Man [**78**].

Servant

e. O. Cullmann's position (-> 1950 and -> 1959) [**79**] is known: from his baptism, Jesus understood his mission as that of the servant of God; the apostle, Peter designated Jesus with predilection by this title (cf. Act 3:13, 26 and 4:27, 30). This primitive Christology of the servant of God is conserved in the liturgy.

Since then, several works have appeared such as Morna Hooker's criticism (**Jesus and the Servant**..., London, 1959) of O. Cullmann and J. Jeremias (art. "παῖς θεοῦ" in **TWNT** 5, Stuttgart, 1954, pp. 676-713).

First of all, we would like to note an article of J. E. Ménard, which appeared in English and in French (-> 1957} and a study by J. H. Roberts (-> 1966). For the former, a professor of Strasbourg, Jesus understood his ministry and fate as the suffering prophet: the Synoptic gospels remind us of this faithfully. Before the problem which the death of Jesus posed, the disciples searched the Scriptures only to find, thanks to Isa 53, that Jesus was not only the Prophet of Dt 18 but also the Messiah, a Messiah who had to suffer (cf. Lk 24:25-27, 44-46; Act 3:12-16 etc.). "This return to the OT prophecies would be the veritable Sitz im Leben of the Messianic title παῖς given to Jesus by the book of the Acts." (p. 214 of the French article). Ménard thinks that the Acts develope in an original way, with respect to the Synoptics, a Christology of the Servant-Messiah. Yet this Christology is not the earliest, for it is the fruit of Christian exegesis of the OT. Two critical remarks are in order: 1) Isa 53, which fits into the prophetic tradition rather than the royal one, could not have given the early Christians the idea of a suffering Messiah. 2) Παῖς Θεοῦ, which is not exclusively a Christological title in the Acts, did not designate Jesus as the Messiah [**80**].

J. H. Roberts defends a strong influence of Isa 53 on the primitive kergyma which is reflected in the speeches in Acts [**81**]. He hardly brings any new arguments and does not effectively counter I. van Irsel's analyses (-> 1961 cf. above, 3, III, b) that demonstrated that Deutero-Isaiah played a secondary role in early Christian preaching. According to the Belgian exegete, it is in the later catechism that the doctrine of expiation, with inspiration from Isa 53, would be applied to the death of Jesus.

It is E. Kränkl who presented the most rigorous study, although he cedes, like several contemporary German Catholic exegetes, to an unexpected scepticism with regard to possible traditions reworked by Luke.

Παῖς Θεου must be translated by servant of God and not Son of God. Inspite of the possible link between Isa 53:11 (link παῖς - δοξάζειν) in Act 3:13, the Christology of the speeches is not impregnated by the theme of the suffering servant. The only two times where Isa 53 is cited in the Lucan corpus, Lk 22:37 and Act 8:32f., the term παῖς does not appear. Furthermore, in these two references Luke does not mention the expiatory suffering of the servant.

Παῖς Θεου does not constitute a Christological title for Luke (neither was it a title especially Messianic in Judaism). According to the OT tradition, into which Luke fits, the servant of God designates a great realizer of the plan of God: "Jesus steht also als 'Knecht Gottes' in einer Reihe mit den Gottesmännern der jüdischen Geschichte, er ist wie Abraham, Mose, David und das ganze Volk Israel ein von Gott erwähltes Werkzeug, dessen er sich bedient zur Ausführung seines auf die Menschen gerichteten Heilsplans (vgl. Apg 13, 17-23)." (p. 127). The servant of God describes a heilsgeschichtlich function rather than a Messianic privilege: the Acts which demonstrate on several occasions that Jesus is the Messiah and Lord, do not seek to prove that he is the Servant. There never was an autonomous Christology of the Servant of God.

Following A. von Harnack ("Die Bezeichnung Jesu als 'Knecht Gottes' und ihre Geschichte in der alten Kirchen" (**SPAW**, Phil-hist. Kl., Berlin, 1026, pp. 212-238), Kränkl sees the liturgy as the primitive Sitz im Leben of the designation of Jesus as Servant.

Son of David

f. Apart from an article from E. Schweizer (-> 1966) [**82**] and a few pages from E. Kränkl [**83**] (-> 1972, pp. 85-87), we must note here the impressive study by Ch. Burger (-> 1970, pp. 107-152) [**84**]. The author arrrives at the results which concern Luke, by following three lines of thought which meet at a focal point: the Lucan reinterpretation of the Marcan data, the announcements of the infancy narratives and the data given in Acts. Gradually from each of the three series of texts, the same editorial conception of Jesus, the Son of David, appears. Luke is wary of a political interpretation of Jesus, the Davidic Messiah. However, he does not reject the royal tradition or the title *υἱὸς τοῦ Δαυιδ*. On the contrary, he recalls the Davidic origin of Jesus to explain the regularity and legitimacy of the Easter enthronement. For it is only at the Easter elevation that Jesus comes into possession of the power which is his right. Thus there is nothing surprising that Ps 2:7 ("today I have begotten you") is cited in Acts 13, in an Easter context.

Luke interprets the three "Davidic" texts borrowed from Mark with reserve: Lk 18:35-43 (Bartimaeus), Lk 19:28-40 (the entry into Jerusalem: Luke modifies the context and deletes the mention of the reign of David to avoid misunderstandings) and Lk 20:41-44 (how can the Son of David be the Lord of David?). Luke, following Mark closely, leaves the question open here. The answer in Acts will be come only after Easter, but it will be an answer which differs from the tradition and from Mark. Act 2:32ff. gives an answer which inverts the question: the Son of David can be the Lord of David, for God has raised him up. Moreover like Matthew, Luke seeks to integrate a genealogy of Jesus (of Judeo-Christian origin). This establishes the Davidic sonship of Jesus. He attaches such an importance that he accepts the risk of entering into contradiction with the account of the virgin birth: does not his genealogy pass through Joseph?

In the three infancy narratives, according to Burger, Luke leans only on one traditional text, the canticle of Zachariah (Lk 1:68-79). The Evangelist is the first to put this hymn in relation with the birth of Jesus. The annunciation (Lk 1:26-38) as much as the nativity (Lk 2:1.10) are free redactional compositions. The Davidic ascendence of Jesus that these texts proclaim is, therefore, a theme that Luke appreciates.

The Acts confirm this interest. According to Luke, Peter, Paul and James, the three main leaders of the Church, elicit in their speeches the promise made to the house of David (Act 2:25-36; 13:23, 32-37; 15:16-18), now fulfilled in the person and resurrection of Jesus.

We subscribe to Burger's theses, with three reserves:

1) Luke does not necessarily remove the royalty of Jesus from the sphere of politics, but he refuses to confuse it with the Jewish Messianic hope. For him, the power of Christ is real and will spread politically over the earth (cf. the article of J. Comblin on peace in Luke, ch 6, -> 1956). By the advances made to the Roman power, the Church is already active in the arena, which is not without political relations.

2) The traditions used by Luke in the infancy narratives are, without the least doubt, more numerous than Burger supposes.

3) The access to the right hand of God, thus to the Messianic power of the Son of David, takes place at the Ascension and not at Easter (with Kränkl -> 1972).

Son of God

g. The first twenty-eight pages of B. M. F. van Iersel's book (-> 1961) brings us up to date on the studies relative to the title, the Son of God. His own view has been presented above in 3, III, b.

Since then, A. George has interested himself in the title and the theme of the royalty of the Christ (-> 1962 and -> 1965). These two studies concern the redactional perspective of Luke. Let us begin with the more recent.

In his gospel, Luke does not augment the references to "the Son" or "the Son of God". He follows the received traditions (the only mention which is his own is in Lk 1:32-35 in the account of the annuciation). The rarity of the title "Son of God" in the Acts confirms this first declaration (Act 9:20; cf. 13:33).

The editorial connotations which are grafted to the common texts, Luke's silence and the passages which are Lucan alone indicate, however, an original thought concerning the divine sonship of Jesus [85]. Here are the particularities:

1) With the Christian tradition, which George takes back to Jesus himself, Luke understands "Son of God" in the Messianic sense. He even accentuates this Messianic character (cf. Lk 1:32, 35; 3:22; 4:41; 10:23f.; 22:67-70; 22:29). This redactional connotation is the Evangelist's own: this royalty, which belongs to Jesus from the beginning, is accomplished by stages in the baptismal investiture, the Easter enthronement and the return in glory.

2) If the baptism constitutes a Messianic investiture (George prefers the Western text of Lk 3:22, i.e. the exact quotation of Ps 2:7 according to the LXX), the preaching in Nazareth (Lk 4:18f.) constitutes a special installation to the ministry of the prophetic servant. The two titles can only be joined later (in the account of the Transfiguration, Lk 9:35) when the disciples will learn that the Messiah must suffer. In respect to Jewish messianism, Luke underlines the mysterious specificity of the Son of God of the Christians, which is the necessary passage he must take in suffering. The innovation of Christian messianism is the concrete exercise of the divine sonship in the obediance and humilty of the Servant.

3) Luke yearns to make another important characteristic of the Son of God precise: the real and absolute sonship with God, the father of Jesus. The double annunciation by the angel clarifies this point: Jesus will be the Messianic "Son of God" (Lk 1:31-33) according to the traditional Jewish hope, but in an unexpected manner by this intimacy with God: thus the announcement of his miraculous birth (Lk1:34f.). The double question of the Sanhedrin, unique to Luke (Lk 22:67-70), takes up this double affirmation of Lk 1. Therefore Luke thinks it is

important: what is at stake is the passing from the Messiah of the prophecies to the Son of the Gospel [86].

4) The demons' utterances (Lk 4:3, 9; 4:41 and 8:28) indicate that the superhuman powers have perceived this mystery of the sonship of Jesus. On the contrary, Luke, parting company with Mk 15:39 and Mt 14:33; 16:16; 27:40-43, avoids putting the title Son of God into the mouths of men (George could have been more precise: before the exaltation of Jesus, for after this event the title will be part and parcel of the kerygmatic baggage if not for the apostles at least for Paul).

5) The words of Jesus himself which use the term Son (and not Son of God; Lk 10:22b; 20:13), those using the Father (certain are peculiar to Luke, like Lk 2:49; 22:29; 24:49), as well as, the prayers of Jesus to his father (a trait which Luke describes with attention) confirm Luke's concern to explain Jesus' messianism in terms of sonship and intimacy. The first and the last words of Jesus are reserved for his Father (Lk 2:49 and 23:46).

6) Finally, Luke insists on the links between the Son and the Spirit (Lk 1:35; 4:1; 10:21 and 24:49).

In his 1962 article, which only partly overlaps with his 1965 one, Father George shows the amplitude which the theme of the royalty of Jesus takes in the Gospel. Six pericopes offer original traits: the announcement of the King-Messiah (Lk 1:32f.: Luke understands the honorific terms in light of Easter);. the parable of the ten minas (Lk 19:12-27: the context reveals a polemic against Messianic impatience and the adherence to a contested and suffering royalty is a Lucan addition); the entry into Jerusalem (Lk 19:28-44: Luke is the only one to use the title "King". He subtly elicits the crowning of Solomon); the promise of the reign at the Lord's Supper (Lk 22:28-30: before being enthroned, Jesus already disposes of the reign; he is the legitimate heir); the confession of royalty before the Sanhedrin (Lk 22: 67- 70) and the promise made to the thief of the cross (Lk 23:40-43). The exegete from Lyon sees a confirmation of his theses in the Lucan usage of the title "Lord" (particularly Lk 1:41, 43; 2:11 and 24:34) and the situation of the royal texts within the Lucan work (divided into three unequal groups: at the beginning of the Gospel where they announce the mystery of Jesus; at the moment of his departure for Jerusalem and especially, at the moment of the last Passover, each time in contrast to the kingdoms of this world).

Here are several critical remarks:

1) We do not believe that Luke contrasts, like John, the reign of Jesus with the reigns of this world. Luke does not say that they belong to the devil (it is the devil who claims them!). Christ's power is exercised on the earth (Act 1:7 refuses to indicate the time, not the place of this reign).

2) Without a doubt, Luke does not esteem that Jesus' royalty is achieved in steps. He juxtaposes the traditional contradictory data concerning the date of the enthronement. For him, the decisive act is the exaltation to the right hand of God.

3) To speak of the Messianic enthronement followed by a prophetic installation, is to underestimate the prophetic element of the baptism and the Messianic import of the predication in Nazareth. The two events mark one and the same beginning (the famous ἀρχή) [**87**].

4) The Christological crescendo which George reads in Lk 22:27-70 seems forced.

Messiah

h. Since H. J. Cadbury's study which remains an example in the genre (-> 1933, pp. 357-359), several authors have studied this title, privileged by Luke: H. Conzelmann (-> 1954, p. 159 footnote 1); J. Dupont (-> 1950, second title, -> 1962, fourth title); U. Wilckens (-> 1961, pp. 156-163); J. C. O'Neill (-> 1962, pp. 119-129); C. F. D. Moule (-> 1966 cf. above 3, IV c); and lastly, D. L. Jones (-> 1970).

For Cadbury, *χριστός* is rarely a proper name in the Acts. If it is, it is in relation to Jesus in a formula used for solemn occasions (Act 2:38; 3:6; 4:10; 10:36, 48; 11:17; 15:26 and 16:18). The usual meaning was Messiah (most often with the article). Luke still knows the etymology of the term (cf. Act 4:27; 10:38; Lk 4:18). Incomprehensible to the Greek, the title is used in the discussions from the Scripture with the Jews. Luke places us in contact with Jewish messianism, but it is not certain that Acts transmits a primitive, apostolic and pre-Pauline usage.

Cadbury's position is important for it will influence several authors who refuse to see anything but an editorial usage, with regard to the data given in the Acts. Conzelmann, Wilckens and O'Neill are in this group; Dupont and Moule do not share this opinion and prefer the idea of an apostolic reminiscence.

Cadbury did not sufficiently elucidate the meaning of the redactional usage of the title *ὁ χριστός*. In a brief note, Conzelmann, who hardly is interested by the titles (for Luke, in his view, uses them indifferently), correctly remarks what follows: ὁ χριστός fits less into a reflection of God and Christ than in a thematic of the promise and fulfillment, a Scriptural promise which, curiously insists more on the suffering than on the glory of the Messiah.

Wilckens, also uninterested in the titles, notes this, nonetheless: 1) the title "Christ" is invested with meaning by the kerygmatic history of Jesus (the contrary is false); 2) it entertains ties with the OT where Luke understands the announcements of the suffering of the Messiah (at this point, ὁ χριστός can be substituted for the "Son of Man" in the Gospel); 3) Luke modifies the traditional Messianic elements in the sense of a subordination of Jesus to God (cf. the various expressions which signal that, with relation to God, Jesus is "his Christ", Act 3:18; cf. Act 4:26f.; Lk 2:29 and 9:20); and 4) the title becomes in Luke eminently heilsgeschichtlich (and no longer eschatological).

For O'Neill, the controversy that the apostles have with the Jews over the Messiah, in the Acts, is anachronous, for the good reason that before A.D. 70 Judaism had no consistent messianism. Therefore, Luke projects into the apostolic age the Christological disputes of his time, which is Justin's time too. "Christ" which began as a title, became a proper name (in Paul for example), and became a title again in the second century. Still it is true that Luke works with ancient materials (Jesus is the Christ from Easter and not before) which he assimilates with more or less success into his own position (Jesus is the Christ from all times and as such, he had to suffer to reach glory and accomplish the prophecies in this way).

D. L. Jones wants to bring the study of the titles [88] into favor again. Unfortunately, he only succeeds in concluding a late Lucan usage of the title ὁ χριστός. The suffering of the Messiah plays no effective role in the early preaching. The meaning of the title and its theological importance rest in the shadow. The most he can say is that the title strongly elicits the anointed one of God of Ps 2:2 (the anointing of the Spirit plays an eminent role in Luke, cf. Lk 4:18; Act 4:27 and 10:38). Jones takes up Moule's idea which distinguishes not the speakers but the occasions: ὁ χριστός, as a title, is related to the polemic and apologetic discussions with the Jews; χριστός, and as a proper name for Jesus, appears in a liturgical and solemn context (Cadbury's thesis). In Act 3:20f., the title does not reflect paleo-Christian thinking (so J. A. T. Robinson -> 1956), but allows Luke to overcome the famous problem of the delay of the Parousia.

Lord

i. The study of the title *κύριος* is indebted to the work of Msgr. Cerfaux [**89**]. The Belgian scholar has observed, for example, that the posterior, post-Easter usage of the title, in a comprehensive move, reacted to evangelical recollections: "we came to speak of the 'Lord Jesus' when thinking of his corporal manifestation. It is so in Luke's and John's gospel. The title no longer has the value of a well determined epithet; it designates Jesus in the concrete representation that the Christians make for themselves of their Savior." (**Le Christ dans la théologie de Saint Paul**, Paris, 1954^2, p. 349; we are obliged to L. Sabourin (-> 1963), p. 249, note1 for the reference).

H. J. Cadbury (-> 1933, pp. 359-363) also notes this stereotyped usage of 'Lord' which designates Jesus without referring precisely to his lordship. In Luke, this use is contrasted with the use of Christ, which always remains a title with internal force. Yet, the author of the Acts also knows how to highlight a term like Lord for example in the glorious expression 'Lord Christ', found in Act 2:36. In Luke, the combination, 'Lord Jesus' corresponds to an appropriate manner to speak within the Christian community. Cadbury concludes with an analysis of the formula, *οὖτός ἐστιν πάντων κύριος* (Act 10:36), unique in the NT. He mentions several Jewish parallels where God is called similarly, and concludes with the translation "Lord of all men".

In his study, "Jesus, Messie et Seigneur dans la foi des premiers chrétiens", J. Dupont (-> 1950) proposes a semantic evolution of the term *κύριος*. From a primitive Messianic significance, which is gradually toned, the succession passes to an eschatological (the Lord who will come) and an anticipatory liturgical sense (the Lord comes in the cult when he is invoked). Here and there, Luke the historian attests to the primitive meaning (so in Lk 1:43 and 2:11) but most often, to the eschatological and liturgical sense. Dupont does not seek to clarify the nuances which are strictly Lucan. He does so briefly in his review of Wilckens' book in order to recall the Easter horizon of Act 2:36. U. Wilckens (-> 1961), who on the contrary, thinks of a Messianic and lordly installation, rebuffs the affirmation of Act 2:36. He sees in it an affirmation of Lucan subordinationism. He takes over an interpretation of H. Conzelmann, who, despite Act 10:36, refuses to enlarge the Lordship of Christ to the cosmos. The angels, and this is an indication, are not submitted to the Lucan Christ. This indeed shows the difference which reigns between the Father and the Son and the subordination of the latter.

The evolution of the positions of J. C. O'Neill attests to the difficulty which we encounter in trying to get too tight a grip on the Lucan meaning of the title κύριος. In 1955, the writer wrote a long article which drew up an inventory and classification of all the uses of the word in Acts. He comes to four conclusions:

1) The term is to be explained with reference to the OT tradition (there is no influence of the Hellenistic κύριος , even in the account of the conversion of Paul: "who are you, Lord?", Acts 9:5). The title picks up connotations from adonai , behind which is the very name of Yahweh. Full divinity is therefore associated to the title.

2) The majority of the cases are ambiguous and when we do not know if God or Jesus is meant by κύριος they refer to Jesus (so the divers references to "the word of the Lord").

3) The Christian originality is that at Easter God gave his name to Jesus. This is the main thesis of the article. The name of the Lord which each Christian can invoke - different from Judaism where only the high priest could invoke Yahweh - is now Jesus. The frightened question of Paul finds its answer: Jesus is the present and definite manifestation of God. He takes on not only the qualities and attributes of God, but his name as well. Cf. the brutal identification of Jesus and the κύριος in Act 10:36.

4) As curious as it may seem, this transfer of κύριος from God to Jesus happened very early after Easter.

O'Neill's theological position, in this article of 1955, is typical of an excessive Christocentricity (is there a Barthian influence?): Jesus deprives God of his name and identity and exaggeratedly is identified with Him. This is an untenable view, for in fact Luke carefully distinguishes the Father and the Son and submits the latter to the former in the economy of salvation. The historical interpretation is hardly convincing: it situates the triumph of the title κύριος in a Palestinian milieu; it is certainly rooted here, but developes only in a Hellenistic environment. On a literary level, O'Neill does not sufficiently distinguish the traditional elements from the redactional rereading.

The author must have felt the weaknesses of his article, for his book of 1965 defends a very different view. O'Neill maintains the Aramaic origin of the title κύριος, but has understood that Luke writes in a period where these distant origins have been forgotten (p. 129). To understand the Lucan usage, it is necessary to accept two anterior influences: a) the

LXX which gives to God the name of κύριος and permits its utilisation for Jesus. Against his own article, he writes, "At this stage there are no indications that there was any confusion between the two Lords, or any attempt to claim divinity for Jesus because he was called Lord." (p. 131). b) The influence of the Hellenistic milieu and its parade of κύριοι. Thus the reaction of Paul at the epiphany "who are you, Lord?" (Act 9:5) cannot be that of a Jew. "We may, then, detect the influence of the Hellenistic environment of the story which Luke retells." (p. 132). Is it to save his anterior thesis that O'Neill adds in the same breath that this Hellenistic influence does not modify the meaning of the word, κύριος? Concerning the significance peculiar to Luke, O'Neill contents himself to say that the Evangelist was perfectly at home in calling Jesus Lord.

The third stage, 1970, the second edition of **The Theology of Acts**, the preface informs us that between the two editions, the author has modified his views on a precise point: throughout his work, Luke uses written sources. This is his new opinion. The chapter he had written on the Christological titles therefore falls by the wayside and, in fact, is not reprinted. Why? It is not easy to see clearly: without a doubt, because the usage of the titles becomes traditional again and does not feed the thesis of a late redaction of Acts (Justin's era).

Because of O'Neill's oscillations and despite the few pages of G. Voss (-> 1965, pp. 56-60, cf. above, 3, IV, b) and I. H. Marshall (-> 1970, p. 166f.), we are still waiting for a good analysis of the term κύριος in Luke. If our expectation persists for Acts, it is now fulfilled for the Gospel.

Father de la Potterie (-> 1970) painstakingly analyzed all the cases where Luke in the Gospel uses κύριος to designate Jesus [**90**]. When Luke clings strictly to history, he avoids the term, but when he mentions it, it is not by chance nor at random. At the beginning of the Gospel (Lk 1:43 and 2:11), he uses it solemnly to characterize he who will be born: κύριος here, like in Lk 7:13 and 19, has a messianic resonance. This same aspect, we will find again at the beginning of the journey (Lk 10:1) and in the narrative of the entry into Jerusalem (Lk 19:31 and 34). This Messiahship of Jesus does not become effective until Easter: it is not surprising that the Risen One in Lk 24:3, 24 bears the title κύριος which henceforth is his full right. But the resurrection and elevation have modified the content of the title, for the Lordship of him who now reigns is quite different from a royal power. It is a Lordship of him who reigns over his Church and who will come again to definitely establish his reign. The reign, de la Potterie reminds, is transcendent.

Related to the cult, the ecclesiastic use of *κύριος* is most frequent in Luke: Luke often uses the term when, surpassing history, he sees in the gospel narration the present activity of the Resurrected One in the Church. "Here is the most characteristic and most frequent usage of *ὁ κύριος* in Luke's gospel: in anticipation, it designates Jesus as the Lord of the Church. He is "the Lord" who liberates his own from the obligations of the Jewish Law (11, 39; 13, 25), "the Lord" who invites the believers to penitence (22, 61) and faith (17, 5-6), "the Lord" whose words they listen to, as perfect disciples (10, 39.41), "the Lord" who exhorts them to practice the distribution of goods (19, 8)". (p. 146, the references are clearly to Lk). The pages the Jesuit scholar consecrates to Martha and Mary (the theme of listening to the Lord) and to Peter (the role of conversion and faith in the Lord and the importance to remember the words of the Lord) are of great quality. He mentions the variety of the activities of the Lord Jesus, which are polemic and provocative, stimulate faith and sustain his Church.

The eschatological parables (Lk 12:42; 14:23; 16:8 and 18:6), evoke, according to tradition, the Lord who will come as judge. Yet, de la Potterie thinks that Luke adds a parenetic note to this eshatological conception: he who will come is already present in his community. We would rather say: he who will come already reigns next to the Father, listen to his voice as the Gospel transmits it to you.

Savior

j. Curiously, G. Voss' book (-> 1965) gives a more sustained attention to the term *σωτήρ* than to the title *κύριος*, which is more frequently cited in the Acts. We have summarized the pages dedicated to Jesus the savior in the general presentation of this work (cf. above ch 3 IV, b). To our knowledge, no other study has completed the picture, with the exception of I. H. Marshall's book (-> 1970, pp. 169-175, et passim, summarized in 5, IV, a).

Guide

k. The dissertation of P.-G. Müller (-> 1973) is the most recent and most stimulating study of the title *ἀρχηγός*. It begins with a state of the question which enumerates the numerous translations and explanations of the term which has been interpreted based on the cult of the sovereign or Heracles, the veneration of a hero, the gnostic myth, the typology of Moses and Judaism in general. To understand this title, it is necessary to situate it in the historical evolution which it has gone through and in the linguistic contexts where it appears. Placed at the crossroads of the diachronic and synchronic, *ἀρχηγός* designates he who guides or leads. This motif of Führung and its divers variations were spread throughout antiquity. Pages 114-128 of Müller's book analyze the different uses with the goal of answering an important question: From where did primitive Christianity, at an oral stage, receive this motif? The Jewish tradition seems to have played a decisive role (p. 113). The fourth part of this monograph is the most original: leaving diachrony aside, it observes the NT appearances of the title in their NT linguistic context, i.e. in their syntagmatic field: Act 3:15 and 5:31 and Heb 2:10 and 12:2. Here is the result of this investigation: "Der Kontext der vier *ἀρχηγός*-Stellen im NT zeigte sich jeweils als 'Kurzpassionsgeschichte'. Nur von diesem Rahmen her kann der Sinn der christologischen Anführerprädikation bestimmt werden: Jesus ist *ἀρχηγός*, weil er dies durch sein Leiden und seinen Tod, durch seine Auferstehung und Erhöhung geworden ist. Die theologisch tiefere Interpretation des Prädikats bietet dabei der Hebr.

Als Unterschied zwischen Apg und Hebr im Gebrauch des Titels wurde folgendes festgestellt: In der Apg wird Jesus Israel als neuer Heilführer angeboten. Der 'Sitz im Leben' des Titels ist die Judenmission. Im Hebr wird Jesus der Gemeinde als Anführer vor Augen gestellt, um die Gläubigen zur Ausdauer in der Glaubensexistenz zu ermahnen. Hier ist der 'Sitz im Leben' des Titels die an die christliche Gemeinde gerichtete Paränese. Trotz dieses Unterschiedes zwischen Apg und Hebr ist der gemeinsame 'Ort' der Christusprädikation *ἀρχηγός* wohl im Judenchristentum zu suchen" (p. 312).

Conclusion

If it was necessary to summarize our interpretation of the Lucan Christ at the end of this chapter, we would insert Christology into redemptive history and begin with the apostolic and ecclesiastic times.

The period which begins with the Ascension is qualified by the life of a once dead man (Act 25:19). In other words, the resurrection confers a specific character to our time. Imposed by the rupture of the irreplaceable rule of death, this mark can be defined as eschatological, since the Risen One is none other that the ultimate envoy of God, the Messiah Jesus.

This present life of the Resurrected One must not, however, be interpreted in the Pauline perspective of the body of Christ. In fact, Luke distinguishes the life and the presence. The Messiah of Israel is risen, but he is not with his people. This absence, which provokes faith and rouses a responsible engagement, the Evangelist expresses in terms of departure: in the Ascension, the Christ left his own and took his place at the right hand of God. We cannot have any doubt about the concrete and material character that this concept takes on in the eyes of Luke.

The Evangelist has little to say about the living Christ: he does not claim for himself any supernatural nor apocalyptic knowledge. He has not crossed the heavens in search of his Lord. His joy is nonetheless great, for he is even taken up in describing the earthly manifestation of the past. Confirming his talent as a historian, he is going to tell this extraordinary adventure, an adventure which humans would be incapable of, but which God, faithful to his Word, has allowed to become reality (Lk 1:37f.).

This story, which articulates humanity's part and God's intervention, is that of a man. This would be nothing extraordinary here, if this man did not go beyond the common. But Jesus united in his person what Israel had longed for and the nations had seen imperfectly. God, who raised him up, can be called his Father. In his case, the fact of being the son of God does not imply submission, but a free relationship because the Father's attitude was free. The good part of sociological schema father-son, is taken over and undergoes a decisive correction. The will of the Son corresponds to that of the Father, without the freedom of the Son being limited and without the exercise of the Father's good pleasure being harmful to his child.

Jesus, for he has a name which singles him out, is the Messiah. It is no longer a question of anguished or dishevelled waiting. The joy and peace are the awaited benefits for the end of suffering which the humble and oppressed endure. They explain the new situation brought on by this coming (Act 10:36).

This Messiah of Davidic origin accomplishes an unexpected activity. He does good (Act 10:38) - this was, of course, anticipated of the Messiah - but he operates differently than foreseen. This difference has a prophetic coloration: to describe it, Luke does not hesitate turning to the category of the inspired one sent of God, herold of the word and protector of the rejected. This figure of the charismatic prophet assumes that of an inspired sage who criticizes the intelligent, the interpreters appointed by the Law.

After having noted the prophetic and didactic role of the Messiah Jesus, Luke advances onto more difficult terrain: to make it understood that the prophetic function can lead to death, for the Lucan Messiah is going to die. He does not die on a battlefield, during a holy war. He dies the death of a martyr, a servant, a faithful prophet.

Luke loves Jesus. He loves the story of this life: the vigorous interventions of Christ for the poor, the parables that attest to the kingdom, henceforth present in the structure of the world. He is happy to recount the healing done by Jesus to reestablish the unhappy. For him, this Messiah is worthy of mention, worthy of the gospel, for he forced no one: the effectiveness of his witness comes from persuasion and not constraint. That Jesus did not adopt the language and claims of the Zealots as his own, does not imply a religious attitude centered on the interior life and hope in a spiritual "sweet bye and bye". The notions of peace and kingdom in Luke never lose their earthly and political connotations. The question is still power, but this power belongs to God. The Messiah, and then those who believe in him, do not yet live this kingdom of God except in a hidden and proleptic manner. However, Jesus and his disciples possess the interior force and exterior courage of those convinced. The latter are persuaded of the final and visible victory of the Christ in whose service they are enrolled.

This is why Luke can speak of the great works of God accomplished in the life of Jesus (Lk 1:49), even if, for the untrained eye, it seems to be only failures and limitations. This is also why he can turn to the same term elevation (Lk 9:51) to describe this life, while it is actually a descent into misery, destitution, suffering and death.

The life of Jesus has a movement: it follows a certain line; it forms a unity. Luke refuses to set aside one event, here the death, in order to attach a salutary virtue to it alone. It is the whole story of this being, which by the faith it arouses and the following it implies, fills a soteriological function. "For the Son of Man came to seek and save that which was lost." (Lk 19:10).

The same movement of the existence of Jesus the Messiah explains an exegetical enigma: Luke's gaze is from the victory of Easter onwards, not at the successes of the victor, but at the combats of his followers. He renounces looking above to the right hand of God in order to hear and then narrate the activity of the witnesses, which is marked by obstacles. The **Protevangelium of James** will seek to complete the story of Jesus: it will do so by going back in time and sacralizing the past. From Jesus, it will pass over to Mary to contemplate the Virgin's birth and miraculous infancy. The Evangelist, on the contrary prolongs the story of Jesus, not in the sphere of the marvelous, but in the often painful reality of the Christians. He refuses to sacralize the past, since he neglects the triumphant apocalyptic.

For Luke the past is in fact marked not by the sacred but by holiness: the sacred can be debilitating; on the contrary, the holiness of Jesus (Lk 1:35) invites his followers to a militant Christian activity. Certainly, it marks a beginning to which we refer and which we venerate., yet this beginning does not beget a conservative ideology. It is a genesis which calls for a 'follow up', a responsibility. The role of the Spirit, according to the Acts, signals that God himself gives his accord to this movement which is the Church. Jesus' free actions and generous attitudes find their prolongation here.

We could say that the Lucan Christology was pascal (J. Dupont) or that it culminated at the Ascension (E. Kränkl). Or then we could maintain that the Passion is central (F. Schütz). One exegete even recalls the Christological importance of Pentecost (O. Betz). These interpretations are partially true, but they all come from the conviction that Luke highlights the stages in salvation history. What is striking, on the contrary, is the accent Luke places on the continuity (a continuity which he assures by doubling, just like we prefer to make two knots instead of one). The whole life of Jesus is a great movement, an *ἀνάλημψις* which takes us up to Jerusalem, up to the cross, out of the tomb and to the right hand of God. Similarly, the history of God, if we dare to express it in this way, is marked by the Father's faithfulness to send messengers whose fates resemble one another by the regular aggressive reaction of the people (Luke, as O. Betz has rightly seen, is not triumphalistic). Jesus fits into this series of envoys and the apostles continue in this movement which Luke describes by faithfulness, not to Judaism (against Jervell), but to what he believes to be the Christian revelation.

For Luke, the word of God was made flesh in Jesus, but not in John's manner: it is the word of God, in the past addressed to the prophets and not preexistent in heaven, which took on a body in Jesus (Act 10:36f.). In Jesus, the word continues to be heard, more than ever. The passage from the Gospel to the Acts represents, we might say, the passage from history to language. The flesh becomes word: Jesus, the messenger, becomes the message. The flesh is not, however, reabsorbed; it is the apostles who henceforth become the human and suffering bearers of what God wants to say to the world. But they do not do this in their own name, but in the name of the one who alone is the Messiah, Lord, Master, Guide, Savior, etc. Thus they bear the word differently than Jesus.

To this could be grafted a theological comprehension of the titles deeper than what has been written: the Christological titles would be signs alerting Jesus' nonconformity. By his life, Jesus conformed to the fate of the prophets. By his titles, he is radically distinct. This means that the incarnation of the word in his life takes on a specificity that the presence of God in the prophets and apostles did not have. The infancy narratives, far from being an appendix to Luke's Christology, would be the focal point. On this point, Luke draws near to John. The theology of Luke would be Christological: it attaches itself to Easter and the Ascension, because of the Passion and especially because of the nativity.

The interminable panning of Lucan studies we have just made seems to manifest a danger to which the Evangelist did not succomb: that is to fix Jesus into a Biblical past and the exegete into a fixed attitude, which would then close the door to the return of the Spirit and neglect all commitment of service to the neighbor.

One last remark and question to end. It seems necessary to us to end with the quarrel concerning the age of Luke's Christology. The double work is Lucan and the Christology which it manifested belongs first of all to the author. Because of who he is and what he wants to do, Luke is a man of the Church and tradition and transmits material which is difficult, but necessary, to distinguish. Now the question: in Luke's eyes, how did the Jews understand Jesus? Did they think to unmask him as a usurper or did they perceive, without wanting to admit it, that he was the Son of God and the Messiah.

CHAPTER IV

THE HOLY SPIRIT

Chronological Bibliography

1926

H. VON BAER, **Der Heilige Geist in den Lukasschriften** (Stuttgart, 1926).

1939

N. ADLER, **Das erste christliche Pfingstfest. Sinn und Bedeutung des Pfingsberichtes, Apg. 2, 1-13** (Münster, 1938).

1948

W. L. KNOX, **The Acts of the Apostles** (Cambridge, 1948), pp. 80-92.

1950

J. DUPONT, **Les problèmes du Livre des Actes d'après les travaux récents** (Leuven, 1950), included in **Etudes**, Dupont, pp. 85-87 and 99-100.

1951

N. ADLER, **Taufe und Handauflegung. Eine exegetisch-theologische Untersuchung von Apg, 8, 14-17** (Münster, 1951).

G. W. L. LAMPE, **The Seal of the Spirit. A Study in the Doctrine of Baptism and Confirmation in the New Testament and the Fathers** (London-New York-Toronto, 1951; London, 1967[2]).

1952

E. K. BROWN*, **An Interpretation of the Holy Spirit in the Acts,** unpublished dissertation, Union Theological Seminary (Richmond, 1952).

L. S. CHAFER*, "The Baptism of the Holy Spirit", **BS** 109 (1952) 199-216.

J. G. DAVIES, "Pentecost and Glossolalia", **JTS**, N.S., 3 (1952) 228-231.

E. KÄSEMANN, "Die Johannesjünger in Ephesus", **ZTK** 49 (1952) 144-154; taken up in **Exeg. Versuche**, I, (Göttingen, 1960[2]), pp. 158-168. We are citing from this volume.

J. A. MARROW*, **The Holy Spirit in the Book of Acts**, unpublished dissertation, Union Theological Seminary (Richmond, Va.,1952).

1953

C. L. CHESHIRE Jr.*, **The Doctrine of the Holy Spirit in the Acts,** unpublished dissertation, Union Theological Seminary (Richmond, 1953).

E. LOHSE, " Die Bedeutung des Pfingstberichtes im Rahmen des lukanischen Geschichtswerkes", **EvT** 13 (1953) 422-436; taken up in **Einheit**, Lohse, pp. 178-192.

1954

H. CONZELMANN, **Die Mitte der Zeit. Studien zur Theologie des Lukas** (Tübingen, 1954, 1960[3]), pp. 167ff. <u>et passim</u> from the 3rd ed.

G. KRETSCHMAR, "Himmelfahrt und Pfingsten", **ZKG** 66 (1954-1955) 209-253.

E. LOHSE, "Lukas als Theologe der Heilsgeschichte", **EvT** 14 (1954) 256-275; included in **Einheit**, Lohse, pp. 145-164.

J. E. L. OULTON, "The Holy Spirit, Baptism and Laying on of the Hands in Acts", **ExpTim** 66 (1954-1955) 236-240.

1955

G. B. CAIRD, **The Apostolic Age** (London, 1955), pp. 57-72 of the 1972 reprint.

G. W. H. LAMPE, "The Holy Spirit in the Writings of Luke", in D. E. Nineham (ed), **Studies in the Gospels. Mémorial R. H. Lightfoot** (Oxford, 1955), pp. 159-200.

C. C. RYRIE*, "The Significance of Pentecost", **BS** 112 (1955) 330-339.

E. SCHWEIZER, "Die Bekehrung des Apollos, Apg 18, 24-26", **EvT** 15 (1955) 247-254; taken up in Schweizer, **Beiträge zur Theologie des Neuen Testaments. Neutestamentliche Aufsätze (1955-1970)**, (Zurich, 1970), pp. 71-79.

1956

E. HAENCHEN, **Die Apostelgeschichte. Neu übersetzt und erklärt** (Göttingen, 1956, 1959^{3}, 1968^{6}, 1977^{7}), p. 83 et passim of the 3rd ed., to which we refer.

E. HAMMAN, "La Nouvelle Pentecôte", **BiViChr** 14 (1956) 82-90.

E. SCHWEIZER, "Gegenwart des Geistes und eschatologische Hoffnung bei Zarathustra, späjüdischen Gruppen, Gnostikern und den Zeugen des Neuen Testamentes", in **The Background of the New Testament and its Eschatology. Mélanges C. H. Dodd** (Cambridge, 1956), pp. 482-508, included in Schweizer, **Neotestamentica. Deutsche und Englische Aufsätze 1951-1963** (Zurich-Stuttgart, 1963), pp. 153-179.

A. C. WINN*, **Pneuma and Kerygma: A New Approach to the New Testament Doctrine of the Holy Spirit**, unpublished dissertation, Union Theological Seminary (Richmond, 1956).

1957

G. HEUTHORST*, "The Apologetic Aspect of Acts 2, 1-13", **Script** 9 (1957) 33-43.

C. F. D. MOULE, "The Post-Resurrection Appearances in the Light of Festival Pil - grimages", **NTS** 4 (1957-1958) 58-61.

G. J. SIRKS, "The Cinderella of Theology: The Doctrine of the Holy Spirit", **HarvTR** 50 (1957) 77-89.

1959

M. H. FRANZMANN, "The Word of the Lord Grew. The Historical Character of the New Testament Word, **ConcTM** 30 (1959) 563-581.

E. LOHSE, "Art. *πεντηκοστή*", **TWNT**, VI (Stuttgart, 1959), pp. 44-53.

E. SCHWEIZER, "Art. *πνεῦμα κτλ.*", **TWNT**, VI (Stuttgart, 1959), pp. 401-413.

1960

J. GOETTMANN, "Le feu du ciel sur la terre", **BiViChr** 33 (1960) 44-61.

1961

R. LE DÉAUT, "Pentecôte et Tradition juive", **Spiritus. Cahiers de spiritu - alité missionnaire**, 7 (1961)127-144; included in **AssSeign**, 1st series, 51 (Bruges, 1963), pp. 22-38.

K. B. WELLIVER*, **Pentecost and the Early Church: Patristic Interpre - tation of Acts 2**, unpublished dissertation, Yale University (New Haven, 1961).

1962

S. MAC LEAN GILMOUR, "Easter and Pentecost", **JBL** 81 (1962) 62-66.

B. NOACK, "The Day of Pentecost in Jubilees, Qumran and Acts", **ASTI** I (1962) 73-95.

1963

S. L. JOHNSON, "The Gift of Tongues and the Book of Acts", **BS** 120 (1963) 309-311.

1964

W. GRUNDMANN, "Der Pfingsbericht der Apostelgeschichte in seinem theolo - gischen Sinn", in F. L. Cross (ed), **Studia Evangelica**, II (Berlin, 1964), pp. 584-594.

G. D. KILPATRICK, "The Spirit, God, and Jesus in Acts", **JTS**, N. S., 15 (1964) 63.

1965

J. ABRI*, "The Theological Meaning of Pentecost", **Kator Shin** 4 (1965) 133-151.

C. CABIÉ, **La Pentecôte. L'évolution de la cinquantaine pascale au cours des cinq premiers siècles** (Tournai, 1965).

C. JOURNET, "La mission visible du Saint-Esprit", **RThom** 65 (1965) 357-397.

E. SAMAIN*, **Le récit de Pentecôte dans le cadre de l'oeuvre luca - nienne**, unpublished dissertation (Leuven, 1965).

M. F. UNGER, "The Significance of Pentecost", **BS** 122 (1965) 169-177.

1966

S. SVEDA et al., "Die Kirche und der Geist Gottes nach dem Zeugnis des Lukas", **BiKi** 21 (1966) 37-53 (series of brief articles).

1967

F. BOVON, **De Vocatione Gentium. Histoire de l'interprétation d'Act. 10, 1-11, 18 dans les six premiers siècles** (Tübingen, 1967), pp. 195-198 and 247-292.

P. BRUNNER, "Das Pfingstereignis. Eine dogmatische Beleuchtung seiner historischen Problematik", in R. Bäumer and H. Dolch (eds), **Das Volk Gottes. Mélanges J. Höfer** (Freiburg-Basel-Vienna, 1967), pp. 230-242.

J. R. BRUTON*, **The concept of the Holy Spirit as a Theological Motif in Luke-Acts**, unpublished dissertation, Southern Baptist Theological Seminary (Louisville, Ky.,1967). Cf. **DissAbstr**, A, 28 (1967) 2322 A - 2323 A.

G. HAYA-PRATS*, **El Espíritu en los Hechos de los Apóstolos. Su influjo en la vida cristiana de la comunidad primitiva**, unpublished dissertation, Greg. Pont. Univ. (Rome, 1967). Cf. G. Haya-Prats -> 1975.

J. H. E. HULL, **The Holy Spirit in the Acts of the Apostles** (Lutherworth, 1967).

1969

E. TROCME, "Le Saint-Esprit et l'Eglise d'après le livre des Actes", in S. Dockx (ed), **L'Esprit Saint et l'Eglise** (Paris, 1969), pp. 19-27 (discussion, pp. 28-44).

1970

J. BORREMANS, "L'Esprit-Saint dans la catéchèse évangélique de Luc. Leçon pour l'annonce de Jésus-Christ dans un monde sécularisé", **LumVit** 25 (1970) 103-122.

J. DANIÉLOU, **L'Eglise des apôtres** (Paris, 1970), pp. 137-153.

J. D. G. DUNN, **Baptism in the Holy Spirit. A Re-examination of the New Testament Teaching on the Gift of the Spirit in Relation to Pentecostalism Today** (London, 1970).

E. EICHELE, "Pneuma Hagion nach dem Verständnis der Apostelgeschichte. Thesen", **Oekumenische Rundschau**, Beiheft 11 (Stuttgart, 1970), pp. 26-31.

K. HAACKER, "Das Pfingstwunder als exegetisches Problem", in O. Böcher and K. Haacker (eds), **Verborum Veritas. Mélanges G. Stählin** (Wuppertal, 1970), pp. 125-131.

J. KREMER, "Die Voraussagen des Pfingstgeschehens in Apg 1, 4-5 und 8", in G. Bornkamm and K. Rahner (eds), **Die Zeit Jesu. Festscrift H. Schlier** (Freiburg-Basel-Vienna, 1970), pp. 145-168.

1971

J. POTIN, **La fête juive de la Pentecôte,** 2 vols. (Paris, 1971), esp. vol. I, pp. 299-322.

E. SAMAIN, "Le Récit de Pentecôte-Actes 2, 1-13", in **Cahiers Bibliques** 10 de **FoiVie** 70 (1971), N°5, 44-67.

R. F. ZEHNLE, **Peter's Pentecost Discourse. Tradition and Lukan Reinterpretation in Peter's Speeches of Acts 2 and 3** (Nashville-New York, 1971).

1973

F. F. BRUCE, "The Holy Spirit in the Acts of the Apostles", **Interpr** 27 (1973), 166-183.

J. KREMER, **Pfingstbericht und Pfingstgeschehen. Eine exegetische Untersuchung zu Apg. 2, 1-13** (Stuttgart, 1973).

S. S. SMALLEY, "Spirit, Kingdom, and Prayer in Luke-Acts", **NT** 15 (1973) 59-71.

G. STÄHLIN, "Τὸ πνεῦμα Ἰησοῦ (Apg 16, 7)", in B. Lindars and S. S. Smalley (eds), **Christ and Spirit in the New Testament. Mélanges C. F. D. Moule** (Cambridge, 1973), pp. 229-252.

1974

J. GIBLET, "Baptism in the Spirit in the Acts of the Apostles", **One in Christ** 10 (1974) 162-171.

J. KREMER*, **Pfingsten-Erfahrung des Geistes. Was sagt darüber die Bibel?** (Stuttgart, 1974).

1975

J. D. G. DUNN, **Jesus and the Spirit. A Study of the Religious and Charismatic Experience of Jesus and the First Christians as Reflected in the New Testament** (London, 1975), pp. 135-196.

G. HAYA-PRATS, **L'Esprit, force de l'Eglise. Sa nature et son activité d'après les Actes des apôtres**, translated from Spanish (Paris, 1975). Cf. G. Haya-Prats -> 1967.

1976

S. SCHULZ, **Die Mitte der Schrift. Der Frühkatholizismus im Neuen Testament als Herausforderung an den Protestantismus** (Stuttgart-Berlin, 1976).

1977

J.-D. DUBOIS, **De Jean-Baptiste à Jésus. Essai sur la conception lucanienne de l'esprit à partir des premiers chapitres de l'évangile**, unpublished dissertation (Strasbourg, 1977).

D. MINGUEZ*, **Pentecostés. Ensayo de Semiótica narrativa en Hch 2** (Rome, 1977).

CHAPTER 4

THE HOLY SPIRIT

Introduction

The Holy Spirit plays a preeminent role in Luke's writings. The third Gospel mentions in fact the Spirit more frequently than the two other Synoptics and chapters 1-12 of the Acts constitutes the portion of the NT where the πνεῦμα appears with the most insistence [**1**].

In the Gospel of Luke, Jesus makes allusion four times to the Spirit: "The Spirit of the Lord is upon me" (4:18, with synoptic parallel); "How much more will the heavenly father give the Holy Spirit to those who ask him" (11:13; in Mt, it is a question of *ἀγαθά* and not of the Spirit); "But he who blasphemes against the Holy Spirit, will not be forgiven" (12:10; with regard to the other Synoptics, Luke disconnects this sin from the pre-Easter miracles to relate it to the rejection of the post-Easter preaching); "For the Holy Spirit will teach you the same hour what you must say" (12:12) [**2**].

The Evangelist also notes the presence of the Holy Spirit in John the Baptist (1:15), Elizabeth (1:41), Zechariah (1:67) and Simeon (2:25-27). The prophecy which had been quiet, awakes.

The Spirit penetrates Mary in a particular manner to permit her to conceive Jesus (1:35). Jesus, begotten by the Spirit, receives it in corporal form at his baptism (3:22). He lives and acts filled by the Spirit's presence (4:1, 14; 10:21) [**3**].

If we turn to the book of the Acts, we see that the word *πνεῦμα* appears about seventy times [**4**]. More than fifty times it designates the Holy Spirit (twenty times Holy Spirit with the article, eighteen times without the article; ten times Spirit without the adjective Holy, twice "my Spirit", i.e. God's; twice "Spirit of the Lord" and once "Spirit of Jesus") [**5**]. Furthermore, other terms like the power and promise designate the same reality [**6**].

The Risen One announces the outpouring of the Spirit, which must happen in Jerusalem. This eschatological eruption took place on the day of the Jewish Pentecost: it provokes a pheno -

menon of speaking in foreign tongues which suggests also an eruption of glossolalia. Moreover, it confers on the apostles the *παρρησία* necessary to preach. It, therefore, suscitates a mission. Henceforth the community organizes itself: its internal life as well as its missionary efforts are determined by the Holy Spirit [7]. Always new, the Holy Spirit gives evangelization a decisive impulsion [8].

Associated to conversion and baptism (Act 2:38), the Holy Spirit sets apart the believer, who enters the Church. In one case (Act10) the Holy Spirit precedes baptism, in the other cases, he comes only after baptism and the imposition of hands (Act 8 and 19).

A counselor, the Holy Spirit inspires the practical decisions of the community (Act 15). A prophetic Spirit, he announces the suffering to come to Paul the witness (Act 20). Intransigent, he does not tolerate that someone trick him (Act 5). Perseverant, he rouses at all times the opposition to the elected people (Act 7:52) [9].

There briefly presented are the references to the Holy Spirit in the Lucan corpus. We shall see that the role, nature and variety of the interventions of the Holy Spirit pose a certain number of questions to the exegete and theologian. Is it a fluid or a person? What happens to the one who receives the Spirit? Does the Spirit live in the believer or does he appear intermittantly? From where does Luke get his conception of the Spirit: the OT, early Christianity, oriental or Greek religiosity? Does he not exaggerate the importance of 'pneumatism' in the early Church in Jerusalem? What function does he attribute to the Spirit in the course of the history of the Church? Does he have a coherent approach or does he let himself be swept along by his disparate sources?

A study of the recent works will permit us to gather a certain number of answers. Sometimes it will be embarassed because of the contradictory character of certain positions. However, this study is to be esteemed for helping us to discover the problems that a superficial reading of the Biblical texts would not.

I. GENERAL CONCEPTION

a. Because of our concern for clarity, we will first present the recent works which illuminate Lucan pneumatology on the whole. Contrary to the rule followed in the other chapters, we will have to go back before 1950, the date of the Lucan renewal.

A book, which in fact has not sufficiently retained the attention of exegetes and antedates the first work of the Redaktionsgeschichtler by twenty years, is von Baer's. Then, we will analyze Lampe's long article, then E. Schweizer's contribution, which appeared in the **Theologisches Wörterbuch zum Neuen Testament**, and finally the book of Hull. Along the way, we will signal what Knox, Dupont, Haenchen and Conzelmann have done.

We will then treat two particular problems: the Pentecost account and the relation between the laying on of hands and the outpouring of the Spirit.

H. von Baer (-> 1926)

b. If he sometimes seeks behind the Biblical text, the historical reality to which the latter refers, von Baer concentrates his attention most often on the Lucan composition. Complaining (and rightly so!) of the lack of interest, in his time, given to the particularities of each Gospel, he determines what the Lucan concept of the Spirit is. He explains that only a comparision of the text of Luke with the traditions and sources used - the Gospel of Mark, first of all - permits such an update (p. 5f.).

From this methodological point of departure, von Baer discovers three Lucan particularities which Conzelmann, who cites von Baer here and there, does not take over, find or specify:

1) Different from Mark's and Matthew's, Luke's theology is a theology of salvation history: "Als Leitmotiv der lukanischen Komposition haben wir den Gedanken der Heilsgeschichte festgestellt." (p. 108) **[10]**.

2) This history of salvation, as the Lucan pneumatology shows, unfolds in three large periods: the OT, time where the Holy Spirit is promised, the life of Jesus, when the Spirit intervenes, but concentrates on the son of Mary and the time of the Church, when the Spirit is poured out in the Church (p.111f.).

3) In the time of the Church, the Spirit is linked to missionary work, according to the relation of cause and effect: so the presence of the Spirit and the missionary activity constitute the leitmotiv of the Lucan work **[11]**.

After having introduced these conclusions, surprisingly contemporary, let us now turn for a closer look at the arrangement of the book.

After an introduction where, he defines the goal of his research and the means of attaining it, von Baer shows the Lucan particularity of the Holy Spirit: distinct from the Johannine 'Paraclete' and the Pauline 'pneuma' the Holy Spirit of Luke is first of all the Spirit of Pentecost who breathes on the Church.

Tied to Christ, who promises (Act 1:8) and who sends (Act 2:33) [**12**] it, the Holy Spirit in his Pentecostal unity, appears in Luke in a variety of manifestations. Faithful to his sources, Luke maintains the diversity of the modes of intervention of the Spirit: glossolalia, prophecy, communal life, act of initiation, etc. More - over, due to the work he is writing and the literary genre of the latter, he places the tangible and visible repercussions of the Spirit in the forefront.

The first section of the book (pp. 43-112) is significantly entitled, the Holy Spirit as one of the leitmotive of the Lucan composition. This part is the most original and sets forth how the notion of the Spirit allows to distinguish the three stages of redemptive history. If chapters 1-2 of the Gospel show us the last manifestations of the Spirit of prophecy with John, Anna and Simeon, they let us get a glimpse of a new stage which commences with the miraculous conception. However, it is the baptism of Jesus which marks the point of departure of the new economy: the Baptist plays no role in it, so to speak. The only thing that counts is the "corporal" coming of the Spirit which answers Jesus' prayer. The parallel with Pentecost, which Luke cannot make nearer because of his sources, is compelling [**13**]. Having the Spirit from birth does not preclude his asking for it.

Von Baer then shows the redactional importance of the initial sermon of Jesus at Nazareth, which differs greatly from Mark. The programatic importance of this predication is confirmed by the quotation of Isa 61:1: "the Spirit of the Lord is upon me".

In Lk 3 and 4, as will be the case in the Acts, the gift of the Spirit is tied immediately with the mission.

In the course of the Gospel, Luke relates the thaumaturgical power of Jesus to his possession of the Spirit. Even if the word Spirit is not used, because of Luke's sources, the pneumatic origin of the miracles is unquestionable for von Baer. In the third period of salvation history, this same force will allow the disciples to preach and heal [**14**].

What interests Luke, besides the presence of the Spirit in Jesus, is the promise of the Spirit which the Christ makes to his disciples. Yet, the gift of the Spirit does not come without obliga - tion: if one can obtain forgiveness before Easter for having sinned against Jesus - as is Peter's case -, after Pentecost the sin against the Holy Spirit is irremissable.

Finally, Lk 10:21 and 11:13 tie prayer and the presence to the Spirit together.

Von Baer then turns toward what he calls the interregnum of the Spirit, the period which separates the resurrection and Pentecost. As Lk 24:44-53 and Act 1:1-14 indicate, this period of forty days is marked by the reiterated promise of the Spirit. The importance which Luke accords to this announcement allows us to sense the preeminence of the Spirit in the book of the Acts.

If the interregnum must be explained historically, it nonethe - less uncovers Luke's intention: to distinguish the second period from the third. Beforehand the Spirit was present in Jesus, but in the future, he will be present in the persons of the disciples. Between the two, he is temporarily absent. As a sign of this provisional absence, von Baer draws attention to - what many will note after him **[15]** - the drawing of lots which designates Matthias the successor of Judas in the circle of the Twelve. When the Spirit of Pentecost will reign, it will not be necessary to turn to such a practice: The Church with the help of the Spirit will be able to decide itself and designate who it wants (cf. Act 13:2 and 15:28).

In his analysis of the Pentecost account, von Baer remarks that Luke is bent on underlining the place of this event in the history of the Church, and so the heilsgeschichtlich importance of the miracle, which will describe the event with precision. Afterwards he notes Luke's affection for the materiality of the presence of the Spirit (the flames of Pentecost correspond to the dove at Jesus' baptism). He also points out that despite a real relationship with the other outpourings of the Spirit, the adventure of Pentecost possesses an intrinsic character **[16]**. "This day possesses for the apostles as well as for the whole Church, a significance of absolute principle." (p. 90).

Finally, Peter's discourse at Pentecost and vs. 36 in particular proves, according to von Baer, that the outpouring of the Spirit coincided with a new revelation: The Church understood this instant that the Christ had been elevated to the right hand of God and that he now possessed Lordship. This deduction can be debated: in return, we can easily accept with von Baer that something new happens at Pentecost: fulfilling the prophecy of Jesus (Lk 22:32), Peter is converted. Pentecost is, moreover, the day when the Holy Spirit allows Christian preaching to take form and become effective.

From this, von Baer shows the way Luke has chosen, when he places the second part of his book under the sign of the Spirit of Pentecost. The Evangelist shows the influence of the Spirit on the exterior diffusion of the Word of God. Von Baer attributes to the Spirit of Pentecost the itinerary which follows the proclamation of the Gospel as well as the reality of the miracles which accompany it. We might emit some doubt to this last idea (Luke ties the miracles to the name of Jesus).

In the second section of his book, von Baer takes up the details - not without repetition - of the study of the texts which he used in the first synthetic section [**17**]. He studies particularly the relations between the Holy Spirit and the initiatory rites (baptism - imposition of hands). We will present his theses when we treat this subject.

Finally, he concentrates his attention to an arduous problem: in insisting on the exterior manifestations of the Spirit, does Luke neglect, as some think [**18**], the impact of the *πνεῦμα* on the interior life of the believer? While recognizing that one must "read between the lines" (p. 183), the writer thinks we must seek the origin of the notions of *παρρησία*, of joy, of the fear of God and of *κοινωνία* in the inspiration of the Spirit. He analyzes Act 2:43-47 and 4:32f. in this way. The action of the Spirit does not limit itself to a few spectacular manifestations reserved for the pneumatic elite: it models the entire existence of the community. If Luke evokes willingly glossolalia and prophecy, it is because of the literary genre of the work he is writing (p. 191) [**19**].

G. W. H. Lampe (-> 1955) [**20**]

c. According to Lampe, Luke's theology, which is not always clear, is expressed generally in the personal rearrangement of material and minute redactional corrections. Yet in one domain the Lucan conception is impressive by its elaboration: pneumatology. The Spirit determines the birth, life, death and exaltation of Jesus. The Spirit also marks the origin, life and mission of the apostolic Church (p. 200). The summit of Luke's work is the eruption of this age of the Spirit which the risen Christ confers to his disciples to act, in the world, as agents of his kingdom. This Spirit, with which Jesus was anointed, allows the evangelization of the world (p. 188) [**21**].

Lampe defines this general concept, which he shares with von Baer [**22**], only at the end of his article. A study of the texts which turns sometimes into paraphrase, leads the author to this conclusion. Before going into this exegetical section, Lampe makes two important declarations:

1) From a pneumatic point of view, the Gospel and the Acts are symmetric: the gift of the Spirit conferred to Jesus from his conception and baptism corresponds to the outpouring of the Spirit on the Church at Pentecost. This Spirit permits preaching to be deployed: the speech of Jesus at Nazareth has its counterpart in Peter's speech at Pentecost (p. 159). The miracles done by Jesus in the Spirit find their match in the healings done by the apostles following Pentecost. Concerning this, Lampe even thinks he is able to establish more precise correspondences between the Gospel and Acts (p. 194ff.). Aside from the problematic aspect of such coupling, we would reproach Lampe for not having sufficiently distinguished the qualitative difference that exists between the presence of the Spirit in the person of Jesus and in the disciples' **[23]**. In return, we will admit readily with him that the death and resurrection of Jesus are at the basis of this passage of the Spirit from the Christ to his Church (p.159).

2) With von Baer and against the religionsgeschichtliche Schule **[24]**, Lampe roots the Lucan doctrine of the Spirit in the OT. The Holy Spirit, according to Luke, corresponds to the ruach of the OT. It is the divine force, most often impersonal **[25]**, which has a double characteristic of power and life.

With regard to this and in an original manner, Lampe points out the relation which exists between the name and the Spirit of Yahweh in Deutero-Isaiah (44:3-5). This connection sanctions the affirmation that by attaching the miracles of Jesus and the apostles to the Name, Luke associates them implicitly to the Spirit: Lk 11:20, which speaks of the finger of God (Lampe evokes Ex 8:19, LXX here because of the parallelism between Moses and Jesus), confirms this thesis, for the Spirit of God and the finger (or the hand, Act 4:28, 30; 7:35) of the Lord are practically synonymous.

Finally, certain texts of the OT and Judaism expect an out-pouring of the Spirit at the end of time.

On two points, Luke's thought is to be distinguished from the OT: a) Luke attaches the presence of the Spirit to the person of Jesus **[26]**; b) he thinks that the eschatological promise of the Spirit contained in the OT is now fulfilled **[27]**.

With these declarations made, Lampe goes throughout the text of Luke and analyzes the relations of the Holy Spirit to 1) eschatology, 2) prayer, 3) Jesus Christ, 4) conversion and 5) the kingdom. Here is a summary of his conclusions:

1) Luke affirms clearly that the Spirit, which went out, was rekindled with force in the times of John the Baptist: the Baptist, who in Luke yields up to Jesus the role of Elijah redivivus, is described with traits which remind us of the inspired heroes of the OT: Samson, Samuel and Jeremiah. The miraculous birth of Jesus fits into this context of the Spirit which permits the accomplishment of God's plan.

The ministry of John the Baptist is the hinge between the time of the promise and the time of Jesus, like the fifty days which separated the resurrection and Pentecost served as the transition between Jesus' era and the Church's. However, there is one difference between the inspiration of John, with a prophetic goal, and the permanence of the Spirit in Jesus from his conception. Luke does not tell us that Jesus grew in Spirit, like he does of John.

2) Lampe notes that Luke inserts a prayer of Jesus between the baptism and the outpouring of the Spirit. It seems that for Luke the coming of the Holy Spirit is the main answer of God to man's prayer. Of course, he cites Lk 11:13, mentions various prayers of Jesus and the apostles (Act 4:25-31) and thinks that the Marcionite version of the second request of the Lord's Prayer ("May your Spirit come upon us and purify us") is Lucan (pp. 169-171) [**28**].

3) Jesus follows in the line of the inspired prophets. Or better, he is like an antitype of Samuel, Moses (cf. Dt 18:15 in Act 3:22f.; 7:37 and perhaps 13:33f.), Elijah and the suffering servant.

Like Elijah was taken to heaven before transferring his spirit to Elisha, so Jesus was taken up at the resurrection before transmitting his Spirit to his disciples (p. 176). This idea would merit an attentive examination; for it is certain that Luke insists on (at the expense of John the Baptist) the typology Elijah-Jesus; it is not evident that the link between the exaltation and Pentecost (which does not appear explicitly except in Act 2:33 and perhaps in Lk 24:49) comes from this typology [**29**].

According to Lampe, Luke distinguishes Jesus from the prophets: what was only a superficial and temporary outpouring on the prophets, becomes a constant indwelling of the Spirit in Jesus [**30**]. Moreover, especially what was the spirit of prophecy becomes the spirit of power.

The Spirit is closely related to Jesus, to the point that Luke can speak of the Spirit of Jesus (in fact, the expression is unique in Acts: 16:7). Thus, Lucan pneumatology is near to Paul's and John's. The Risen One appears as the master of the Spirit, since he can announce its outpouring on the disciples (Lk 24:49 and Act 1:4: "promise" is the term used) (p. 193).

4) If he does not distinguish enough the indwelling of the Spirit in Jesus and the outpouring on the apostles and believers, Lampe underlines the rapport which Luke establishes between the gift of the Spirit and conversion. He indicates that since Pentecost conversion and faith are associated to the baptism and gift of the Spirit. The time of repentence corresponds to the period of the Spirit's activity in the apostolic mission (p. 186). It is the same for forgiveness which is obtained now by the calling on the name of Jesus in the close relation with the Spirit.

Lampe correctly insists on these relationships. However, we must regret that he has not clarified them enough [**31**]. Particularly, he does not mention that the Spirit in Luke is always the answer to a first movement by man [**32**]. Luke is bent on maintaining if not the freedom of man, at least his responsibilty in the act of faith.

The notions of life (Jesus Christ as the prince of life) and peace (Jesus Christ announcing peace) in Luke refer to the kindness of God in Jesus Christ. Lampe would like to go further and see in them the effects of the power of the Spirit. Does he want to make us admit that in Luke the Spirit is already at work in the conversion of man? This would be to project an Augustinian problematic onto Luke. When Luke says that conversion is given to men, he means that the Passion and resurrection offer to guilty man the possibilty to turn toward God [**33**].

5) Chapter 1 of the Acts brings two great things together: the kingdom of God (1:3, 6f.) and the Spirit (1:2; 5:8): the disciples were waiting for a national restauration, and Jesus commands them to wait for the power of the Holy Spirit. It seems that Luke reinterprets the notion of kingdom: the kingdom, according to Lampe, is defined no longer in political terms, but in terms of the preaching of the Gospel in the power of the Spirit. Lampe points out, as we have said, what he believes to be the second request of the Lord's Prayer according to Luke: not "your kingdom come" but "may your Spirit come upon us...". Here we might wonder if Lampe does not neglect the relations in Acts which join the king - dom to the earthly ministry of Jesus. When it is said of Paul, in the last verse of Acts, 28:31, that he preaches the kingdom and teaches concerning the Lord Jesus Christ, the two expressions presuppose that Luke has the terrestrial ministry of Jesus in mind rather than his eschatological consequence [**34**].

In his analysis of the Acts, Lampe insists manifestly on the Spirit relation to baptism and the laying on of hands. We will describe his views in the section consecrated to this delicate problem [35].

E. Schweizer [36](-> 1959)

d. Written by five authors, the article *πνεῦμα* of the **Theologisches Wörterbuch zum Neuen Testament** appeared in 1959 (ET, 1968). It is divided into five parts (Greece, OT, Judaism, Gnosticism and NT). The fourth and fifth sections are from E. Schweizer's pen. He broaches the Synoptics and Acts before turning to Paul and John. This approach, which offers the possibility to study Mark and Luke in their similarity and diversity, hinders the author from analyzing the possible influence of Pauline pneumatology on Luke. This is a regrettable lacuna, for if Luke depends on the Synoptic tradition, he is not a complete stranger to the ideas of the apostle.

After several pages on the Spirit in Mark and Matthew, Schweizer approaches the work dedicated to Theophilus. Luke, in his opinion, manifestly reinterprets the Synoptic conception of *πνεῦμα*. This rereading is felt particularly in that the Spirit, in Luke, ceases to be a charistmatic force conferred provisionally to a few "pneumatics" in order to become a power offered in a stable manner to the entire community.

An obscurity in Schweizer's position must be pointed out here. On p. 403 (ET, p. 404), the exegete from Zurich refuses the thesis, often defended, according to which the predominance of the Spirit in the Lucan corpus originates from a Greek influence. In his opinion, the development of this notion, undergone in rapport with Mk, comes mainly from Jewish influences [37]. Yet in the course of his presentation, if we have understood correctly, he, nonetheless, brings this evolution (that we can summarize as the passage from an animistic conception to a dynamistic view) back to Greek influence. In any case, we can wonder if the distinction between an animistic perspective of Jewish origin and a dynamistic influence of Hellenistic does not force the texts. Luke seems to have a uniform concept of the Spirit.

These reservations which concern the origin of Lucan pneumatology must not diminish our interest in Schweizer's presentation of the Lucan doctrine.

With a comparative analysis of the Synoptics, Schweizer determines first the ties Luke establishes between the Spirit and Jesus. While Jesus is presented as a pneumatic in Mk and Mt, in Lk he appears not submitted to the Spirit but as its master [38]. It is not, for example, the Spirit who pushes Jesus into the desert and into Galilee, but Jesus, accompanied by the Spirit, goes to these places (Lk 4:1 and 14; Mk 1:12). If Schweizer is right to show that Jesus is not submitted to the Spirit, he surely goes too far when he speaks to Jesus' domination of the Spirit. The heilsgeschichtlich perspective must be respected: Jesus will not be the master of the Spirit until the hour of his elevation; it is at this moment that he will be able to transmit it to his disciples. For the moment - Luke does not say more - the Spirit dwells constantly on Jesus, as the citation of Isa 61:1 in Lk 4 testifies.

Speaking of the ties which unite the Spirit and Jesus Christ after the resurrection, Schweizer tends, on the contrary, to bring the two together exaggeratedly. Thus he can write that the believer meets the Risen One in the gift of the Spirit. This seems to strike a blow to the transcendence and independence of the Risen One, so evident in Luke.

Schweizer, therefore, exaggerates the power of the historical Jesus over the Spirit and minimises the Lordship of the Christ elevated over the *πνεῦμα*. On these two points, von Baer and Conzelmann seem to have better defined the Lucan perspective.

Schweizer's main intention is to show how Luke overcomes a naive and animistic conception of the Spirit (cf. the second section consecrated to "The Abiding of the Spirit with the Community"). Certainly, Luke keeps certain traditional allusions to a capricious Spirit who suddenly alights on a hero only to leave him later. However, he refuses to be held to this conception and defines the Spirit as a force determining the whole human existence. In taking this path, Luke sometimes avoids the gnostic danger where the Spirit becomes the natural possession of the elect. Schweizer wonders why Luke some times keeps the animistic conception: more than faithfulness to the sources, he discovers a theological concern: to affirm that man can never consider the gift of God as his own. For God always comes anew as a gift [39]. This preoccupation appears even there where Luke uses a dynamistic terminology: along side the expression *πλήρης πνεύματος*, filled with the Spirit, he uses the passive verb *πλησθῆναι πνεύματι* [40] to be filled with the Spirit and maintains the initiative and prerogative of God.

Aside from the doubts which we have expressed concerning the animistic - dynamistic distinction, we think that Schweizer perhaps makes Luke say more than he really does. Only the general intention can be defined with certitude: the Holy Spirit remains the free master with regard to the community.

In his third part, entitled "The Outward Manifestations of the Spirit", Schweizer insists, like many others, on the visibility which Luke confers of the presence of the Spirit. Yet he goes further, esteeming that Luke, with his Hellenistic mentality, cannot conceive of a force, the Holy Spirit's in particular, other than as a substance. He deduces that for Luke, consciously or unconsciously, the Spirit is a fluid. One might wonder if this reasoning does not rest on the outmoded categories of the history of religions. Here again, Schweizer recovers: in Luke, it is but a reflex of thought. The conscious intention of Luke is not to determine the modalities of the spiritual outpouring on man, but to note the outward manifestations of the Spirit (p. 404; ET, p. 406f.).

As outward manifestations, there are orders which God transmitted to believers. Luke, according to Schweizer, esteems that the Holy Spirit could not tolerate any contradiction here: understood ad malem partem, such an affirmation must be corrected by other NT data (Schweizer is thinking no doubt of the discerning of spirits which Paul proposes): understood ad bonam partem, this means, for Luke, the Spirit of God desires to reach the human being all the way to his corporality. Here again, we wonder if Schweizer, by his hermeneutical concern, does not go beyond what Luke naively tells us, i.e. that the Holy Spirit comes truly upon man and can really transmit to him the orders of God. This movement of the Spirit, according to Luke, does not crush humanity.

The fourth section deals with "The Works of the Spirit". Here, the influence of Jewish tradition on Luke is evident: the Holy Spirit manifests himself, first, if not exclusively, in prophecy and preaching, so in human speech. Schweizer shows that Luke adds the verb "prophesy" to the quotation of Joel in Act 2:18. Moreover, he holds that Luke consciously avoids attaching the miracles of Jesus to the accomplishment of the prophecy of Isa 61 in Lk 4:23-27 [41]. Not once in his work, does Luke seek the origin of the miracles in the Spirit's power. Beside that Schweizer does not indicate the theological consequences of such a statement, we wonder if the word *δύναμις* used for the miracles and the Spirit does not serve as link between the two. Furthermore, the OT and Judaism do not discard the thaumaturgical power of the Spirit. On the contrary, an effective and inspired sermon is accompanied with signs: Acts, Paul and Hebrews accept this thesis which goes back to the OT. It suffices to agree on the demonstrative import of these "miracles": in Luke they seem to respond to a call of faith and do not become possible except in the realm of faith.

This conception of the Spirit as a prophetic spirit hinders Luke from defining the moral life of the believers as a life in the Spirit. Clearly, as Schweizer notes, the Spirit does not appear in the summaries in the beginning of Acts which describes the life of charity of the first believers. Is it however erroneous to believe that Pentecost suscitated this communion and love?

Schweizer then analyzes the role of the Spirit in certain decisions made by the ecclesiastical authorities in Acts: Peter's striking down Ananias and Sapphira; the setting apart of Barnabas and Paul; the resolution of the conference in Jerusalem: the author rightly notes there is the danger of believing that all ecclesiastic decisions are inspired. He thinks that the texts of Acts rather emphasize the prophetic nature of the Church whose inspiration depends on the will of the divine *πνεῦμα*.

The author concludes this paragraph: "Hence, even though the Hellenist Luke is strongly interested in the visibility of the Spirit's works, the limitation of these works to prophetic proclamation is completely Jewish." (p. 407; ET, p. 409).

In the fifth section entitled "The Spirit as a Feature of the Age of the Church", Schweizer again distinguishes Luke from Mark and Matthew. If the Spirit is an eschatological gift, it remains, for the two latter, something extraordinary which comes to the aid of believers in exceptional circumstances. For Luke, on the other hand, the Spirit is offered to all the members of the community [**42**] and is given to them in a lasting manner [**43**]. The Pentecost narrative, which opens the third period of salvation history, shows this fulfillment of the promises. Moreover, according to Schweizer, the Pentecost episode and, through it, the gift of the Spirit, is not of an eschatological nature: it opens a new time and not the last times [**44**]. The outpouring of the Spirit could be repeated during the enduring period of the Church. Schweizer seems to us here to underestimate the eschatological nature of Pentecost: furthermore, does not Luke add the words "in the last days" to the text of Joel [**45**]? That these last days persist, does not take away their eschatological character [**46**].

Schweizer goes even further into the problem of the Spirit in the Church. First, he points out that neither faith, moral life nor salvation are explicitly provoked by the Spirit in Luke. Faith can exist and even subsist before the coming of the Spirit. Prayer is a request to obtain the Spirit. Salvation is offered in the name of Jesus Christ. The role of the Spirit, certainly indispensible to the Church, is more limited: it allows the Church to receive messages from God and to transmit the gospel with *παρρησία* [**47**]. The Spirit is therefore not necessary for salvation. It is a fortunate comple-ment to supererogatory acts. We can wonder if this restrictive conception of *πνεῦμα*, faithful without doubt to the letter of the Lucan work, corresponds to its spirit.

The sixth and last part deals with "The Reception of the Spirit". Conscious of the variety of texts, Schweizer thinks as a general rule, that the Spirit is received at baptism, but that Luke considers conversion, expressed in prayer, more important than baptism in provoking the Spirit's advent. We think that Luke would have rejected this alternative.

J. H. E. Hull (-> 1967)

e. J. H. E. Hull's book interests and irritates at the same time. It interests by the clear questions that it poses to the Lucan work, and often, the solutions marked by faith, offered. It irritates for two main reasons. Instead of delivering as the title promises, a pneumatology of Acts, it often proposes a description of what the Spirit's activity was in the nascent Church: parting from the con - viction that Luke is more historian than theologian Hull pays more attention to history, which he believes he is able to reconstruct from the texts which we have in hand. Thus the Lucan specificity is sometimes hidden behind harmonizing constructions. Furthermore, the author does not really enter into dialogue with contemporary exegesis: he ignores certain important contributions, like von Baer's book and in those which he knows he often retains only what pleases him [**48**]

The work is divided into six chapters: 1) The Promise of the Spirit. 2) The Expectation of the Spirit. 3) The Promise Fulfilled. 4) The Later Dispensations of the Spirit. 5) The Meaning of the Gift. 6) Several Conclusions. The author thus follows the un - folding of the work of Luke, which corresponds to the historical succession for him, before investigating the nature of the Spirit.

In Hull's opinion, while alive, Jesus spoke rarely of the Spirit. He only did it when constrained to by his adversaries [**49**]. The early Church, on the contrary, does not hesitate to speak of the Spirit which it received. This difference appears in the dispro - portion of the references to the Holy Spirit in the third Gospel and the Acts. Hull explains this surprising fact in the following manner: the teaching of Jesus concerning the Spirit, inspite of the Gospel of John which situates it at the last supper, was dispensed to the apostles during the period which separates the resurrection and the Ascension (p. 40) **[50]**. This is summarily the first chapter.

The second, consecrated on the period mentioned above, analyzes the end of the Gospel and the beginning of Acts. According to Hull, at this time, the Risen One gives his teaching concerning the Holy Spirit: this Spirit will fulfill a quadruple mission. Perfecting the baptism of John, he will regenerate men, create a community, serve as a sign of the new times and finally, permit an effective witness of the Christ. These four elements which are found throughout the Acts, originate in the teaching of the Resurrected One. The author believes he can affirm this by an analysis of Act 1:4f. which sets forth the first three elements and Act 1:8 which gives the last **[51]**. The baptism of John implied the renewal of the person, the constitution of a community and the signaling of the new age. The baptism of the Spirit, placed in parallel here by the Risen Jesus, contains these three elements. Moreover, in Act 1:8, the Resurrected Lord draws the reception of the Spirit near to the proclamation of the word .

We wonder if Luke's intention is well presented in this way. We prefer to say that Luke insists on the promise of the outpouring. He does not wish to affirm that the Resurrected Lord taught concerning the Spirit. The mention of the logion concerning the baptism of the Spirit does not indicate that the Spirit renews man, but anounces that the baptism of the Spirit will be administered: *οὐ μετὰ πολλὰς ταύτας ἡμέρας* (Act 1:5).

This chapter has, nonetheless, the quality of bringing to light a curious fact: in the Acts, Luke describes a community determined by Holy Spirit which the Jesus of the third Gospel had promised without precision. Does Luke think that every reader of the OT knows what the Holy Spirit is? Or is his Church so charismatic that no definition of the Spirit was necessary? Luke 24:49, which does not refer directly to the Spirit but to the promise, furnishes the answer: for Luke, the Spirit was promised in the OT. Jesus serves as relay: he reiterates the promise and specifies the date of its fulfillment. Moreover, he dares to link this Spirit to his own person. The Spirit, that he will offer himself, will come on Pentecost. The teaching on the Holy Spirit, according to Luke, goes back more to the OT than to Jesus.

In chapter 3, Hull analyzes the Pentecost account. This Jewish feast, which he gives the sense, offers a providential occasion for the largest possible number of Jews from the entire world to become aware of the coming of the Spirit (p. 56). He then studies the signs of the presence of the Spirit (noise, fire, tongues). If these images originate in the OT or with John the Baptist, it would be wrong to deny the objectivity of what happened: the coming of the Spirit upon man is a supernatural experience; he who has received it cannot doubt. The signs serve to describe the indescribable (p. 59). Hull discovers in what follows in ch. 2 of Acts, the effects of the outpouring of the Spirit: Jesus predicted the four repercussions mentioned above. Finally, to reconcile the Johanine and Lucan traditions, the author proposes the following: the disciples received the Spirit at Easter, but they realized it only at Pentecost. The author does not tell us how he reconciles this harmonizing solution with his thesis of the pneumatic experience which cannot be doubted!

Chapter 4 analyzes the later dispensations of the Spirit in the Acts. He says first of all - and he is exact - that Luke does not tell us what are the conditions a man must fulfill to receive the Spirit. If Act 2:38f. indicates conversion and baptism as the normal conditions, there are exceptions to this rule, as we know. Hull esteems that conversion and faith are the conditions sine qua non. Baptism and the imposition of hands as such do not confer the Spirit.

This interpretation , which neglects the direct link that Luke establishes between the laying on of hands and the outpouring of the Spirit, gets bogged down in speculation when the author explains that Luke does not impose baptism as a condition to the reception of the Spirit, but the disposition of the man to be baptized! The conditions would be three in number: repentence, faith, and a disposition to baptism [52]. This arbitrary solution permits Hull to affirm that there is no "inconsistency" between the cases where the Spirit is offered before and after baptism (p. 98). We are not surprised when the author says, after Protestant fashion, that the imposition of hands was only a prayer to receive the Holy Spirit [53]. He adds that often in Acts, what Luke calls the coming of the Spirit is only the outward and visible manifestation of the Spirit. The laying on of hands provides only supplementary charisms.

At the end of the chapter, Hull thinks he is able to show that, in the Church, the Holy Spirit is a permanent gift and not a pro - visional loan. Admitting that the Acts sees the Spirit sometimes animistically as a personal being and sometimes in a dynamistic manner as an impersonal fluid, the author thinks that the spe - cifically Lucan conception is one of a force given to all believers in a permanent way **[54]**.

The Holy Spirit is a power which empowers the Christian to preach with effectiveness, accomplish miracles and become like Christ. This is the content of the fifth chapter.

The Holy Spirit permits the apostles to centralize their preaching on the Christ. They do not forget the Spirit in their sermons: it is he who inspires the Scriptures, anointed Jesus, and became the sign of the present glory of Christ. He now illuminates believers in their reading of the OT (p. 131).

Hull's expression "The Spirit gives the power to become like Christ" is certainly not Lucan, But the conviction that the Spirit influences the ethic of the believer, corresponds, despite Schweizer, to the Evangelist's intention. If the apostles display *παρρησία* (Act 2:29), if Stephen is filled with wisdom (Act 6:10), if the disciples believe (Act 6:5 and 11:24) **[55]**, if the community lives in joy (Act 13:52), it is because the Spirit is at work in the Church.

Hull then attacks all interpretations which conceive of the Spirit as an impersonal force. The Spirit in the Acts is also a person who intervenes and gives orders. He could have, with the fathers, cited the texts of Acts, 10:19f. for example, where the Holy Spirit seems to intervene in as personal way as the Christ **[56]**.

The author finally sets forth the role of the Spirit in ecclesiastic decisions: the Spirit indicates those the Church can accept into its circle. He also chooses the ministers of the Church (Act 13:2 and 20:28) and inspires the decisions that the ecclesiastical authorities must make (Act 15:28) **[57]**.

In his conclusion in chapter 6, Hull, first of all, makes himself Luke's apologist. Inspite of his disparagers, the Spirit in Luke is not only the originator of the ecstatic phenomena; he is no longer an occasional loan or a force solely impersonal. He is an objective, personal, permanent and ethical reality. The reproaches made against Luke neither consider the literary genre of the work, a historical account, nor Luke's underdeveloped theology (or rather developing). As a theologian, Luke has but two things to say: the Spirit is at work in the evangelization of the world and in the edification of the Church [58].

Conclusion

After this survey, we would like to first note the results which seem the most solidly buttressed, make a few remarks about the present state of research and suggest several tasks for the future.

1) The relations which Luke establishes between the Holy Spirit and salvation history are clear: after Pentecost, all believers receive a gift which in the OT had only touched a few prophets and then during the second stage of salvation history was centered on Jesus alone.

2) The pre-Easter Jesus lived in a relationship with the Holy Spirit that the disciples will never know. He alone was conceived by the Holy Spirit: Luke wants this distinction to be clear.

3) Despite the outpouring of the Spirit on all believers, who are then indelibly marked, this divine force can still arise from time to time with a precise and particular goal, which is most often prophetic.

4) The Holy Spirit is not an impersonal power for Luke; he gains a personal stature comparable to God or Christ.

5) The links between the exalted Christ and the Spirit are difficult to determine. The Spirit appears frequently distinct from the Risen One (cf. the Pentecost narrative where Luke does not explicate that the Risen Lord sends the Spirit himself; cf. Kilpatrick's philological statement in note 78). However, Luke knows that the risen Christ in the place of God will pour out the Spirit and that this outpouring will be conditioned by the exaltation (cf. Lk 24:45 and Act 2:33).

6) Like the Word, the Spirit is independent of man and earthly contingencies. Yet, he appears here and there dangerously at the disposition of the apostles.

Exegetes have come to these conclusions, because they have known how, for twenty years or so, to delimit and discern the specific character of each NT author. The literary analysis of Lucan redaction, set forth by von Baer already in 1926, favorized the study of the theology of the third Evangelist.

Nonetheless, as the section on Pentecost will show, the embarrassment of the exegetes arises, when they seek to determine the historical origin of Christian pneumatism, and more precisely Luke's. The study of ancient Judaism, particularly the targumim, forces the scholar to relativize the influence, accepted until now by so many, of Greek spiritualism on the esctastic phenomena described in Luke. But other writings, much more Jewish than Luke, ignore such dispensations of the Spirit. Could it be that Luke is marked - oh the irony! - by a Jewish apocalyptic tendency? Our chapter consecrated to Christology has already provided a few indications in this direction. Briefly, if the OT has made its mark on Lucan pneumatology, the task is now to find out how this influence was transmitted and to examine the possibility of other contributions, especially Greek.

Further doubts arise when reading our last section, centered on the imposition of hands. Where must Luke's thought be placed in the evolution of the Christian doctrine of the ministry and sacraments? Certain elements make us place Luke in the protoCatholic era, such as the tendency to intrust the Holy Spirit to the apostles. Then others invite us to project Lucan thought into an earlier period, for example, the lack of rigor which Luke manifests in his sacramental vocabulary and the lordly freedom which the Spirit enjoys in his thought.

In conclusion we think that the philological, literary and theological exegesis of Lk-Act has given all it could offer. Real progress will not be made until two tasks have been accom - plished. The first is to specify with all the precision necessary the original environment and nature of the traditions which influenced Luke and the second is to determine where Luke fits in (at the intersection of the Synoptic tradition and Pauline theology?) and the conditions which provoked the writing of his work (was it an anti-gnostic polemic? or anti-Jewish one? or internal ecclesiastical quarrels? or the weakening of the initial enthusiasm?).

II. THE PENTECOST ACCOUNT

N. Adler (-> 1938)

a. Here, it is suitable to begin with N. Adler's monograph. After summarizing the interpretation of the text throughout the ages, the author presents and criticizes the position of the literary critics who distinguish, in Act 2:1-13, the presence of two sources, one which describes a glossolalia and another younger one a "xenolalia" **[59]**. He maintains himself the unity of the narrative constructed in two symmetrical parts, one calling upon audition and the other, sight (vss. 1-4 and 5-13: each part contains an introduction, the main event and the mention of the effects of the event). A comparison of the vocabulary and style show the Lucan origin of the account. What had been called doublets, e.g. vss. 7 and 12, are in fact not. Therefore, the existence of written sources which Luke used can be shown,.

Secondly, Adler rejects all foreign influence on the composition of Luke: the rabbinic legend, which tells the story of the outpouring of the law of God in seventy languages on Mount Sinai, is too late to have influenced Luke **[60]**; the text of Philo often evoked is too different from Luke's to have influenced its elaboration.

A third negative conclusion is that Form criticism does not permit us to imagine what the oral preliterary stage of the narrative was like.

Eventhough the conclusions of this investigation are negative **[61]**, they at least are to be admired for having sent exegetes back to the text and to Luke's theology **[62]**. We will realize this in reading E. Lohse's article.

E. Lohse (-> 1953)

b. Having enumerated the problems raised by this pericope **[63]**, Lohse takes up Adler's negative conclusion. Against the Literary critics, he also refuses a dissection of the text and differing from the Religionsgeschichtler, he rejects the parallels with Philo and the rabbis **[64]**. After this, he is ready to study the text, himself and to ask the proper question: what did Luke, the author of the Acts, want to express by this account of the story of Pentecost (p. 430)?

Luke's intention seems to have been double. On the one hand, with the expression "when the day of Pentecost came" (2:1), parallel to Lk 9:51 ("when the time of his *ἀνάλημψις* came"), Luke wants to signal the beginning of a new stage in redemptive history. The time which begins is the one the Christ announced in Act 1:8 ("you will receive the power of the Holy Spirit who will come upon you"). Thus, Luke's perspective is salvation historical.

Furthermore, the second part of the promise of the Resurrected Lord is fulfilled, too: "you will be my witnesses in Jerusalem, in all Judea and Samaria, and to ends of the earth" (Act 1:8). The Spirit, distributed at Pentecost, will allow the missionary proclamation and the constitution of an eschatological people. The list of peoples is explained by this universalistic perspective of Luke's theology. According to his theological project, Luke ends chapter 2 of Acts with a description of the life in this 'latter days' community (2:42-47) [**65**]. The account of Pentecost serves as the monu-mental gateway to the story of the Church [66].

G. Kretschmar (-> 1954-1955)

c. The historical study of Kretschmar has theological implica - tions which interest our subject. It concerns an analysis of the origins of the Ascension and Christian Pentecost. At the begin - ning, the following declaration is made: despite the indications in Act 1:3 (forty days) and 2:1 (on the fiftieth day, the outpouring of the Spirit), certain eastern churches in antiquity celebrated the Ascension on the fiftieth day after Easter. To explain this fact, one must imagine a Christian Pentecost which primitively celebrated the Ascension and the gift of the Spirit at the same time. Moreover, divers NT texts bring the Ascension and the gift of the Spirit close together: Jn 20, Eph 4:7-12 (where, one must admit, the word *πνεῦμα* is lacking) and Act 2:33. The hypothesis of an ancient tradition according to which the Spirit is the gift God through the Son makes to his Church [**67**] is not unlikely. This perspective would be more ecclesiastic than missionary: Christ transfers his power to the twelve disciples. This tradition is distinguished from the appearance accounts where the perspective is cosmic and where the Spirit remains absent. It must be Palestinian for several reasons: particularly, the quotation of Ps 68:19 in Eph 4 originates from a Jewish interpretation and not from the Hebrew or the LXX. This Christian tradition goes back, no doubt, to a Jewish interpretation: only from the second century of our era, does the rabbinic literature establish a relation between Pentecost and the gift of the Law at Sinai; while certain sectarian milieus, like those of the book of **Jubilees** and perhaps the writings from Qumran, seem to have linked them earlier. In these writings, earlier than Christianity, Pentecost has lost its agrarian attraction and has taken on a second historical signification: it recalls the covenant concluded at Sinai and the gift of the Law. A Jewish influence on the Christian conception of the Ascension is even confirmed by iconography: in the oldest representations of the Ascension, Christ resembles Moses. He has a scroll in his left hand which recalls the Torah. Several details do not come from

Acts but from the Jewish interpretation of the Sinai event (p. 218) [68]. Thus in the early Palestinian Church the Ascension was celebrated on the day of Pentecost [69].

The account of Pentecost (Act 2:1-13) has several points in common with this tradition: the gift of the Spirit at Jerusalem (the typology of Zion-Sinai is not unknown) and the "people of God" outlook. Two traits distinguish it, however: the Ascension is not the topic and it is not said that the Spirit comes from the Christ.

Yet, Luke's narrative has a story. Inspite of the important redactional contribution, Kretschmar thinks we can recover a primitive account, where the miracle of foreign languages was the center: as in Jn 20, the Spirit does not provoke any ecstatic aspects. He descends on the Twelve. Because the link between the Spirit and mission cannot go back to the origins of the Church, Kretschmar imagines that the primitive version of the account had no connection with the mission: it referred to an outpouring of the Spirit which transmitted the total power of the Risen Lord to the Twelve.

This original account would not be without relation with the Jewish tradition of Sinai: Kretschmar notes in priority the link between Pentecost and the Holy Spirit (the date would be therefore traditional).

According to the author, the primitive narrative probably reflects a historical event: during the Jewish Pentecost which followed the first Christian Easter, an outpouring of the Spirit, marking the eschatological renewal of the Covenant, would have only happened when Christ was taken up into the sky. Three reasons militate in favor of this idea: 1) this explains the fact that the Jewish feast of Pentecost was taken over by the Christian Church, while the feast of Tabernacles, for example, was not; 2) the relationships established between the first chapters of Acts and the texts of Qumran favor this hypothesis; 3) the appearances in Galilee and the life of the nascent Church in Jerusalem are explained: the first Christians went up to Jerusalem for the Jewish Pentecost [70], to participate in the accomplishment of the new covenant on Mount Zion (the antitype of Sinai).

Before coming down to Luke, the account would have under - gone a first rereading in Antioch: still in the flow of the Jewish interpretation of the gift of the Law, the perspective would have become universalistic: the divine voices, in the form of tongues, related, despite Adler, to those in Ex 19:16 and 20:18 [71], would have evoked the languages of different peoples God wanted to integrate, henceforth, into his covenant [72].

Luke's contribution is twofold: by the context in which the story is situated, Luke insists on the gift of the Spirit to the whole Church and not to the Twelve alone. With the citation from Joel and several modifications in the narrative, he underlines the ecstasy provoked by the presence of the Spirit (p. 247). He particularly resorted to a scholarly polysemia in the use of the word *γλῶσσα* (tongue): the prophecy of Joel is accomplished, glossolalia appears, the foreign languages are mastered for the mission (p. 234f.).

This prehistoric reconstruction of Act 2:1-13 shocks our practice: it situates glossolalia at a posterior level to the gift of tongues. It offers much to tradition and, despite the author's claim, little to redaction.

From our point of view, we would like to retain the following positive elements: the polysemia as a literary technique of Luke is a useful operating concept [73]. The ambiguities and implications, which escape the unbelieving reader of Acts, could also seduce and edify the Christian reader (like the term *γλῶσσα*). Moreover, the links the author establishes between Act 2 and the old Pentecostal tradition seem valid: they permit a more assured religionsgeschichtlich insertion than the efforts of the beginning of the century: the first Pentecost would have thus been tied to the establishment of the New Covenant [75]. The presence of the eschatological people of the Covenant in chapter 2 could confirm this idea. That the Spirit was not linked to the mission in the tradition, but rather to the transmission of a power to the Twelve is not unlikely either. Finally, the date of Pentecost could well be traditional.

On other points Kretschmar is less convincing: his reconstruction of the prehistory of Act 2 seems improbable. Without going further than Haenchen in his commentary [76], we think that Luke's part in the elaboration of the account is more important that Kretschmar admits. It is probable that the universalisitic aspect of the text comes from the author of Acts rather than from an Antiochean milieu. Furthermore, we could imagine that Luke desintegrated - to make a succession of the events - a traditional unity which had combined the Ascension and the gift of the Spirit as Act 2:33 suggests. Moreover, it highly improbable that the allusions to glossolalia come from Luke. Kretschmar, moreover, does not explain why the Evangelist situated the Ascension on the fortieth day. In compensation, he must be right, against Haenchen, to consider the date of Pentecost as a traditional element [77].

E. Haenchen (-> 1956) **[78]**

d. The way Haenchen explains the genesis of Act 2:1-13 is typical of the method he uses to specify Luke's intentions and manners. It is also characteristic of the scarcity of traditions which the German exegete discovers behind the Lucan work.

Luke wants to describe, according to Haenchen, one of the most important events which has happened since Jesus' depar - ture: the coming of the Spirit. This description must be easily perceptible and intelligible. In order to compose it, Luke disposes of no ancient tradition, as the sole account of an outpouring of the Spirit in the Gospels, Jn 20:22, proves. Since he took up the notion of the forty days from tradition, he simply situates the coming of the Holy Spirit at the next feast day, Pentecost.

To describe the Spirit, who comes from heaven, he naturally turns to the image of the wind. To explain how the Spirit effects the disciples, Luke takes up the Jewish Pentecostal tradition. Haenchen does not doubt the great age of the latter: from where the flames of fire and tongues come. Luke's taking over, however, is not mechanical: Luke excludes the idea of a new law and enlarges the gift of the Spirit to all the faithful.

Luke could have insisted on the story of the Tower of Babel, antithetical parallel of the Pentecost account, but he does not; the history of the Christian mission forbids him to speak of the unity of humanity as yet. Therefore, the Jews alone can witness this first Christian Pentecost. The spectators are Jewish: it is not even the pilgrims but the Jews of the Diaspora established in Jerusalem. The list of the countries of origin of these Jews allows Luke to express the objectivity of the outpouring of the Spirit.

The author of Acts does not indicate the content of this speaking in tongues, because he reserves for Peter the honor of the first Christian proclamation. He resorted to the phenomenon of glossolalia which permits him to establish two stages: the glossolalia which arouses embarrassment will be followed by a predication which provokes conversion.

Haenchen is to be admired for having attempted to explain the genesis of this narrative, located at the level of Luke's conscience. We can, however, raise a few questions: Did Luke reflect as logically as Haenchen suggests? Furthermore, if Luke tells of one of the most important events which happened since Jesus' departure, it is because he knows this story. To be transmitted it must have been recounted. And we do not tell a story without describing: an elaborate tradition, influenced by the Jewish Pentecost, must have existed. It must have told of the first outpouring of the Spirit. Glossolalia must have played a role, as well as the wind and flames. The role of Luke who must have been more limited on the literary level than Haenchen believes, was more important on the theological level. With scholarly ambiguity, Luke succeeds in making an allusion to the universality of the Christian mission and Church [78].

P. Brunner (-> 1967)

e. Frequently historically shaky, the interventions of Systematic theologians into the biblical sciences, are almost always stimulating. Such is the case with the analysis of P. Brunner.

Brunner first of all notes that different from the work of Christ, the gift of the Spirit is reiterated. After this he insists on the dogmatic importance of the first of the outpourings (p. 233). This first manifestation of the Spirit marks a passage, the passage from the Old to the New Testament. It also expresses a beginning. From this first gift, the Church, the people of God, is constituted. We would suppress the Church and the eschatological newness, if we denied the historical event which is this first gift.

To say that there is a first dispensation of the Spirit, is to say as well that there is a date. The date is far from being without importance. The one proposed by Luke merits our confidence [79]. The dogmatic impact is not only in the exactitude of the date given by Luke, but in that only one date is proposed (p. 237).

This date is related to a place: Jerusalem, thus, plays a dogmatic role.

What happened? Here, the difficulties come forth, for from the interventions of God in history, we can note only the exterior aspects (Aussenseiten). In the case of Pentecost, the important tangible consequences are the proclamation of the Christ, his death and resurrection and the constitution of a community. But these are not all the repercussions. Were there more immediate manifestations? There were, no doubt, but the gift of the Spirit can only have as Aussenseite an Innenseite, an interior event. Outwardly, the spectator can only speak of the ecstasy or glossolalia (p. 238).

Other aspects signaled by Luke, the wind and flames, incite Brunner to speak of a 'Pneumatophany'.

Brunner summarizes the kerygmatic content of the Pentecost story: God intervenes extra nos. He gives signs which point to the Spirit. The Spirit is received by all the disciples. The Spirit creates a new word, which is the praise of God for his merciful acts. The promises are fulfilled: a new people is constituted. The proclamation begins.

These primitive traits have been taken over by Luke and stylized in an intelligent movement of faith. The Evangelist transformed, for example, glossolalia into speaking in foreign languages. Moreover, he understood that Pentecost marks the foundation of the Church, the beginning of the Mission and the departure point of the Christian cult [**80**].

J. Potin (-> 1971)

f. A recent book allows us to continue this presentation of the Pentecost account. It analyzes afresh the origins of the Jewish feast of Pentecost and its evolution. With an impressive study of the most ancient targumim, Potin points out the influence of the Sinai tradition on the progressive historicization of the feast. He concludes that if the Pharisaism of the second century accentu - ated in a characteristic manner, the theme of the gift of the Law, Judaism contemporary with the apostles, especially Essene Judaism, emphasized the theme of the renewal of the covenant. The Jewish exegesis of Sinai, therefore, influenced the Jewish Pentecost and then the Christian one: in a theophany, God as - sociates himself to his regenerate people. As Act 2 unfolds with a ideal portrayal of the community of the new covenant, this exe - getical influence is confirmed.

Why in Act 2 Luke insists on the Spirit rather than the Word remains to explained. Certainly, the two realities went together in Judaism, but texts relative to the outpouring of the Spirit, like Num 11 and Joel 3, no doubt marked the eschatological reflection of the first Christians as well.

J. Kremer (-> 1973)

g. J. Kremer's work wants to be an essay on the interpretation of the Pentecost narrative which corresponds to the actual state of affairs (p. 5). It opens with a presentation of the Jewish feast of Pentecost (chapter one) and an analysis of the first Christian experiences of the Spirit (chapter two). Since Jewish hope expected for the end of time an outpouring of the Spirit on the Messiah and the people, the first Christians, persuaded in having found the Messiah, could resort to the category of the Holy Spirit.

The third chapter constitutes the major part of the book and is subdivided into three: first, the author analyzes the text of Act 2:1-13 in a sober and profound manner. He starts withvss. 1-4 which contain an ancient tradition (vss. 2 and 3 are reminiscent of the accounts of theophanies and apocalypses; vs. 4 is the most important). This tradition brings two historical elements to the verifiable origins: the presence of Jesus' disciples united at Jerusalem and a speaking in foreign languages (as we can see, Kremer refuses to see in the "foreign tongues", a redactional rereading of glossolalia. The other elements of the account are not historical , but express a certain biblical and metaphorical faith (p. 126).

Verses 5-13, editorial, report the effect which Pentecost produces on the Jewish pilgrims present in Jerusalem. Verse 6 and 7a fulfill the function of Chorschluss of the evangelical narratives (but - we ask - should not this literary element be traditional if we want to maintain the unity of the primitive literary genre?). Verses 7b-11 explain vs. 6 in a long period. Luke inserts the famous list of peoples at vss. 9-11. Verses 12 and 13, which could follow vs. 6 immediately, repeat in another manner the astonishment of the spectators. In fact, vss. 5-13 do not explain the phenomena noted in vss. 1-4. They do not accord any importance to tongues (p. 165) - an affirmation which seems disputable to us. What interests Luke is that the message of the Galileans, the disciples of Jesus, is understood by the Jews, come from all over.

Secondly, the writer illuminates the account in Act 2 with other Lucan texts. The result of these comparisons is, what is important for Luke, less the date of Pentecost than a heilsgeschichtlich beginning, the *ἀρχή* to which Luke often refers (cf. Act 11:15 etc.). Another important conclusion in our opinion, is that Luke tends to materialize the intervention of the Spirit without renouncing his understanding that these formulations are typical of a metaphorical approach. On this, he does not sense the alternative, that we set forward between metaphor and reality.

Finally, in a third step, Kremer thinks an influence of the Sinai tradition on the Pentecost account is likely.

In its richness, this work, which uses a linguistic, historical and theological method, marks an important step in the research of the Holy Spirit in Luke's writings.

III. THE HOLY SPIRIT AND THE LAYING ON OF HANDS

a. The affinities which unite the Holy Spirit to baptism and the imposition of hands have been analyzed many times. Yet we doubt that the debates of the last few years have made much progress toward understanding Lucan theology on this point. Two reasons help to explain this failure: first, the obscurities of the Lucan work and second, the confessional allegiance of the exegetes. Contrary to what G. B. Caird [**81**] recommends, we must not neglect the controversies of late antiquity concerning the sacraments: for the history of the effects of a text, the Wirkungsgeschichte can help to understand it better.

It is not unfruitful to recall the premises of the problem, and the texts cited in the dispute. In Act 2:38, Peter exhorts the audience at Pentecost : "Repent and each one of you be baptized in the name of Jesus Christ for the forgiveness of your sins; and you will receive the gift of the Holy Spirit." In Act 5:3 and 8, Peter rebukes Ananias for having lied to the Holy Spirit, and Sapphira for having tempted the Holy Spirit. These declarations strike the couple down. In Act 8:14-17, the apostles, Peter and John, go to Samaria where Philip has preached. "They arrived to where the Samaritans were, prayed for them, so that they could receive the Holy Spirit. For he had not yet descenced on any of them: they had only been baptized in the name of the Lord Jesus. When Peter and John laid hands on them they received the Spirit." In Act 8:18-20, "when Simon [the magician, who had believed and had been baptized, Act 8:13] saw that the Holy Spirit was given by the laying on of hands of the apostles, he offered them money." He desired to be able to lay hands on and so, transmit the Spirit. Peter condemns him for wanting to buy the "gift of God" and calls him to repent. In Act 9:17, the Lord appears to Ananias, a Christian in Damascus, and sends him to seek for Saul who has just been converted. "Ananias went out; and when he arrived at the house, he laid hands on Saul, saying, 'Saul, my brother, the Lord Jesus who appeared to you on the road which you were taking, sent me so that you might recover your sight and be filled with the Holy Spirit'. In the same instant, the scales fell from his eyes and he recovered his sight. He got up and was baptized." In Act 10:44; the Holy Spirit "falls" on Cornelius and his household in the middle of the sermon of Peter, who then exclaims, "Can we refuse the water of baptism to those who have received the Holy Spirit like us?" (Act 10:47). A bit later, in Jerusalem, Peter defends what he has just done: he leans on the words of Jesus "John baptized with water, but you will be baptized in the Holy Spirit." (Act 11:16). In Act 13, during a service, the Holy Spirit intervenes and demands that Barnabas and Saul be set aside for the mission. "So after having fasted and prayed, they laid hands on them and let them leave." (Act 13:3). Finally, after the episode of Apollos (Act 18:24-28), Paul meets the mysterious "disciples" at Ephesus and asks them, "Did you receive the Holy Spirit when you believed? And they answer him, 'We have not even heard that there was a Holy Spirit.'" (Act 19:2). After declaring that they had received only John's baptism, Paul teaches them John the Baptist's function in salvation history. "With these words, they were baptized in the name of the Lord Jesus. When Paul had laid hands on them, the Holy Spirit came upon them and they spoke in other tongues and prophesied." (Act 19:5f.).

In reading these texts, we note that Luke established a link between the outpouring of the Holy Spirit and certain human rites. However, if these links appear certain, they are never explained. So the problems, we know: does the baptism confer the Holy Spirit? Or is it the laying on of hands? Or is the laying on of hands more a human affirmation than a divine intervention? Is it necessary to be an apostle or minister to administer these rites?

H. von Baer (-> 1926)

b. In pp. 169-182 of his book, von Baer treats the problems which presently preoccupy us. He thinks that the event of Pentecost modified in an instant the baptism of John: Christian baptism appeared immediately as a baptism of the Spirit accom - panied by a baptism of water in the name of Jesus. The free outpouring of the Spirit, which was not related exclusively to the baptismal rite or the laying on of hands, preceded the rite historically.

Nonetheless, from the beginnings, believers felt that a relationship existed between the gift of the Spirit and the act of initiation. This was an empirical establishment and not a theoretical reflection. This is why, they associated the gift of the Spirit and the regeneration of the believer, in general, with the act of baptism and the laying on of hands.

As always, when we begin with practical experience, excep - tions exist: some became conscious of the Holy Spirit before baptism and others after. For von Baer, Act 2:38 would be the general rule and Act 8 and 10, the exceptions. The Acts would then reflect the practice and thought of the first Christians.

N. Adler (-> 1951)

c. After his book on Pentecost, Adler wrote a second work, on Act 8. After a brief history of the interpretation of this text, the author defends the unity of the pericope and its Lucan character: vss. 14-17 do not constitute a secondary addition. He also shows that, from a theological point of view, the Samaritan adventure is not exceptional, since baptism does not offer the totality of the Holy Spirit to the believer. According to Luke, it is necessary for an apostle to come and confirm the baptized by laying hands on him. Only at this moment, the fullness of the Spirit rests on him. This imposition of hands confers the Holy Spirit. If Peter and John came to Samaria, it was to see that what Philip had done was according to the plan of God and to establish a relation with the mother Church in Jerusalem. After having verified that the Holy Spirit had not yet descended upon the Samaritan converts, they first prayed and then laid hands on them. Slightly neglecting the role of this prayer, Adler insists particularly on the effectiveness of the imposition of hands which truly transmits the Spirit. It is not to be deduced from this action that man can magically transmit the Holy Spirit, for it is God who gives it by the intermediary of men that he has chosen for this purpose. Adler remarks that Luke seems to restrict the laying on of hands to superiors, while baptism can be done by lower ministers. The Spirit received by the Samaritans was not only an outpouring of supplementary charisms, but the Holy Spirit himself in his fullness.

This solution to the problem is faithful, as we can see, to the Catholic theology of baptism and confirmation **[82]**. It also corresponds to Lucan doctrine in many areas, except that Luke does not distinguish two manifestations of the Spirit, the one, elementary, and the other, perfect, at the imposition of hands. Luke seems to relate the total gift of the Spirit to the imposition of hands. Furthermore, it seems to us that normally for Luke baptism with water in the name of Jesus, with a view to forgiveness, and the imposition of hands do not form two acts, two sacraments, as Catholic theology would like, but a unique rite of initiation into the community.

E. Käsemann (-> 1952)

d. Käsemann's position can be defined in the following manner: the anomalies in Act 8 and 19 do not reflect historical recollections but rather theological redactional preoccupations. Taken up in conflicts with heresy, Luke chooses the way of Frühkatholizismus [**83**]. He makes the Hellenists' mission, to the Samaritans, submissive to apostolic authority. Peter and John's imposition of hands in Samaria as well as Paul's in Ephesus are the literary and redactional indication of this theological option.

If Luke is constrained to separate baptism from the gift of the Spirit from time to time, it is not that he is innovating a sacramental theology. He is guided by a certain doctrine of the Church: the Una sancta catholica centered in Jerusalem and directed by the Twelve.

Käsemann does not explain clearly the signification of this imposition of hands. He speaks sometimes of an apostolic blessing (p. 166) [**84**], and sometimes of the transmission of the Spirit (p. 163). He seems to be torn between the presupposition that baptism and the Spirit are always tied together in early Christianity and the reality of the Lucan texts which sometimes separate them.

In a certain measure, Käsemann's position is neighbor to Adler's: 1) despite the connections which unite the Spirit and the laying on of hands, Luke does not completely detach the out - pouring of the Spirit from baptism; 2) the imposition of hands, reserved for the apostles, is a mark of the centralizing authority of the hierarchy. However, he deviates from Adler in three points: 1) Luke's intention is more ecclesiological than sacramental; 2) the Lucan position is an innovation in the sense of Frühkatholizismus and not a traditional doctrine resting on historical facts; 3) this position must be corrected and criticized by older theologies, like Paul's, which were not yet tinted by catholicism [**85**].

Käsemann is to be praised for recognizing the exegetical weakness of traditional Protestant positions, like the one which conceives of the imposition of hands as a prayer to obtain supplementary charisms. Yet, he is, no doubt, wrong to conceive of Luke's ecclesiology as the one of Una sancta catholica with a centralized hierarchy. This is not yet the case with Luke, for the danger of heresies is less than has been said [**86**]. Luke is more concerned with a salvation history tied to Jerusalem than an actual unity of the Church [**87**]. Finally, it is not certain that Luke innovates. We know early Christianity too badly to say that Luke connects the gift of the Spirit to the imposition of hands because of an ecclesiological caprice with no sacramental importance. A Christian milieu could have existed where the gift of the Spirit was signified by the laying on of hands rather than by baptism.

G. W. H. Lampe (-> 1955, **J. E. L. Oulton** (-> 1954-1955), **G. B. Caird** (-> 1955)

e. In the same year, three British authors presented a Protestant solution to the problem at hand.

For Lampe, there is no doubt, Luke ties the gift of the Spirit to baptism. Act 2:38 would be the proof, as well as the parallel, established by Luke between the baptism of Jesus and the baptism of believers (p. 197f.). Yet, this Holy Spirit does not manifest himself always in an ecstatic form. This explains why Luke does not always mention the descent of the Spirit on the baptized. The mention of joy which fills certain newly baptized could suggest the presence of the Spirit (e.g. in the case of the Ethiopian eunuch and the Philippian jailer in Act 8 and 16).

How can one explain the three cases where the Holy Spirit is linked with the laying on of hands (the Samaritans, Paul and the Ephesian disciples? Lampe refuses to see here a confirmation in the later sense of the term (p. 199). It is unlikely that a rite of imposition of hands was administered regularly at baptism. "In the three cases, it is a special gift." (p. 199). In the case of the Samaritans, the apostles assure the converts of their belonging to the Church, inspite of the racial hindrances [**88**]; in the case of Paul, Ananias heals the apostle and transmits a power with a view to preaching; in the case of the Ephesian disciples, the laying on of hands provokes gifts of glossolalia and prophecy.

Oulton begins by noting the importance of the logion concerning the baptism of water and the baptism of the Spirit (Act 1:5; 11:16) which seems to tie the various parts of Acts together. After mentioning the main texts relative to the Holy Spirit in Acts, he presents a precise thesis [**89**]: the Holy Spirit normally comes to the believers at baptism and provokes an interior renewal which suscitates an exemplary communal life. One must distinguish this invisible gift and the visible manifestations of the Spirit which cease from the second half of the book of Acts on. These manifestations were necessary to put the mission in place. This is what happens three times in the first half of Acts, in order to overcome three obstacles: the first speaking in tongues (Act 2) takes place at the conception of the Christian community, issued from Judaism; the second at the admission of the Samaritans (Act 8); and the third when the Gentiles are accepted into the Church (Act 10).

The imposition of hands, mentioned in one of the cases (Act 8), did not provoke the habitual and invisible gift of the Holy Spirit, but rather an extraordinary dispensation. As Luke indicates, it was accompanied by a prayer. The laying on of hands, according to Oulton, does not transmit the Spirit ex opere operato, but it symbolizes the act of God which we ask for in prayer **[90]**.

Act 19:1-7 is not in contradiction with what preceded. As in Act 8, the visible manifestation of the Spirit provoked by the imposition of hands demonstrates that an irregularity has been committed. The laying on of hands offers only exterior signs of the Presence of the Spirit granted at baptism.

As for Act 6, it is an ordination by prayer and the imposition of hands, whereas in the case of Paul in Act 9, the laying on of hands is first linked to healing **[91]**.

The thesis is coherent and yet,we think that it does not correspond to the coherence of the Acts. In fact, Luke never affirms explicitly that baptism bestows the Spirit, while he does for the imposition of hands. Furthermore, when he speaks of the gift of the Spirit provoked by the laying on of hands, Luke is speaking of the Spirit and not of the exterior signs. Finally, if the Spirit plays an obvious role in the progressive expansion of the mission, he occupies a different place in the case of the Ephesian disciples, as Oulton has noticed. However, the author's explanation of Act 19 does not convince: for it is indeed the Spirit and not only spiritual charisms which the imposition of hands bestows.

Caird also accepts as a general rule thathe Spirit descends on the believer at baptism, but - this is his originality and the strength of his position - the baptismal rite included an imposition of handsrelated to the gift of the Spirit, as the case of Paul (Act 9) and the Ephesian disciples (Act 19) **[92]** show. This last part of thebaptismal act was not reserved for the apostles, thus for the hierarchy. If the apostles, Peter and John (Act 8), lay hands on in Samaria, exceptional reasons pushed them to do so **[93]**. It had to do with the success of the mission to the non-Jews and the unity of the Church. Luke is unaware of a ceremony of confirmation distinct from baptism, which only an apostle could celebrate.

E. Schweizer (-> 1959) **[94]**

f. According to Schweizer, Luke takes over, from the Christian tradition, the relation which unifies the Spirit and baptism. However, he gives more particular attention to the rite: without being a spiritualist attached to the baptism of the Spirit alone, he considers conversion, faith and prayer as the most important conditions for receiving the Holy Spirit. In any case, the Spirit remains free and can act independently of the sacrament.

The case of Act 8:14-17 does not permit us to detect a nascent catholicism. Luke's attention is given more to the relations with Jerusalem than to the respect of an ecclesiastic ordinance [95].

In conclusion here are several personal remarks:

1) It is to beg the question to claim that Luke, because he is a Christian, necessarily joins the Holy Spirit and baptism. Despite several authors, Act 2:38 does not impose this affirmation: Baptism has a explicit function: εἰς ἄφεσιν τῶν ἁμαρτιῶν ὑμῶν "for the forgiveness of your sins". The words "and you will receive the gift of the Holy Spirit" do not indicate that this happens necessarily at the baptism in water. The parallel of Jesus' baptism often invoked as support for the thesis criticized here, confirms, on the contrary, our position: Jesus is already baptized when during a prayer (note the difference in tenses: βαπτισθέντος in the aorist and προσευχομένου in the present), the Holy Spirit descends on him. The account of Jesus' baptism therefore distinguishes the baptism of water and the outpouring of the Spirit. It is the same for Christian baptism: the baptism of water is an effective sign of forgiveness and the invocation of the name; the laying on of hands, that of the gift of the Spirit: cf. Act 10: 47-48.

2) Luke affirms that the gift of the Spirit is related to prayer and the imposition of hands: They "prayed for them, so that they might receive the Holy Spirit" (Act 8:15); "So Peter and John laid hands on them and they received the Holy Spirit" (Act 8:17). "Paul having laid hands on them, the Holy Spirit came upon them" (Act 19:6). If Peter condemns Simon the magician, it is not because the former joined the gift of the Holy Spirit to the imposition of hands, but because he wanted to buy this power (Act 8:18-20). Ananias was sent to heal Paul and bestow the Spirit on him by laying on hands (Act 9:17).

3) Normally, water baptism in the name of Jesus for the forgiveness of sins and the imposition of hands for the outpouring of the Holy Spirit form two moments of one

ceremony. Vss. 5 and 6 of Act 19 reflect the general rule: "With these words, they were baptized in the name of Jesus. When Paul laid hands on them, the Holy Spirit came upon them..." (Act 19:5f.).

4) The imposition of hands is not always mentioned. It is not present in the case of the converts at Pentecost, Act 2:41, nor in the account of the Eunuch, Act 8:38 (several manuscripts however read in Act 8:39: "when they came out of the water, the Holy Spirit fell upon the Eunuch and the angel of the Lord took Philip away."). Is the verb "to baptize" to be taken in a wide sense (water baptism in the name of and the imposition of hands)?

5) It is not impossible that the laying on of hands was reserved for the leader of the community or an apostle (if one of the two was present). It is clear that Ananias is simply called disciple, but then the elders of the non-Jerusalemite communities do not appear until Act 14:23. It is significant that in ch. 19 (vss. 5-6) the active and personal form "Paul having laid hands on them" succeeds the impersonal passive "they were baptized in the name of the Lord Jesus."

6) What is related to the imposition of hands is not, as too many Protestants claim, the visible charisms of the Spirit, but the Holy Spirit himself. We must not presuppose a presence or activity of the Spirit before this imposition of hands.

7) Luke does not say that the laying on of hands transmits the Holy Spiritex opere operato. He takes the pain to say: a) the Holy Spirit is a gift of God (we cannot buy it) (Act 2:38; 8:20; 11:17); b) a prayer accompanies the imposition of hands to recall the divine origin of the outpouring of the Spirit (Act 8:15); c) the Holy Spirit remains free. He can transmit himself in other ways than the laying on of hands (Act 10:44).

The imposition of hands is more than a prayer or a symbol of the act of God in Zwingli's sense. Luke thinks - whether we call it naive or frühkatholisch - that God has intrusted a power to those who belong to him, i.e. those who live as servants of the word and not in an autonomous manner. They know this power can be transmitted to new converts when the latter have been baptized and received, after a prayer, the imposition of hands.

Different from certain contemporary theologians, Luke does not distinguish Spirit baptism which is the work of God, preceding or following man's action from water baptism, understood as a response or sign. He distinguishes two movements: the first is baptism, in which both collaborate and which offers forgiveness and the invocation of the name, and a second, the laying on of hands which triggers the outpouring of the Spirit.

8) It is proper to note the social character of the rites studied here. The imposition of hands, in particular, points out to the gathered assembly that a new member is henceforth integrated in the Church.

Conclusion

J. D. G. Dunn (-> 1975) considers Luke's work as a faithful reflection of the enthusiastic and inspired experience of the first Christians. S. Schulz (-> 1976) sees in the third Evangelist a typical witness to developing catholicism. We cannot follow one or the other.

In our opinion, Luke, like the author of 1 Peter, wants to conserve and transmit the Christian heritage in a living way. The Holy Spirit holds a double role in this operation: he was active in the origins; this must not be forgotten. Furthermore, he is at work in the transmission itself (Act 1:2), so that the heritage does not congeal. It is proper therefore to live in the Holy Spirit.

In the interpretation of the Scripture as in the transmission of the Word, the Spirit and Christ fulfill complementary and yet distinct functions. In the past the Christ explained the promises to his witnesses (Lk 24:27 and 44f.) and taught them the content of the message (beyond the Gospel, cf. Act 1:3). Today the Spirit inspires the preacher and interpreter (cf. the words "filled with the Spirit" which qualify the witnesses when they intervene: Act 4:8; 7:55).

Luke's historic enterprise is that of a Christian, a man particularly mindful of the presence of the Spirit. His project respects the double mission of the Spirit, mentioned above, in the measure that it remains voluntarily limited. Refusing to be the only Christian word of his time, or the only experience, he opts for a description from the outside: narrative, which leaves to others the task of proclaiming the kerygma and the care of describing the Spirit's activity within the believer.

When he evokes the Holy Spirit, Luke speaks from the observer's point of view. This exteriority has as its correlative the recollection of the past interventions of the Spirit. This excludes an enthusiastic intuition, but does not necessarily imply a proto-catholic conception. If Luke goes so far as to visualize the Spirit and by this "materialize" it, he neither inserts it into the sphere of creation nor submits it to ecclesiastic authority. He takes care to recall the divine origin and sovereign freedom: by calling it a gift (cf. Act 2:38; 8:20; 11:17) and by representing it as a person (cf. Act 10:19f.).

This exteriority also responds to other exigencies: a) apolo - getic, in that the Evangelist shows the world that Christians are not deprived of this divine presence so dear to the Greeks; b) catechetical, in that he popularizes an early Christian conviction: the activity of the Spirit in the communities in the last days.

While Paul thought of the role of the Spirit, Luke affirms and describes it. If the apostle envisaged the interior transformation of believers by the Spirit, Luke watches the *πνεῦμα* come to them. By doing this, he does not think he is unfaithful to his master: he accomplishes another task. In this effort which is of a literary order, he resorts to a historiographic model of the OT. Inspite of the visible character of the Spirit's interventions that this manner of writing implies, Luke, with Paul, refuses to place the Spirit in the forefront. It is the Word, stimulated and accompanied by the Spirit, which is the most important. The Book of the Acts does not recount the success of enthusiastic experiences, but the diffusion of the Word supported and followed by the offer of the Spirit. The issue is the growth of the Word (Act 6:7), and never that of the Spirit. It is the Name, confirmed by the kerygma, which saves (Act 4:12), and not the manifestation of the Spirit. Henceforth, it is not important that the Christian experience in its Lucan formulation does not have a particular character. The Acts do not primarily report the history of the Church (Conzelmann -> 1954) or the time of the Spirit (Bruce -> 1973). They narrate the diffusion of the Word. This conclusion strengthens the results of our first chapter: the insertion of salvation into history and the active presence of the Spirit here below, two of Luke's convictions, do not fit into the framework of a theology of glory.

CHAPTER 5

SALVATION

Chronological Bibliography

1938

A. WIKENHAUSER, **Die Apostelgeschichte übersetzt und erklärt** (Regensburg, 1938, 1951^{2}, 1956^{3}).

1939

J. GEWIESS, **Die urapostolische Heilsverkündigung nach der Apostelgeschichte** (Breslau, 1939).

1947

J. T. ROSS*, **The Conception of σωτηρία in the New Testament,** unpublished dissertation, University of Chicago (Chicago, 1947).

1953

J. A. T. ROBINSON, "The One Baptism As a Category of New Testament Soteriology", **ScotJT** 6 (1953) 257-274; included in J. A. T. Robinson, **Twelve New Testament Studies** (London, 1962), pp. 158-175.

1954

H. CONZELMANN, **Die Mitte der Zeit. Studien zur Theologie des Lukas** (Tübingen, 1954, 1957^{2}, 1960^{3}, to which we refer, 1962^{4}).

D. M. STANLEY, "The Theme of the Servant of Yahweh in Primitive Christian Soteriology, and Its Transposition by St. Paul", **CBQ** 16 (1954) 385-425.

1955

G. W. H. LAMPE, "The Holy Spirit in the Writings of Luke", in E. Nineham (ed), **Studies in the Gospels. Mémorial R. H. Lightfoot** (Oxford, 1955), pp. 159-200.

1956

J. COMBLIN, "La paix dans la théologie de Saint Luc", **ETL** 32 (1956) 439-460.

S. N. STANLEY, "The Conception of Salvation in Primitive Christian Preaching", **CBQ** 18 (1956) 231-254; summarized under the title "What the First Christians Meant by Salvation", **TDig** 5 (1957) 137-142.

1957

J. HAMAIDE and P. GUILBERT*, "The Message of Salvation in the Acts of the Apostles: Composition and Structure", **LumVit** 12 (1957) 406-417.

J. HAMAIDE and P. GUILBERT*, "Résonnances pastorales du plan des Actes des apôtres", **EglViv** 9 (1957) 95-113 and 368-383.

W. C. VAN UNNIK, "L'usage de σῴζειν 'sauver' et des dérivés dans les Evangiles synoptiques", in J. Coppens (ed), **La formation des Evangiles** (Bruges, 1957), pp. 178-194; taken up in **Sparsa**, Van Unnik, pp. 16-34.

1959

J. DUPONT, "Le salut des Gentils et la signification théologique du livre des Actes", **NTS** 6 (1959-1960) 132-155; included in **Etudes**, Dupont, pp. 393-419.

1960

W. C. VAN UNNIK, "The 'Book of Acts' - the Confirmation of the Gospel", **NT** 4 (1960) 26-59, included in **Sparsa**, Van Unnik, pp. 340-373.

1961

N. BROX, **Zeuge und Märtyrer. Untersuchungen zur frühchristlichen Zeugnis-Terminologie** (Munich, 1961).

E. LÖVESTAM, **Son and Saviour. A Study of Acts 13, 32-37. With an Appendix: 'Son of God' in the Synoptic Gospels** (Lund, 1961).

J. C. O'NEILL, **The Theology of Acts in Its Historical Setting** (London, 1961, 1970[2]).

U. WILCKENS, **Die Missionsreden der Apostelsgeschichte. Form- und traditionsgeschichtliche Untersuchungen** (Neukirchen, 1961, 1974[3]).

U. WILCKENS, "Das Offenbarungsverständnis in der Geschichte des Urchristentums", in W. Pannenberg (ed), **Offenbarung als Geschichte** (Göttingen, 1961), pp. 42-90, esp. pp. 71-77.

1962

J. DUPONT, "Les discours missionnaires des Actes des apôtres d'après un ouvrage récent", **RB** 69 (1962) 37-60; included in **Etudes**, Dupont, pp. 133-155.

K. STALDER, "Die Heilsbedeutung des Todes Jesu in den lukanischen Schriften", **IntKiZ** 52 (1962) 222-242.

1963

J. BIHLER, **Die Stephanusgeschichte im Zusammenhang der Apostelgeschichte** (Munich, 1963).

M. CAMBE, La *χάρις* chez Saint Luc", **RB** 70 (1963) 193-207.

The Saviour God. Comparative Studies in the Concept of Salvation. Mélanges E. O. James, S. G. F. Brandon (ed), (Manchester, 1963).

1964

W. FOERSTER and G. FOHRER, "Art. *σῴζω κτλ.*", **TWNT** 7 (Stuttgart, 1964), pp. 966-1024.

1965

H. FLENDER, **Heil und Geschichte in der Theologie des Lukas** (Munich, 1965, 1968[2], to which we refer).

W. OTT, **Gebet und Heil. Die Bedeutung der Gebetsparänese in der lukanischen Theologie** (Munich, 1965).

G. VOSS, **Die Christologie der lukanischen Schriften in Grundzügen** (Paris-Bruges, 1965).

1966

U. WILCKENS, "Interpreting Luke-Acts in a Period of Existentialist Theology" in **Studies**, Keck, pp. 60-83; in German included in U. Wilckens, **Rechtfertigung als Freiheit. Paulus Studien** (Neukirchen, 1974), pp. 171-203.

1967

W. MUNDLE et al., "Art. Erlösung", in L. Coenen et al., **Theologisches Begriffslexikon zum Neuen Testament**, I (Wuppertal, 1967), pp. 258-272.

1969

M. RESE, **Die Alttestamentlichen Motive in der Christologie des Lukas** (Gütersloh, 1969).

F. SCHÜTZ, **Der leidende Christus. Die angefochtene Gemeinde und das Christuskerygma der lukanischen Schriften** (Stuttgart-Berlin-Köln-Mainz 1969).

R. F. ZEHNLE, "The Salvific Character of Jesus' Death in Lucan Soteriology", **TS** 30 (1969) 420-444.

1970

I. H. MARSHALL, **Luke: Historian and Theologian** (Exeter, 1970).

P. H. MENOUD, "Le salut par la foi selon le livre des Actes", in M. Barth et al., **Foi et Salut selon S. Paul. Colloque Oecuménique à L'Abbaye de S. Paul hors les murs, 16-21 avril 1968** (Rome, 1970), pp. 255-276; included in **Jésus-Christ**, Menoud, pp. 130-149.

1971

L. SCHOTTROFF, "Das Gleichnis vom verlorenen Sohn, **ZTK** 68 (1971) 27-52.

1972

J. DE KESEL*, **Le salut et l'histoire dans l'oeuvre de Luc** (typed thesis), Pont. Greg, Univ. (Rome, 1972).

1973

F. BOVON, "Le salut dans les écrits de Luc. Essai", **RTPhil**, 3rd series, 23 (1973) 296-307.

B. H. THROCKMORTON, "*Σῴζειν, σωτηρία*: in Luke-Acts", in E. A. Livingstone (ed), **Studia Evangelica**, VI, (Berlin, 1973), pp. 515-526.

U. WILCKENS, "Das christliche Heilsverständnis nach dem Lukas-evangelium", in P. A. Potter (ed), **Das Heil der Welt heute. Ende oder Beginn der Weltmission? Dokumente der Weltmissionskonferenz Bangkok 1973** (Stuttgart-Berlin, 1973), pp. 65-74.

1975

R. GLOECKNER, **Die Verkündigung des Heils beim Evangelisten Lukas** (Mainz, n.d. (1975?)). Cf. E. Schweizer's book review, **TR** 72 (1976) 373.

1976

A. GEORGE, "L'emploi chez Luc du vocabulaire de salut", **NTS** 23 (1976-1977) 308-320.

CHAPTER 5

SALVATION

Introduction

Lucan studies have long preferred Christology to soteriology [1]. When interested in salvation, they considered most often the subjective aspect alone: conversion. The objective nature of the redemptive work of God in Jesus Christ, which is nonetheless central to Luke's thought, escaped them. This chapter analyzes the contributions, especially recent, which are the exceptions to this rule [2]. We will precede our presentation with a precision concerning the adjective "objective" and a rapid inventory of the Lucan material, then we will follow this with a synthetic and per - sonal conclusion.

The reader is mistaken regarding our intention if he takes the term "objective" in a positivistic sense. "Objective" does not signify here that which can be verified, grasped or controlled. Salvation can be said to be objective without placing God within the reach of our senses or intelligence. What we mean by this adjective is the real character of redemption which precedes us and remains foreign to us. Henceforth, the present chapter does not deal with what a directly accessible God would have done for us. Furthermore, the next chapter is not interested in the subjective and autonomous answer of man. Chapter 5 evokes the intervention of God into human history before us (we specified this type of salvific action at the end of ch 1). Chapter 6 will describe the living relation which is established between the believer and his God. If history of salvation precedes us, it continues today and God reminds us to be integrated in it.

Luke knows almost all the traditional Christian vocabulary which notes or evokes the saving work of God: pardon of sins (*ἄφεσις ἁμαρτιῶν*, Lk 24:47; Act 2:38), redemption (*ἀπολύτρωσις*, Lk 12:28: the sole usage of this term in the Gospels), life (Act 11:18), eternal life (Lk 10:25; 18:18, 30; Act 13:46, 48), gospel (Act 15:7 and 20:24; if the substantive is rare, the verb *εὐαγγελίζεσθαι* is frequent), grace (Lk 1:30, etc.), message of peace (Lk 19:42; Act 10:36) etc.

As the statistics and Synoptic comparison show, Luke gives his preference to the specific vocabulary of salvation: neglecting verbs like ῥύομαι and λύω (cf. however, λύτρωσις, Lk 1:68 and 2:38), he concentrates on s1(zv and the substantives in this family of words: διασώζω, ἐκσώζω, σωτήριον, σωτηρία and σωτήρ [3].

Two examples witness to this preference of Luke. In his presentation of John the Baptist (Lk 1:1ff.), Luke, in imitation of Mark, conceives the ministry of the prophet as the accomplishment of a prophecy of Isaiah. Yet instead of limiting the quotation of Isa 40:3, as Mark does (cf. Mk 1:2f. which cites Mal 3:1 as well), Luke carefully lengthens the prophetic text to vs. 5. In this way, he can close his OT quotation with an allusion to salvation: "And all flesh will see the salvation of God" (Lk 3:6).

A similar phenomenon occurs in the Pentecost account (Act 2). After the miracle of the tongues, Peter explains the event to the surprised crowd with the help of a Scriptural argument. The gift of tongues is the fulfillment of the prophecy in Joel 3: "I will pour out my Spirit on all flesh..." (Act 2:17ff.). If Luke cites Joel beyond vs. 2, it is not because of the apocalyptic description of the Day of the Lord that it contains (Joel 3:3-4 cited in Act 2:19-20) [4]. It is to come to vs. 5 of Joel where is salvation mentioned: "And whoever calls on the name of the Lord will be saved" (Act 2:21). Luke carefully stops the prophetic text here, for vs. 5b, related to Jerusalem, is too particularistic. We will sense the subtlety of the Lucan composition at the end of Peter's speech, in the presence of an allusion to the last words of the same verse in Joel (vs. 5c): "The promise is for you and your children and for all who are far away, in as great a number *as the Lord,* your God, *will call them*" (Act 2:39; the words in italics come from Joel 3). Here again Luke's interest in salvation appears: with the help of a formula taken from Isa 57:19 [5], Luke evokes the redemption to the Jews and pagans. Finally this interest arises again in the next verse, in Luke's summary of Peter's speech: "With many other words, he warned and exhorted them: 'Save yourselves (σώθητε) from this corrupt generation'" (Act 2:40).

As the evidence from the infancy narratives shows (Lk 1-2) [6], the salvation the apostles preach in the Acts is more related to the coming than to the death of Jesus, the Messiah and Lord: cf. Lk 2:11 ("a savior is born to you") and 2:30 ("my eyes have seen your salvation") [7]. In Jesus Christ, the God of the fathers, manifested his mercy (this is the main virtue of God in Lk 1-2: cf. Lk 1:50, 54, 58, 72, 78). The *Magnificat* (Lk 1:47-54) and the *Benedictus* (Lk 1:68-79) are witnesses to a soteriology which, because expressed in OT terms, assures the continuity of God's project in the history of Israel.

Beside the allusion to salvation in the pericope consecrated to the ministry of John the Baptist, of which we spoke above [8] it is necessary to mention that Luke then summarizes the future ministry of the hero of his book in soteriological terms borrowed from Isa 61:1: proclamation of salvation to the poor, healing for the blind, deliverance for the captives, liberation for the oppressed, in one word "a year of grace of the Lord" (Lk 4:18).

For Luke the life of Jesus accomplishes this salvation: "The Son of Man <u>has come</u> to seek and <u>to save</u> what was lost" (Lk 19:10). His ministry, summarized in this way, is marked by the coordination of action and word. The importance of the proclamation of salvation, and so of the word (in the form of the predication of the kingdom), permits Luke to remove from the notion of salvation anything which it might be automatic. The response man gives to the offer of salvation is necessary. In Luke, it is called *πίστις* and *μετάνοια*. Luke cannot conceive of a miracle where the faith of man is absent (the "your faith has saved you" is more frequent in Luke than in the other Synoptics, cf. Lk 7:50; 8:48 etc.). We also know that Luke gives importance to conversion. The illustration he gives in the parable of the prodigal son (Lk 15:11-32) is proof.

After Easter, which confirms Jesus' function as Messiah, Lord and Savior, the witnesses of the Resurrected Lord, the Twelve, Stephen and Paul become the proclaimers and agents of salvation (Act 11:14; 13:26 and 28:28 associate the notion of the word with salvation). However, they will only be messengers of a salvation which is not their work: here we see the importance of the name of Jesus. It is this name, i.e. this person, who was given to men for their salvation (cf. Act 4:12).

Throughout and following our presentation of the recent contributions on the subject we will ask several questions which come forth from what has just been said: Is salvation a present or future reality? If the law was the way to salvation, why was Christ necessary? If Jesus' power is salvific, what about his weakness and death? Does the cross of Christ have no expiatory function for Luke?

I. THE MESSAGE OF SALVATION

a. Even if 1950 is the departure point of our investigation, the history of Lucan studies of soteriology obliges us to go behind this date. In 1939, in fact, J. Gewiess published an important work of biblical theology with a revealing title: **Die urapostolische Heilsverkündigung nach der Apostelgeschichte** [9]. Of course, Gewiess' intention is not to present Lucan theology, but rather that of the apostles, which is more important for him. This theology of the apostles, following M. Dibelius and C. H. Dodd, he believes he is able to discover in the speeches of Act 1-12. Inspite of this perspective which is today outdated, Gewiess' analysis remains nonetheless valuable if we accept that soteriology, updated in this fashion, is work the editor of Acts and not the early Church.

The work, criticized for its systematic presentation of a too homogenous tableau [10], embraces all the contents of the apostolic message, describes the movement of faith and concludes with an analysis of the doctrine of the sacraments. We will only mention several highlights of the chapters on salvation.

After underlining that in Acts, God is the originator of the work of salvation and of the life of Jesus with the Church's expansion [11] - too many authors neglect to mention this [12] - Gewiess presents "Jesus the Messianic mediator of salvation" [13]. Of course, the death of Jesus is rarely described as an effective sacrifice: all the same, by the crucifixion, humanity has not destroyed the plan of salvation willed by God (cf. Act 4:27): "Der Leidenstod Jesu spricht nicht gegen, sondern für seine Messianität" (p. 27). More important than the resurrection, Durchgangsstadium (p. 27) like the death, the exaltation allows Christ to exercise henceforth his Messianic and salvific power (p. 30).

Concerning the Parousia, Gewiess antedates Conzelmann in noticing that Acts is turned less toward the future than contemporary Jewish texts. Two reasons explain the decline of eschatology: 1) the Messiah is not only a future reality: in fact he has already come and human beings can already know him (p. 31); 2) the allusions that Acts makes to the future (Act 3:19ff. and 10:42) have no value in themselves: they serve rather to incite the Jews to conversion and faith in the Messiahship of Jesus (p. 31); in short, they incite the acqusition of salvation (p. 33).

The fourth part of the book is consecrated to the benefits of salvation. Correctly, Gewiess insists first on the benefits the believer already receives from Christ. He points out, differing from Jewish theology, the theology of Acts associates these benefits with the person of a mediator, Jesus Christ (p. 71). If man responds positively to the Chrisian proclamation, he obtains the forgiveness of his sins (total remission, not partial).

This pardon originates from God himself, like in the OT. Since this pardon is obtained in the name of Jesus and Jesus is the Messiah of the end times, the forgiveness in Acts receives an eschatological coloring (p. 74) - later certain exegetes will deny this. Gewiess thinks that forgiveness is not yet tied to the death of Jesus [**14**]. Furthermore, Acts interprets the death and resurrection of Jesus in a more Christological than soteriological perspective. The resurrection only confirms Jesus' Messiahship. Thanks to his title Messiah, Jesus is able to transmit pardon.

Now, the Resurrected One also has the power to bestow on every believer, on every baptized person, the Holy Spirit, the great eschatological gift announced by the prophets. The πνεῦμα ἅγιον is, however, less an individual gift than the gift offered by the Christ to his Church with a view to its edification and mission (p. 95).

Salvation is not exhausted in the present moment: the book of Acts knows of blessings for Christians which are still expected: the resurrection [**15**], eternal life and belonging to the kingdom of God [**16**]

Gewiess' work [**17**] presents an interesting synthesis of the theology of the Acts. We think its principle merit lies in the setting forth of the notion of salvation, around which divers theological loci are organized. Its weakness comes from the false conviction that the speeches in Acts coincide with the Christian theology of the early days. This error of perspective prevents Gewiess from correctly situating the thought of Acts in its true environment (Sitz im Leben), and with this, from distinguishing tradition from redaction. In particular, he is able neither to see how much the evangelical material has aged nor how Luke reinterprets the primitive kerygma in a historicizing manner.

Thirty years will have to pass before the appearance of a large scale study that chooses salvation as the center of Lucan thought [**18**]. The difference between these two books remains important, for Gewiess' is attached to the preaching of salvation, and Marshall's retains the reality of salvation. Between the two, H. Conzelmann's **Die Mitte der Zeit** opts for salvation history.

b. Before introducing this last monograph, let us indicate several authors who, despite the avatars of Lucan studies, have not lost sight of the importance of soteriology in the theology of Acts. In 1955, G. W. H. Lampe set out that salvation is a Lucan theme of capital importance [**19**]. It no longer deals with the deliverance from enemies, as in the OT, but with the pardon of sins and the gift of repentence. It is more the glorification than the death of Jesus, which is at the origin of this redemption. The story of the gospel of salvation begins with the message of the angel to Zechariah and terminates in Rome when the offer of salvation reaches the pagans. In 1959, J. Dupont presented his conference on the salvation to the Gentiles and the theological signification of Acts. In this study, centered on the fate of the pagans and Luke's intention, Dupont recalls the importance of salvation for the Jews and pagans: "It does not seem rash to seek here one of the keys of the work: the history that Luke wants to recount is defined as that of the manifestation of the salvation of God in favor of all flesh." [**20**] Finally, in 1960, W. C. van Unnik entitled one of the sections of an article consecrated to Acts [**21**], the "leading idea is σωτηρία - σῴζω. For the Dutch professor, the second book of Luke does not tell the story of the Church (against Käsemann), but continues the narrative of the Gospel. Thus Luke's intends to make a bridge between the salvific activity of Jesus and the people who had no direct contact with him: this bridge is the message of salvation proclaimed by the apostles, a message which <u>confirms</u> the salvation brought by Jesus. Both the Gospel and the Acts insist, therefore, on the same reality of salvation [**22**], a salvation that, whatever is said, has not lost its eschatological character: "Ultimately all these sermons [in Acts] serve to insist upon the same fact: the need of salvation, the Man of salvation, the way of salvation." (p. 53) [**23**].

II. SALVATION HISTORY

The famous monograph of H. Conzelmann (-> 1954) explains first of all the Lucan conception of history. But, as this history is a history of salvation, the German exegete approaches the question of salvation on several occasions and from different angles.

Contrary to the interpretation of certain of his adversaries, Conzelmann does not think that Luke substitutes the historical account for the evangelical kerygma. The narration is no longer to be identified with the kerygma, as was the case in Mark, but neither does it replace the latter. The account serves rather as a justification, a foundation, a presupposition of the kerygma. Conzelmann never says that Luke demands faith in the history of salvation or that he imposes salvation by history (cf. p. 3).

What Luke consciously does however is to historicize the saving events, considered until then as belonging to an escha -

tology which was unassimilable to history. By this insertion into the historical, the eschatological is necessarily betrayed: it be - comes the objectivation of verifiable truths. God's plan is then as follows: God, according to Luke, decided in advance a plan of collective salvation (individual salvation is not the object of such a developed divine solicitude: Luke is unaware of the predestination of believers (p. 144)).

To fulfill this plan, God uses the mediation of Jesus Christ. Jesus' ministry is no longer immediately eschatological: far from being the eruption of the kingdom in Luke, it is no longer but the fleeting foretaste. Salvation had been present, but now this present has taken on the consistency of the past (p. 158). Situated in the middle of salvation history, it can no longer be at the end. Lk 4:18ff. speaks of this "today" of salvation; Luke considers it as completed (p. 182) **[24]**. The rupture between the peaceful time of the life of Jesus (the absence of Satan between Lk 4:13 and 22:3, p. 146) and the period of the Church, troubled by the *πειρασμοί* (p. 90 and 219) is deep. Long live the future salvation in the kingdom, whose coming is more certain than imminent!

A "Typos des Heils" (p. 173) **[25]**, type of salvation, the activity of Jesus is more so by the salvific acts of the Lord than by his words (the opposite of Matthew) (p. 177ff.). But, the word actually takes its revenge, for the contemporary Church has access to this privileged period by the word (p. 174) which is fortunately accompanied by a dispensation of the Spirit (p. 179). Yet, this divine gift is no more eschatological than the word about Jesus. It had simply become - with regard to the first Christian writings - the Ersatz [replacement] of the eschatological benefits (p.87).

In Conzelmann's perspective, we can see how believers and the Church are far from true salvation, a salvation which is both past and future simultaneously. An analysis of the vocabulary of salvation would have constrained Conzelmann to modify his interpretation. It would have shown him that, in fact, the moat between the time of Jesus and that of the Church is not as deep as he thinks. Eschatology, far from evaporating at the first contact with history, in Luke, gets along quite well with it. Without being first marked by trials, the period of the Church is above all the time of the joyful possession of salvation to which the end times will bring fullness **[26]**.

Conzelmann also deals with the problem of the Law. In his view, Luke does not attack directly the Law, which is the old pathway to salvation. Far from being at its *τέλος* in Christ (Rom

10:4), it subsists for one generation: the Paul of the Acts is its venerable defender. However, Luke does not transform - differing from Frühkatholizismus - the Gospel into a new law. The Law is a high point of the history of salvation, which belongs to the past. The apostolic decree has come to supplant the law which linked the first generation of Christians to the Israel of the OT. Conzelmann thinks that Luke does not develope a theological concept of the Law: an allusion to justification without resorting to the Law is exceptional for him (Act 13:38).

We wonder if Conzelmann is right on this last point. Luke is conscious of the difference of the economies: the Jerusalem conference - the center of Acts like the parable of the prodigal son is the heart of the Gospel - is concerned with the problem of salvation (cf. Act 15:1, 11). For Luke, this decisive event in the history of the Church allows for a radical transformation in the access to salvation. As Peter says, according to Luke, it is now by faith and no longer by the works of the Law, that human beings come to salvation (Act 15:11). Without having the depth of Pauline theology, the Lucan conception of the Law is quite theological and related to salvation. We might summarize it in the following: God offers us salvation in Jesus Christ; we can acquire it by a personal movement which is called conversion to God and faith in the Lord Jesus.

With this we come to the last section of Conzelmann's book: "Man and Salvation", a title followed, by the way, by the significant word "the Church". For Conzelmann, Luke has shattered the original unity of salvation (Conzelmann often believes in the myth of the joyous origin!), to abusively separate the subjective perspective from the objective. Salvation for him has an objective side, the doctrine of Christ the savior, and a subjective one, the appropriation of salvation, the Nachfolge. In the next chapter, we will speak of the Lucan concept of conversion and faith. Let us simply note here that Conzelmann rightly affirms that the individual finds his insertion into salvation history in the heart of the Church. Access to salvation which begins with an individual act is continued in the community experience of forgiveness. But, Conzelmann concludes, - a conclusion necessary considering the premises announced above - wrongly that salvation remains particularly a future reality connected to the individual resurrection. Clearly, in Luke the content of hope is the resurrection (cf. Act 23:6; 24:15; 26:6ff.; 28:20). However, Lucan hope is not the only expression of present salvation: joy, peace, with all that the summaries describe - which is equal mutatis mutandis to the present

Church as well - and all that the verb σῴζω contains are present eschatological realities **[27]**. To project salvation into the future, as Conzelmann does, is to judaize Luke: "Wie das Eschaton nicht mehr gegenwärtige, sondern ausschliesslich künftige Sachverhalte bezeichnet, so ist auch das ewige Leben in die Ferne gerückt. Jetzt besitzen wir nicht das Leben, sondern die Hoffnung darauf." (p. 216).

III. THE SAVIOR AND HIS COMING

The books, we open now, have all been influenced by Conzelmann's ideas, that they take over, modify or reject accordingly. Without having made Lucan soteriology the principle subject of their research, the writers of these monographs, a new generation of exegetes, all consecrate a chapter or section to the subject.

U. Wilckens (-> 1961, first title) **[28]**

a. U. Wilckens accepts Conzelmann's basic problematic, but the study of the speeches in Acts, which he undertakes and the allegience which he gives to the group of W. Pannenberg, leads him to modify a few of Conzelmann's views and go beyond him from time to time.

Whereas Conzelmann hesitates calling the epoch of Christ a time of salvation and prefers to qualify this period as a type of salvation **[29]**, Wilckens affirms categorically that, for Luke, salvation remains in the past, in the past of salvation history whose grandiose conception is less original that has been said **[30]**. Projected by Luke into the past, salvation obligatorily loses the eschatological nature that it had in the thought of the first Christians (p. 202f.) **[31]**.

From now on, for Luke the theological difficulty consists in building bridges between this past salvation and the believer's acquisition today (p. 203). To resolve this difficulty, Luke would have been badly armed and gone about it wrongly. Wilckens thinks that by projecting Christ into history (Historie), Luke would have, so to speak, let him escape: he would no longer possess a true conception of Christ, the elevated Lord, presently active in the life of the believer and the Church (p. 205f. and 210). Without a living Christ at his side, Luke could only throw a few meager cords across the chasm which separated the Gospel and Acts, i.e. the Mitte der Zeit and the poor contemporary period: the continuity of history (Geschichte) of salvation (p. 204), the kerygma concerning Jesus to which the speeches witness [32] and the name of Jesus [33] would be the only elements allowing an access - an indirect one - to the past salvation. The insufficiency of these bridges are because of two of Luke's theological weaknesses: his incapacity to confer a soteriological value to the cross [34] and the closure of a salvation history influenced by Hellenistic historiography rather than by Jewish apocalyptic [35]. "Die Heilsteilhabe in der christlichen Gegenwart ist hier also nicht als jeweils unmittelbares Widerfahrnis aus der Transzendenz heraus beschrieben, sondern vielmehr konsequent als geschichtlich vermittelte Teilhabe an einer bestimmten Vergangenheit." (p. 207).

These theses which form the book's last chapter, a chapter which is more systematic than exegetical, have suscitated the thunder of J. Dupont [36]. The affirmations in these pages are in fact badly supported exegetically, the generalizations often abusive and contradictions frequent.

In particular, we wonder how Wilckens can reconcile his thesis of a salvation in the past with the results of the analysis of the ordo salutis [37] which lead him to accept the present nature of salvation offered by God [38] to the believer: "In Taufe, Sündenvergebung und Geistempfang handelt es sich im Zusammenhang der Predigten eindeutig um den Empfang des Heiles" (p. 183) [39]. It seems that one excludes the other. Unless, of course, we admit with van Unnik and Marshall [40] that the time of the Church follows without interruption the time of Jesus. Provoked by God in Jesus Christ, the era of salvation follows the activity of the Risen One until the Parousia. The present period is more marked by the *χαρά* than by the *πειρασμοί*. But, Wilckens refuses such an interpretation.

J. Bihler (-> 1963)

b. The ambitions of J. Bihler in his chapter of **Die Heilsvorstellungen in der Stephanusrede** (pp. 97-134) are more modest. He limits his investigation to the speech in Act 7, and in counterpoint, to the one in Act 3. The analysis gains in exactitude what it loses in volume.

As the entire Lucan work, the speech of Stephen, which Bihler attributes to Lucan composition (p. 86), situates salvation in the past. But, - Bihler is thinking precisely of Wilckens and in a certain measure Conzelmann - this salvation, originating from God, is already accomplished in the history of Israel by the intervention of Moses, the λυτρωτής (Act 7:35) (p. 98, note 2). The ancient covenant is, therefore, not uniquely the time of the promise, but also the time of the fulfillment: cf. Act 7:17 : καθὼς δὲ ἤγγιζεν ὁ χρόνος τῆς ἐπαγγελίας.

This offer of salvation to Israel is, nonetheless, only one of the facets of salvation history: the attitude of the addressees forms the other side of the coin. Israel reveals itself as the people who reject Moses the mediator of salvation, the prophets after him and finally the Righteous One, i.e. Jesus (Act 7:39, 51ff.). Act 7 shows in a typical manner the constancy of God who wants to save, the hardening of a people who refuse salvation and the tragic fate the messengers of the Lord suffer. The history of redemption unfolds in distinct periods; but these periods can be structurally related. The salvation in Jesus has as its antecedent, but also as its model the σωτηρία (Act 7:25) which Moses, the rejected prophet, brought in his time (pp. 97-99).

According to Bihler, this is the contribution of Act 7 to the understanding of Lucan soteriology. Some will reply that Stephen's speech is not specifically Lucan and reflects traditions peculiar to the Hellenists. For the German exegete, this is not so as the traditions that Luke uses in this chapter (Bihler does not deny that he possesses some) largely overlap those of the rest of Lucan corpus [**41**]. The speech in Act 7 does not correspond to Stephen's theology. It is the work of Luke who situates it half way between Peter's speeches (in particular Act 3) where the Jews are still invited to repent and Paul's (Act 13) where the opening up of salvation to the Gentiles takes place (p. 111).

Admitting the important part Luke takes in the composition of this speech, we ask ourselves if Luke - following a verifiable custom in Act 13 [**42**] - does not seek to highlight the particularity that he believes to have been the theology and soteriology of the Hellenistic wing of the early Church.

H. Flender (-> 1965)

c. We have presented Flender's work in our first chapter [**43**]. Here, we will just retain the developments concerning salvation. The German exegete, as we have seen, is bent on whitewashing Luke from any suspicion of Offenbarungspositivismus, positivism of revelation, that Conzelmann's monography placed on him. He thinks that he can do this by claiming that Conzelmann's views reflect only one of the faces of Luke's theology. Salvation history, as Luke conceives it, is not a closed system of cause and effect. The Evangelist allows history to open up to transcendency - that Wilckens seems to have refused him **[44]**. Thus, the principle of duality which appears in the Lucan composition **[45]**, asserts itself in the conception of history , a history with two faces, one where humanity triumphs, and the other where God wins out: the death of Jesus, human work and fulfillment of God's design, is the privileged example of this perspective (p. 141). Flender thinks that this duality, valuable at a historical level, is found in Christology and soteriology. Luke took up an early Christian schema called Zweistufenschema, a Christological schema according to which Jesus Christ possessed a double mode of existence, one, earthly and another, heavenly (pp. 43-55). In soteriology, Flender thinks he is able to break out of the blind alley into which we had been cornered by Conzelmann and Wilckens. These two exegetes thought that salvation had now left the scene to find refuge in either the past or the future, or even the two at the same time. This present absence of salvation because of this historicization, collides with an indubitable exegetical verification: the verb *σῴζειν* in Luke has a present value. Flender thinks he can do justice to these two apparently irreconcilable theses. His original solution can be summarized here: present on the earth in past times in Jesus of Nazareth, salvation remains perpetually present - the eschatological character which Conzelmann could not find in Luke - because of the exaltation of Christ (like Gewiess, Flender attributes a great importance to the elevation) (pp. 85-98). But this salvation has left the earth, so to speak (Luke, according to Flender, willingly transfers into space what had happened in time: so the earthly blessings of the Parousia of early Christianity are transformed in Luke into celestial benefits of the Ascension) (pp. 85-91, especially p. 90f.). Salvation is installed in heaven. This "heavenizing" of salvation is the price that Flender must pay in order to obtain an infinite duration. The problem is therefore not to rejoin the past of salvation, but to reach the heavenly position. How do we get "up there"? Flender considers the risen Christ much more active in Luke than Wilckens believes [46]: thanks to him, the human word of the apostles can become the Word of God and history can regain its kerygmatic note. The believers and the Church can have access to the heavenly salvation in this way (p. 122ff.). However, they do not become angels for that, for because of the ethical demand **[47]**, they have the mission of diving into the profanity of human structures and situations **[48]**. Believers are invested with salvific or heavenly blessings (for Flender this word becomes synonymous with eschatological) **[49]**: the Holy Spirit and the communion of the Risen One **[50]**. Yet they continue to live a historical existence.

This is a summary of Flender's subtle approach which we have tried not to betray. But, does it conform to Luke's intention? Doubts begin to appear when we verify the exegetical foundations of this beautiful construction. They often seem shaky or fragile. Because of lack of space let us take but one example: Flender understands one verse from Luke in the following way: "Das Heute des Heils gilt, wenn auch Jesus in die unsichtbare Ferne des Himmels entrückt ist." p. 59). Whereas the verse in question is Lk 19:11, a redactional verse which links the episode of Zacchaeus to the parable of the pounds: "As the people were listening to all this, he told them another a parable, because he was close to Jerusalem and they imagined that the Kingdom of God was going to appear immediately." This verse, far from assuring the continuity of salvation, incites the believer not to believe in the imminence of the Parousia. It introduces the parable of the pounds which concerns the Christian life here below **[51]**.

Only a cavalier treatment of the texts allows Flender to elaborate his theory of heavenly salvation. He is perhaps right, against Wilckens **[52]**, to insist on the activity of the ascended Christ, but he is wrong to orient our eyes to the sky. The word of the angel to the disciples should be applied to him: "Why are you all looking at the sky?" (Act 1:11). This reference is not a joke: Luke throws us back down to the earth and, different from the author of Hebrews, does not speculate on the heavenly world. He believes in salvation here and now, a salvation which Marshall describes in the most convincing manner **[53]**. We nonetheless recognize Flender is to be praised for having revalorized the present salvation history by opening it up to what might be called the contingency of God.

G. Voss (-> 1965)

d. Three sections of the book which Voss consecrates on Luke's Christology concern soteriology. Here are the titles: **Das Wirken Jesu als Offenbarung der Gottesherrschaft** (pp. 24-45), *σωτήρ* **und** *κύριος* **als Herrscherliche Jesus - prädikate** (pp. 45-60) and **Der Tod Jesu als Offenbarung von Schuld und Erlösung** (pp. 126-130) [**54**]. These contributions, both philological and theological, have been influenced by Catholic dogmatics. The dialogue with Conzelmann is here not always fruitful.

According to Voss, the Gospel of Luke brings near the ministry of Jesus and the manifestation of the kingdom of God. "Now" (Lk 4:21), the promises of God and the hope of Israel are fulfilled in Jesus. The miracles of Jesus are signs of the coming kingdom.

With a careful analysis of the terms *ἐπισκέπτεσθαι*, *ἄφεσις* and *λύτρωσις*, the author shows us the Evangelist in his theological effort: in Jesus the Messiah, God comes to visit his people, free them from Satan and offer them pardon. By the usage of this OT vocabulary, Luke succeeds in focalizing the Messianic and es - chatological hopes of the OT and ancient Judaism on Jesus (pp. 25-28) [**55**]. We are then not surprised that the Lucan Christ is portrayed often with the royal characteristics which are suitable for the Messiah [**56**].

In examining the privileged addressees of the ministry of Jesus that we can regroup under the denomination of "the poor", Voss notes that the eschatological "visitation" in Jesus Christ is the expression neither of distributive justice nor of the vindicative justice of God ("nicht Belohnung oder Strafe", p. 35),but the manifestation of the love and grace of God which seeks and finds the lost (pp. 35-38).

Jesus has the right to be called Savior, "to save" is the verb Luke uses to summarize the work of Jesus which by healing, removes the victims from the sphere of the demons and by forgiveness takes away the power of Satan. In Acts, we often move from the sign to the reality: the verb *σῴζειν* is less used for healings than for redemption: the relation between salvation and faith becomes more explicit (cf. Act 16:31).

The title *σωτήρ*, which Voss analyzes in a deeper manner than *σῴζειν* or *σωτηρία* is attributed to God and Jesus by Luke (pp. 45ff.) [**57**]. In the rest of the NT, this title appears in the writings most influenced by the Greek mentality. It seems certain that such an influence is evident in Luke as he also uses terms like *εὐεργέτης* (Lk 22:25), *εὐεργετεῖν* (Act 10:38) and *εὐεργεσία* (Act 4:9), whose religious sense is originally Greek. Voss attempts nonetheless to show that if *σωτύρ* recalls the titles given to the healing gods and potentates of the Hellenistic world, the link with Greece remains formal. The concept of Savior, in fact, has its roots in the Biblical compost (cf. eg. Isa 45:21), although this title, reserved for God, was not attributed to the Messiah in the OT and Jewish traditions.

By applying this divine title to the Resurrected One, Luke has maintained two major Biblical elements: he, who is the savior, creates and guarantees the liberty of the people he protects, from the interference of foreign powers; and furthermore, he, who is savior, forgives sinners who in turning from God give themselves up to servitude.

Because he comes from God and yet is not God himself, Jesus detains royal power which he shares with no other savior or lord. Far from being syncretistic, the use of the word *σωτύρ* is rather more polemic.

By distinguishing the (Hellenistic) form from the (OT) sub - stance, Voss perhaps underestimates the Greek impact of the word *σωτύρ*. Related to *ἀρχηγός*, this title recalls, at least for Greek ears, the blessings analogous to the gifts of the healing gods. The tenderness and goodness of the Lucan Jesus may partly originate from the pagan homologues of the Christian Savior [58].

If Jesus is *σωτύρ* by his preaching of the kingdom and the healings he does, what then is his death? We know that, for several exegetes, Luke confers no soteriological worth to the cross. The two sole Lucan allusions to an efficacious death (and one is not even clearly attested in the text) would be traditional stereotyped formulas. The little interest Luke has for the redemptive death of the Lord would receive a confirmation e silentio of the absence of Mk 10:45, in the third Gospel. Voss does not completely share this view, which, following Gewiess, is proposed by Conzelmann, Wilckens, Kaestli [59] and others.

Voss' explanation is subtle: the guilt of humanity before the death of Jesus poses more a theological than historical problem. Luke, as we know, speaks on this occasion of the fault of men and their ignorance, and if they have been guilty without knowing it, it is because they were not the only artisans of Jesus' death. The power of darkness guided them and held them captive as well. By accepting the death voluntarily, the Son of God suffered a judgment which he did not merit. From now on his death is not simply exemplary nor substitution either. It is the gateway to salvation, the victory over the enemy. Human beings, following Christ can henceforth, (in this "henceforth" resides the soteriological import of the cross) have access to salvation by the appropriation of the kerygma in faith. If they refuse, their ἄγνοια then becomes unpardonable.

This dogmatic explanation is unconvincing: it comes more from theological intuition than exegetical analysis. M. Rese, we will see, sets us in better direction. Voss is certainly right to seek for a middle way between the doctrines of imitation and substitu - tion, but his proposition which offers a Christ "working" for salva - tion corresponds better to the epistle of Hebrews than to the third Gospel. Finally, his explanation in fact confers a redemptive value to the resurrection and not to the crucifixion, for when he speaks of the victory over death, he implies the redemptive import of the resurrection rather than the cross. This was not the intended goal.

M. Rese (-> 1969)

e. Two reasons spur us to mention again M. Rese, whose work we have already presented [**60**]. First, this author is to be recommended for laying out in the open the interest that Luke, as an exegete of the OT, has for the theme of salvation. Furthermore, he has drawn our attention to the quotation of Isa 53, inserted into the Lucan account of the Passion, which permits us to better understand the salvific value Luke attributes to the death of Christ.

According to Rese, numerous are the editorial references to the OT, which deal with eschatological salvation in Luke's work [**61**]. Their number even shows that Luke attributed a particular importance to them for theological and apologetic reasons: in Lk 1:69, for example, Luke adds the word "salvation" to the OT promise of a Davidic messiah: "<u>he will raise up a horn</u> of salvation in the house <u>of David</u> his servant." (p. 180). Rese wonders if this soteriological interpretation of Davidic messianism is not a Lucan creation. Luke is at least pleased to bring the notions of Davidic Messiah and Savior together (cf. Lk 2:11).

Moreover,when he cites Isa 40:5 "all flesh will see the salvation of God" (Lk 3:5), the Evangelist already indicates the universal import and universalistic nature of Christian salvation.

The Biblical quotations in the speech of Peter in Act 2 and 3 hold Rese's attention for a long while. In his view, their point is more soteriological than Christological (p. 76). The proof is in the invitations to salvation which concludes them. Joel 3:5

("whoever calls on the name of the Lord will be saved") quoted in Act 2:21 serves as the cornerstone of the speech (p. 64). The later evocation of the "times of refreshing" (Act 3:21) functions as the basis of the call to conversion (p. 76).

Finally, in Paul's speech in Antioch of Pisidia, the reference to Isa 55:3 (*δώσω ὑμῖν τὰ ὅσια Δαυὶδ τὰ πιστά*) is not uniquely Christological: the resurrection itself (even if we must discard the interpretation of Dupont **[62]** who thinks of the benefits which flow from the resurrection) is one of the gracious gifts God makes to men (pp. 86-89).

Let us go on to his second point. In the Lucan narrative of the Passion, the Evangelist refers to Isa 53:12: "he was counted among the transgressors (*ἄνομοι*)." As the introduction to the quotation indicates, we are in the presence of the promise-accomplishment schema. The presence of the thieves at the sides of the crucified Christ (Lk 23:32) signals the fulfillment of the prophecy.

This citation, absent in the other Synoptics, must be redac - tional. The solemnity by which it is introduced and the central place it occupies within the Passion account calls attention to its importance for Luke. The Evangelist gives it a meaning which goes beyond the description of Jesus' sad fate. As the dialogue with the thieves shows (Lk 23:39-43) (pp. 157-159), Luke can understand the cross as "the foundation and the point of departure of salvation" (p. 158). Rese then proposes to see another allusion to the savific value of the cross (pp. 157-159) in the allusion to Isa 53:12 .

However, Rese stops along the way. He declares that the Isa 53 quotation in Lk 22, like the one from the same chapter in Act 8, does not precisely contain a reference to the death of the servant <u>for our sins</u> (pp. 154f. and 97-103). He then concludes with Conzelmann and others **[63]**, that Luke refuses to speak of the death of Jesus in terms of redemption or expiation.

It seems by following the beginning of Rese's reasoning, we cannot accept his conclusion. For us, the allusion to Isa 53 is capital: Jesus, for Luke, rejoins on the cross those who are lost, impious and unrighteous (cf. Lk 5:31f.; 19:10). He, the Righteous One (cf. the centurion at the cross, Lk 23:48, and the speeches of Peter and Stephen, Act 3:14 and 7:52), suffered the fate of the *ἄνομοι* **[64]**. Why? This is where the soteriological import of the cross comes forth: so that the lost sheep might rejoin the flock and the joy in heaven be great.

Our hypothesis receives confirmation from the very concept of salvation history. For in fact, without reversing the decision on it, we cannot take away the death of the Messiah from the Master of history. It is one of the most important events. As F. Schütz [65] has shown, the general theme of the plan of salvation of God invites us (and him, too) to give a positive value to the cross.

Why, in these conditions, do we find only two meager explicit allusions to the expiatory nature of Jesus' death? To our know - ledge, no one has known how to explain this yet. J. Dupont's explanation [66] seems insufficient: the early Church would have reserved this *theologoumenon* to the esoteric teaching of the community: hence the absence of ὑπὲρ ἡμῶν in the missionary speeches in Acts and its appearence in Paul's ecclesiastic discourse to the elders in Ephesus (Act 20:28). No, it seems another explanation is necessary. The reason of Luke's silence is his love for μετάνοια. To insist on the redemptive death, on the *extra nos*, would be to risk interference with human personal engagement, the decision of faith and conversion. We think that Luke accepted that the cross was also (aside from the ministry of Jesus and the resurrection of the Lord) a saving event and not only an accident by the way. Yet, he did not explicitly draw all the soteriological conclusions, so as to prevent the Christians of his time from going to sleep [67].

These frequently divergent theses, just presented [68], reveal the limits and dangers of a *Redaktionsgeschichte* pushed to the limit. The results are obtained at the term of too subtle and subjective analyses. The small signs become proofs of the redactional intentions; texts refractory to the theory [of the scholar] are declared traditional; and a contemporary theological problematic is projected into the texts. The horizon is perhaps not as dark as we paint it, but, nonetheless, a reaction against the excess of the *redaktionsgeschichtliche Methode* is in order. The best remedy consists in an interpretation which exchanges the microscope for the eye. A contemplation of the *totality* of the work within its proper structure , where the traditional elements also have redactional importance, must serve as an access to the interpretation. This is what I. H. Marshall has attempted.

IV. SALVATION

a. I. H. Marshall, a Reader in NT in Aberdeen, published a work on the whole of Luke's theology [69]. Marshall uses only moderately the *redactionsgeschichtlich* method in his studies of

Luke. If he often defends conservative positions, he is to be appreciated for demonstrating that the theme of salvation forms the center of Lucan thought.

After having summarized several recent works [70], the author attempts to show that the Evangelist merits the title of historian. The work of Luke, one of the best historians of antiquity, even fulfills the exigencies of modern historiography.

But, since the Christian revelation is historical, the fact that he reasons as a historian, far from being a weakness, guarantees the quality of Luke's theological work. Kerygma and history go hand in hand and have since the origins of Christianity [71]. Luke could not have "historicized" a Christian message whose ties with history were constituent [72]. Luke's theological characteristic is not salvation history - at this point the author of Acts continues the effort of his predecessors -, but the elaboration of a theology of salvation [73]. For Marshall, Luke is above all an evangelist and his work, which does not have as its primary objective, history or apologetic, is essentially kerygmatic (p. 84) [74]. This is the central thesis of his work, which, as we can imagine, is constantly in polemic with Conzelmann's [75].

The exegete supports his idea in two ways: first, in a philolo - gical manner and then, in a literary one. He has no difficulty in showing that the verb σῴζειν and its derivatives occupy a privileged position in Luke. Of course, the rest of the NT knows the vocabulary of salvation, but σωτηρία takes on a particular coloring and place in Luke. Lk 1-2, soteriological chapters <u>par excellence,</u> provide the theme of the symphony which Paul's friend composes [76].

Following van Unnik [77], Marshall deems that the Lucan work in two books, forms but one literary unit, marked by the constant saving activity of God in Jesus Christ. Inspite of the discontinuity the Ascension produces, the Lucan Christ continues his work in the Acts of the Apostles. The time of the Church is therefore not scarred by only one negative sign (in fact, the time of the historical Jesus was already so) [78]: it is particularly characterized by salvation which continues on its way in human history.

Opting for a dogmatic scheme, Marshall then treats the major theological subjects in the perspective of salvation: God the Savior (ch. 5), the work of salvation accomplished in Jesus Christ according to the Gospel (ch. 6), the preaching of salvation in Acts (ch. 7) and humanity's access to salvation (ch. 8) [79].

The OT already says that God is a savior, but Luke specifies what the Biblical source offered him: the God of Luke saves according to a plan which embraces the whole of human history: "The main feature of Luke's teaching about God thus lies in the thought of His plan, announced in the Old Testament and presently being fulfilled in history by His obedient servants." (p. 106f.).

Against Conzelmann's two theses, Marshall thinks that the theme of the plan of God and the notion of salvation history do not contradict early eschatology. History and eschatology are but two sides of the same coin.

The theme of the project of God neither implies the idea of necessity nor fatality. The Lucan notion of election does not rest on a pagan foundation: like in the OT, election is a call to a precise task rather than a non-differentiated incorporation into the Church.

Lk 19:10 ("the Son of Man is come to seek and save what was lost") is the condensation of the evangelical message and the summary of Jesus' life. Thus begins the chapter on the ministry of Jesus in the Lucan perspective **[80]**. The soteriological activity of the Messiah fits into eschatology: the references to Isa 61 in Lk 4:18f. and to Isa 35 in Lk 7:22 show this. It is not possible to speak of a "past" ministry, as Conzelmann does. Luke does not deeschatologize the ministry of Jesus by separating it from the end times: "It is more correct to say that Luke has broadened out the time of the End so that it begins with the ministry of Jesus, includes the time of the church, and is consummated at the parousia." (p. 121). The epoch of salvation has begun and continues **[81]**.

What then is the content of salvation brought by Jesus Christ? What are the "blessings of salvation"? The content is the presence of the kingdom whose healings and preaching to the poor are the signs. This manifestation of the kingdom goes hand in hand with the forgiveness of sins. The scenes of Jesus' supping with sinners witnesses to this.

An analysis of the Lucan beatitudes shows nevertheless that the salvation offered to believers has not yet attained its fullness. "Happy are you who are hungry <u>now</u>, for you will be satisfied." (Lk 6:21). There is a tension between the beatitudes, which oppose the present misfortune with the salvation to come and certain <u>logia</u> concerning the kingdom which note the actual eruption of salvation. There is however no contradiction between these two series of texts, for the present salvation must, in Luke, attain its completion (p.141ff.).

The opposition between the rich and poor that is found in the beatitudes and in other passages of Luke must not make us believe in a limitation of the universality of salvation (p. 141ff.).

Marshall then goes on to analyze the theological content of Acts. The principle theme of the second book of Luke is the same as that of the Gospel: the good news of salvation (p 157). It is with regard to this theme that Luke chooses his materials. The number and importance of the sermons in Acts is to be explained by this redactional perspective. The notion of the Word of God guarantees the continuity between the Gospel and the Acts. The apostles succeed Jesus as the ministers of the word.

The discontinuity appears at the level of the content of this word (p. 160f.). The kingdom gives place to the exalted Lord (p. 161ff.). Yet the crevice is not as deep as it seems, for the resurrection does not establish the Messiahship and Lordship of Jesus, but, in fact, manifests these existing realities to the disciples who had been blind to them until now. Behind this predication of the kingdom, the Christ and Lord was already present (p. 161f) **[82]**.

Salvation is a gift of God, but transmitted by Jesus **[83]**. Jesus has the ability to offer it - in the Gospel as well as in the Acts - for he is the Lord. There is really no other name by which we can be saved (Act 4:12).

Luke is not the only to relate salvation to the resurrection, Ascension and Lordship of Jesus. Marshall points out the exis - tence of several NT traditions which give priority to the resurrection in the establishment of salvation. The slight soteriological impact that Luke accords the cross is not the expression of a redactional intention, but rather the reflection of a primitive Christology (p. 174f.).

Like in the Gospel, salvation in the Acts is first of all present, even if the future will see its fulfillment (cf. the analysis of Act 3:20 on p. 170). The Christ of the Acts is not inactive, he intervenes by his name and the Holy Spirit. It follows that the word of God and the salvation which it entails, are spread from Jerusalem to Rome and passes from the Jews to the pagans (pp. 182-187).

"What must I do to be saved?" The question of the Philippian jailer (Act 16:30) serves as the title for the last chapter that insists on the kind grace of God **[84]**, repentence, faith and the conversion of humanity, and the baptism conferred by the church and its fruits.

Conclusion

At the end of this overview, we would like to add a few personal opinions.

The most frequent Lucan use of σῴζειν and σωτηρία designates a present reality: Jesus has already intervened, the era of salvation has already begun, eschatological peace and joy are present throughout the Acts as much as in the Gospel.

Luke realizes nevertheless that this present salvation must still come to its fullness. So σῴζειν sometimes aims at the future. Moreover, the apocalyptic texts which evoke the ἀπολύτρωσις (Lk 21:28) or the ἀποκατάστασις πάντων (Act 3:21), thus the future, are not eliminated by Luke.

The notion of the word permits an explanation of this tension found in the whole of the NT. Salvation is manifested presently in oral form. In several texts (Act 11:14; 13:26 and 28:28) Luke emphasizes the link between the word and salvation. The word which forgives and saves requires a response. Luke's insistance on πίστις, with regard to Matthew and Mark, points out that this answer belongs first to an order other than ethical. Yet Luke preserves, if not the freedom of man, at least his involvement and responsibility in the salvific process. Destined for humanity, salvation cannot be accomplished without them.

Since this word comes from God, it is more effective and creative that human word. This is why Luke can show, if we can say so, the dynamic and factual side. Lk 1-2, where salvation is almost imposed by God, shows that the Christ event surges forth into history according to the will of this merciful God. The healings signify in their way that salvation (the verb is ambiguous, to Luke's great joy) reestablishes human integrity.

Since Luke's God is the same as the OT's, we might wonder why the coming of Jesus was necessary. Without Luke dealing with this question explicitly, we can induce what follows from dispersed texts. God had made provision for a way of salvation for his people: the Law. On two occasions (Lk 10:25-28 and 18:18), the Lucan Jesus points out that obedience to the Law is a condition for access to salvation. But, "this perverse generation", from which it is fitting to "escape" (Act 2:40), has not known how to respect the will of God. From being a way of salvation, the Law has become an unbearable burden (Act 15:10).

Neither does the apostle Paul deny that the Law leads to salvation (cf. Gal 3:13, a verse too neglected in the discussions concerning the Law in Paul). But, he knows that the Law can incite to sin and encourage the proliferation of evil. Luke, who does not know this conception, is therefore unaware of the expression "Christ, the end of the Law" (Rom 10:4). If this generation is being lost, it is, for Luke, because of human disobedience. His illustration is the gypsy prodigal son. Stephen's speech (especially Act 7:51-53) reveals a Luke who is a theologian of the history of perdition.

This perdition of humanity, of the elected people in particular, makes the savior Jesus necessary. Davidic Messiah, he was sent by God to reestablish a people. By the power of "the finger of God" (Lk 11:20), he casts out demons and brings us nearer to the kingdom. With his Word, he calls upon men and announces salvation and peace to them (Act 10:36).

On two points, Luke remains silent. He does not articulate the notion of conversion in Christology. Why is the kerygma of Jesus, dead and resurrected, now necessary for humanity to be converted? Why does God use the elevation of Christ to offer conversion to Israel (Act 5:31)? Could not this return to God have taken place already before Easter?

To this question which we already noted in the previous chapter, another must be added. This one recalls the discussions of Protestant liberalism: why pass from Jesus who preaches the kingdom to the Church which preaches Jesus? Luke certainly thinks that salvation originates from the contact of the word of God, who forgives and justifies. But, how does he understand this "evolving" word and the transformation of its contents. Is this not a more important change than simply a legitimate adaptation of the kerygma to a new situation?

Whatever his limits, Luke is the witness to a quadruple connotation of salvation.

a) Salvation is not first addressed to the individual. It expresses the voluntary movement of God in favor of his people and, through it, the whole of humanity. The verb "to be saved" is conjugated in the plural. The ecclesiological element of salvation appears (the lost sheep is saved when it is reintegrated into the flock Lk 15:4-7), as much in the Gospel as in the Acts (in the gift of his Son, God acquired a church and not an aggregate of individuals; cf. 2:47).

This Lucan conviction does not contradict the urgent call addressed to each person with a view to faith and conversion. But, it attests at the beginning that salvation suscitates a series of new relations, not only with God and Christ, but also with brothers and sisters in the faith. Luke shares a Hebrew faith: the gift, the God of the fathers offers to everyone, is a place within the community, a cluster of affective relations, a sharing.

b) The OT conceived of salvation as deliverance given to the people and entry into a communal existence offered to the believer. Luke actualizes this concept and retains the concrete and visible trait of this Hebrew heritage. The terms, joy and peace, have a human depth: they express the fruits of the sending of the Son, the spiritual and material blessings which the believers get from their involvement. The Book of Acts narrates how this salvation, offered and received, is lived out now. The Gospel, by the rays of light it sends out here and now to those invited to the Kingdom, also gives the feeling of the concrete and historical character of salvation. In our opinion, the notion of salvation offers an exit to the quarrel which opposes the adherents of salvation history and those of eschatology. Lucan salvation attests that eschatology does not evaporate at contact with history, but is clearly stated in it. Without being triumphalistic, the Church lives out its salvation from now on.

c) There is no triumphalism because salvation is not here to satisfy some lacuna with tangible benefits. God does not respond to the human call with quantifiable gifts. Salvation is not expressed in terms of possession but in terms of relation. Resorting to the Hebrew hope of reestablishment, now fulfilled, it describes this event with a familiar metaphor: the return of the fathers to their sons (cf. Lk 1:17 referring to Mal 3:23f.). Whether it is with God or the brethern, the believer experiences salvation in a relational mode. This is the real but contingent savor of the eschatological joy and peace recovered . The savor is contingent for it is continually threatened: Ananias and Saphira knew something about this. The salvation received can be lost if it is not cared for by the community and the individual. Luke strongly articulates salvation with responsibility: thus the order of our chapter five and six.

Another reality forbids all theology of glory: the unfinished character of salvation, the "not yet" accompanied by the "already". The lack, or gap, provoked by evil still at work, accompanies the eruption and history of salvation. Luke does not erase the tribulations, which flank and stake out the access to Kingdom (Act 14:22). Without being sated, believers with the benefits of new relations are able to persevere.

The figures of Jesus, in the Gospel, and Paul, in the Acts, illustrate in a narrative manner dear to Luke, this constellation of the present and incomplete salvation. The last trip of the one and the other attests to the joyous assurance of those who walk toward the fulfillment by way of poverty and suffering. Without recommending an ideal of poverty or succombing to dolorism, Luke describes the witnesses of God's plan detached from material goods and ready to bear insults.

d) The articulation of ethics with regard to soteriology must be specified. Indeed, we would take the wrong road in limiting the consequences of salvation to responsibility. This would be to omit the confession of faith. Lk 12 makes evident the first responsibility of the believers: the public adherence to Jesus (*ὁμολογέω*, Lk 12: 8). This confession is the first expression of those saved, the gest, from which all others flow, and which integrates, orients and motivates the rest.

CHAPTER 6

THE RECEPTION OF SALVATION

Chronological Bibliography

1933

A. D. NOCK, **Conversion. The Old and New in Religion from Alexander the Great to Augustine of Hippo** (Oxford, 1933; many reprints, 1952, 1961, 1963).

1938

A. WIKENHAUSER, **Die Apostelgeschichte übersetzt und erklärt** (Regensburg, 1938, 1951[1], 1956[1]).

1939

J. GEWIESS, **Die urapostolische Heilsverkündigung nach der Apostel-geschichte** (Breslau, 1939), pp. 106-115.

1942

J. BEHM, E. WÜRTHWEIN, "Art. *νοῦς κτλ.*", **TWNT** IV (Stuttgart, 1942), esp. pp. 994-1004.

1949

J. T. ROSS*, **The Conception of** *σωτηρία* **in the New Testament**, unpublished dissertation, University of Chicago (Chicago, 1947).

1950

R. SCHNACKENBURG, "Typen der Metanoia-Predigt im Neuen Testament", **MüTZ** I (1950) 1-13.

1951

A. RÉTIF, "Témoignage et Prédication missionnnaire dans les Actes des apôtres", **NRT** 73 (1951) 152-165.

A. RÉTIF, "La foi missionnaire ou kérygmatique et ses signes", **RUnOtt** 21 (1951) 151-172.

1952

F. F. BRUCE, "Justification by Faith in in the Non-Pauline Writings of the New Testament", **EvQ** 24 (1952) 66-77.

1953

A. RÉTIF, **Foi au Christ et Missions d'après les Actes des apôtres** (Paris, 1953).

1954

H. CONZELMANN, **Die Mitte der Zeit. Studien zur Theologie des Lukas** (Tübingen, 1954, 1957[2], 1960[3],1962[4]), pp. 193-220 of the 1960[3].

H. G. WOOD, "The Conversion of St Paul: its Nature, Antecedents, and Consequences", **NTS** I (1954-1955) 276-282.

1955

E. SCHWEIZER, "Die Bekehrung des Apollos, Agp. 18, 24-26", **EvT** 15 (1955) 247-254; included in E. Schweizer, **Beiträge zur Theologie des Neuen Testaments. Neutestamentliche Aufsätze (1955-1970)** (Zurich, 1970), pp. 71-79.

1956
J. COMBLIN, "La paix dans la théologie de saint Luc", **ETL** 32 (1956) 439-460.
A. MEUNIER, "La foi dans les Actes des apôtres", **RELiège** 43 (1956) 50-53.
D. M. STANLEY, "The Conception of Salvation in Primitive Christian Preaching", **CBQ** 18 (1956) 231-254; summarized under the title "What the First Christians Meant by Salvation", **TDig** 5 (1957) 137-142.
1957
M. MEINERTZ, "'Dieses Geschlecht' im Neuen Testament", **BZ**, N. F., I (1957) 283-289.
1959
M. H. FRANZMANN, "'The Word of the Lord Grew'. The Historical Character of the New Testament Word", **ConcTM** 30 (1959) 563-581.
R. KOCH*, "Die religiössittliche Umkehr [Metanoia] nach den drei ältesten Evangelien und der Apostelgeschichte", **Anima** 14 (1959) 296-307.
W. LANGE*, "L'appel à la pénitence dans le christianisme primitif", **ColctMech** 44 (1959) 380-390.
I. DE LA POTTERIE, "L'onction du chrétien par la foi", **Bib** 40 (1959) 12-69; taken up in I. de la Potterie and S. Lyonnet, **La vie selon l'Esprit. Condition du chrétien** (Paris, 1965), pp. 107-167.
1960
J. DUPONT, "Repentir et conversion d'après les Actes des apôtres", **ScEccl** 12 (1960) 48-70; included in **Etudes**, Dupont, pp. 421-457.
J. DUPONT, "La conversion dans les Actes des apôtres", **LumVie** 9, N° 47 (1960) 137-173; taken up in **Etudes**, Dupont,1967, pp. 459-476.
D. SQUILLACI, "La conversione dell'Etiope (Atti 8, 26-40)", **PalCl** 39 (1960) 1197-1201.
D. SQUILLACI, "La conversione del Centurione Cornelio (Atti 10)", **PalCl** 39 (1960) 1265-1269.
1961
J. ALFARO, "Fides in terminologia biblica", **Greg** 42 (1961) 463-505.
J. C. O'NEILL, **The Theology of Acts in its Historical Setting** (London, 1961, 1970^2).
D. SQUILLACI, "Saulo prima della conversione", **PalCL** 40 (1961) 139-147.
D. SQUILLACI, "La conversione di San Paolo (Atti 9, 1-19)", **PalCl** 40 (1961) 233-239.
U. WILCKENS, **Die Missionsreden der Apostelgeschichte. Form- und traditionsgeschichtliche Untersuchungen** (Neukirchen, 1961, 1974^3).
1962
S. MACLEAN GILMOUR, "Easter and Pentecost", **JBL** 81 (1962) 62-66.
1963
P. AUBIN, **Le problème de la "conversion". Etude sur un terme commun à l'hellénisme et au christianisme des trois premiers siècles** (Paris, 1963).
M. CAMBE, "La *χάρις* chez saint Luc", **RB** 70 (1963) 193-207.
J. GIBLET, "Art. Pénitence", **SDB** 7, (Paris, 1963), col. 671-683.
1964
W. BARCLAY, **Turning to God: A Study of Conversion in the Book of Acts and Today** (Philadelphia, 1964).
1965

R. MICHIELS, "La conception lucanienne de la conversion", **ETL** 41 (1965) 42-78.

P. TERNANT*, "'Repentez-vous et convertissez-vous', Ac 3, 19", **AssSeign**, first series, 21 (1965) 50-74.

1967

W. S. UDICK*, "Metanoia as found in the Acts of the Apostles. Some Inferences and Reflections", **BiTod** 28 (1967) 1943-1946.

1968

F. X. HEZEL*, "'Conversion' and 'Repentance' in Lucan Theology", **BiTod** 37 (1968) 2596-2607.

1969

H. D. BETZ, "Ursprung und Wesen christlichen Glaubens nach der Emmauslegende (Lk 24, 13-32)", **ZTK** 66 (1969) 7-21.

S. BROWN, **Apostasy and Perseverance in the Theology of Luke** (Rome, 1969).

1970

I. H. MARSHALL, **Luke: Historian and Theologian** (Exeter, 1970).

P. H. MENOUD, "Le salut par la foi selon le livre des Actes", in M. BARTH et al. **Foi et Salut selon S. Paul (épître aux Romains, 1, 16). Colloque Oecuménique à l'Abbaye de S. Paul hors les murs, 16-21 avril 1968** (Rome, 1970), pp. 255-276; taken up in **Jésus-Christ**, Menoud, pp. 130-149.

1971

E. DES PLACES, "Actes 17, 30-31", **Bib** 52 (1971) 526-534.

H. JASCHKE "'λαλεῖν' bei Lukas. Ein Beitrag zur lukanischen Theologie", **BZ**, N. F., 15 (1971) 109-114.

J. JEREMIAS, "Tradition und Redaktion in Lukas 15", **ZNW** 62 (1971) 172-189.

L. SCHOTTROFF, "Das Gleichis vom verlorenen Sohn", **ZTK** 68 (1971) 27-52.

1973

B. DA SPONGANO, "La concezione teologica della predicazione nel libro degli 'Atti'", **RBiblt** 21 (1973) 147-164.

J. WANKE, **Die Emmauserzählung. Eine redaktionsgeschichtliche Untersuchung zu Lk 24, 13-35** (Leipzig, 1973).

1974

J. KODELL, "'The Word of God grew'. The Ecclesial Tendency of Λόγος in Acts 1,7; 12,24; 19,20", **Bib** 55 (1974) 505-519.

C. P. MÄRZ, **Das Wort Gottes bei Lukas. Die lukanische Worttheologie als Frage an die neuere Lukasforschung** (Leipzig, 1974).

Y. REDALIÉ, "Conversion ou libération, Actes 16, 11-40", **Bulletin du Centre Protestant d'Etudes**, Geneva, 26 (1974), N^{O} 7, 7-17.

1975

G. ANTOINE, et al. , **Exegesis, Problèmes de méthodes et exercices de lecture (Genèse 22 et Luc 15)**. Published under the direction of F. Bovon and G. Rouiller (Neuchâtel, 1975). (ET, **Exegesis. Problems of Method and Exercises in Reading (Genesis 22 and Luke 15)** (Pittsburgh, 1978).

C. E. CARLSTON, "Reminiscence and Redaction in Luke 15, 11-32", **JBL** 94 (1975) 368-390.

A. TOSATO,*, "Per una revisione degli studi sulla metanoia neotestamentaria", **RBiblT** 23 (1975) 3-46.

1976

M. DUMAIS, **Le langage de l'évangelisation. L'annonce missionnaire en milieu juif (Actes 13, 16-41)** (Tournai-Montreal, 1976).

A. GEORGE, "L'emploi chez Luc du vocabulaire de salut", **NTS** 23 (1976-1977) 308-320.

R. P. MARTIN, "Salvation and Discipleship in Luke's Gospel", **Interpr** 30 (1976) 366-380.

1977

JEANNE D'ARC, **Les pélerins d'Emmaüs** (Paris, 1977).

CHAPTER 6

THE RECEPTION OF SALVATION

Introduction

It may seem arbitrary to the reader that we distinguish salvation from its reception; an objective soteriology from a subjective one. Beside the practical interest that this separation offers, we think that Luke himself makes a distinction between the kerygma and the acceptation of the word, between the salvation effected by Christ and the movement of man toward this salvation [1]. It seems to us that the Evangelist has a bit of a struggle to tie together theologically what God has accomplished (the schema of salvation history) and what man is called to do (the schema of conversion).

In this chapter, we will present the principle works of the past few years concerning the appropriation of salvation in Lucan theology. Should we not begin with the themes of election, grace, the gift of the Spirit and vocation? This is not certain, for Luke speaks little of an prevenient intervention of God other than the ministry of Jesus Christ (cf. our preceding chapter) and the preaching of Church (cf. our chapter on the Church). Here we retain only what concerns the hearer of the word, the man who will become Christian: his repentence, conversion, coming to faith, in one word his salvation. We will deal with repentence and conversion and signal in footnotes what touches faith.

As we know, Luke confers a great importance to repentence and conversion. With the word faith, these terms designate a movement and a manner by which one becomes a Christian. Richer in the Lucan corpus than in the rest of the NT (with the exception of Revelation), this vocabulary, however, is not used in a stereotyped or technical way. A certain fluctuation in the use of this word provokes a number of questions: must all men repent in order to come to faith? Are repentence and conversion synonymous in Luke? Does Luke know of an _ordo salutis_ by which man passes from repentence through forgiveness, baptism, faith and the gift of the Spirit to glory? Is conversion the work of man, the gift of God or both? How is repentence to be articulated with regard to the work of Christ (mainly the resurrection, the Parousia or the crucifixion)? Are repentence and forgiveness in a relation of cause and effect? And what about the relations between conversion and faith?

The contributions which we will present all begin with one conviction: Luke is a theologian who gives an answer to these questions, but perhaps only implicitly. His understanding of faith is lively enough to sense the problems and give them a solution adapted to his time and his community.

They diverge, however, on the degree of originality that they find in the Lucan writings. Differing from J. Behm (-> 1942) who still deals with the whole Synoptic block in the article *μετάνοια* of the **Theologisches Wörterbuch zum Neuen Testament**, these exegetes are persuaded that Luke must be studied alone. Yet this analysis of Lucan redaction leads some to disconnect the Evangelist from his hagiographic frame while others find the reflection of the early Christian doctrine of conversion in the Lucan work.

For the sake of memory, we would like to mention two relatively old contributions which have not lost all their interest. J. Gewiess (-> 1939) discusses the "path which leads to salvation" in the fifth part of his classic **Die urapostolische Heilsverkündigung nach der Apostelgeschichte**. The first chapter of this part is dedicated to conversion and faith, the second, to baptism and the third, to the controversies between the new way of salvation and the old, marked by the Temple and the Law [**2**]. If the author is no doubt wrong in identifying repentence (*μετάνοια*) and conversion (*ἐπιστρέφειν*), on the other hand, he is right in saying that conversion, the first requirement of the apostolic message, is not the same for all in the Lucan writings. He believes - and on this point, he has been followed by many - that Luke distinguishes the conversion of the Jews, who must repent of the murder of Jesus, from that of the Gentiles, who must repent from their idolatry. The nature of conversion, common to all, is the attachment to Jesus, the Messiah and Lord. For all must see in the death of Jesus the reversal of a failure and accept the resurrection of the Messiah. By leaving their various situations, believers place themselves under God's unique domination.

R. Schnackenburg (-> 1950) accepts variety in the NT use of the term *μετάνοια* , but he makes this diversity depend, not on different theologies, but on divers stages in salvation history. The preaching of repentence in the early Church, as we encounter it in Acts (pp. 7-9) represents a type, which because of the time, differs from John the Baptist's (centered on the imminence of judgment) and Jesus' (marked by the eruption of the kingdom). In Acts (i.e. for Schnackenburg, in early Christianity), the center of the message moves and passes from the Kingdom of God to the person of the resurrected Jesus. Furthermore, the imminence of the Parousia gives way to a longer period. These two changes do not suppress the requirement of conversion, but modify it. The moral aspect (to turn from evil) is accompanied by a religious value (to turn toward God) which is more and more pronounced. This religious value is specified from the resurrection on: it includes faith in Jesus Christ (Act 20:21 and 26:18-20), a Jesus Christ indissociable from his eschatological work, marked by his death, resurrection and exaltation (Schnackenburg's proposed link between conversion and eschatology will later be the subject of vibrant discussions). Finally, conversion acts as the condition of baptism. This is to say that it also involves the will of the believer to be part of God's people [**3**]. Schnackenburg's article and Gewiess' book are mainly amiss in identifying the data in Acts with the realities of primitive Christianity, as if Luke reproduced faithfully the theology of the apostles.

I. H. CONZELMANN (-> 1954) AND U. WILCKENS (->1961)

a. Our interest in the pages which Conzelmann consecrates to conversion is mainly because of the manner which the author organically inserts this theme into the whole of Lucan theology. Having analyzed Luke's understanding of eschatology (the future) and salvation history (mainly, the past of the OT and the story of Jesus), the German exegete logically explains the Lucan interpretation of the present.

For Luke, how can the ties between the believer and the salvation events be established today? His answer is: in an objective manner by doctrine and in a subjective way, by the Nachfolge. In both cases, the Church gains importance that it did not have when objective and subjective salvation formed a unity. At the same time, the Church transmits the message and opens the doors to converts. This role of mediator which it fills explains this thesis, surprising at first, which accompanies the title of the last part of his book: "Man and Salvation: The Church".

Man finds his insertion into the history of salvation only through the Church. "Der Einzelne steht in der Kirche und dadurch in einer bestimmten Phase der Geschichte." (p. 194). We cannot deal with the problem of man's access to salvation without a preliminary analysis of the mission of the Church (the Church, pp. 209-215; the bearers of the message, pp. 215-218.; the message, pp. 218-225, ET). The Church permits the individual to reach past salvation in Jesus Christ and future salvation in the kingdom. It is thanks to the diffusion of the Spirit in the Church that this double contact can be made (and not because, for example, of a practice of the sacraments). This double relation with salvation does not however exclude the historical distance: the Church has its own history (the Urgemeinde differs, for example, from the churches born from the Pauline missions). Access to the saving message and insertion into its time are the two principle characteristics of the Church.

By detaching objective salvation from the subjective version and coupling them at the same time with ecclesiology, Luke opens up the two themes of man's coming to faith and Christian perseverence to reflection. Without stereotyping them, the Evangelist fixes, on the one hand, a series of steps by which man enters into the Church and salvation. But, on the other hand, he makes the Christian life problematic. For it becomes difficult by reason of the protracted time period until the Parousia.

From these preliminary remarks, Conzelmann shows how the original unity of conversion disintegrates and how conversion being eschatological, receives an increasingly ethical coloring (pp. 225-231, ET). In his demonstration, the author does not argue according to a linear logic. Like an impressionistic painter, he presents Luke's opinion with several brush strokes: without developing a psychology, Luke, he tells us, tends to understand the access to faith in a psychological manner, even if he understands conversion and faith as the works of God. In his view, psychology and ethics get along quite well in Luke: different from Mark, Luke distinguishes forgiveness from *μετάνοια* which then becomes the condition. Salvation, then, does not coincide with the forgiveness of sins, but succeeds it. Conversion, itself, is subdivided into two: it is both the return to oneself and an action: cf. Act 3:19 and 26:20. The call to conversion no longer rings out because of the imminence of the end but because of the existence of the Church (preaching and baptism) and the personal future of the believer (hope of individual resurrection). Conzelmann finally notes two limits to this process of disintegration and 'psychologization': a) Luke describes the stages of the coming of man to faith, not the steps of Christian existence; b) repentence and conversion have certainly become the conditions but for all this they are not transformed into meritorious works.

Different from Schnackenburg (whom he does not cite), Conzelmann is right to abandon the identification of Lucan conversion with that of early Christianity. It is precisely the con - sciousness of the distance separating the first times and Luke's own, which permits Conzelmann to rightly deny the impact of eschatology on the Lucan doctrine of conversion. Yet we must note two of Conzelmann's weaknesses: first, he offers no serious semantic analysis of the terms *μετάνοια* and *ἐπιστρέφειν* (he exaggeratedly schematizes their relations) [**4**]; and secondly, he does not use the narrative of the prodigal son to define man's access to salvation [**5**]: this oversight leads him to intellectualize the procedure. We think on the contrary that the first step toward conversion, repentence is not uniquely the taking of the doctrine seriously. While being a declaration by man of his sinful state, it is also the awareness of a possible salvation. Similarly, the second stage is not an ethical act alone, but also and especially an existential movement toward God.

b. U. Wilckens (-> 1961) could not analyze the theological discourses in Acts without considering the call to conversion which concludes many of them. In his method, theological sense and, sometimes, arbitrariness, Wilckens resembles Conzelmann. The exegete from Hamburg thinks that the schema of the access to salvation is both more complete and more precise than the author of **Die Mitte der Zeit** thought. He determines six steps: 1) *μετάνοια* , 2) baptism (note the role of the name which relates baptism to the kerygma centered on Jesus Christ), 3) the forgiveness of sins, 4) the reception of the Holy Spirit, 5) the placing among all believers (insertion into salvation history) and 6) the access to salvation.

Wilckens has no difficulty admitting that the complete schema occurs only once: in Act 2:38-40. However, he thinks that these first conversions to the Christian faith, at Pentecost, are of such a programmatic nature that they confer a normative value to the schema.

The author then wonders if Luke imagined this ordo salutis or if he depends on a tradition. For Wilckens, the schema corresponds basically to the missionary reality of the Hellenistic church to which Luke belongs. Luke's originality lies in the projection of this schema into the beginnings of the Church and adapting it to what he believes to be the situation of the very first converts. In this way, the particular meaning of *μετάνοια* in the first chapters of Acts (repentence from the death of Jesus) would have been invented by Luke.

Like for Conzelmann, Wilckens thinks the Lucan *μετάνοια* has a double coloration: a) moral and b) heilsgeschichtlich. Whether Jew or pagan, all must repent of their faults and be inserted, no longer into the eschatological situation but, into the history of salvation. According to this definition of the first step of the diagram, Wilckens does not go beyond Conzelmann. In one area, he even remains behind him: he thinks it is evident ("offenbar", p. 180!) that *μετάνοια* and *ἐπιστρέφειν* are interchangeable expressions, while Conzelmann was right in distinguishing them.

Wilckens is not clear on another point: he analyzes the tradition-redaction rapport for the entire outline, but hardly notices when the double coloration mentioned above comes on the scene. No doubt, he considers these particular connotations as Lucan: he is only repeating Conzelmann.

Concerning another element, Wilckens lacks the wisdom, Conzelmann had shown. The latter, considered in fact that it was not necessary to follow the Lucan expressions too closely. He thought the ordo salutis and the psychology, which are necessarily related, are not found in Luke except in embryonic form. On the contrary, Wilckens does not hesitate to develope an outline so rigid that it does not respect the diversity of the texts. Cornelius is, nevertheless, there to show us that the Holy Spirit can descend before baptism, and the Samaritans recall the existence of the imposition of hands (on which Wilckens remains mute) between baptism and the effusion of the Spirit.

Other criticisms come to mind: what proves that the schema, valid for the Gentiles, was projected into the past of the early Church, with regard to the Jews? Could not the contrary be true if we imagine that the tendency to make the Jews guilty (and consequently, to incite them to conversion when they desire to enter the Church) is older than Luke? Saying that the rapport between conversion and baptism is typical of Luke (and the author of Hebrews), is this not to underestimate the influence of the ministry of John the Baptist on primitive Christianity? Finally, to suppose that the moral coloration of conversion is redactional, is this not to neglect the phenomenology of all access to salvation and underestimate the contribution of Qumran (Essene conversion is as moral as religious) **[6]**. Willingly, we would admit that Luke tends to conceive of the liberation from sin in a more moral manner than, say, a Paul, but this is because the Parousia is getting farther and farther away and individualism is setting in.

II. J. DUPONT (-> 1960, both titles), J. GIBLET (-> 1963) AND R. MICHIELS (-> 1965)

a. The discussion continues in the French-speaking world. Dom Dupont consecrated two articles to the subject; they testify to an analytical mind and a sense of synthesis at the same time. In a nuanced manner, the Belgian exegete distinguishes repentence from conversion, including all the while repentence into the global process of conversion.

There is no hope of conversion for man except when he senses that he is a sinner before God and desires to obtain for - giveness. Luke distinguishes three sorts of repentence: 1) that of the Jews in Jerusalem, who are responsible for the death of Jesus and must repent of this crime, 2) that of the Gentiles, submitted to idolatry, whose first task is to detach themselves from their false gods and 3) that of the Jews of the Diaspora and the "Godfearers", who must simply believe (this faith, as the example of Cornelius shows (Act 10:43), offers forgiveness to good people who have no explicit reason to be called to repentence) **[7]**. By establishing this third path of access to salvation in an original way, Dupont respects the Lucan texts, but, at the same time, does not forget to bring the three categories together: for Luke is conscious of the universality of sin, sin more or less spectacular according to the human situations. "The call to faith always implies the consciousness of sin and the desire for forgiveness." (p. 461) **[8]**. Dupont refuses therefore to imagine an access to faith that could do - for lack of sin - without forgiveness. Is Luke as explicit on this point as Dupont supposes?

A precise analysis of the vocabulary of repentence and con - version makes Dupont underline the <u>movement</u> toward God. It would be false, we are told, to insist only on the fact of <u>turning</u>. Of course, for the human being this means to turn toward God, but this rotation must be followed by a step toward him. In Acts, conversion therefore implies an ethical movement toward God as well as the decision to look to him. In a detailed fashion, Dupont also notes that for Luke we are not converted to a doctrine, be it Christianity or other, but to a person, God or the Christ.

What can provoke this renunciation of a guilty past and this step toward God? To answer this question, J. Dupont has the kerygma intervene, a kerygma with salvation historical dimensions. "Concretely, to enter into the perspective in Acts, it is necessary to envisage conversion in the relation which unites it to the decisive moments of salvation history: the Passion, resurrection and last judgment." (p. 421) **[9]**.

The Christian regime is here to be distinguished from Judaism. Turning to the Lord is no longer synonymous to turning toward God, as Jesus is henceforth also Lord. One must therefore turn toward him.

Christ is alive. His past resurrection possesses a present force: as Act 5:31 says, Jesus is risen and exalted in order to give *μετάνοια* to Israel. He now offers it through the kerygma of the apostles which accompanies the miraculous signs (cf. Act 4:33) and the interior action of grace. Of course, the signs do not convert man: they only surprise or unsettle him. However, when the Christian message explains the signs (as is the case at Pentecost), they manifest an intervention of the living Christ with a view to conversion. Aside from this visible effort, the Risen One intervenes inwardly, too: he opens, for example, Lydia's heart (Act 16:14). "In order for a conversion to take place, a meeting with God is necessary, a meeting impossible for man, if God does not manifest himself to man." (p. 449) **[10]**.

The future of Christ, i.e. the Parousia and Judgment, also plays a role in man's decision. Several Lucan texts, of which Act 17:30f. (Paul's speech to the Athenians) is the most famous, warn men who are reticent toward the Gospel. Christian preachers note the risk these men run: to be rejected at the last judgment. "A sign preceding the end time, the resurrection of Jesus invites sinners to examine their consciences, repent and believe in order to gain forgiveness of their sins before the great assizes of the last judgment." (p. 472) **[11]**.

Dupont considers that the divers aspects of conversion which he has highlighted from Acts correspond to what the first Christians meant by the term. He seems thus to refuse an evolution of the Christian doctrine of conversion. For him, the evolution precedes Christianity: this Christian theme comes from the OT and Judaism. It undergoes a reinterpretation in Christian circles and it is here that there is evolution (Dupont outlines the main differences between Jewish and Christian conversion) **[12]**. Normally a defender of the redaktionsgeschichtlich method, Dupont minimizes the semantic evolution which goes from the origins of the Church to the time and person of Luke. The most he can say, without being more precise, is "This simple summary [of the Lucan texts mentioning μετάνοια where Mark does not signal it] makes us think that the calls to "repent" and "be converted" must be explained not only by way of the context of the apostolic preaching but also by the personal preoccupations of Luke, as much in the Gospel as in Acts." (p. 423). The legitimate insistance which he places on the linking of conversion to salvation history should have incited him to underline more forcefully the tensions between the Lucan redaction and the traditions he uses.

Several critical remarks force to correct certain of Dupont's views and to better distinguish Luke's thought from the other NT authors.

a) Dupont no doubt exaggerates the psychological nature of conversion: his interpretation of repentence seems to be marked by the centuries of penitential exercises which are behind us [**13**]. It is our opinion that the Lucan repentence is less a moral mea culpa than an existential statement concerning one's own situation (the situation of the human being, who is more lost than guilty).

Inversely, Dupont seems to overestimate the role of God in conversion. For us, Luke leaves man with the care of his own fate. The prodigal son goes home by himself. If Luke can say that God gives conversion, we must understand this expression - Michiels has understood it - as the corresponding Jewish topos: God offers man the possibility to be converted (cf. Act 17:30; Conzelmann caught a glimpse of it) [**14**]. Too many authors especially Protestant, joyfully share Dupont's opinion: for them, Luke knew how to defend the prevenient grace of God [**15**]. Certainly Luke reminds us of the initiative and intervention of God, but refuses to transform man into a puppet of grace. The work of God is situated on another level than that of μετάνοια .

b) Having said this, Luke occupies a special place within early Christianity. His concept of sin, repentence and forgiveness differs from Paul's or Mark's. In Mark, μετάνοια contains the work of God and the decision of man, the beginning of this relationship as well as the whole of salvation. Luke clearly restricts conversion to the first steps of man toward God. Paul speaks little of repentence or forgiveness: for him, God frees us from the hold of sin (in fact, he has already freed us) and does so by the cross of Christ and not by our decision.

b. P. Giblet's article (-> 1963) appeared in the **Supplément au Dictionnaire de la Bible** and analyzes the majority of the Lucan texts relative to repentence and conversion. Here we will communicate only a few of the dominating ideas and original remarks.

As we know, Luke insists on the vocabulary of repentence and conversion (these terms are not synonymous in his work). By doing this he underlines the anthropological aspects: repentance and conversion go neither without initial faith and humility nor without a subsequent personal change of life. He also relates the attachments with the kerygma: this is Giblet's main thesis, which rejoins Dom Dupont's analyses on this point. The formal link between the salvific events and the call to conversion, within the kerygma of Acts, depends upon the theological articulation between the work of Christ and conversion of man. "If we study here only the aspect of repentence and conversion, we cannot forget that they are organically related on the one hand, to the salvation events, and on the other hand, to faith and baptism. Conversion is not possible and has meaning only with regard to the Easter event." (col. 679). Father Giblet thinks that by this junction concerning salvation history, Luke enriches the theme of conversion he inherited from Hellenistic Judaism (col. 680) **[16]**.

c. R. Michiels' article (-> 1965) seems to be the most striking of the last twenty years. Dialoguing with Conzelmann, Descamps, Schürmann and Wilckens **[17]**, the author analyzes with great rigor all the Lucan texts relative to conversion. He applies the redaktionsgeschichtlich method with success.

In his introduction, Michiels presents the actual positions concerning eschatology (Conzelmann and Schürmann) and conversion (Conzelmann and Wilckens) in the Lucan work. He accompanies these summaries with an NT inventory of the vocabulary of conversion (*μετάνοια* , *ἐπιστρέφειν*, etc.).

A first section of the first part deals with conversion as it appears in the context of the Christological speeches addressed to the Jews in the first half of Acts. In these first sermons, Luke insists on the offer of repentence which is made to the Jews. Despite the gravity of the fault committed, the murder of Jesus, God gives the inhabitants of Jerusalem an (last?) occasion to buy themselves back. By repentence and baptism, they can still receive forgiveness for their sins **[18]**. The time of the Church is thus distinctive by divine mercy. The quotation of Isa 6:9f. concerning the hardening of Israel finds its legitimate place neither in the framework of the drama of the Passion, nor even at the time of the first Christian proclamations, but at the end of the last chapter of Acts [19].

Contrary to the early Christian message, the eschatological motivation of conversion is toned down. Here, Michiels' analyses confirm Conzelmann's intuition: it is no longer the imminence of the Kingdom which incites man to repent but the actual manifestation in the kerygma of risen Christ. The perspective is heilsgeschichtlich and not eschatological: the Christian description of ethics and the Church in terms of "path" (*ὁδός*) is there to show this [20]. *Μετάνοια* is no longer the condensation of the whole Christian life, but the designation of the first step of the believers. In the case of the Jews, this beginning is decisive and consists in repentence. However, as Luke realizes that this beginning is not enough, he can apply the vocabulary of conversion to the Jews also: *ἐπιστρέφειν* (cf. Act 9:35). Unleashed from eschatology and placed in relation with the forgiveness in the Church, the notion of *μετάνοια* has a clearly moral character. We cannot draw an argument from the affirmation that God gives conversion to Israel (Act 5:31) or the Gentiles (Act 11:18), to question this moral note. Michiels shows forcefully that this expression does not mean that God diffuses his prevenient grace, but that he offers the occasion to be converted (cf. Act 17:30). By using this formulation, Luke takes over an old topos of Hellenistic Judaism with a sapiential tendency (p. 46).

The second section of the first part points out that if the access to salvation is structured in the same way for Jew and Gentile alike, the importance of the stages varies according to the case. Concerning the Gentiles, Luke emphasizes *ἐπιστρέφειν*: turning toward God, after detaching themselves from their idols. Michiels refuses here to oppose Luke to Paul, as if Act 14 and 17 represent a "liberal" solution in the face of the "orthodox" position which Paul would hold in Rom 1. In Luke, the universality of salvation goes hand in hand with the universality of sin. Even if by captio benevolentiae, Luke does not inculpate the Gentiles, he hardly imagines them as innocent. Since idolatry is an error, they must also repent (the vocabulary of *μετάνοια* applies occasionally to them as well: cf. Act 11:18; 17:30; 20:21 and 26:20).

Finally, Michiels analyzes briefly what traditions Luke might have taken over: for him, the schema of conversion of the Gentiles existed before Luke (with Wilckens and others) (p. 54). It is the same for the offer of *μετάνοια* to Israel: this is an archaic theme (against Wilckens) (p. 48) [21]. This traditional foundation must not however, hinder us from grasping the importance of the redactional rereading, a rereading which has an ethical sense and which, consequently, subdivides the process of access to faith and salvation into steps.

Michiels' argumentation manifests its strength in the second part of the article: the author confirms his ideas in a stunning way in interpreting the Gospel of Luke. He does it in three stages: first, he analyzes conversion in Luke's **Sondergut** [ET, "own property"] (Lk 5:32; 15:1-32; 17:3b-4; 13:3 and 5; 16:19-31; 24:47 and 22:32), then in the Lucan reinterpretation of the Synoptic tradition (Lk 3:1-20; 11:32; 10:13.15; 8:10b and Act 28:25-27); finally, he studies the Marcan texts where the conversion theme occurs, which are not taken up by Luke (Mk 1:15b and 6:12).

In his analysis of the Gospel's texts, Michiels finds a middle position between the extreme interpretations of Descamps and Jeremias [**22**]. Msgr. Descamps interprets several Lucan texts parenetically: they would be an invitation addressed to guilty Christians (and not to Jews and Gentiles) to be converted a second time. On the contrary, Jeremias discovers in the same texts the original eschatological conception of conversion with regard to the kingdom of God. In a convincing manner, Michiels points out that a kerygmatic perspective is indeed at stake, but a kerygma which had been modified: the Lord proclaimed by the Church now holds the position occupied previously by the kingdom of God, whose coming was imminent. In the Gospel like in Acts, *μετάνοια* is the benevolent and merciful offer of God, which is made to Jew and Gentile by the intermediary of the Christian Church.

Michiels affirms in conclusion that the Lucan vocabulary of conversion reflects a certain evolution. If several texts maintain the original relation between conversion and the Parousia (Lk 3:7-9; 10:13-15; 11:32; 13;3, 5; 16:19-31; Act 3:19-21; 10:42 and 17:30-31), the majority disconnect *μετάνοια* from its eschatological frame [**23**] "according to a history of salvation, which sees conversion offered everywhere and to all, thanks to the apostolic proclamation, and which considers consequently the promises of salvation as essentially fulfilled and accomplished in medio Ecclesiae. In this manner, the Evangelist shrinks the notion. It no longer expresses conversion in its totality. Luke dismembers the de-eschatologized process of conversion. Metanoia signifies henceforth for him the moral aspect of conversion.. Metanoia has become the condition for the remission of sins. In several texts, Luke seems even to forsee metanoia as a permanent moral disposition of Christian life." (p. 76). Concerning this, Michiels could have related this last extension to the logion concerning the import of the cross (Lk 9:23) where Luke alone adds "every day": "If someone wants to follow me, he must deny himself and take up his cross every day and follow me." **[24]**

On the whole, Michiels' study has won our adhesion by the rigor with which it draws out Conzelmann's intuitions.

III. W. BARCLAY (-> 1964)

The little book from the professor of Glasgow is the presentation of the A. S. Peake Memorial Lecture, given in 1963. It is not a scientific approach in the strictest sense. Aside from the oral character of the account, we must note the harmonizing and conservative attitude of the author: what Acts tells us about conversion is true for early Christianity and harmoniously fits into the whole of the Biblical message.

Nonetheless, Barclay's explanations are quite interesting. They emphasize the coherence of Acts by placing the theme of conversion in its proper place into the ensemble of Luke's theological system. The differences between the Christian system and the other ancient religious systems of wisdom - and Barclay knows them well - becomes even more evident.

After a philological chapter centered on the verbs *ἐπιστρέφειν* and *στρέφειν* (the passing from a literal to a figurative sense, from a profane to a religious sense, from a Hellenistic to a semitic context), the author describes conversion as a passage from ignorance to knowledge, from evil to good, from Satan to God. As a Protestant theologian, Barclay studies first the movement toward God, then the rupture with past sins. Concerning this, he makes two interesting remarks: a) conversion is a passage from the oscillation of the will to a calm state in faith; b) what man leaves behind amounts to things, dead objects (idols, for example).

The third chapter analyzes the phenomena which conversion produces. Here of course, first we have the proclamation, a proclamation which varies with its location and at the same time, remains identical to itself because of its Christological contents **[25]**. Miraculous signs, the exemplary life of the Christians and the Holy Scriptures can also lead a man to conversion. Yet, more than the others, Barclay rightly insists on the role of dialogue: Acts points out numerous conversations and disputes which were at the origin of several conversions [26].

The Church demands three requirements or rather proposes three gests to those who welcome the word: μετάνοια, baptism and faith (chapter 4). Repentence [27] is not only regretting the annoying consequences of a past sin: it is renouncing the guilty act and even the intention which precedes it. Baptism, as the baptism of adults, destined for the Jews as well as the Greeks, is a pledge of the man who on this occasion experiences the intervention of God. Faith holds for true what the message pro - claims. It goes beyond the intellectual conviction to become total acceptance of the person.

Chapter five demonstrates that conversion is but a beginning and it imposes certain general demands (holiness is understood as being different from the world and as an engagement in the world) and particular ones, too (ethics). Conversion leads to a life of obedience, but a free and joyous obedience. The reference is no longer a legal sanction but the love of God. Here, Barclay examines first of all the apostolic decree (Act 15:23, 29), showing the moral importance at the time (even understood in its original formulation which is ritual), and then the summary of Act 2:42-47.

The Church must not consider its task terminated once a convert has been baptized. Its permanent mission is to teach, fortify, exhort and encourage those who have found asylum with its ranks. Conversion fits into a community project.

As we see, Barclay is unaware of the actual problematic. He says nothing of the ties which bind conversion to eschatology and he minimizes the difference between the conversion (to the kingdom) proposed by Jesus and the one proposed by the Church (to the Lord). This does not diminish the fact that here and there, he notes important aspects of conversion that other exegetes have too often left in the shadow.

IV.L. SCHOTTROFF (-> 1971)

Luise Schottroff is active in contemporary discussions relative to the historical Jesus. She attempts to show that the concept of salvation developed in Lk 15:11-32 is in no way distinct from the soteriology of the Gospel of Luke on the whole or from that of the book of the Acts. She thinks that no doctrinal theme constrains us to attribute the parable of the prodigal son to tradition [**28**]. Other arguments are added to this one, in particular the rooting of this story in the Greco-Roman rhetorical tradition [**29**]. The author concludes that the parable of the prodigal son does not help us to recover the teaching of Jesus.

J. Jeremias (-> 1971) rejected this conclusion for philological reasons. What interests us here is the emphasis on Lucan soteriology to which L. Schottroff is attached (by soteriology, she means subjective soteriology which the present chapter is dealing with).

First, she treats (pp. 29-31) the soteriology of Acts: in this work, salvation is closely associated to repentence and the forgiveness of sins, to the point that Luke cannot describe the Pauline conception of justification (cf. Act 13:38) without understanding it as a proclamation of repentence and forgiveness (which it is not in the authentic Pauline writings) [**30**].

Luke insists on the universal necessity of repentence (*πάντας πανταχοῦ*, Act 17:30), yet all the while distinguishing from case to case the guilty past from which one must turn [**31**]."So generell es gilt, dass der Heilsvollzug Abkehr vom Vorausliegenden ist, so speziell ist jeweils die Bestimmung des Vorausliegenden." (p. 30). Differing from Paul, Luke does not understand sin as a power holding all men in the same grip of slavery.

In return, conversion toward God is always understood in the same manner: to turn to God and subsidiarily to Jesus.

Forgiveness cannot be granted without being preceded by the double movement of repentence and conversion. This call to personal initiative and responsibility does not however preclude the gratuitousness of pardon, since Luke can interpret repentence as a divine gift.

This presentation, which leans on the contributions of Conzelmann and Wilckens, is not unattackable: we cannot admit that Luke does not consider guilty, the past from which the believer must detach himself (this sin is certainly understood differently from Paul: it is personal guilt and not super-human force). Neither can we concede that conversion toward God for Luke does not imply adhesion to the Lord Jesus Christ.

The interest of Mrs. Schottroff's work resides rather in the elaboration of the soteriology of the third Gospel, and more particularly of the parable of the prodigal son.

Lk 5:32; 17:3f. and 15:7 are the editorial passages of the Gospel which manifest a close relation between salvation and *μετάνοια*. If the point of the traditional parable of the lost sheep was in the shepherd's joy at the reunion, it is modified in the lesson that the final editor draws (Lk 15:7). The accent moves from the shepherd to the sheep: the latter incarnates the true convert, while the ninety-nine others become people who think themselves righteous [**32**].

What was still embryonic unfurls in the parable of the lost son. The parable forms a unity: none of the literary, juridical redactionsgeschichtlich or theological arguments invoked by other exegetes can cast a doubt on the original coherence of the whole parable. In this text, Luke's subjective soteriology comes to the light [**33**]: the prodigal expects nothing from his father. He has nothing to offer. He lives the μετάνοια as Luke perceives it and reacts in two steps: first, he talks to himself and then he goes and confesses his sins to his father. He turns from his past to come to God. Without being an allegory, the account reflects precisely Luke's soteriology where μετάνοια is at the heart. The elder son is not a reply to the historical Pharisees, but the Lucan incarnation of the one who thinks himself righteous. The words "my son who was dead has returned to life, he who was lost is found" (Lk 15:24; cf. 15:32) confirms this soteriological interpretation.

We are thankful to L. Schottroff for having recalled the impor - tance of Lk 15 in the study of Lucan soteriology. We share most of her views: Lk 15 reflects the convictions of the Evangelist, convictions according to which salvation is lived out by personal μετάνοια. We also think that conversion is detached from eschatology to a large degree.

Yet our reservations concern three points:

a) It is not certain that the Greco-Roman rhetorical tradition is the background of Lk 15:11-32. The themes of the return from a trip, the father who forgives and the rivality between two brothers are much too anchored in the Biblical tradition to make us venture into another tradition. Luke could adapt an authentic parable of Jesus to his theology.

b) At the end of the article, the author insists, in a manner a bit too Pauline and Lutheran for us, on the gratuity of salvation. "Ist hier nun das Sündenbekenntnis, die Busse, Bedingung des Heiles? Nur in dem Sinne, dass das Heil dem geschenkt wird, der es sich schenken lässt,..." (p. 48f.). For Luke, μετάνοια is the work of man, the way to enter salvation history (on p. 31, Mrs. Schottroff hesitates on the meaning to give to words δοῦναι μετάνοιαν: the offer of salvation or the possiblity to be saved? She seems to have settled the question at the end of her article).

c) The author does not emphasize enough the relation that Luke establishes between conversion and Jesus Christ, between subjective and objective soteriology [**34**]. Even if Luke does not perfectly reconcile the two, he does not prefer one over the other. True μετάνοια is not fulfilled except within a Christian regime. Therefore it seems proper to us not to point out the absence of Christology in Lk 15:11-32, unless we recall its presence in Lk 15:1-8 (the shepherd) and especially in the narrative of the disciples of Emmaus (Lk 24:13-35). If, as L. Schottroff says, the parable of the prodigal son invites to conversion (toward God) [**35**], the parallel account of the disciples of Emmaus leads toward the Resurrected One [**36**].

Conclusion

Luke clearly insists on man's responsibility. Repentence and conversion are his task and responsibility. It is what he must do: a priority ποιεῖν which involves him entirely. It is a task which bears fruit (Act 26:20: ἄξια τῆς μετανοίας ἔργα πράσσοντας; cf. Lk 3:7). Compared to this ethical necessity, the eschatological motivation is toned down. When it appears, it is integrated into the moral side, as is attested in the famous verses of Act 3:19ff., for which Luke must not be made entirely responsible. It is a Jewish conviction that conversion allows or provokes the end time; Luke has inherited this from tradition and has not felt the need to eliminate it.

Let us not accuse Luke of having emphasized the moral aspect of μετάνοια. By maintaining the individual reponsibility, even if he justifies it differently, he remains faithful to one of Jesus' requirements, rooted in the OT.

It is better to understand these calls, by situating them with regard to perdition and life, and then to the evangelical message and Church life.

Let us place in parallel Lk 13:3, 5 ; Lk 5:31, and 15:7 and 10: in one case perdition precedes conversion, in the other, it follows. In each case, death is not a fatal issue but the consequence of an error. This state of perdition, which represents the approbation of a life, recalls the gravity with which God considers what we do. It suppresses all divine indifference with respect to us and forbids a "laisser aller" on our part.

Between the present perdition and death to come, God offers the possibility of a history: that of μετάνοια which shakes the static situation, the negative immutability. The message which is heard offers the possibility to change the situation that men tend to believe is unchangeable. A grammatical game illustrates and explains this offer: *ὁ θεὸς τὰ νῦν ἀπαγγέλλει τοῖς ἀνθρώποις πάντας πανταχοῦ μετανοεῖν.* (Act 17:30). The dative *ἀνθρώποις* attests that the initiative is not their own. God is the grammatical and real subject of the innovation (*ὁ θεός*). But immediately called into question, men are called to act, to become in turn the subjects of this *μετανοεῖν* in the syntax of life.

The action of God does not exclude the action of man, for the gift *τοῦ δοῦναι μετάνοιαν τῷ Ἰσραήλ*, Act 5:31 and *ἄρα καὶ τοῖς ἔθνεσιν ὁ θεὸς τὴν μετάνοιαν εἰς ζωὴν ἔδωκεν*, Act 11:18) is not an object, but a relation where the movement of the one provokes the reaction of the other. This action is said, according to a performative discourse of a particular genre. It is not effective in itself but after it is given: hear and obedience (*ἀκούω* may already have this double connotation; cf. Act 28:28: the pagans *ἀκούσονται*).

It would be too simple to say that God's call precedes the answer of man. The relation between the two is more complex and dialectical. The strange expression "to be converted *εἰς τὸ κήρυγμα*" (Lk 11:32; that we have here a sermon of Jonah changes nothing) suggests that the human being must give proof of certain dispositions and witness to an interior *μετάνοια*, in order to understand the saving message which God addresses to him. Inversely, a text like Lk 24:47 attests that the kerygma must be proclaimed and *μετάνοια* proposed before conversion takes place and the new life begins. The meeting between God and the believer thus will take place and open up onto a living relation, if the two partners decide to start on their way one toward the other.

If we are attentive to the content of the message, we will see that Luke respects the stages of salvation history. In the body of the Gospel, which recounts the time of Jesus, God alone and his kingdom explicitly constitute the good news. In the Acts, which evokes the time of the Church, the message concerns not only the Father but the Son, too. Summarizing his missionary activity, Paul recalls that his testimony "called both Jews and Greeks to be converted to God and believe in our Lord Jesus " (Act 20:21).

Let us now look at the ties which Luke established between the Word, the Spirit and conversion: Luke's theological project confers a fundamental function to the Word. The role of the Spirit rests secondary in the emergence of *μετάνοια* within the sphere of sin. In one text however Luke associates the offer of *μετάνοια* to the gift of the Spirit: it is when for the first time the

Spirit is poured out on the Gentiles, as it had on the circumcized Chistians (Act 11:16-18).

Conversion to God establishes a new relation between the believer and his God, the faithful and his Lord. But it also intro - duces the Christian into a communal activity where repentence toward God and forgiveness among the brethern is lived out in an analogous fashion. As man returns to God, he repents with regard to others: "If your brother offends you, rebuke him and if he repents, forgive him; and if seven times a day, he offends you and seven times he comes back to you, saying 'I repent', forgive him." (Lk 17:3-4).

In conclusion, we would like to give attention to a Biblical metaphor which expresses in Luke the phenomenon of conver - sion: the passage of the blindness to sight: "I am sending you to open their eyes, to turn them away from darkness to the light, from the empire of Satan toward God..." (Act 26:18). The image used suggests that the convert becomes a seer. Paul himself blinded by the appearance of the Lord, will gain his sight. Inevitably he will have a new view of reality. The believer will see not only differently but other things: the Risen One said to Ananias concerning Paul, "I will show him all that he will have to suffer for my name." (Act 9:16). The convert of the Damascus road will henceforth have another conception of reality. More exactly, he will construct in another fashion the reality he perceives.

What sociologists teach us concerning the construction of reality can help us to extend our explanation of the metaphor and our interpretation of conversion. Going beyond the explicit content of the Lucan texts and the psychological lineaments which underlie it, we would propose the following: a conversion to Christ represents a critique of a certain conception of reality, a calling into question of the social structures and an attack of the reification of functions. A conversion moreover fits into the project of a new society as a counter-model which claims to be applicable. To endure, conversion - Luke seems sensitive at this point - is not limited to a rupture. If it implies an attachment to Christ, it also needs a reasonable and realistic insertion in the society. What we know today of the evolution of ideologies, their concrete implications and the decisive role of the founder should help us to overcome a psychologizing and individual interpretation of conversion in Luke [37], to attain a social and ecclesiastic definition. In this case, Luke's view of the reality of his time and his Church served as a model and permitted verification. Has he not too passed from "darkness to the light"?

CHAPTER 7

THE CHURCH

Chronological bibliography

1925
L. CERFAUX, "'Les Saints' de Jérusalem", **ETL** 2 (1925) 510-529; taken up in **Recueil L. Cerfaux** (= **Receuil**, Cerfaux), II (Gembloux, 1954), pp. 389-413.
1932
O. LINTON, **Das Problem der Urkirche in der neueren Forschung. Eine kritische Darstellung** (Uppsala, 1932; reprint Frankfurt, n.d.).
1933
H. J. CADBURY, "Names for Christians and Christianity in Acts", in **Beginning**, Foakes Jackson, 5, pp. 375-392.
K. LAKE, "Proselytes and God-fearers", in **Beginning**, Foakes Jackson, 5, pp. 74-96.
K. H. RENGSTORF, "Art. *ἀποστέλλω, κτλ.*", **TWNT**, I, pp. 397-448.
1936
B. S. EASTON, **The Purpose of Acts** (London, 1936); taken up in B. S. Easton, **Early Christianity. The Purpose of Acts and Other Papers** (London, 1955).
1939
L. CERFAUX, "La première communauté chrétienne à Jérusalem (Actes 2, 41-5,42)", **ETL** 16 (1939) 5-31; taken up in **Recueil**, Cerfaux, II , pp. 125-156.
1942
H. STRATHMANN, "Art. *μάρτυς, κτλ.*", **TWNT**, 4, pp. 495-498.
1943
L. CERFAUX, "Témoins du Christ d'après le livre des Actes", **Ang** 20 (1943) 166-183; taken up in **Recueil**, Cerfaux, II , pp. 157-174.
L. CERFAUX, **La communauté apostolique** (Paris, 1943, 1956^{3}).
1944
O. CULLMANN, **Urchristentum und Gottesdienst** (Zurich, 1944, 1950^{2}), (FT, Neuchâtel-Paris, 1944, 1945^{2}).
1946
R. LIECHTENHAN, **Die urchristliche Mission: Voraussetzungen, Motive und Methoden** (Zurich, 1946).
E. PETERSON, "Christianus", in **Miscellanea G. Mercati**, I, Città del Vaticano, 1946; pp. 355ff.; taken up in E. Peterson, **Frühkirche, Judentum und Gnosis. Studien und Untersuchungen** (Rome-Freiburg-Vienna, 1959), pp. 64-87.
J. R. PORTER, "The 'Apostolic Decree' and Paul's Second Visit to Jerusalem", **JTS** 47 (1946) 169-174.
1947
H. VON CAMPENHAUSEN, "Der urchristliche Apostelbegriff", **ST** I (1947) 96-130.

M. DIBELIUS, "Das Apostelkonzil", **TLZ** 72 (1947) 193-198, taken up in (ed) H. Greeven, **Aufsätze zur Apostelgeschichte** (Göttingen, 1961^4), pp. 84-90.

1948

H. W. BARTSCH, "Die Taufe im Neuen Testament", **EvT** 8 (1948-1949) 75-100.

P. GAECHTER, "Jerusalem and Antiochia. Ein Beitrag zur urkirchlichen Rechtsentwicklung", **ZKT** 70 (1948) 1-48: taken up in P. Gaechter, **Petrus und seine Zeit. Neutestamentliche Studien** (=**Petrus**, Gaechter), (Innsbruck-Vienna-Munich, 1958), pp. 155-212.

H. MOSBECH, "Apostolos in the New Testament. Two Lectures Given at the University of Uppsala", **ST** 2 (1948) 166-200.

B. REICKE, "Die Mahlzeit mit Paulus auf den Wellen des Mittelmeers Act. 27, 33-38", **TZBas** 4 (1948) 401-410.

G. SCHRENK, "Urchristliche Missionspredigt im 1. Jahrhundert", in (ed). M. Loeser, **Auf dem Grund der Apostel und Propheten. Festscrhift T. Wurm**, (Stuttgart, 1948), pp. 51-66; taken up in G. Schrenk, **Studien zu Paulus** (Zurich, 1954), pp. 131-148.

1949

E. J. BICKERMANN, "The Name of Christians. Act 11, 26", **HarvTR** 42 (1949) 109-124.

P. GAECHTER, "Die Wahl des Matthias", **ZKT** 71 (1949) 318-346; taken up in **Petrus**, Gaechter, pp. 31-66.

M. GOGUEL, **Les premiers temps de l'Eglise** (Neuchâtel-Paris, 1949).

O. LINTON, "The Third Aspect. A Neglected Point of View. A Study in Gal 1-2 and Act 9 and 15", **ST** 3 (1949-1950) 79-95.

P. H. MENOUD, **L'Eglise et les ministères selon le Nouveau Testament** (Neuchâtel-Paris, 1949).

E. PETERSON, "La λειτουργία des prophètes et des didascales à Antioche", **RecSR** 36 (1949) 577-579.

R. SCHNACKENBURG, "Episcopos und Hirtenamt. Zu Apg 20, 28", in **Episcopus. Festschrift M. von Faulhaber** (Regensburg, 1949), pp. 66-88.

E. SCHWEIZER, **Gemeinde nach dem Neuen Testament** (Zollikon-Zurich, 1949).

1950

P. BENOIT, "Remarques sur les sommaires des Actes 2, 4, 5", in **Sources**, Goguel, pp. 1-10; taken up in P. Benoit, **Exégèse et Théologie**, 2 (Paris, 1961), pp. 181-192.

H. VON CAMPENHAUSEN, "Die Nachfolge des Jakobus", **ZKG** 63 (1950-1951) 133-144.

G. DUTERME*, **Le vocabulaire du discours d'Etienne (Act 7, 2-53)** unpublished thesis, University of Leuven (Leuven, 1950).

P. GAECHTER, "Petrus in Antiochia, Gal 2, 11-14", **ZKT** 72 (1950) 177-212; taken up in **Petrus**, Gaechter, pp. 213-257.

P. H. MENOUD, "La mort d'Ananias et de Saphira (Actes 5, 1-11"), in **Sources**, Goguel, pp. 146-154.

C. F. D. MOULE, "Sanctuary and Sacrifice in the Church of the New Testament", **JTS**, N. S., I (1950) 29-41.

J. MUNCK, "Discours d'adieu dans le Nouveau Testament et dans la littérature biblique", in **Sources**, Goguel, pp. 155-170.

D. T. ROWLINGSON, "The Geographical Orientation of Paul's Missionary Interests", **JBL** 69 (1950) 341-344.

1951

N. ADLER, **Taufe und Handauflegung. Eine exegetisch-theologische Untersuchung von Apg 8, 14-17**, (Munster, 1951).

M. BARTH, **Die Taufe ein Sakrament? Ein exegetischer Beitrag zum Gespräch über die kirchliche Taufe**, (Zolliken-Zurich, 1951).

M. BLACK, "The Doctrine of the Ministry", **ExpTim** 63 (1951-1952) 112-116.

S. G. F. BRANDON, **The Fall of Jerusalem and the Christian Church. A Study of the Effects of the Jewish Overthrow of A.D. 70 on Christianity** (London, 1951, 1957[2]).

M. DIEBELIUS, **Aufsätze zur Apostelgeschichte** H. Greeven (ed) (Göttingen, 1951, 1961[4]).

S. GIET, "Le second voyage de Saint Paul à Jerusalem (Actes 11, 17-30; 12, 24-25), **RevSR** 25 (1951) 265-269.

S. GIET, "L'assemblée apostolique et le décret de Jérusalem. Qui était Siméon?", **RevSR** 39 (1951) 203-220.

F. R. KLING*, **The Council of Jerusalem** unpublished thesis, Princeton Theological Seminary (Princeton, N.J.,1951).

G. W. H. LAMPE, **The Seal of the Spirit. A Study in the Doctrine of Baptism and Confirmation in the New Testament and the Fathers** (London, 1951, 1967[2]).

L. P. PHERIGO, "Paul's Life After the Close of Acts", **JBL** 70 (1951) 277-284.

A. RÉTIF, "Témoignage et prédication missionnaire dans les Actes des Apôtres", **NRT** 73 (1951) 152-165.

J. M. ROSS, "The Appointment of Presbyters in Acts 14, 23", **ExpTim** 63 (1951-1952) 288-289.

M. SIMON, "Saint Stephen and the Jerusalem Temple", **JEH** 2 (1951) 127-142.

1952

O. CULLMANN, **Saint Pierre, disciple-apôtre-martyr** (Neuchâtel-Paris, 1951).

P. GAECHTER, "Die Sieben (Apg, 6, 1-6)", **ZKT** 74 (1952) 129-166; taken up in **Petrus**, Gaechter, pp. 105-154.

H. GREEVEN, "Propheten, Lehrer, Vorsteher bei Paulus. Zur Frage der 'ÄMTER' im Urchristentum", **ZNW** 44 (1952-1953) 1-43; taken up in (ed) K. Kertelge, **Das kirchliche Amt im Neuen Testament** (Darmstadt, 1977), pp. 305-361.

K. HEUSSI, "Galater 2 und der Lebensgang der jerusalemischen Urapostel", **TLZ** 77 (1952) 67-72.

E. KÄSEMANN, "Die Johannesjünger in Ephesus", **ZTK** 49 (1952) 144-154; taken up in E. Käsemann, **Exegetische Versuche und Besinnungen**, I (Göttingen, 1960[2]), pp. 158-168.

P. H. MENOUD, **La vie de l'Eglise naissante** (Neuchâtel-Paris, 1952).

P. H. MENOUD, "L'Eglise naissante et le judäisme", **ETRel** 27 (1952) 1-52; taken up in **Jésus**, Menoud, pp. 276-313.

D. T. ROWLINGSON, "The Jerusalem Conference and Jesus' Nazareth Visit: A Study in Pauline Chronology", **JBL** 71 (1952) 69-74.

E. STAUFFER, "Jüdisches Erbe im urchristlichen Kirchenrecht", **TLZ** 77 (1952) 201-206.

W. C. VAN UNNIK, "Tarsus of Jeruzalem, de Stad van Paulus' jeugd", Mededeelingen der Koninklijke Nederlandse Akademie van Wetenschappen, Afd. Letterkunde, N. R. Deel 15, 5, Amsterdam, 1952, pp. 141-189 (ET, **Tarsus of Jerusalem. The City of Paul's Youth**, translated by G. Ogg

(London, 1962); taken up in **Sparsa**, van Unnik, pp. 259-320 (cf. pp. 321-327).

A. WIKENHAUSER, "Die Wirkung der Christophanie vor Damaskus auf Paulus und seine Begleiter nach den Berichten der Apostelgeschichte", **Bib** 33 (1952) 313-323.

1953

C. K. BARRETT, "Paul and the 'Pillar' Apostles", in (ed) J. N. Sevenster and W. C. van Unnik, **Studia Paulina. Mélanges J. de Zwaan**, (Harlem, 1953), pp. 1-19.

F. F. BRUCE, **The Spreading Flame. The Rise and Progress of Christianity.** (Grand Rapids, 1953).

H. VON CAMPENHAUSEN, **Kirchliches Amt und geistliche Vollmacht in den ersten drei Jahrhunderten,** (Tübingen 1953, 1963[2]).

L. CERFAUX, "Saint-Pierre et sa succession", **RecSR** 41 (1953) 188-202; taken up in **Recueil**, Cerfaux, II , pp. 239-251.

C. CHARLIER, "Le manifeste d'Etienne (Actes 7). Essai de commentaire synthétique", **BiViChr** 3 (1953) 83-93.

W. FOERSTER, "Stephanus und die Urgemeinde", in (ed) K. Janssen, **Dienst unter dem Wort. Festschrift H. Schreiner**, (Gütersloh, 1953), pp. 9-30.

S. GIET, "Les trois premiers voyages de Saint Paul à Jerusalem", **RecSR** 41 (1953) 321-347.

M. GOGUEL, "Quelques observations sur l'oeuvre de Luc", **RHPhilRel** 33 (1953) 37-51.

E. LOHSE, "Ursprung und Prägung des christlichen Apostolates", **TZBas** 9 (1953) 259-275.

C. MASSON, "Le baptême, un sacrement?" **RTPhil**, 3rd series, 3 (1953) 21-30, taken up in C. Masson, **Vers les sources d'eau vive. Etudes d'éxègese et de théologie du Nouveau Testament** (Lausanne, 1961), pp. 216-227.

P. H. MENOUD, "Les Actes des apôtres et l'eucharistie", **RHPhilRel** 33 (1953) 21-35; taken up in **Jésus**, Menoud, pp. 63-76.

W. MICHAUX, "De la communauté de Jérusalem aux Eglises Pauliniennes (Act 1 à 12)", **BiViCar** 3 (1953) 72-82.

D. C. MOORE*, **The Theology and Polity of the Jerusalem Church in Their Relation to Primitive Christianity,** unpublished thesis, Southern Baptist Theological Seminary (Louisville, Ky., 1953).

E. PERCY, **Die Botschaft Jesu. Eine traditions-kritische und exegetische Untersuchung** (Lund, 1953), pp. 40-108.

J. A. T. ROBINSON, "The One Baptism as a Category of New Testament Soteriology", **ScotJT** 6 (1953) 257-274; taken up in J. A. T. Robinson, **Twelve New Testament Studies** (London, 1965[2]), pp. 158-175.

Saint Paul's Mission to Greece. Nineteenth Centenary, A.D. 50-1951. A Volume of Commemoration, (ed) H. S. Alivisatos, (Athens, 1953).

J. SCHMITT, "L'Eglise de Jérusalem ou la 'Restauration' d'Israël d'après les cinq premiers chapitres des Actes", **RevSR** 27 (1953) 209-218.

G. SEVENSTER*, "De wijding van Paulus en Barnabas", in (eds.) J. N. Sevenster and W. C. van Unnik,**Studia Paulina. Mélanges J. de Zwaan**, (Harlem, 1953), pp. 188-201.

D. M. STANLEY, "Paul's Conversion in Acts: Why the Three Accounts?" **CBQ** 15 (1953) 315-338; taken up in D. M. Stanley, **The Apostolic Church in the New Testament** (Westminster, 1966), pp. 285-311.

1954

L. CERFAUX, "L'unité du Corps Apostolique dans le Nouveau Testament", in **L'Eglise et les Eglises 1054-1954. Neuf siècles de douloureuses séparation entre l'Orient et l'Occident . Mélanges L. Beauduin**, I (Chevetogne, 1954), pp. 99-110; taken up in **Recueil**, Cerfaux, II, pp. 226-237.

H. CONZELMANN, **Die Mitte der Zeit. Studien zur Theologie des Lukas** (Tübingen, 1954, 1957^2 1960^3, which we are using, 1962^4).

P. GAECHTER, "Jakobus von Jerusalem", **ZKT** 76 (1954) 130-169; taken up in **Petrus**, Gaechter, pp. 258-310.

S. E. JOHNSON, "The Dead Sea Manual of Discipline and the Jerusalem Church of Acts", **ZAW** 66 (1954) 106-120.

E. LOHSE, "Missionarisches Handeln Jesu nach dem Evangelium des Lukas", **TZBas** 10 (1954) 1-13; taken up in **Einheit**, Lohse, pp. 165-177.

E. LOHSE, "Zu den Anfängen der Mission in Samarien", **TZBas** 10 (1954) 158.

S. LYONNET, "La *κοινωνία* de l'Eglise primitive et la sainte Eucharistie", in : **La Eucaristía y la Paz. XXXV Congresso Eucarístico internacional. Sesiones de Estudio**, I (Barcelona, 1954), pp. 511-515.

P. H. MENOUD, "Le plan des Actes des apôtres", **NTS** *I* (1954-1955) 44-51 taken up in **Jésus**, Menoud, pp. 84-91.

J. PRADO, "La Eucaristia foco de irradiación misionera (Act. 13, 1-4)", in **La Eucaristía y la Paz. XXXV Congresso Eucarístico internacional. Sesiones de Estudio**, I (Barcelona, 1954), pp. 503-507.

B. REICKE, "Die Verfassung der Urgemeinde im Lichte jüdischer Dokumente", **TZBas** 10 (1954) 95-112 (ET in (ed) K. Stendahl, **The Scrolls and the New Testament** (New York, 1957), pp. 143-156).

1955

R. BULTMANN, "The Transformation of the Idea of the Church in the History of Early Christianity", **CanJT** I (1955) 73-81; taken up in German in R. Bultmann, **Glauben und Verstehen. Gesammelte Aufsätze**, III, (Tübingen, 1960), pp. 131-141.

T. H. CAMPBELL, "Paul's Missionary Journey's as Reflected in His Letters", **JBL** 74 (1955) 80-87.

J. DANIELOU, "La communauté de Qumrân et l'organisation de l'Eglise ancienne", **RHPhilRel** 35 (1955) 104-115.

J. DUPONT, "La prière des apôtres persécutés (Act 4, 23-31)", in "Notes sur les Actes des apôtres", **RB** 62 (1955) 45-47; taken up in **Etudes**, Dupont, pp. 521-522.

J. DUPONT, "'Parole de Dieu' et 'Parole du Seigneur'", in "Notes sur les Actes des apôtres", **RB** 62 (1955) 47-49; taken up in **Etudes**, Dupont, pp. 523-525.

J. DUPONT, "Chronologie paulinienne", in "Notes sur les Actes des Apôtres", **RB** 62 (1955) 55-59; taken up under the title, "Les trois premiers voyages de saint Paul à Jerusalem", in **Etudes**, Dupont, pp. 167-171.

O. EGGENBERG, "Die Geistestaufe in der gegenwärtigen Pfingstbewegung", **TZBas** II (1955) 272-295.

E. FASCHER, "Zur Taufe des Paulus", **TLZ** 80 (1955) 643-648.

H. M. FERET, **Pierre et Paul à Antioche et à Jérusalem. Le "conflit" des deux apôtres** (Paris, 1955).

I. FRANSEN, "Paul, apôtre des païens, Actes 12, 20-19, 20", **BiViChr** 9 (1955) 71-84.
E. HAENCHEN, "Tradition und Komposition in der Apostelgeschichte", **ZTK** 52 (1955) 205-225; taken up in E. Haenchen, **Gott und Mensch. Gesammelte Aufsätze**, (Tübingen, 1965), pp. 206-226.
A. KRAGERUD, "Itinerariet i Apostlenes Gjerninger", **NorTT** 56 (1955) 249-272.
C. MASSON, "La reconstitution du collège des Douze (d'après Actes 1, 15-26, **RTPhil**, 3rd series, 5 (1955) 193-201; taken up in C: Masson, **Vers les sources d'eau vive. Etudes d'exgésèse et de théologie du Nouveau Testament** (Lausanne, 1961), pp. 178-188.
I. MIRCEA, "L'organisation de l'Eglise et la vie des premiers chrétiens d'après les Actes des apôtres" (in Rumanian), **Studii Teologice** 7 (1955) 64-92.
W. PRENTICE, "St. Paul's Journey to Damascus", **ZNW** 46 (1955) 250-155.
J. N. SANDERS, "Peter and Paul in the Acts", **NTS** 2 (1955-1956) 133-141.
J. SCHMITT, "Sacerdoce judaïque et hiérarchie ecclésiale dans les premières communautés judéochrétiennes", **RevSR** 29 (1955) 250-261; taken up in (ed) J. Guyot, **Etudes sur le sacrement de l' 'ordre'** (Paris, 1957), pp. 77-96 (German translation, Mainz, 1961).
F. STAGG*, **The Book of Acts: The Early Struggle for an Unhindered Gospel** (Nashville, 1955).
D. M. STANLEY, "Kingdom to Church: The Structural Development of Apostolic Christianity in the New Testament", **TS** 16 (1955) 1-29; taken up in D. M. Stanley, **The Apostolic Church in the New Testament** (Westminster, 1966), pp. 5-37 (Spanish translation, Santander, 1968).

1956

E. BARNIKOL, "Das Fehlen der Taufe in den Quellenschriften der Apostelgeschichte und in den Urgemeinden der Hebräer und Hellenisten", **Wissenschaftliche Zeitschrift der Martin-Luther-Universität, Halle-Wittenberg**, 6 (1956-1957) 593-610.
O. BAUERNFEIND, "Die erste Begegung zwischen Paulus und Kephas, Gal 1,18-20", **ZNW** 47 (1956) 268-276.
J. DUPONT, "La mission de Paul 'à Jerusalem' (Actes 12, 25)", **NT** 1 (1956) 275-303; taken up in **Etudes**, Dupont, pp. 217-241.
J. DUPONT, "Le nom d'apôtre a-t-il été donné aux douze par Jésus?", **OrSyr** I (1956) 261-290 et 425-444.
J. DUPONT, "*Λαὸς ἐξ ἐθνῶν* (Actes 15, 14)" **NTS** 3 (1956-1957) 47-50; taken up in **Etudes**, Dupont, pp. 361-365 (with an additional note).
L. E. ELLIOTT-BINNS, **Galilean Christianity** (London, 1956).
E. GUENTHER, "Zeuge und Märtyrer", **ZNW** 47 (1956) 145-161.
E. HAENCHEN, **Die Apostelgeschichte neu übersetzt und erklärt** (Göttingen, 1956, 1968[6], 1977[7]) (we are citing the 3rd ed. of 1959).
E. HAMMAN, "La nouvelle Pentecôte (Actes 4, 24-30)", **BiViChr** 14 (1956) 82-90.
E. F. HARRISON, "The Attitude of the Primitive Church toward Judaïsm, **BS** 113 (1956) 130-140.
E. M. KREDEL, "Der Apostelbegriff in der neueren Exegese. Historisch-kritische Darstellung", **ZKT** 78 (1956) 169-193 and 257-305.
J. LOWE, **Saint Peter** (New York-Oxford, 1956).
G. SCHULZE-KADELBACH, "Die Stellung des Petrus in der Urchristenheit", **TLZ** 81 (1956) 1-14.
H. J. SCHOEPS, **Urgemeinde, Judenchristentum, Gnosis** (Tübingen 1956).

1957

P. BONNARD, "L'esprit saint et l'Eglise selon le Nouveau Testament", **RHPhilRel** 37 (1957) 81-90.

A. CABANISS, "Early Christian Nightime Worship", **JBR** 25 (1957) 30-33.

L. CERFAUX, Fructifiez en supportant (l'épreuve), à propos de Luc 8, 15", **RB** 64 (1957) 481-491; taken up in **Recueil**, Cerfaux, III, (Gembloux, 1962), pp. 111-122.

J. CREHAN, "Peter according to the D-text of Acts", **TS** 18 (1957) 596-603.

M. A. DAHL, "A People for his Name (Acts 15, 14)", **NTS** 4 (1957-1958) 319-327.

J. DANIELOU, "L'Etoile de Jacob et la mission chrétienne à Damas", **VigChr** II (1957) 121-138.

A. P. DAVIES, **The first Christian: A Study of St. Paul and Christian Origins** (New York, 1957).

J. DUPONT, "Pierre et Paul dans les Actes", **RB** 64 (1957) 35-47; taken up in **Etudes**, Dupont, pp. 173-184.

J. DUPONT, "Pierre et Paul à Antioche et à Jérusalem", **RecSR** 45 (1957), 42-60 and 225-239, taken up in **Etudes**, Dupont, pp. 185-215.

S. GIET, "Nouvelles remarques sur les voyages se saint Paul à Jérusalem", **RevSR** 31 (1957) 329-342.

J. JEREMIAS, "Πρεσβυτέριον ausserchristlich bezeugt", **ZNW** 48 (1957) 127-132.

A. F. J. KLIJN, "Stephen's Speech - Acts 7, 2-53", **NTS** 4 (1957-1958) 25-31.

R. KOCH, "Die Wertung des Besitzes im Lukasevangelium", **Bib** 38 (1957) 151-169.

D. J. McCARTHY, Qumran and Christian Beginnings", **TDig** 5 (1957) 39-46.

M. MEINERTZ, "Σχίσμα und αἵρεσις im Neuen Testament, **BZ**, N.S., I (1957) 114-118.

P. H. MENOUD, Les additions au groupe des douze apôtres d'après le livre des Actes", **RHPhilRel** 37 (1957) 71-80; taken up in **Jésus**, Menoud, pp. 91-100.

O. MOE*, "Actas misjonsteologi", **TsTKi** 28 (1957) 148-161.

C. F. D. MOULE, **Christ's Messengers. Studies in the Acts of the Apostles.** (New York, 1957).

W. PROKULSKI, "The Conversion of St. Paul", **CBQ** 19 (1957) 453-473.

B. REICKE, **Glauben und Leben der Urgemeinde. Bemerkungen zu Apg. 1-7** (Zurich 1957).

D. RIMAUD, "La première prière liturgique dans le livre des Actes (Actes 4, 23-31)", **MaisD** 51 (1957) 99-115.

H. RUSCHE, "Gastfreundschaft und Mission in Apostelgeschichte und Apostelbriefen", **ZMissRelWiss** 41 (1957) 250-268.

J. SCHMITT, "Contribution à l'étude de la discipline pénitentielle dans l'Eglise primitive à la lumière des textes de Qumrân", in **Les manuscrits de la Mer Morte. Colloque de Strasbourg, 25-27 mai 1955** (Paris, 1957), pp. 93-109.

J. SCHWARTZ, "A propos du statut personnel de l'apôtre Paul", **RHPhilRel** 37 (1957) 91-96.

M. SMITH*, "The Ecclesiological Consciousness of the Early Church: A Study based Primarily on the Book of Acts", in **Ecclesiology in the New Testament. Papers presented in the New Testament Theological Seminar**, unpublished, Yale University Divinity School (New Haven, Conn, 1957-1958).

1958

G. R. BALLEINE, **Simon whom He surnamed Peter. A Study of his Life** (London, 1958).
R- BOWLIN *, **The Christian Prophets in the New Testament**, unpublished dissertation, Vanderbilt University (Nashville, 1958).
E. EHRHARDT, "The Construction and Purpose of the Acts of the Apostles", **ST** 12 (1958-1959) 45-79.
P. GAECHTER, **Petrus und seine Zeit. Neutestamentliche Studien**, Innsbruck-Vienna-Munich, 1958.
S. V. McCASLAND, "The Way", **JBL** 77 (1958) 220-230.
H. B. MATTINGLY, "The Origin of the Name 'Christiani' (Act II, 26)", **JTS**, N. S., 9 (1958) 26-37.
C. F. D. MOULE, "Once More, Who Were the Hellenists?" **ExpTim** 70 (1958-1959) 100-102.
M. SIMON, **St. Stephen and the Hellenists in the Primitive Church** (New York-Toronto-London, 1958).

1959

E. BAMMEL, "Art. πτωχός, κτλ.", **TWNT** 6, pp. 885-915.
J. BIHLER, "Der Stephanusbericht (Apg 6, 8-15 und 7, 54 - 8,2)", **BZ** N. F., 3 (1959) 252-270.
G. BORNKAMM, "Art. πρέσβυς, κτλ.", **TWNT** 6, pp. 651-683.
D. BOSCH, **Die Heidenmission in der Zukunftsschau Jesu** (Zurich, 1959).
F. F. BRUCE, "The True Apostolic Succession: Recent Study of the Book of Acts", **Interpr** 13 (1959) 131-143.
M. CARREZ "Le Nouvel Israël. Réflexions sur l'absence de cette désignation de l'Eglise dans le Nouveau Testament", **FoiVie** 58 (1959), N° 6, pp. 30-34.
J. DUPONT, "Le salut des Gentils et la signification théologique du livre des Actes", **NTS** 6 (1959-1960) 132-155; taken up in **Etudes**, Dupont, pp. 393-419.
E. FASCHER, **Sokrates und Christus. Beiträge zur Religions-geschichte** (Leipzig, 1959), passim.
M. H. FRANZMANN, "The Word of the Lord Grew. The Historical Character of the New Testament Word", **ConcTM** 30 (1959) 563-581.
P. GEOLTRAIN, "Esséniens et Hellénistes", **TZBas** 15 (1959) 241-254.
J. GOETTMANN, "La Pentecôte, prémices de la nouvelle création", **BiViChr** 27 (1959) 59-69.
H. H. GRAHAM*, **"The Reflexion of the Church in Mark, Matthew; Paul's Letters, and Acts"**, unpublished dissertation, Union Theological Seminary of New York, (New York, 1959).
A. HAMMAN, **La prière, I, Le Nouveau Testament** (Tournai, 1959), pp. 59-169, passim, and 170-213.
P. E. HOWARD*, **The Book of Acts as a Source for the Study of the Life of Paul**, unpublished dissertation, University of Southern California (Los Angeles, 1959).
J.D. McCAUGHEY, "The intention of the Author. Some Questions About the Exegesis of Acts 6, 1-6", **AusBir** 7 (1959) 27-36.
L. S. MUDGE, **"The Servant Lord and His Servant People"**, **ScotJT** 112 (1959) 113-128.
B. REICKE, "The Risen Lord and His Church: The Theology of Acts", **Interpr** 13 (1959) 157-169.

R. D. RICHARDSON, "The Place of Luke in the Eucharist Tradition", in (eds.) K. Aland, F. L. Cross, J. Daniélou, H. Riesenfeld and W. C. van Unnik, **Studia Evangelica**, I, (Berlin, 1959), pp. 663-675.

G. SCHILLE, "Die Fragwürdigkeit eines Itinerars der Paulusreisen", **TLZ** 84 (1959) 165-174.

J. Schmitt, "L'organisation de l'Eglise primitive et Qumrân",, in (ed) J. van der Ploeg, **La secte de Qumrân et les origines du christianisme** (Bruges, 1959), pp. 217-231.

E. SCHWEIZER, **Gemeinde und Gemeindeordnung im Neuen Testament** (Zurich, 1959) (ET **Church Order in the New Testament**, 1961).

L. TURRADO, "La Iglesia en los Hechos de los Apóstoles", **Salmant** 6 (1959) 3-35.

A. C. WINN, "Elusive Mystery: The Purpose of Acts", **Interpr** 13 (1959) 144-156.

1960

W. A. BEARDSLEE, "The Casting of Lots at Qumran and in the Book of Acts", **NT** 4 (1960-1961) 245-252.

E. BEST, "Acts 13, 1-3", **JTS**, N.S., II (1960) 344-348.

L. CERFAUX, "Pour l'histoire du titre 'Apostolos' dans le Nouveau Testament", **RecSR** 48 (1960) 76-92; taken up in **Recueil**, Cerfaux, III, pp. 185-200.

E. HAENCHEN, "Petrus-Probleme", **NTS** 7 (1960-1961) 187-197; taken up in E. Haenchen, **Gott und Mensch. Gesammlte Aufsätze** (Tübingen, 1965), p. 55-67.

E. HAENCHEN, "Quellenannalyse und Kompositionsanalyse in Act 15", in (ed) W. Eltester, **Judentum-Urchristentum-Kirche. Festschrift J. Jeremias**, (Berlin, 1960, 1964^2), pp. 153-164; taken up in E. Haenchen, **Gott und Mensch. Gesammelte Aufsätze** (Tübingen, 1965) pp. 206-226.

R. G. HOERBER, "Galatians 2, 1-10 and the Acts of the Apostles", **ConcTM** 31 (1960) 482-491.

E. KÄSEMANN, "Amt und Gemeinde im Neuen Testament", in **Exeg. Versuche**, I, Käsemann (Göttingen, 1960), pp. 109-134.

G. KLEIN, "Galater 2, 6-9 und die Geschichte der Jerusalemer Urgemeinde", **ZTK** 57 (1960),275-295; taken over in G. Klein, **Rekonstruktion und Interpretation. Gesammelte Aufsätze zum Neuen Testament** (Munich, 1969), pp. 99-128 (pp. 118-128: Nachtrag).

T. W. MANSON, "**Ethics and the Gospels**, (London, 1960, 1962^2), pp. 69-103.

P. H. MENOUD, "Jésus et ses témoins. Remarques sur l'unité de l'oeuvre de Luc", **Eglise et Théologie. Bulletin trimestriel de la Faculté libre de théologie protestante de Paris**, 23 (1960), N° 68, pp. 7-20; taken up in **Jésus**, Menoud, pp. 100-110.

H. H. PLATZ*, **Paul's Damascus Experience. A study in the History of interpretation**, unpublished dissertation, University of Chicago (Chicago, 1960).

J. S. RUEF*, **Ananias and Saphira; a Study of the Community-Disciplinary Practices Underlying Acts 5, 1-11**, unpublished dissertation, Harvard University (Cambridge, Massachusetts 1960).

G. SCHULZE*, **Das Paulusbild des Lukas. Ein historisch-exegetischer Versuch als Beitrag zur Erforschung der lukanischen Theologie**, unpublished dissertation, University of Kiel (Kiel, 1960).

B. SCHWANK, "'Und so kamen wir nach Rom' (Apg 28, 14). Reisenotizen zu den letzten beiden Kapiteln der Apostelgeschichte", **ErbAuf** 36 (1960) 169-192).

H. ZIMMERMANN*, "Die Wahl der Sieben (Apg 6, 1-6). Ihre Bedeutung für die Wahrung der Einheit in der Kirche", in **Die Kirche und ihre Ämter und Stände. Festschrift Cardinal Frings** (Copenhagen-Köln, 1960) pp. 264-287.

1961

N. BROX, **Zeuge und Märtyrer. Untersuchungen zur frühchristlichen Zeugnis-Terminologie** (Munich, 1961).

J. CAMBIER, "Le voyage de S. Paul à Jerusalem en Act. 9, 26 ss et le schéma missionnaire théologique de S. Luc", **NTS** 8 (1961-1962) 249-257.

G. DELLING, **Die Zuegnung des Heils in der Taufe. Eine Untersuchung zum neutestamentlichen "Taufen auf den Namen"** (Berlin, 1961).

J. DELORME, "Note sur les Hellénistes des Actes des apôtres", **AmiCl** 71 (1961) 445-447.

G.. DOWNEY, **History of Antioch in Syria from Seleucus to the Arab Conquest** (Princeton, 1961), pp. 272-316.

J. DUPONT, "Aequitas Romana". Notes sur Actes 25, 16", **RecSR** 49 (1961) 354-385; repris in **Etudes**, Dupont, pp. 527-552 (with a few complementary notes).

O. GLOMBITZA, "Der Schluss der Petrusrede Acta 2, 36-40. Ein Beitrag zum Problem der Predigten in Acta", **ZNW** 52 (1961) 115-118.

J. GNILKA, **Die Verstockung Israels. Isaias 6, 9-10 in der Theologie der Synoptiker** (Munich, 1961).

P. GRELOT, "La pauvreté dans l'Ecriture Sainte", **Christ** 8 (1961) 306-330.

E. HAENCHEN, "Das 'Wir' in der Apostelgeschichte und das Itinerar", **ZTK** 58 (1961) 329-366; taken up in Haechen's **Gott und Mensch. Gesammelte Aufsätze** (Tübingen, 1965), pp. 227-264.

G. KLEIN, **Die Zwölf Apostel. Ursprung und Gehalt einer Idee** (Göttingen, 1961).

H. KRAFT, "Die Anfänge der christlichen Taufe", **TZBas** 17 (1961) 399-412.

J.C. O'NEILL, **The Theology of Acts in its Historical Setting** (London, 1961, 1970[2]).

K. H. RENGSTORF, "Die Zuwahl des Matthias", **ST** 15 (1961) 35-67.

W. SCHMITHALS, **Das kirchliche Apostelamt. Eine historische Untersuchung** (Göttingen, 1961).

R. SCHNACKENBURG, **Die Kirche im Neuen Testament. Ihre Wirklichkeit und theologische Deutung, ihr Wesen und Geheimnis,** (Freiburg-Basel-Vienna, 1961) (FT Paris, 1964).

G. S. SLOYAN, "'Primitive' and 'Pauline' Concepts of the Eucharist", **CBQ** 23 (1961) 1-13.

C. SPICQ, "Ce que signifie le titre de chrétien", **ST** 15 (1961) 68-78.

H. ZIMMERMANN, "Die Sammelberichte der Apostelgeschichte", **BZ**, N.F., 5 (1961) 71-82.

1962

J. BLINZLER, "Rechtsgeschichtliches zur Hinrichtung des Zebedäiden Jakobus (Apg 12,2), **NT** 5 (1962) 191-206.

M. DUJARIER, **Le parrainage des adultes aux trois premiers siècles de l'Eglise. Recherche historique sur l'évolution des garanties et des étapes catéchuménales avant 313** (Paris 1962).

E. DUMONT, "La Koinonia en los promeros cinco capitulos de los hechos de los Apóstoles", **RBíbArg** 24 (1962) 22-32.
E. DUPONT, **Le discours de Milet, testament pastoral de Saint-Paul (Actes 20, 18-36)** (Paris, 1962).
E. J. EPP, "The 'Ignorance Motif' in Acts and Anti-judaic Tendencies in Codex Bezae", **HarvTR** 55 (1962) 51-62.
B. GÄRTNER, "Paulus und Barnabas in Lystra, zu Apg 14, 8-15", **SvExAb 27** (1962) 83-88.
B. GERHARDSSON, "Die Boten Gottes und die Apostel Christi", **SvExAb** 27 (1962) 89-131.
O. GLOMBITZA, "Der Schritt nach Europa. Erwägungen zu Act 16, 9-15", **ZNW** 53 (1962) 77-82.
O. GLOMBITZA, "Zur Charakterisierung des Stephanus in Act 6 und 7", **ZNW** 53 (1962) 238-244.
V. KESICH, "The Apostolic Council at Jerusalem", **StVlSemQ** 6 (1962) 108-117.
B. LIFSHITZ, "L'origine du nom des chrétiens", **VigChr** 16 (1962) 65-70.
P. H. MENOUD, "La Pentecôte lucanienne et l'histoire", **RHPhilRel** 42 (1962) 141-147; taken up in **Jésus**, Menoud, pp. 118-124.
M. MIGUÉNS, "Pietro nel concilio apostolico", **RBiblt** 10 (1962) 240-251.
B. MOREL, "Eutychus et les fondements bibliques du culte", **ETRel** 37 (1962) 41-47.
F. MUSSNER*, "Die Bedeutung des Apostelkonzils für die Kirche", in **Ecclesia. Festschrift M. Wehr,** (Trier, 1962), pp. 35-46.
E. RAVAROTTO, "Die Hierosolymitano Concilio (Act. Cap. 15)", **Anton** 37 (1962) 185-218.
H. SCHÜRMANN, "Das Testament des Paulus für die Kirche (Apg 20, 18-35)", in (eds.) O. Schilling and H. Zimmermann, **Unio Christianorum. Festschrift L. Jaeger** (Paderborn, 1962), pp. 108-146; taken up in H. Schürmann, **Traditionsgeschichtliche Untersuchungen zu den synoptischen Evangelien** (Düsseldorf, 1968), pp. 310-340. We are citing the collection.
O. SOFFRITTI, "Stefano, testimone del Signore", **RBiblt** 10 (1962) 182-188.
G. STRECKER, "Die sogennante zweite Jerusalemreise des Paulus (Act 11, 27-30)", **ZNW** 53 (1962) 67-77.
T. WIESER, **Kingdom and Church in Luke-Acts**, unpublished dissertation, Union Theological Seminary (New York, 1962).

1963

G. R. BEASLEY-MURRAY, **Baptism in the New Testment** (New York 1963), pp. 93-122.
J. BIHLER, **Die Stephanusgeschichte im Zusammenlang der Apostelgeschichte** (Munich, 1963).
F. F. BRUCE, "St. Paul at Rome", **BJRylL** 46 (1963-1964) 326-345.
H. CONZELMANN, **Die Apostelgeschichte erklärt** (Tübingen, 1963, 1972^{2}).
J. CRETEN, "Voyage de Saint Paul à Rome", in **Studiorum Paulinorum Congressus Internationalis Catholicus, 1961,** 2 (Rome, 1963), pp. 193-196.
E. DABROWSKI, "Le prétendu procès de S. Paul d'après les recherches récentes", **Studiorum Paulinorum Congressus Internationalis Catholicus, 1961,** 2 (Rome, 1963), pp. 197-206.
J. DUPONT, "La première Pentecôte chrétienne (Act 2, 1-11)", **Assemblées du Seigneur**, 1st series, 51 (Bruges, 1963), pp. 39-62; taken up in **Etudes**, Dupont, pp. 481-502.
T. FAHY *, "The Council of Jerusalem", **IrTQ** 30 (1963) 232-261.

P. GAECHTER, "Geschichtliches zum Apostelkonzil", **ZKT** 85 (1963) 339-354.
E. HAENCHEN, "Judentum und Christentum in der Apostelgeschichte", **ZNW** 54 (1963) 155-187; taken up in E. Haenchen, **Die Bibel und Wir. Gesammelte Aufsätze**, 2 (Tübingen, 1966), pp. 338-374.
F. HAHN, **Das Verständnis der Mission im Neuen Testament** (Neukirchen, 1963).
G. JASPER, "Der Rat des Jacobus (Das Ringen des Paulus , der Urgemeinde, die Möglichkeit der Mission unter Israeld zu erhalten, Apostelgeschichte Kap. 21-28)", **Jud** 19 (1963) 147-162.
F. M. LOPEZ-MELUS, **Paupertas et divitiae in Evangelico sancti Lucae.** Pars dissertationis ad lauream in Facultate S. Theologiae apud Pontificiam Universitatem "Angelicum" de Urbe (Madrid, 1963).
V. MANCEBO, "Gál 2, 1-10 y Act. 15. Estado actual de la cuestión", **EstBib** 22 (1963) 315-350.
W. SCHMITHALS, **Paulus und Jakobus** (Göttingen, 1963).
B. SCHWANK, "'Setze über nach Mazedonien und hilf uns!' Reisenotizen zu Apg 16, 9-17, 15", **ErbAuf** 39 (1963) 399-416.
1964
A. W. ARGYLE, "Acts 19,20", **ExpTim** 75 (1964) 151.
T. BALLARINI, "Collegialità della chiesa in Atti e i Galati", **BibOr** 6 (1964) 255-262.
F. W. BEARE, "Speaking with Tongues. A Critical Survey of the New Testament Evidence", **JBL** 83 (1964) 229-246.
J. H. CREHAN, "The Purpose of Luke in Acts", (ed.) F. L. Cross, **Studia Evangelica**, II (Berlin, 1964), pp. 354-368.
J. DUPONT, "La parabole du semeur dans la version de Luc", in (eds.) W. Eltester and F. H. Kettler, **Apophoreta. Festschrift E. Haenchen**, (Berlin, 1964), pp. 97-108.
M. GOULDER, **Type and History in Acts** (London, 1964).
F. V. FILSON, **Three Crucial Decades. Studies in the Book of Acts** (London, 1964).
E. HAENCHEN, "Acta 27", in (ed.) E. Dinkler, **Zeit und Geschichte. Festschrift R. Bultmann** (Tübingen, 1964), pp. 235-254.
P. H. MENOUD, "Le peuple de Dieu dans le christianisme primitif", **FoiVie** 63 (1964) Cahiers Bibliques, No. 2, pp. 286-400; taken up in **Jésus**, Menoud pp. 337-346.
P. S. MINEAR, "A Note on Lk. 22, 35f.", **NT** 7 (1964) 128-134.
E. REPO, "Der 'Weg' als Selbstbezeichnung des Urchristentums. Eine traditionsgeschichtliche und semasiologische Untersuchung", Suomalaisen Tiedeakatemian Toimituksia. Annales Academiae scientiarum Fennicae, B series, vol. 132, 2 (Helsinki, 1964).
W. RORDORF, "Was wissen wir über die christlichen Gottesdiensträume der vorkonstantinschen Zeit?", **ZNW** 55 (1964) 110-128.
W. RORDORF, "La thélogie du ministère dans l'Eglise ancienne", **VerbC** 18 (1964) 84-104.
E. SCHLINK, "La sucession apostolique", **VerbC** 18 (1964) 52-86.
1965
D. C. ARICHEA*, **A Critical Analysis of the Stephen Speech in the Acts of the Apostles**, unpublished dissertation, Duke University (Durham, N. C., 1965); cf. **Dissertation Abstracts**, A 26 (1966) 4838.
H. J. DEGENHARDT, **Lukas, Evangelist der Armen. Besitz und Besitzverzicht in den lukanischen Schriften. Eine traditions- und redaktionsgeschichtliche Untersuchung** (Stuttgart, 1965).

J. DUPONT, "Saint Paul témoin de la collégialité apostolique et de la primauté de Saint Pierre" in (ed) Y. Congar, **La collégialité épiscopale**, (Paris, 1965), pp. 11-29.

H. FLENDER, **Heil und Geschichte in der Theologie des Lukas** (Munich, 1965, 1968[2]) (we are citing the 2nd ed).

D. GEORGI, **Die Geschichte der Kollekte des Paulus für Jerusalem** (Hamburg-Bergstedt, 1965).

T. HOLTZ, "Beobachtungen zur Stephanusrede Acta 7" in (ed) H. Benkert, **Kirche-Theologie-Frömmigkeit. Festschrift G. Holtz** (Berlin, 1965) pp. 102-114.

J. JERVELL, "Das gespaltene Israel und die Heidenvölker. Zur Motivierung der Heidenmission in der Apostelgeschichte", **ST** 19 (1965) 68-96; taken up in English in J. Jervell, **Luke and the People of God. A New Look at Luke-Acts** (= **People**, Jervell) (Minneapolis, 1965), pp. 41-74.

G. LOHFINK, **Paulus vor Damaskus. Arbeitsweisen der neueren Bibelwissenschaft dargestellt an den Texten Apg 9, 1-19: 22, 3-21: 26, 9-18** (Stuttgart, 1965) (FT, Paris, 1967).

G. LOHFINK, "Eine alttestamentliche Darstellungsform für Gotteserscheinungen in den Damaskusberichten", **BZ**, N.F. 9 (1965) 246-257.

R. E. OSBORNE, "St. Paul's Silent Years", **JBL** 84 (1965) 59-65.

W. OTT, **Gebet und Heil. Die Bedeutung der Gebetsparänese in der lukanischen Theologie** (Munich, 1965).

J. RIEDL*, "Sabed que Dios envía su salud a los gentiles (Hch 28, 28)" **RBíbCalz** 27 (1965) 153-155, 162.

J. ROLOFF, **Apostolat-Verkündigung-Kirche. Ursprung, Inhalt und Funktion des kirchlichen Apostelamtes nach Paulus, Lukas und den Pastoralbriefen** (Gütersloh, 1865).

1966

H. BRAUN, **Qumran und das Neue Testament**, I-II (Tübingen, 1966).

J. P. CHARLIER, **L'Evangile de l'enfance de l'Eglise. Commentaire de Acts 1-2** (Brussels-Paris-Montreal, 1966).

J. FENTON, "The Order of the Miracles performed by Peter and Paul in Acts", **ExpTim** 77 (1966) 381-383.

J. A. FITZMYER, "Jewish Christianity in Acts in Light of the Qumran Scrolls" in **Studies**, Keck, pp. 333-357.

E. FUCHS, "Kanon und Kirche", **ZTK** 63 (1966) 410-433.

A. GEORGE, "Art. pauvre" in **SDB** 7 (Paris, 1966), col. 387-406.

E. R. GOODENOUGH, "The Perspective of Acts" in **Studies**, Keck, pp. 51-59.

J. VAN GOUDOEVER, "The Place of Israel in Luke's Gospel", **NT** 8 (1966) 111-123.

E. HAENCHEN, "The Book of Acts as Source Material for the History of Early Christianity" in **Studies**, Keck, pp. 258-278; taken up in German in E. Haenchen, **Die Bibel und wir. Gesammelte Aufsätze**, 2 (Tübingen, 1966), pp. 312-337.

O. G. HARRIS*, **Prayer in Luke-Acts: A Study of the Theology of Luke**, unpublished dissertation, Vanderbilt University (Nashville, 1966); cf. **Dissertation Abstracts**, A, 27 (1967) p. 3507 A.

G. LOHFINK, "'Meinen namen zu tragen...' (Apg 9, 15)", **BZ**, N.F. 10 (1966)108-115.

R. PESCH, **Die Vision des Stephanus. Apg 7, 55-56 im Rahmen der Apostelgeschichte** (Stuttgart, n.d. (1966).

G. RINALDI, "Giacomo, Paolo e i Giudei (Atti 21, 17-26)", **RBiblt** 14 (1966) 407-423.

J. T. SANDERS, "Paul's 'autobiographical' Statements in Galatians 1-2", **JBL** 85 (1966) 335-348.

G. SCHILLE, **Anfänge der Kirche. Erwägungen zur apostolischen Frühgeschichte** (Munich, 1966).

1967

K. BARTH, **Das christliche Leben (Fragment): Die Taufe als Begründung des christlichen Lebens, Die kirchliche Dogmatik** IV/4 (Fragment) (Zurich, 1967).

F. BOVON, **De Vocatione Gentium. Histoire de l'interpretation d'Acts 10. 1-11. 18 dans les six premiers siècles** (Tübingen, 1967).

F. BOVON, "L'origine des récits concernant les apôtres", **RTPhil**, 3rd series 17 (1967) 345-350.

E. C. DAVIS*, **The Significance of the Shared Meal in Luke-Acts,** unpublished dissertation, Southern Baptist Theological Seminary (Louisville, Ky., 1967); cf. **Dissertation Abstracts,** A 28 (1967), p. 2324 A.

J. DUPONT, "La communauté des biens aux premiers jours de l'Eglise (Actes 2, 42. 44-45; 4, 32. 34-35)" in **Etudes** Dupont, pp. 503-519.

C. EXUM AND C. TALBERT, "The Structure of Paul's Speech to the Ephesian Elders (Act 20, 18-35)", **CBQ** 29 (1967) 233-236.

S. GIET, "Exégèse", **RevSR** 41 (1967) 341-348.

H. LUZ*, "Cristo y la Iglesia, segun Hechos", **RBíbCalz** 29 (1967) 206-223.

C. M. MARTINI, "La figura di Pietro secondo le varianti del codice D negli Atti degli Apostoli" in **San Pietro. Atti della XIX Settimana Biblica** (Brescia, 1967), pp. 279-289.

F. MUSSNER, "Die Una Sancta nach Apg 2, 42" in **Praesentia Salutis. Gesammelte Studien zu Fragen und Themen des Neuen Testaments** (Düsseldorf, 1967), pp. 212-222.

J. K. PARRATT, "The Rebaptism of the Ephesian Disciples", ExpTim 79 (1967-1968) 182-183.

L. PERETTO, Pietro e Paolo e l'anno 49 nella complessa situazione palestinese", **RBiblt** 15 (1967) 295-308.

M. PHILONENKO, "Le décret apostolique et les interdits alimentaires du Coran", **RHPhilRel** 47 (1967) 165-172.

E. RAVAROTTO*, "La figura e la parte di Pietro in Atti 8-15" in **San Pietro. Atti della XIX Settimana Biblica** (Brescia, (1967), pp. 241-278.

C. H. TALBERT, "Again: Paul's visit to Jerusalem", **NT** 9 (1967) 26-40.

1968

J. BEUTLER, "Die paulinische Heidenmission am Vorabend des Apostelskonzils. Zur Redaktionsgeschichte von Apg 14, 1-20", **TPhil** 43 (1968) 360-383.

F. CASA, "La Iglesia de los Hechos de los Apóstoles y la Iglesia del Vaticano II", **TCatArg** 6, 13 (1968) 195-208.

A. GEORGE, "Israël dans l'oeuvre de Luc", **RB** 75 (1968) 481-525.

C. GHIDELLI*, "I tratti riassuntivi degli Atti degli Apostoli" in **Il Messagio della Salvezza, V, Scriti apostolici** (Turin, 1968), pp.137-150.

V. HASLER*, "Judenmission und Judenschuld", **TZBas** 24 (1968) 173-190.

J. JERVELL, "Paulus - der Lehrer Israels. Zu den apologetischen Paulusreden in der Apostelgeschichte", **NT** 10 (1968) 164-190; taken up in English in **People,** Jervell, pp. 153-183.

P. JOVINO*, "L'Eglise, communauté des saints dans les 'Acts des Apôtres' et dans les 'Epîtres aux Thessaloniciens'", **RBiblt** 16 (1968) 497-526.

M. MASINI*, "La testimonianza cristiana. Spunti dal libro degli Atti", **Servitium** 26 (1968) 165-184.

B. NOACK*, **Pinsedagen. Litteraere og historiske Problemer i Acta Kap 2 og droftelsen af dem i de sidste artier** (Copenhagen,1968).

E. RASCO, **Actus Apostolorum. Introductio et exempla exegetica** (photocopied course from the Pont. Univ. Gregoriana), fasc. II (Rome, 1968), pp. 271-330 (concerning the summaries).

M. H. SCHARLEMANN, **Stephen: A Singular Saint** (Rome, 1968).

P. SCHUBERT, "The Final Cycle of Speeches in the Book of Acts", **JBL** 87 (1968) 1-16.

1969

S. BROWN, **Apostasy and Perseverance in the Theology of Luke** (Rome, 1969).

L. C. CROCKETT, Luke 4, 25-27 and Jewish-Gentile Relations in Luke-Acts", **JBL** 88 (1969) 177-183.

J. DUPONT, "L'union entre les premiers chrétiens dans les Actes des apôtres", **NRT** 91 (1969) 897-915.

J. KODELL, "Luke's Use of Laos, 'People', especially in the Jerusalem narrative (Lk 19, 28-24, 53)", CBQ 31 (1969) 327-343.

M. LETURMY, **Le Concile de Jérusalem** (Paris, 1969) (This is in fact a novel!)

R. J. MAC KELVEY, **The New Temple. The Church in the New Testament** (London, 1969).

C. M. MARTINI, "L'esclusione dalla comunità del popolo di Dio e il nuovo Israele secondo Atti 3, 23", **Bib** 50 (1969) 1-14.

P. ORTIZ VALDIVIESO, **'Υπομονή en el Nuevo Testamento** (Bogota, 1969).

I. PANAGOPOULOS, ***'Ο Θεός καὶ ἡ Ἐκκλησία. Ἡ θεολογική μαρτυρία τῶν Πραξεων Ἀποστόλων*** (Athens, 1969).

R. PESCH, "Der Christ als Nachahmer Christi. Der Tod des Stefanus (Apg 7) im Vergleich mit dem Tod Christi", **BiKi** 24 (1969) 10-11.

B. PRETE, **Il Primato e la Missione di Pietro. Studio esegeticocritico del testo di Lc 22, 31-32** (Brescia, 1969).

P. RICHARDSON, **Israel in the Apostolic Church** (Cambridge, 1969).

L. F. RIVERA, "El nacimiento de la Iglesia: Hch 1, 1-2, 41", **RBíbCalz** 31 (1969) 35-45.

L. F. RIVERA, "De Cristo a la Iglesia (Hch 1, 1-12)", **RBíbCalz** 31 (1969) 97-105.

A. SCHULZ, "Wer mein Jünger sein will, der nehme täglich sein Kreuz auf sich! Meditation", **BiKi** 24 (1969) 9.

M. SIMON, "The Apostolic Decree and its Setting in the Ancient Church", **BJRylL** 52 (1969) 437-460.

B. TRÉMEL, "La fraction du pain dans les Actes des Apôtres", **LumVie** 94 (1969) 76-90.

E. TROCMÉ, "Le Saint Esprit et l'Eglise d'après le Livree des Actes" in (ed) S. Dockx, **L'Esprit Saint et l'Eglise. Catholiques, orthodoxes et protestants de divers pays confrontent leur science, leur foi et leur tradition: l'avenir de l'Eglise et l'oecuménisme** (Paris, 1969), pp. 19-27 (discussion on pp. 28-44).

1970

R. BARTHES, "L'analyse Structurale du Récit. A propos d'Actes 10-11", **RecSR** 58 (1970) 17-37; taken up in (ed) X. Léon-Dufour, **Exégèse et herméneutique** (=**Exégèse**, Léon-Dufour) (Paris, 1971) pp. 181-204 (round table pp. 239-265).

O. BETZ, "Die Vision des Paulus im Tempel von Jerusalem - Apg 22, 17-21 - als Beitrag zur Deutung des Damaskuserlebnisses" in (eds.) O. Böcher and K. Haacker, **Verborum Veritas. Festschrift G. Stählin** (= **Verborum**, Böcher) (Wuppertal, 1970), pp. 113-123.

F. BOVON, "Tradition et rédaction en Actes 10, 1-11, 18", **TZBas** 26 (1970) 22-45.

P. B. BROWN*, **The Meaning and Function of Acts 5, 1-11 in the Purpose of Luke-Acts** unpublished dissertation, Boston University School of Theology (Boston, 1970); cf. Dissertation Abstracts, A 30 (1970) 4531 A.

C. BURCHARD, **Der dreizehnte Zeuge. Traditions- und kompositionsgeschichtliche Untersuchungen zu Lukas' Darstellung der Frühzeit des Paulus** (Göttingen, 1970).

J. COPPENS, "Miscellanées bibliques, LVIII. La Koinônia dans l'Eglise primitive", **ETL** 46 (1970) 116-121.

J. DANIÉLOU, **L'Eglise des apôtres** (Paris, 1970).

E. E. ELLIS, "The Role of the Christian Prophet in Acts" in **Apostolic History**, Gasque, pp. 55-67.

F. V. FILSON, "The Journey Motif in Luke-Acts" in **Apostolic History**, Gasque, pp. 68-77.

B. GERHARDSSON, "Einige Bemerkungen zu Apg 4, 32", ST 24 (1970) 142-149.

K. HAACKER, "Das Pfingstwunder als exegetisches Problem" in **Verborum**, Böcher pp. 125-132.

E. HAULOTTE, "Fondation d'une communauté de type universel: Act 10, 1-11, 18. Etudes critique sur la rédaction, la 'structure' et la 'tradition' du récit", **RecSR** 58 (1970) 63-100; taken up in **Exégèse**, Léon-Dufour, pp. 321-362.

E. HAULOTTE, "L'envoi de Paul aux nations (Actes, chapitres 9, 22 et 26)", **Vie Chrétienne**, No. 132 (1970), 11-15 and 19.

A. J. B. HIGGINS, "The Preface to Luke and the Kerygma in Acts" in **Apostolic History**, Gasque, pp. 78-91.

I. H. MARSHALL, **Luke: Historian and Theologian** (Exeter, 1970), pp. 188-215.

L. MARIN, "Essai d'analyse structurale d'Actes 10. 1-11. 18", **RecSR** 58 (1970) 39-61; taken up in **Exégèse**, Léon-Dufour pp. 213-238.

G. RINALDI, "Comunità cristiane nell' età apostolica", **BibOr** 12 (1970) 3-10.

G. SCHNEIDER*, "Die Zwölf Apostel als 'Zeugen'. Wesen, Ursprung und Funktion einer lukanischen Konzeption" in (eds.) P. -W. Scheele and G. Schneider, **Christuszeugnis der Kirche. Theologische Studien** (Essen,1970), pp. 39-65.

Y. TISSOT, "Les prescriptions des presbytres (Act 15, 41, D)", **RB** 77 (1970) 321-346.

A. VÖÖBUS, "Kritische Beobachtungen über die lukanische Darstellung des Herrenmahls", **ZNW** 61 (1970) 102-110.

1971

C. BRIDEL, **Aux seuils de l'espérance. Le diaconat en notre temps** (Neuchâtel 1971), pp. 16-26.

H. VON CAMPENHAUSEN, "Taufen auf der Namen Jesu?", **VigChr** 25 (1971) 1-16.

S. CIPRIANI, "La preghiera negli Atti degli Apostoli", **BibOr** 13 (1971) 27-41.

J. COURTÈS, "Actes 10, 1-11, 18 comme système de représentations mythiques" in **Exégèse**, Léon-Dufour, pp. 205-211.

J. D. M. DERRETT, "Ananias, Saphira and the Right of Property", **DowR** 89 (1971) 225-232.

J. DUPONT, "Les pauvres et la pauvreté dans les Evangiles et les Actes" in A. George et al, **La Pauvreté évangélique** (Paris, 1971), pp. 37-63.
J. DUPONT, "Renoncer è tous ses biens (Luc 14, 33)", **NRT** 93 (1971) 561-582.
B. B. HALL, "La communauté chrétienne dans le livre des Actes. Actes 6, 1-17 et 10, 1-11, 18 (15, 6-11)", **FoiVie** No. out of series: **Reconnaissance à Suzanne de Dietrich** (Paris, 1971), pp. 146-156.
H. JASCHKE, "λαλεῖν bei Lukas. Ein Beitrag zur lukanischen Theologie", **BZ**, N.F. 15 (1971)109-114.
J. JERVELL, "The Law in Luke-Acts" , **HarvTJ** 64 (1971) 21-36; taken up in **People**, Jervell, pp. 133-151.
A. LEMAIRE, **Les ministères aux origines de l'Eglise. Naissance de la triple hiérarchie: évêques, presbytres, diacres** (Paris, 1971).
S. LUNDGREN, "Ananias and the Calling of Paul in Acts", **ST** 25 (1971) 117-122.
D. J. MC CARTHY, "An Installation Genre?", **JBL** 90 (1971) 31-41.

1972

P. C. BORI, **Κοινωνία. L'idéa della comunione nell'ecclesiologia recente e nel Nuovo Testamento** (Brescia, 1972), pp. 100-102 et passim.
W. DIETRICH, **Das Petrusbild der lukanischen Schriften** (Stuttgart-Berlin-Köln-Mainz, 1972).
W. ELTESTER, "Israel im lukanischen Werk und die Nazareth-Perikope" in E. Grässer et al, **Jesus in Nazareth** (Berlin, 1972), pp. 76-147.
G. FORKMAN, **The Limits of the Religious Community. Expulsion from the religious community within the Qumran Sect, within Rabbinic Judaism and within primitive Christianity** (Lund, 1972).
J. HADOT, "L'utopie communautaire et la vie des premiers chrétiens de Jérusalem", **Problèmes d'histoire du christianisme** 3 (1972-1973) 15-34.
H. HÄRING, **Kirche und Kerygma. Das Kirchenbild in der Bultmann-schule** (Freiburg-Basel-Vienna, 1972).
J. JERVELL, **Luke and the People of God. A New Look at Luke-Acts** (Minneapolis, 1972).
J. MÁNEK, "Das Aposteldekret im Kontext der Lukastheologie", **ComViat** 15 (1972) 151-160.

1973

Amt und Eucharistie, (ed) P. Bläser,* (Paderhorn, 1973).
P. J. BERNADICOU, "The Lucan Theology of Joy", **SciEspr** 25 (1973) 75-88.
J. DUPONT, **Les Béatitudes, III, Les Evangélistes** (Paris, 1973), pp. 17-206.
J. DUPONT, "Les ministères de l'Eglise naissante d'après les Actes des apôtres" in **Ministères et célébration de l'Eucharistie** (Studia Anselmiana, 61 = Sacramentum I) (Rome, 1973), pp. 94-148.
R. H. FULLER, "The Choice of Matthias" in (ed) E. A. Livingstone, **Studia Evangelica.** VI, (Berlin, 1973), pp. 140-146.
J. L. HOULDEN, **Ethics and the New Testament** (Harmondsworth, 1973), pp. 55-60.
A. JAUBERT, *L'élection de Mathias et le tirage au sort", (ed) E. A. Livingstone, **Studia Evangelica.** VI, (Berlin, 1973), pp. 274-280.
J. A. JAUREGUI, **Testemonio Apostolado-Misión. Justificación Teológica del concepto Lucano Apóstol-Testigo de la Resurrección. Analisis Exegético de Act 1, 15-26** (Bilbao, 1973).

L. E. KECK, "Listening To and Listening For. From Text to Sermon (Acts 1, 8)", **Interpr** 27 (1973) 184-202.
K. LÖNING, **Die Saulustradition in der Apostelgeschichte** (Münster, 1973).
H. J. MICHEL, **Die Abschiedsrede des Paulus an die Kirche, Apg 20, 17-38. Motivgeschichte und theologische Bedeutung** (Munich, 1973).
P. T. O'BRIEN, "Prayer in Luke-Acts", **TyndB** 24 (1973) 111-127.
Peter in the New Testament. A Collaborative Assessment by Protestant and Roman Catholic Scholars, (ed) R. E. Brown **et al** (Minneapolis-New York-Toronto, 1973), pp. 39-56 and 109-128 (FT Paris, 1974).
P. DA SPONGANO*, "La concezione teologica della predicazione nel libro degli 'Atti'", **RBiblt** 21 (1973)147-164.
J. WANKE, **Beobachtungen zum Eucharistieverständnis des Lukas auf Grund der lukanischen Mahlberichte** (Leipzig, 1973).
S. G. WILSON, **The Gentiles and the Gentile Mission in Luke-Acts** (Cambridge, 1973).

1974

C. BORI, **Chiesa Primitiva. L'immagine della comunità delle origini - Atti 2, 42-47; 4, 32-37 - nella storia della chiesa antica** (Brescia, 1974).
F. BOVON, "L'importance des médiations dans le projet théologique de Luc", **NTS** 21 (1974-1975) 23-39.
H. FLENDER, "Die Kirche in den Lukas-Schriften als Frage an ihre heutige Gestalt" in **Lukas Forschung**, Braumann, pp. 261-286.
A. GEORGE, "L'oeuvre de Luc: Actes et Evangile" in (ed) J. Delorme, **Le ministère et les ministères selon le Nouveau Testament** (Paris, 1974), pp. 207-240.
D. GILL, "The Structure of Acts 9", **Bib** 55 (9174) 546-548.
J.D KODELL, "'The Word of God Grew'. The Ecclesial Tendency of Λόγος in Acts 1, 7; 12, 24; 19, 20" **Bib** 55 (1974) 505-519.
K. LÖNING, "Die Korneliustradition", **BZ**, N.F. 18 (1974) 1-19.
C.-P. MÄRZ, **Das Wort Gottes bei Lukas. Die lukanische Worttheologie als Frage an die neuere Lukasforschung** (Leipzig, 1974).
A. M. RITTER*, "Die frühchristliche Gemeinde und ihre Bedeutung für die heutigen Strukturen der Kirche" in (eds) H. W. Schütte and F. Wintzer, **Theologie und Wirklichkeit. Festschrift W. Trillhaas** (Göttingen, 1974), pp. 123-144.
J. A. SANDERS, "The Ethic of Election in Luke's Great Banquet Parable", in (eds) J. L. Crenshaw and J. T. Willis, **Essays in Old Testament Ethics. Memorial J. Ph. Hyatt** (New York, 1974), pp. 245-271.
J. Y. THERIAULT*, "Les dimensions sociales, économiques et politiques dans l'oeuvre de Luc", **SciEspr** 26 (1974) 205-231.
P. ZINGG, **Das Wachsen der Kirche. Beiträge zur Frage der lukanischen Redaktion und Theologie** (Fribourg, Switzerland-Göttingen, 1974).

1975

C. BURCHARD, "Paulus in der Apostelgeschichte", **TLZ** 100 (1975) 881-895.
O. CULLMANN, **Der johanneische Kreis. Sein Platz im Spätjudentum, in der Jüngerschaft Jesu und im Urchristentum. Zum Ursrung**

des Johannesevangeliums (Tübingen, 1975) (FT. Neuchâtel-Paris, 1976).

J. T. LIENHARD, "Acts 6, 1-6: A Redactional View", **CBQ** 37 (1975) 228-236.

G. LOHFINK, "Der Losvorgang in Apg 1, 26", **BZ**, N.F., 19 (1975) 247-249.

G. LOHFINK, **Die Sammlung Israels. Eine Untersuchung zur lukanischen Ekklesiologie** (Munich, 1975).

J. M. MC DERMOTT, "The Biblical Doctrine of *κοινωνία*", **BZ**, N.F, 19 (1975) 64-77 and 219-233.

E. NELLESSEN, "Tradition und Schrift in der Perikope von der Erwählung des Mattias (Apg 1, 15-26)", **BZ**, N.F, 19 (1975) 205-218.

W. RADL, **Paulus und Jesus im Lukanischen Doppelwerk. Untersuchungen zu Parallelmotiven im Lukasevangelium und in der Apostelgeschichte** (Bern-Frankfurt, 1975).

H. J. SIEBEN*, "Zur Entwicklung der Konzilsidee. 10. Teil: die Konzilsidee des Lukas", **TPhil** 50 (1975) 481-503.

1976

F. BOVON, "Orientations actuelles des études lucaniennes" **RTPhil**, 3rd series 26 (1976) 161-190.

M. DUMAIS, **Le langage de l'evangélisation. L'annonce missionnaire en milieu juif (Actes 13, 16-41)** (Tournai-Montreal, 1976).

J. KILGALLEN, **The Stephen Speech. A Literary and Redactional Study of Acts 7, 2-53** (Rome, 1976).

P. S. MINEAR, **To Heal and to Reveal. The Prophetic Vocation According to Luke** (New York, 1976).

L. MONLOUBOU, **La prière selon saint Luc. Recherche d'une structure** (Paris, 1976).

E. NELLESSEN, **Zeugnis für Jesus und das Wort. Exegetische Untersuchungen zum lukanischen Zeugnisbegriff** (Köln-Bonn, 1976).

W. POPKES, "Art. Gemeinschaft", **RAC** 9 (Stuttgart, 1976), col. 1100-1145.

G. STEIMBERGER, "Die Stephanusrede (Apg 7) und die jüdische Tradition" in (ed) A. Fuchs, **Jesus in der Verkündigung der Kirche** (Linz, 1976), pp. 154-174.

1977

JEANNE D'ARC, **Les pèlerins d'Emmaüs** (Paris, 1977).

D. L. MEALAND*, "Community of Goods and Utopian Allusions in Acts 2-4", **JTS**, N. S., 28 (1977) 96-99.

CHAPTER 7

THE CHURCH

Introduction

If the fifties permitted us to discover a theologian in Luke, the seventies reminded us that Luke was also a historian and maybe more than a theologian, an evangelist or a pastor. Nevertheless, if Luke did not abstractly develope doctrines, he was still guided by a theological project, certainly subjacent, but coherent. In this project, which the very existence of Acts already attests, ecclesiology occupies a high position. Transmitted at first by Jesus, the message of the kingdom, reworked in the light of Easter in a Christological direction, is transmitted by the Twelve apostles, who are reorganized into a unique college. Setting out from Jerusalem, this proclamation gains the then universal empire step by step. Gradually during this march which often changes into conquest, the mission is joined with a variable, not to say evolutive, phenomenology, the Church. Diverse by its members, it is diversified by its ministries as well. Jewish, Hellenistic, and then Gentile Christians walk in a procession in front of the scene, in a scenario directed by the Holy Spirit and animated by the Twelve, Stephen and then Paul. The diversity of the requirements follows the risks of the initial conditions as well.

In his state of the question, Dom J. Dupont (-> 1950) presented several interpretations of Lucan ecclesiology. He distinguished certain Catholic contributions, marked by the official doctrine of the Church, and the Protestant studies of M. Gogel and J. L. Leuba [1].

The published works since then have been innumerable. Without being exhaustive, we have examined thirty monographs or so and more than two hundred articles. At the risk of simplify - ing, we can say that research has been directed in four major directions.

One series of scholars have dealt with the nature of the Church, as Luke presents it. They studied the traits of this

Church (people of God, way, body of Christ, local communities, the universal Church, etc.). Some, more historical, sought in Luke-Acts the primitive image of the Church, beyond Luke and Paul. More theologically, others were interested in the notae of the Lucan Church and sought to discern the ecclesiological intentions of the editor of Acts. The analysis of the Pentecost account and more generally, Act 2 on the whole, often served as their guideline [2].

A second group of exegetes thought the relations between the Church and Judaism as well as the links between Jewish Christianity and the Gentile version, merited particular attention. They think that a proper understanding of Lucan ecclesiology depends on a correct interpretation of these rapports. Unfortunately, despite the work of authors as eminent as J. Dupont, E. Haenchen, A. George and J. Jervell no consensus came forth. Their views are even antagonistic: for some, Acts marks the Church's progressive and ineluctable disengagement from Judaism; for others, it constantly reminds us of the Church's pretention to remain the Israel of God. These authors clearly have each their own view toward certain texts in Acts: the story of Cornelius (Act 10:1-11, 18), the conference of Jerusalem (Act 15), the rupture between Paul and the Jewish leaders in Rome (Act 28). Moreover, they think that the very structure of the Lucan corpus as well as the author's principle intention, permit a redactional solution to the problem posed.

Other researchers, which we have classed with some violence in a third group, placed the organization of the Church on the first row of their investigations, be it the early Church described by the Evangelist, or Luke's own which filters through certain editorial indications. The college of the twelve apostles has been thrown into the center of the debates: Is Luke the first to bring the Twelve and the apostles together? Does he have a special conception of apostleship which would place Paul's ministry on a second level? Several contributions considered the theme of the "witness" which Luke appreciates and does not limit to the Twelve. Others choose the themes of the "elders" or "prophets". The general question of the ministries, recently dealt with by A. Lemaire and other French exegetes, cannot be dissociated from the question of the people who, in Acts, incarnate the apostles and witnesses. Many monographs present Peter, Stephen and even more Paul according to the Lucan perspective (Act 2; 7; 9; 22 and 26 are analyzed in the greatest detail). The jurisdictional power of the apostles has not escaped the attention of the exegetes: several articles examine the episode of Ananias and Sapphira. Other scholars, pushed by Qumranian research, seek to determine what the concrete organization of the primitive community was like. Several studies, distinguishing tradition from redaction, go back to the origins of Christian liturgy, while others set forth the Lucan elaboration of baptism and the Lord's Supper.

A last group of exegetes were sensitive to the daily life of the Church and particularly, the communal ethic proposed by Luke in the name of Jesus and the Christian tradition. The summaries in Acts have been the object of various genetic, structural and theological studies. The themes of communion and sharing have been located and dissected. A few dissertations began with the redactional coloration of the teaching of Jesus to attain the particular aspect of Luke's ecclesiastic ethic: poverty, perseverence, prayer, suffering, imitation and union in turn have been closely examined.

I. THE NATURE OF THE CHURCH, GENERAL PRESENTATIONS

Historical Perspective

a. Two declarations, taken as arguments, stimulated certain authors to reconstitute, more or less critically, the ecclesiology of the first Christians based on Acts: 1) Luke is first of all a historian and 2) the style and vocabulary helps to locate the sources in the first chapters of Acts. Since our investigation aims at the Lucan theological project, we will go briefly through these contributions.

It is first of all necessary to mention various studies of L. Cerfaux. In one of them (-> 1925), he thinks to have established that the expression the "saints" designates the primitive cell of the Church, i.e. the leaders of the first community in Jerusalem. The expression would go straight back to Palestinian Judaism. Another article (-> 1939) seeks to determine that the section Act 2:41-5:42 forms a traditional literary unit, also rooted in Judaism of the Palestinian type. These and other studies have permitted the Belgian scholar to write a small book called **La communauté apostolique** (-> 1943, second title). In our opinion, the author is a little too overconfident concerning Luke's historical faithfulness and sometimes projects certain later ecclesiological conceptions onto the primitive community; they have since become normative in Catholic theology. Here is the division of the chapters: Pentecost, the Apostles (with Peter at the helm), the life of the community (L. Cerfaux demonstrates that ethics were anchored in pneumatology), liturgy (Act 2:46f. and 4:24-31), the expansion of the Church thanks to Stephen [3], Peter, the Church in Antioch (which frees itself from the Jewish framework), the council of Jerusalem which marks the end of the role of Jerusalem (a historically questionable affirmation in our view) [4].

Such a traditional approach is also found among certain Pro - testant exegetes. The author of a commentary, whose philological information is precious, F. F. Bruce wrote (-> 1953) a popular work on the primitive Church where the ecclesiological indications of Luke are taken for objective descriptions of the mother community and the churches of the Diaspora (cf. chapters 6: the new community; 9: the expansion in Palestine; 10: the council of Jerusalem; 11: toward Europe). We conserve the following affirmations: the first Christians did not call themselves Nazarenes . They preferred the vocabulary of the OT and called themselves the holy people, the poor and the brethren. They formed a separate synagogue in the larger Jewish community. The term 'church' had the advantage of being understood by all because of its background which was Jewish (religious) and Greek (political).

Identifying the information of Luke as the historical reality of early Christianity, C. F. D. Moule, in a popular work (-> 1957) proposes a distinction without separation of the three types of testimony in the book of the Acts: by <u>action</u>, the first Christians witnessed to the present activity of the Holy Spirit in individuals and in the Christian community; by <u>word</u>, they presented not a moral code but a recollection of the acts of God in history; and by <u>communal life,</u> they rendered glory to God and testified among men.

Two contributions present a more critical position, but in a strictly historical perspective. The first by L. E. Elliot-Binns (-> 1956) following E. Lohse [5], examines the relations between the Church at Jerusalem and the Christian communities in Galilee. For the author, Galilean communities existed which were interested in Jesus' teaching rather than his life. Their Christology and soteriology were but little developed. Narrow ties linked them to Judaism. The Church in Jerusalem rapidly ceased, to be dominated by the Galilean group, which corresponded to the twelve princes of Israel, and had for principle mission to testify to the resurrection. Becoming an institution, because of the delay of the Parousia, this church took on a sacerdotal and dynastic form under the influence of the Judean converts. We do not understand clearly how such an affirmation is reconcilable with the ascension of James to the head of the Jerusalem Church, an ascension which Elliot-Binns accepts. Was not James Galilean, too? Does it suffice to say that he was persona grata in the eyes of the Jewish authorities and that in Christian circles the differences between Galileans and Judeans were toned down? Why, if we follow the author, did they not put one of their own at the head of this institution?

The other work which is unusually constructed, is A. P. Davies' (-> 1957). The writer critically analyzes the NT sources to resolve the crucial question, among others, which is dear to him: how can the fulgurating development of the early Church in Jerusalem be explained? His answer is original: parallel to the Essenes or even identical to them, an important messianic group existed in Jerusalem before the resurrection of Jesus. This pre-Christian community, directed by a group of twelve men with James at their head, were perhaps called Nazarenes. Returning from Galilee after the appearances, Jesus' disciples, with Peter at their head, announced the resurrection and Messiahship of Jesus. This preaching had a rapid and decisive success among the so-called Nazarene messianic community. We think that the Qumranian parallels can be explained in a simpler manner than Davies proposes (cf. the prudent methodological remarks of J. Schmitt and H. Braun) [6]. Furthermore, the numbers which Luke mentions concerning the initial success of the Christian mission are certainly excessive and therefore do not require such an adventurous hypothesis [7].

Theological Perspective

b. From 1950 on, a new problem appeared, which rejoined the intention of the Tendenzkritik of the 19th century. What is the ecclesiology of the author of Acts? This redactional approach is more delicate with regard to the Church than to the Spirit or the Christ, for more than anywhere else, the exegete must know how to read between the lines and distinguish in Acts what is archaic ecclesiologically from what is Lucan interpretation. This question, coming forth from Formgeschichte has been proposed and imposed by German exegesis. Before exposing some of their fruit, it is fitting to introduce an earlier American work, which concerning several points, anticipated the research. The opuscule of B. S. Easton is entitled **The Purpose of Acts** (-> 1936).

Aside from the main thesis which sees Acts as a work intended to present Christianity as a Jewish sect, i.e. as a part within a religio licita, this essay contains two chapters relative to our subject. One concerns Paul and the other deals with the government of the Church. First of all, the author demonstrates that Luke tends to submit Paul and, with him, Gentile Christianity, to the Twelve and, with them, the mother Church in Jerusalem. He points out with finesse, for example, that the Pauline preaching in Acts leans on the appearances of the Risen Lord to the Twelve and not on the Damascus Road experience (cf. Act 13:30f.). The apostolic college possesses the authorized testimony and holds the government of all of the communities in its hands. Its existence is decisive for the constitution of the Church. Easton continues by saying that the group of the Twelve serves as a model for the different Churches. The elders, installed by Paul according to Act 14:23, take on the form and function of the college of the Twelve. Here and there, the responsibility is collegial, which does not exclude individual charisms [8]. This type of organization goes back to Judaism which knew the great Sanhedrin of Jerusalem, the model of the college of Elders of all synagogues. Like the Sanhedrin of Jerusalem was directed by the High Priest, different from the local elders, James, in the same way, obtained an important position in the mother Church. Yet at two points the Christian system differed from the Jewish one. 1) Instead of taking the tradition back to Moses, the early Christians made it depend on the apostles. 2) The Christian Church was more democratic than the Jewish community, since all the brethren took part in the election of Matthias and the deliberations concerning circumcision. Easton seems to suppose at the same time that this presbyterian system is ancient (he notes that Luke introduces the Elders in Jerusalem without warning for they were known to his readers) and that Luke generalized its existence. Moreover, he thinks that in his time, Luke knew of deacons, side by side the elders. Unable to make the Seven into a second presbytery, he sees them as deacons. This view does not really correspond to their historical activity. Easton, as we see, presses here and there what could be called a Redaktionsgeschichte, but does not succeed in clearly distinguishing Luke's ecclesiology from the tradition's.

The Redaktionsgeschichtler, like H. Conzelmann and E. Haenchen, have worked in the shadow of R. Bultmann. The master from Marburg summarized in a brilliant way his views on NT ecclesiology in a conference which appeared first in English (-> 1955). He distinguishes four stages in the development of the ecclesiological consciousness of early Christianity: 1) that of the first community which, under the impetus of the Word understands itself as the true Israel of the end times, within Judaism; 2) that of the Pauline churches which, while maintaining the eschatological consciousness, separate themselves from Judaism; 3) the one marked by the passage from the eschatological perspective to the sacramental one (ministers become constitutive); 4) the fourth stage, of which traces are found already in Luke, is distinguished by the relation that the Church entertains with the past and the present rather than the future. By this historization, the transcendent character of the Church appears more in the institutions than in the Word: The Church is well installed in the world. Furthermore, the individual's fate is more important than the universe's. In summary, four expressions help to qualify this evolution: the people of God, the body of Christ, the institution of salvation and the new religion.

We can criticize this conception of a certain schematization. Later research has shown that ecclesiology varied from one milieu to the other. It could have remained archaic in some places or, on the contrary, be transformed with more or less rapidity in Asia or Rome. The Bultmannian model is nonetheless interesting in that we can confront it with the reality of the texts; it thus allows to illuminate the darker corners, and then it can be modified in turn by the analysis of the information.

c. H. Conzelmann (-> 1954), is the first after Bultmann, to have attempted to situate the Lucan conception of the Church. First of all, he brings to our attention a post-Pauline break between objective salvation in Christ and its subjective appropriation by the believer. Luke's effort consists in turning over to the Church, which is thus valorized, the function of leaping over this gap. He writes: "Damit gewinnt der Faktor der Übermittlung, die Kirche, gesteigerte Eigenbedeutung." (p. 193).

The Church occupies the third step in salvation history. The individual does not fit directly into this history but must pass by the intermediary of the Church to find his place. The time of the Church is marked by the departure of the Risen Lord, the granting of the Holy Spirit to believers and the preaching of the Gospel centered on Jesus Christ.

Luke describes the Church with the traits of the primitive Church: he prefers the ἀρχή to the atemporel image of an ideal

Church or the concrete figure of the community of his time. "Das Leben der Kirche im Geist mit seinen Faktoren, Verkündigung, Gemeinschaft, Sakrament, Gebet, Bestehen in der Verfolgung, wird paradigmatisch in der Schilderung der Urgemeinde vorge - führt." (p. 194).

As this quotation shows, Conzelmann perceives a paradox in Luke: the early Church is a great historic event of the past; it is by that inimitable and not repeatable; but it is, at the same time, exemplary in its organization, selfconsciousness and concrete life. We can already sense: Conzelmann, differing from E. Käsemann [9], refuses to consider Luke as a representative of Frühkatholizismus: "Die Ämter der Frühzeit sind nicht Modell der späteren; sie sind nicht wiederholbar." (p. 201). The ministers do not found the Church for the Word still does this. In Luke, the apostles are witnesses more than pillars. They do not worry about the apostolic succession which is assured. The historical perspective is typical of Luke's ecclesiology, according to Conzelmann. Luke is unaware of the themes of the preexistence and transcendence of the Church. On the contrary, Luke does not hide that the Church evolved with the heilsgeschichtlich circumstances. The Urgemeinde is succeeded by the Church of the Gentiles, which is universalistic and detached from the Law. Of course, the idea of the universal mission was already present in Mark (cf. Mk 13:10). "Aber erst Lukas gestaltet das Bild vom äusseren planmässigen Ablauf." (p. 199f.) [10].

What distinguishes the early community from the actual Church is the particular notion of peace: the early Church had no divisions and lived in harmony. A continuity is however not to be excluded: persecution characterizes the Church past and present. Conzelmann deems that for Luke, the Church is necessarily an ecclesia pressa. E. Grässer and S. Brown have rejected this perspective. Namely these authors remind us that according to Luke, the Church also has the characteristics of an ecclesia militans, perseverans and triumphans [11].

For Conzelmann, the importance lies elsewhere: it is that Luke became (the first) conscious of the distance and duration. The Church has a history and it is no longer what it was. The entire question now concerns the continuity. Conzelmann thinks that this continuity is still guaranteed, as in Paul, by the Word and the Holy Spirit. Other researchers, after him, will see the pledge of the institution's survival and the sign of its faithfulness in the institution itself and its ministries and sacraments. As for us, we believe that Luke was sensitive to the collaboration of

God and man. This means we prefer to refuse this alternative and see in Luke, a disciple of Paul, attached to the divine initiative in the form of the Word and the Spirit, and a representative of Frühkatholizismus, attracted by human mediation of ministries and sacraments or rather the ministers within their community.

In rejecting the term Frühkatholizismus (p. 204), Conzelmann often makes himself the advocate of exegesis: he asks us to notice that Luke does not signal the institutions of the Elders by the Twelve, and that with one or two exceptions, Luke means the local Church, not the universal Church when he uses the term *ἐκκλησία*. E. Käsemann and G. Klein do not always use the same exegetical prudence [**12**]. In his brief summary of Lucan ecclesiology [**13**], Haenchen holds positions close to Conzelmann's [**14**].

d. E. Schweizer (-> 1959) also leans on the heilgeschichtlich conception disengaged by Conzelmann: in order to discover in an original manner Luke's various intentions which have remained in the shadow or penumbra until now. He first analyzes the terms "Israel" and "people" to conclude that they still designate for Luke, Judaism, the heir of the OT. We are still far from a frühkatholisch perspective, in which the Christian Church will claim for itself the title of Israel and refuse it for the Jews. Nonetheless, on two occasions, Luke uses, without contradicting himself, the term, *λαός* (Act 15:14 and 18:10) to designate the group of Christians chosen by God [**15**]. The historical perspective allows Luke to reconcile this continuity Judaism - Church, and the innovation of a community formed of Jews and Christians. Schweizer deems furthermore that Luke insists on the responsibility of the rebel Jews in the Church's decision to open up to the Samaritans, and then the Gentiles. Not without reason, Jervell will attempt to fit the election of the Gentiles into the project of God and the faithfulness of the Jewish Christians, rather than in the refusal of the Jews.

If the pre-Lucan tradition could conceive of the annexation of the Gentiles in a Judaizing perspective (after Zech 2:15), i.e. as a grafting of the pagan converts into the old trunk of Israel, the editor of Acts has lost sight of this conception and sees the Church (Schweizer prefers to speak of community) as a tertium genus, distinct from Judaism and paganism [**16**]. Several authors (P. H. Menoud and M. Carrez) have refused to speak of a tertium genus concerning Luke-Acts, because the author does not use this expression and does not think that Israel after the flesh is rejected. As for us, we agree with Schweizer that the

Church does indeed form in Luke an intermediary and original body between the Synagogue and paganism. The terms used to name the Church, "disciples", "brothers", "believers" etc. point out a great innovation. But, Schweizer admits that this is still a fluctuating definition of the Church.

The ecclesiastic ordonnance corresponds to this conception of community. This is to say that the ministries remain a subin - feudation of Judaism, while being adapted to the innovations provoked by history and God. Continuity and discontinuity are very close. Moreover, the installation of the new organs, like the Seven, does not suppose the setting up of structures, henceforth intangible and sacred, but a legitimate response to a new situation. Therefore, order and freedom are not mutually ex - clusive. The Spirit is still the master and organizer of the com - munity. The Church is a path, a way. But, Schweizer asks, in describing the Christian community as part of Hellenistic Judaism, open to the evangelical innovation, does not Luke underestimate the discontinuity effected by the radical intervention of God in Jesus Christ?

e. If Schweizer regroups the NT ecclesiologies according to several large types (the conception of the early community, the Pauline conception, the Johannine conception, the conception of the apostolic Fathers) and inserts Luke's, with the Pastorals', into the line of the early community rather than in Paul's, R. Schnackenburg (-> 1961) first evokes the reality of the NT Church, marked by the post-Easter gathering of the faithful, the outpouring of the Spirit and communal life. To do this, he first speaks of the differences, which in his view, come forth at the level of awareness rather than the ecclesiastic reality. Having recalled the ecclesiastical reflection of the primitive community, Schnackenburg, following a surprising order, treats Luke's and Matthew's conceptions before sketching Paul's

The author recognizes "the remarkable contribution that Luke provided in his double work to a theology of the Church, mainly in the relation "Church" and "history" he establishes and in situating the time and tasks of the Church between Jesus' exaltation to heaven (...) and his return to earth (...)." (p. 72, FT). Thus with Conzelmann, he specifies the mandate the Church received from the Resurrected One: the mission to the ends of the earth and not a feverish and static awaiting of the Parousia. The author then points out the Church's place in salvation history and the geographical milieu where it unfolded. After noting that "the Church in the world is the domain of the Lordship and the organ of the glorified Christ until he returns in glory" (p. 75 in FT), Schnackenburg rightly draws attention to Jesus' farewell speech (Lk 22:21-38), borrowing from the book which H. Schürmann wrote on this pericope (1957). Luke, no doubt, gathered in this passage valuable prescriptions for the Church, a Church in the direct line with the pre-Easter group of disciples. For the German exegete, at the heart of the life of the Church, Luke places the Eucharist, link with the Lord and source of eschatological joy. The Eucharist has an ethical function for it demands faithfulness to the Lord, steadfastness in trials and brotherly communion. With Conzelmann, Schnackenburg accepts the role that Luke attributes to tribulations during the time of the Church: Satan is again at work and will sift the disciples (cf. Lk 22:31). The "saints" of Jerusalem will not be protected from backsliding. Fortunately, the Christ instituted the apostolic college, with Peter at the head, to fortify the brethren. The scenes of the Acts confirm the prophecies contained in the farewell speech.

Schnackenburg's merit is to have considered the Protestant criticisms with respect to the heirarchical structure of the Roman Church and to have recalled that, for Luke, the authority in the Church is defined by service [17].

f. To move from Schnackenburg's book to J. Daniélou's (-> 1970), is to progress in time but regress in science. Under the title, **L'Eglise des apôtres**, the Cardinal provides a conservative commentary of Acts. The Lucan proto-catholic perspective becomes Roman Catholic. The author believes he is able to demonstrate (affirming more than he shows) that Luke borrows from archaic traditions, anterior to Paul and complimentary to the apostle. Fortunately, here and there the Jesuit scholar throws some new light on a particular aspect.

After a chapter consecrated to the Jewish political and religious context, Danéilou underlines the aristocratic, hierarchical and institutional character of the group of the Twelve, installed by the historical Jesus. He does not hesitate to consider historical the Lucan tendency to limit the apostles to the Twelve and to concentrate the breath of the Spirit on them. Despite the absence of Pauline or Johannine affirmations, he also accepts as historical Luke's effort to transmit the apostolic ministry and tradition from the Twelve to the Elders (a tendency which we think is Lucan, but which some think is badly attested in Acts).

A third chapter allows the author to assail Wilckens (ch. 3, ->1961) and save the traditional character of the Christological speeches. Chapter 4 (the Jerusalem council and the mission to the Gentiles) and 5 (James and Paul and the alimentary prescriptions) offer the author the occasion to take more critical positions: Luke, in his opinion, tends to minimize the tensions between Jerusalem and Antioch. He puts together in Act 15, the ecumenical council, which positively regulated the admission of the Gentiles, and a regional council which treated the ritual prescriptions. Correctly, he points out Luke's effort to harmonize the views of Peter and Paul. It is precisely the Lucan image of Paul which is the subject of chapter 6: the author admits that Luke amplified Paul's first stay in Jerusalem to mark a continuity between the apostles and Paul and minimized the quarrels between Paul and the Judaizers, disputes toned down by Luke's time. That which is dramatic in the Epistles becomes a har - monious development in Acts. Daniélou closes his work with an analysis of the Gentile humanity in the speech in Act 14 and 17. Paul, in the hand of Luke, recognizes a spiritual preoccupation in the pagans, but this religious research has gone astray and conversion is necessary [18].

g. We should here present G. Lohfink's book (-> 1975) which came too late for us to consider. Entitled **Die Sammlung Israels**, this work defends the thesis that, according to Luke, Jesus did not found the Church. It existed only after Easter and Pentecost. Without forming a new religious community beside Israel, the Church was progressively constituted of Jews and then Gentiles. This gathering of the true Israel, at the approach of the Kingdom of God, not only corresponds to God's will, but is brought about by God's grace. Progressively the Church separates itself from those who until then represented Israel.

Titles and Images of the Church

In this section, we will draw attention to several contributions which have studied titles or images with regard to the Church.

Christian

h. Several writers, E. Peterson (-> 1946), E. J. Bickerman (-> 1949), J. Moreau (-> 1949), H. B. Mattingly (-> 1958), E. Haenchen (-> 1956), C. Spicq (-> 1960), B. Lifshitz (-> 1962) and P. Zingg (-> 1974, pp. 217-222) have sought for the origin of the term "Christian". We know that according to the Acts (Act 11:26), the term appeared in Antioch, perhaps in a context of persecution. We also know that the translation of the verb form (*χρηματίσαι*) is difficult and words ending in *-ιανος* have been formed after the latin model -ianus. Yet who gave this name to Christians and in which circumstances? Was it the Roman officials to designate a political movement distinct from Judaism and attacked by Herod Agrippa (E. Peterson)? Or was it the Antiochean population who felt that the movement was clearly distinct from Judaism (H. B. Mattingly, E. Haenchen)? Or even the Christians themselves to affirm, with regard to the Roman authorities, that they depended on the Messianic King and would be his agents in the eon to come (E. J. Bickerman and, on the whole, J. Moreau)? B. Lifshitz follows partially E. J. Bickerman: it was the Christians who gave themselves this name, but it was to claim kinship with the crucified Messiah and not to declare themselves servants of the anointed King. If, in Palestine, the Christians are called Nazarenes, in reference to Jesus of Nazareth, in Antioch, because of the election of the Gentiles, they separated themselves from the Synagogue and bore the name which evoked the Christ, the Savior on the cross. In any case, the appearence of this name in Antioch is linked with a certain ecclesiastic consciousness: the believers are a communal entity, distinct from Judaism and foreign to paganism. A community suscitating interest or hostility, it depended on the Christ and referred to him: 'Christ' in the word 'Christian' can be a proper name or a title. In this case, it may call forth either the Messianic glory or the humbling of the cross.

Let us conclude here: the traditional use of the term has attracted special attention. It would be necessary to understand the redactional nuance that Luke gives it. For us, Luke thinks that the title, 'Christian', appeared at a moment when the persecution organized by the Jewish leaders is developing and when the Gentiles are accepted into the Church.

The Way

i. The Qumran discoveries, where the term 'way' appears, have often made several scholars study the passages in Acts which contain the word ἡ ὁδός (especially 9:2 and 19:9). S. V. McCasland (-> 1958) states that Acts alone in the NT, uses the term in an absolute sense. He thinks that this usage is found in Qumran and that Christians and Essenes took it over from the prophet Isaiah (40:3). It is probable that the Christians derived their use from the Qumranian sect by the intermediary of John the Baptist. In the course of the transfer, the term's connotations were modified: in Qumran, believers have not yet taken 'the way', understood as the 'way of the Lord', but for Christians the march has already begun.

Without exactly departing from the same Essene texts, E. Repo (-> 1964) arrives at similar conclusions at the end of a long monograph, criticized intelligently by M. Hengel in **TLZ** 92 (1967) 361-364.

What interests us here, is perhaps less the prehistory of the term (Essene or Jewish, according to Repo, and without a doubt Hellenistic Jewish, according to Hengel) [20] than the theological meaning that it receives in Christian literature. According to Repo, the primitive Church wanted to designate itself by this term. It conferred three connotations on the term, a Christological or soteriological, an eschatological and an ethical.

The tie between the way and the Christ (the Hodoschristology of Repo) goes back to the historical Jesus, whom we know was an itinerant minister. This link would have been reinforced by the Church's first Christology, which sees in the Christ, the only way to salvation. It would have finally come to light in the Gospels and Acts, which insist on the itinerancy of Jesus and the apostles, frequently using the term ὁδός. Is there really a link between the Way and the Christ in Luke? Theologically, we have no doubts but philologically, a question mark remains [21].

The rapport which is established according to Repo between the way and eschatology also seems foreign to the Lucan per - spective. In return, the ethical content of the "way", assured by the OT roots of the term, must correspond to Luke's preoccupations.

It is a pity that Repo wanted to disengage a conception of the "way" common to all primitive Christianity. He would have done better to specify the particular orientations of the Biblical writers. So a redaktionsgeschichtlich analysis of the Lucan notion of the way is still lacking [22]. Such an investigation should explain the technical and absolute usage of the term in particular. It should allow us to answer two questions: does Luke voluntarily take over an archaic expression? If not, how do we explain the scarcity of the term in the literature posterior to Luke? [23]

j. In his thesis which we analyze below (cf. 7, IV, 1, d), S. Brown consecrates a dozen pages to the theme of the "way" (pp. 131-145). With W. C. Robinson (ch 1, -> 1962, cf. 1, III, e), Brown understands this term in a dynamic fashion: it concerns the believers' march toward the kingdom. During the ministry of

Jesus, it was a real accompaniment; in the time of the Church, it is faithfulness to the kerygma and obedience to the commandments of the Lord (cf. Act 18:25f.). Is this supposed spiritualization of the concept not in contradiction with the objectivation and materialization of the inner life that the author discovers in Luke? We think so, and deem that the "way" is the daily path which the disciples and believers take in an existence where the spiritual and the material are not yet separated. S. Brown adds two statements: a) by declaring itself the "way" of the Lord, the Christian religion supplants Judaism; b)we can distinguish two times in this walk along the "way" of the Lord: the setting out, in the form of the acceptation of the message (the "way" signifies here the mission) and the faithful continuation of the walk (the "way" here designates the Christian religion). Are schemas (p. 142) necessary to express such a common thing? In any case, the author is right, against E. Repo, to understand ὁδός in Luke in an ecclesiological sense and not a Christological one.

II. ISRAEL AND THE CHURCH: MISSION AND EXTENSION

In the following pages, we would like to present the recent works centered on the relations that the Church and Israel entertain, in Luke's eyes. The subject has attracted several authors, because it is central and controversial at the same time. Acts in fact seems to be paradoxically the book of the NT which is the most universalistic and favorable to Judaism. Luke describes the Jewish roots of the Church with the same love he paints the geographical expansion of Christianity beyond the racial and religious borders of Judaism.

H. Conzelmann and F. Stagg

a. Three authors pose (or repose, for the history of exegesis is long!) the problem, at about the same time: H. Conzelmann (-> 1954) whose solution we can imagine with no problem: Luke can conceive of a Judaizing Church centered in Jerusalem and a Gentile Christian one dispersed in the whole earth because of his conception of salvation history; F. Stagg (-> 1955) that we know from E. Grässer's summary [**24**]: the Acts is dominated by one major theme: the Gospel frees itself from all national, social and religious fetters; P. Menoud (-> 1954; -> 1960; -> 1962; ->

1964) who rectifies, in the name of Luke's theological project, the commonly accepted outline of Acts (the acts of Peter, Act 1-12, followed by the acts of Paul, Act 13-28). As Menoud deals with the subject on several occasions and from divers angles, we will begin with him.

P. H. Menoud

b. For Menoud, we should not fret over the personages of Peter and Paul in order to understand the Lucan view. The main interest of the editor lies "in the extension, the Spirit gives to the Church through the apostolic testimony..." (-> 1954, p. 45). According to Act 1:8, the Risen Lord gives the order to his witnesses to announce the Gospel in Jerusalem, Judea, Samaria and to the ends of the earth. Menoud has no difficulty showing that the book of Acts in its very composition, describes the accomplishment of this missionary program. This realization, nonetheless, is wrought not only on a geographical level, but also on an ethical and theological level: in turn, it is the Jews, then the Samaritans, the sort of half Jews, and finally the Gentiles who are converted. It follows that the main break of the book is not between chapters 12 and 13 but in Act 15, which thus occupies a central place. Indeed, if the Gospel was already announced to the Gentiles in chapter 10 and if a first typical missionary trip had already taken place (Act 13-14), it is not until chapter 15 that the definitive structure of the Church is adopted: the Church is one, but formed of Jews and Gentiles. Having then attained its perfect stature on the theological level, the Church can now strive to achieve geographical extension. This task falls first on Paul, who, according to Menoud's vision, from chapter 16 on undertakes only one great missionary voyage before being taken prisoner provisionally in Rome where he will carry the apostolic testimony, which, from the capitol, will ring out to the ends of the earth **[25]**.

We have not been convinced by all of Menoud's arguments. In particular, we are not sure that, understood as one sole tour, the second and third missionary journeys of Paul are centered on Jerusalem rather than Antioch. Nevertheless, the exegete from Neuchâtel (Switzerland) has proposed with vigor a plan of the Acts which corresponds to Luke's ecclesiology. He has in this way clarified the Lucan image of the Church.

J. Dupont

c. In a conference which has become famous (-> 1959-1960), Dom J. Dupont attempted to explain why Luke gave a follow-up to his Gospel. For him, the main reason is of a theological order: "Similarly, in the Acts, by spreading out progressively from Jerusalem to Rome, the expansion of Christianity is not purely geographical: it passes from the Jewish to the Gentile world at the same time. This is precisely what interests Luke. With a remarkable insistance, he underlines that the evangelization of the Gentiles is not simply the result of fortuitous circumstances; willed by God, it fulfills the prophecies announced that the Messiah would bring salvation to the pagan nations. It is therefore an integral part of the program assigned to the Christ by the Scriptures. This is the reason Luke wanted to add the account of the apostolic mission to that of Jesus' life; without it, the work of salvation described by the Messianic prophecies would not be complete. The history reported in the Book of the Acts appears thus as charged with theology." (p. 135f.).

To demonstrate this idea, the author halts at the great declarations of the Lucan work. Enlightened by Lk 3:6, the final intervention of Paul (Act 28:25-28) reminds us that God wills the salvation of the Gentiles. The last words of the Risen One, situated by Luke at the end of the Gospel (24:46f.) and at the beginning of Acts (1:8) move in the same direction. The expression "until the ends of the earth" (Act 1:8) must be understood with the help of Act 13:46f., which itself refers to Isa 49:6; the notation aims beyond geography, to the Gentiles whose the initial status differs from the Jews. The climax of several speeches of Lk-Act confirms the importance accorded by Luke to the salvation of the Gentiles: so the discourse-programs of Jesus of Nazareth (Lk 4) and Peter's speech at Pentecost (Act 2; cf. also the one in Act 3). The case of Cornelius (Act 10) which permits the decision of principle in Act 15 shows that Peter and through him, the early Church, knew how to take the decisive turn. Henceforth, God suppresses the difference between Jew and Gentile, since he purifies the hearts of both by faith (Act 15:9). Paul will accomplish the mission to the Gentiles which the Church has theoretically accepted: the important place that Luke gives to the apostle testifies to the interest he has in the salvation of the nations. The kerygma of Paul (Act 26:22f.) corresponds to the Risen One's (Lk 24:46f.) and contains three stages: the death of the Messiah, his resurrection and the evangelical proclamation to all men. The three evocations of Paul's conversion all have a universalistic note. It is the same for the speech in Athens.

We are perhaps surprised at reading this article, by Dupont's lack of attention here concerning Act 15, the true turning point of the book, as Menoud noted [26]. We also regret that the author did not seek to specify the function of the hardening of Israel in the vocation of the Gentiles. We rejoice in return in the majestic manner with which he emphasizes Luke's universalistic perspective: the Lucan Church no longer has any scruples in counting the Gentiles among its midst: the prophecies announced salvation to the pagans; the Resurrected Lord willed that they be evangelized; God himself provoked their conversion; the apostles accepted without condition their grafting into the community (the only reserve: the apostolic decree is to be respected) and Paul made himself the champion of their evangelization to the ends of the earth.

J. C. O'Neill

c. Another exegete, J. C. O'Neill (-> 1961) [27], recognizes that the relations between Jew and Gentile hold a considerable place in the plan of Luke. But instead of underlining the acceptance of the nations, he insists on the rejection of Judaism (in the two senses of the expression). In his contribution, which is in its second edition (1970), the author mixes historical and theological research. By situating the "historical setting" of the book in the second century in an environment close to Justin's, he thinks he can discern Luke's main theological preoccupations.

We have already mentioned chapter 5 of this work, consecrated to the titles of Jesus, in our chapter on Christology [28]. We can pass rapidly over chapter 1 which attempts - without success in our opinion - to situate the Lucan work around 115 A.D. to 130 A.D. by a comparison of the early patristic works, mainly that of Justin (same integration of the mission of the apostles into the work of Christ; related conceptions of the resurrection of the Messiah; and neighboring solutions to the problem of Israel and the nations) [29].

Chapters 2 (the structure of Acts and its theology), 3 (the attitude with respect to the Jews), 4 (Jewish Christians and Gentile Christians), 6 (the debt with regard to Hellenistic Judaism) and 7 (the principle theological goal of Acts) will retain our attention now.

Accepting with J. Dupont and H. Conzelmann that in Luke the historical accounts and geographical information have theological importance, O'Neill sets Jerusalem against Rome. As the central location where the Gospel drew to a close and where the Church is born, Jerusalem symbolizes the refusal of the Jews, whereas Rome, the goal of the apostolic race, marks the acceptation of the Gospel by the nations. Yet Jerusalem is not only the city which killed the Messiah, it is also the guarantee of the mission to the Gentiles, the center from where a new emphasis in evangelization arises. "The spiritual conquest of the Empire depended on Jesus' death and resurrection in Jerusalem, not on Paul's death in Rome." (p.63).

Having defined an outline of Acts, based on the geography, in five parts which offer less theological indications than the author claims, O'Neill shows - it is one of his main theses but in fact is a repetition of F. Stagg (-> 1955) which he is unaware of - that the flow of the narrative is more the progressive detachment from Judaism than the implantation of the Gospel in the world. In Rome, as in other cities, the Christian communities existed before Paul's arrival. If Luke, nonetheless, concentrates on Paul, it is because he wants to report something other than the evangelization of the world: the installation of Christianity which has broken its ties with the Synagogue. For the Evangelist, it is Paul who was the first to liberate the Gospel from the old goatskin bottles: he naturally becomes the hero of the book of the Acts.

Stephen's speech helps to clarify Luke's attitude with regard to the Jews. It is not an isolated discourse, for it could be that Luke does not wed all the words he places in the mouths of his characters, but it is the speech inserted into the thread of the account. In O'Neill's eyes, Luke rejects the complaint lodged against Stephen of a criticism of the Temple, and then rebukes the Jews for having disobeyed the Law. He does this in Hellenistic Jewish manner, leaning on the Scriptures. Even if Jesus and the first Christians - and Luke knows it - respected the Temple, the actual Christianity is right to detach itself from it. It is the same for the Law: according to Luke, the communities rightly rejected the ritual prescriptions to retain the moral law alone. O'Neill thinks he has won on two accounts: this conception of the Temple and the law corresponds to the situation of second century Christianity. He thinks that his proposed late date of Lk-Act is thus confirmed. Furthermore, a rupture in the history of primitive Christianity is discerned: from the death of Stephen, the mission to the Jews in Jerusalem is terminated. It is now the

Jews of the Diaspora and then the Gentiles who will be called. Unfortunately, the author lacks nuance: he does not distinguish the Jews from the Jewish leaders, the principle guilty ones in Luke's eyes: he sometimes forces the texts to discover, for example in Act 21, that God hinders Paul from completing the purification in the Temple and that Luke indicates, with this, that Christians must cease to go to the Sanctuary (p. 77)! The patristic distinction between moral law and ritual law is also more eisegesis than exegesis (p. 78). Finally it is incorrect to say that "Acts presents a theology in which the church has abandoned the People and appropriated the Book" (p. 90). Only his view of a late date allows him to affirm that Luke has abandoned his care for Israel.

We get his major thesis from chapter 4: a comparison of Paul and Luke shows that the attitudes of these two writers with regard to Jewish Christians is very different. Luke, differing from Paul, is unaware of the division of the mission fields among Peter and Paul (in Gal 2:7f.). He resolves the lancinating question of the fellowship which appears from the incident of Cornelius (ignoring thus - we might add - the incident in Antioch). The apostolic decree does not deal with this problem which is already resolved: it resolves the one of the ritual law, typical of the second century. He, finally, limits Judea as the territory of the Judaizers (these are a sort of rare bird and in Luke's time, it is almost necessary to protect the species). The theological differences which come forth from these factual differences are not negligible: for Luke, the question of circumcision of the Gentiles is no longer even asked; the mission to the Jews has lost its theological necessity which it still had in Paul; symmetrically the mission to the pagans has its own legitimacy: "The mission to the Gentiles was to him [Luke] not an unorthodox diversionary operation, authorized at the insistence of a brilliant subordinate commander, but the inevitable and unmistakable direction of the campaign, in which all the leaders had played their part from the beginning." (p. 105).

We will not enter into discussion with these views for we will have the occasion to present J. Jervell's critique. The issue is to decide between these two extreme solutions.

Chapter 6 rightly shows that Luke is marked by the Judaism of the Diaspora. Hellenistic Judaism and Luke are sure that history is apologetic and kerygmatic, that the Church and the pagan state can get along, that a certain natural theology is possible, that conversion implies a renunciation of idols and a movement toward the living God. O'Neill thinks he can deduce from this argument a late date for Acts, for only the later writings of the NT, - so he thinks - have undergone influence from Hellenistic Judaism. In fact, this consequence hardly imposes itself, since nearly all these themes are already found in Paul (cf. Rom 13; 1:20; I Thess 1:9f., etc.), who is influenced by the Judaism of the Diaspora.

The last chapter serves as a conclusion: Luke is unconsciously catholic: the time of the apostles has become normative for him; the visible work of the Spirit is substituted for an eschatological consciousness. Luke has opted for Rome and the Gentiles: to convert the cultivated Romans is his main intention. Acts is thus an apologetic book (inspite of B. S. Easton, Luke does not seek official recognition, but spiritual adherence from the pagans). Read by Christians, the book of the Acts - O'Neill does not deny this internal usage - exhorts the Church of its time to avoid apocalyptic enthusiasm. For us, these affirmations would merit some nuance: for by taking them in the reverse order, we can reply that Luke knew the apocalyptic traditions (several recent works have shown this); that he addresses himself also to the Jews (like Justin!); and that his catholicism is not yet evident (for him, the apostolic times are as outdated as they are normative), etc.

J. Gnilka

d. J. Gnilka's objective, a study of the hardening of Israel, is more limited that O'Neill's . The German Catholic exegete ana - lyzes the quotations from Isa 6:9-10 in the Gospels and the Acts. Our attention is drawn to the third part of the work, pages 117-154 consecrated to Lk-Act.

First of all, the author studies the Lucan version of Mk 4 and arrives at the conclusion that Luke reserved the explicit citation of Isa 6:9-10 for the end of his double work. However, the Evangelist feels obliged to already mention in Lk 8 (taken from Mk 4) the theme of hardening (it is true that he presents it even more truncated than Matthew, without the reader necessarily remarking the allusion to Isa 6). Gnilka thinks that Luke's affection for phrases with a predestinatarian tonality is the main reason for this mention. This Lucan tendency should be even stronger as the Evangelist hardly likes to place the disciples over against the crowd or esoteric teaching against public teaching. Furthermore, at this spot in his Gospel, the hardening of Israel is ahead of schedule in salvation history. Gnilka notes that Luke, however, presents a text which is softer than Mark's: he suppresses a difficult theological problem by deleting the last words of Mk 4:12 (no forgiveness possible).

The hardening of Israel, the object of the second part of the investigation, is progressive or rather it is accomplished in counterpoint with the stages of redemptive history. In the Gospel, salvation is offered to the Jews alone. Despite their refusal, or rather their leaders' refusal of the Savior, they benefit from the delay after Easter and are offered a last chance to turn from their guilty ignorance. Because of this ultimate offer, the book of Acts regularly presents a sermon addressed primarily to the Jews, "Lukas hält das endgültige Urteil über Israel möglichst lange hinaus." (p. 132). Alas, the people of Israel, inspite of the double proclamation of Jesus and the apostles, remain deaf: the citation of Isa 6:9-10 then enters into play in the last verses of Acts. A new time begins: as an entity, Israel will no longer be the addressee of the message, nor the major beneficiary of the mission. The scheme set out by Paul on three occasions (Act 13:44-52; 28:5-11 and 18:23-29) definitely fits into the history of the Church: the acceptation of the nations follows the refusal of Israel.

Luke, according to Gnilka, does not definitely close the door to the Jews: as a people, they will certainly be cut off, but as individuals, access to the Church is still possible.

Gnilka's views concerning the hardening of Israel confirm H. Conzelmann's concerning salvation and history. As we will see, J. Jervell is resolutely opposed. As for us, we would make the following reservations: Luke, contrary to what Gnilka says, never indicates that Israel after the flesh has lost its election. Nor does he think that the Church, a new Israel, replaces the old. Jerusalem, furthermore, is not uniquely the symbol of the hardening and rejection in Luke. Gnilka underestimates the role the capital plays until the end of the book of Acts: the new missionary enterprises still maintain contact with Jerusalem. With other exegetes, he neglects the last words of Isa 6:9-10 (LXX): "and I will heal them" (future and not conjunctive!) and he does not notice that the citation is addressed to the Jews (*γνωστὸν οὖν ἔστω ὑμῖν*) in a kerygmatic manner (cf. Act 2:14: *τοῦτο ὑμῖν γνωστὸν ἔστω*).

E. Haenchen

e. In a long article (-> 1963), E. Haenchen reunited the scattered information of his commentary relative to the Church and Judaism. The problem of the relations between the two is also set out in the Pauline epistles and the other Gospels, but for him, Luke gives a new and original theological answer. Luke is unaware of the Pauline solution (failure with the Jews -> success with the Gentiles -> conversion of the Jews -> Parousia). For him, the opposition between Christian and Jew does not emerge concerning the Law: the Jewish Christians continue to observe the Law, a Law which does not, as in Paul, incite to sin. In fact, the apostolic decree requires a certain observance for the Gentile Christians as well. Therefore, the Law is, for Jew and Christian, the sum of the divine commandments and to respect it is indeed difficult (Act 15:10). The shibboleth of the matter is the message of the resurrection, Christ's in the first place. Once it is understood that in Luke the Christian faith in the resurrection and the Jewish Law do not exclude one another, the outline and composition of the Acts becomes clear even in the smallest detail.

Luke uses the tradition of the forty days to make the preaching of the resurrection believable (Act 1). The limitation of the Kingdom of God to Israel and the consciousness of the eschatological imminence are corrected by Luke (Act 1) with a prudence which must help the readers to understand the slowness with which the mission to the Gentiles is accomplished. The Church until Act 5 remains confined to Judaism: Pentecost does not immediately take away the difference between Jew and Gentile. The choice of Matthias is not associated to a mission (against K. H. Rengstorf, cf. below 7, III, 2, f). The Twelve play a primary role (they alone can give a valid testimony). They incarnate all the Church's activity. Their function is terminated at the Jerusalem council (and not, as for Rengstorf, at the death of James). Their activity is normative for the Church.

Stephen's speech (Act 7) manifests a triple attack with respect to Judaism, it is accused of not having recognized Moses (vs. 25), having sacrificed to idols (vs. 42f.) and having constructed the Temple (vs. 47f.). Far from reflecting traditions with which Luke did not agree, this speech is redactional. Anachronistically, it witnesses to the situation between the Church and Judaism of Luke's time.

The Evangelist can be the author of Stephen's speech and the first five chapters, for he sometimes presents the true Israel (the continuity from the OT to the primitive Church) and sometimes Judaism, hostile to the Holy Spirit (and hostile to the

Hellenistic Christianity of Luke who understands the Book in an allegorical and Christological manner).

Haenchen continues the analysis of Acts from this particular point of view: Act 10 is the main turning point of Acts, the passage from Judeo-Christianity to the Christian mission to the pagans; Act 11:1-18 testifies to the legitimacy of this mission, recognized by Jerusalem (this argument differs from Paul's direct interventions of God): Act 10:35, a revolutionary word, dismisses the privileges of Israel. Luke thinks God would be unjust to elect Israel alone. Act 13:46f. marks the summit of Paul's first missionary journey: because the Jews do not show themselves worthy of eternal life, the apostle turns to the Gentiles. Act 15 appears quite pale after the account in Act 10: men simply ratify God's decision and accept the election of the Gentiles. Forced to take this decisive turn in the Church, the twelve apostles can disappear. Henceforth, Paul alone accomplishes the evangelization of the world, in the East and then in the West: but his evangelization is not accomplished without a constant discussion with Judaism. The narrative schema is thus: Paul's missionary success, the Jews' aggressivity and the continuation of the journey. After Act 21, Judeo-Christianity disappears from the scene and Paul finds himself confronted with Palestinian Judaism alone: with this, Luke wants to show that Chris-tianity is the true Judaism and must be tolerated. Luke's adversaries are then Jews and not Gnostics (against G. Klein, cf. below 7, III, 1, h). After the condemnation of the Jews in Asia (Act 13:46f.) and Greece (Act 18:5f.), it is the Italian Jews who are rejected because of their callousness (Act 28:25-28): Haenchen even thinks that Luke thus rejects definitely Israel and substitutes it with Gentile Christians as the people of the covenant **[30]**. Later we will criticize this view taken up by S. G. Wilson (cf. below, 7, II, h).

A. George

f. The Lucan perspective of the reality and mystery of Israel is the topic of the important article of Father George (-> 1968). Here is the conclusion: "For us, Luke's view of Israel, its values and fate, appear many times quite different from Paul's. Several motifs are easy to discern. Luke is writing late, at the time when the rupture between the Church and Judaism is consummated. Above all, he is not a Jew. He is less preoccuppied with Israel's destiny than Paul was (Rom 9:1-5); his interest lies more in the mission to the pagans,in which he was active. It is even more remarkable that he gives such a place to the mystery of Israel in his work." (p. 525).

To set forth this mystery, the author takes up the divisions of salvation history elaborated by Luke.

First of all, for Luke, what is Israel before Jesus' appearance? With the help of Stephen's speech and Paul's at Antioch of Pisidia and then with the terms, Israel, the people and the fathers, and finally aided by the oft typological references to the great figures (Moses, Solomon, Elijah) of the sacred history, George summa-rizes the Lucan solution: Israel is the object of God's election and custodian of the covenant and the promises; but it has not always faithfully responded to these signs of the divine favor. This crack within Israel, this infidelity mixed with faithfulness, will be one of the principle characteristics noted by Father George. It will reappear at each step of redemptive history with more and more clarity only to reach a conclusion in a radical division.

The Israel of the infancy narratives and the time of John the Baptist still belongs to the OT (we doubt this thesis, taken up from Conzelmann). The division of Israel is mended: the friends of God, to whom the germinal revelations are confided, form a group of elite, clearly distinct from the people. Father George correctly notes that Luke desires to describe these trustees as faithful to the Law and this for an apologetic reason: the Jewish roots of Christianity go deep into the unadulterated faithfulness to the Law. Here we would like to note another typical aspect: this privileged group with relation to God is precisely a group of poor and marginals with regard to the riches of this world and even the traditional religion.

The strongest part of Father George's article concerns Israel's relation to the historical Jesus. Here, the author testifies to the fruitfulness of the redactional method: he distinguishes three steps in the life of Jesus, in order to discern a crescendo of hostility toward the Messiah. Despite Jesus' Jewish roots, legalistic observance (stricter than in Mark), and exclusive concern for Israel, he is attacked more and more: in Galilee, the people still follow him and the opposition of the leaders is not yet tragic; during the journey, the confrontation becomes more precise; the group of disciples is formed and receives a crash training course. The number of adversaries increases, which practically makes the beautiful name of λαός [31] disappear. It is not surprising that in Jerusalem, the third and final stage of Jesus' ministry, the enemies occupy the forefront. Yet even here, the rupture is not final: it is the political leaders who bear the weight of responsibility for the death of Jesus: the Pharisees are not named, while the good dispositions of the people continues to be mentioned. If the fall of Jerusalem is the punishment of those who killed Jesus, Luke removes the eschatological character of the event: judgment of God, yes, but it is not the last judgment. In his universalistic perspective, Luke was turned toward the Gentiles and attaches but limited import to this event: it is a historical event which concerns Judaism. Since the Acts is turned toward the nations, Luke would have no occasion to tell of the fall of Jerusalem.

Despite all this, Luke does not rush to the Gentiles. The tragic hardening of Israel is not irreparable before the end of the book of Acts. Forgiveness is still possible: Luke underlines that the apostles who still belong to Israel begin their mission among the Jews of Judea and continue among those of the Diaspora. Moreover, this evangelization is not a failure. Until the death of Stephen, the Church recruits only Jews from Judea. Nonetheless, the mass of Judea bristles up and the Church developes more into a new people, emerging from Judaism, but now autonomous. Luke has no word concerning the good judgment of the Jews of the Dispersion with respect to the evangelical message. The opening up to the nations is done and racial adherence to Israel ceases to be a condition for entry.

Israel, in Luke's eyes, is a profane people, like the others, and the elected people of God at the same time. This fundamental information is disparaged throughout the account, to the point that at the end of the book, Israel is only a secular people. Individually, the Jews can join the Church, but nothing is said in Lk 21:24 or in Lk 13:35 which indicates that Luke shares the optimistic views of Paul concerning the general conversion of Israel in the last hour. Paradoxically, Luke does not go as far as Paul in the transfer of the titles: he never speaks of the Gentiles as the children of Abraham (as Paul does in Gal 3); neither does he ever give them the title of Israel. At the most, twice (Act 15:14 and 18:10; cf. above our summary of E. Schweizer), he calls them *λαός* **[32]**.

J. Jervell

g. For several years, this Norwegian exegete has been attacking certain popular interpretations in Lucan theology. He particularly refuses the widespread image of a universalistic Luke, who is hostile to Jewish particularism **[33]**. He thinks Luke is on the contrary a most ardent defender of the Jewish character of the Church: he ignores the succession of covenants, maintains the function of the Mosaic law in the Church, is interested in Jewish Christianity and inserts the mission to the Gentiles into the context of Israel. For Luke, the Church is not the new Israel, but Israel restored. It is hard to imagine a greater contrast than these theses and the positions presented above.

Several important articles were gathered together and supplemented by others in a book (-> 1972). Jervell now could elaborate this new conception from different angles: the notion of the Church, the function of the Twelve, the Samaritans' adherence to Israel, the image of Paul and of James and the conception of the Law.

The Church (-> 1965) is not the new Israel for Luke. It does not achieve its true identity when it "lets go" of Judaism. The Gentiles are not integrated because of the hardening of Israel. On the contrary, the Church belongs to Israel: it is the good part; the people of God regenerated, it lives out the promises and covenant and believes in a Jewish Messiah, i.e. circumcized; it is formed primarily of Jews, who are particulary scrupulous [34].

Israel according to the flesh is therefore a divided people (George and Jervell are agreed on this point): one part of Israel is faithful to the promises and the Law and believes the Christian message; but this is not the case for all: thus the slow process of exclusion of the rebel Jews from Israel.

As for the Gentiles' participation in salvation, it is not a Christian innovation as it was already inscribed in the OT and proclaimed by the risen Christ. It is thus not necessary to expect a new intervention by God nor the resistance of the Jews in order to accomplish it. To evangelize Israel is already to preach to the Gentiles, by intermediary. It is because the Jews believed in the Christ that the Gospel can go to the pagans and not the contrary.

The Jewish Christian faith is thus the source of the mission to the Gentiles. The Church is not the new Israel made up of Jewish and Gentile Christians, but rather it is the faithful part of Israel, which the Gentile converts join. The book of Acts' main objective is the mission to the Jews; the mission to the Gentiles is but a complement, legitimate of course but, secondary. It is not the Church which separates itself from Israel, but the hardened Jews who withdraw from it.

What are the arguments which Jervell advances in favor of these ideas? The first concerns the success of the mission to the Jews: Jervell thinks that the Lucan arithmetic (cf. Act 2:41;

4:4; 5:14; 6:7; and 21:20) serves Jewish Christianity and not simply Christianity. The second deals with the fidelity of the early Church to Judaism in all its obligations and customs. The third is the very use of the word 'Israel' which never designates the Church. The fourth is taken from the speech of Peter in Act 3 (σπέρμα (Gen 12:3 cited in vs. 25) is neither the Christ nor the Church but Israel) and James' in Act 15 (the tent of David restored (Am 9:11 cited in vs. 16) is the Jewish Church whose existence is necessary for the adherence of the Gentiles).

Let us make four reservations:

1) Contrary to what Jervell thinks, the conversion of Cornelius and the Jerusalem council concern the very notion of the admission of the Gentiles and not merely the conditions to be imposed. The innovation, for there is innovation for Luke, is that God has given his Spirit to the Gentiles (Act 11:17) and from now on it is faith, not the Law, by which God purifies the heart (Act 15:9), that is the condition of access to the Church.

2) We think it is inexact to say that until the end of the book of Acts, only one section of Israel is condemned. Clearly, in the beginning the Church was composed of Jews, but finally, it is not the carnel affiliation to Israel which typifies Christians: it is faith in the Lord Jesus. The privileges of Israel are henceforth abolished.

3) To say that Luke orients his attention toward the mission to the Jews rather than toward the Gentiles, seems to go against the very movement of the work of Luke.

4) Finally, to claim that access into the Church for the Gentiles poses a problem for Luke seems inaccurate to us: this integration manifests on the contrary the triumph of God which Luke applauds. At the limit, Jervell's system would function better if no pagan was converted. The Scandinavian exegete would be right if Luke were perfectly Judaized. However, he must admit that Luke's love for the OT and Judaism hardly excludes the adherence of the Gentiles (and it does not imply submission to the Law). The decision in Act 15 (circumcision is not necessary) seems to be the most decisive reply to Jervell's position.

Yet Jervell admits that henceforth Gentiles are accepted without the condition of circumcision. Thus his views are perhaps less revolutionary than they seem: an early stage of salvation history where the Jews - who remain Jews - become Christians, is succeeded by a second stage where the Gentiles - who remain Gentiles - come into the Church. Is this not the traditional thesis?

The virulence of our criticisms originates in the stimulation which Jervell's argumentation arouses. On one point, we think he is right: the theological motivation in favor of the Gentiles does not fit into Israel's obstination but rather into the plan of God, the promises of the OT and the command of the Risen One. Yet it is necessary to distinguish the theological motivation and the historical realization: here, it is difficult not to accept that Luke, with Paul, places the evangelization of the nations in relation with the hardening of the Jews: cf. Act 13:46 (*πρῶτον-ἐπειδή*); 18:5f. and 28:28. The concrete accomplishments, the praxis, interest Luke as much as the motivations or the theoretical intentions.

In another study (-> 1972) [**35**], Jervell analyzes the function of the Twelve. Curiously, he hardly insists on their mission as witnesses: "Even the public nature of Jesus' ministry in Luke runs contrary to the view that the task of the Twelve is to be the eyewitnesses to guarantee the Jesus-tradition." (p. 87). He must, however, admit that their testimony exists, but that it is uniquely to the Messiahship and resurrection of Jesus. Moreover, Jervell accepts that in the Gospel the apostles are closely associated to the life of Jesus. But then - Jervell affirms without giving probing arguments - Luke is following the tradition. Whatever the case, Jervell underestimates the evangelizing function of the Twelve.

By giving excessive weight to the traditional verse, Lk 22:30, he emphasizes the eschatological function of the Twelve as regents of Israel, of the regenerated Israel which is the Church. In doing this, he rightly notes the importance of the number Twelve and the divine origin of the vocation of the apostles (not only a call of Jesus). He thinks that the verse concerning the apostles on thrones (Lk 22:30) and the one on the apostolic task (Act 1:21) are related by the notion of the kingdom, a notion which Jervell - it is not to surprise us - understands in an exclusively Jewish sense. "The meaning is that the basileia Jesus proclaims is precisely the 'kingdom' Israel waits for, that which has been promised to the people of God." (p. 90f.). The Twelve apostles are therefore not bearers of an ecclesiastic ministry, since there is no Church beside Israel. They have become the new leaders of Israel, betrayed by its old ones: "In other words, there is no basis for claiming that Luke traces the ecclesiastical offices back to the Twelve. The reason is that Luke's ecclesiology, coupled with his view of history, has no room for ekklesia as a specific religious institution." (p. 96).

Another article (-> 1971), swifter and more apodictic, concerns the Lucan notion of the Law. Luke cannot reject the Law, for it plays an ecclesiological as well as soteriological role. To abandon the Law would be for the Evangelist to cause the Church to lose its identity. To accept the Gentiles into the Church was not the solution to the problem of the Law. Luke gives a personal solution to the problem. He does not belong to a kind of ecclesiastical "establishment" of which he is the messenger (p. 24). His solution is extremely conservative: the Law given by God at Sinai remains the law of Israel (let us note that this expression is foreign to Luke!). "The law is to him not essentially the moral law, but the mark of distinction between Jews and non-Jews. The law is the sign of Israel being the people of God." (p. 25). Jervell, to underline the eulogious qualifications which the Law receives and the Christians' respect for the observances, begins with Jesus.

Unfortunately for Jervell, the Lucan Church does not remain a Jewish Church and the hereditary sign of belonging to Israel, circumcision, is not imposed upon Christians of Gentile descent, as favorable as they might be to Judaism. Certainly, Jervell invokes the Jewish conception of the people of God who take on the Gentile converts as associates: so the reason of the present importance of the apostolic decree. But is this not a first answer given by Judeo-Christianity, with the help of Zech 2:15, to the problem of the conversion of the Gentiles? Is not Luke's solution rather that the function of the Law is overcome by the regime of salvation by faith? Jervell underestimates the redactional import (which for him is traditional!) of Act 13:38 and 15:10. Once the soteriological importance of the Law disappears - and Jervell admits that Luke is not a partisan of salvation by works - can we maintain its eschatological function? In the same manner, can the Law be subdivided? Can we take away the obligation of circumcision, without making the Law something different from the Law of Israel? These are a few questions that we ask ourselves after reading this article, which is to be appreciated at least for having sensibly distinguished the Lucan conception of the Law from the Pauline.

Below **[36]** we will indicate the place which Jervell accords to Paul and James in Lucan ecclesiology. Not to neglect anything, let us say that the Norwegian exegete published an article concerning Samaria in Luke in his book (-> 1972) **[37]**. For him, the Samaritans must be classed side by side with the Jews and not the Gentiles. For Luke, they are all converted to the gospel and are exemplary of the Israel regenerated by the faith in the Messiah Jesus. "Thus, for Luke Samaria is a Christian territory. This in turn implies that for Luke all Samaria has also become 'orthodox' Jewish territory. The reason for the obvious interest in the Samaritans should be located here." (p. 125). Thus the Church brought the Samaritans into the bosom of Judaism! He guards himself from insisting on the heretical weaknesses of Simon the Samaritan magician!

S. G. Wilson

h. Jervell renewed Lucan studies with as much brilliance as arbitrariness. We cannot say as much for S. G. Wilson (-> 1973) whose exegetical prudence is to be praised. Yet his angles are often conventional. If Dupont interests himself in the salvation of the Gentiles, the Canadian exegete, a disciple of C. K. Barrett, gives attention to the mission to the Gentiles.

After a chapter on Jesus and the pagans (summarized on p. 18), which is basically J. Jeremias' position, Wilson analyzes the manner which Luke presents the Gentiles in his Gospel. The Evangelist frequently walks in the steps of Mark, who, already has a heilsgeschichtlich position: the mission to the Gentiles is established though it will unfold after Easter. Nonetheless a particular Lucan accent appears here and there: the faith of the centurian of Capernaum is not paralleled in Israel (Lk 7:9); the Jewish virtues, like those of Cornelius, do not invalidate universalism. On the contrary, the Gentiles, for Luke's pragmatic mind, are not worse than the Jews: there is therefore no reason to refuse them the Gospel. In the parable of the banquet (Lk 14:16-24), Luke adds a second invitation which symbolizes the election of the Gentiles: the parable passes from the apocalyptic to the historical, since the Church will do the inviting. Discarding certain texts as irrelevant (Lk 11:33; 2:10), he explains others with more or less contentment: Lk 2:30-32 (Luke understands Isa 49:6 in a universalistic sense); Lk 3:1-6 (Wilson is wrong to affirm that Luke replaces δόξα with σωτήριον from the LXX: Luke simply jumps over the beginning of vs. 5 of Isa 40 to quote the rest correctly); Lk 3:23; 4:16f. (Luke may imply that the rejection of Jesus allows the inclusion of the pagans); 9:51-18:14 (here we find a curious affirmation: "We conclude that the whole section 9:51f has no direct or exceptional significance for Luke's view of mission." (p. 45)); 24:46f. (the first explicit allusion to the mission to the Gentiles which relates this mission to Jerusalem, the Holy Spirit and the testimony). Two conclusions impose themselves on the author: the mission to the Gentiles fits into the schema (OT), promise - accomplishment, and this mission is separated from its apocalyptic framework in which Mark still inserts it (with Conzelmann).

We have already evoked chapter 3 ("Lukan Eschatology") in speaking of eschatology [**38**]. The following chapters deal with the order of the principle texts of the Acts. The lacunas in Wilson's information are unpleasantly surprising: concerning Act 1, the author is unaware of G. Lohfink's book on the Ascension; concerning Act 2, J. Potin's; concerning Act 7, J. Bihler's; concerning Act 9, 22 and 26, C. Burchard's and so on, to cite but a few works concentrated, like his own, on the redactional perspective.

From Chapter 4, especially the beginning of Acts, we retain several conclusions: if Act 1:6-8 does not attack the eschatological imminence (the contrary seems to be true), these verses at least make allusion to the Gentile mission. Furthermore there are tensions in Luke between the explicit orders of the Resurrected Lord to go and evangelize the world (Lk 24 and Act 1) and the difficulty that the apostles had in getting to work (Act 10). The Church in fact did not immediately fulfill the potentiality of its missionary essence. Luke did not want to make the doctrine and the facts correspond, for he is historian and pastor, more than theologian. Neither did he discard the inequalities which subsist between the received traditions and his personal intentions. Concerning Act 1:15ff., Wilson believes that Luke is not interested in the term 'apostle' (he correctly notes that the idea of the twelve apostles, against Klein, is anterior to Luke). What preoccupies the Evangelist is to establish, thanks to the apostles, a bridge between Jesus and the missionary Church of his time. As for the account of Act 2,. Wilson does not consider the targumic traditions of Pentecost enough: if he had, he could not have said that the date of the first outpouring of the Spirit was of no theological importance (p. 127), nor that the Pentecost narrative concerns the Jews alone.

In his fifth chapter, consecrated to Stephen, Wilson rightly remarks that Luke does not dogmatically justify the mission to the Gentiles by the condemnation of the Jews. This universal evangelization is rooted doctrinally in the project of God. The hardening of Israel is only the second cause , the historical impulsion, of the mission to the nations, as is attested in the famous texts, Act 13:46f.; 18:5f. and 28:25-28.

We can survey more rapidly the three following chapters which offer nothing very new. Chapter 6 on the conversion of Paul is a criticism of Klein's interpretation which we will speak of later on. The author insists on three famous texts (Act 9; 22; 26): the main mission of Paul will be the vocation of the Gentiles; this mission is proposed in OT terms at the very heart of Judaism (vision in the Temple) and it will not be fulfilled without suffering (like Paul, Luke ties apostleship to martyrdom). Chapter 7 deals with Cornelius and the Jerusalem council: "Apart from the historical question, Luke clearly sees the Apostolic Council as a confirmation of the momentous turning point in chs. 10-11, when the Gentiles are accepted as equal members of the church." (p. 192). Chapter 8 presents Paul's speech in Athens: Act 17:22f., like Act 14:15-17, has considerable importance for Wilson, in understanding how Luke conceived the preaching to the Gentiles: since the morality of the pagans is not worse than the Jews', their religiosity is not negligible either. Evangelizing them is compelling because of this springboard of natural piety and because of their ignorance of the heart of the Christian faith (the resurrection; should not we say the resurrection of Jesus, the Messiah of Israel?).

Perhaps the most topical of the book, chapter 9 analyzes the programmatic assertions of the Acts in favor of the universal mission. Having discarded Act 2:39 ("those who are afar" are the Jews of the Diaspora; with Dupont, we believe on the contrary that Luke already has the Gentiles in mind), Wilson stops at Act 3:25-26: against Jervell, he concludes that the title σπέρμα of Abraham by which the families of the earth will be blessed designates not Israel but Christ. Nonetheless, Wilson's main argument is hardly cogent: if there were a distinction between Israel and the nations, Luke would have used πάντα τὰ ἔθνη concerning the latter and not πᾶσαι αἱ πατριαί (cf. Eph 3:15). The decisive argument, rapidly noted by Wilson, is elsewhere: in the taking over of the word "to bless" and the pronoun "you" and in the interpretation of σπέρμα and αὐτόν, i.e. "his servant", i.e. "the Christ". The πρῶτον, despite Jervell's opinion, does not contradict this view which sees the resurrection of Jesus as the source of blessing, first reaching the Jews and then the Gentiles: the πατριαὶ τῆς γῆς includes Jew and Gentile alike.

Next Wilson studies three texts, Act 13:46-48, 18:6 and 28:26-28 [**39**]: he comes to the conclusions that we have already mentioned concerning Stephen. We have accepted them with two exceptions: 1) it is sure that the hardening of the Jews (Luke uses this name in Act 28 and not, as Wilson thinks, Israel) goes hand in hand with the annexation of the Gentiles. Yet to speak of substi-tution is awkward, for according to salvation history, the Gentiles are indeed substituted for the Jews as the present adherents of the Church. Yet the Church remains one from its Judeo-Christian origins, which are hardly denied and which Luke delights in describing. 2) Elsewhere, Wilson, like the majority of exegetes, does not pay attention to the three words, perhaps laden with hope, which punctuate the terrible quotation of Isa 6:9-10: καὶ ἰάσομαι αὐτούς (Act 28:27).

In his last chapter, Wilson summarizes what can be called a theology of the Gentiles. The project does not lack bite since for the author, Luke is hardly a theologian and "the most striking characteristic of Luke-Acts is precisely the lack of any consistent theology of the Gentiles." (p. 239). He insists on the function of Jerusalem, from where the various missionary movements depart (in our opinion, Antioch must not be neglected; cf. Act 13); on the role of the Twelve (the mission to the Gentiles comes from them and not from the marginals of the Church); on the Spirit who accompanies the mission (Wilson should have developed this); on the miracles which signal God at work (Wilson thinks that the God of Luke is too active; we think the contrary, that he never acts without resorting to mediations); on Jesus who ordained the mission after Easter and promised it already before the Passion; on the impartiality of God (Act 10: 34 and 15:9) who accepts Gentiles and Jews alike; and on the OT prophecies, the signs of a God with a universal plan.

In short, Luke belongs to a Church where Gentiles predominate, but because of a Jewish environment, he must recall the Jewish roots of the Church and of Paul, in particular. The work comes to a close with a comparison of Luke and Paul.

P. Zingg

i. P. Zingg (-> 1974) does not enter directly into the discussion of the relations of the Church to Israel. His interest is rather of the growth of the Church in Lucan theology. His first chapter from a stylistic point of view, distinguishes the general notices concerning this growth in the imperfect (Act 2:47b; 5:14; 6:7; 9:31; 11:21; 12:24; 13:49; 16:5; 19:20) from the incidental remarks which are in the aorist (Act 1:15b; 2:41; 4:4; 6:1; 8:6, 12; 9:35, 42; 11:24b; 13:48; 14:1, 21; 16:14b, 15; 17:4, 11b, 12, 34; 18:8 (10); 28:24; cf. 19:10 and 21, 20bc). All of the notices are from Luke's pen. Those which deal with growth of the word are without parallel **[40]**, whereas the texts mentioning the multiplication of the believers stem from OT texts. Luke is thinking particularly of the promise made to Abraham. He wants it to be known that the Church's growth is both extraordinary and durable, but above all, that it is God's work. This growth is manifested invisibly by faith and visibly by the number of believers. Whereas up to this point, the notices had been seen as indicators in the historical unfolding or settings in the narrative account, Zingg confers a chiefly theological value on them: they articulate the narratives in giving them a common denominator [41]. At this point, we would like to criticize the author for not sufficiently distinguishing the growth of the Word and the growth of the community. For Luke, does the growth of the Word always imply an ecclesiastic activity of preaching?

Chapter 2 (pp. 75-115) deals with growth parables and Luke's interpretation of them (while the growth theme is not primary in these parables, it is not negligible either; generally, Luke is faithful to the tradition. We nonetheless can discern a rift: the eschatological perspective tends to become ecclesiological, however, it is the triumphal activity of God, which continues to be celebrated).

After this, Gamaliel's speech (Act 5:35-39) retains the author's attention (ch 3). This redactional text suggests that the development of the Church originates in God's active will.

Chapters 4 and 5 successively treat the growth of the communities of Jerusalem and Antioch. The writer recalls the theological function of the Jewish capital, the bonds which unite the mother church to the Jewish people. The astounding progress of this community expresses God's blessing on the first Christians. Antioch, which is closely linked to Jerusalem, is less the Church of continuity than the Church opening up to the new mission to the Gentiles. A new name sanctions this stage: "Christians" (Act 11:26). It is from this city that the missionaries Saul and Barnabas depart for Asia Minor where Jewish hostility strengthens the invitation to the Gentiles (Act 13-14) (the author only occasionally dialogues with J. Jervell here). Using these places and people, Luke makes us sensitive to the continuity and growth of the Church.

Thus is the summary of this balanced book which does not stand out by its novel contributions. In our view, the two original offerings are, first, the stylistic analysis of the growth sayings (notices) and, second, the interpretation of the role of Antioch. In his conclusion, the author thinks that the theme of the organic growth indeed appears in Luke's thought, but it is not an innova - tion of the third Evangelist. The OT and Jesus had already used this theme [42].

III. THE ORGANIZATION OF THE CHURCH

Numerous are the recent authors who have studied the organization of the Church in Luke. Their task has not been easy, for to grasp the redactional intention does not signify an understanding of the ecclesiology of Luke's time, nor the life of the primitive Church. Since Luke is a historian, the Church he describes is not necessarily the Church of his time and since he is also a theologian, his views of the Church often escape history in the narrow sense of the word. One must have a lot of adroitness to do justice to the historical and the ideological.

We have regrouped the studies which we have read in three series: the persons who fulfilled an office; the organization of the ministries and discipline; and the cult and sacraments. In each series, we have selected the authors most attentive with regard to the Lucan contribution. So as not to prolong this chapter beyond measure, we have had to restrain our desire for exhaustivity.

1) The Persons

The figure of Peter

a. To evoke the apostles and witnesses is to think first of persons, and especially Peter. Numerous have been the studies concerning Peter since O. Cullmann's book (-> 1952). However, few have dealt with Luke's work in a redactional perspective. The majority of the exegetes pursued historical (a biography of Peter: the leader of the Church or the missionary?) [**43**] or dogmatic (the question of primacy) [**44**] goals. They naturally turn to the "great" Petrine texts in the Lucan corpus, especially on the Jerusalem conference, whose version in the Acts compared to the one in Gal 2, has been and remains the occasion for countless exegetical acrobatics. Even M. Dibelius (-> 1947), who desires to detach himself from all influence of Gal 2 is content with the following results: the account in Act 15 is the work of Luke, who heard of a conflict concerning circumcision in Antioch. Luke sets this conflict in Jerusalem. One should not even seek the sources of this account which is secondary compared to Gal 2. Dibelius is thus interested in Luke's historical method and literary technique, but rather little in the theological preoccupations of the author of the Acts. His study does not illuminate the Lucan figure of Peter. It is the same for most of the contributions that we have read on the subject [**45**]. The rare allusions are quite banal: Luke insists on the person of Peter. With respect for Mark, he immediately associates Peter's mission to his vocation (cf. Lk 5:1-11) and mentions, already at the Passion of Jesus, the apostle's leadership function in the community (Lk 22:31f.), a function which will be confirmed in the Acts [**46**].

b. In 1972, a monograph concerning the person of Peter in the Lucan writings appeared. Its author, W. Dietrich (-> 1972) set as his goal, to discover the Lucan characteristics of the apostle, detach a portrait and finally situate the function of the texts relative to Peter in the unfolding of the entire work. Practically Dietrich successively analyzes all the texts and concludes in the following manner: it is clear that Luke gives a prominent place to Peter. This becomes evident in a comparison of Luke's Gospel with Mark's and a reading of the Acts. Peter occupies an intermediary position between Jesus and the disciples in the Gospel and the Acts, he becomes the apostle *par excellence*, the missionary witness.

It would however be false to draw from these assertions the conviction that Luke yielded to a personality cult. The Evangelist does not forget Jesus' condemnation of Peter and underlines that Peter becomes the representative of the Twelve only after the intervention of the Holy Spirit. It is here that the main conclusion of Dietrich's study appears: Peter neither decides nor directs except when the Holy Spirit has set up a new situation and thus prepared the way. Moreover, as the interventions of the Spirit multiply, the apostle is taken up in an *understanding process*, which from the denial, leads him to the confession of faith and finally, to his acceptance of the Gentiles. The image of Peter confirms the exist-ence of a *heilsgeschichtlich* schema in Luke: for him, there are three Pentecosts in Acts: one for the Jews, another for the Samaritans and a third for the Gentiles. Luke is not interested in Peter except in that he is related to these three foundational events. It is thus necessary to speak of theological not biographical attention that Luke gives to the apostle.

We would form two criticisms of this interpretation: a) we do not understand what the phrase "Peter is the apostle *par excellence*" means. Should we understand priority of the apostle *par excellence*? b) The link established between Peter and the out-pourings of the Holy Spirit seems real to us, but still Dietrich should have insisted on the notion of ἀρχή: Peter is only associated to the beginning of the life of the Church, which is made up of Jews, Samaritans and Gentiles. This is a limitation and a privilege at the same time from which certain theological conse - quences flow. W. Dietrich has hardly disengaged these [47].

Stephen

c. Through several studies and particularly by his book of 1958, Marcel Simon (-> 1951 and -> 1958) gave new impetus to the studies concerning Stephen [48]. For the former dean of the Faculty of Philosophy of Strasbourg, the word "Hellenist" must have been forged and used in a pejorative manner to designate one of the movements of Judaism of that time (cf. Act 9:29f.), influenced by Hellenism, hostile to the Temple and antiritualistic. This movement draws from the old prophetism (e.g., Nathan, 2 Sam 7), but also from the Greek spiritualistic criticism with regard to the cults. Certain Hellenists were converted to Christianity and Stephen was one. If the account concerning Stephen and the Hellenists has undergone a strong Lucan influence, the speech, without being historical, is not Luke's work: it reflects basically the theses of Stephen and the Hellenists concerning the role of Moses, the importance of the Law and the criticism of the Temple as well as all that accompanied the episode of the Golden Calf. Luke does not share Stephen's critical ideas concerning the Temple and Stephen's theological position will remain marginal and isolated in early Christianity. The mission of the Hellenists did not have as its primary objective, the Gentiles but Samaria. These audacious propositions concerning the origin of the Hellenists have been criticized by not a few (cf. e.g., C. F. D. Moule -> 1958 and T. Holtz -> 1965).

Ties between the Hellenists, Samaria and the Gospel of John were already recognized by O. Cullmann who since then has not ceased to consider that this current of early Christianity depends on a marginal branch of Judaism, attested at Qumran [49].

d. The contemporary works on Stephen are oriented in two irreconciliable directions. According to some, the information in the Acts conceals traditions of certain historical value. On the contrary, for the others, Luke's concerns override. The former lean on Acts to reconstitute the history of the Hellenistic Christian movement. The latter, less numerous, seek the redactional intentions of Luke. Among the former, we would like to mention P. Gaechter (-> 1952) who imagines that under the jurisdiction of the apostles, there were two groups of seven, one responsible with the assistance to the Hebrews and the other, to the Hellenists. The Seven were not deacons, but men solemnly consecrated to a ministry, who beside the assistance they offered, also engaged in pastoral counseling and mission. The ordination of the Seven will later serve as a model for the consecration of bishops. These groups of Seven were formed under the influence of the Jewish organization of civil communities. Afterwards, the seven Hebrews will be called presbyters or elders. These strange theses lead to the following consequence: upon his departure from Jerusalem, Peter leaves in place a presbyterial body lead by James, a monarchical bishop! **[50]**

e. More recently M. H. Scharlemann (-> 1968) believed himself able to reconstruct the historical figure of Stephen. Accompanied with a good bibliography (especially pp. 190-191 and 198-199) and a brilliant presentation of the state of the question (p. 1-11), this work analyzes the material relative to Stephen, in particular the famous speech in Acts 7, whose thematic content seems historical. A study of Stephen's inter - pretation of the OT follows. Then a comparison of this speech with contemporary Jewish literature and the first Christian texts allows the singling out of the special features of the "Protomartyr". Here in summary fashion are the author's conclusions: "Stephen is an authentic figure from the history of the primitive church; his discourse is a very distinctive piece of work, containing some highly original theology, which, on the one hand, owes much to contacts with the Samaritan tradition and is indebted, on the other hand, to Jesus both for its radical opposition to the temple and for its understanding of the Old Testament, Luke included a description of Stephen and his theology at the point where he introduces that section of Acts which deals with the mission of the church in Jerusalem to Samaria, and he did so because Stephen had in fact dealt with the problem of Samaria in his various discussions at the synagogues of Jerusalem." (p. 11).

Scharlemann, it is clear, sees Luke as more a historian than a theologian: Luke's effort is, for him, to paint the historical situation of the community in Jerusalem in the beginning of Christianity.

f. It is difficult to find a more marked contrast than between Scharlemann and Bihler (-> 1963). The latter thinks he can demonstrate the redactional character of the speech in Acts 7, which men like E. Haenchen and H. Conzelmann, in their com -

mentaries, still believed traditional. After having evoked the history of research, J. Bihler shows that Stephen's story (Act 6:8-15 and 7:54-8:2) bears the obvious mark of Luke who does not follow one unique source, but is inspired by divers traditions (a tradition concerning persecution, the saying concerning the temple and one concerning the Son of Man, the list in Act 6:9 and a remembrance of ecstatic phenomena). In this account, Luke compares Stephen's fate to Jesus'. Their martyrdoms result in the same human refusal of the project of God. If exegetes have noted already for a long time, the parallel Jesus-Stephen, they have not noted, according to Bihler, what distinguishes the two destinies: responsible for the death of Jesus, the Jews were still excusable; guilty of Stephen's stoning, they become unpardonable. The general culpability of Judaism leads Christians to open the Church to the Samaritans and then to the Gentiles. As for us, we can accept, with Bihler and against Jervell, a relation between the hardening of the Jews and the mission to the non-Jews, but we hesitate to say that in condemning Stephen, the Jewish people have refused forever the call to conversion: on the contrary, until the last chapter of Acts, Luke evokes Christian efforts to convert the Jews.

J. Bihler then dedicates the essential part of his work to the speech in Acts 7. He sees three sections: 1) a history of Israel centered on Abraham, Joseph and especially Moses (vss. 2-37), 2) a description of the fall of Israel, idolatrous and builder of the Temple (vss. 38-50) and 3) a declaration of the hardening and guilt of Israel (vss. 51-53). The style of the discourse as well as the themes dealt with reflect Luke's theological and literary intentions rather than Stephen's. From the Abrahamic period Luke retains, like in the rest of his work, the promise and not circumcision: this time already announces the entire history of Israel. At the time of Joseph, the prophecies made to Abraham begin to be fulfilled: a tribulation, understood in the Lucan way, i.e. non-eschatological. Moses' period witnesses to the fulfillment of the promise of deliverance. This story corresponds to the salvation history of Lucan theology. The same is true for the criticism of the Temple (vss. 38-50) and the allusion to Jesus' death (vss. 51-53). The Lucan side of the speech does not exclude the use of various traditions which Bihler stakes out: an apocalyptic tradition concerning the history of Israel; a messianism, supported by Dt 18, which originates from heterodox Judaism. As for the criticism of the Temple, it goes beyond all that Judaism and early Christianity dared to say. Is it then a tradition? Bihler thinks that Luke sometimes plays on the favorable affirmations to the Temple and sometimes on slashing attacks on the sanctuary. The Evangelist thus can assure a providential continuity and discontinuity between Judaism and Christianity.

Acts 7 is one of the hinges of the Lucan work: "Genau an der Stelle des Umbruchs hat Lukas die Stephanusgeschichte im Zusammenhang einer Geschichte der Sieben (Hellenisten) ein - geordnet," (p. 182f.). Samaria lies between Jerusalem and the Empire; the Seven are going to evangelize it, as the Twelve had preached in Jerusalem and Paul will in the Empire.

Bilher concludes that Luke submits the Seven to the Twelve and refuses them the titles, witnesses or apostles, that indeed they should have born. This ecclesiological effort nonetheless butts into traditions that the Evangelist never dared to openly counteract.

It is difficult to choose between Scharlemann and Bihler. Methodologically, our preference is with Bihler who seeks the Lucan sense of the texts, relative to Stephen. Yet we wonder if the German exegete does not exaggerate the redactional impulsions of Luke and minimize the contemporary Jewish exegesis (concerning Act 7). As for the Hellenists, it seems to us that he has not resolved the age old problem: chosen for the service of tables, the Seven do not fulfil this function but go to evangelize. Why? He resolves it even less for he thinks the description of Philip and Stephen as missionaries is redactional [51].

g. R. Pesch in a small book (-> 1966) shares several of Bihler's ideas, in particular as to the role of Stephen in the economy of the book of the Acts. Pesch's personal contribution concerns Stephen's vision (Act 7:55-56). He thinks that the mission to the pagans is not provoked by persecution alone. It is above all the will of God, which finds its illustration precisely in the appearence of the Risen Lord to Stephen. The well.known fact that the Christ is presented <u>standing</u> is the hermeneutical key of the vision (the *ἑστῶτα* takes the place of an explanatory hearing): if he is standing, it is because he comes as an angry judge, to sentence his hardened people. Indirectly, this vision is a sign of favor for the mission to the Gentiles. The vision, influenced perhaps by Isa 3:13 (LXX), is thus in relation with the speech in Act 7 which it confirms.

While we do not necessarily share the interpretation which Pesch gives to the vision, we nonetheless grant that 1) the mission to the Gentiles is not the hazardous fruit of persecution and 2) the Stephen incident is an important step in the unfolding of God's plan.

Paul [52]

h. Because of space, we have placed in the footnotes, the references to the numerous works which deal with the Lucan texts concerning Paul from a strictly historical point of view. For the authors of these contributions, Acts is a bone which has to be broken open to reach the marrow [**53**].

In our chapter on eschatology, we described P. Vielhauer's position. He concludes there is a radical difference between the Lucan Paul and the historical Paul. To be honest, the author compares above all the theological ideas of the two. The controversy which he provoked concerned mainly the theology (and more particularly the eschatology) of Luke and Paul [**54**].

What must retain our attention here is the Lucan figure of Paul. We must say at the first that no entire work has appeared on the subject, with the exception of an unpublished dissertation [**55**]. On the other hand, uncountable particular studies have come to general conclusions which are often contradictory. The most numerous concern Paul's conversion and the Athenean speech, but the most recent deal with his attitude at the end of the book of Acts.

What material did Luke have at his disposition to narrate the conversion of Paul? Why does he tell this event three times in Acts? These are the two principle questions which authors have asked themselves. G. Klein's (-> 1961) position is clear: Luke undertakes a double rescue operation against the Gnostics. He limits to twelve the number of the apostles, and then submits the missionary to the Gentiles to them. The subordination of Paul to the Twelve is the price Luke has to pay to save the apostle from the hands of the Gnostics. For G. Lohfink, C. Burchard and K. Löning (-> 1965) it is better first to discern the tradition of the Lucan redaction. G. Lohfink (-> 1965) thinks that Luke resorts to a literary genre found in the OT: the dialogue with a divine ap - parition (Act 9:4-6; 22:7-10 and 26:14-16). Luke, using the LXX, presents an anthology of Biblical texts in Act 26:16-18: he places on the lips of Jesus a series of sayings attributed in the OT to the Lord God (this has definite Christological repercussions). Lohfink also discerns a double Greek influence: he perceives, following A. Wikenhauser (**Bib** 29 (1948) 100-111), the Greek literary genre of the double vision and, after many others, the Greek origin of the proverb of the goad (Act

26:14). For the German exegete, the Lucan accounts of the conversion of Paul serve to underline 1) the irresistible power of the Christ; 2) the divine origin of the mission to the Gentiles and 3) the accomplishment of the Scriptures which this evangelization constitutes. They also witness to the literary art of the Evangelist and permit a favorable comparison with the epistles. If the historical Paul thinks that all comes from God, Luke adds that these gifts pass through the mediation of men and Jerusalem.

i. Full of nuances, C. Buchard's book (-> 1970) is difficult to summarize. It is composed of two sections which are unequal in length. The first analyzes the traditional and redactional elements of the Lucan texts consecrated to the first period of Paul's life: before his conversion, his conversion and his first missionary activity. Rightly, he thinks that a traditional element is not necessarily historical. Furthermore, he distinguishes the solid traditions from the more informal and less precise knowledge (we wonder if this distinction is justified?). Sometimes, without being able to give arguments, he notes his personal impressions: Luke, for example, must have known of Paul's double citizenship, just like he must have heard of the apostle's profession (*σκηνοποιός*) and pharisaical commitment. In certain cases, he suspends judgment; he is unsure if the presence of Saul at the stoning of Stephen is purely redactional or not. On other occasions, he thinks he can come to certain results: if the mention of Saul, the persecutor, in Act 26:9-11 and 22:4f. is redactional, in Act 8:3, it is traditional and rests on a formulation of the apostle himself (Gal 1:23). Against Klein, the portrait of Paul the persecutor is not voluntarily darkened in order to save the apostle from the hands of the Gnostics. If Luke underlines Saul's opposition to the Church, it is to better emphasize his conversion. Moreover, this opposition to the Christ comes from, as in I Tim 1:13, a failure to recognize the exact nature of the Gospel.

Precisely concerning the conversion reported in Act 9, Bur - chard takes us on perilous paths and because of vertigo, we cannot follow him. He thinks that the narrative schema used is related to the one used in the Hellenistic Jewish novel <u>Joseph and Aseneth</u>, which itself has undergone influence from the religion of Isis. The German exegete believes he discovers an indication in favor of his hypothesis in the fact that the redactional reminders of Act 22 and 26 either break or abandon this schema. Act 22 and 26 are <u>vocations</u> to become a witness while Act 9 reports a <u>conversion</u> which leads to martyrdom. In its present form, Act 9:3-19a is at the source what a text from Luke's Gospel is to the Marcan original. Yet Paul himself is not at the origin of the narrative. Without the influence being as clear, it is in Act 26:12-18 that Luke depends on the apostle himself. Luke thus knew how to combine a traditional account of the conversion and the Pauline concept of vocation.

In the account of the missionary beginnings of Paul (Act 9:19b-30), Burchard believes he uncovers a conglomerate of two traditions: the one relative to the incident of the escape in the basket over the walls of Damascus and the other recalling the presentation of Saul to the other apostles by the intermediary of Barnabas.

Concerning the sending of Paul to the nations, ordered by Christ during a vision in the Temple (Act 22:17-21) **[56]**, Burchard thinks that he has discovered a tradition from unknown origin (in any case not Pauline). We prefer to think that the totality of these verses are the work of Luke. We do not believe that the appearance of Christ is as solid as Burchard thinks or that Luke must be refused the origin.

In the much briefer second part of his book, Burchard first rehabilitates Luke as a historian. He writes with regard to Act 8:3: "Der Vers spricht gegen den Schriftsteller, aber für den Historiker." (p. 169). Luke makes judicious use of his documentation. Unfortunately, it is difficult to gauge the quality of his traditions. "Die crux ist Lukas' Traditionsbasis." (p. 172f.).

Luke is also a theologian: for sure he is little interested in Paul's theology, but he does not limit his attention to the person of the apostle. He confers a historical role to the one Burchard calls the thirteenth witness who is on the same level as the Twelve (and not below them, as many would like). Paul is a witness of Christ. He is even the only witness to accomplish the program laid out by the Resurrected One (Act 1:8). In contrast, his mobility is underlined by the stability of the Twelve. Furthermore, like the Twelve, Paul will have no successor. If one must divide the time of the Church into two, the division must be placed <u>after</u> the death of Paul, not between the time of the primitive Church and that of the Gentile mission marked by Paul. In fact, the time of the witnesses does not succeed properly speaking a period but rather the present moment characterized by the expectation of the end, patience and suffering, and this, despite many exegetes.

In closing this book, we have the impression that the author could neither define the different genre of the traditions used by Luke nor specify their mode of communication. It is perhaps a difficult task, but until it is accomplished we cannot appreciate Luke's original contribution [57].

j. Following M. Dibelius, K. Löning (-> 1973) judges that there is but one tradition behind the three accounts of Paul's conversion. Act 9 represents the main Lucan redaction of this tradition and Act 22 and 26 are only variants. He believes he can discern several indications of a pre-Lucan written redaction of the account in Act 9, in particular in Act 9:15-16 (the non-Lucan image of Paul which Luke can tolerate). In his redactional adaptations, Luke modified the tradition by leaning on Pauline soteriological teaching of a autobiographical nature, attested in Gal 1:13f.; I Cor 15:8f.; Phil 3:6 and the post-Pauline literature (the motif of Paul's zeal for the Law, for example). At the end of this section consecrated to source criticism (Literarkritik), the author limits the tradition to Act 8:3; 9:1-12 and 17-19a and then passes on to an analysis of the literary genre of the tradition. Here, in his opinion, is the structure of the account: a) the exposition (Act 8:3; 9:1f.): the persecutor plans to eliminate the community in Damascus; b) the first part (Act 9:3-9): the persecutor just before reaching his goal is thrown to the ground by the Lord; c) the second part (Act 9:10-12, 17-19a): mandated by the Lord, a disciple heals the persecutor. The correspondence of the two parts is highlighted in vs. 18f. by the inversed resumption of elements from vs. 9: blindness and fasting (vs. 9) are transformed into healing and a meal (vs. 18f.). The antithetical structure of the two sections is confirmed by other indications. The central idea which imposed the structure of the narrative is that heaven coordinates earthly events. Various motifs permit us to bring together the conversion of Paul and the legend of Heliodorus, hindered by God to pillage the treasure of the Temple (2 Mac 3), as well as various texts of synogagal propoganda (Löning citing Joseph and Aseneth, fortunately, does not venture as far as Burchard). Nevertheless, by the structure of its literary genre, Act 9 is closer to certain legends and short stories found in the NT (Löning curiously limits his investigation to the accounts in Act 9:32-35, 36-42 and Act 10:1-11, 18). The author thinks he can establish that Paul's conversion, primitively a short story centered on the intervention of Christ, became by the will of a pre-Lucan editor a legend consecrated to the vessel of election. The story must have intentionally used the image of the adversary, miraculously conquered by the Lord (Lönig faithfully applies the terminology and method of M. Dibelius).

In the second part of his book, Löning studies the Lucan redaction of this tradition. Luke transforms the legend into a narrative (diegesis), in pursuing his programmed formula in Lk 1:1-4. Luke's effort to transform the conversion legend into a narrative of vocation (so Ananias' progressive receding from view) is typical. Furthermore, the Evangelist reinterprets the figure of the adversary: confined to Judaism and attached to an erroneous messia-nism, Saul represents the official Jewish opposition with respect to the whole Church. The intervention of the Risen One transforms this man and provides him with a veritable interpretation of the Messianic prophecies. Understood as a vocation, the appearance of the Resurrected One is not, for Luke, to confer apostleship on Saul, and thus align the new witness with the Twelve, but on the contrary, to highlight the specificity of the vocation and missionary work of Paul according to God's plan. If the contents of the testimony always remain the same, the paths this witness follows vary from the apostles to Paul. The Twelve are servants of the word for the people of Israel and Paul, for all men.

Löning terminates his work with the important pages concerning the theological function of the last Pauline discourses in Acts. He thinks that the triangle, accusers (Jews) - accused (Paul) - judge (Romans) allows Luke to resolve the doctrinal question which preoccupies him and the community he addresses. Luke succeeds in showing in the last interventions of Paul that the actual trench between Christianity and Judaism was dug by the Jews and that in fact a continuity exists in the project of God, continuity assured precisely by the testimony of the Twelve and Paul's missionary activity. Luke thus does not seek to save Paul from the hands of the Gnostics (Klein), nor judaize him (Jervell), but rather he uses Paul to resolve the identity crisis of the Lucan community. The apostle's indisputable authority permits Luke to legitimize the existence of the Hellenistic communities, irremediably separated from Judaism.

This interpretation encounters two problems: why does the Lucan Paul so cling to Judaism if he must justify the actual rupture between the Church and the Synagogue? Moreover, is it true that the figure of Paul is so incontestable at Luke's time?

Let us mention several other works consecrated to Paul's life before his first Christian mission:

k. In a remarkable study, W. C. van Unnick (-> 1952) interests himself in Paul's youth and shrewdly analyzes Act 22:3, the only text which speaks of the place Paul lived his childhood and adolescence. The Dutch exegete shows how this text resorts to a tripartite schema used often by Greek writers: birth - first education (ἀνατροφή) - instruction (παιδεία). Understood correctly, Act 22:3 signifies that if Paul was born in Tarsus, it is in Jerusalem that he received his first education. It is also in Jerusalem, at the feet of Gamaliel, that he was instructed. With this view, van Unnick attacks an exegetical consensus which situates the youth of the apostle in Tarsus. In our opinion, van Unnick has given the right meaning to Act 22:3, but it is not sure that this Lucan text corresponds to the historical reality. In the perspective which interests us, we can conclude that at least for *Luke*, Paul received in his youth a *Jewish* formation in the holy city itself.

l. D. M. Stanley (-> 1953) was one of the first to study the three accounts (Act 9, 22 and 26) from a *redaktionsgeschichtlich* point of view. Curiously, the author thinks that Act 22 depends on Paul and Act 9 on Luke. Having chosen as doctrinal theme, the progressive accomplishment of the universal character of the Christian faith, Luke retains *narration* as literary genre and *Paul* as the main character. All three show Paul's apostolic character and intimacy with the Christ.

m. Influenced by the courses and works of D. J. McCarthy (-> 1971), Father E. Haulotte (-> 1970, second title) thinks that to describe Paul's conversion, Luke uses an OT scheme of *investiture*.

n. Finally, S. Lundgren (-> 1971) attacks the most prevalent interpretation of the role of Ananias. For him, Ananias does not intervene to humanly mediate Paul's apostleship. He appears on the contrary 1) to heal and baptize the apostle and 2) to witness with Paul that the Lord alone converted and called the persecutor of the Christians.

o. Before dealing with the figure of Paul the accused, let us note several contributions concerning Paul the missionary and leader of the Church (Act 13.20). J. Cambier (-> 1961-1962) analyzes the first missionary journey of Paul to Jerusalem in the theological framework of Luke's missionary schema. Because of his conception of the history of the Church, Luke brings Paul close to Jerusalem and attaches his ministry to the apostles'. Thus this trip neglects Gal 1:17.

p. Concerning the second journey (Act 11:27-30), we can read the article of G. Strecker (-> 1962). Vss. 29 and 30 are editorial even if Luke uses two recollections, the one of a trip common to Saul and Barnabas to Jerusalem, and the other concerning the collection. The literary construction of this journey, which did not happen historically at that moment, responds to a theological need: to link Antioch and Jerusalem in salvation history. The fulfillment of a prophecy, this journey takes place under the action of the Spirit. The unity of the Church is thus legitimated pneumatically.

q. B. Gärtner (-> 1962) and J. Beutler (-> 1968) [**58**] interest themselves in Act 14 , so often neglected and O. Glombitza (-> 1962) in Act 16:9-15 (the importance of the accusative after the verb "to evangelize" which signifies the insertion of the converts into a new existence). Concerning the speech of Paul in Athens, the reader can refer to our article in the **Revue de Théologie et de Philosophie** [**59**]. Three principle works concern the Paul's speech in Miletus: the exegetical and pastoral book of J. Dupont (-> 1962), the excellent article by H. Schürmann (-> 1962) and the thesis of H. J. Michel (-> 1973), which is solid but not very original [**60**].

r. To conclude, let us mention Paul the prisoner. Two important articles have recently attracted attention to the last chapters of Acts. The first is the work of P. Schubert (-> 1968). This writer first summarizes the form and function of the speeches in Acts: all of them, even the last ones, serve Luke's theological project, a project which can be summarized as a theology of promise and fulfillment. This theological project includes a second theme, closely associated to the first: the plan of God accords a prominent place to Saul (without being an apostle, Paul is not for all that lesser than the Twelve). A first cycle of speeches spoken by Peter alone (chs 1-5) has as its counterpart a second cycle in which Paul is the main orator (chs 6-20): throughout these two series, the whole design of God is presented. What then is the function of the last speeches? The theology of the project of God remains central, but here more than before, Luke is bent on spec-ifying the role of Paul, who becomes the only spokesman (cf. the importance of the "I" in these chapters).

Schubert then analyzes the sequence of chapters 21-28 and the interaction of the accounts, speeches and dialogues. He sees in the speech of Act 26 the summit of the sequence and the accomplishment of a prophecy of the Lord (Act 9:15). The article reaches its end with a thematic analysis of these last discourses: 1) Paul and the whole sect of the Nazarenes are innocent. 2) Luke's theology is summarized in the following: Luke skillfully transforms the process into a doctrinal dispute centered on the resurrection, the object of hope for the Pharisees and Christians. Act 24:25 proves to be a good summary of Luke's theology and ethics. 3) Paul's conversion is recalled twice. If the first recollection (Act 9) was centered on the double vision, the second (Act 22) insists on the mission to the Gentiles and the third (Act 26), submitted to the entire work of Luke, summarizes the theology of the plan of God, a theology which includes the function of the witness (Paul's) and the ethical demand (for converts).

P. Schubert arrives thus at the following conclusions: the last chapters do not present an original theological preoccupation. They fit into Luke's coherent theological program. The figure of Paul remains the same, that of a witness to Christ. The speeches hold a considerable place because of Luke's project, which is to narrate the proclamation of the Word of God. At the end of this article, inspite of the approbation which we accord the majority of the author's declarations, we are a bit disappointed: in underlining Luke's theological coherence throughout his work, does not Schubert eliminate what is at stake in the trial of Paul at the redactional level? Having seen above the historical context in which K. Löning situates these last chapters **[61]**, let us now look at what they become in the other important article by J. Jervell (-> 1968).

s. Let us say at the first that Jervell's article fits into the whole of his original research **[62]**. As we have seen, far from breaking with Judaism and from being be Hellenized, the Lucan Church rests faithful to the unique covenant of God and remains an integral part of the one holy people. From this, it is not surprising that Jervell conceives of the Lucan Paul as the master of Israel, Jew and Christian at the same time: Christian because he is a son of Abraham and Jew because attached to the Scriptural promises concerning the resurrection.

Having said this, let us take a look at the argumentation of the subtle Scandinavian exegete. He first of all notes that the last speeches of Acts, neglected by scholars, are different from the missionary discourses (Schubert here on the contrary tended to minimize the differences). In the company of many exegetes, Jervell calls them apologetic, but against the majority, he deems that Paul does not defend Christianity in general nor the political innocence of the Church, he defends his person.

Against whom is he fighting? With the voice of Paul, Luke does not lay blame on the Romans, nor the Greeks nor even the Christians' Gnostic or Judaizing adversaries. No, his target is the Jews. Up to the last chapter, Paul's companions and adversaries are the Jews. What does this former persecutor accuse them of? They have betrayed Israel.

With his OT conception of the Church, Luke is forced to avoid the ambiguities which Paul's historical attitude might have aroused. He must, if we can say so, rejudaize Paul to show that he is the adversary neither of the Law nor of the Temple nor even of the people. The Evangelist's entire effort is thus directed toward rectifying and asserting this image of Paul. Paul is of course a Christian, but he nonetheless remains a faithful partisan of the Law even after his conversion. If chapters 22 and 26 give the impression that Paul's Pharisaism belongs to the past, it is because traditional elements predominate. In the most redactional and most Lucan speeches, those in 23 and 24, Paul is presented with no hesitation as an orthodox Jew of the strictest observance, i.e. a Pharisee (cf. especially Act 23:6 and 24:14-16).

To believe in the resurrection is for Luke to be faithful to the Law, the Scripture and the people of God. Paul is not an Irrlehrer (false doctor, heretic) of Israel, but a better rabbi.

The picture of Paul Jervell discovers is that of a man with a firm gaze fixed on Israel. It is clear that Jervell attempts to discard the argument which jumps out at the exegete: what about the mission to the pagans? His weak answer shows where the shoe pinches: Act 22:17-21 (the apparition of the Christ in the Temple) is a traditional text which Luke could not eliminate. Elsewhere, he adds that the mission to the Gentiles was not a problem, for it was foreseen by the plan of God. It was the conditions of entry into the people of God which brought forth difficulties (cf. the Lucan solution in Act 15).

From this Jervell thinks he is able to situate the work of Luke; for him, it fits into a community where the Jewish Christians are very strong and Gentile Christians appear not as the successors of the Jewish ones but, as their proselytes (this differs from a Justin for whom the Judeo-Christians are a minority). Even if the mission to the Jews is finished (this declaration seems correct to us, but is contrary to the spirit of the article), the Church is directly confronted with a Jewish milieu, which accuses the apostleship of Paul. Far from being forgotten, as will be the case in the year 100 A.D., the activity of Paul is the source of criticism and worry. This is reason for Luke's magisterial clarification.

In our opinion, Jervell is right to indicate the Jewish permanence of the Lucan Paul, but he is wrong to imagine that the Lucan community clings to Judaism. The entire thrust of Luke's work moves toward the Gentiles: he is attached to the figure of Paul because the latter received the mission to leave a certain Judaism in order to go and convert the nations. The apologetic effort consists henceforth in showing that in doing this, this privi - leged witness of Christ does not betray the Jewish heritage. We understand that to the reproaches of having reviled the Law and Temple, Paul responds with his hope in the resurrection . Yet the Law and Temple do not interest Luke. The value of the Scriptures is in their Messianic prophecies and promise of the resurrection.

We have one more grievance with Jervell when he says the innovation which overthrows Paul on the road to Damascus, loses its importance. The heilsgeschichtlich continuity exaggeratedly wins over the discontinuity. Luke seems to have been judaized to the limit [63].

2) The ministers and discipline

The apostolate

a. Center of the missionary irradiation, founders of the edifice and successors of Jesus, the apostles have evidently held a primary place for exegetes.

1) Two states of the question facilitate our task and permit us to jump a few steps: one which remains a model in the genre is O. Linton (-> 1932, pp. 69-101) which evokes in a precise and lively manner the critical consensus of the 19th century Protestants , the Catholic position, the contribution of J. B. Lightfoot, the developments caused by the discovery of the Didache and the positions at the beginning of the 20th century, for example, those of A. Harnack, K. Holl and F. Kattenbusch.

The other by E. M. Kredel (-> 1956) goes back even further to H. S. Reimarus and brings us closer to our period with W. G. Kümmel, H. von Campenhausen, P. H. Menoud, A. M. Farrer, A. Fridrichsen and O. Cullmann.

These two studies, despite their merit, lead us only to the edge of the arena, for with one or two exceptions, the redaktionsgeschichtlich method became dominant only after their writing [64].

2) H. von Campenhausen and E. Lohse are the exceptions. In an important article (-> 1947), the former, a historian from Heidelberg was the first to distinguish with clarity the Lucan conception of the apostolate from the Pauline one. With this, he inaugurates the redactional method which men like H. Conzelmann, P. Vielhauer and E. Haenchen will refine. The Lucan apostle is set off from the Pauline one in two manners:

first of all, the apostolate is limited to the Twelve (Act 14:4 is an exception and Act 14:14, an inauthentic gloss) and secondly, to be an apostle, it is not enough to have seen the Risen Lord, one must also have been a witness to the earthly Jesus.

Typical of Luke, the first point is not however the Evangelist's invention (the limitation to the Twelve is already felt in other places than in Luke and before him). G. Klein will wrongly criticize this balanced view. Von Campenhausen's last remark concerning Luke is that the Lucan apostolate is not yet catholic, for the apostles have no jurisdictional powers.

b. E. Lohse (-> 1953) distinguishes two great stages in the history of the Christian apostolate. There is a first stage during which the apostolate remains a function corresponding to the Jewish shaliah and a second during which the apostolate, once a temporary function, becomes an institutional ministry. The author thinks that the passage from one stage to the other corresponds to the passage from Aramaic Jewish Christianity to the Greek-speaking Gentile brand. By reducing the notion of the Twelve and the advantage being given to the concept of apostle, Paul favorized this evolution. If Act 13:1-3 reports a tradition which allows the old functional conception to come through, the Lucan perspective on the whole corresponds to the more recent ministerial doctrine. For Luke, the Church reposes on the Twelve, the plenipotentiary messengers of the historical Jesus [65].

3) The account of the election of Matthias is an important text for the understanding of the Lucan apostolate. It is then not surprising that it has drawn the attention of not a few [66].

c. P. Gaechter (-> 1949) consecrated a long article to this event and defends conservative positions which hardly distinguish tradition from editing. Yet he shows a sensitivity to the juridical problems which is often lacking in exegesis. Matthias' election responds to a need to complete the group of the Twelve. This is indispensible because of the mission confided to the Twelve in the past and because of the task which awaits them in the future (participation in the last judgment). A collegial group which symbolizes the whole people, the apostles have not lost all individuality. They are antitypes of the twelve patriarchs: the people of God are constituted by their existence. Since the end times began with the Ascension, their lordly function (to judge on twelve thrones) has already begun! To accomplish this mission, this collegium must be complete: the catalogues of the apostles militate in favor of the exclusivity of the Twelve. In the Greek-speaking churches, the Twelve are perceived according to their present and future function. They are the authority of the universal Church, the spiritual Israel. Jesus did not abandon his carnal people, but based it upon a new foundation, Peter and, through him, the other apostles. A twelfth apostle is thus chosen to serve with the others as the foundation of the Church (it is noticeable that like many Catholic exegetes, Gaechter insists on the apostles who are invested with a ministry rather than a mission. They are the irremovable basis rather than itinerant missionaries). Gaechter then exegetes Act 1:15-26 ("eine kunstlose, schlichte Erzählung", against O. Bauernfeld in his commentary). Vss. 18-19 are an addition to the source and vss. 20-21, a summary (the two conditions to be an apostle complete one another: it is necessary to have known the earthly Jesus in order to know that he is the Resurrected Lord). Against popular opinion, the choice of the twelfth apostle was not imposed by the holy Scripture cited in vs. 20b: in the NT, the Scripture is never the origin of concrete actions. It is Peter who took the initiative himself, concerning the order that the risen Jesus did not forget to give him! The article ends with several considerations concerning the place (not in the Temple), the time (it was pressing) and the persons (the ones likely to be candidates were few, since Peter did not have the time to convoke them from Galilee). While according to many exegetes, Matthias was chosen in a particular manner, even exceptional (the Holy Spirit not yet being able to give his aid), this choice, according to Gaechter, represents the Ur-wahl, the norm of all later elections, beginning with the Seven's [67].

d. The exegete from the canton of Vaud (Switzerland), C. Masson (-> 1955), who was unaware of the article of P. Gaechter, thinks Luke's redactional work did not hinder the discerning of the traditional materials used. There is a tradition concerning the reconstruction of the college of the Twelve and a tradition concerning the death of Judas [68]. The first tradition confirms the pre-Easter existence of the group of the Twelve chosen by Jesus himself. For this tradition, as for Jesus himself, the Twelve were not the representatives of Israel, but missionaries of the kingdom. The reconstruction of the group finds, at a traditional level, its place in the eschatological and missionary perspective of the early days of the Church. However, the period of the Church which continued modified the function attributed to the Twelve. Concerning the redaction of Luke, i.e. at the time of a universal Church, the reconstituted college of the Twelve no longer regroups the missionaries to

Israel, but the witnesses of the resurrection of Christ in the Church and before the world. The new function confided to the Twelve is to serve as the basis of the apostolic preaching and the source of the Evangelical tradition. To effect this modification of perspective, Luke composes Peter's speech: "It is necessary to recognize that Luke places on the lips of Peter his conception of the apostolate, a conception which does not agree with the reality, since no one could fulfill the condition imposed on Judah's successor." (p. 180).

e. P. H. Menoud (-> 1957) criticized certain theses of his collegue mentioned above. For the exegete from Neuchâtel (Switzerland), the whole pericope must be considered Lucan. The text forms a literary unit of which the citations in vs. 20 form the heart. The Scripture justifies and explains the downfall of Judas as well as the election of Matthias. Luke attributes great importance to the reconstitution of the college of the Twelve which has hardly lost all signification in his view. Thus he pays more careful attention to the choice of the obscure Matthias than to that of James, the brother of the Lord. Why? It is because of his doctrine of salvation history: the life of the Church could not be based on an initial unbalance. It is of utmost importance that the apostolic circle be completed and limited at the same time. This allows the testimony to be valid and assures its transmission. Nonetheless, Paul's function is not darkened: Luke's Paul, like Stephen, is <u>not</u> an apostle but he <u>is</u> a witness.

f. Less exegetical than expected, K. H. Rengstorf's article (-> 1961) navigates between refined nuances and dogmatic judg - ments. Distinguishing little between tradition and redaction, the German exegete asks stimulating questions: why does the Church in choosing Matthias organize itself, although it has not yet received the Spirit? Furthermore, why does Luke not place the episode during the forty days of the presence of the Resurrected Lord? For E. Haenchen, like P. H. Menoud, Luke is interested in the reconstitution of the college of the Twelve because of his salvation history: Luke shows how the Church learned to endure. Rengstorf thinks, on the contrary, that the Matthias episode embarasses Luke who makes no allusion to it in the rest of his work. He discards the thesis of the Lucan originality of the Twelve apostles, by claiming that the idea of the "Twelve apostles" is pre-Easter! The election of Matthias fits into the same pre-Easter context, since the resurrection occupies only a little space: "Die Zuwahl des Matthias erweist sich damit ihrem Wesem nach als ein Ausdruck ungebrochener messianischer Zuversicht zu Jesus im Kreise seiner Jünger zwischen Himmelfahrt und Pfingsten." (p. 51). Rather than clinging to the number twelve, the Church decided to maintain the link with the ministry of Jesus. The incident is typical of the period separating Easter from Pentecost: the disciples know that they must prepare themselves for the shocks after Pentecost, but they still do not dare to set up the structures promised by Jesus for the time of the Church. Thus, they have not yet grasped the radical innovation of the resurrection. In a rather obtruse manner, they imagine a mission still limited to Israel. This is the reason for the tension Rengstorf discovers in this text, particularistic in his opinion, and the rest of Acts where univer - salism triumphs. The theology of the pericope is thus not Luke's. If Luke nonetheless keeps this text, it is that he believes that God continues to say yes to the people of Israel, though they have hardened their hearts. Fortunately, Pentecost comes to foil human projects which are turned toward the past and reform the structure set up by men.

In our view, Rengstorf does not succeed in showing that this text embarasses Luke. He is equally wrong to situate the entity of the "twelve apostles" in a pre-Easter period. If the narrative has no continuation in Acts, it is because it is unique, as Rengstorf thinks. However, Luke, who has the sense of history, is interested in what is unique: far from contradicting his theology, the account of the election of Matthias is necessary to his concepts of the testimony and the apostolic college [**69**].

g. 4) In 1961, two works appeared almost at the same time. They both know and criticize each other. The first is the work of G. Klein (-> 1961). His project is to find the original setting of the doctrine of the Twelve apostles. A historical investigation, this book has a theological section as well, since it results in the dis - covery of a proto-catholicism within the NT: "So gewiss die Apostel 'früher' als die Kirche sind, sind "die zwölf Apostel" (...) 'später' als die Kirche, nämlich ganz und gar ein Produkt kirchlicher Reflexion" (p. 13): Luke's reflection, he clarifies.

To arrive at this conclusion, the author must nimbly sidestep numerous obstacles. His attack is first directed at K. H. Rengstorf (-> 1933): the conservative consensus, which takes the origin of the apostolate back to the Jewish shaliah and the idea of the Twelve apostles to Jesus himself, does not resist a critical analysis of the Gospels (the usage of the term 'apostle' appears in redactional passages). At this point, Klein is right. However what he calls the critical consensus does not find any more grace in his eyes: if it is correct to say that the Twelve were not apostles in the beginning, but inexact, in his opinion, to confer on Paul a role in the movement of the Twelve toward apostolicity. The writer then arrives at the most contestable part of his book: he attempts to set apart all traces of a doctrine of the Twelve apostles from the Christian literature up to Justin, with the exception of Luke. To do this, he is constrained to abuse texts as explicit as Mk 6:30, Barn 8:3 and Rev 21:14. Klein's goal is simple: to show the originality of Luke, who is declared the ingenious inventor of the theory of the Twelve apostles at the proto-catholic epoch. Luke does this to fight against Gnosticism and to domesticate Paul without abandoning him to the adversaries nor disqualifying him. It is Paul more than the Twelve who will be the center of the rest of the book and the title of the third section is significant: "Das Verhältnis zu Paulus als Schlüssel-Problem für die Frage nach dem Ursprung des Zwölferapostolats". Without always helping the cause they should serve, certain of Klein's discoveries merit our attention. The author indeed demonstrates a keen sense with regard to the Lucan redaction. He first analyzes the Lucan presentation of Saul before his conversion: if Luke avoids the idea that Saul in his person stands out, he highlights on the other hand the exceptional side of his activity. Moreover, he is not content to simply designate Saul <u>in statu persecutoris,</u> he goes on to describe him as such. Like in Paul's epistles, Luke levels his activity as persecutor (?) and accentuates the quality of his Judaism. The apostle to the Gentiles is not at the origin of the image Luke paints of his Jewish existence. We have a great deal of trouble conceding this. Since other influences are hardly discernable, Klein concludes that the Lucan image of Saul is an erratic block (p.143).

The three repetitions of Paul's conversion are not dependent either on the authentic epistles or a personal contact with the apostle [**70**]. Whatever we make of this thesis, Klein correctly remarks that Luke shuns all of Paul's independence with respect to the Church as well as all institutive immediacy with the Risen Lord: "Das lukanische Bild von der Bekehrung des Paulus lässt sich wie folgt zusammenfassen: schlechthin konstitutiv ist die Idee der Mediatisierung. Lukas arbeitet sie konsequent in den gesamten Stoff seiner Darstellung ein, was sich nur deswegen dem ersten Blick verborgen hält, weil er sich dabei variabler Modi der Verschlüsselung bedient. Im ersten Bericht mediatisiert er das Amt des Paulus über einen <u>Menschen</u>, im zweiten ausserdem noch über einen <u>Ort</u>, im dritten über die <u>Zeit</u>." (p. 158f.). We know that these conclusions have been disputed (in particular by S. G. Wilson, cf. above 7, II, h), and, we too admit that Klein sometimes confers a hidden intention to texts perhaps inoffensive. Nevertheless, his general thesis of an important but domesticated Paul in harmony with the Twelve and dependent on them, seems to correspond to the intentions of Luke. Klein shows this with the help of the sections in Acts which evoke the relations of Paul and the Church in Jerusalem.

The author no doubt thinks Luke's proto-catholic ecclesiastical system more developed than it is: with the role of ordination, apostolic succession, consciousness of the universal catholic Church (with Jerusalem as the sedes apostolica). If this was Luke's perspective, Barnabas and Paul would have been ordained in Jerusalem and not in Antioch (Act 13:1-3) and the elders would have been installed in the communities, by the Twelve rather than by Saul (Act 14:23). Less the juridical and canonical aspect of the succession (Klein correctly remarks that Luke is insensitive to hierarchy), it is the pragmatic continuity of the Church, which interests Luke, i.e. the mediation of ministers (more than the ministries), the firm transmission of the message and the canalization of the Spirit.

h. Since it deals less with Luke, W. Schmithals' book (-> 1961) will not hold our attention very long. After having drawn a composite picture of the Pauline apostle (his first section) which corresponds to that of the early Christian apostle (the second part), the author concludes that two conceptions of the apostolate ('apostle' in the narrow sense and in a wider sense) did not exist. The apostles were a relatively restrained group, distinct from the Twelve and from Syria. Schmithals has thus cleared the way for the third part of his book, which finds the origin of the Christian apostolate in Syrian gnosticism. We can neither present nor discuss this thesis here; we send the reader to the often pertinent criticisms of B. Gerhardsson (-> 1962), whose views we share only partially. The last section of the book is closer to our subject (pp. 233-238 on Luke): "Die Übertragung des Apostolats auf die Zwölf und seine Beschränkung auf die Zwölf und Paulus." The writer thinks that it is necessary to distinguish between a first stage where the title apostle was applied to the Twelve and a second during which the title was reserved for the Twelve. This development did not happen uniformly, since we must distinguish various branches in Hellenistic Christianity, in particular a Pauline branch and a Synoptic one. In the one, the apostolate maintains its gnostic characteristic. In the other, the Twelve receive rapidly the title, apostle. Ireneaus regroups these traditions by putting the

Twelve and Paul together: the later Church will follow. Luke did not invent the doctrine of the Twelve, for it emerges simultaneously in different places in early Christianity. For Luke, the task of the apostles is missionary (Act 1:8). Their vocation goes back to the pre-Easter period. They knew Jesus and learned his teaching. Bearers of the Holy Spirit, they dominate the Church. Paul has no authority apart from them, but, against Klein, he is not particularly submitted to them. Luke is uninterested by the principle of apostolic succession.

i. J. Roloff's study (-> 1965) which studies Paul, Luke and the Pastorals, is without a doubt the most complete and most nuanced account concerning the Lucan apostolate. The author begins by refusing an exclusive programmatic value to the election of Matthias. On the one hand, this text is not the only to deal with the apostolate, and on the other hand, it conveys traditional elements which are hardly typical of Luke.

One must begin with the Gospel to witness the election of the Twelve emerging from the disciples (election is not installation), notice their evangelical formation by Jesus and finally, analyze particularly the account of the institution of the Lord's Supper. Roloff underlines that it is here that Jesus, according to Luke, installs the apostles in their function. Two theological motifs appear: the symmetry with the mission of the Son and the choice of a heilsgeschichtlich place and a heilsgeschichtlich time (Jerusalem for the Passion). Lk 22:29 serves as the key to the understanding of the Lucan apostolate. The apostles' mission was to make the covenant sealed by the death of Jesus endure in the Church. They also received the order to live this mission as a *διακονία*.

The accounts of the resurrection (Lk 24) demonstrate how the Christ progressively eliminated the incomprehension of the disciples, an incomprehension willed by God, and how he initiates them to the fullness of the revelation. This latter formation will be continued during the forty days of Act 1.

In the light of what preceded the election of Matthias loses its exceptional character. The apostolate does not lean solely on the participation in the ministry of Jesus and is not imposed in priority by the Scripture, as a superficial reading, disregarding the rest of Lk-Act, might suggest. Act 1:15-26 simply signals that the witnesses of the Resurrected One must also have been the witnesses to the words and works of the earthly Jesus. Willed by the Scripture, the installation of an apostle is above all ordained by Christ.

Roloff thus singularly achieves a rapprochement of the Lucan apostolate and the Pauline version. However, if Luke, differing from Paul, limits to twelve the number of the apostles, it is because he desires to avoid the Gnostic temptation of a decrease of the apostolic level.

Roloff then analyzes the Lucan image of Paul (Luke weaves relations between the Twelve and Paul, avoiding a subordination of the latter and is unconcerned about establishing an apostolic succession). He ends his study with the paragraph, "Die Apostel und die Ämter der werdenden Kirche." We would like to retain the following: at the installation of the Seven, we see the passage from an apostolic ministry to an ecclesiastic one (Luke no doubt conceives of it in the form of ordination); it can be noted as well that the new servants must be formed as the apostles were (Roloff establishes a parallel between the speech in Lk 22 and the one in Act 20). This does not yet signify that Luke is frühkatholisch nor that his concern is juridical. On the contrary, Luke's ecclesiology is closer to Paul's than to the Roman Clement's: the Spirit is not yet submitted to the ministry and the Gospel is not accessible through the institution alone. The elders of Ephesus (Act 20:28) are not the successors of the apostles but the elect of the Kyrios (p. 235).

Let us note for our part, that the elders of Ephesus, according to Act 20:28, were established by the Spirit and not by the Lord, and furthermore, Luke indeed confides the Spirit to the apostles (cf. Act 8 and 19). We thus think that it is difficult to deny an institutional aspect in Luke as well as a certain attraction to the idea of a succession (de facto more than de jure) **[71]**.

The witnesses

j. The notion of the witnesses in the Acts is associated to that of the apostles. With the Twelve, only Paul (Act 22:15; 26:16) and Stephen (Act 22:20) receive this title and have seen the Risen Lord (of course, differently than the Twelve, since it was after the Ascension, Act 22:14; 26:16; 7:55f.).

Several authors have studied this notion of *μάρτυς* in Luke. H. Strathmann (-> 1942) shows that the Lucan usage goes beyond the current use (witness of events where the person was personally present). For the events in question must be believed and proclaimed: "Tatsachenzeuge und Wahrheitszeuge fallen zusammen..." The consequence is that the Gospel is neither a raw fact nor a doctrine, but a historical revelation. It requires elected and qualified witnesses. Lk 24:48

summarizes the specific characteristics of the Lucan witness. Act 13:31 notes that for Luke the testimony of the resurrection rests more on the Twelve than on Paul. Strathmann thinks that the unexpected application of the term μάρτυς for Paul (Act 22:15 and 26:16) and Stephen (Act 22:20) is an indication of a semantic evolution which disintegrates original unity confered by Luke to the concept (for Paul and Stephen are not Tatsachenzeugen (witnesses to the facts), like the Twelve: they can only be Wahrheitszeugen (witnesses to the truth).

k. L. Cerfaux (-> 1943, first title) proposed another distinction: he sets testimony over against kerygma. The testimony, centered on the resurrection of Christ, is given in Jerusalem. It is destined to the Jews and has a juridical character. The Holy Spirit confirms it. The kerygma's contents are more ample (all the life of Jesus) and its destination more universal. A. Rétif (-> 1951) pertinently criticized this distinction. The testimony of the Twelve is more than a testimony concerning the facts in a juridical framework: it is also a witness of faith which is supported by the Scripture. Rétif nonetheless maintains a certain difference between the terms: "kerygma" is the testimony "informed" by a mission.

l. E. Günther (-> 1956) radically distinguishes witness from martyr and thinks he can root the latter (absent in the Acts) in an apocalyptic tradition.

m. As for P. H. Menoud (-> 1960), he insists on the limitation of the title witness to the Twelve, Paul and Stephen in the Acts. The Lucan μάρτυς is more than an eyewitness. Elected and specially formed, the witness is an intermediary between Christ and the Church. He still belongs to the time of the revelation. All those who have seen the Risen Lord and, with greater reason, all believers are not witnesses. In fact, only the Twelve apostles are witnesses. If Matthias, Paul and Stephen become witnesses, it is because they have seen the Christ and received an election and a special preparation. Luke prefers this title to that of apostle, for it is clearer and more decisive. Thus in his work he mentions three main witnesses: Peter, the mouthpiece of the Twelve who testifies to the Jews; Stephen, the witness to the half-Jews; and Paul, to the non-Jews. So the program in Acts 1:8 is fulfilled. With N. Brox, we think that the case of Stephen is the most shaky stone of Menoud's otherwise solid edifice.

n. Despite the title, the article of O. Soffritti (-> 1962) is more interested in the witnesses in general than Stephen in particular. Rightly so, the author refuses to understand Act 22:20 (Stephen, my witness) in the sense of a martyr. The Lucan testimony implies for him, the direct experience of the facts and their scriptural understanding. Invested with a higher authority, the witness is the protector of the evangelical truth. In turn, the Holy Spirit guarantees the testimony, which rests on a vision of the exalted Christ. Stephen indeed fills the conditions in order to be a witness by the sides of the Twelve and Paul. Finally, he notes that God (Act 14:16f.), the Scripture and Christ himself (Act 14:3) witness in their own way.

o. The monograph of N. Brox (-> 1961), despite certain weaknesses, is the most important contribution relative to the Lucan concept of the witness. The author defined his task: to define the NT sense of *μαρτ-* and detect the hazard which led to the signification of martyr in the second century. At the end of his study, he concludes with the conviction that the title of martyr comes neither from philosophical language nor directly from OT or NT traditions, but from a polemical use, first occasionally directed against the Docetics: "Den doketischen Irrlehrern wurde - vielleicht zum ersten Male von Ignatius - das Martyrium der Christen als Beweis für die Leidensfähigkeit Christi und die Tatsächlichkeit seines Leidens vorgehalten." (p. 234).

Our attention will not be drawn to the pages which Brox consecrates to the profane usage of the word witness nor those which treat the popular use among the first Christians. Only Luke and John know a specifically religious usage of the term, a use which moreover varies considerably from one to the other.

Brox first mentions that Luke consciously restrains the number of witnesses (all the eyewitnesses of the Passion are not accredited witnesses in Luke's view). Three conditions are necessary to make a Christian a witness: he must 1) have participated in the life of Jesus and seen him risen; 2) have been chosen and established a witness by the Christ and 3) have received the Holy Spirit. The twelve apostles are then the witnesses par excellence. With regard to later studies, the precisions concerning the election of the witnesses by Christ and the gift of the Spirit are sensible complements to point 1) accepted today by all Biblicists. So far so good.

Paul's case necessarily attracts Brox' attention since Luke twice calls him witness (Act 22:15 and 26:16). What we have is not unreflected uses but the conscious attribution of a prestigious term to the missionary of the Gentiles. Luke judges that Paul has filled the three required conditions: he is thus without restriction an accredited witness.

Brox then expresses his conviction that apostle is a title and witness is not: μάρτυς fills in Luke the functional role which ἀπόστολος holds in writings anterior to early Christianity. This does not mean that the circle of the witnesses is larger than that of the apostles: Paul is a witness, and consequently an apostle (even if the use in Act 14:4 and 14 is due to tradition and a Lucan distraction). Stephen, on the other hand, despite Act 22:20, is not a witness in the strong sense of the word, for Luke nowhere affirms that Stephen fills the three required conditions.

It is here that Brox' work seems disputable: he gives too much to Paul and not enough to Stephen. P. H. Menoud was right to distinguish apostle and witness: Stephen and Paul are both witnesses but they are not apostles.

However, Brox is correct to underline, following Conzelmann, the mediating role of the witnesses. An indispensible link in the historical project of Luke, the witnesses assure the presence of the saving act of God in Jesus Christ in the Church. At this point, the Lucan notion of the testimony with its conjugation in the eschatological and historical separates itself from the other theological interpretation of μάρτυς, John's, to which Brox dedicates the next chapter of his book [**72**].

The other ministries

p. Two reasons explain the renewal of interest that exegetes have given recently to the organization of the primitive Christian communities, an organization in which Luke is less interested than in the missionary success and the extension of the Church [**73**]: first, the discoveries of the Dead Sea Scrolls and then the acuity of the problem in the current ecumenical conjuncture.

Without being worried by the concern of exhaustivity, we have placed in the footnotes, several studies which have both the advantage and inconvenience of essays of synthesis [**74**]. Neither we will linger long over the numerous comparisons between the Essene hierarchy and the early Christian one, for they are historical works which most often neglect the Lucan perspective. Let us simply note that the discoveries of Qumran provided arms for the defenders of the antiquity of ecclesiastical discipline and hierarchy. Yet the interest of the argument is limited, for one must admit that this organization is only valid for the Jewish Christian communities. It should not be taken for granted that the rigidity of this organization is primitive. It may even represent a regression with regard to the instructions of Jesus. For the latter, in short, recommended a community where freedom should reign, limited by love and an authority founded on a redistribution of power. The first community in Jerusalem could respect this heritage and underwent no Jewish influence except in a formal or secondary manner, which can now be verified. Some suppose, but it is not sure, that the Pauline communities were organized according to Jewish models. Thus the relation between the early Church and Qumran is not "biological" and the organization of the early Church, as we can now discern it, is not necessarily normative for the contemporary communities.

Of the articles we read concerning this subject [**75**], the most balanced remains one of the first which appeared, B. Reicke's (-> 1954). The NT furnishes indications in favor of a varied ecclesiastical organization: we meet monarchical, oligarchical and democratic aspects. The book of Acts especially insists on the various collegial authorities (the Twelve apostles, the Seven and the elders), but it does not ignore the authority which the whole community enjoyed: in Judaism, 120 were necessary for the election of a member of the Sanhedrin; if 120 people are noted in Act 1:15, it is so that Matthias' election be juridically valid. The presence of the entire community, according to Act 15:22, gives the decisions of the Jerusalem council the strength of law. Finally, in one or two texts, Peter or James appear to act like monarchical princes of the Church. Thus in primitive Christianity we encounter an organization of authority which gives the force of law to the decisions made with accord of the people, who have *different* rights: a group of leaders and, below them, the whole of the community which is conscious of its unity. Therefore, we are far from the Greek system, according to which an assembly can validly legislate only if all the members have the *equal* rights. Reicke's effort consists in showing that this operation of authority in early Christianity, which surprises the heirs of a Greek democratic system, which we are, corresponds to oriental and particularly Jewish customs. It is here that the study of the texts from Qumran, mainly the *Rule of the Community* and the *Damascus Document*, intervene. The author finds again in Qumran this mixture of strict hierarchy and communitarian spirit. By what must be called a miracle of the Holy Spirit, the opinion of the leaders corresponds to the intentions of the community. If only it was still this way in our Churches! - we might add.

Before specifying the nature of the local ministry in the book of Acts, that of the elders, let us first mention several other functions (we hesitate to call them ministries).

The Seven

q. In our presentation of Stephen, we already indicated research's hesitation concerning the Seven [76]. In Act 6:1-6 do we have an installation of the Seven to a ministry which still exists at the time of Luke, or is it simply an occasional disposition? Should we see the Seven as deacons, like Ireneaus and a long exegetical tradition? Or must we recognize in these men, the first elders of the Jerusalem community? C. Bridel (-> 1971) clearly presents the arguments in favor of the many options and summarizes the positions of several contemporary exegetes [77]. As for us, we think that Luke has in mind a ministry peculiar to the first community. This ministry is not meant to last. Yet the type of election and installation which proceeds the placement of the Seven remains normative in his eyes. It will be confirmed by the installation of the elders in the Pauline commmunities in the Acts. No doubt one must consider the tension between the Lucan redaction, which insists on the diaconal function of the Seven, and the tradition which leans on the historical importance of the Seven as leaders of the Hellenistic branch of early Christianity.

The Prophets

r. The Acts mention on several occasions the activity of Christian prophets. E. E. Ellis (-> 1970) who analyzes these reports comes to the following results: if he sometimes accords the gift of prophecy to simple disciples (Act 2:4, 11, 17f.; 19:6 and 9:10), Luke applies the term prophet, most often in a restrictive sense, to a certain number of leaders in the communities: a group of prophets from Jerusalem visiting Antioch (Act 11:27f.); another group resides in Antioch (Act 13:1); Judas and Silas (Act 15:22, 32). Peter in several passages where he is not called apostle has the traits of a prophet (Act 5:3; 8:12f.; 10:10). Finally, the four daughters of Philip are prophetesses (Act 21:9).

The prophet in Acts often resembles the OT prophet and fulfills divers missions. He intervenes in a concrete situation with a symbolic act (Act 21:11) or, more often, with a word. His intervention bears on the future which he predicts (Act 11:21; 20:23, 25; 27:22), the present which he judges in the name of God (Act 13:11; 28:25-28) or the past of the Scriptures or Jesus which he explains. His activity is summarized in the verb: *παρακαλέω*.

It is difficult to situate the prophet with regard to the other ministries and Luke hardly worries about dissipating a certain haze. Since Jesus is both prophet and teacher in the Gospel (Lk 7:39f.; 6:6 and 13:10), filled with authority and wisdom, the prophet in the Acts often fulfills an educative role (Ellis does not seem to share H. Schürmann's view (-> 1962), according to which Luke mistrusts teachers). If it is fitting to distinguish the prophets from the elders, it is nonetheless necessary to note that they both accomplish a teaching chore. The most important ministerial difference concerns the apostles: an apostle can, like Peter, accomplish a prophetic mission; the prophet on the other hand, cannot become apostle.

In short, the Christian prophet is the instrument of the Lord, one of the ways, he leads his Church [**78**].

The Elders

s. It is clearly difficult to imagine the place Luke gives to teachers and evangelists in his ecclesiology. He mentions both of them but once (Act 13:1: teachers and Act 21:8: evangelist, concerning Philip). Should one then think that he mistrusts the teachers whose ideas might become subversive and thus prefers elders (H. Schürmann, -> 1962)? Even if we accept É. Trocmé's thesis (-> 1969) for whom the extension of the Church in Luke is more important than the organization of the communities, it is queer to note that the title 'evangelist' appears but one time. Without a doubt, Luke wants to tell the story of the missionary activity of the <u>first</u> missionaries: so he gives them the title, witnesses or apostles.

The elders of Jerusalem appear suddenly in Act 11 and Luke makes no effort to describe their installation (no editorial indica - tion, in our opinion, permits us to identify them with the Seven). With G. Bornkamm (-> 1959), we see them in Act 11:30 and 21:18 as the local authority (here there is synagogal influence), presided by James after the apostles' departure. On the other hand, the professor from Heidelberg thinks that in Act 15 and 16, the apostles and the elders form a college and serve as a counterpart to the Sanhedrin: "oberster Gerichtshof und massgebliche Lehrinstanz für die Gesamtkirche" (p. 663). He judges that what we have here is a judaizing of the ecclesiastical organization with the disappearance of the Twelve. The presbyterian system, first influenced by the organization of the synagogue then the Sanhedrin, exists at Luke's time in Palestinian Christianity and begins to be implanted in the communities of the Diaspora under the pres - sure of Hellenistic Judaism. This system progressively competes with the Pauline principle of the multiplicity of gifts and slowly but surely installs a firm tradition confided to the guarantors, who lead the community. As Luke mentions the elders in the Pauline communities (cf. Act 14:23 and 20:17-38), we can think that the evangelist endeavors to bring the presbyterian system closer to the episcopal system, known from Phil 1:1 **[79]**.

Our project is not to study historically the birth of the presby - terian system, but to set the limits of its role in the communities presented by Luke. This is why we shall leave aside the work of A. Lemaire (-> 1971) whose historical interest is evident, but remains overshadowed by traditional information with loss to the redactional intention of Luke. The author concludes from his analysis of Acts that in the early Church, two sorts of ministries existed: the general ministry, missionary and itinerant (the Twelve, the Seven, then the other missionaries going two by two, accompanied by servants. The titles used for them are apostles, then prophets, teachers and finally evangelists) and local ministries of the elders, leaders and representatives of the community **[80]**.

Today we can distinguish three interpretations of the ministry of the elders which Luke mentions:

1) Luke points out the existence of the group of the elders, but personally maintains a flexible, functional, and charismatic concept of ecclesiastic organization (E. Schweizer, -> 1959).

2) Representing Frühkatholizismus, Luke defends the unity of the universal Church which he defines as a fixed heirarchical organization. He holds that the elders were installed by the apostles or Paul. This traditional Catholic position has found support in men like E. Käsemann (-> 1960) **[81]** and G. Klein (-> 1961) **[82]**, who of course denounce this ministerial concretion, contrary to Paul and, all the while, note that Luke insists more on continuity than on hierarchy.

3) Catholic exegetes like H. Schürmann (-> 1962) **[83]**, H. J. Michel (-> 1973) **[84]** and A. George (-> 1974) **[85]** propose a middle way which seems more respectful of the texts and the ecclesiastic situation of Luke's era. At the risk of being schematic, we can summarize it in the following manner: conscious of the time which has passed since the apostles, Luke is convinced that the word of God and the Spirit of the Lord do

not exclude the responsibility of the Christian, whose mission is to protect the tradition against betrayal. This responsibility is realized in the determining of an evangelical doctrine and the organization of the communities. The role of the first witnesses (the Twelve and Paul) was decisive for the fixing of the tradition like for the constitution of the ministries: for Luke, they had the wisdom to transmit faithfully the message and install men who could be relied upon. Having said this, it would be wrong to think that Luke speculated on the powers of these leaders and their juridical status. The Evangelist mentions the laying on of hands but does not confer the value of a sacrament of order to this gest. Neither does Luke seem to be any more preoccupied by the conception of the apostolic succession [86].

Discipline

t. We thought we would find several studies concerning ecclesiastic discipline. In fact, this was to create false hopes, for Luke is more interested in the communities' success than in the problems which require the application of a rigorous discipline. The only texts which mention disciplinary interventions are Act 3:23, in the form a prophecy, Act 5:1-11, Ananias and Sapphira, and Act 8:18-24, the attempt of Simon the magician.

C. M. Martini (-> 1969) considers Act 3:23 in the Lucan perspective ("And every person who does not listen to this prophecy will be cut off from the people."). He comes to the con - clusion that this verse, an OT quotation forcefully reworked by Luke, has important redactional import. But it deals with the mission to the Jews rather than ecclesiastic discipline. Having described the success of the evangelical proclamation in the first chapters of Acts, Luke notes that the plan of God, as Deuteronomy (18:19) presents it, foresaw the Jewish opposition to Jesus Christ, an opposition which will emerge from Act 4 on. To be cut off from the people does not signify to die physically (the death of Ananias and Sapphira is not an accomplishment of this prophecy) but - which is even more serious - to lose the heritage of Abraham, the messianic blessings, the gift of the Spirit, in short, salvation. Luke thus redefines the notion of the people of God.

u. The condemnation of Ananias and Sapphira has roused three principle treatments. In the Mélanges offered to Maurice Goguel, P. H. Menoud (-> 1950) attempted to show that this ac - count was born as the result of a crisis in the early community: because of the doctrine of the new life in Christ, the death of the first Christians must have caused problems. To explain this death, Christian reflection imagined a fault which could explain it. Professor Menoud's solution seems improbable to us, for it presupposes a primitive Christianity affected by an enthusiasm which is not attested in our texts.

v. J. Schmitt's study (-> 1957) seems to be more convincing. It highlights the archaic allure of the narrative which reflects a Judeo-Christian organization, inspired by the commandments of the Law and related to the communal discipline of Qumran. This account of Scriptural inspiration evokes the extermination of the sinner (cf. Lev 7:20f.) and the intimidation of the people at the sight of the guilty one punished (cf. Dt 13:11). Its objective is "to contribute to the formation of the faithful to the main requirements of communal life." (p. 103).

w. If J. Schmitt insists on the sense which this account had in the catechetical tradition of the primitive community, P. B. Brown, in his dissertation manuscript, which we know of by a summary in **Dissertation Abstracts** (-> 1970), analyzes the function of Act 5:1-11 in the economy of the Acts. In his opinion, Luke inserts this narrative not because of interest for ecclesiastic discipline but because of the attention he gives to the Holy Spirit in his relations with the Church. The moral fault and death of the couple as well as the intervention of Peter are not the main elements in his view. "In short, from Lukan perspective, Ananias' and Sapphira's sin is the veritable denial of the existence of the Holy Spirit in the Christian community." (p. 4531 A). The agent who communicates the Gospel today is neither an active mystical Jesus nor an ecclesi-astical structure, but the Holy Spirit. Act 5:1-11 manifests the presence of the Spirit in the community and his lordship over the Church. It would be necessary to read the entire thesis to know if the author, in a non-Lucan manner, sets the intervention of the Spirit over against the activity of the witnesses and ministers [87].

3) Worship and sacraments [88]

a. In the flood of recent publications, certain contributions concerning the worship in the Acts of the Apostles must have escaped us. Since the older works of O. Cullmann (-> 1944) and P. H. Menoud (-> 1952, first title), we have identified only a few articles which, furthermore, are interested in Acts only in an occasional way. A. Cabaniss (-> 1957) thinks that with other ancient witnesses, the Acts supposes a <u>nocturnal</u> practice of the first Christian worship services. W. Rordorf (-> 1964, first title) is interested in the first rooms of service. If the places of evangelization vary, the locations where the Eucharistic ceremonies were celebrated must have been quickly fixed . For him, the Acts testify to this attachment to house churches. John Mark's, for example (Act 12:12), served as the first meeting place of the Christian community. It had a court or a porch (*πυλών*, Act 12:13f.) and an upper room. One could enter directly from the street. Act 12:17 specifies that there were other Christian meeting places in Jerusalem and apparently, even more in the various cities where Christian communities were established.

B. Morel (-> 1962) begins with an analysis of Act 20:7-12 to distinguish two parts of the first Christian services as Luke presents them: the word related to the Scripture, seen here in the speech of Paul before the fall of Eutychus, and the breaking of the bread which was reserved for the members of the community which we see following the accident. The author then proposes the following hypothesis: the fate of Eutychus, who falls dead and then is raised up living is not without an analogical rapport with the movement of the Easter liturgy which goes from the death to the resurrection of Christ. The contrast night-light would theoretically confirm this idea.

Baptism

b. The interest of theologians for the origin of Christian baptism has not weakened, as is evident in consulting the bibliography of A. J. and M. B. Matill [89]. On the other hand, we can count of our fingers the works relative to Chirstian baptism as Luke conceives and describes it. Moreover, they are more interested in the tradition than the redaction.

As the title of his contribution indicates, E. Barnikol (-> 1956-1957) thinks that the sources of the Acts were unaware of a baptism of water and knew only of the baptismal outpouring of Spirit. It is Luke who introduced the numerous baptisms in his description of the first communities to offer an apostolic basis to the sacramental practice of his time. This redactional effort was fed by a double polemic: against those who saw in baptism, a simple gest of penitence and against those who appealed to the only baptism of the Spirit. This hypothesis of a primitive Christianity hostile to ritualism which is superseded by a Church favorable to sacraments is unlikely. Appearing in the nineteenth century, this conception corresponds more to the aspirations of a certain spiritualizing Protestantism than to historical reality.

Moreover, the source criticism which Barnikol practices is arbitrary and outdated.

c. In his book on baptism, G. R. Beasley-Murray (-> 1963) gives his attention to Rom 6. However, he does consecrate a chapter to what he calls "The Emergence of Christian Baptism: The Acts of the Apostles" (pp. 93-122). In these pages, he attacks precisely the thesis of a primitive Christianity hostile to rites. Even if the Acts do not note the baptism of the apostles or Apollos', it seems evident that the very first community practiced Christian baptism from the beginning. The witness of the Pauline epistles is indisputable at this point. The baptism of the converts at the day of Pentecost is far from being improbable. "Whether or not Luke's sources imply a development of thought on the nature of baptism it is doubtful that they imply a development in the practice of baptism, from its disuse to its application in the churches." (p. 95). Luke's doctrinal development is not very advanced, for compared to Paul's baptismal theology, the Lucan conception of the sacraments is still primitive: the baptism is confered in the name of Jesus and not, as in Mt 28:19, in the name of the Father, Son and Holy Spirit. The idea of participation in the death and resurrection of Christ (Rom 6) is absent in the Lucan texts.

Beasley-Murray of course analyzes the formula in the name of Jesus Christ or in the name of the Lord Jesus (Act 2:38; 8:16; 10:48 and 19:5). He leans toward the interpretation of the transfer of the authority of Christ [90] to the believer.

This baptism of the Acts was conceived as an act of God and an act of man. One fact will attest this: the invocation in the name of Jesus was probably pronounced by baptizer and by the one baptized. Here the rite receives its full signification from the person of Jesus and the relation it establishes with him.

Baptism refers to salvation through the name of Jesus and the preaching of this name. It is the sacrament of the good news, proclaimed and received. The Lord, who takes possession of the newly baptized, accords him privileges: he takes away his sins, incorporates him into the messianic people and offers him the Holy Spirit.

The author terminates this chapter with an analysis of the ties which link baptism and the Holy Spirit. He takes up one by one the texts which we have analyzed in our excursus on the laying on of hands [91]. He tends to distinguish (without dissociating) the effusion of the Holy Spirit from the rite. When he brings them near, he attaches the Holy Spirit - wrongly, in our opinion - to baptism rather than to the imposition of hands [92].

In our opinion, many questions still remain [**93**]. Why has Luke not been influenced by the Pauline view of baptism? Can Luke as historian describe a rite which as a theologian of his time, he can no longer tolerate as such? Is it not more probable to think that the Pauline conception comes from an isolated thinker and that Luke's reflects a more widespread practice (A. Benoit has shown that the second century did not know Paul's position) [**94**]? Yet it would be inexact to say that the Lucan description of baptism fits with no problem into the perspective of the Church at the end of the first century, for there was not only one conception of baptism nor only one practice. Luke normally relates the gift of the Spirit to the laying on of hands, and forgiveness and the invocation of the name to baptism. This is hardly attested by other texts of the end of the first century. The symbolism of this conception is easily understood: life follows death. Finally, it would be erroneous to infer a purely symbolic conception of the sacraments from the dissociations, which Luke makes between the gift of the Spirit and the rite. We rather perceive a realism which finds its explanation in the Lucan theology of the mediations.

The Lord's Supper

d. Many years have passed since H. Lietzmann [**95**] matched the Palestinian information of the Acts (a joyful meal which extended the fellowship of Jesus and his disciples in the expectation of the Kingdom) against the Greek convictions of the apostle, Paul (the Eucharist as a memorial of the death and resurrection of Jesus). G. S. Sloyan (-> 1961) took up these arguments and came to the following conviction: "Much of Lietzmann's theorizing fell with the researches of the last three decades, which provide enough Semitic background for every element in Paul's eucharistic teaching to establish it as a possible genuine Aramaic tradition that he had got 'from the Lord', that is, from Palestinian communities." Consequently, the solution which obtrudes itself is a unique primitive tradition with two distinct emphases, anchored in the intervention of Jesus at the last supper (the eucharistic prayer itself was not conserved). "On the basis of the NT itself it can be held that the tradition which Paul received and passed along to the Corinthians was fully in spirit of the first layer of gospel tradition, and was both eschatological and joyous despite its reference to the supper and the redemptive death..." (p. 12).

Concerning the Lucan interpretation of the breaking of bread mentioned, we now have four studies from P. H. Menoud (-> 1953), E. C. Davis (-> 1967), B. Trémel (-> 1969) and J. Wanke (-> 1973) [**96**].

e. Having noted that Luke does not use the specific terms of the ancient Christian literature to evoke the Supper (the meal of the Lord, the Eucharist, etc.), P. H. Menoud (-> 1953) analyzes the Lucan texts which mention a breaking of bread or a prepared table. What defines the Church in the first summary (Act 2:42 and 46) is not the meal - everyone eats - but the eucharistic meal: this is the meaning of the expression the "breaking of bread". Yet this Eucharist was celebrated during a real meal. That the breaking of bread in vs. 46 precedes the meal in the syntax does not signify that the former preceded the latter in reality. It is even probable that the opposite is true. The fraction is mentioned first in vs. 46 because of its theological and spiritual priority.

To set the table in Act 16:34 (following the baptism of the Philippian jailer), as in Act 6:2, is to prepare a eucharistic meal. Associated with baptism, this Eucharist was celebrated in joy. This *ἀγαλλίασις*, in Act 2:46, evokes the eschatological nature of the meal. The expression "to set the table" allowed Christians to designate their holy meal in covert manner. Why the discretion? Was it because of the discipline of the arcana? Or because the Christians distinguished themselves, by their weekly sacred meals, from the Jews who celebrated their Passover annually?

It is the first day of the week that is mentioned in Act 20:7-11 (the incident with Eutychus). For Luke, there is nothing extraordinary in this dominical meeting for the breaking of bread. Whether it is Saturday or Sunday is of little import, what matters is the nocturnal character of the meeting, to which is intentionally contrasted the profusion of lamps. Here the Eucharist precedes the agape (the practices must have varied from one region to the other).

Following B. Reicke (-> 1948), P. H. Menoud thinks that the meal ordained by Paul during the storm was not ordinary. Without identifying it as the Eucharist (the sailors and soldiers were not Christian), the author gives it a religious import because of the *σωτηρία*, the salvation (a term voluntarily ambiguous), which results.

Menoud concludes as a historian rather than theologian: the mention of the Supper, which are voluntarily imprecise, are found in the oldest texts of Acts. They evoke the Jerusalem type of Eucharist (Menoud maintains Lietzmann's distinction). In the presentation of his 1952 book [**97**], Menoud insists more on the religious and theological sense of the Supper: the Eucharist, whose existence is necessary between Easter and the Parousia, recalls the last supper of Jesus before his death and the meal the Lord ate with his disciples after his resurrection (Luke underlines this Easter fellowship). By its joy, it anticipates the eschatological banquet.

f. The dissertation manuscript of E. C. Davis (-> 1967) is known to us only by the summary in **Dissertation Abstracts.** It is an analysis of all the meals mentioned in Luke's work. For the author, Luke conceives the actual meals in the perspective, inherited from Judaism, of the apocalyptic feast. Jesus' meals with the marginals of the Jewish society actualized the banquet of the Kingdom and at the same time reveal the Messiah to those who want to receive him. The same dominating eschatological idea is found again in the meal of Jesus with his disciples. Having signaled that at a redactional level, the parables and the teaching of Jesus insist on the meals, E. C. Davis comes to the meals mentioned in Acts. The communion of the first Christians also anticipates the joy of the banquet of the Kingdom. The writer nevertheless indicates the evolution of the participants at this supper: they are first Judeo-Christians, then Christians from Judaism and paganism and, finally, a Gentile Christian community.

By transforming in this way the Jewish theology of the eschatological feast, Luke developes his theology of the continuity (and could we add of the presence?). This doctrinal position helps the Evangelist to resolve two main problems: the delay of the Parousia and the annexation of the Gentiles to the Church.

One should read the whole thesis to see how the author distinguishes and relates the meals of Jesus with the crowds and those with the disciples. Does Luke put them all on the same level of anticipation of the Kingdom? Furthermore, does the Lucan perspective of salvation history not better distinguish the meanings of the meals which punctuate the earthly ministry of Jesus and those which mark the life of the Church?

g. Father Trémel (-> 1969) studies the allusions along with the explicit texts. Act 2:42 and 46 are made to carry the accent of perseverance and joy. According to Act 20:7-12 and with B. Morel (-> 1962) and J. Wanke (-> 1973), the resurrection of Eutychus symbolizes what the breaking of bread produces effectively. Act 27:35 places the salvation of the crew in relation with the food eaten liturgically. Among the numerous allusions,

Act 16:34 (the set table) and 9:19 (the food eaten) must be included. These texts confirm the link between the reestablishment and the Eucharistic meal. At the editorial level, "between the last meal of Jesus, the breaking of bread in Jerusalem and that of the Churches in the Greco-Roman world, there is continuity of a tradition, a tradition he [Luke] evokes in his prologue (Lk 1:1-4)." (p. 82). Luke seems to reproduce faithfully traditions which did not separate the two types of meals. The breaking of bread has the same meaning: next to the proclamation of the word, this action is constituitive for the Church (it is "at the heart of this 'communion' which is the whole Church of God", p. 85); it is also the source as well as the term of the universal mission. Retaining its eschatological angle, it also invites us to understand the power of Christ at work. Now, the account of the disciples of Emmaus witnesses to this lordly presence in the Supper. "Thus the fraction of the bread appears intimately linked to a period of the Church when the presence of Christ is experienced as both a gift of the eschatological life and as a requirement of fraternal communion." (p. 89).

h. If the heilsgeschichtlich continuity brings B. Trémel close to Davis, the theme of the saving presence situates the professor from Fribourg (Switzerland) close to J. Wanke. The latter in an excellent little book (-> 1973) deals amply and precisely with the theme of the Eucharist, limited to the Lucan redaction alone. He successively analyzes 1) the meals in the Acts and the Eucharistic allusions (pp. 11-30); 2) the meal at Emmaus (pp. 31-44); 3) the Eucharistic connotations in the Gospel of Luke (pp. 45-59); and 4) the account of the Supper and its context (Lk 22:7-38) (pp. 60-65). He does seem to contradict himself at least once (p. 15 and p. 17 concerning the daily or weekly frequency of the meals widened into the Eucharist) and here and there, his redactional analysis vacillates with hypersensitivity (especially in ch 4, where Judah and Peter take on a typological stature, the parenetic virtue of which is far from evident). However, this does not hinder Wanke from being right in at least one or two of his theses: 1) the redactional framework of several narratives testify to the salvific virtue that Luke attributes, if not to the breakings of bread, then to the Lord they point to (this thesis was already sketched out by B. Trémel); 2) Luke distinguishes the fraction of the bread from the meal itself but does not separate the two realities: at regular intervals, the meals terminate with the liturgical breaking of bread (in this term the presence of the cup is also included); 3) the principal thesis is less evident for us: the fraction of bread, especially because of the context Luke regularly places it in, refers less to the Passion of Jesus or the Parousia (despite the "joy" which accompanied the meals) than to the active presence of the Savior. Is it because J. Wanke and B. Trémel are Catholic or is it the content of the Lucan texts which lead the two to the same conclusion: the presence of the Lord in the communion? We would say that the account of Emmaus orients our thinking in this direction, but it is to reveal the absence as much as the presence of the Risen Lord. The liturgical meals are the substitutes as well as the supports of the presence of the Lord. They attest to a mediated presence [98].

IV. THE ETHICS OF THE COMMUNITY

a. The NT ethics which we consulted [99], H. Preisker's, R. Schnackenburg's and H. D. Wendland's are little interested in the moral teaching of Luke. Only the work of T.W. Manson (-> 1960) offers a few stimulating pages. In ch 5 of his **Ethics and the Gospel**, the Scottish exegete analyzes the beginning of the Acts. According to Act 1, the apostles follow in the steps of Jesus: they exercise their authority in service; Act 2:42 enumerates the four elements of the Christian life: the faithfulness of the nascent Church to teaching, communion and prayer reminds us of the Jewish ethic of a Simon the Just who declares that the Torah, the mutual affection and adoration of God are the three pillars of piety. These four elements (Act 2:42) mark the life of the community and are found throughout the first chapters of the Acts. As the Christian community carries on, it is distinguished from the synagogue, the religious associations which flourish and then from the second century Church. It claims to live as the people of God in full exercise of its communitarian activities. Refusing to be a closed circle of believers, a saved remnant, the first community was above all, by its missionary activity a saving remnant. Nonetheless little by little the teaching of Jesus received a new coloration: it becomes the carta of the community. The gaze turns toward the interior of the Church and eschatology yields to ethics.

b. The monographs consecrated to Lucan theology as a whole grant little place to the ethics of the one the NT introductions call "social". H. Conzelmann (-> 1954, pp. 217-219) briefly notes that Lucan ethics are born and develope logically from an eschatology which is historicized. I. H. Marshall (-> 1970) offers a chapter called "What must I do to be saved?" (pp. 188-215). He tarries over repentence, faith and conversion before aligning the expected references on prayer, the fraction of bread, the sharing of goods and persecution. The originality of his presentation is that the moral life, for Luke, is determined by the action of the Holy Spirit in the Church. J. Jervell (-> 1971) wrote an article concerning the Law in Luke. Yet it is to emphasize the ecclesiological and not ethical connotation (cf. above 7, II, g). In his work with an exaggerated typological schematization, M. D. Goulder (-> 1964) believes he discovers a recurrent structure in the third gospel and the book of the Acts. He entitles it thanatos-anastasis. Jesus as much as the disciples and believers go through life, which from election leads to the resurrection through a suffering ministry. Without being directly consecrated to the ethics of the believers, one chapter of H. Flender's book (-> 1965) offers an interesting new position. Refusing to lock up the message of Jesus in a religious and transcendent shell, disconnected from social engagement, Flender shows how Luke attempts to do justice to the absolute of the demand which refers to the kingdom and the fragmentary and contingent fulfillment, which is bent on remaining concrete. It is what he calls "das Eingehen der Christusbotschaft in die weltlichen Ordnungen" (pp. 69-83) [**100**]. The German exegete has put his finger on the conscious effort of Luke who does not want to let go of the faithfulness to the message he received nor the present responsibility.

If we lack a general study, which shows in particular, the roots of the Lucan ethic in the homologesis, we must mention several articles and monographs which scrutinize one aspect or another. Perseverance, detachment from material goods, the brotherly communion and prayer have all retained the attention of the exegetes [**101**].

1) Perseverance

a. More than twenty years ago, P. H. Menoud clearly set forth for the sisters of the Grandchamp community the content of the Christian life (-> 1952, first title). He did this with a historical, theological and spiritual exegesis of Act 2:42 which led him to summarize the ethics of the first Christians as a quadruple perseverance. According to the Acts, it is necessary to persevere in the cultic life as well as in practice which fulfills the requirements formulated by the liturgy. The four chapters of his well-known opuscule successively deal with each of the forms of Christian perseverance: perseverance in the apostolic teaching (a deepening of the initial predication destined for believers); perseverance in communion (one should understand this in the wide sense of communion with the apostles, fraternal communion in Christ and sharing in the material domain); perseverance in the breaking of bread (the Eucharist, food for the salvation of believers, took place within a real meal) and perseverance in prayer (by prayer, the first Christians accepted with thanksgiving the place God assigned them in the history of redemption. Prayers were not confined to the Eucharistic service and were not limited to requests).

b. From the Gospel of Luke (Lk 8:13, 15) and the terms *πειρασμός* and *ὑπομονή*, L. Cerfaux (-> 1957) approaches the theme of perseverance and by it, Lucan ethics. The result of his investigation confirms H. Conzelmann's position: *πειρασμός* (Lk 8:13) no longer designates exclusively the great final persecution but all trials of the Christian life. We thus assist in a "sliding of Christian thought which mitigates eschatology, or rather introduces into eschatology - without transforming it [**102**] - a new element, that of a Christian life lived out until death in a bearable environment for the faithful." (p. 119). Ἡ *ὑπομονή* underwent a parallel evolution: the term no longer designates in Luke the constancy in the final trial, but the perseverance in the midst of tribulations of all sorts (cf. the well-known redactional addition of "every day" in Jesus' saying concerning the bearing of the cross, Lk 9:23) [**103**]. His conclusion is optimistic: while remaining faithful to the words of Jesus, Luke adapts them to a situation of the evolving Church. From our point of view, it would be good once and for all to establish the criteria which permit us to speak of a legitimate adaptation. Too often we have the impression that the exegetes accept the Lucan adaptations when, for the Catholics, they fit into a harmonious evolution of the thought and Christian morals and, if the exegete is Protestant, in the framework of the canon. Could it be that the "every day" of Luke removed the radicality of Jesus' demand and helps us sidestep the obstacle of absolute obedience? The martyrs must have heard the voice of Jesus rather than Luke's, for we venerate them and not the bourgeois Christians who tranquilly bear their cross of the difficulties of daily life. It seems to us that Luke did not hear the rigor of the call and did not prolongate it into the continuity of daily existence.

c. The extract of the thesis of Father Ortiz Valdivieso (-> 1969), written in Spanish, contains a good bibliography concerning per-severance (in particular, C. Spicq, **RScPhil** 19

(1930) 95-106; A. M. Festugière, **RechSR** 21 (1931) 477-486; F. Hauck, **TWNT** 4, 1942, pp. 585-593; and P. Goicoechea, a dissertation at the Antonianum (Rome, 1965), on *ὑπομονή* in Paul). In twenty pages, the author summarizes the first three chapters of his dissertation manuscript (*ὑπομονή* in Greece, in the LXX and the Jewish literature). He then presents the integral text of his study of *ὑπομονή* in the NT. We will draw out the analysis of the two Lucan texts (Lk 8:15 and 21:19) [**104**].

Concerning Lk 8:15 (pp. 28-34), he says: the fourth category of auditors, the believers, are opposed to each of the precedent: thus the *ὑπομονή* of the believers is contrasted with the short-lived and easily shaken faith of the second group (vs. 13). This *ὑπομονή* has thus to do with faith (we think this is an important remark which brings Luke close to Paul, for whom *πίστις* is also an *ὑπακοή*). The trial in vs. 13 is not eschatological (Luke does not speak of *θλίψεις* in these verses). It designates the satanic activity in the life of believers. To face up to this, faith is manifested in a particular attitude: the author is right to conceive of this *ὑπομονή* not as an expectation or constancy but as the perseverance of the one who endures with steadfastness. Ortiz Valdivieso introduces here the notion of strength: *ὑπομονή* gives strength to faith so that it does not vascillate. This force has the effect which Luke calls "fruit" (*καρποφορέω*), without specifying its nature [**105**].

Lk 21:19 (pp. 34-37) uses an expression unknown to the LXX and the rest of the NT: "to save his soul". Luke expresses this not as the promise of a rescue in extremis, but as the evangelical paradox: by losing oneself, one finds himself [**106**]. The *ὑπομονή*, through which one saves himself, is associated here with eternal life which the believer attains by accepting persecutions. Thus we witness to a certain de-eschatologization (Luke suppresses the "until the end" of Mk 13:13), but the ethical accent does not eliminate all eschatological coloring (against Conzelmann -> 1954, p. 211 note 1 and p. 217).

In short, *ὑπομονή* for Luke, is the virtue of the believers who must "hold out" during the long period which continues until the Parousia. For the author, Lk 8:15 and 21:19, isolated texts in the Synoptic tradition, reveal a reflected and posterior theological perspective.

On the whole, the comments of Ortiz Valdivieso seem pertinent to us. However, we wonder why Luke, if he thinks the *ὑπομονή* is typical of Christian ethic, uses this term so little. There is not a doubt that he resorts to other expressions like *καρτερέω*. We think a study of the Lucan ethic must be conducted differently and should not be limited to an isolated analysis of any one virtue.

d. From this point of view, S. Brown's book (-> 1969) is not entirely satisfying, for it often lingers on the polemic with Conzel - mann to no great profit. Furthermore it is a rather curious construction. The title **Apostasy and Perseverance in the Theology of Luke** is inadequate, for the two first sections deal with *πειρασμός* and the Lucan qualification of the blessed time in which Satan does not intervene (as we know that Satan withdraws in Lk 4:13 and reappears on the eve of the Passion, Lk 22:3). Despite the arguments of Brown for whom Satan continues his activity during this period (does not Act 10:38 say that Jesus snatched men from Satan during his earthly ministry?), Conzelmann put his finger on an important redactional particularity. Between Lk 4:13 and Lk 22:3, Satan no longer attacks Jesus. This truce even has beneficial effects on the disciples who, at a loss, will be able to exercise their mission without running any danger (from the Passion on, they will need to be equipped, since Jesus will again be attacked by the devil: this is the reason for the redactional verses concerning the swords, Lk 22:35-38).

Let us see the development a bit closer. The first part defines the meaning of *πειρασμός* (the author, who wants to account for the philological level, constantly makes incursions into biblical theology, which provokes ambiguities and misconceptions).

Luke - this is the thesis set forth against Conzelmann in the first section - does not give *πειρασμός* the usual NT meaning, a sense inherited from the LXX. *Πειρασμός* is the trial to which apostates succomb. Believers are confronted with *θλίψεις* which they go through successfully! If the temptations of Jesus by Satan are called *πειρασμοί* it is exceptional! We have a Messianic temptation overcome successfully . The *πειρασμοί* that Jesus had to go through, according to Lk 22:28, were of human, not diabolic, origin. The Passion of Jesus is not a new *πειρασμός* (against Conzelmann). Furthermore, the time of the Church is not the time of the *πειρασμοί* of the believers (still against Conzelmann). This part seems laborious to us and of limited interest: the usage of an isolated word is not sufficiantly revealing; only the meanings of several expressions and the realities they manifest count. Perhaps Luke does not call the tribulations which await believers *πειρασμοί* (Conzelmann is no doubt wrong), but he certainly thinks that the Church will suffer (Conzelmann is right). This is what is important.

The same fault is found again in the second part: the author interests himself excessively in what Luke omits: the habitual semantic field of πειρασμός in the NT. The oscillations of desire and the inclination to coveting hardly interest Luke (yet the role Luke confers on the "heart" and the διαλογισμοί, which preoccupy him, should be emphasized). According to Brown, the Evangelist projects the dangers and temptations in exteriority (could this not be for reasons of literary genre rather than theological?). Lucan ethics thus become ethics of the act, rather than the intention. It is clear that Luke does not associate the term πειρασμός with the idea of a valorizing trial imposed upon Christians and yet the Acts describes narratively the trial of Paul which is overcome in faith and faithfulness (cf. especially Act 27).

Passing again from the philological to theological level - this fluctuation is tiring - the author places an *excursus* here con-cerning faith in Luke and an analysis of the perseverance in a section entitled: the absence of the characteristic vocabulary of πειρασμός in Luke-Acts! Faith is important in Luke, but never related to πειρασμός for Brown. Not only is this inexact at a formal level (cf. Lk 8:13), but it also seems contestable to us at the level of content. This aside, the excursus is interesting. S. Brown notes a tendency to objectivize faith: with the article, πιστίς, in Act 6:7; 13:8 and 24:24, comes to mean *fides quae creditur* or better *fides quae praedicatur*; this confers on faith an ecclesiastical and missionary connotation. In Lk 18:8 (that the Son of Man find faith on the earth when he comes), πιστίς could almost be rendered "Christianity". If not, πιστίς - this was known - designates faith in the power of Jesus or his name; this charismatic faith, Jesus can impart; faith in Jesus' messiahship (this sense, rare in the Gospel, becomes frequent in the Acts). The following declaration is original: faith in Luke designates the *beginning* of the Christian existence. From the moment one *has believed* ("those who believed" 22:19 is an exceptional expression), one must demonstrate *perseverance*. To persevere (ὑπομένειν Lk 2:43 and Act 17:14) has a local sense - we remain in the objectivizing externality: it means not to go away, thus not to apostosize. Agreeing with Conzelmann to say that ὑπομονή is not eschatological, Brown separates company with the German exegete by perceiving in this virtue an ecclesiastic rather than a moral connotation. The Lucan ἐλπίς does not have the habitual NT meaning which associates it with πειρασμός. It designates the article of faith which is the resurrection from the dead. From eschatological and ethical, hope in Luke has become dogmatic and apologetic.

With these analyses, we have in fact already entered into the third part which S. Brown, however, does not come to until their end. It is entitled: "Positive Findings: The Lucan Conception of Apostasy and Perseverance." With this we find ourselves in the midst of theological analysis or more precisely in the midst of re - dactional thematic. We wonder why the author does not introduce this part with a section on the vocabulary of perseverance (Brown does not cite P. H. Menoud's work on the quadruple perseverance -> 1952, cf. above 7 , IV, 1, a).

Brown wants to show that Luke described the apostles as perseverant in faith, a faith in Jesus' messiahship, during the ministry of their master. To make legitimate apostles, the Evan - gelist is not content with a physical presence with Jesus. He elaborates a believing and morally perseverant presence of the Twelve: the continuity of salvation history is consequently not assured by virtue of the apostolic witness alone but also by the faith and commitment of the small circle of disciples. One might make a few objections to this thesis: the author himself notes that the attitude of the apostles in the Gospel is not without failures but he gets around this by saying that the disciples doubted not Jesus' messiahship, but his suffering messiahship. Is not the essential then misunderstood? Then again, it is clear in the Passion narrative that others, different from the Twelve, understand what is happening. Peter will have to be the first to be converted (Brown gives an embarassed explanation of Lk 22:32, p. 71). The continuity which Luke is fond of - we accept this willingly - is more subtle than the author conceives: at Jesus' time, it was assured by Jesus himself. The disciples certainly accompanied the Master, but they do not understand the deep intention (Brown should have insisted more on the post-Easter teaching which Jesus gave the Twelve, Lk 24:44-49, concerning the suffering messiahship and Act 1:3ff., concerning the resurrection and the kingdom). We will not speak of the progressive growth of the apostles' faith (p. 60). What seems right is that the continuity is not assured by the witness alone (an idealistic danger). It is accomplished concretely by the faith and ethical commitment of the apostles (we would add, since Pentecost). Before this, it is Jesus who incarnates it.

Judas is the type of the apostate. Since he was part of the col-lege of the Twelve, Luke has a problem because of his theory of continuity. The answer comes: like the disciples in general, Judas was <u>called</u>, but he could then refuse the call by reason of his liberty. The other apostles were elected and their agreement was foreseen by God. What counts is not the name of the apostles, but that they formed a group of twelve: Judas will be replaced by a disciple called and elected. Ananias and Sapphira (Act 5:1-11), with Simon the Magician (Act 8:9-24), are other examples of apostates. In these two cases, like for Judas, money-mammon plays a role. Moreover, the sin of the couple is a danger not only for them but for the community.

If at the time of Jesus, perseverance signified a physical presence by the side of the Lord, during the time of the Church, it designates faithfulness to the Christian kerygma. This fidelity is favorized by the Spirit who is poured out on believer. Brown is right to note that the ecclesiastical parenesis aims more at the community than at the individual. To be perseverant is to remain in the Church, a Church centered on Jerusalem and directed by the Twelve with whom the Holy Spirit sometimes identifies himself in a functional manner.

Without our knowing why the book ends with twenty pages or so on the theme of the "way" which we have considered above.

2) Poverty and the Sharing of Goods

a. No one can ignore the attention Luke gives to the poor, nor Jesus' rebukes directed at the rich, which he reproduces. Such a solidarity with the deprived had to awaken interest among contemporary exegesis. In fact, it was Catholic theologians, and most often monks concerned about their own vow of poverty, who dealt with the subject.

1953 opened the renewal of theses studies. A. Gélin published in Paris a beautiful book called **Les pauvres de Yahvé**, while E. Percy (-> 1953) dedicated about sixty scholariy pages of **Die Botschaft Jesu** (Lund) (pp. 40-108) to the first beatitude and its Hebrew background. The conclusion of the Scandinavian scholar is different than Gélin's: the perspective called Ebionite in Luke goes back historically to Jesus, who believed in an absolute incompatibility between the possession of goods and access to the Kingdom of God.

b. Here we would like to mention a suggestive article by P. Grelot (-> 1961) where doctrinal balance rivalizes easy formulations. The Bible offers a progressive revelation of the virtue of poverty, which is distinct from the state of poverty; and yet they are not without relation. Even with the Evangelist's variety of interpretations the essential idea is left intact: Jesus gives an eminent place to poverty in his Gospel of the Kingdom. The idea of poverty no more overturns the state of the world than it canonizes established situations. It is yeast deposited in the world, as the detachment of the first Christians, their communal spirit and support given to the poor, attests.

c. A. George's article (-> 1966) is more erudite, as is fitting for a scholarly dictionary (**SDB**). Alas, the exegetical or theological appreciations are not always at the same level as the philological and historical knowledge. The author, a specialist in Lucan thought, is wrong to speak of the poverty of the apostles and the satanic character of money. To define the early Church as a Church of the poor (col. 402) [**107**] is not better. He should have been even more prudent as he himself had noted the surprising absence in the Acts of the vocabulary of poverty, so emphasized in the Gospel and the LXX. Father George explains the social interpretation that Luke gives to the first beatitude by the personal sensitivity of the Evangelist and by the atrocious misery of the poor in the Greco-Roman world. He concludes that the Jerusalem Church had organized communitarily an assistance to the poor and practiced a facultative sharing of goods (the redactional summaries generalize).

d. Four authors of unequal importance, approached the subject of poverty as extolled in Luke: R. Koch (-> 1957), F. M. Lopez-Melus (-> 1963), but especially H. J. Degenhardt (-> 1965) and J. Dupont (-> 1967; -> 1971, first and second title). The article of Koch is prudent and banal. Luke is not an exception within the Bible: the criticism he brings toward riches in fact deals only with their abuse. Instead of underlining Luke's particularity, the author strives to align Luke with a pre-established orthodoxy. Despite the parable of the rich man and poor Lazarus (Lk 16:19-31), it is not material poverty which assures access into the Kingdom. The Lucan Jesus' point of view is "rein religiös" (p. 168). Menaced by his possessions, the rich man must learn to give alms!

e. Author of a book on poverty and riches in the Gospels (Madrid, 1962), F. M. Lopez-Melus (-> 1963) published an extract of his dissertation, written in Spanish, with the Latin title, **Paupertas et Divitiae in Evangelico Sancti Lucae**. He walks on the well-trodden paths of the official doctrine, already tread by R. Koch. Luke's main principle and the common patrimony of the Gospels is: to those who seek the Kingdom, the rest will be given (Lk 12:31). This principle is at the basis of a new and transcendent world vision. Wisely, the author introduces the idea of instrumentality: for Luke, this life ceases to be an end in itself; it and the goods, which accompany it, must be taken as instruments which one must use for good. Thus, Luke is not an Ebionite.

f. The thesis of H. J. Degenhardt (-> 1965) is the most exhaustive work in the last few years on the subject. It is unfortunately contaminated by an unbearable interpretation of the term "disciple" as Luke uses it in his Gospel (not in the Acts): the term μαθητής does not designate each believer who joins himself to the Lord Jesus, but only the leaders of the community. Of course, Luke distinguishes the disciples from the people who listen to the teaching of the Master, but is it this group of Twelve, a circle narrower than the disciples, who represent the leaders. In our opinion, the disciples in the Gospel like in the Acts designate the members of the community distinct from the crowds who hesitate to adhere. Another problem which comes up here and there is the Catholic distinction between praeceptum and concilium: so Lk 12:33a (sell your possessions), could we have perhaps advice more than a command of the Lord (p. 87)! Having said this, one must admire the exhaustivity of this work which leaves no Lucan text relative to poverty and riches in the shadow.

In a few words here is the outline of the work: an introduction shows that Luke's heilsgeschichtlich project or more specifically the elaboration of a time of the Church, necessarily opens the chapter on ethics [**108**]. Luke writes this chapter resorting to the sentences of Jesus which he interprets in the light of the contem - porary situation. Degenhardt then describes the situation of the poor within the people of Israel and the different forms private and public assistance had taken. After the unfortunate chapter on the Lucan sense of the word "disciple", the writer analyzes the texts following the Lucan order. The texts are few but decisive in the Galilean period, then increase in the instructions given during the journey before diminishing during the Passion in Jerusalem and reappearing in the Acts.

The first beatitude does not bless the poor in general, but the modest community which is attached to Jesus ("you"). Exegetes forget too often the literary character of the passage. It is not a general call to poverty necessary for salvation. The curse directed toward the rich reproduces an old Palestinian tradition which aimed not at all rich, but those who are close to Jesus' teaching. By taking up this text, Luke may be thinking of the rich sectarians! Lk 6:27f. with Lk 11:39-41 proves that the Evangelist does not expect a vow of poverty of each faithful follower but liberality without restriction.

The texts in the account of the journey - the majority of the crop - comport a more radical demand. Degenhardt is to be praised for not having dilluted them, but he is wrong - as has been said - to reserve them for an elite. Let us mention a tension which we have found in several redaktionsgeschichtlich contributions consecrated to Luke: the exegete believes to have found ecclesiastic preoccupations in the story of Jesus (a heritage of the Formgeschichte) and yet while he must respect the unfolding of the stages of salvation history, he refuses to see in the Gospel a mirror of Church life (a perspective of the Redaktionsgeschichte). Luke himself forbids this. The equipping of the Twelve in Lk 22:35-38 loses the sobriety it had in Lk 10:4. What should be maintained for the time of the Church? Degenhardt does not retain the later solution alone as we might expect, but both! The severe requirement of Lk 10 is foreseen for the better days; the more accomodating dispositions of Lk 22 will be for the time of persecution! Can this be serious?

It is impossible to summarize all of this section of the book so we will mention several results: the missionaries (cf. Lk 9 and 10) will limit their needs to the extreme ("Bedürfnislosigkeit"); they must not necessarily work. The communities must care for them; Lk 12:13-34 defines what their attitude with regard to possessions should be: if greed and/or worries threaten them they will recall that Jesus expects of them involvement or availability accompanied by uncaring poverty. Lk 14:7-35 indicates the four initial conditions to be fulfilled by each leader of the community: leave his family, carry his cross, know his possibilities and renounce his possessions. Lk 16:1-31 contains a summary of the ethics with a view to those responsible. In the parable of poor Lazarus (Lk 16:19-31), Luke implies that the rich man receives his punishment because he lacked love. The episode of the rich man (Lk 18:18-30) shows that Jesus' new requirement goes beyond the Law and criticizes the old Jewish principle according to which a heritage was a visible sign and an anticipation of the eschatological reward. To sell his goods is related here to Christology: it is not an isolated ascetic action but the condition for following Jesus. In a Catholic perspective, Degenhardt believes that the effort of man in Lk 18:17-23 and the grace of God in Lk 18:24-27 collaborate harmoniously!

The work terminates with two chapters concerning Acts and repetitions are inevitable. The summaries in Act 2:42-47 and

4:31c-35 are naturally elucidated. Although he takes over semitic traditions, Luke interprets and completes them (Act 2:43-45 less vs. 44a; 4:32b and c) from a Greek point of view. Thus *κοινωνία* (Act 2:42), concerning the poor, comes to mean a spirit of communion: for Luke it is fraternal assembling. The breaking of bread goes beyond the liturgical frame to include the common meal, a form assistance to the poor. Act 2:44 and 4:32 are Greek formulations: the ideal which is never accomplished in Greece finds its spontaneous application in the Christian communities (cf. Dupont, -> 1967). What we have is not communism, but a volontary mutual disposal of possessions [**109**]. These redactional expressions complete not without contrast the traditional information which evokes the great liberality of the first Christians. God is concerned about the poor and so requires alms: this is the traditional data which Luke takes up to instill charity into his readers of Greek origin surprised by this benevolence which their society neglected. Luke however does not want to speak here of organized charity but of fraternal communion, within the early Church, between 'the haves and the have-nots'. Dt 15:4 is fulfilled: there are no needy in the people of God. Practically, the Christians had to take over the form of the Jewish assistance (daily help to foreigners and widows; weekly for the poor of the city). Cf. Act 4:35 and 6:1. Basically this charity leaned on the Christian conception of the will of God (a more universal love for one's neighbor), the sayings of Jesus, the example of the apostles and the communal conscious. Luke - and it is significative - does not resort to the motif of retribution nor the idea of the imminent Parousia. Act 20:28-35 (Paul's speech at Miletus) sketches what should be the ministers attitude toward material goods (the guideline: it is better to give than to receive).

To conclude Degenhardt's careful interpretation, let us retain that for Luke, the community is a heart and soul when it shares its material riches. "Für Lukas ist die Stellung des Christen zum Besitz ein Testfall seiner gläubigen Existenz." (p. 185). It is not simply a question of ethics, but above all an ecclesiastic pre-occupation. Without sharing nor charity, the Church denies what it is.

g. The first article of J. Dupont (-> 1967) corresponds in the main lines with the two last chapters of Degenhardt's book (even if, and so it seems, it was written independent of this work). Participating in the same spiritual possessions, the first Christians actively share what they possess. To describe this attitude, Luke transposes several Greek literary themes relative to friendship. To avoid all ambiguity, he does not use the name "friends". He prefers the word "believers" showing that in Christ this *κοινωνία* is founded on faith . It is rather the tradition that evokes the OT idea of the absence of needy in the community (cf. Act 4:34).

The second article concerns Lk 14:33 (-> 1971, second title; we are surprised the little space given to the parallel. Lk 12:33 in this article). The verse which invites to give up all possessions is editorial. The vocabulary ("goods") and themes (the insistence on all goods) are in fact Lucan. The form of this saying originates from the traditional verses, vss. 26-27 of the same chapter. Rightly, Dom Dupont refuses to water down the verse: the demand is radical. However, the tense of the verb (present) as well as the general perspective shows that it is not an imperative addressed to men on the verge of acceding to faith. It is an instruction unique to Luke's time - the time of perseverance - addressed to Christians who have already gained access to the faith. What is asked of them? Not to make a vow of poverty, but they must be disposed to renounce their possessions. This denial finds its signification not in itself but "in the relation which it establishes between the disciples and their Master" (p. 581). To conclude with Dupont, "he who is not able to accept these dispositions cannot consider himself a true disciple of Jesus Christ." (p. 582). The investigation of the Belgian scholar impressed us. Yet we wonder if Luke evokes principally the interior dispositions ("if someone does not desire to renounce his possessions", p. 575). Does he not want to fulfill concretely the requirements of the Lord?

The third article (-> 1971, first title) rightly notes that Luke-Acts does not speak of poverty, but of the poor. It is divided into four parts: 1) the needy: without aspiring to share their fate, Luke asks that charity be practiced with regard to them; 2) the community of possessions: Dupont takes up the arguments of this earlier article (-> 1967); the ideal which the summaries in Act 2 and 4 recommend is an ideal of brotherly charity and not voluntary poverty; 3) the privilege of the poor (Lk 4:18; 7:22 and 6:20f.). In this suggestive section, Dom Dupont spurns the moralizing interpretation of A. Gélin. The texts and their context do not incite such a spiritualization. The privilege accorded to the poor is not because of the spiritual dispositions of the poor themselves, but the content of the message which is announced to them. In proclaiming the Kingdom of God, the Lucan Jesus affirms God's imminent exercise of power. Far from being a possession, poverty is a situation which shocks God, the reign which will be installed will provoke the reestablishment of the deprived poor. The announcement of this reign cannot be good news for the oppressed and deprived alone. Here again the issue is not an ideal of poverty, but of justice and charity rooted in God. 4) Significantly, the fourth section is not entitled poverty but detachment. The author shows that for Luke the response to the Good News implies a total availability, acceptance of the denial of all earthly security. From Easter on, to follow Jesus - a demand which is maintained - takes on a new meaning: to participate in the cross (a particularly Pauline perspective). Luke accepts not a compromise, but an adaptation of the requirement, as the second pericope concerning the equipping (Lk 22:35f.) indicates. Along the way, the hunger for riches and the confidence placed in money remain real dangers for Christians.

The studies of Dupont on this subject culminate in the first part of the third volume of the Beatitudes (-> 1973, first title) **[110]**.

3) Brotherly Communion

a. In the first of C. Bori's two books (-> 1972), the reader will find a bibliography on the theme of Biblical κοινωνία and a summary of the various interpretations **[111]**. We might add four brief studies respectively by S. Lyonnet (-> 1954) **[112]**, G. Gerhardsson (-> 1970), G. Rinaldi (-> 1970) **[113]** and B. B. Hall (-> 1975) **[114]**, which escaped the author. Since then a study by J. M. McDermott (->1975) and the article "Gemeinschaft" in the **RAC** by W. Popkes (-> 1976) have appeared.

It is again J. Dupont (-> 1969) who seems to have studied the suject most appositely. His article concentrates on the relations of Christian to Christian and is divided in two: 1) the Jerusalem community; 2) Jerusalem and the other churches. The κοινωνία of the Mother Church (Act 2:42) is presented first (cf. Act 2:44-45) as a common sharing of all possessions. Dupont then summarizes the interpretation which we have analyzed above (cf. just above 7, IV, 2, g). This communion is also spiritual as the expression "of one heart and soul" (Act 4:32) demonstrates. The words "one soul" come from the same Greek literary friendship tradition as the common sharing of goods. Dupont opts rather for a solution other than B. Gerhardsson's. The evocation of "the heart" originates from Biblical reminiscences (LXX). Heart and soul are two ways of describing the same anthropological reality in which brotherly communion is accomplished. Ὁμοθυμαδόν (Act 1:14; 2:46; 4:24 and 5:12) signals that κοινωνία is first of all a spiritual union. But the unanimity evoked by this adverb must not delude us into believing that the first Christians shared the same opinion on all points. The three texts where the word appears all deal with prayer: the unanimity of the believers is total only in adoration (ὁμοῦ in Act 2:1 could have the same sense). Another expression of this communion of heart is ἐπὶ τὸ αὐτό whose meaning is sometimes local (cf. Lk 17:35; Act 2:1 and 4:26), can have a "global" sense, as in Act 2:44 and 47 (it is necessary to keep in mind the difficult lesson in this last verse: "Every day, the Lord united 'together' those who were being saved."). This "global" acceptance which is translated by the expression "in all" or "together" in Luke, seems to be earmarked by the OT: it takes on an ecclesiastic connotation: the Christians are "together", as they form a yahad, a community. Faith is the foundation of this spiritual communion which is incarnated in the sharing of temporal goods.

The second part of the article moves quicker. It surveys the relations which are established between Jerusalem and the other communities. It must be noted that Luke did not explicate this communion between communities. For Dupont, certain facts attest to this reality nonetheless: "New communities cannot be born except in communion with the Jerusalem community." (p. 910). Yet in the case of Samaria as with Cornelius, the communion takes another coloration, which is for us, new: there is hardly exchange or sharing. It is the apostles who bring the benefits of the Gospel and the Spirit to the populations of Palestine. We can even feel a certain superiority of the Jerusalem community and perhaps even an aspiration of the apostles to control the missionary work of Philip (Act 8). In Act 11, the Jerusalem community condescends, under the pressure of Peter who evokes the intervention of the Holy Spirit, to recognize the validity of the integration of Cornelius into the Church. It is hard to see what the new converts offer in exchange to the Christians of the capital (the Pauline argument of the collection in favor of the poor in Jerusalem is not used by Luke in the sense of an exchange). Certainly, as Dupont notes, a shuttle is organized later between Jerusalem (who sends Barnabas, Act 11:19-21) and Antioch (who sends help to Jerusalem, Act 11:27-30; 12:25). But Luke does not say what interest the Mother Church pursues in sending Barnabas to a community, born by chance because of a persecution. He deals with the gest of *διακονία* of the Antiochean community (Act 11:29).

Dupont then notes the "co-responsibility" of the laymen in the Jerusalem conference. Clearly laymen intervene, but - it seems to us - they do not take the initiative: they wisely adhere to the opinion of the apostles. Moreover, are not the two communities placed on the same level by Luke: it is in Jerusalem where the fate of Antioch is decided. Against Dupont, we would not say that the communion between the churches reflects the communion which reigns within the Jerusalem community. In our view, the lack of place Luke gives to the collection (a vague allusion in Act 24:17) confirms this. For if Paul, upon his arrival at Jerusalem, conforms his attitude to that of the Jewish Christians, it is more for peace than a free sense of sharing. At least, this is the impression Luke gives. Moreover, Dom Dupont mentions his deception with respect ot Luke who draws an imperfect image of the *κοινωνία*, which according to Paul, united the Christian Churches among themselves and their center, Jerusalem (p. 913). Personally, it is in the other direction that we would seek a complement and confirmation to the communal life of the early Church of Jerusalem: in the Lucan allusions to the spiritual and material communion which is manifested within the young local churches (hospitality, care for the missionaries, Paul's attention for new converts, etc.) **[115]**.

b. B. Gerhardsson (-> 1970) adopts a different position: there is no need to attach the "one soul" of Act 4:32 to a Greek com - munal ideal. The whole verse fits into the Jewish tradition of the schema. For the "force" mentioned in the first commandment ("with all your force", Dt 6:5) was often interpreted by Jewish exegesis as material possessions. In Act 4:32 we find the same order, heart, soul and force, at the beginning of the schema. Since the text concerns here the community ethic, we could read in it a commentary of the second commandment, Lev 19:18. By allusion, Act 4:32 would indicate that the Christian community obeys the double commandment of love. The early Church would accomplish the requirements of the Law, summarized by Jesus, and fulfill the oracles of the prophets (the Law written in the hearts). The latter recalled that the heart had to be bare and simple (Jer 32:39; Ezek 11:19f.).

Since Lk 10:27 cites four and not three anthropological terms in the commandment of love for God, the formulation of Act 4:32 is without a doubt traditional. It must fit into a context also anterior to Luke which Gerhardsson characterizes in two manners: 1) inter-ested by an idealistic image of the Mother community and 2) hostile to the Samaritans (in the Synoptics, it is the Pharisees who are the target).

Gerhardsson wonders at the end of the article if his different hypotheses can be held. They are in any case stimulating. We doubt that Luke consciously had this Jewish background in mind. Moreover, the sharing of possessions, as Dupont has shown (-> 1967), is expressed in a typical language of the Greek tradition relative to friendship. We have seen that "one soul" fits well into the Hellenistic ideal. The hypotheses of the Scandinavian exegete become shaky.

c. In reading the brilliant introduction to the first contribution, we expected much of the two books of C. Bori (-> 1972 and -> 1974). Let us here avow that we were disappointed by the first: the work opens with an interesting section which takes stock of contemporary ecclesiological research with a rich bibliography worthy of praise: it concludes that there is an influence of the contemporary idealogical setting on the communal renewal in the Churches and recommends a return to the Biblical sources (pp. 13-77). The second part analyzes summarily the Biblical passages where the term *κοινωνία* appears (as if a lexicographical inventory sufficed to understand a Biblical thematic system!). Other terms with their particular semantic field, which describe church life as well as the accounts of the communal events, would permit us to paint a complete and precise image of NT *κοινωνία*. The author realizes this on pp. 115-116. What he says concerning Act 2:42 remains hypothetical: since vs. 42 constitutes a unity with vs. 41 and serves as a conclusion of the speech at Pentecost, the *κοινωνία* of which it is question does not express itself by the sharing of goods until vss. 44-45. One should not seek Eucharistic content. It designates a communion of faith, the unanimous agreement which the newly baptized give to the teaching of the apostles. Let us note the general conclusions of the exegetical part: *κοινωνία* receives three meanings in the NT: a Christological sense (communion with Christ), an ecclesiological sense (communion with the Holy Spirit in the teaching of the apostles) and a moral sense (concrete collaboration and mutual service of the believers). This notion is not directly derived from the OT. Formally, it finds its origin in Greece, and more particularly, in the juridical, sociological and religious context of Hellenism. Finally to avoid ambiguity of the Jewish communitarian legalism, the Hebrew equivalent of the root *κοιν-* was not used to describe the rapport between Jesus and his disciples. However, from the appearance of the Gospel in the Greek world, the supple vocabulary of κοινωνία was adopted and adapted. The originality of the Christian κοινωνία: the communion with God is now mediated; the communion is related to the Church: it must be seen and become effective. It manifests the communion of the Father and the Son. It is finally dialectic, in the measure that it is not transformed into fusion nor separation.

The second work (-> 1974) is a history of the patristic exegesis of the summaries of Act 2:42-47 and 4:32-37 which concentrates successively on Origen (East, third century), Cyprian (West, third century), Eusebius, Basil and Chrysostom (East fourth and fifth centuries), Hilary, Ambrosius, Jerome and especially Augustine (West, fourth and fifth centuries) and finally, the ancient monachism. The writer judges that the ideal description of the vita apostolica was read at three different levels: ecclesiological, spiritual and monastic. Each in turn the Church, the believer and the monastic community found in the summaries of Acts the norm and source of their faith and behavior. The Fathers resorted to the summaries of Acts in the elaboration of ethical themes like peace or charity as well as in the trinitarian and Christological discussions. The second and last part of the book provides an impressive patristic file.

4) Prayer

a. Luke, as we know, insists on prayer. Divers studies have thus centered on this redactional characteristic. What is surprising is the recent date of the profound monographs on the subject.

In all circumstances it is necessary to pray. The Lord's Prayer is one of the prayers which the Acts mentions. The first Christians address indifferently the Father or the Son. Prayer was above all the act by which the believer accepts with thanksgiving the place God assigns him in salvation history. Then and only then, can it become request. This is the essential idea of the chapter which P. H. Menoud (-> 1952, first title) dedicates to perseverance in prayer (Act 2:42).

b. D. Rimaud (-> 1957) interpreted the first liturgical prayer in the Acts (4:23-31) in a study which did not awaken the attention it merited. This prayer is divided in three: 1) the invocation "Master" and the qualification of this master as the creator with the help of Ps 145, designate God as the author of the healing of the paralytic. It is furthermore necessary to mistrust the instigators of persecution. 2) The citation of Ps 2 demonstrates that the first Christians did not invent their liturgical texts. 3) They found inspiration in the Scripture which they gave an actualizing interpretation. This "Biblical" reading of their present or this "contemporary" adaptation of the Scripture is pursued in ulterior Christian liturgy with more or less success. We would reproach the author for imagining that the entire texts of Pss 145 and 2 were present in the minds of the authors of this first Christian prayer. This leads him to the false conclusion that the Church applied the vss. 7-9 of Ps 2 especially to itself (filial engendering, which Luke, in our opinion, reserves for the Son, cf. Act 13:33) [116].

c. After Father Hamman amply presented the texts of Luke-Acts in his mongraph on the subject (-> 1959), the first monograph concerning the Lucan conception of prayer appeared in 1965. Its author, W. Ott (-> 1965) no doubt has not taken stock of all the aspects of the subject, but he has discovered an unquestionable parenetic tendency. The work is alas not without weaknesses: disproportioned, it paints the picture too nicely for the two parables in Lk 18:1-8 and 11:5-10 to the detriment of the Acts. Moreover, he disheartens the reader with scholarly digressions and picky exegesis and then certain of his hypotheses are not convincing. Nonetheless, the cluster of support gathered in favor of his general thesis wins acceptance . Differing from Matthew who promises answers to prayers because of divine goodness, Luke exhorts his readers to pray without ceasing so as not to succomb during the time of the Church which continues and in order to be able to present oneself before the Son of Man. This parenesis is even more necessary as the present (not eschatological!) tribulations and worry (worldly preoccupations) may harrass the believer. Even if Luke and Paul express the same requirement of incessant prayer, they do not give it the same justification. In Paul, prayer is the thankful expression of salvation already received in faith and hope. In Luke, what is at stake is avoiding the final loss of eschatological possessions (the writer implies that in the chapter on the Acts that prayer favorizes salvation, which seems an exaggeration to us).

The indications in favor of his thesis are: 1) the Lucan interpretation (Lk 18:1 and 8) of the traditional rereading (Lk 18:6-7) of the primitive parable of the unjust judge and the widow (18:2-5); using an <u>a minori ad maius</u> reasoning, the tradition dealt with the answering of the perseverant prayer. 2) The same phenomenon concerning the parable of the untimely friend (Lk 11:8 is a traditional interpretation of the primitive parable in Lk 11:5-7; the Lucan context, Lk 11:9ff. takes the eschatological edge from the parable. Ott imagines that the tradition had coupled the two parables, the one of chapter 11 preceding the one in chapter 18. Luke would have separated them). 3) Like Lk 18:1-8, Lk 21:34-36 follows an apocalyptic discourse: the vigilance which the Marcan parallel knows also, is accompanied here with an invitation to constant prayer which does not match with the second Gospel; 4) Lk 22:31-34: an impressive illustration of the necessity of prayer to avoid falling (but we would say, be careful here; for J. Gnilka, **TR** 64 (1968) 218, it is a prayer of Jesus and not Peter); 5) Lk 22:39-46: at Gethsemane, the warning is given at the very place where Jesus is praying; Ott wrongly interprets the *πειρασμοί* of Lk 22:28 as present and future tribulations! 6) Lk 11, the chapter where Jesus, a man of prayer, teaches on prayer (different from Matthew, it is not the manner of prayer, but the necessity to pray). Luke rejects (Lk11:11-13) the idea that one prays to obtain material possessions (differing again with the Matthean parallel). The request for the Holy Spirit alone counts; Ott thinks that the second request of the Lucan Lord's Prayer - the Lucan abbreviation of the Our Father of the Matthean text is a literary and not liturgical text - comports the weakly attested reading of the request for the Holy Spirit. 7) Perseverance in prayer which the community in Acts demonstrates (Act 1:14; it is necessary to give a strong meaning to the verb "they remained", corresponding to the "they persevered" of Act 2:42. This last verse describes the life and not the liturgical activity of the first Christians: continual prayer finds its proper place). The prayers of the Acts are generally oriented toward the mission. They can also fight against backsliding and favorize access to faith and salvation. Never do they contain requests in favor of material goods.

d. W. Ott set forth an important element of the Lucan doctrine on prayer, but as P. T. O'Brian (-> 1973) reproaches him, he clearly has failed to notice the relation which prayer has with the unfolding of redemptive history. It is this particular aspect which yet another dissertation manuscript developes. The writer is O. G. Harris (-> 1966) and we know only of a summary of his work.

For this author, the regularity of prayer is important, particularly owing to the delay of the Parousia. However, this ethical slant is secondary with respect to salvation history: "His essential idea of prayer is shown to be as a means by which God guided the course of redemptive history, both in the life of Jesus and in the period of the church's expanding mission."

Prayer has its role until the decisive stage of the annexation of the Gentiles is cleared. From then on (from Act 13:1-3) it loses its importance, for there is no longer any special revelation to expect of God in prayer. Certainly, prayer keeps its importance in fighting against temptations and receiving the Holy Spirit [**117**].

e. P. T. O'Brian (-> 1973) walks in the footprints of O. G. Harris. He presents the vocabulary of prayer in Luke and notes several examples of prayer. In the Gospel, Luke often shows Jesus in prayer: with the exemplary Christ, he encourages all believers to pray without ceasing: to obtain spiritual possessions (the coming of the Son of Man - this is the sense he gives Lk 18:1, against Ott; the Holy Spirit, Lk 11:13; avoiding falling away or temptation, Lk 22:39, 46; etc.). Prayer particularly appears at decisive moments of salvation history. The book of Acts confirms this in a striking way [**118**].

Conclusion

The Book of Acts does not tell primarily the history of the Church, or the Holy Spirit's either. It situates in the foreground the diffusion of the Word of God. For Luke, the human mediations which his theology claims and the concrete character every intervention of God takes, incites him to include the accounts of conversion and describe the birth and growth of Christian communities.

Since God has been speaking for a long time, the notions of Israel and the people have a long past behind them. The begin - ning of the Gospel attests that the Church is not to be substituted for Israel. Coming from Judaism, Jesus attempts, with the help of the Holy Spirit, to renew it. The marginals, Galileans and women accept this questioning more easily than the Judeans and their leaders. The salvation which Jesus announced and accomplished consists precisely in being brought back to God and everyone must be.

Jesus' great saving effort coincides, for Luke, with a first regrouping of disciples (Lk 6:12-16). But what does Jesus do with them? Lucan ecclesiology - this would be one of our own theses - depends on the riches of Christology. Luke's Christ is "a teacher", he will form his disciples with a teaching which integrates thought and life. Such a ministry confers an ethical note on the activity of the Twelve and the seventy. These disciples are called to walk in the footprints of the Christ, whose life and especially Passion become exemplary (Luke signals thus his own coordinates: he is a theologian of the third generation, situated in a Greek environment).

Jesus is the Messiah, but what are the ecclesiological repercussions of this affirmation? One negative consequence is that the Church, which could not detach itself from the OT, is constituted as the reestablished people of God, within Israel. Since Luke does not dissociate Jesus from Davidic Messianism, does he not cut the Church off from its Jerusalem roots? A positive but banal consequence is that a king cannot do without his subjects: the believers will become the subjects of the Messiah. Here, Luke demonstrates a great desire for assimilation. He opens his universalistic perspective from the beginning of his work (cf. 2:32). The title "Messiah" applied to Jesus confers thus to the Church a centripetal vigor and a centrifugal mission.

It would be illplaced to try to knit relations too narrow between such a Christological title and such a mark of the Church, although it is tempting, for example, to link the Son of Man with the forgiveness of sins. More than the titles, it is the elements of the person of Jesus which count. Two of these elements are essential for Luke: power and service. Without them, the community cannot be saved or safeguarded. From the service Christ, the "suffering Messiah" (this is particular to Luke), accomplishes, the salvation of the people and the nations comes. The obedience of the disciples, the involvement of believers, depends on the power exercised by the Christ Jesus, exalted and sovereign.

All this, the disciples, gathered by the Master and Guide, foresee and experience already. Henceforth, they constitute a community, but the great crisis is still to emerge. After Good Friday, everything is to begin again. The disciples themselves, will have to be converted again (this is at least the interpretation of Lk 22:32) and the call of salvation will ring again one more time, a last time, for the ears of Israel. From Easter and Pentecost, the Holy Spirit, poured out on the believers and not on Jesus alone, gives the group sufficient consistency and cohesion that the word church appears from the pen of Luke.

At the time when the Evangelist composes his work, a type of ecclesiology appears which situates the Jews and the Gentiles at the same threshold before the Church. The Christian community is formed of Jews and Gentiles, who in past were enemies. The priority of Israel tends to be toned down. This is the interpretation of the epistle of Ephesians and 1 Peter. In Luke, on the contrary, salvation is offered and proclaimed first to

Israel, who need it as much as the nations. This gift and call do not exclude an offer to the Gentiles: on the contrary, if the former precede the offer, they permit it as well. Fundamentally, by the conversion of certain Jews; historically, by the hardening of others: "He is for the fall and rise of many in Israel and to be a contested sign" (Lk 2:34). There is no other Biblical book which underlines with the same vigor the vocation of Israel and the Gentiles' as well. If Luke takes over Jewish Christian traditions of centripetal tendency which integrate the pagans into the history of the Messianic people, he interprets this information in the light of Pauline universalism of centrifugal force which shatters the false barriers of Israel to maintain their identity.

The book of Acts permits us then to define three exemplary characteristics for Luke of the first community: instrumental, fundamental and dynamic.

First is the instrumental role of the primitive Church. Not that Luke means to accord a mediating mission to the Church in the order of salvation, for it is Jesus and he alone who can deliver. Yet, taking the exaltation literally, recognizing the absence of the Risen Lord, Luke confers on the Church a double function as vehicle of the Word and as bridge between the present and the *ἀρχή*. In one case, it allows God to reach man and in the other, it offers to man the possibility to go back to the founding events.

Since the word of God is related, for Luke, to the events which concern a person in the past, Jesus, it is logical, secondly, that the witnesses play a considerable role. They are not the first in a series, but a separate group, impossible to enumerate. At time zero of the Church, as X. Léon-Dufour has said, the apostles fulfill a founding and normative function which Luke designates with the term *ἀρχή*. It is clear that Luke does not apply this word to the men themselves, but to the events of which they are the beneficiaries. Irreplaceble contemporaries of the *ἀρχή*, their mission is to transmit the flame and serve as a norm. So it is with the two figures of the Acts: Peter and Paul. The presence of Peter is normative: without evangelizing the Gentiles, he is nonetheless, by his vision, their protector and defensor. By his mobility, Paul effects the diffusion of the Word or rather, offers the indispensible human support to this divine operation.

Lucan ecclesiology has yet a third characteristic: it is dynamic, doubly dynamic. First in space, since it breaks through barriers and then in time, since growth takes place and gradually, the new converts are added to the group of the faithful.

Chapter 21 of Acts permits finally a study of the relations which are established between the leaders of the Church and the simple faithful. Paul wants to go up to Jerusalem. In doing so he believes that he is conforming to the directives of the Holy Spirit. He knows that he is running great risks. Yet Luke adds without embarrassment that the disciples in Tyre oppose this project and they too are inspired by the Spirit of God (Act 21:4).

Thus a rapport of forces is established. Moreover it already appeared in a veiled manner in ch. 20: Paul had convoked the elders of Ephesus in Miletus. His speech on this occasion attested that he was leaving them by regulating definitely - he thought - his relation: he had nothing to reproach himself of, for he had accomplished his task, a task in their favor. Free from obligations with regard to them, he could henceforth leave them: "Now I know that none of you will see my face again..." (Act 20:25). It was to ignore their tears, the force of their cries. Paul, who thought he had smoothed out everything, in his relations with them, by his speech, provoked a reaction. "Everyone broke into tears and threw themselves on Paul to kiss him - their sadness came especially from the phrase where he had told them that they would not see him again -..." Act 20:37f.). Their tears constituted a way to pressure him to stay.

In ch. 20 as in ch. 21, Paul's will imposes itself despite the reaction, first, of the elders in Ephesus and then, of the divers communities. We could think that the authority in the Church functions like in society in the end: the strongest triumphs and here the heirarchically superior, Paul, enriched by his knowledge and his status as a witness.

Of course, the psychological actions and reactions obey, in the Christian domain, rules which are not at all distinct from the mechanisms analyzed by the theory of communication. Nonetheless, if the logic of the interactions between persons, like the operations of knowledge, are identical, here and there, a decisive difference exists. Luke notes it in the gest of prayer, the mention of the Holy Spirit and the heartbreak.

These three indications show that the relation of force is more complex than a simple opposition of two parties. By getting on their knees to pray (Act 20:36), both attest that they are fitting their desires into the ecclesiastic space where God himself intervenes. The affection ceases to be appropriation of the other (to hold Paul back for self) to become fraternity with a project which is beyond us all (the will of God). If finally the disciples cannot convince Paul, they will not be bitter for this defeat, for it is not equal to a human victory, but rather to the triumph of the plan of God. So the phrase: "May the will of the Lord be done." (Act 21:14).

Yet does this result not equal a lost battle, or a cause trans - mitted to superior instance? We could fear so and then assist the triumph of the one who is truly the strongest, God and, men would be only puppets or pawns. This is not the case, for two other indications emerge in the text: the apparent contradictions of the Holy Spirit, who slowly but surely provokes the desire for the journey (Paul) and the concern to keep him (for the communities), and the will of God still known incompletely. If God revealed his plan in a tyranical manner and imposed a preestablished largely diffused will, he himself would enter into the logic of a closed system of interpersonal relations marked by oppressions and brutal victories. But what follows in the Book of the Acts, by the surprises it reserves, shows that the will of God is also ahead and not exclusively behind, taken in the letter of a known law. Paul himself ignores that Jerusalem, where he is ready to die, is not the place of his martyrdom. The story goes on to Rome. There is thus a margin of the unknown and liberty in which the wills and desires of the apostle and the disciples navigate. All, in good faith, calling upon the Spirit to propose legitimate but contradictory hopes and projects: to keep the witness of Christ and to continue the testimony elsewhere.

The third pole, God, in this non-tyranical and not completely unveiled form, modifies the type of communication between the leaders and the faithful. Paul's intention is certainly realized, but it does not crush the disciples: the dialogue, which unfolds according to the logic of persuasion, replaces the decision transmitted in an authoritative manner, thus the tears, thus the hearts which may be broken, Paul's first of all.

At the term of the exercise, each could have grown in the faith: left to themselves, the communities could have matured without having lost Paul. And the apostle faithful to his Lord, would not have submitted himself to a God favorable to the death of those dear to him. Ready to be tied and die in Jerusalem for the name of his Lord, he will not endure - as Abraham and Isaac - the test to which he gives himself up to, or better to which he offers himself. In a certain unexpected manner, the communities will find him who they accepted to lose: in the communion of the saints, a spiritual reality, which Luke, faithful to his theology of mediations, suscitates through his writing, the book of the Acts. Thus the thing they feared to lose is restitued to them in the figure of Paul. So they will understand the last phrase of the farewell speech: "there is more pleasure in giving than in receiving" (Act 20:35). This type of Scriptural restitution also has a secondary effect: it offers Paul, like Jesus, to later generations, attesting that in the communication among Christians, others are included in the relation of affection. For in the dialogue between the author and the readers resides in seed form a call to others, to "them", that they might join the Christians. The Lucan ethic, like all Christian ethic, proposes a relation to one's neighbor which arouses a hope in others. This capacity of integration draws its strength in the Father and the Son who want to associate men in their knowledge and their mutual love: "As has been committed to me by the Father, and no one knows who the Son is, except the Father, and no one knows who the Father is, except the son and those to whom the Son chooses to reveal himself." (Lk 10:22).

APPENDIX

CHRONICLES IN LUCAN STUDIES [1]

The student who wants to initiate himself to Lucan studies [2] will do well to first read the classics. Without going back to F. Overbeck and A. Loisy, he should discover H. J. Cadbury, M. Dibelius, H. Conzelmann and E. Haenchen [3].

If he then desires to inform himself concerning recent works, there are a series of bulletins at his disposal: for example, those of C. H. Talbert [4], A. del Agua Pérez [5], M. Cambe [6], J. Guillet [7], M. Rese [8], E. Rasco [9] and E. Grässer [10].

More durable than these precious relays of knowledge, two works concern the history of research over a longer period of time, of course, in differing manners. W. Gasque [11] describes the history of research concerning the Acts from the beginning of the nineteenth century. Faithful to a British tradition, the North American exegete thinks Luke a historian worthy of confidence which the Germans refuse him by overemphasizing his literary talent and theological strength. E. Rasco [12] has a theological mind and the sensitivity of an artist: his account of the history from the beginning, the developments and actual orientations of Lucan theology is remarkable. He is able to disengage a coherent evolution from what too often appears as a bloated amalgam of bibliographical lists. He even discovers a forerunner of the disciples of the Redaktionsgeschichtliche Schule: W. Hillmann. The second section of his book is more personal; let us mention three particular chapters 1) on Jesus, 2) on Jesus, the Holy Spirit and the Church and 3) on history, salvation history and eschatology which we considered elsewhere [13]. For Rasco, the time of the Church is not qualitatively distinct from the time of Jesus. On the contrary, it is intimately related (against Conzelmann). Neither is eschatology eliminated or historicized. Finally, the Lucan schema of redemptive history is not unique to Luke (with O. Cullmann). At the end of this survey, the author rejoices that Luke, of course, with his own glasses, transmitted to us both Jesus and Paul. At the end of this paragraph, let us mention the very precious bibliography (pp. XV-XL).

In the last few years new instruments for the work on Luke have appeared. 1) An annotated translation of the third gospel has appeared by a professor of Greek, E. Delebecque [**14**]. The reader will admire his philological knowledge, but regret the absence of exegetical lore and the conservative doctrinal positions of the author. 2) The last gift of J. Jeremias [**15**] to the world of scholars was his analysis of the language of Luke (in the sections with non-Marcan parallels), which attempts to distinguish the redactional nuances and the traditional expressions in each pericope. Thanks to this study, exegetes will taste again (let us hope) the savor of Luke's language and discover its subtleties. They will also learn that Jeremias maintained several of his own positions: the Lucan account of the Passion is not an adaptation of Mark and on the whole Luke is faithful to the traditions he takes over, particularly in the case of the sayings of Jesus. 3) Finally, specially for regional translators, the Universal Biblical Alliance planned a series of manuals. Appearing first in English, the volume consecrated to Luke has been adapted in French [**16**]. It is first of all a meticulous work which renders help; alas, faced with the difficulties of the text, the reader who is used to Bauer and the erudite grammars, will hardly find supplementary aid. He will nonetheless read with interest the options already taken by the different translators, mainly from Asia, who are abundantly cited.

To present the monumental work of H. Schürmann [**17**], I waited for the second volume of his commentary, but since it delays in coming, here are several notes concerning the first which appeared in 1969. It comments Lk 1:1-9:50: the infancy accounts and the ministry in Galilee. The erudition of the professor from Erfurt is immense and his historical and philological competence very certain. These qualities serve a very sensitive theological appreciation of the Gospel of Luke for which he testifies an authentic sympathy. Luke appears as an evangelist whose theology is rooted in the tradition of his community. His gospel is not to be explained without reference to the life of the Church of his time. Schürmann's exegesis insists regularly on the ecclesiological elements of the Lucan editing, sometimes to the detriment of the individual challenge (this can be felt in the exegesis of the Sermon on the plain, Lk 6:17-49).

If we could deplore, not so long ago, the absence of new commentaries, such a regret is no longer justified: four German popular, but high quality commentaries appeared one on top of the other. The thickest, J. Ernst's [**18**] which replaces J. Schmid's in the "Regensburger Neues Testament", leans heavily on the work of Schürmann. The same ecclesiological perspective and the same reserve with respect to an ethical reading of the third gospel is present. As for W. Schmithals, he adopts drastic measures for the most complex literary problems and finds help in the theory of the two sources and a certain theological approach of Luke (Luke fights against a form of pre-Marcionism) [19]. G. Schneider [20] is to be thanked for providing a up-to-date bibliography for each pericope; but little space is left to justify his critical literary options and exegetical choices. The last born is the commentary of E. Schweizer in the "Neues Testament Deutsch" series. The professor in Zurich thus terminates his synoptic trilogy [21]. Parallel to his commentary, he offered his theological interpretation of the whole Lucan corpus in a little book which appeared this year in the United States [22]. Without neglecting the ties between history and eschatology, he affirms that Luke insists on the presence of God in the person of Jesus (we are quite far from the ecclesiological views of a Schürmann and an Ernst). Schweizer judges Luke's theology sufficiently actual to permit us to go beyond the Protestant and Catholic positions. In his commentary, a coherent exegesis developes in compact form. If philology takes up little space beyond a careful translation, the literary problems always emerge with clear theological positions. For example, the explanation of Lk 13:1-9 ends with these words, "they are told that God cannot be explained, but can be experienced." (p. 220, ET).

With his numerous contributions on Luke, I. H. Marshall prepared himself to write a large commentary on the third Gospel. It appeared in a new series [23], "The New International Greek Testament Commentary", which is conservative in orientation, but honestly open to critical problems. The exegete often affirms that nothing contradicts the historicity of such and such event. Furthermore, he is sensitive to textual criticism and discusses, of course with more exhaustivity than originality the numerous problems of establishing the text (e.g. in the Lord's Prayer or the episode with Martha and Mary). The commentary examines also the questions of historicity and enters with competence into the theological debate (Marshall knows German exegesis well). It is perhaps the examination of the language, style and literary form which demonstrates the most borrowing. Should we regret that so many commentaries are written with so little sensitivity to the linguistic and stylistic problems? [24]

The first commentary in French to appear in a very long time is a work of collaboration, one might even say a community effort. The concern of Ph. Bossuyt and J. Radermakers [25] is catechetical and pastoral: these authors desire to facilitate the preacher's task. In a first fascicule, they present a structured French version of the third Gospel, a version which should grant the private reader access to the original language and perception of the flavor of Lucan nuance nonetheless. The commentary itself, which - because of prudence? - bears the subtitle Lecture continue, forms a thick tome of 551 pages. The authors begin by situating each pericope in its context, advance to a redaktionsgeschichtlich analysis and then move on to an explanation which highlights the theological and spiritual questions of the text. The philological (apart from the analyses of vocabulary) and historical questions are moved into the background. Valuable footnotes furnish an abundant bibliography and present the different scientific postions. From cover to cover the text remains very readable. The title given the volume **La Parole de la Grâce selon saint Luc** summar - izes the essential message of the authors.

It is not a commentary on Luke which R. Meynet [26] wrote, although he can affirm "The goal of this study has not been to portion the Lucan text into units, or to discover an outline. It is to seek to understand the text" (I, p. 139). This comprehension is global: the second section of Luke (Lk 4:14-9:50), for example, articulates first two themes: the teaching and healings of Jesus, on the one hand, and the question of his identity, on the other. Moreover, this section shows that the power of God becomes Jesus' before passing on to the Twelve. These doctrinal affirmations result in an analysis called rhetorical. From ancient rhetoric, the author retains principally the dispositio: the organization of the matter. To discover it, he rejects an examination of the sources, as well as a semiotic analysis. He prefers to locate rhetorical models, three in particular: the paradigmatic model (e.g. the couplet "teach-heal" which occurs with the "question of the identity of Jesus"), the syntagmatic model (more particularly that of the wide chiasm, the chiasm of discourse) and the model we would call scriptural, which relates the text of Luke with OT passages. This rhetorical analysis, which emerges in declarations relative to the global sense of the literary units, constitutes the majority of the work, but it touches only ten chapters of Luke (if the composition of the whole is so important, we do not understand why the author does not complete his enterprise, nor why he discards Lk 9-19, the most

Lucan part of the third Gospel). This formalization of the texts opens up onto a series of plates grouped into a second volume, which with typographical astuteness, attempts to clarify the structure of the various units (often chiastic!). Finally let me note that in the first volume, the analysis is intersected with precise theoretical and comprehensible chapters concerning the rhetorical models, the problems of translation and the history of research relative to the chiasm. I can feel that the author is well instructed in linguistics and able to expose clearly.

Alas I am not sure if the conclusions of R. Meynet will find a wide audience. First because the author ignores or wants to ignore all the exegesis which went before him; and then because he does not sufficiently establish the existence of the chiasms in the discourse in ancient literature (moreover, he hesitates between the international or Hebraic character of this rhetorical construction). Finally, because the presence of all these figures in the Gospel is not assured.

The collective works, Festschriften and Mélanges, can be a curse. When they are centered on one author or theme, they have their value. No less than six collections appeared recently on the Lucan corpus [**27**]. The two series of "Journées Bibliques of Leuven" (in 1968 and 1977) produced two corresponding volumes [**28**]. A contribution offered as essays to professor Paul Schubert in 1966, met with such a lively success that the editors decided to republish a new paperback edition in 1980 [**29**]. G. Braumann [**30**] did the same with a selection of articles or extracts of books for the series "Wege der Forschung". The choice, which corresponds to a state of the question in 1970 is judicious, with the exception that only a few Anglo-Saxon contributions (translated into German) have the honor of appearing next to the articles of the German exegetes. The following volume originates from a work group of the Society of Biblical Literature [**31**]. A first part regroups historical and literary studies (semitisms, synoptic problem, prologues of Luke and Acts, etc.). An interesting article of R. J. Karris [**32**] arrives at the conviction that Luke attacks the rich Christians who consider their possessions as a mark of divine blessing (concerning riches and poverty in Luke, we can read, beside the studies summarized above [**33**], the long chapter by Luise Schottroff and W. Stegemann [**34**], as well as the article of G. W. E. Nickelsburg [**35**] which shows that Luke reworked apocalyptic traditions concerning the fate of the rich and the poor). The second part of the American collection is more exegetical. The annunciation accounts, ch. 9 of Luke, the miracles, the journeys, the pleadings, the vocations or divine interpellations are successively examined according to a method which combines the Redaktionsgeschichte and a socio-cultural analysis in vogue in the U. S. A. Finally, a series of exegetes of French expression (why this limitation?) honored, alas, in a posthumous manner, Father Augustin George, an eminent specialist of the Lucan work [**36**]. The majority of the contributions are exegetical (Lk 6:43-49; 10:19; 17:33; 22:29; 22:54-23:25; 24:49; Act 1:4-8; 2:1-41; 6:8-8:2; 15:19-20; 16:4; 17:16-34; 21:27-26:32); several articles deal with Biblical themes (the humanity of Jesus, prayer, the "way", Jerusalem). In a schematic manner, we mention that French exegesis maintains its attention on a rereading of the traditions and I sense a discreet and above all understandable presence of semiotics.

Father George died before finishing his much awaited commentary on the Gospel of Luke. Yet he still had the time to prepare a collection of his articles, which two of his students, J. P. Lémonon and G. Coutagne, edited [**37**]. The reader will find several new authoritative articles (the construction of the third Gospel, the parallel between John the Baptist and Jesus in Lk 1-2, Israel in the Lucan work, etc.) and will discover nine unpublished articles (concerning the Christology, eschatology, miracles, angels, conversion, prayer and the mother of Jesus). A precious index of the texts and then the Lucan themes appears at the end of the volume. The work does not take up again all the articles of Father George relative to the Lucan writings. To be convinced one must only consult the **Bulletin des Facultés catholiques de Lyon**, number 51, April 1978, pp. 31-49, which recently published, thanks to the care of Father G. Etaix, an exhaustive bibliography of Father George's work. The studies gathered are characterized by their method and perspective. The method, which has imposed itself in the last thirty years, is the study of the history of redaction. The perspective is theological, even if Father George rightly thought that the evangelical message and the theology which it implies is expressed in literary forms to be analyzed and in the historical circumstances to be known. As these studies go right to the heart of the Gospel of Luke and the Acts, they constitute a reference work as well as an initiation.

As for introductions, I would like to note the nice article of E. Plümacher on the Acts of the Apostles in the **Theologische Realenzyklopädie** [**38**], and M. Hengel's [**39**] work which invites exegetes, on the one hand, not to separate history from preaching and, then, to qualify Luke as a historian as much as a theologian. Concerning Luke, the two syntheses of Ph. Vielhauer and H. Köster are welcome, but depend a bit too much on H. Conzelmann [**40**].

Finally, I have before me a series of monographs. We wonder if so many are needed. Two of them come from the United States. The one tries to situate Jesus [**41**] within his time and milieu and the other, Luke [**42**] (renewal of interest for history in the slant of social ethics and the socio-cultural analysis). An Italian one [**43**] deals with the sharing of goods (confrontation of the practices in the primitive Church and the Essene sect); and yet another [**44**], Canadian, concerns the speech of Paul at Antioch of Pisidia (an interesting essay which goes beyond exegesis and asks the hermeneutical problem of the cultural adaptation of the evangelical proclamation). There are two volumes in the "Lectio Divina" series. In the one [**45**] on prayer in Luke, the author perceives a structure in the prayer in the third Gospel. His principle starting point is Lk 1-2 (seeking God, meeting the Word, listening and praise, placing faith and life in relation). The other [**46**] concerns the account of the annunciation (Lk 1:26-38). This beautiful thesis which is a little too long, fits the account not into the genre of the vision but into that of the annunciation, an apocalyptic rather than prophetic annunciation. This apocalypse emerges onto history, which in turn becomes good news, to which the faith and consequently the maternity of Mary responds [**47**]. Two books issued from the pen of U. Busse, one on what is called the manifesto of Jesus in Nazareth (Lk 4:16-30) [**48**] and the other [**49**], already in its second edition, on the miracles of Jesus in the third Gospel. Except for the unpublished dissertation by M. H. Miller (Berkeley, 1971), it is the first work on the whole concerning the subject. The essential part, pp. 57-337, is exegetical; each miracle is analyzed with much finesse; the end of the work disengages the doctrinal elements of Luke, the dimensions he calls Christological (the accomplishment of the prophetic promises), theological (God's role in hindering Jesus from becoming a *θεῖος ἀνήρ*) and soteriological of the miracles which illustrate, like a mosaic, the salvation offered by Jesus Christ [**50**]. F. G. Untergassmair [**51**] examines Jesus' Passion narrative, and more particularly Lk 23:26-49, and J.-M. Guillaume [**52**] the resurrection of Jesus (Lk 24-Act 1), more precisely the very personal manner by which Luke reworks the old traditions he inherited: "While rejoining the primitive information with tradition, especially those of the kerygma, Luke fits them into a coherent and well composed totality. The unity of time and place are a part of the redactional process. The progression in faith, the gradual presentation of the message, the discovery of the resurrected One and the internal evolution of the witnesses are intentionally marked off. For Luke the Easter message itself is not the only thing important, but above all, the way which it is received, assimilated, lived and transmitted by the first members of the Christian community" (p. 8). Several formal imperfections (the absence of summaries, spelling errors, misprints) mar this serious study.

It should be noted here that the Lucan sector has naturally been touched by the renewal of the studies relative to the parables of Jesus, especially by the contemporary works of H. Weder [**53**] and H.-J. Klauck [**54**] and the articles and then book of J. D. Crossan **55**] (particulary his analyses of the good Samaritan: at the origin, a parable and not an exemplary account, in **NTS** 18 (1971-1972) 285-307 and in **Semeia** 2 (1974) 82-112; this whole issue of **Semeia** is consecrated to the good Samaritan) [**56**]. All of these authors have been influenced by the systematic reflection of P. Ricoeur and E. Jüngel concerning the parables as metaphors [**57**]. G. Sellin wrote a thesis, which remains in manuscript form, on the parables in the Sondergut of Luke (Munster, 1973); his long article also appeared in two deliveries in **ZNW** [**58**]: after a general presentation, he deals with the good Samaritan. Since K. E. Bailey [**59**] lived for an extensive period in the Middle East and interrogated the inhabitants of these regions, his socio-cultural remarks merit the attention of the "office exegetes" which the majority of us are (cf. the section entitled "The contemporary Middle Eastern peasant and his oral tradition as a tool for recovering the culture of the parables"). This exegete believes that he can discern several oral literary genres (the chiasm, the seven poetic forms, poetry incrusted in prose and the parabolic ballad). He finally analyzes several parables (Lk 16:1-13; 11:5-13 and 15) [**60**].

This brings us to mention that the flood of publications on eschatology in Luke has subsided. Above I considered the book by Ruthild Geiger [**61**] which was sent to the editor of our Review. I can signal the work of A. J. Mattill [**62**], who after a series of articles, binds the whole and maintains that Luke believes in the imminence of the end of time. Two works deal with the lordship of Christ in its rapport with eschatology [**63**].

The Lucan theme of salvation retains the attention of R. Glöckner [**64**] (cf. the severe review of E. Schweizer in the **ThR** 72 (1976) 373) and M. Dömer [**65**]; J. M. Nützel [**66**] interests himself in Luke's Christology (six chapters: 1. Jesus' activity, especially his coming; 2. the Kingdom of God preached by Jesus, the revealer of God; 3. the "Johannine" logion, Lk 10:22; 4. salvation provoked by the encounters with Jesus; 5. the experience of salvation through the miracles; 6. Jesus' activity after the parables, Lk 15 and 18:9-14). Another contribution concerns a particular ethical point [**67**]; the prohibition made to the missionaries to greet those passing by on the way (Lk 10:4b). Little has appeared concerning the Church since 1975, except an italian book [**68**]. On the other hand, a study of the Eucharist by W. Bösen [**69**] was published.

The Holy Spirit continues to arouse, if we might say so, enthusiam and moderation: Pastor B. Gillièron [**70**] consecrated two chapters to the work on Luke in his book which is a good popular work. These chapters present and analyze the texts, insisting, in a "reformed" manner, on the relations between the Spirit and the Christ. The Spirit enters into the service of the Word. M.-A. Chevallier's work [**71**] is more ample as well as more historical: it places the Biblical witness before the Jewish antecedents (at the verge of the Christian era, Num 11, Ezra 36 and Isa 11 are present in the Jewish consciousness) as well as the Greek. In conlusion of the chapter reserved to Luke, the professor from Strasbourg notes 1) the links between the Spirit and salvation history (this has been accepted since the book of H. von Baer appeared in 1929); 2) the rapport between the Spirit, experience and faith (Chevallier and Gillièron join each other here). Translating πνεῦμα by breath/wind (French "souffle"), Chevallier dares to speak of faith in the breath/wind (p. 222), which signifies : "Based on experienced lived [of the Holy Spirit], Luke believes in a general and durable outpouring announced for the eschatological people" (p. 222). Contrary to many, Chevallier refuses to attribute a specific role to the Holy Spirit in exorcisms and healings. He thinks that Luke's originality is to have made of the Spirit a grandeur of the next-to-end times, i.e. Luke's time: the Evangelist thus confers a dynamic note to the Church ("The Church and mission are made into one by the breath/wind", p. 224). Finally, one must not detach the Holy Spirit from Christology: "And the eschatological outpouring of the wind as it is experienced in the first communities is itself related to the risen and glorified Christ and the baptism of the faithful is related to his baptism" (p. 238) [**72**].

As C. Burchard in **ThLZ** 106 (1981) 38 noted, one subject has hardly been approached: Luke's anthropology; it is now done with the dissertation of J.-W. Jaeger [**73**]. A first section defines the adressees of the proclamation (man before faith) and a second deals with conversion (toward the believing man). We find again the schema of Bultmann's chapter on the theology of Paul. Yet correctly, the second part is entitled "conversion" and not "faith"; Jaeger thinks that Luke is optimist and the Lucan man is responsible, and thus able to get out by a decision of his will. In my opinion, the writer is right to insist on the responsibility of the human being, but I would say the believer's responsibility, for according to Luke, Satan holds non-believers under his power more than Jaeger is willing to admit **[74]**. In a significant manner, the author is almost mute when it comes to Act 10:38 (read the embarrassed note 282 on p. 72f.).

At the end of these pages **[75]**, two things surface: first, Luke remains enigmatic. The diversity of themes in presence underlines the insatiability of all the intentions of the Evangelist. Does he want to resolve the problem of the delay of the Parousia with a theology of salvation history; encourage the worn out people of God and exhort the leaders; fight against an antinomian Paulinism, a form of pre-Marcionism or a dualistic gnosticism; evangelize the favored classes; force the Roman authorities or a cultivated Greek public to recognize Christianity; maintain ties with Judaism? Personally, I believe that he is bent on taking into consideration the ultimate announcement of the Word of God in Jesus Christ, whose resurrection sets the apostolic witness in movement.

Secondly, the most stimulating theological interpretations hardly facilitate the work of the exegete, nor do they necessarily enrich. The numerous readings I have done with a view to a state of the question concerning the theology of Luke have not always helped me to write a commentary. What can be said? That the reader attentive to a particular text should dread contamination from a general perspective; or rather that the globalizing interpretations, because of a doctrinal simplification betray the particulars? On the level of the NT on the whole, this danger has long been perceived. Exegetes have, in fact, renounced explaining a passage of an epistle from a gospel or a portion of a gospel from a Biblical coherence in the wide sense. Yet few are the scholars who have complained of the tension which emerges between the interpretation of the whole of the corpus, here Lk-Act, and the reading of a sole passage. Does the parable of the salt (Lk 14:34-35), to take but one example, become less enigmatic when we fit it into the redemptive historical perspective? Being always clarified from the outside, a pericope finally risks being misunderstood **[76]**.

NOTES

FOREWORD

1. We have explained this starting point in the beginning of our article, "Orientations actuelles des études lucaniennes", **RTPhil**, 3rd series, 26 (1976) 176f.

2. Cf. the lines we have given to the subject in the article mentioned in the note above (p. 176f.).

3. To the works mentioned in the article cited above in n.1 (p. 188, n. 1) and the study entitled "L'origine des récits concernant les apôtres", **RTPhil**, 3rd series, 17 (1967) 345-350, it is fitting to add S. E. Johnson, "A Proposed Form-Critical Treatment of Acts" **AnglTR** 21 (1939) 22-31.

4. In the article mentioned in note 1.

5. W. Gasque, **A History of the Criticism of the Acts of the Apostles** (Tübingen, 1975); E. Rasco, **La teología de Lucas: origen, desarrolo, orientaciones** (Rome, 1976); E. Grässer, "Acta-Forschung seit 1960", **TRu** 41 (1976) 141-196; 259-290; 42 (1977) 1-68.

6. F. F. Bruce, "The True Apostolic Succession. Recent Study of the Book of Acts", **Interpr** 13 (1959) 131-143; C. S. Williams, "Luke-Acts in Recent Study", **ExpTim** 73 (1962) 133-136; J. Rhode, **Die redaktions-geschichtliche Methode** (Hamburg, 1966) pp. 124-183; I. H. Marshall, "Recent Study of the Acts of the Apostles", **ExpTim** 80 (1969) 292-296; I. Panagopoulos "*Αἱ Πράξεις 'Αποστόλων καὶ ἡ κριτικὴ αὐτῶν ἔρευνα*" *θεολογία* 42-43 (1971-1972); H. Conzelmann, "Literaturbericht zu den Synop-tischen Evangelien", **TRu**, N. F., 37 (1972) 220-272, especially 264-272; C. H. Talbert, "Shifting Sands: The Recent Study of the Gospel of Luke", **Interpr** 30 (1976) 381-395 (the whole issue is dedicated to the Gospel of Luke).

7. In the bibliography of ch 1, -> 1977 and -> 1978, we mention three new commentaries of the Gospel of Luke.

CHAPTER 1

1. Cf. above 1, I, a and b.

2. Cf. R. Bultmann, "Weissagung und Erfüllung", **ST** 2 (1949) 22-44; taken over in **ZTK** 47 (1950) 360-383 and in R. Bultmann, **Gauben und Verstehen II** (Tübingen, 1961[3]) pp. 162-186.

3. E. Rasco (-> 1976) has recently shown what P. Vielhauer and H. Conzel-mann owed to R. Bultmann. It is necessary to recall the role Käsemann played

between the end to the war and the first articles of Conzelmann and Vielhauer. We owe this information to Käsemann, who affirms his dependence on the commentary of the Acts of A. Loisy (1920).

4. H. Conzelmann (-> 1952), p. 31.

5. Cf. K. Löning (-> 1969) and E. Kränkl (see ch 3, -> 1972).

6. God's foresight finds its basis in his essence and no longer in his revelation.

7. S. Schulz offers as indications the Greek proverb "one can not kick against the goads" (Act 26:14), the texts Act 13:46 and 10:8ff. and the theme of *θεομαχία* (Act 5:39).

8. The "events" take place before their "accomplishment among us". G. Klein recommends a distance between the time of salvation and the ulterior time.

9. Cf. E. Haenchen (-> 1956), p. 679f. of the 1968 edition and p. 134 f. of the 1977 one.

10. The reader can consult a second article by G. Klein (-> 1967) which shows how Luke posed and resolved the problem of syncretism.

11. The first thesis is: Paul is a theologian of salvation history too. Of course, he understands it differently than Luke (p. 686f.). The second thesis is that Paul is not unaware of the traditions relative to Jesus' life, as U. Wilckens would like, but voluntarily neglects them for a theological reason. In fact, he conceives of Jesus' resurrection eschatologically (p. 687f.). The majority of these developments disappear in the 1977 edition (p. 140f.).

12. J.-D. Kaestli comes to this conclusion even for certain texts for which Conzelmann maintains an apocalyptic point like Lk 12:49-59.

13. P. 72. Kaestli thinks that the entrance into the Kingdom occurs at the death of the individual rather than at the Parousia of the Son of Man. How can this be reconciled with Lk 21:31, if we decide to follow the exegesis which Conzelmann offers for this verse (on p. 53, the author does not decide).

14. A last chapter asks the question of Luke's protocatholicism, i.e. the ecclesiological question: we cannot say that Luke fights a Gnostic front, nor that he establishes a succession guaranteed juridically or sacramentally.

15. Concerning Lk 17:24 (the image of lightning), R. Geiger notes that the Evangelist shifts the focus, from what in tradition dealt with the day or the coming of the Son of Man, to the person of the Son of Man. This eschatological manifestation of the Son of Man gained inspiration from the OT and Jewish tradition concerning the apparition of the hypostasized glory of Yahweh.

16. At the redactional level, Lk 17:34f. concerns the final sorting out, which should not be confused with the non-eschatological divisions which the believers' involvement introduced into society.

17. Especially Kaestli. Concerning the work of A. Salas (-> 1967), she says "mir nicht zugänglich". She does not know the work except by the review of J. Schmid (**BZ**, NF., 14 (1970), pp. 290-292). This is hardly acceptable, for it is a book which concerns the very subject she is studying. The author could have borrowed it from Professor Schmid or made a trip to Rome (to the Pontifical Biblical Institute) where it can be found!

18. E. Trocmé (-> 1957) and J. C. O'Neill (-> 1961) seem to accept the delay of the Parousia and the Lucan displacement of eschatology. In the chapter consecrated to the unity of the work of Luke, Trocmé takes over four of Conzelmann's ideas which are found in Luke-Acts: 1) the eschatological recoil; 2) salvation history; 3) the importance of the preaching of the Gospel, and 4) the central role of Jerusalem. The French exegete's work is an important contribution to the study of Acts, for it is analyzed from a historical, literary and theological point of view. The double work is apologetical ad extra, as well as ad intra, not against Gnostics but rather against the Judeo-Christians. As for the title of O'Neill's study the should be inversed: the work deals with the historical setting of Acts from a theological perspective. The result is that the Lucan work, thematically and literarily, is near to Justin. It is thus proper to situate it in the second century. Among the subjects not treated, the author mentions at the end of the book 1) the delay of the Parousia; 2) the normativity of the time of the apostles, and 3) the protocatholicism, still unconscious, of Luke.

19. O. Cullmann (-> 1965), pp. 214-225.

20. Here the author (p. 222, note 1) can lean on the book of E. Grässer (-> 1957).

21. G. von Rad, **Theologie des Alten Testaments**, I-II (Munich, 1957-1962) (FT. Geneva, 1963-1967 and ET. London, 1962-1965).

22. On the subject of this chapter, we can read from the same author 1) a state of the question (-> 1966); 2) an article which rejects the thesis according to which salvation history would be in Luke a anti-Gnostic rampart (-> 1967); 3) a study of the verb *σήμερον* in the Synoptics (ch 5 -> 1957). These articles are assembled in the fist volume of **Sparsa Collecta. The Collected Essays by W. C. van Unnik** (Leiden, 1973).

23. For a deeper presentation of I. H. Marshall's book, cf. below 5, IV, a.

24. In this article, J. Kodell presents basically the positions of Conzelmann (-> 1954) and H. Flender (-> 1965). With the latter, it seems he opts for the eschatological character of the present period and the continuity of salvation history from Jesus' time to our own (p. 146).

25. According to this writer, the time of salvation is subdivided into a period of Jesus and a time of the Church; but it is a secondary subdivision with respect

to the larger rupture of the OT and the NT. G. Lohfink indicates (p. 255) several authors who share his opinion. Concerning Act 3:19-21 and the Lucan conception of history which transpires in these verses, cf. G. Lohfink (-> 1969), summarized below 3, I, h.

26. W. G. Kümmel (-> 1970, second title). We are refering to the reedition of this article in the 1973 volume of **Memorial L. Cerfaux**, p. 101.

27. 1) the text of Luke-Acts; 2-3) the literary genre (Luke with regard to the historians and religious writers of his era); 4) the language; 5) the traditions which Luke takes over; 6) the ecclesiastic roots.

28. M. Dibelius; B. Gärtner; A. Ehrhardt; R. Morgenthaler; H. Conzelmann and E. Haenchen.

29. Cf. below 1, III, q.

30. Cf. an article of the same author concerning the anti-Gnostic character of the Christology, noted in the bibliography of ch 3 (-> 1967, second title) and the contents are taken up in the most recent contribution of the author (-> 1974), summarized below 1, III, q.

31. In an article concerning the fall of Jerusalem (of the same year -> 1963, second title). G. Braumann accepts the thesis of Conzelmann: the fate of the city is dissociated with eschatology, but the author opts for another cause for this dissociation than the one proposed by Conzelmann. The fall of Jerusalem is historical, for it is the punishment God inflicts, in time, on those who reject Jesus. The destiny of the believers alone remains associated to the Parousia, which will witness the reestablishment of the present martyrs. Jerusalem suffered because it was unfaithful. The believers, we might add, suffer because of their infidelity.

32. Author of a commentary on the Acts which appeared in 1939 (reprint 1980), O. Bauernfeind intervened in the debate on several occasions (-> 1953; -> 1954; -> 1963).

33. Cf. p. 270 has a few lines on the subject.

34. H. J. Cadbury, **The Book of Acts in History** (London, 1955).

35. R. Bultmann, **Die Geschichte der synoptischen Tradition** (Göttingen, 1957[3]) p. 391f.

36. F. Mussner (-> 1961) defends the authenticity of "in the last days" (Act 2:17a) and draws several conclusions concerning the eschatological perception which Luke has of the present time. By the same author (-> 1962) we can read an analysis of Lk 17:20b-21; verses we know are important for the interpretation of Lucan eschatology: neither predictable by signs, nor exclusively future, the Kingdom is among you in the form of enigma which only those, who place it in relation with the person of Jesus, can decipher. As for W. Eltester (-> 1961), he published an article entitled "Lukas und Paulus". The first part brings Lucan studies up to date (it is particularly a controversy with A.

Ehrhardt (-> 1958)). To understand Luke's theology, it is necessary to place the Evangelist within his own time period: in the eighties and not in the second century (against G. Klein). The precise traits of Frühkatholizismus are lacking (against E. Käsemann). The polemic against Judaism is still intense. The corpus of the Pauline letters is not yet constituted. The author of Luke-Acts is Greek and did not want to do the work of a historian, but of an evangelist. The arguments evoked against the identification of the author with the companion of Paul are not all binding. In particular, those based on theological differences, for Paul's theology is that of a converted Jew. As a Greek, Luke could not understand the apostle's approach. The circumstances more than the times have changed: while the Pauline kerygma renounced the Synoptic tradition, Luke, with a clear theological will, inserts this tradition: this is why the Gospel is placed before the Acts. In placing Acts after the Gospel, Luke pays tribute to history, whereas John telescopes the exalted Christ and the historical Jesus. However, in Luke, the history remains a salvation history. The Lucan particularity of the apostolate is not unfaithful with regard to the apostle Paul, but rather the consequence of the adoption of the Synoptic tradition. Similarly, the relation between Judaism and Christianity is no longer Paul's, not because the times have changed, but because Luke's point of view is different. It is the approach of a Gentile, who is bent on explaining that all the chances for conversion have been given to the Jews. The "Judeophilic" character of the Lucan apostles originates from an ecclesiastical preoccupation of a Gentile Christian: to show the continuity between the Israel of the promises and the early Church. The OT reveals to Luke the God, who is creator of the world and regulator of history. Furthermore, he presents the prophecies relative to the Christ. All that Paul could have read in them, escapes Luke. A new and important contribution to the work of Luke was provided by W. Eltester (-> 1972).

37. This important work contains: 1) a good state of the question which insists on the consensus of C. H. Dodd - M. Dibelius (the speeches take up an archaic traditional schema); 2) a first section on the recurrent structure of the speeches; 3) a second section shows that the redactional frame corresponds admirably to the speeches; the scheme of these latter is redactional as well as a good part of the material used; 4) a last part situates the Christology of the speeches in Hellenistic Christianity and ends with a theological evaluation which we speak of in the text. J. Dupont (-> 1962) wrote an excellent summary and critique of this work.

38. To oppose, as Wilckens does, the solutions which Luke and "popular Christianity" (this unfortunate term designates 2 Pet, the Pastoral epistles, etc.) give to the problem of the apostolic heritage seems to be a simplification which exaggerates the theological merit of Luke.

39. J. Dupont (-> 1962) and E. Haenchen (-> 1956) expressed sharp reserves with regard to the last pages of Wilckens' book. In his evaluation of present research (-> 1966), Wilckens corrects some of his theses. He insists on the distance which separates Luke from his sources and on the fact that the framework of salvation history is already indissolubly associated with the primitive Christian kerygma which Paul makes his own. The attacks against Luke come from a contestable existentialist understanding of the apostle Paul.

40. S. G. Wilson (-> 1969-1970) also thinks that Luke does not remove all eschatological value from John the Baptist.

41. The reader may not grasp why the word "take up" (Lk 9:51) and the verb "to take up" (Act 1:2, 11, 22) might indicate that the life of Jesus would unfold in two stages.

42. Another thesis: the ministry of Jesus has a normative value as the representation of the reign of God. From here the Church draws its confidence in the divine plan which stretches toward the last realization of this reign. The Church draws its legitimation from the time of Jesus; for it is the present proclamation centered on the Kingdom and the authority of the apostles which have been given to the Church. It would be exaggerated to say that Luke ela - borates his concept of the apostolate in order to offer a historical guarantee to the tradition on Jesus. Luke's preoccupation is more that of a pastor who takes care of his flock than that of a historian or archeologist (pp. 28-30).

43. G. von Rad, **Theologie des Alten Testaments**, I (Munich, 1958^2) pp. 127ff.

44. To our knowledge, few periodicals have presented the work of W. C. Robinson. Cf. the review of H. C. Waetjen in **JBL** 84 (1965), p. 300f. W. C. Robinson also wrote an article (-> 1960) concerning the theological sense of the journey of Jesus to Galilee in Judea; the trip is one step on the way of the Lord. The length of the journey is explained by the fact that Luke wants to solidly install the apostles in their function as witnesses. In our opinion, the presence of the witnesses at the side of Jesus is important for Luke. However it does not explain the length of the trip.

45. To present H. W. Bartsch's position (-> 1963; cf. before this -> 1959), we can do no better that cite the good summary given by J.-D. Kaestli (-> 1969, p. 56). "H. W. Bartsch refuses to speak of the extinction of the apocalyptic expectation in Luke. He lifts out of the third Gospel a series of affirmations concerning the proximity of the judgment and the Kingdom, which Conzelmann cannot integrate into his conception without doing them violence (Lk 3:9, 17; 10:9, 11; 21:32). In fact, Lucan eschatology must be understood from a double opposition. On the one hand, it is a systematic correction of a primitive concept which in leaning on Gnostic speculations, identifies the resurrection of Christ with the coming of the Kingdom of God. Luke answers this by underlining that the eschaton is linked to no determined event (the resurrection of Jesus or the destruction of Jerusalem: cf. Lk 19:11; 21:9, 12). On the other hand, he combats an easing of the eschatological expectation. This is the reason for his insistance on the sudden and unpredicatable nature of the end, and his numerous exhortations to vigilance (cf. Lk 9:27; 21:32, 34-36). It is the "watch at all times" of Lk 21:36 that best summarizes the intention of Lucan eschatology: each moment of the life of the community is found immediately in relation with the eschaton and placed under judgment.

46. D. P. Fuller - if we have read properly - is wrong in saying that Paul founded the Christian community in Ephesus. As Act 18:24ff. attests, there were already Christians in Ephesus when the apostle arrived in the city.

47. We will continue our presentation and critique of this book in our chapter on salvation (cf. below 5, III, c). The reader can read three critical presentations of H. Flender: J.-D. Kaestli (-> 1969, passim); H. Kodell (-> 1971) and R. A. Edwards (-> 1969): The last article presents the articles of L. Keck (-> 1967) and O. Betz, as well as the English version of H. Flender's book (Philadelphia, 1968).

48. Against P. Vielhauer, P. Borgen (-> 1966) shows that the theology of Luke remains in the furrow of Paul's. The continuity concerns particularly es - chatology: "Auf eine klarere Weise als Markus interpretieren sowohl Lukas als auch Paulus die Zeit der Heiden auf Grund einer eschatologischen Interims - periode, welche die historischen Ereignisse mit dem Eschaton verbindet. Lukas interpretiert auf diese Weise das Ausbleiben der Parusie innerhalb des Rahmens einer eschatologischen Perspektive, die schon bei Paulus bezeugt ist." (p. 157). The book of A. Salas (-> 1967) does not touch directly our subject, since he attempts to detect behind Lk 21:20-36, along side of Mark, a second source. He then seeks to define its theology.

49. The first pages of the article provide a brief presentation and a rich bibliography on this subject.

50. J. Reumann summarizes here the conclusions of an earlier article (-> 1966-1967).

51. J. Reumann seems to be unaware of S. Schulz thesis (-> 1963), summarized above 1, I f. Otherwise he is remarkably informed.

52. K. Baltzer, **Das Bundesformular** (Neukirchen, 1960, 1965[2]).

53. J. Reumann published other articles concerning the notion of *οἰκονομία* which he mentions in the notes (they appeared in **JBL** 77 (1958), pp. 339-349; **NT** 3 (1959) pp. 282-299; F. L. Cross (ed), **Studia Patristica**, III (Berlin, 1964) pp. 370-379).

54. Luke could have written a salvation history, O. Betz judiciously remarks, because of the persistant presence of evil as well as the delay of the Parousia.

55. We can join to these authors, C. E. B. Cranfield (-> 1963) who speaks of imminence but for him it is an imminence associated to the decisive event of the cross, and H. W. Bartsch (-> 1963). The latter is summarized above in note 45.

56. A. J. and M. B. Mattill, **A Classified Bibliography of the Literature on the Acts of the Apostles** (Leiden, 1966). For the articles, cf. ->1970, -> 1972 (second title) and -> 1975.

57. In Lk 18:8 *ἐν τάχει* appears once, but the translation of these words is not sure: "suddenly" or "soon"?

58. Cf. above 1, II, c and note 40.

59. H. D. Betz (-> 1969) analyzes the legend of Emmaus (Lk 24:13-32) and indicates what henceforth is the mode of the presence of the Resurrected One: it is in the interpretation of the Scriptures and the communal meals. It is a presence related to the event of the cross and accessible to faith. This article, without being an explicit contribution to the study of Lucan eschatology, sets forth some important elements to define the time of the Church. The year after, R. Schnackenburg (-> 1970) presented his interpretation of the first apocalyptic discourse of Luke (Lk 17:20-37). He attributes to the redactional work of Luke the following: the double frame vss. 20a and 22a, perhaps vs. 21b, vs. 22, the reminder in vs. 25 of the suffering of the Son of Man, the insertion into vs. 31 of a saying taken from Mk, which should instill faithfulness in the hour of the end, vs. 32 and the question of the disciples in vs. 37a (the "vs. 34a" on p. 230 should be corrected). The redactional work allows several particularities of Lucan eschatology to emerge: 1) the bending of the apocalyptic expectation of the end; 2) the accentuation of sufferings, persecutions and tribulations; 3) a gaze on the coming of the Son of Man which motivates the parenesis and encourages the community. By the sensitivity, he witnesses to the theme of vigilance, Luke remains faithful to Jesus' intention. Lk 21, the second apocalyptic discourse, will open the space necessary for the mission and the Church.

60. J. Panagopoulos expresses himself curiously on this subject. He uses the adjective "secondary" in an inhabitual sense (p. 144). This term must mean traditional for him.

61. After having forbidden the distinction between the tradition and redaction in Acts (p. 140), the author makes it nevertheless (without providing sufficient justification, he declares these verses redactional) on p. 144f.

62. The translation of Act 20:32 which is proposed (p. 149) reflects this rejection of mediation; it links directly the words "able to edify" with the "Lord", whereas, if we follow the order of the words, they should be made to depend on the "word of grace", i.e. the instrument to which the Christ must resort in order to reach the Church. Cf. F. Bovon (-> 1974).

63. The author explains why he studied ch 21 before ch 17.

64. So it is with H.-J. Degenhardt (see bibliography of ch 7, -> 1965), cf. below 7, IV, 2, f.

65. G. Schneider notes that Luke places before the parables of the flood and the heavenly fire (Lk 17:26-30), a historical allusion to the crucifixion (vs. 25 is redactional), which provokes a delay in the eschatological program. These two parables, in their actual formulation, declare the questions of the date and the place of the Parousia as illegitimate. The chapter ends with the exegesis of verses in which a belief of Q and Luke in the imminency have been seen: the judgment announced by John the Baptist (Lk 3:9, 17) would be historical and not eschatological. The preaching of the seventy (Lk 10:9, 11) draws the proximity of "the being" and not the "date" of the Kingdom (the author becomes a bit confused here).

66. G. Schneider offers an unprecedented parallel to vss. 7b-8a which must consequently be taken as a unity: Bar 4:25.

67. Luke must have understood the ἐν τάχει in the sense of "suddenly" and not "soon".

68. On p. 3, note 2 we find the names of E. Stauffer, R. Bultmann (in their NT theologies) and E. Grässer (-> 1957, p. 211). We could add C. K. Barrett (-> 1964). Later notes add other names (W. Pesch, A. Descamps, G. Gaide).

69. J. Dupont, **Les Béatitudes. Le problème littéraire, le message doctrinal** (Bruges-Leuven, 1954) p. 211f.

70. Above, 1, II, d.

71. W. C. van Unnik (-> 1967).

72. From E. Rasco, we know a long critical review of Conzelmann's book (-> 1965) and two polycopied fascicles concerning the beginnings of the Acts (Pontifical Biblical Institute); cf. bibliography of ch 7, -> 1968.

73. E. Franklin (-> 1975) clearly distinguishes himself from Conzelmann. The end is not neglected or pushed back, for history is determined by eschatology. While transcendent, the Kingdom nonetheless exercises an influence on history. The Ascension becomes, for this author, the central eschatological event which gives meaning to the whole of salvation history. The theological reinterpretation of Luke does not consist in substituting salvation history for eschatology, but in making salvation history serve eschatology. The goal of this reinterpretation is that the readers of the Lucan work recognize in Jesus, the Lord, i.e. the place of the eschatological action of God.

CHAPTER 2

1. Cf. Lk 7:22, 27; 8:10; 10:27; 13:35; 18:20; 19:38; 20:17, 28, 37, 42.

2. Cf. P. Benoit, "L'enfance de Jean-Baptiste selon Luc I", **NTS** 3 (1956-1957), pp. 169-194.

3. Like in the other Synoptics, the Lucan account of the Passion often uses OT expressions, most frequently from the Psalms. Luke adds another important quotation from Isa 53, which is peculiar to him: "and he was counted among the impious" (Lk 22:37).

4. Three studies present a list of citations (the second is the most complete): L. Venard, art. "Citations de l'Ancien Testament dans le Nouveau Testament", **DBS** 2 (Paris, 1934), col. 24 (Lc) - 25 (Ac); J. Dupont (-> 1953), p. 281f. of **Etudes** (see note 9 below) of 1967; P. S. White (-> 1973), p. 155f. Cf. book by book and for the whole NT, K. Aland, M. Black, B. M. Metzger and A. Wikgren (eds), **The Greek New Testament**, (Stuttgart, 1966) 897-920.

5. The reader will find a list of references in F. Bovon, "Le Christ, la foi et la Sagesse dans l'épître aux Hébreux", **RTPhil**, third series, 18 (1968), pp. 135-136. Cf. K. Kliesh (-> 1975).

6. Concerning the divers types of citations which M. Rese distinguishes, cf. below 2, III, e.

7. The publication of C. H. Dodd's book **According to the Scriptures. The Substructure of New Testament Theology** (Digswell Place, 1952) has perhaps not been foreign to this renewal of theological interest for the OT quotations in Luke.

8. The end of the article (pp. 178-186) show the importance of the proof-from-prophecy argument in the rest of the Gospel of Luke and in the last scene of the Acts, the counterpart to Lk 24.

9. All of these studies have been regrouped in J. Dupont, **Etudes sur les Actes des Apôtres** (Paris, 1967), pp. 243-390. They form the third section of the book. All our references are to the book.

10. And not the traditional usage of the apostles, as S. Amsler thinks (-> 1960).

11. Here J. Dupont adds two annex remarks. The first seems contestable: Luke sometimes abbreviates his sources. The second is that Luke draws the consequences from the OT context from where the verse is taken.

12. Such as M. Wilcox (-> 1956 and 1965).

13. J. D. Barthelemy, "Redécouverte d'un chaînon manquant de l'histoire de la Septante", **RB** 60 (1953), pp. 18-29.

14. J. Dupont (-> 1961, first title) sees in Psa 69:26 (Act 1:20a) the Scripture mentioned in Act 1:16 and now fulfilled in what follows the death of Judah and in Psa 109:8 (Act 1:20b) the point of departure of the drawing of lots for the successor of Judah.

15. However, at Qumran we can note that the actualization, different from the NT, concerns the community, not the Messiah.

16. Thus Luke distinguishes himself from Frühkatholizismus, for he does not use the notion of the new Law (p. 148).

17. In Lk 10, the double commandment of love is perceived as the norm of evangelical ethics, not as the foundation of the call to conversion. S. Amsler (-> 1960) shares our view on this point.

18. Cf. see the two preceding pages.

19. H. Conzelmann refers to the Lucan particularities of the quotation of Isa 40 in Lk 3:4ff. (with regard to Mk 1:2f.). He should have mentioned here the first sermon of Jesus and the recourse to Isa 61:1f. it contains (Lk 4:16-30).

20. The only accepted exception, but which has no consequence: Act 3:21 (p. 151, note 1).

21. Valid for the Jews, is this conclusion valid in the same manner for the Gentiles? Were not the Jews the beneficiaries of the divine election? It would be necessary to see if the *ἄγνοια* of the Jews in Jerusalem, guilty of Jesus' condemnation (Act 3:17), corresponds to the *ἄγνοια* of the Gentiles (Act 17:30).

22. Cf. M. Dibelius, "Die Reden der Apostelgeschichte und die antike Geschichtsschreibung", **Sitzungsberichte der Heidelberger Akademie der Wissenschaften, Phil.-Hist. Klasse**, 1949/I; taken up in M. Dibelius, **Aufsätze zur Apostelgeschichte** (Göttingen, 1951), pp. 120-162 of the 1961[4].

23. 1) The notion of testimony (Act 10:42); 2) the Scrip-ture more prophetic (Act 1:16; 3:18; 7:52) than normative; 3) the notion of fulfillment; 4) it is necessary to add one point to the program detected by Dupont: the coming of the king-prophet (Act 3:22; 7:37; 13:22, 34).

24. Cf. Act 2:30f. and 26:22f.

25. N. A. Dahl seems to be unaware of J. Bihler's book (-> 1963), which on pp. 38-46, comes to similar conclusions.

26. This point is also demonstrated by M. H. Scharlemann (-> 1968), pp. 58-63.

27. "Here God's word to Abraham is seen as the beginning of a history in which partial realizations are interconnected with new promises, until the coming of the Righteous One, of whom all the prophets spoke (cf. 7, 52)." (p. 144).

28. N. A. Dahl signals the modification of the end of the quotation of Gen 15:14 (Luke substitutes the words "and will offer me worship in this place", from Ex 3:12, at the end of the verse). The place of this worship is more important than the conquest of Canaan. It allows us to explain the apparent tension between Act 7:47 (Solomon built him a dwelling place) and Act 7:48 (But the Most High does not live in constructions made by men). There is no contradiction (between Stephen and Luke, for example), but Luke has a firm conception: the Temple of Jerusalem was only the provisionary place of worship which would be fulfilled in the risen Christ. It was not itself the fulfillment of the prophecy of David: the heaven is my throne... (Act 7:49). N. A. Dahl sees a confirmation of this interpretation in the Benedictus (Lk 1:68-75).

29. "In Stephen's speech Moses and, to some extent, Joseph are seen as types of Christ, but the typology is subordinated to the recurring pattern of prophecy and fulfillment." (p. 144).

30. N. A. Dahl adds: not an eschatological interpretation either. In our opinion, everything depends on what we place under these words. If Luke means that the Church, open to the Gentiles, lives at the end of time, he gives an eschatological sense to the promise God made to Abraham (Gen 21:18) which he cites in Act 3:25. Cf. J. Dupont (-> 1953), p. 251 of **Etudes**.

31. For M. H. Scharlemann (-> 1968), the speech is traditional and reflects the theology of Stephen himself, influenced by Samaritan conceptions.

32. At the end of his article, Dahl draws several conclusions concerning the Lucan theology of history: Abraham remains the father of the Jews. He is never called the father of believers (this is different from what happens in Paul). The Gentiles are not substituted for the Jews.

33. S. Sandmel, "Philo's Place in Judaism", **HUCA** 25 (1954), p. 237.

34. Concerning the figure of Joseph, cf. J. Bihler (-> 1963), pp. 46-51, who shows a) that a prophecy fulfilled at the epoch of Joseph (the descendence must go to a foreign country) and b) that Luke places the accent on Joseph who escapes tribulations. M. H. Scharlemann (-> 1968), pp. 63-69, thinks of a certain typology: "Stephen's interest can be accounted for by the fact that he saw an inner connection between the experiences of Joseph and those of God's Righteous One. Joseph had been rejected by his brothers and sold into Egypt as a slave. By this very act, however, the brothers unwittingly became the instruments for carrying forward God's gracious concern of His people. In this development Stephen noted an element of Messianic prefigurement. In a very real sense, therefore, he understood Joseph to be something of a type of Jesus, who had recently suffered in Jerusalem but now stood at the right hand of God." (p. 68). We would like to be as confident as Scharlemann!

35. Beside the authors mentioned in the text, let us signal F. Gils (cf. ch 3 bibliography, -> 1957). pp. 30-42, and R. F. Zehnle (cf. ch 3 bibliography, -> 1971), pp. 47-52 and 75-89, who both insist on a typology Jesus-Moses in the Lucan corpus.

36. We might wonder if J. Bihler, when insisting on the redactional nature of the rereading of the personage of Moses, does not underestimate the work of reinterpretation which was already practiced in the Hellenistic Jewish synagogue.

37. Cf. Lk 1:27, 32, 69; 2:4, 11; 3:31; 6:3; 18:38f.; 20:41, 42, 44; Act 1:16; 2:25, 29, 34; 4:25; 7:45; 13:22, 34, 36; 15:16.

38. One should note God's affection for David. Act 7:46 indicates that, in his relations with David, God takes the initiative .

39. J. Dupont, "'Filius meus es tu'. L'interprétation de Ps 2,7 dans le Nou - veau Testament", **RechSR** 35 (1948), pp. 522-543, and Dupont (-> 1961, second title).

40. Cf. the book reviews of R. H. Fuller (**JBL** 81 (1962), pp. 295-296) and T. Holtz (**ThLZ** 88 (1963), col. 202-203).

41. "In the light of what has been shown above, there can be no doubt that the words cited from Isaiah in Acts 13, 34 refer to the covenant promise to David." (p. 72).

42. Cf. note 40.

43. With E. Lövestam, p. 5, against E. Lövestam, p. 81 (noted by T. Holtz, cf. note 40)!

44. L. Cerfaux (-> 1950) notes: "The second citation reacted to the first [Isa 55:3], *δώσω* (cf. *δώσεις*) replacing *διαθήσομαι* of the LXX." (p. 48). This confirms our hypothesis.

45. Cf. the pre-Pauline idea (cf. Rom 1:3-4) of the adoption of Jesus as the Son on Easter day.

46. Cf. concerning Elijah, J. D. Dubois (-> 1973).

47. Only a partial rehabilitation, since Cerfaux maintains the primacy of the Egyptian text in several passages. What he refuses is to discard systematically the Western variants

48. These tendencies have been studied successively by P. Menoud and E. J. Epp. Cf. P. H. Menoud, "The Western Text and the Theology of Acts", **SNTS Bulletin** 2 (1951), pp. 19-32: included in French in P. H. Menoud, **Jésus-Christ et la foi. Recherches néotestamentaires** (Neuchâtel-Paris), 1975, pp. 49-62; and E. J. Epp, **The Theological Tendency of Codex Bezae Catabrigiensis in Acts** (Cambridge, 1966).

49. **The Greek New Testament**, .K. Aland, M. Black, B. M. Metzger, A. Wikgren, (eds) (Stuttgart, 1966), p. 423 indicates the other variants.

50. Cf. from the same author, a later article (-> 1956).

51. Cf. E. Hatch and H. A. Redpath, **A Concordance to the Setuagint and other Greek Versions of the Old Testament (Including the Apocryphal Books)**, I (Oxford, 1897); (reprint Graz, 1954), pp. 602-603.

52. J. Dupont (-> 1961, second title, p. 346, note 38 of **Etudes**; and -> 1962, p. 285, note 8 of **Etudes**) noted the hypothetical character and some - times unlikely propositions of M. Wilcox, set forth in his 1956 article.

53. Cf. furthermore, eventually, Dt 33:3-4 to which Act 20:32 and 26:18 seem to make allusion.

54. This distance of four years hinders the author from integrating the contribution of the studies of M. Wilcox (-> 1965) and M. Rese (-> 1965) into his work. Moreover, certain bibliographical lacunae are surprising: W. Beyse (->

1939), L. Cerfaux (-> 1950), P. Schubert (-> 1954), J. Dupont (partially), S. Amsler (-> 1960), H. Rusche (-> 1961).

55. With the exception of the summaries of the history of Israel contained in Act 7 and 13 which he includes in his work, the author limits his investigation to the citations and leaves aside the allusions to the OT as well as the Biblical expressions.

56. This does not mean that all the selbständig quotations are redactional. It could be that Luke received some of them from tradition, which he then verified and reestablished according to the scroll of the LXX at his disposition.

57. The first part analyzes the following quotations: Joel 3:1-5a (Act 2:17-21); Amos 5:25-27 (Act 7:42f.); Hab 1:5 (Act 13:41); Amos 9:11f. (Act 15:16f.); Hos 10:18 (Lk 23:30); Isa 66:1f. (Act 7:49f.); Isa 53:7f. (Act 8:32f.); Isa 49:6 (Act 13:47); Isa 6:9f. (Act 28:26f.); Isa 40:3-5 (Lk 3:4-6); Isa 61:1f. (Lk 4:18f.); Isa 53:12 (Lk 22:37); Psa 68:26 and108:8 (Act 1:20); Psa 15:8-11 (Act 2:25-28); Psa 109:1 (Act 2:34f. and Lk 20:42f.); Psa 2:1f. (Act 4:25f.); Psa 90:11f. (Lk 4:10f.); Psa 30:6 (Lk 23:46).

58. In Act 7:50, for example, the text which is an affirmation in the LXX becomes a rhetorical question (p. 30).

59. Cf. below 2, III, e. T. Holtz does not emphasize the theological impor - tance of the prolongation of the citations of Isa 40:3-5 in Lk 3:4-5 (pp. 37-39).

60. T. Holtz sometimes claims the contrary: the quotation of Ex 22:27 in Act 23:5, which corresponds exactly to the text of the LXX must be traditional.

61. The exception is a curious quotation of Ex 22:27 (Act 23:5). Cf. the preceding note.

62. "Mit dieser positiven Auswahl steht Lukas in dem grösseren Kreis einer bestimmten Frömmigkeit des Spät-judentums, eine Erscheinung, der hier nicht näher nachgegangen werden kann." (p. 170).

63. Cf. P. M. Barnard, **The Biblical Text of Clement of Alexandria in the Four Gospels and the Acts of the Apostles** (Cambridge, 1899), p. 62.

64. An expression which, according to T. Holtz, would have in any case the same meaning.

65. Cf. above 1, III, b.

66. Cf. J. Bihler (-> 1963).

67. The aspects which Holtz considers clearly redactional are in fact also found in Jewish tradition; the critique of the Temple and the hardening of the people.

68. For example, one can read the recension of M. A. Chevallier, **RHPR** 51 (1971), p. 391.

69. M. Rese has little new to offer us concerning Luke's choice of the cita - tions and their textual form.

70. "Schriftbeweis im Schema von Erfüllung und Weissagung".

71. "Schriftbeweis im Schema von Weissagung und Erfüllung "

72. In an introductory note (p. 40, note 125) and in his conclusion (p. 209), M. Rese delimits a much rarer fifth type, called typological, which would be close to the first. In his review, M. A. Chevallier **RHPR** 51 (1971), p. 391, reproaches him for not having deepened this typological interpretation.

73. In the recension mentioned in the preceding note, M. A., Chevalier regrets that Rese did not take into consideration enough these traditions.

74. On p. 98, Rese even thinks that Isa 53:7f. including vs. 8d, was cited in the tradition and that Luke shortened the quotation and eliminated in this way the mention to the expiatory value of the death in the name of his soteriology.

75. E. Lövestam (-> 1961), as we have seen (cf. above 2, II, g) has a diametrically opposed view.

76. We will return to this in our chapter on salvation, below, 5, III, e.

77. Cf. below 5, III, e.

78. On this point, M. Rese (p. 145 and 151) follows E. Schweizer, "art. *πνεῦμα κτλ.*", **TWNT**, VI (Stuttgart, 1959), p. 405.

79. Here let us mention an interesting article of G. Delling (-> 1973). At the end of an analysis of the verbs which express the relation, Christ established between Christians and the Scripture, mainly the verb "to open", the author concludes: "Indem die frühe Christenheit auf solche Weise Jesu Tod und Auferweckung von der Schrift her verstand und die Schrift auf Kreuz und Auferstehung hin auslegte, gab sie nach Lk das weiter, was sie ihrerseits vom Auferstandenen her empfangen hatte: er hatte den Seinen 'das über ihn' im Alten Testament aufgezeigt, hatte ihnen die Schrift aufgeschlossen. Damit spricht Lk in seiner Weise aus, was sich anderweit von historischen Überlegungen her ergibt: dass die Schriftauslegung der Urchristenheit mit Ostern beginnt. Er sagt darüber hinaus, dass die frühe Christenheit die Schriftauslegung in ihren grundlegenden Sätzen empfängt als eine Gabe ihres auferstandenen Herrn." (p. 82).

80. Cf. J. W. Bowker (-> 1967) and E. E. Ellis (-> 1970).

81. Concerning this subject, see the few lines of L. Marin, offered as a conclusion to "Sémiotique narrative: Récits bibliques", **Langages** 22 (1971), pp. 123-125.

82. We are surprised that no one to our knowledge has analyzed the citations with consideration to the order in which they appear in Luke.. This

order is important the moment we want to make a redaktionsgeschichtlich investigation.

The redaction of this chapter was finished when we heard of the dissertation of P. S. White, defended at the Protestant Faculty of Theology in Strasbourg. The absence of the presentation should not prejudge this work. The author limits his quest to the citations contained in the speeches. He successively studies the citations in the speeches of Peter, Stephen and Paul. "Our method will be to clarify the citations by: 1) the contextual considerations in the OT; 2) the study of the textual situation; 3) the contextual considerations of the NT; 4) the study of the parallels in the NT and finally; 5) the development of the hermeneutic of each citation", p. 168f.

CHAPTER 3

1. And we have discarded several articles which have remained inaccessible to us, or belong more properly to edification or vulgarization. The reader who wants to find these works can go to the bibliography of A. J. and Mary B. Mattill, **A Classified Bibliography of Literature on the Acts of the Apostles** (Leiden, 1966), pp. 274-281 (Numbers 3814-3919), for the works before 1961 and to the **Elenchus Bibliographicus** of **Biblica**, **IZBG** and **NTAbstr** for the more recent studies.

2. Concerning preexistence in Luke, cf. R. G. Hamerton-Kelly (-> 1973), pp. 83-87, and C. F. D. Moule (-> 1966).

3. These last two books are presented and evaluated by J. Dupont in his state of the question (-> 1950, first title), pp. 43-47; pp. 98-101 and 105-107 in **Etudes**. As for the work of Gewiess, we will summarize if in our chapter on salvation, below 5, I, a.

4. P. Vielhauer (ch 1, -> 1950).

5. J. Weiss, **Das Urchristentum** (Göttingen, 1914-1917), p. 23. U. Wil - ckens (-> 1961), p. 36, note 1 and p. 171, note 2 indicate other adherents to this interpretation.

6. A. C. Winn (-> 1959) thinks that Luke resolves a major problem: the rejection of the Christ by the Jews. The answer is that the Lord foresaw and willed the hardening of the Jews and the vocation of the Gentiles. The Lucan Christ gains a particular trait: he does not evangelize the pagans yet (Luke respects the tradition), but he has a (redactional!) soft spot for them. On U. Luck's article (-> 1960), cf. above 1, III, c.

7. On this work, cf. below 5, III, a.

8. I. H. Marshall (-> 1970, first title), p. 72.

9. We would prefer to say the author of the epistle to the Ephesians.

10. On this work, cf. below 5, III, b.

11. Only vs. 20a is traditional. However, it is not important enough to have constituted a tradition alone. Moreover, Luke reinterpreted it. On these verses since,cf. R. F. Zehnle (-> 1971), pp. 71-75 who concludes: "Luke has adopted a Jewish appeal for repentance and placed it in congenial surroundings in a discourse directed to the Jews. The use of source material seems evident, but because of the possibility of successful archaizing the question of its primitive nature must remain open." (p. 75).

12. H. J. Cadbury (-> 1933, second title).

13. Beside the schema, E. Kränkl enumerates the following traditional elements: a) "of the seed of David"; b) the baptism of Jesus by John; c) the miracles of Jesus; d) the burial of Jesus; e) the resurrection by God; f) the apparitions; g) the sitting at the right hand of God; h) "judge of the living and the dead"; i) the allusion to the kerygma of salvation and its addressees; j) the requirements of faith.

14. Cf. E. Samain (-> 1973, second title).

15. Kränkl correctly notes that Luke establishes his important synchronism (Lk 3:1f.) concerning John the Baptist's, not Jesus', entry on the scene: the baptism of Jesus by John, from the Gospel of Luke on, is an important step.

16. In his detailed analyses, Kränkl often runs counter U. Wilckens (-> 1961).

17. Here is a summary of the second part of the book: pp. 85-87: the Davidic sonship (Act 13:22f.) is typical of Luke; it describes not the incarnated Jesus (so Paul, Mk and Mt) but the exalted Christ; pp. 86-97: John the Baptist and Jesus (Act 1:22; 10:37f.; 13:24f.) (cf. see above note 15); pp. 98-101: the public ministry of Jesus (Act 2:22 and 10:37-39: the miracles are no longer the beginning of the end, but the attestation of God's designation of Jesus); pp. 102-124; the death of Jesus (Act 2:23; 3:13-15, 17-18: the theme of ignorance is found later in Justin; the time of ignorance ceases as soon as the Christian preaching rings out; Act 4:10f.: the responsibility of Herod and Pilate is not a Lucan element; this tradition is found also in Justin; Act 5:30 and 10:39b (Dt 21:22f. is understood differently in Gal 3:13); Act 7:51: Jesus fits into the larger framework of salvation history; one can sense the next passage of the Gospel from the Jews to the Gentiles; a contrast between the guilty Jews and the innocent Jesus is noted; Act 8:32-35: vs.33a: the humbling is transformed into exaltation; vs. 33b: the spiritual descendence of Jesus? vs. 33c: the ascension to the right hand of God. It is not necessary to draw an expiatory value of Jesus' death from Isa 53. Luke is not the only one of his time to identify Jesus with the Servant; Act 13:27-29: the ignorance of the Jews, the fulfillment of the Scripture and the innocence of Jesus are Lucan elements; pp. 125-129: an excursus on παῖς θεοῦ which we summarize below 2, VI, e; pp. 130-148: the resurrection of Jesus: the work of God, firmly attested by the Scripture (Act 2:24-32: Psa 16:8-11; Act 13:32-37: Psa 2:7; Ia 55:3; Psa 16:10; the apparitions of Act 10:40f. and 13:31: God is the author of the apparitions; the bodily presence of the Risen One is a typical trait of writings at the end of the first century). The resurrection is heilsgeschichtlich like the death: Scriptural proof shows this. One must note the contrast between the

Jews who killed and God who raises (in ignoring the account of Emmaus, Kränkl deems that until the Ascension the resurrection was first a reviving); pp. 149-166: the exaltation: a) to the right hand of God: one must translate Act 2:33 and 5:31 by "at he right hand" and not "by the right hand" (this locative sense given to the dative seems contestable to us). Luke isolates here the exaltation from the humbling, a later phenomenon which is found also in John; Act 2:34f.: a traditional usage of Psa 110:1 which corresponds to Luke's idea; Act 7:55b-56, cf. below 2, VI, d; b) other witnesses from the Scripture: Act 2:30 (Psa 132:11: the Messianic sense of the oath of God is presupposed: it is indeed attested at Qumran and must be traditional; the frame is redactional); Act 4:11 (Psa 118:22); Act 15:16-18 (Amos 9:11f): the rising up of the house of David is identified by Luke with the exaltation; pp. 167-175: the witnesses (cf. above); pp. 176-186: the salvific value of the exaltation (cf. above); pp. 187-205: Jesus and eschatology: Kränkl analyzes Act 2:17-21 (Joel 3:1-5), Act 3:19-26 and 4:12 (in speaking of future salvation, the author does not notice on p. 202 that *σῳζόμενοι* (Act 2:47) is a present participle), Act 10:42f.; Act 17:30f. There is a recoiling of future eschatology, but it is because the exaltation has become the central event in Luke's theology. Pp. 206-214 are a summary of the author's theses.

18. Kränkl thinks (p. 169) that the exaltation was aimed more at Jesus' function with regard to the community than to his person. Is he right on these two points?

19. Cf. F. Bovon (ch 1, -> 1974-1975).

20. Concerning this insertion of the Church in the credo, cf. F. Bovon, "L'origine des récits concernant les apôtres", **RTPhil**, 3rd series, 17 (1967), 345-350.

21. After a precise formal investigation, E. Schweizer (-> 1957) also concludes in the Lucan character of the speeches. He is followed by D. L. Jones whom we know only by the summary of his dissertation (-> 1966) and an article concerning the title Christ (-> 1970), cf. below 2, VI, i.

22. U. Wilckens (-> 1961), pp. 19-25.

23. For C. S. C. Williams, the problem is to find out if Luke consciously "archeologized" or if he repoduces his oral or written sources (p. 44). A summary analysis of the Christological content of the speeches led him to conclude: "Each of the early speeches of Peter and Paul reflects the ideas of the primitive kerygma, but they are often found to have an individual flavour in keeping with the speaker." (p. 47). Luke's faithfulness also appears in other indications than the primitive character of the speeches: a) Luke, in his time (cf. the Pastorals), should have used the title savior often. He seems to avoid it because of faithfulness to the primitive kerygma which did not apply it to Jesus; b) a Christological development, which recalls the Epistles, does not appear in the Acts except in the conersion of Paul: so Luke transmits correctly the evolution of primitive Christology (with W. L. Knox (-> 1948), p. 77f.).

24. O. Cullmann concentrates his attention on the archaic nature of the Christology of the servant, which he sees attested in the Acts.

25. In a later article, S. S. Smalley (-> 1973) seeks new arguments in favor of the great age of the Christology of the speeches. He finds them especially in certain parallels between Acts and 1 Peter (the same usage of the title Christ and the same relation between the Christ and suffering).

26. As specific traits of the Jesus of the third Gospel (which originates partially from the Sondergut), V. Taylor also notes: a) Jesus does not like flattery; b) he knows the trial of desires which are not fulfilled (Lk 22:15; but here we object to Taylor, Jesus can fulfill the desire to eat the Passover once more with his disciples) and he is oft tempted (Lk 4:13 and 22:28); c) he is compasionate with the most despised (Lk 7:36-50; 19:1-10), Samaritans (Lk 9:51-56; 17:11-19), sinners (Lk 18:9-14); d) Messiah of the Jews, Jesus has however broken his attachments with the Jewish world; e) the title Son of Man becomes almost a synonym for Jesus; f) he prefers the title Lord; g) the work of the Spirit is more important than in Mk: he intervenes from the birth of Jesus, and not like in Mk, from the baptism (at this point Luke takes up, rather than innovates, a traditional development); h) he is the Son of God by virtue of his birth.

27. We only know of this work by the review given by W. Klassen in **JBL** 81 (1962), 96f.

28. On p. 105 we can find a summary of the conclusions, which is included on pp. 25-26 of the second volume.

29. In his chapter on the Christ, the author exaggerates the role of the anointing. Luke, in our opinion, hardly connnects the title Christ with the anointing of the Holy Spirit. Concerning the anointing, cf. I. de la Potterie (-> 1958).

30. In the same sense, J. Dupont (-> 1950, second title).

31. Cf. I. H. Marshall (-> 1973).

32. Cf. E. Des Places (-> 1971), pp. 532-533.

33. The reader can find a summary of Marshall's book (-> 1970, first title), in particular chapters 5 ("Jesus in the Gospel") and 6 ("Christ in the Acts"), in our chapter consecrated to salvation, below, 5, IV, a. In fact, the author insists on the soteriological mission of the Messiah.

34. We renounce giving the bibliographical references to these well known works in order to save space.

35. We have reviewed, in our second chapter (cf. above 2, III, c), certain contributions which dealt with the traditional Scriptural argumentation encountered in Acts.

36. In the rest of the work, the author attempts to take the use of the title, Son, back to Jesus himself. Rightly, he proposes a distinction between this title and that of Son of God, whose usage goes back to the early Church.

37. Later we will speak of the important contributions of R. Laurentin (-> 1957) and G. Lohfink (-> 1971), Cf. below 3, V, a and 3, V, c. We should note the redactional modifications to the portrait of Christ from Scriptural arguments. Cf. our ch 2.

38. We have summarized in the first chapter the thesis of W. C. Robinson (-> 1962), above 1, III, e.

39. On this title, cf. below 3, VI, k.

40. Cf. below 7, IV, 4, a-e.

41. We will consecrate several pages to this book in our chapter on salvation, below 5, III, d.

42. J. Dupont (-> 1962, first title).

43. Cf. A. W. Wainwright (-> 1957).

44. Here we must mention the important article of O. Betz (-> 1968). The author sets himself against the current interpretation which the Bultmannian exegetes give to Luke. Writing the Gospel and the Acts, Luke did not betray the kerygma, for being more involved than the ancient historians, he did not write Christian Antiquities, but a Gospel of Jesus Christ and a mission of the apostles. At the center of Luke's faith is Christology not anthropology nor ecclesiology. To describe the kerygma of Jesus, Luke used traditions which the monks of Qumran knew. Jesus appears (cf. Lk 4) anointed by the Spirit as the proclaimer of good news for the whole earth: he announces the heavenly defeat of Satan and a year of liberation. Satan is clearly still at work on the earth. We must wait for the kerygma of the Church in the Acts, for the proclaimer - still following the Jewish tradition - to be enthroned according to the Davidic messianism of 2 Sam 7. The relation of the speeches of Peter (Act 2) and Paul (Act 13) is expressed in that the two preachers, according to Luke, shared the same Christological faith. It is at Pentecost that the Church realizes this exaltation. The Kerygma of Luke is faithful to Jesus' and the apostles'. However, it has three characteristics: a) Easter and the Ascension are distinct (the exaltation does not yet signify the end; we must wait until the last reestablishment); b) to respond to the Greco-Roman aspirations of a child savior, Luke did not apply the title Son of God and the anointing of the Spirit after the old formula (Rom 1:3-4), along with the Jewish material coming from the messianic exegesis of 2 Sam 7, to the resurrection but to the nativity. c) To show that Jesus prepares the end in heaven, the Acts use a prophetic tradition concerning Moses. Conclusion: 1) the kerygma of the apostles is a kerygma concerning the Kingdom, for the Kingdom has been revealed by Jesus; 2) Luke is not frühkatholisch; 3) the historical framework did not transform the saving virtue of eschatology; 4) Luke did not understand the Pauline theology of the cross. But he shares the paschal Christology of the apostle; 5) Luke has a dynamic conception of the ministers; 6) the gospel has an existential import for the Evangelist.

45. The context of Act 3 as well as 4 is Petrine. If Luke had been free to dispose of his materials as he wished, he would certainly have used the title παῖς in the speech of Paul.

46. Cf. F. Bovon (-> 1973).

47. This is also the opinion of W. Eltester (cf. E. Grässer et alii -> 1972, p. 108, note 65).

48. Let us note here several of the conclusions of G. W. MacRae (-> 1973); 1) there is a relation between the questions of introduction and the Christology of Acts. The Christology is Lucan, but Luke is not totally free : he reworks traditions. The three accounts of the conversion of Paul in the Acts show that Luke inscribes a theological or rather Christological motif of Paul's career in history. 2) We sense no influence of the doctrine of Wisdom on Luke's Christology: so the absence of preexistence. If Luke distinguishes the exaltation from the resurrection, it is to say that now the Christ is in another world. 3) The Christology of the Acts is indeed marked by the absence of Christ. Jesus had an terrestrial history and he will have another one on the earth. His "present" is somewhere else. 4) Without being present among his own in the form of corporate personality, he re-mains attached to them by his Name and by his Spirit (the author follows Conzelmann here, ->1954), by the traces he left in history (so the importance of the evangelical accounts and the summaries of the life of Jesus in Acts) and for example those which he gave: the structure of the Acts shows that Paul follows Jesus. Since Jesus preceded his followers, theirs is not a pure imitation.

49. In his book review, **RTPhil**, 3rd series, 9 (1959) 90-91. C. Masson is right to reproach him this hypothesis.

50. The work of the German exegete is not to be found in the bibliography of Laurentin and is, unless we are mistaken, not mentioned in the notes.

51. The commented bibliography of Laurentin includes 500 titles! Among the works which have appeared since then, cf. H. H. Oliver (-> 1963-1964), P. S. Minear (-> 1966), J. K. Elliot (-> 1971: Jesus in the Temple = a prefiguration of the resurrection), G. Schneider (-> 1971: Lk 1:35 is not an interpolation; vss. 34-37 are Lucan. They were added to a traditional account which included vss. 26-33 and vs. 38. Vss. 34-35 develope a traditional Christologoumenon of Hellenistic Jewish origin, older than the account) and R. E. Brown (-> 1973, -> 1975, -> 1976 and -> 1977).

52. Concerning the baptism of Jesus according to Luke, cf. I. de la Potterie (-> 1958: messianic anointing at baptism and not at the incarnation) and F. Lentzen-Deis (-> 1970).

Concerning the temptations of Jesus according to the third Gospel , cf. J. Dupont (-> 1962, first title; dialogue with R. Schnackenburg, [Tüb] **TQ** 132 (1952), 297-320, and A. Feuillet, **Bib** 40 (1959), 613-621; against these exe - getes who emphasize the exemplarity of the temptations (to eat, see and hear), thus the parenetic nature of the narrative, J. Dupont gives it its Messianic dimension: the account is attached to the baptism; the first temptation: abuse of the Messianic miraculous power; the second temptation: exercise of power and not the apppropriation of benefits alone (Satan is thus for Luke the prince of this world); the third temptation: as usual, Luke is more interested in the questions of the devil than Jesus' answers (the opposite is true of Mt). Henceforth Jesus will no longer be tempted in Luke, he will be tried: at the cross, by the same enemy (cf. Lk 22:53), at Jerusalem which is a theological place. Because of Jerusalem where the temptations culminate in Luke, Luke inverses the last two. The editorial modifications often function only to make the account more believable. On the speech-program of Lk 4, cf. E. Grässer, A. Strobel, R. C. Tannehill, W. Eltester (->1972) and J. Delobel (->1973). In these works, abundant bibliography is to be found. On the ministry in Galilee, cf. C. H. Talbert (-> 1967, first title). On the transfiguration, cf. J. G. Davies (-> 1955 and -> 1958: Lk 9:1-34 prefigures the Ascension (Act 1:1-12) and not as has been said (for example, by A. M. Ramsey, **The Glory of God and the Transfiguration** (London, 1949)) the Parousia; H. Baltensweiler (-> 1959: ignores Davies and is interested little in Luke's redactional work; besides seeing the pedagogical modifications noted by H. Riesenfeld (**Jésus Transfiguré**... (Copenhagen, 1947), p. 291), and the heilsgeschichtlich strokes perceived by Conzelmann (-> 1954, pp. 50-52 of the 3rd ed.), he perceives psychologizing and dramaticized developments; G. Voss (-> 1965), without being always convincing, is more sensitive to the redactional per - spective properly speaking (cf. above 3, IV, b).

Concerning the journey, J. Starky (-> 1951: analyzes στηρίζειν in the OT perspective where two expressions are found: to set one's face to do something (never translated by στηρίζειν in the LXX) and to set one's face against someone (translated by στηρίζειν in the LXX): with intention or hostility. Has Luke confused the two formulas or does he discretly make allusion to the Messianic text of Isa 50:7? The author then analyzes the term ἀνάλημψις and proposes not to limit it to the Ascension. The Passion is also included in it. In short, Luke uses the phraseology of the LXX to express Jesus' firm resolution); E. Lohse (-> 1954: in salvation history, the second stage of Jesus' life is marked by the missionary effort of Jesus, which is frequently opposed); J. Schneider (-> 1953: a didactic and parenetic tendency of the journey); W. Grundmann (-> 1959: a Christology of a Jesus, traveller and guest: he visits his people in the name of God and eats with with those he meets. Other Christological notes of this journey are: the mystery of the sufferings of the Messiah which are necessary for his glorification, and the invitation of the disciples to follow the master's way); W.C. Robinson (-> 1960: the journey, whose fullness we must note, is Luke's work: it marks an important step on the way of Jesus; the role of the witnesses who participate in this step); D. Gill (-> 1970: good bibliography; analyzes the Reisenotizen which fit into a certain pattern. Jesus teaches on the true disciple who knows how to suffer and evangelize. He also shows how to faithfully obey the will of God by going to Jerusalem while continuing to exercise his mission, a mission which prefigures the mission to the Gentiles); P. von der Osten-Sacken (-> 1973: the account of the journey brings a Christological clarification. Jesus is indeed the Messiah which the first part of the Gospel confesses, but the very nature of the journey which he is undertaking shows that this Messiahship, escaping the Jewish canons, is a suf-fering Messiahship. This perspective modifies hope, which from a nationalistic hope becomes an expectation of the universal royalty of God); E. Samain (-> 1973, first title); G. W. Trompf (-> 1973); M. Miyoshi (-> 1974).

53. J. Weiss, **Das Urchristentum**, Göttingen, 1914-1917, p. 84 cited by Lohse (-> 1955, p. 188, note 1 of 1963^2 ed.). L. Cerfaux, **Le Christ dans la théologie de saint Paul**, Paris, 1954^2, p. 22ff., takes up this thesis.

54. Ph. Vielhauer (ch 1, -> 1950), pp. 10-12; H. Conzelmann (-> 1954), p. 175 of 3rd ed.; E. Käsemann (ch 1, -> 1954), p. 199 from the collection; E. Haenchen (-> 1956), p. 82 of the 3rd ed.; U. Wilckens (-> 1961), p. 216; J. D. Kasestli (ch 1, -> 1969), p. 87.

55. Numerous authors use these last two arguments. But it is more often to define Christology of the early Church from the Acts and not Luke's.

56. We could invoke against this idea which is too general the witnesss of 1 Clement (1 Clem 7:4; 21:6; 49:6 etc.). Cf. A. Jaubert, **Clément de Rome. Epître aux Corinthiens. Introduction, texte, traduction, notes et index** (Paris, 1971), pp. 60-74.

57. Cf. above 3, IV, c.

58. This is what B. Klappert demands, in his introduction to the article of G. Bornkamm and L. Goppelt in his contribution: B. Klappert, ed., **Diskussion um Kreuz und Auferstehung. Zur gegenwärtigen Auseinandersetzung im Theologie und Gemeinde** (Wuppertal, 1967), p. 183ff. and 207ff.: cf. B. M. F. van Iersel (-> 1963), summarized above , 3, III, b.

59. Cf. R. F. Tannehill (-> 1961); K. Stalder (-> 1962); R. Zehnle (-> 1969); F. Bovon (-> 1973); A. George (-> 1973).

60. M. Dibelius, **Die Formgeschichte des Evangeliums.** Dritte, durchgesehene Auflage mit einem Nachtrag von G. Iber, herausgegeben von G. Bornkamm (Tübingen, 1959), p. 202.

61. He makes a subtle distinction between the secular form of Jerusalem (for the present time of the Church) and the sacred form (for Jesus' Passion and resurrection and the first period of the Church).

62. On the account of the Lucan Passion narrative, cf. since the work of G. Schneider, the posthumous work of V. Taylor (-> 1972) and the article of P. W. Walaskay (-> 1975).

63. Cf. above 3, Intro and ff. The reader can go to J. Schmitt (-> 1949 and -> 1951); P. Schubert (ch 2, -> 1954), presented above 2, I, a; A. R. C. Leaney (-> 1955-1956: Lk 24 confirms the hypothesis of traditions common to Luke and John; vss. 12, 36-43, 48-49 of Lk 24 come from only one tradition, which John knows (cf. Jn 20:3-10 and 19-22). Is it really one tradition divided by the two Evangelists as Leaney proposes? We would prefer to think that there are two distinct traditions, which John and Luke know. On this last point, the center of the argumentation, Leaney must be right); C. F. D. Moule (-> 1957-1958, second title: one must consider the movement of the Galilean disciples, provoked by the feasts. Having gone up to Jerusalem for the Passover, they

go home immediately and return to the capital as pilgrims for Pentecost. Lk 24:36.49 happened just after Passover. The author proposes to read *συναυλιζόμενος* (lodging for a feast) in Act 1:4), cf. below note 69; J. Dupont (-> 1959: analyzes 1 Cor 15:4 and Act 10:40. The precision of the third day is based on the Scripture and can only be related to Hos 6:2. The Biblical reference is never indicated, for in a Jewish Christian environment everyone knew it came from Hosea); A. George (-> 1969: analyzes Lk 24:36-53. At vs. 53, we must keep the words *καὶ ἀνεφέρετο εἰς οὐρανόν*, which propose another date for the Ascension. Three sections: a) vss. 36-43: scene of thanksgiving; b) vss. 44-49: teaching in two periods; c) ascension. The function of the account is to conclude the Gospel (adoration, joy and separation) and announce the Acts (vss. 46-48 "enumerate one by one the articles of the apostolic kergyma" (p. 81)). Concentration on the day of Easter (the chronology is voluntarily imprecise): the Lucan will to make everything begin at Easter. The contradiction with the forty days of the Acts does not shock Luke. The role of Jerusalem and the witnesses (not limited to the Eleven). The Resurrected One and the Scripture lead men and women to faith who had been only perturbed by the empty tomb. Mystery: Jesus is is henceforth alive: he is the same and has a body (in this new condition he can appear as God or an angel). No materialism: the massive traits are destined for the Greeks who often sink into spiritualism. Henceforth Savior (in permitting conversion), the risen Jesus becomes God's lieutenant and the custodian of the Spirit. The Ascension shows the disciples that their master is from now on enthroned as Lord at the right hand of God. New period of salvation history. A second part of the article compares Lk 24:36-53 with the parallel narratives in Mt and Jn. A third recontructs an ancient tradition of the apparitions, which developed from the apparition to the Eleven and the doubt of the disciples (the tradition is of the "scene of thanksgiving" type, it is hidden behind vss. 36-43; vss. 44-45 are redactional; vss. 46-49 are a redactional rereading of the old kerygmatic schema of the Acts; vss. 50-53 are very Lucan); H. D. Betz (->1969: analyzes Lk 24:13-32 which represent a cultic legend. The text is the product of a reflection particular to the Christian community: the knowledge of the Scriptures, the relation of the historical Jesus and the events of the crucifixion do not suffice to understand the cross. This aporia leads Christians to dialogue. Christ thus becomes present, since he is in the understanding of the Scripture and the common meals. With this, a new understanding of oneself and the the cross come); X. Léon.Dufour (-> 1971, p. 123ff.: analyzes the Jerusalemite tradition taken over by Luke in Lk 24:36-53: a traditional schema: initiative - thanksgiving - mission (cf. in a different sense, G. Lohfink (-> 1971), p. 147ff.);149ff.; analyzes the empty tomb, especially the tradition taken over in Lk 24:1-11; p. 199f.: the Easter message according to Luke: Easter is not the constitution of the Church, but the expectation of Pentecost: with the conviction, for the disciples, that Jesus is henceforth living (or rather resurrected)); I. H. Marshall (-> 1073); J. Wanke (-> 1973) and Sister Jeanne d'Arc (-> 1977).

64. Conclusions: 1) the traditions is unanimous to confirm the heavenly triumph of Christ after the resurrection. The most ancient documents are content to tell this truth of faith without worrying about telling what took place. 2) It is only in the fourth century that the tradition of the Ascension after forty days is established indisputably in the Church. 3) A tendency of exegesis criticizes wrongly that the resurrection in the beginning was perceived in a

spiritual form. The primitive affirmation of the corporal resurrection of Jesus implies a corporal elevation, too. 4) However, one must distinguish the invisible mystery from the elevation to the right hand of God - decisive for faith - and the last declaration of the Risen One at his last appearance, attested by the accounts of the Ascension (p. 198), which go back to a tradition of the primitive Church (p. 194).

65. We mention them below in note 69.

66. There is also the departure of an angel in ch 4 of the long version of Test Abr (ἀνῆλθεν).

67. Here the author rests on the article of P. A. van Stempvoort (-> 1958-1959), summarized in note 69.

68, F. Hahn (-> 1974) wonders if Lohfink does not underestimate the traditional elements of the two accounts of the Ascension.

69. Here is the summary of other articles which appeared in the past few years concerning the Ascension: P. H. Menoud (-> 1954: the beginning of the Acts (vss. 1-5) and the last verses of Luke's Gospel (vss. 50-53) do not belong to the primitive work. Lightened of this later addition, the work of Luke presents a coherent witness of the Ascension. Cf. below the partial retraction in 1962); J. G. Davies (-> 1955: cf. above note 52); J.Haroutunian (-> 1956; the Ascension is indispensible to the credo; it witnesses to the Lordship of Jesus who can thus intervene for his own, and because he is heavenly, can be present on the earth by preaching and the sacraments); C. S. Mann (-> 1957: can we speak of the Ascension as an event distinct from the resurrection? Yes, but what is most often the concentration on one event, e.g. in Jn, becomes a series in Luke); C. F. D. Moule (-> 1957, first title: is interested in the chronology of the events of Easter and Pentecost (cf. above note 63) and maintains his confidence in the forty days. There were apparitions in Galilee and in Jerusalem. Just before Pentecost, the disciples went up to Jerusalem and there received the order to stay (Luke neglected to correct Lk 24:49f in this sense). Then something happened which Luke describes in the narrative of the Ascension without taking all the exterior signs he indicates literally. The Ascension is an end for Luke and at the same time the affirmation that a new chapter begins); J. G. Davies (-> 1958: important book for the history of the dogma of the Ascension. After a chapter concerning the prefiguration of the theme in the OT and LXX, the author establishes that the whole NT believes in the ascension of the Risen One (Davies consciously confuses elevation and ascension). He then studies the accounts of Luke, the only in his opinion which indicate the occasion and circumstances. Luke disposed of two traditions which he does not seek to harmonize. He adds the forty days on his own. The narrative in Lk 24 finds its inspiration in the ascension of the angel Raphael in Tob 12:19-21, that of Acts 1, in the translation of Elijah (2 Kgs 2). The Ascension took place the day of the Passover. The forty days have a typological, not chronological, value. As for the sense of the Ascension, it is multiple for Luke: by this act, God breaks the verdict pronounced against Jesus by men and he glorifies his servant. The Ascension is the necessary prelude to the gift of the Spirit and the attestation that Jesus henceforth dwells with the Father. The book then studies the meaning of the Ascension for the rest of

the NT and Christian tradition); R. Russel (-> 1958: presentation of V. Larrañaga, F. M. Braun, **Jesus, histoire et critique**, Tournai-Paris, 1941, ch13; and P. Benoit (-> 1949)); P. A. van Stempvoort (-> 1958-1959: criticized on one point by Dupont (-> 1962, third title), this article is nonetheless precious: he judiciously distinguishes the redactional value of each account (Lk 24:50-53 and Act 1:9-11). G. Lohfink (-> 1971) will follow him a great deal); J. F. Jansen (-> 1959: behind the Ascension accounts, there was an appearance during which the disciples learned that the experience of Easter was terminated and a new period was beginning. The reality of the Ascension was thus attested to the disciples by a distinct sign, but which was inseparable from this reality); P. Miquel (-> 1959: wants to penetrate into the mystery of the Ascension. Following P. Benoit (-> 1949), he distinguishes the parting sequence from the paschal elevation. It is an article of reflection and meditation, rich in patristic and liturgical citations. It meditates on the themes of the descent and ascension with the absence and presence. It establishes a series of correspondences; the departure of the Christ to the place where the glory of God went in 587 B.C. (cf. Ezek 11:23); Parousia which would correspond to the Ascension); H. Schlier (-> 1961: not mentioning the ancient kerygmas, the Ascension takes a predominant place in Luke. Lk 24: the mode of being of Jesus (resurrected and dominating space and time) constitutes the basis of the Ascension. A radical distance will henceforth exist between Jesus and his followers, but the Risen One leaves his blessing behind. Thus the joy of the disciples is explained: the Ascension is not only an end but also the beginning of the time of the Church, which descends from heaven (where does he read this in the text?). Act 1: Luke dares to present a new version of the event to offer a solution to the problem of the end of time: before the end, there is the time of the Spirit and the Church. The author speaks of a beginning of the Parousia (is this not to excessively valorize the time of the Church?); J. Dupont (-> 1961: refuses to understand, with P. A. van Stempvoort (1958-1959), ἀνελήμφθη (Act 1:2) as a euphemism to speak of death. The verb designates the corporal Ascension of Jesus to heaven); P. H. Menoud (-> 1962: renounces his 1954 thesis on the primitive unity of Luke-Acts. The mention of the forty days finds its origin in the reflection of Luke who interprets it symbolically: 1) the restrained circle of the witnesses is thus designated as authorized depository of the Resurrected One (others who also saw the Risen Lord are not included in the group). 2) It is the disciples, not Jesus, who need these forty days of preparation. To repeat his teaching forty times, was for a rabbi to have truly transmitted it. 3) The mention of the forty days is not related to the Ascension. Luke is precise as to the date of the resurrection (Passover) and the sending of the Spirit (Pentecost). He is not for the Ascension. Generally the Fathers understood Luke's intention and did not relate the forty days with the Ascension); R. D. Kaylor (-> 1964 which we know by the summary in **DissAbstr**, A, 25 (1965), p. 6792, right column: "Luke-Acts contains two accounts of the Ascension. Luke ends with an abreviated ascension story which points to the exaltation of Jesus, while Acts begins with an account which shows the decisive connection between the beginning of the church and the exaltation of the church's Lord. Motivations for narrating the ascension in this unique way may include a desire 1) to place a decisive end to the resurrection appearances; 2) to seal the identity of the earthly Jesus with the risen Lord; 3) to emphasize that while 'times and seasons' are in God's hands, and are not to be subject of speculation, the parousia will definitely occur; 4) to stress the fact that until the parousia, the present age is the time in which the church is to carry out its mission of proclamation." This dissertation studies also the motif of the Ascension in Heb and Jn; B. Metzger (->1966: insists for a large public on the metaphorical value of the language of the Ascension: its signifies the end of the operation, the return to the father and the omnipotence of the King Christ); G. Schille (->1966: sees in the tradition taken over by Luke the etiological legend of a cultic meeting of the Jewish Christian community of Jerusalem on the Mount of Olives 40 days after Easter. In our opinion the indications are too tight in order that Schille's hypothesis ceases to shake), S. G. Wilson (->1968: first criticizes the hypothesis of Schille. He then deems that in primitive christianity there was a consciousness sufficiently lively of the difference between the resurrection and the Ascencion that Luke in his narration deals separately with these two events (G. Lohfink (->1971) is convinced of the contrary). For Wilson the two accounts of the Ascension responds to different preoccupations: Lk 24 is doxological and heilsgeschichtlich (the event distinguishes and relates the time of Jesus and the time of the Church). Following a pastoral orientation, Act 1 straightens out two antagonistic Christian attitudes, provoked by the delay of the Parousia: vss. 6-8 criticizes a return to apocalyptic concerns and vs. 11 no longer believes in the Parousia at all); E. Franklin (->1970: Luke concentrates his attention on the Ascension-Elevation and not on the Parousia. The Ascension is the decisive eschatological event, preceeded by the cross and followed by the sending of the Spirit. Luke signals this interest for the Ascension by series of modifications which he brings to the Synoptic tradition. The expectation of the Parousia does not disappear for all that); since the appearance of the thesis of the G. Lohfink (-> 1971), cf. G. Friedrich (-> 1973: proposes to understand the ἀνάλημψις of Lk 9:51 as an allusion to the death of Jesus and not to his ascension. It is in the course of his Gospel that Luke resorts to the vocabulary of the translation for his Greek readers, especially in Lk 24 and Act 1 (Lk 24:1-11: the tie between the fact of not finding a body and the doctrine of the translation/ lifting up is absent in Mk and Mt; vss. 13-35: the appearance of Jesus to the disciples of Emmaus; "enter into glory" (vs. 26, a unique expression in the NT), not to confused with entering into life, and "become invisible" (vs. 31) are expressions peculiar to the translation accounts; vss. 36-43: these verses recall an apparition of Apollonius after his translation; vss. 50-53 (maintain the long text): this first account of the Ascension must not be understood exclusively from Sir 50:20-22, as has been the custom; to read rather as the adieus of one who is going to be translated/ lifted up; Act 1:1-11: Luke uses the category of translation to show the difference between the historical Jesus and the exalted Christ: eg. the relation between translation and last instruction; between translation and promise; Act 2:25-36: David was not translated since his tomb can be seen. The lifted one of the Psalm is thus another, Jesus; Act 3:20f.: one should not think uniquely of an Elijah tradition, but more generally of the relation which the Jews established between translation and the eschatological task. Curiously, while insisting on this vocabulary of translation/ lifting up, known to the Greeks and the Jews, G. Friedrich thinks that Luke used it only as an instrument to render the kerygma of the resurrection, the preamble of eschatology, intelligible to Greek ears. The translation of Jesus is not a major theme of Lucan theology (the summaries in Act 10:40ff. and Act 13:30ff. confrount only the death and the resurrection). According to the author, Luke is not interested in the chronological distinction of the stages the resurrection and the Ascension. Without grasping clearly if Friedrich distinguishes translation and exaltation, we oppose the author on this point; in our opinion, Luke distinguishes the stages and puts the exaltation forward. It is distinct from the resurrection. To present the exaltation, he uses the translation vocabulary. We concede that Luke does not describe the translation as such: he is interested in the result, the sitting at the right hand of God.

70. F. Schnider's book (-> 1973) contains eight chapters and the most important deals with Jesus, the prophet, in the Synoptics. The writer thinks especially that Luke used the motif of the tragic fate of the prophet for Jesus' journey to Jerusalem (Lk 13:33 would be redactional with regard to Lk 13:33f.). On the contrary, the pericope of Jesus' rejection at Nazareth, Luke valorizes Jeusu messiahship more than the tragic prophetic destiny (Lk 4:16-30). No doubt because of the language, I. Panagopoulos and F. Schnider do not use F. Gils' work enough. For an interpretation of hte figure of Jesus as prophet, cf. recently P. S. Minear (-> 1976).

71. A good summary of M.-E. Boismard in **RB** 66 (1959), pp. 612-613.

72. Particularly, the later prophets like David interprets earlier oracles. With this suggestive remark, the author sets himself against Greek influence.

73. Cf. more recently, H. Jaschke (ch 7, -> 1971).

74. Exception: Lk 17:13 where *ἐπιστάτης* is used by the lepers.

75. F. Norman (-> 1967) notes on p. 47, note 11 that it is not evident, for the **Life of Pythagoras** 21:99 applies this term to Pythagoras.

76. This term could signify official, inspector, leader and tutor (cf. A. Oepke, "art. *ἐπιστάτης*", **TWNT**, 2, p. 619f.).

77. Concerning this individual eschatology, cf. see above 1, III, p.

78. For Moule's position (-> 1966), cf. 3, IV, c.

79. On the worksearlier than 1950, cf. J. Dupont (-> 1950, first title), pp. 108-111 of the collection.

80. Cf. J. E. Ménard (-> 1959).

81. 1) *Παῖς θεοῦ* in the Acts designates Jesus as the Messiah who must suffer as a servant and be exalted up as a heavenly being. 2) The sufferings of Jesus lead to his exaltation. 3) Jesus the servant represents his people by substitution.

82. E. Schweizer begins with Act 13:33: the begetting of the Son of David prophetized in Psa 2:7 took place on Easter day. He then studies the history of interpretation of the prophecies made to David, in Judaism and primitive Christianity. He distinguishes two trends: a) one accentuates the individual figure of the Messiah, son of David (so the NT which proposes different applications to Jesus of these prophecies, cf. tradition and redaction of Rom

1:3-4; cf. Act 2:25-26 etc.). b) the other insists of the sonship of the eschatological Israel (so a good part of Judaism).

83. E. Kränkl studies Act 13:22f.: cited just after David, Jesus is a the most important link in the chain of salvation history. "Dem Bemühen des Verfassers, Jesus in die Heilsgeschichte einzuordnen, kommt die traditionelle Ansicht von der Davidssohnschaft Jesu sehr entgegen ..." (p. 85f.). Different from Paul, Mk and Mt, the text of the Acts does not describe through this conception of the Davidic descendence Jesus' earthly status but rather his heavenly. Basically the author takes over C. Burger's position (-> 1970) and insists too much on the Kontinuum of salvation history (Act 13 rightly shows that from a Davidic point of view, this history makes jumps).

84. As we do not know Polish, we are unable to summarize the work of J. Lach (-> 1973), which has no summary in French.

85. This is H. Conzelmann's view (-> 1954), p. 159, note 2 of the third edi - tion: the rarity of the title in the Acts must not hide its importance for Luke.

86. Along the same line, cf. P. von der Osten-Dacken (-> 1973).

87. Cf. E. Samain (-> 1973, second title).

88. D. L. Jones is also the author of an unpublished dissertation (-> 1966); we found its summary in **DissAbstr**, A, 27 (1967), p. 3925 A.

89. These works have now been gathered into a first volume, **Receuil L. Cerfaux** (Gembloux, 1954).

90. Cf. before the brief article of R. C. Nevius (-> 1966).

91. Cf. G. A. Galitis (-> 1960), which E. Neuhäusler summarizes and presents in the **BZ**, N.F., 5 (1961), pp. 311-313; and T. Ballarini (-> 1971), summarized in **NTAbstr** 17 (1972-1973), p. 56.

CHAPTER 4

1. Cf. E. Schweizer (-> 1959), pp. 401-402; "Die Neubewertung des Geistes in diesem Kreis zeigt sich schon, dass πνεῦμα als Bezeichnung des göttlichen Geistes gut dreimal so oft bei Lukas steht wie bei Markus." And p. 402: "Vor allem aber weist Apg 1-12 mit 37 Stellen das relativ häufigste Vorkommen im NT auf."

2. Certain have wondered if the rare reading "may your spirit come upon us and purify us", with the second request of the "Our Father" (Lk 11:2), was not original. If it is, this would confirm the theme of the Spirit in favor of Luke. Cf. below note 28.

3. Cf. J. H. E. Hull (-> 1967) pp. 185-188.

4. Cf. Hull (-> 1967), pp. 189-193.

5. Cf. G. Stählin (->1973).

6. Cf. H. von Baer (-> 1926), pp. 38-43.

7. Cf. Act 10:19; 16: 6-7 etc.

8. It is one of the points on which F. F. Bruce (->1973) insists.

9. G. W. H. Lampe (-> 1955) paraphases Lk-Act based on the notion of the Spirit. One unique case must be mentioned: Act 8:39 (the translation of Philip by the Spirit).

10. "Die grossen Ereignisse, in denen das Pneuma Hagion epoche - machend in die Geschichte der Menscheit eingegriffen hat, lokalisiert Lukas in genauen Zeitpunkten der Geschichte." (p. 109).

11. "Als Ursache und Folge gehören *πνεῦμα ἅγιον* und *εὐαγγελίζεσθαι* zu den Elementen der lukanischen Theologie und bilden das Leitmotiv für das Doppelwerk." (p. 2).

12. On this important point (ties between the Christ and the Spirit), the author is opposed to W. Bousset, **Kyrios Christos. Geschichte des Christusglaubens von den Anfängen des Christentums bis Irenaeus** (Göttingen, 1913, 1921[2]) and H. Gunkel, **Die Wirkungen des Heiligen Geistes nach den populären Anschauungen der apostolischen Zeit** (Göttingen, 1888).

13. Here against E. Schweizer (-> 1959), p. 403.

14. The same position for Hull (-> 1967). Here against E. Schweizer (-> 1959).

15. For example Hull (->1967), p. 42f. and 162f., who never refers to this work.

16. In the same sense P. Brunner (-> 1967).

17. 1) He presents the role of the Holy Spirit in the virginal conception of Jesus and shows that Luke reads the semitic tradition with a Greek mentality: the title Son of God describes a physical quality. 2) He studies the Holy Spirit as a force which permits Jesus to exorcise (this is the meaning of the expression "the finger of God" (Lk 11:20)). 3) He analyzes the pericope concerning the sin against the Holy Spirit.

18. H. von Baer is thinking of H. Gunkel (cf. above footnote 12). H. Gunkel thinks that the Spirit only provokes surprising acts. The absence of the word *πνεῦμα* in the summaries might indicate that the first Christians did not place ethics in relation with pneumatology.

19. Between H. von Baer and G. W. H. Lampe, one must situate the pages (pp. 80-92) which W. L. Knox (->1948) consecrates to the Holy Spirit. J.

Dupont summarizes them in this state of the question (-> 1950) taken up in his **Etudes**, pp. 99-100. We would like to correct his summary on one point: "He [W. L. Knox] does not invisage the question of a possible progress of this doctrine in the different parts of the book." (p. 99). On the contrary, Knox distinguishes in an interesting way two periods in Acts: when Luke depends on his Judeo-Christian sources, he insists on the visible charisms of the Spirit (p. 88). Whereas, when he follows other sources, the situation changes: "In the later chapters of Acts we find that the action of the Holy Spirit is modified." (p. 90). Luke affirms the prophetic nature of inspiration and even relates the Spirit to sanctification (pp. 90-91).

20. Appearing just before Lampe's work we must mention Conzelmann's contribution (-> 1954, particularly pp. 171-172) who nevertheless concerning the Spirit adds little to what von Baer had discovered.

21. "It is a gospel of the work of the Spirit, whose continuous activity before the birth of the Saviour, in him and , then, as a unifying theme through these Lucan summaries." (p 165). "In the Old Testament dispensation, God revealed his purposes through the prophetic Spirit; during the ministry of Jesus the Spirit works in him as the power in which the Kingdom of God is already operative among men; and after his death and exaltation the same power, as the Spirit, poured out by the Lord Christ, is the guide driving force of the apostolic mission to evangelize the whole world," (p. 167).

22. Did Lampe know of H. von Baer's work? He does not quote him.

23. This is a distinction noted by E. Schweizer (-> 1959), p. 403. Believers are regenerated and, different from Jesus, they are not born of the Spirit. Not having sensed this difference, Lampe says that after the exaltation of Jesus and the outpouring of the Spirit, the apostles "will in a sense, replace him as the servant's continuing antitype." (p. 179).

24. We can cite H. Leisegang, **Der Heilige Geist. Das Wesen und Werden der mystisch-intuitiven Erkenntnis in der Philosophie und Religion der Griechen, 1: Die vorchristlichen Anschauungen und Lehren vom Pneuma und der mystisch-intuitiven Erkenntnis** (Leipzig-Berlin, 1919); and from the same author, **Pneuma Hagion. Der Ursprung des Geistbegriffs der synoptischen Evangelien aus der griechischen Mystik** (Leipzig, 1922), and H. Gunkel, op. cit., above note 12.

25. J. H. E. Hull (-> 1967), pp. 171-172, rebukes Lampe for speaking of an impersonal force.

26. This link is rarely explicit, perhaps because the influence of the OT notion of ruach on Luke.

27. Cf. The citation of p. 167 above in footnote 21.

28. We have several doubts as to this. The sanctifying function of the Spirit is hardly underlined by Luke. Concerning this reading of the "Our Father" which he proposes to discard, cf. J. Carmignac, **Recherches sur le**

"Notre Père" (Paris 1969), pp. 89-91. Concerning the role of prayer, cf. below 7, IV, 4, a-e, esp. the presentation of W. Ott's book 7, IV, 4, d (ch 7, ->1965).

29. Cf G. Kretschmar (-> 1954-1955), who thinks rather of a Moses typology.

30. The "in bodily form" (Lk 3:22) which Luke mentions concerning the descent of the Spirit at the baptism of Jesus allows the distinguishing of this outpouring from the more frequent manifestations of the Spirit in the OT (p. 168). We can doubt the strength of this statement: the corporality of the Spirit does not prove his permanence.

31. "Repentance is evidently regarded as the primary mode of the Spirit's operation in the converts, and it is natural to find repentance, together with faith in Jesus as Messiah, is associated from the day of Pentecost onwards with baptism in his name and the reception of the gift of the Spirit." (p. 186).

32. E. Schweizer (-> 1959), p. 410, noted that Luke takes neither faith nor individual salvation back to the initial intervention of the Spirit.

33. Act 11:18 and 3:26.

34. This point was illuminated by M. H. Franzmann (-> 1959), p. 568f.

35. In the year when Lampe's study appeared, J. E. L. Oulton (-> 1954-1955) published an article which we have summarized below in 4, III, e. Let us simply mention a general perspective of this study: to the three stages of the history of the Church announced by the Risen One (Act 1:8), would correspond three distinct manifestations of the Spirit. In the introduction of his commentary, E. Haenchen (-> 1956) furthermore, consecrates a chapter of the theology of the Acts. Here is a brief but dense excerpt which deals with the Holy Spirit: "In his teaching concerning the Holy Spirit,...likewise, Luke does not yet show the balance attained by later theology in the doctrine of the Trinity. He links together the three predicates of different provenance. Firstly, he presents the Spirit as the gift which every Christian receives at baptism ... its ecstatic effects afford Luke the welcome opportunity of making the reality of the gift visible.... Secondly, Luke describes the Spirit as the equipment possessed by individual Christians for a given task at a particular moment...; it was already possible for Judaism to speak of the Spirit in this manner. Thirdly, according to Acts, the Spirit gives specific directions for the Christian mission at important junctures...- like a 'bath qol' in Jewish traditions; but in such cases the Spirit could as well be replaced by 'the angel of the Lord' ... or a 'vision'..." (p. 92f. of ET 1971).

36. On p. 402, note 462, E. Schweizer rightly notes that the primitive commmunity knew pneumatic phenomena. The appearance of the Spirit in the Church is thus not explained by influence from the Hellenistic milieu. It is significative that the prophets in the Acts are all of Jewish origin.

36. There are two other articles by the same author. Cf. E. Schweizer (-> 1955 and -> 1956).

38. Cf. Lk 4:1 compared to Mk 1:12. Thus the relation of Jesus to the Spirit differs from that which is established between the disciples and the Holy Spirit (p. 402f.).

39. P. 403, line 8ff. and p. 404, line 4ff.

40. In fact, Luke uses the verb with the genitive: πλησθῆναι πνεύματος.

41. In this pericope, we think Luke does not refuse miracles in an absolute manner. He simply thinks that they will take place elsewhere, there where we receive them in faith.

42. E. Schweizer quotes Act 2:38f.; 8:16-19; 9:17; 10:44; 11:16f.; 15:8f.; 19:2, 6: Is he right to say that the community is a community where everyone is prophet (p. 406, line 11 and p. 409 line 26)? We do not think so: Luke has a narrower conception of prophet.

43. "Das bedeutet, dass der Geist allen Gemeidegliedern und dass er ihnen dauernd gegeben ist." (p. 408). Does E. Schweizer contradict himself? For he says in another place (p 406, lines 11-13) that Luke insists little on the durable aspect of the Spirit on believers.

44. P. 409, lines 11ff. and p. 413, lines 23-28.

45. On this text and the textual critical problem which is posed, cf. above 1, III, b; ch 1, note 36; 2, III, d; ch 5, note 54.

46. Cf. E. Franklin (ch 1, -> 1970), p. 194.

47. P. 410, lines 28-32 and p. 413, line 14f.

48. Concerning the permanent presence of the Spirit, we can wonder if J. H. E. Hull has understood Schweizer properly.

49. The few allusions ot the Spirit in the Gospels confirm this fact and demonstrates that the Church did not project its pneumatic experiences into the pre-Easter past.

50. The promise of the Spirit which the disciples received (Act 1:4) refers, according to the author to the teaching of the Resurrected One (Lk 24:49) and not to the historical Jesus.

51. "These two references may well be important for the light they throw on what the author of Acts considered to be the purpose of Spirit-baptism." (p. 43). Cf. p. 47.

52. "It may well be nearer the truth to say that the conditions as understood by both Peter and Luke, were (i) repentance, (ii) faith in Jesus, and (iii) lthe readiness to be baptized." (p. 93).

53. In the analysis of the case of the Samaritans (Acts 8), Hull gets caught in a web of contradictions. He affirms then he denies that one must distinguish the outpouring of the Spirit and the consciousness of having received the Spirit, consciousness which can appear later.

54. Above in his book (p. 68f.), the author has distinguished the presence of the Spirit in the Old covenant and that which fills Christians. Elizabeth and Zachariah (Lk 1:41 and 67) must have received individually the Spirit for limited period of time, whereas the disciples (Act 2:4) are filled forever. Hull can set forth this last statement even if Luke uses in both cases the same expression.

55. Hull correctly mentions the social import of faith in both these cases.

56. F. Bovon (-> 1967) pp. 195-198).

57. Hull interprets the drawing of the lot of Matthias like H. von Baer (-> 1926): this manner of election was then necessary, for the Spirit had not yet been poured out on the Church.

58. In the year that Hull published his book, an American exegete, J. R. Bruton (-> 1967) finished his doctoral dissertation, which remains unpublished, concerning the Lucan pneumatology. A summary of this work appeared in **Dissertation Abstracts**, A, 28 (1967), pp. 2322A-2323A. Since then J. Daniélou has consecrated a chapter to the Holy Spirit in the Acts at the end of his work **L'Eglise des apôtres** (-> 1970). His is a conservative Catholic interpretation, which emphasizes the frühkatholisch aspects of Luke. Let us mention several original or typical remarks: 1) the Acts may contain a polemic against the pneumatology of the Essenes; 2) Foreseen for all men, the spirit is directed first toward the apostles. 3) "More than a baptism, Pentecost is an ordination." (p. 143). 4) The Holy Spirit confers on the apostles a power to teach infallibly. 5) In Samaria and at Ephesus, the Holy Spirit given by the apostles is not far from the spiritual gift of baptism: "Here again it appears that there is a gift of the Spirit distinct from baptism and given by the apostles alone." (p. 147). 6) The Spirit not only constitutes the mission, but he directs it as well. 7) The idea of the Spirit as the principle and agent of new life is not absent in the Lucan work. Cf. E. Eichele (-> 1970) who presents a few theses concerning the Holy Spirit in the Acts. Among these let us mention: the Acts tell the stories of the Spirit in activity: in activity in the preaching of the apostles and in the lives of the believers. It is most often a particular gift, which does not become the property of the faithful but remains sovereignly free. The laying on of hands cannot be understood in a ritual manner in the frame of an ecclesiastic discipline. Cf. finally G. Haya-Prats (-> 1975) which we have not been able to consider.

59. N. Adler rebukes the Literarkritiker of the beginning of the century for three abuses of method: a) an initial prejudice: the Pentecost event could only have been glossolalia; b) an injurious intention: because of the miracle, to establish the non-historical side of the story; c) a deficient demonstration: all that deals with foreign languages - the phenomenon which was thought impossible - could not be original and must be declared secondary. These criticisms remain valid with respect to certain partisans of the Redaktionsgeschichte, when they determine what must be traditional.

60. Today we do not exclude that Luke might have been influenced by Jewish traditions which associated the feast of Pentecost and the gift of the Law at Sinai, cf. E. Samain (-> 1971).

61. On pp. 60-61, Adler summarizes the results of his literary analysis: "1. Der Pfingstbericht stammt nicht aus einer von Lukas übersetzten aramaïschen oder einfachhin übernommenen griechischen Quellschrift. 2. Beim Pfingstbericht lässt sich nicht ohne weiteres eine Quellenscheidung vornehmen, d.h. eine Zerlegung in schriftliche Quellstücke oder mündliche Traditionsschichten, auf denen er fusst und die als solche leicht erkennbar wären. 3. Der Pfingstbericht ist vielmehr echt lukanisch, d.h. Lukas hat die ihm über das Pfingstereignis vorliegenden Nachrichten oder Berichte in der ihm geläufigen sprachlichen und literarischen Form wiedergegeben. Dass Lukas dabei schriftliche Aufzeichnungen verwertet habe, lässt sich nicht beweisen. 4. Eine literarische Abhängigkeit des lukanischen Pfingstberichts von jüdischen oder sonstigen ausserbiblischen Erzählungen, die gewisse Aehnlichkeiten mit der Pfingsterzählung aufweisen, liegt nicht vor." Without mentioning N. Adler, W. L. Knox (-> 1948), pp. 80ff., takes up the theory of the influence of the Jewish Pentecost and supposes an original version, reworked by Luke, who would have told the proclamation of the new Torah to the nations by the intermediary of their representatives, the proselytes.

62. J. G. Davies (-> 1952) also defends the unity of the account in com - parison with the texts of Gen 11:1-9 (tower of Babel). He mentions a relationship in the vocabulary and a series of symmetrical contrasts.

63. Summarized on p. 426.

64. He criticizes the others for confusing the historical problem and the literary problem. He says to the latter: the account of Pentecost has little relationship to the theophany of Mt. Sinai. As for the new interpretation of the Jewish feast of Pentecost, in the sense of the recalling of the Law, E. Lohse thinks that it was provoked by the destruction of the Temple in 70. He takes up this hypothesis in his article in **TWNT** (-> 1959) p. 48, l. 3ff.

65. "Es ergibt sich also, dass Lukas die Pfingstgeschichte streng von dem Thema der sich erfüllenden Verheissung her aufgebaut hat." (p. 433). "Die Pfingstgeschichte ist also im Rahmen der lukanischen Geschichtswerkes fest verankert und kann nur im Zusammenhang des lukanischen Theologie ver - standen werden." (p. 434).

66. E. Lohse terminates his article with an analysis of the traditions, no doubt oral, which Luke could have had at his disposition: the story of the first eruption of the Spirit, in the form of glossolalia, and the list of the peoples.

67. Rather than to the individual believer (p. 215).

68. Cf. since then R. Le Déaut (-> 1961), W. Grundmann (-> 1963) and especially J. Potin (-> 1971).

69. R. Cabié's book (-> 1965) allowed a correction of this thesis in specifying that the first Christians appear to have celebrated annually a feast of fifty days which commemorated joyfully and without chronological care the New Covenant, the resurrection of Christ, the Ascension and the gift of the Spirit. This solemnity was assimilated with Sunday and the Christians prayed standing up.

70. An idea taken up without mentioning G. Kretschmar, by C. F. D. Moule (-> 1957).

71. N. Adler (-> 1938) refuses the contacts with Ex 19-20. He refers to Psa 68:19 and Jer 23:29. But we must mention against Adler, these last two texts only reflect the Sinai tradition.

72. "Danach hätte die Vorlage des Lukas also vor allem von der Herabkunft des Geistes auf die Zwölf und von einem Sprachenwunder gehandelt. (p 236).

73. G. Kretschmar does not use the term polysemia, but this is indeed what we have, p. 234.

74. In the same sense, R. Le Déaut (-> 1961), B. Noack (-> 1962) and E. Samain (-> 1971).

75. E. Haenchen (-> 1956), pp. 137-139 of the 1959 edition.

76. G. J. Sirks (-> 1957) makes several suggestive remarks concerning the Holy Spirit. If, in the Gospels, man first meets Jesus Christ in order to later make contact with the Spirit, in the time of the Church, the contrary is true. Furthermore, whereas the relation with Jesus is more individual, the Holy Spirit in the NT is more attached to the community. After this, the author proposes a translation and interpretation which is in our view untenable of the word *γλῶσσα* in the Pentecost account: "Clearer insight is obtained when we translate 'glossai' as 'pericopes', chosen passages of Scripture - with or without a commentary." (p. 85).

77. Pp. 137-139 of the 1959 edition.

78. S. Mac Lean Gilmour (-> 1962) takes up the old idea according to which the tradition, hiding behind Act 2:1-13, corresponds to the apparition of the Risen One to the 500 brothers (I Cor 15:7). Conjointly, he defends the following theory: while Paul and John tend to confuse the activity of the exalted Christ and that of the Holy Spirit, Luke is the only NT author to distinguish them, for he is the only one to separate them in time, Easter from Pentecost. Without quoting this author, G. D. Kilpatrick (-> 1964) defends the same theory philologically: "Thus Acts probably fails to associate the Holy Spirit with God or Jesus by means of a dependent genitive." (p. 63). In Act 5:9; 8:39 and 16:7, the text is uncertain. W. Grundmann (-> 1964) wonders if even the Pentecost tradition does not come from environments hostile to Paul's apostolate. Paul in fact never speaks of this event and appears to be ignorant of the limitation of time to forty days for the appearances. In his analysis of the

event, Grundmann offers nothing new. Concerning Lucan theology, he does not go beyond what von Baer had written (-> 1926).

79. The reasons advanced by P. Brunner, which give this confidence, are unequal in value.

80. K. Haacker (-> 1970) resolutely defends the unity of Act 2:1-13. If we accept that the account evokes a miracle of foreign tongues, this unity imposes itself even more. This interpretation gains in probability, if Paul in I Cor 14 thinks of a phenomenon of speaking in foreign tongues. From a literary and phenomenological point of view, the presence of the foreign tongues (Act 2:6, 11) and enthusiasm (Act 2:13), side by side, poses no problem at all. The exegetical problem which was found in this juxtaposition has been introduced into the text.

81. "We must try, therefore, to find a simpler explanation of the episode in Samaria, unencumbered by later controversies about church order." G. B. Caird (-> 1955), p. 71.

82. "Apg 8,14-17 stellt die älteste klare biblische Urkunde für die Spendung jener geistmitteilenden Handauflegung dar, die der Christusjünger nach seiner Taufe empfängt und die wir heute Firmung nennen." (p. 111).

83. Unless we are mistaken, Käsemann does not yet use this term in this article.

84. "Wenn sie wenigstens nachträglich den apostolischen Segen empfangen hatten und von Jerusalem legitimiert worden waren." (p. 166).

85. We have intentionally neglected Käsemann's exegetical analysis in order to retain only his theological conclusions. The point of Act 19:1-7 for him is: "die Aufnahme kirchlicher Aussenseiter in die Una sancta catholica." (p. 162). Luke thus veiled the historical reality, i.e. the existence of a rival Baptist community , so as not to render suspect the Christian interpretation of the role of John the Baptist. E. Schweizer (-> 1955) critcized this exegesis: Apollo was not a marginal but a Jew.

86. Cf. above 1, III, q.

87. This is E. Schweizer's view (-> 1955).

88. In the same direction, see G. W. H. Lampe (-> 1951) and F. F. Bruce (-> 1973).

89. Luke does not tell us if the men invested with the Spirit at Pentecost have been baptized. Why? He thinks that either they were baptized by John and that was enough, or their participation in Jesus' fate replaced baptism.

90. "The human symbolic act answering to the Heavenly act prayed for." (p. 238).

91. J. E. L. Oulton concludes: "When in repentance and faith new members are added to the Christian Church by baptism, they receive the gift of the Holy Spirit. This gift is an immanent power, manifest in the character of the individual member who is sometimes spoken of as 'full' of the Spirit, and manifested in the Church by its unity of doctrine and worship, by its joyfull fellowship, and by its expanding life. But the gift of the Holy Spirit is sometimes an illapse upon a person or persons, frequently accompanied by outward sign, such as speaking with tongues or prophesying. This occurs on special occasions, or for a special purpose." (p. 239f.).

92. "Baptisms and the laying on of hands are mentioned together in Hebrews, but without anything to show how they were related [Heb 6:2]. Twelve men at Ephesus received the Spirit by the laying on of Paul's hands, but the conversation which preceded shows that Paul believed baptism to be the occasion on which the Spirit was given, so that the laying on of hands must be regarded here as a part of the baptismal rite [Act 19:1-6]." (p. 69f.).

93. G. B. Caird seems to insinuate that this imposition was not the one foreseen in the baptismal rite. It should have confered the exteriors signs of the Holy Spirit which the Samaritans lacked and whose absence risked to provoke a crisis in the Church. This typical Protestant interpretation seems inexact to us. Nevertheless it does not annul the interest of Caird's main thesis.

94. It is the sixth paragraph of the chapter consecrated to Luke in the article *πνεῦμα* of **TWNT** (-> 1959) pp. 410-413.

95. In our view, the pages Hull gives to the question which preoccuppies us here makes no progress in our understanding of Lucan theology. Cf. J. H. E. Hull (-> 1967), pp. 87-120. According to the author, there are three conditions to fulfill to obtain the Holy Spirit (cf. above 4, I, e). Baptism is not one of these conditions. Nor is it the obligatory canal by which the Spirit is poured out either. The laying on of hands is not either. Hull undertstands the latter as a prayer to receive the *πνεῦμα* or better the visible signs of his presence. It can also be destined to appoint someone to a particular office. Finally, Hull refuses to make the laying on of hands a part of the baptismal rite.

CHAPTER 5

1. The bibliography of A. J. and M. Matill, **A Classified Bibliography of Literature on the Acts of the Apostles** (Leiden, 1966), pp. 274ff. and 282f. has 106 titles concerning Christology and 10 concerning Soteriology.

2. Our next chapter of is dedicated to humanity's access to salvation.

3. *σῴζω* appears 30 times, *διασῴζω* 6 times, *ἐκσῴζω* once, *σωτήριον* 3 times, *σωτηρία* 10 times, *σωτήρ* 4 times (once for God and 3 times for Jesus).

4. This description (sun which becomes darkness and the moon which is transformed into blood) seems illplaced since nothing of this sort happens at present.

5. Cf. Eph 2:13-17.

6. H. Conzelmann (-> 1954) is wrong to exclude these two chapters from his investigation. Thus several aspects of salvation, as Luke perceives it, escape him.

7. Does Luke know the meaning of the Hebrew word Yehôchoua (Yahweh saves)? It is difficult to know. Different from Mt 1:21, the evangelist is content with the Greek transcription Ἰησοῦς which he does not translate.

8. Cf. the preceding page.

9. J. Gewiess(-> 1939).

10. J. Dupont, **Etudes**, pp. 41 and 136.

11. The second part is entitled: "Das Heilswerk und Gott als Urheber".

12. J. Bihler (-> 1963), p. 97f. does not ignore this aspect.

13. This is the title of the third part which contains: 1) Jesus Christ: a) the resurrection; b) the death; c) the exaltation; d) the parousia; 2) Jesus the servant; 3) Jesus the Lord.

14. For Gewiess, the theology of the speeches is anterior to Paul's.

15. Gewiess notes on p. 96, that the Acts do not express the Pauline idea according to which the Christian has the right to expect his own resurrection because of Jesus'.

16. Gewiess (p. 100) mentions that the notion of the Kingdom of God is hardly noted in Acts.

17. "Der Weg zum Heil" is the title of the fifth section: it deals with first *μετάνοια* (ch 1) and baptism (ch 2). We will come back to this below (cf. 6, Intro). Let us simply note that believers are attached to Jesus Christ by conversion, whose precise contents depend on each individual life, and by baptism. The Jews must revise their conception of Jesus and the pagans must detach themselves from their idols (p. 113f.). The Risen One covers the converts with eschatological blessings. Ch. 3 of this fifth part treats the only way to salvation: "Die Auseinandersetzungen mit dem alten Heilsweg (Tempel und Gesetz)". Stephen's speech, which Gewiess then analyzes, does not contain an accusation of the Law considered in its essence. The zeal for Jesus allows Stephen to direct his attack against the Temple which opens the way to a criticism of the Law.

18. It is I. H. Marshall's work (-> 1970). Normally well informed, he seems to ignore Gewiess' study.

19. G. W. H. Lampe (-> 1955), p. 179f. For a general presentation of this article, cf. above 4, I, c.

20. J. Dupont (-> 1959-1960), p. 400f. in the compilation.

21. W. C. van Unnik (-> 1960). We are refering to pp. 45 and 50-53. From the same author, there is a later study of the verb *σῴζειν* in the Synoptics which examines to see if the verb is used by the apostolic preaching. He notes that it does not gain new connotations with its insertion into the main flow to the Synoptic tradition. Cf. van Unnik (-> 1957).

22. van Unnik remarks that the word *σωτηρία* can have in Luke a double meaning: healing and salvation. He then notes that the healings (still in the 1960 study) are signs of the Kingdom and must be understood from the angle of eschatological salvation.

23. In his article (-> 1953), J. A. T. Robinson wants to "explore the extent to which this conception of the work of Christ as a single, prevenient and all-in - clusive baptism is in fact to be found in primitive Christianity." (p. 159 of the collection). After an investigation which analyzes particularly the Acts (pp. 166-168 of the collection), the author answers that this soteriological conception of the unique baptism of Christ includes the whole work of Christ from his baptism in water until the baptism of the Spirit at Pentecost, and that it is present in all the NT writings.

24. We could thus not speak of a unique and punctual conception of the activity of Jesus. Like the whole of salvation history, it draws out and is organized into three stages also: Galilee - journey - Jerusalem.

25. H. Conzelmann can say elsewhere: "Die Taten Jesu sind ihm [Lukas] das Indiz der Heilszeit, die mit Christus 'erschienen' ist." (p 179). Cf. p. 116. Is there not an ambiguity here?

26. This is what I. H. Marshall (-> 1970) will show, with a few excesses.

27. Cf. in this sense B. H. Throckmorton's study (-> 1973). Here are the conclusions: "In Luke-Acts *σῴζειν* , *σωτηρία, σωτήριον* point, almost exclusively, not to the future, not to the End-time or the consummation, but to historical reality met or received during Jesus' life and experienced in the apostolic and post-apostolic church. (The one clear exception is the implication of Luke 18, 26 which Luke takes over verbatim from Mark).

Salvation, for Luke, assumes faith and repentance. (Forgiveness, closely related to salvation, also assumes repentance.)

Salvation is appropriated by hearing the words of the apostolic preaching.

Salvation connotes the following: Rescue or deliverance from humilation, from ennemies, from the powers of nature, from death. Physical healing, including exorcisms. Gratitude. Health or safety. Forgiveness of sins." (p. 526).

28. Cf. from the same (-> 1961, second title) and (-> 1966).

29. Cf. the preceding pages.

30. For U. Wilckens, the evangelical kerygma never existed outside of the framework of salvation history: "In this respect, Luke with his concept of redemptive history stands indeed within a broad Christian tradition." (-> 1966, p. 75). Wilckens will go as far as to say that the fullness of salvation, present in Jesus and established forever by the resurrection, forms the center of Lucan thought (-> 1966, p. 66).

31. With H. Conzelmann and E. Käsemann.

32. This kerygma is centered on the past: "Der christliche Glaube [in Luke] ist darum prinzipiell rückwärts auf das vergangene Leben Jesu gerichtet." (p. 206; the italics are in text).

33. "Der 'Name' Jesu ist gerade in diesem wesenhaften geschichtlichen Rückbezug die einzige Weise [the author notes others!] der ständigen Gegen - wart Jesu." (-> 1961, first title, p. 206).

34. (-> 1961, first title), p. 216ff. U. Wilckens goes as far as to say that Luke indicates no soteriologcal function to Jesus (p. 216).

35. U. Wilckens (-> 1961, second title), p. 77.

36. Cf. above, ch 1, footnote 39 and 3, II, f.

37. Cf. p. 178ff. are subtitled "Bussruf und Heilsverkundigung". Cf. especially the analysis of the verb, to save and the noun, salvation on p. 185, note 1.

38. P. 183f. which insists on this point.

39. Cf. further, p. 184f.

40. van Unnik (-> 1960), pp. 50-53, and Marshall (-> 1970), p. 157ff.

41. In the third Gospel, the vocabulary of salvation appears mainly in what is peculiar to Luke, especially in the first two chapters. This vocabulary of OT and non-Hellenistic origin reflects a particularistic perspective, in which salvation is closely tied to Israel and Jerusalem. Outside of Israel there is no salvation. But Zacchaeus and the true converts can become children of Abraham (cf. Lk 19:9-10). These traditions do not establish as close a link between salvation and a precise messianism: Lk 1-2 associates salvation with the Davidic Messiah, whereas other texts relate it to the Son of Man (Lk 19:10, 21and 27f.) or the prophet (Lk 24:13-27). Cf. J. Bihler (-> 1963), p. 100ff.

42. Whether he understands it well or badly, Luke makes allusion in this chapter to the heart of Pauline theology, justification by faith. Cf. P. H. Menoud (-> 1970) who corrects the thesis of P. Vielhauer (ch 1, -> 1950).

43. Cf. above 1, III, g.

44. Cf. above 1, III, d.

45. The first part of the book of H. Flender, who was influenced by R. Morgenthaler's mongraph [**Die lukanische Geschichtsschreibung als Zeugnis. Gestalt und Gehalt der Kunst des Lukas**. 2 vols. (Zurich, 1949)], is consecrated to the "dialektische Darstellungsweise des Lukas" (pp. 14-37).

46. Cf. above 1, III, d.

47. Cf. below 7, IV, 1, a-c.

48. Cf. the important chapter entitled "Das Eingehen der Christusbotschaft in die weltlichen Ordnungen." (pp. 69-83).

49. Cf. among others, concerning the Holy Spirit, p. 127.

50. Cf. the two sections, p. 126ff. and 131ff. In perhaps too formal a way, H. Flender distinguishes clearly the gift of the Spirit from the presence of the Resurrected Lord (p. 122).

51. Cf. J. -D. Kaestli (ch 1, -> 1969), p. 38f.

52. Cf. above 1, III, d.

53. Cf. below 5, IV, a.

54. We should add the two pages (p. 147f.) that the author consecrates to the outpouring of the Spirit: this renders intellible to the believer the redemption realized in Jesus Christ. By becoming prophets in turn, like Jesus and the seers of the OT, the first Christians obtain a new comprehension of themselves. By the power of the Spirit, they can among other things, henceforth take the path marked out by the fate of Jesus, the way of salvation. The time the Church is a part of the last days (Act 2:17).

55. We are permitted to wonder if the author does not exaggerate the importance of the family *λυτρ-* in Luke, when he affirms that "*λυτροῦσθαι* und seine Derivate gehören also dem von Lukas bevorzugten Wortschatz an." (p. 27). In fact Luke concentrates rather on the vocabulary *σωτ-*, more religious and less commercial or military than *λυτρ-*. Why does not Voss in these pages, deal with the Lucan notion of *σωτηρία*?

56. Cf. ch 2 entitled "Jesus, der messianische König" (p. 61ff.), which borrows from the article of Father George (ch 3, ->1962).

57. Lk 1:47 (God), 2:11; Act 5:31 and 13:23 (Jesus).

58. G. Voss on p. 54f. evokes this possibility only to discard it immediately.

59. J. -D. Kaestli (ch 1, -> 1969).

60. Cf. above 2, III, e.

61. We have mentioned several in the introduction of this chapter.

62. Cf. J. Dupont (ch 2, -> 1961, second title).

63. Cf. above 2, III, e.

64. Lk 23:41 which insists on the innocence of the Righteous One who dies.

65. Cf. G. Schütz (-> 1969), p. 89ff. The pages this author gives to the suffering Christ are important: different from Conzelmann, he notes that the ministry of Jesus constantly unfolded in an atmosphere of criticism and rejection (p 54). Jesus' passion does not oppose his ministry as a failure to a victory (p. 89). Even if Luke hardly says so explicitly, God is active during the drama of the Passion (p. 86f.). The use of *δεῖ*, the kerygma which inserts the death of Jesus into the plan of God, the Lucan announcements of the Passion and certain Scriptural proof show it. "(...), so ergibt sich, dass die lukanischen Aussagen über das Herrsein Gottes über die Passionsereignisse in einem grösseren Zusammenhang einzuordnen sind. Dieser ist dadurch gegeben, dass Jesus von Anfang an von Gott zum Leiden bestimmt ist." (p. 90). And further: "In den lukanischen Schriften bildet die Passion jedoch einen festen Bestandteil der Geschichte als Geschichte Gottes mit der Welt, dh als Offenbarungsgeschichte." (p. 96). In Luke, the idea of an expiatory death clearly loses ground. Salvation originates rather from Jesus' Messiahship. Yet this Messiahship is provoked or confirmed by the death and resurrection. The death and resurrection are thus indirectly salvific. This tie between the ministry and the suffering is found in the life of the Church. Far from benig discouraged in the face of suffering, the Church must see in it the sign of her faithfulness. The reader can read the two chapters where Schütz shows how Jesus is the savior of the rejected ones (of women and sinners) and Israel's (pp. 113-122 and 123-126). Persecuted for her activity, like her master, the Church must nonetheless continue her mission to the marginals and Jews.

66. J. Dupont, **Etudes**, p. 145, note 27 and **Le Discours de Milet. Testament pastoral de saint Paul**. Paris, 1962, p. 182ff.

67. Cf. F. Bovon (-> 1973).

68. Inspite of its title, **Gebet und Heil**, the work of W. Ott (-> 1965) is consecrated exclusively to prayer in Luke.

69. I. H. Marshall (-> 1970).

70. Ch 1: "The Modern Approach to Luke-Acts", pp. 13-20.

71. Ch 2: "History or Theology", pp. 21-52 and ch 3: "Luke as a Historian", pp. 53-76. Without going into the heat of the topic history and theology, let us however mention that the Christian faith as the NT presents it, in our opinion, is not faith in historical events as Marshall supposes, but faith in a person whose manifestation was accomplished in history.

72. Marshall does not do justice to what Conzelmann (-> 1954) has shown and what Käsemann (ch 1, -> 1954), p. 199 of the collection of essay, summarized in saying that before Luke history was a chapter of eschatolgy and with him eschatology becomes a chapter of history. We would say rather that from a history integrated into the kerygma, with Luke we pass to a kerygma integrated into history, salvation history.

73. "This means that Luke's purpose was not so much to reframe the Christian message in terms of 'salvation history' as to make the way of salvation plain to his readers." (p. 84).

74. Ch 4: "The Theology of Salvation", pp. 77-102.

75. The delay of the Parousia does not play the determinative role in that some want to give it. The history of salvation is a common motif in the whole NT. The periods of salvation history are too schematic in Conzelmann. The gap which separates the time of Jesus and that of the Church is too deep: Act 1:1 shows the continuity of the intervention of the Lord (p. 84ff.).

76. Rightly, Marshall reproaches Conzelmann for having discarded these chapters in his investigation.

77. van Unnik (->1960), cf. above 5, I, b.

78. Marshall rejects Conzelmann's thesis according to which the time of Jesus is marked by an absence of Satan. On this point, he joins himself with the analysis of F. Schütz (-> 1969).

79. Ch 5: "God my Savior", pp. 103-115; ch 6, "To save the Lost", pp. 116-156ff; ch 7: "The Word of this Salvation", pp. 157-187; ch 8: "What must I do to be saved", pp. 188-215.

80. Here it is ch 6 which the preceding note indicates the title.

81. The Lucan notion of the Kingdom is not clearly distinct from that of the other Synoptics. Luke does not create the idea of a present Kingdom, an idea which the tradition knew already. Nor does he develope the theory of a Kingdom pushed into the far future. Luke's originality concerning the Kingdom is that he integrated this notion with that of the Word. Cf. pp. 128-136.

82. "The disciples came to recognize Him as Lord only at the resurrection, but what they recognized was not a new status, but one already possessed by Jesus." (p. 167). This explanation is too easy. The rupture between the gospel that Jesus preached and the gospel which proclaimed Jesus is deeper. Furthermore, we can remark that Luke has hardly overcome the problem.

83. This is the import of Act 2:21: "(...) and whoever will invoke the name of the Lord will be saved."

84. Certainly Luke insists on grace, but the interpretation which Marshall gives reminds us more of Pauline grace than Lucan.

CHAPTER 6

1. H. Conzelmann (-> 1954), p. 193, is of the same opinion.

2. J. Gewiess (-> 1939), pp. 106-143.

3. R. Schnackenburg then distinguishes the conversion of the Jews and that of the Gentiles. He motivates the latter by the last judgment without mentioning idolatry. He ends by signaling the gracious offer of *μετάνοια* God gives to men. We will come back to this graciousness. The article terminates with two sections: one on the recoil of the term *μετάνοια* in Paul and John, and the other on *μετάνοια* in Revelation.

4. J. Dupont (-> 1960, first title, pp. 423, note 8 and 426, note 10 in the collectionof essays) rebukes him of it. He notes particularly the too skillful way which Conzelmann gets rid of Act 20:21.

5. L. Schottroff (-> 1971) will be attentive to this parable. Cf. below 6, IV.

6. Concerning conversion in Qumran, cf. the bibliography mentioned by Dupont (-> 1960, first title, p. 429, footnote 16 of the collectionof essays), in particular R. Noetscher, "Voies divines et humaines selon la Bible et Qumrân", in J. van der Ploeg (ed), **La Secte de Qumrân et les origines du christianisme** (Bruges, 1959), pp. 135-148.

7. Cf. Act 13:38-39 and 26:17-18.

8. Dupont (-> 1960, second title), p. 461 of the collectionof essays.

9. Dupont (-> 1960, first title), p. 421 of the collectionof essays.

10. Dupont (-> 1960, first title), p. 449 of the collectionof essays.

11. Dupont (-> 1960, second title), p. 472 of the collectionof essays.

12. Here he rejoins Schnackenburg (-> 1950), cf. above 6, Intro.

13. Cf. K. Stendahl, "The Apostle Paul and the Introspective Conscience of the West", **HThR** 56 (1963), pp. 199-215.

14. Cf. Conzelmann (-> 1954), p. 214, footnote 1 and R. Michiels (-> 1965), which we will present below.

15. Cf. Wilckens (-> 1961), A. Rétif (-> 1951, first title) and W. Barclay (-> 1964).

16. J. Giblet is wrong to say that it is the idea of *μετάνοια* which permits Luke to enrich the Jewish Hellenistic schema by attaching salvation history to it. It is neither *μετάνοια* nor the verb *επιστρέφω* which hooks conversion to the

saving events. What then is it? This a question to elucidate? It could be that Luke brings conversion close to salvation history without being able to articulate one on the other.

17. H. Conzelmann (-> 1954), A. Descamps, **Les Justes et la Justice dans les Evangiles et le christianisme primitif** (Leuven-Gembloux, 1950), pp. 98-109; H. Schürmann, **Jesu Abschiedsrede. Lk 22, 21-38.** III. Teil (Münster, 1957); U. Wilckens (-> 1961).

18. "Eventhough the Jews rejected Jesus, thanks to the apostolic prea - ching, they conserve the possibility to be converted to him." (p. 48).

19. The remark is valid even if Act 13 indicates a turning point i.e. the movement of Paul who addresses from then on the pagans.

20. "Since Luke presents Christianity as a *ὁδός*, he deals with Christian existence at the heart of the Church, and he seems then to foresee the time with follows conversion. In the speeches of Act 2-13, Luke has manifestly de-eschatologized the notion and emphasized its moral content." (p. 49).

21. As an argument, R. Michiels uses the presence of the teme of the guilt of the Jews in the speeches in Act 10 and 13 where at the redactional level, it has no "raison d'être".

22. A. Descamps, op. cit., above note 17; J. Jeremias, **Die Gleichnisse Jesu** (Zurich, 1958[6]).

23. The author could have specified here that the imminency of the Parousia was toned down.

24. Cf. the good note in the **Traduction oecuménique de la Bible. Edition intégrale, Nouveau Testament** (Paris, 1972), p. 225, note y.

25. According to W. Barclay, preaching, in Luke's eyes, is a joyous message of divine origin, transmitted by men who collaborate with God. It brings life (Act 5:20), peace (Act 10:36), grace (Act 14:3; 20:24, 32) and salvation (Act 13:26; 16:17) to the convert. Barclay notes the contents of the predication: a) the crime of the cross; b) the glory of the resurrection; c) the accomplishment of prophecies; d) the offer of forgiveness (liquidation of the past) and the gift of the Spirit (equipping for the future); e) the decision of dwelling place for heaven or hell. Concerning preaching in Luke, cf. M. H. Franzmann (-> 1959), H. Jaschke (-> 1971), B. Da Spongano (-> 1973), J. Dupont (ch 2, -> 1973), J. Kodell (-> 1974) and especially C. P. März (-> 1974) and M. Dumais (-> 1976).

26. To our knowledge, we lack a formal analysis of the dialogues which punctuate the book of Acts. This literary genre is only a little less important than that of the speeches. Cf. for the OT, R. Lapointe, **Dialogues bibliques et dialectique interpersonnelle. Etude stylistique et théologique sur le prodédé dialogal tel qu'employé dans l'Ancien Testament** (ParisTournai-Montreal, 1971).

27. Barclay opposes μετάνοια to πρόνοια, and then shows that this "second thought" becomes repentance, thus a different critical appreciation of our past. Is he right to insist on the sense of "after" for μετά, rather than the meaning "transformation"? He is no doubt wrong to explain the text of Act 5:31 (the gift of pardon) in the Pauline and Augustinian sense of prevenient grace. Cf. above 6, II, c.

28. "Die inhaltliche Übereinstimming der Soteriologie des Lukas mit der des Gleichnisses ist evident." (p. 51).

29. L. Schottroff is the first, to our knowledge, to put forth this hypothesis. She bases it essentially on a case presented in the fifth **Declamatio** of Pseudo-Quintilian ("Aeger redemptus"). Cf. G. Lehnert (ed), **Quintiliani Declamationes** XIX, 1905, pp. 88-110.

30. P. H. Menoud (-> 1970) is of another opinion.

31. We do not see why the author refuses to call sin, the past of which the believer must repent: "...hier 'Sünde' zu sagen, wäre unlukanisch." (p. 29). Ignorance does not exclude guilt.

32. "Lk 15, 7 muss also paraphrasiert werden: Ich sage euch, so wird Freude im Himmel sein über einen büssenden Sünder, und nicht über 99 Scheingerechte, die keine Busse nötig zu haben meinen (oder behaupten)." (p. 35).

33. "Das Gleichnis will am Beispiel dreier menschlicher Verhaltensweisen (des Vaters und der zwei Söhne) eine soteriologische Konzeption verdeut - lichen." (p. 43).

34. On the last page, L. Schottroff certainly evokes in six lines the implica - tions of the parable. She refers exclusively to Lk 15:1-3 to say, and rightly so, that the return of God takes place in Luke by an adherence to Jesus. This contradicts what she affirms above in the soteriology of Acts, to her Lucan eyes, according to which conversion to God is not "primär" (p. 30) a conversion to Jesus.

35. "Sie [the parable] ist insgesamt eine Einladung zur Busse,..." (p. 49).

36. Concerning the parable of the prodigal son, cf. the different works gathered by F. Bovon and G. Rouiller (-> 1975, ET Pittsburgh, 1978) and concerning the Emmaus account, H. D. Betz (-> 1969), J. Wanke (-> 1973) and Sister Jeanne d'Arc (-> 1977).

37. Cf. F. Bovon (ch 1, -> 1974-1975) and Y. Redalié (-> 1974).

CHAPTER 7

1. M. Goguel, **L'Eglise primitive** (Paris, 1947); J. L. Leuba, **L'institu - tion et l'événement. Les deux modes de l'oeuvre de Dieu selon**

le Nouveau Testament. Leur différence, leur unité (Neuchâtel-Paris, 1950).

2. According to E. Trocmé (-> 1969), Luke especially relates the spirit to the progress of the mission and is little concerned about the ties which bind the Spirit and the life of the Church. The only important element - which moreover is traditional - of the latter is the presence of the Spirit in the Church, a conception related to that of the community understood as a new Temple.

3. Different from M. Simon (->1958), cf. below 7, III, 1, c, L. Cerfaux perceives of Stephen as the first Christian to have completely broken off with his Jewish past.

4. Fortunately, L. Cerfaux has published since then other more critical articles concerning the Acts: one concerns the unity of the apostolic Church (-> 1954); and another concerns the title apostle (-> 1960).

5. E. Lohmeyer, **Galiläa und Jerusalem** (Göttingen, 1936).

6. J. Schmitt (-> 1957; -> 1959) and H. Braun (-> 1966).

7. We could evoke here other historical contributions. Let us note only those of K. Heussi (-> 1952) on the primitive community, in particular concerning Peter (cf. the critique of E. Haenchen (-> 1961).

8. The prophets and doctors had to be elders with particular spiritual gifts.

9. Cf. above 1, I, e and below the next page.

10. Cf. the criticisms of Jervell (-> 1971). This article is summarized below 7, II, g.

11. E. Grässer, "Die Apostelgeschichte in der Forschung der Gegenwart", **TRu** 26 (1960), p. 112, note 1, and S. Brown (-> 1969).

12. Cf. above 1, I, e and below 7, III, 2, g.

13. E. Haenchen (-> 1956), p. 83f. of the 3rd ed.

14. Concerning the ecclesiology of Bultmann and his disciples, cf. H. Häring, **Kirche und Kerygma. Das Kirchenbild in der Bultmann-schule** (Freiburg-Basel-Vienna, 1972).

15. Cf. F. Zehnle (ch 3, -> 1971), pp. 63-66.

16. E. Schweizer notes that this tertium genus is "preformed" by the Galileans in the Gospel and the God-fearers in the Acts who are neither Jew nor pagan: Christians in power.

17. Our efforts to get D. M. Stanley's book (**The Apostolic Church in the New Testament** (Westminster, Maryland, 1966)) were not rewarded. Far from being an original work consecrated to subject announced in the title, the volume is a collection of disparate articles. No subtitle warns the reader of

this fact, which is hardly acceptable. Moreover, the two articles which concern our topic were known (-> 1953 and -> 1955).

18. Before concluding this part, we would like to draw attention to several articles, without pretention but often full of finesse. L. S. Mudge (-> 1959: analyzes from a Biblical point of view the title of an ecumenical conference ("The Servant Lord and His Servant People"). He comes to the following conclusions: to believe in the Messiah Servant goes hand in hand (sometimes not without difficulty) with the realization that the Church is a servant; cf. the first chapters of Acts); Mrs. B. B. Hall (-> 1971: Luke is sympathetic toward women and poor; one of the goals of the Acts is to show that the desire of the community can find a solution; there is a close link between the Jewish Church and the Gentile one; Act 6:1-7 is modeled after Num 11; the presence of éthe Spirit is a certain sign of the Church; God acts directly in history (this thesis, in our opinion, is disputable)); L. Turrado (-> 1959: a long article on the Church in the Acts; his perspective is that of the old Catholic exegesis. Lucan ecclesiology confirms the Roman Catholic ecclesiology. The article contains three sections: a) the new community in Jerusalem (a paraphrase of the first chapters of Acts and an analysis of the voacabulary of the Church); b) the internal life of the community (the spiritual, eschatological and trinitarian nature of the community centered on the Eucharist); c) the hierarchy and ministries (even prophetism is institutional). The articles of W. Michaux (-> 1953) and J. Goettmann (-> 1959) are of lesser importance. T. Wieser (-> 1962) was kind enough to lend us a copy of his dissertation manuscript entitled **Kingdom and Church in Luke-Acts**. At the beginning of this study is the problem of continuity, continuity between the origins and today. What struck us was the "cosmic" perspective of salvation history and the "secular" responsibility which comes forth from it, for the Church. "Thus Luke does not blur the 'worldly' aspect of redemptive history, so evident in the Old Testament. The world remains the object of God's saving purpose." (p. 145). We prefer the author's summary to our own: "This thesis examines the relation of the Kingdom of God to the church in the Lukan writings, with particular emphasis on Acts.

It has recently been recognized that Luke's work is distinguished from other New Testament writings by its attempt at setting forth the ministry of Jesus and the history of the church as two periods in redemptive history. The former period is characterized by Jesus' proclamation of the kingdom of God while the latter period is marked by the apostolic witness and the emergence of the church. At the juncture between the two periods stands the resurrection of Jesus. This event, it would follow furnishes the clue to the relationship between the two periods.

The resurrection reveals to the disciples that Jesus of Nazareth is the Kyrios of the world and in the world. In him the kingdom is present in history. At the same time the disciples are made witnesses. Witness is understood by Luke as the response to the presence of the Kyrios. Furthermore, the continuity of this presence is assured by the gift of the Holy Spirit.

Luke has a dynamic understanding of this presence of the Kyrios. His kingdom manifests itself as a history of redemption. This history is world history because it centers in the universal Lordship of Christ. Luke shows, especially in the mission of Paul, how this whole world, symbolized by the Roman authorities, is confronted with the claim of the Kyrios and asked to acknowledge his Lordship.

Luke's view of the church is closely related to his understanding of redemptive history. It is not the role of the church in redemptive history to take the place of Israel but to proclaim to the Jews that in Jesus of Nazareth the destiny of Israel has been fulfilled: Jesus is the Kyrios of Israel. His Lordship over the world does not exclude but includes his Lordship over Israel. Hence the church must remain open toward the Jews. In fact, it carries out its world-wide mission in behalf of the Jews, waiting for them to take their meaningful place in it.

The church fulfills its role as a witnessing community and as an itinerant people. In its life it exhibits the presence of the Kyrios in the world. In its mission from Jerusalem to the end of the earth it follows the Kyrios on the way with that of Jesus from Galilee to Jerusalem.

Luke answers: therefore, the question of the relationship between the kingdom and the church in terms of the continuity of Jesus' way in the world." (p. 254f.) Concerning the book of P. S. Minear (-> 1976), cf. our review in **The Ecumenical Review** 31 (1979) pp. 207-208.

19. On the names given to the Christians, the best presentation remains H. J. Cadbury's (-> 1933).

20. H. Conzelmann (-> 1963), p. 57, mentions the Greek origin of the concept of the way which W. Jaeger proposes in **Die Theologie der frühen griechischen Denker** (Stuttgart, 1953), p. 122ff., only to reject it.

21. S. Brown (-> 1969), p. 142, says no.

22. We know from Father S. Lyonnet that the Uruguayan exegete, Father P. Barriola, is going to publish a dissertation on the notion of the Way.

23. We wondered if Luke used other images to evoke the Church, in particular that of the new Temple. Taking on the whole NT, C. F. D. Moule (-> 1950) judges that the Christians elaborated a doctrine of the cult and the spiritual Temple, taught to the catechumens, to answer the Jews who reproached them for neither having sacrifices nor sanctuaries. R. J. Mac Kelvey (-> 1969) probably commits the error of dissociating the study of Luke which he regroups with Mt and Mk and that of the Acts. He is certainly wrong also in not analyzing Lk 1-2 in the perspective of R. Laurentin (cf. above 3, V, a). This said, we must praise the author for his prudence: in his view, Luke did not elaborate in Acts a doctrine, be it Christological or eccesiological, of the New Temple. At the most, he notes the role of Jerusalem and the sanctuary in the accomplishment of the prophets and the progressive detachment from the Temple. From being centripetal in Jewish theology, the mission becomes centrifugal with the Christians, for there is henceforth a cult and sanctuary where the Church gathers and where the Lord is present. Neither the speech of Stephen (Act 7:48ff. particularly) nor James' (Act 15:13ff.) permits however to establish explicitly a doctrine of the New Temple, be it Christ or his Church. Mac Kelvey is opposed to A. Cole's discussion of Act 15:13ff. (**The New Temple. A Study in the Origins of the Catechetical 'Form' of the Church in the New Testatment** (London, 1950)) which we could not consult. On the new Temple, cf. E. Trocmé (-> 1969), summarized above in note 2. Concerning the metaphor of the column, taken eschatologically and

then institutionally in primitive Christianity, as a part of the new sanctuary, cf. C. K. Barrett (-> 1953).

24. Reference above note 11.

25. P. H. Menoud has always been interested in the relations between the Church and the Synagogue. Cf. -> 1952, second title (the first part: the love of Israel and anti-Judaism; the second part: the theological conflict). Luke's position is not particularly analyzed; (-> 1960), cf. our pages concerning the witnesses below 7, III, 2, j-o; (-> 1964: an article on the Peole of God. For the NT, if there is a new covenant, a new man, and a new commandment, there is no new people: God does not have two successive peoples. The Church is not a new Israel. The universalism of the work of Christ could not tolerate the expression: "New Israel": this would be to reject the old Israel and transform the Church into a sect. Menoud also has written an article on the Lucan Pentecost (-> 1962) and a commentary on Act 2:42 (-> 1952, first title).

26. J. Dupont does not ignore the importance (cf. ch 1, -> 1950; and 1956-1957, included in the collection with an additional note relative to N. A. Dahl (-> 1957-1958). For J. Dupont not only is the citation of Amos (Act 15:15f.) redactional but also the allusion in Act 15:14 (" God has taken care to choose among the Gentiles a people reserved for his Name."), this against J. N. Sanders (-> 1955-1956). In the words of vs. 14, the Belgian exegete thinks he can discern the echo of a Biblical expression, particular to the LXX version (Dt 14:2 etc.). But if, in the LXX where we read *ἀπό*, the idea is that of a people distinct from the nations, in Luke, where the prepostion *ἐξ* is used, the people which God constitutes is not opposed to the nations, but is constituted from them. In an additional note, Dupont leans toward the solution of N. A. Dahl who thinks that behind Act 15:14 there is an "Aramaism" rather than a "Septuagintism": issued from Zech 2:15. This would be a first Judeo-Christian solution to the conversion of the Gentiles, considered as added, aggregated people to the Jewish people. If, for us, we think that Zech 2:14-17 is perhaps in the traditional background of Act 15, we think that Luke understood this tradition in the sense which Dupont means in the body of the article: as the constitution of a people from all the nations.

27. Cf. the two critical recensions of H. Conzelmann: the one of the first edition, in the TLZ 87 (1962) 753-755; the other, of the second, ibid. 96 (1971) 584-585.

28. Cf. above 3, VI, i.

29. A long excursus allows the author to affirm that Justin did not know the Gospel of Luke.

30. On p. 184, Haenchen, one of the only to have noted the words *καὶ ἰάσομαι αὐτούς* (Act 28:27), proposes not to take them as a sign of hope addressed to the Jews: the future and conjunctive can be substituted one for the other in koinè Greek. Is he right?

31. H. Strathmann, "Art. *λαός*", TWNT 4 (Stuttgart, 1942), p. 49, already remarked this.

32. Concerning Israel in the Lucan work, cf. J. van Goudoever (-> 1966) and W. Eltester (-> 1972).

33. J. Jervell can lean on certain of the works of N. A. Dahl (cf ch. 2, ->1957-1958 and -> 1966), who also avoids the clichés of the rejection of Israel and the substitution of the Church.

34. Before Jervel, J. Schmitt (-> 1953) had drawn attention to the ecclesiology of the beginning of the Acts which, influenced by Dt, understands the Jerusalem Church as Israel restored.

35. "The Twelve on Israel's Thrones. Luke's Understanding of the Apostolate", an article which appeared for the first time in the collectionof essays -> 1972, on pp. 75-112.

36. Cf. below 7, III, 1, s and ch 7, note 63.

37. "The Lost Sheep of the House of Israel. The Understanding of the Samaritans in Luke-Acts", an article which appeared for the first time in the collection of essays (-> 1972)on pp. 113-132.

38. Cf. above 1, III, k.

39. S. G. Wilson explains Act 15:14-17 in the following manner: the "rebuilt tent" could well be the salvation of Israel which precedes the entry of the nations (with Jervell -> 1966, p. 51ff. of the 1972 collection of essays).

40. The most we can say is a theological and not stylistic influence of the parables of Jesus dealing with growth.

41. P. Zingg compares theses notices with the sayings of the infancy narratives which speak of the growth of John the Baptist and Jesus (Lk 1:80; 2:40, 52). On pp. 61-73 there are three excursus, one concerning *ὄχλος*, another concerning *πλῆθος*, and a third concerning *λόγος* in Luke.

42. We have put in the notes the mention of certain texts which, without being necessarily of lesser importance, treat less directly with the subjects being studied here: R. Liechtenhan (-> 1946: studies mission in the primitive Church from a historical point of view. Historically, the conversion of Cornelius (Act 10) must have happened after the discussions in Jerusalem (Gal 2)); E. Lohse (-> 1954, two articles: with the account of Jesus' journey across Samaria (Lk 9:51ff.), Luke wants to indicate that Jesus continued his way, conformed to the plan of God, preaching the Kingdom to the Samaritans who were divided between hostility and approbation. The historical Jesus thus offers a theological justification to the Christian missonaries in their evangelization of Samaria and the nations); D. M. Stanley (-> 1955: the relation between the Kingdom and the Church. There is parallelism as well as continuity between the Gospel of Luke and the Acts. In the Gospel, the conception of the cult is modified; in the Acts, that of the Kingdom (Pentecost takes place instead of the Parousia). Act 1-5: we have the ideal community. Yet the liberation of Christianity from Judaism as well as the election of the Gentiles was necessary

for the total fulfillment of the Kingdom (the role of Antioch grows, while Jerusalem's diminishes). The Church becomes the path toward the Kingdom); E. F. Harrison (-> 1956: were the relations between the Church and Judaism an affair of conviction or opportunity? The Church conserves its Jewish heritage. Then there is the attitude of Stephen and Paul before Judaism. Inspite of the adherance of the Gentiles, the Lucan Church remains loyal to Judaism); O. Moe (-> 1957, which we know only in its summarized form in **IZBG** 6 (1958-1959) p. 115: the foundation and contents of the mission in Acts. The messengers and the message); N. A. Dahl (-> 1957-1958: "a people for his name" is a current idiom in the Palestinian targumic literature. Thus Act 15:14 does not depend solely on the LXX (against Dupont, -> 1956-1957, third title, which makes him right in an additional note in the 1967 collection). Zech 2:15 is the background. The article ends with important considerations concerning the mission and the idea of the people of God in Luke. Luke has not yet reach the stage where the Gentile-Christian Church is the New Israel. The evangelist again leans on the old Judeo-Christian concept according to which the converted pagans are integrated into the Jewish believers, who have remained faithful to Israel. Λαός in Act is still dependant on the Biblical sense (against H. Strathmann's distinction between a specific and a popular meaning, "art. λαός", **TWNT** 4 (Stuttgart, 1942), pp. 33 and 50ff.); M. Carrez (-> 1959: despite the fall of Israel and the application of the term of Israel for the Church in 1 Pet 2 and Gal 6:6, the Jews remain in a certain manner the elected people, Israel. The Church is never called the New Israel in the NT. The people of God is larger that the Israel of the OT and the Church of the NT); M. H. Franzmann (-> 1959: analyzes the expression "the word of God increased" (Act 6:7; 12:24; 19:20). The Word is active and powerful. The Acts tell the story of the Church understood as the story of the Word of God. The Risen Christ is active in his Church. Then there is the role of the Spirit in the Church and the apocalyptic atmosphere. Finally there is a harmonizing solution to the proclamation of the Kingdom by Jesus and the kerygma of the Christ by the apostles); on the same texts, cf. since, J. Kodell, ch 6, -> 1974; B. Reicke (-> 1959, pp. 162-169, on the Church in Acts: a) Israel; b) the Spirit (no contradiction between the Spirit and the ecclesiastical organs); c) the expansion of the Word in concentric circles, with a gradual expansion throughout the classes and races; d) the interpretation of history); A. C. Winn (-> 1959: the principle intention of Luke is to show that the rejection of the Christ by the Jews was not an unseen catastrophe, but he reversal of the welcoming of the Gentiles which corresponds to the project of God, announced in the Scripture and fulfilled by the Spirit); F. Hahn (-> 1963, p. 111ff.: the missionary theology of Luke: the role of the resurrection in the passage from a latent universalism to a patent universalism. The important function of Act 10: a decisive turning point in favor of the mission to the Gentiles under the impact of God and by the agent of the apostles); G. Rinaldi (-> 1966: studies the reaction of the three groups, Jewish Christians of Palestine, the Jewish Christians of the Disapora and the Gentile Christians, according to Act 21:17-26); L. C. Crockett (-> 1969: the redactional function of the words "over the whole earth" (Lk 4:25) which relates this famine to the one in Act 11:28: in the two cases, the trial reunites people, here Elijah and the widow, and there the Jewish and Gentile Christians. Lk 4:25-27 points not only toward the pagan mission, but also toward the reconciliation in the Church between the Jews and the Gentiles. The author sometimes overinterprets certain parallels, for example the parallel he thinks between Elijah and the widow on the one hand and Peter and Cornelius on the other);

P. Richardson (-> 1969: in this thesis centered on Pauline theology, a chapter studies the post-Pauline developments, in particular in Lk-Acts (p. 159ff.). Act 28 seems to seal the rejection of the Gospel by the Jews. The Church thus takes over the relay of Israel. The Jews are called Israel until the beginning of the Gentile mission, the Jews hence. However Luke does not apply the title Israel to the Church. He does however dare to use the term λαός twice (Act 15:14 and 18:10). The Acts express the tension at the time of Luke between the continuity and the novelty); L. F. Rivera (->1969, two articles: in the first, the role of the summaries in the editing of Acts. The insistance on the continuity of salvation history and eschatology. The proposition of an outline of Act 1-5 based on the summaries. The election of Matthias and Pentecost: Christian midrash and haggada at the same time. It is the preaching and not the glossolalia which provokes the reaction of the Jews. In the second article (-> 1969, second title), the author proposes an outline of the Acts and insists not only on the continuity but also on the redactional parallelism between the life of Jesus and that of the Church in the book of the Acts. Jesus and the Church receive a baptism of the Spirit and a servant's mission to accomplish. The same Spirit guarantees the preaching of Jesus and the the Church's. Luke fights against the apocalyptic idea and a particularistic view).

43. O. Cullmann (-> 1952); L. Cerfaux (-> 1953, a critical analysis of Cullmann's book); J. Lowe (-> 1956, the image of Peter, according to Luke, is confirmed by the one which the Pauline epistles give); G. Schulze-Kadelbach (-> 1956: the Acts confirm the postition of Peter in Primitive Christianity, as the rest of the NT attests); G. R. Balleine (-> 1958: the author applies a precritical method); E. Fascher (-> 1959); E. Haenchen (-> 1960-1961, first title: basically a critique of Cullmann). On the historical Peter, cf. the bibliography of W. Dietrich (-> 1972), p. 7, note 1 and p. 335ff.

44. Even if the question is more often approached in relation to Mt 16, a few Catholic authors think they are able to lean on Luke (so B. Prete (-> 1969)), principally concerning the figure of Peter in the Acts: cf. P. Gaechter (-> 1963) and E. Ravarotto (-> 1962).

45. J. R. Porter (-> 1946, suggestive); S. Giet (-> 1951); D. T. Rowlingson (-> 1952: a conference of Jerusalem during the stay mentioned in Act 18:22-23; Act 15 is a free composition of Luke in the sense of the Spirit in expansion toward Rome); E. Haenchen (-> 1960, second title); G. Klein (-> 1960: especially on Gal 2:6-9: thinks he is able to discern a diminishing of Peter's power at the time Paul is writing the Galatians); R. G. Hoerber (-> 1960: a good presentation of the differing hypotheses; for Gal 2 = Act 11); V. Kesich (-> 1962: the reports of the conference do not reflect the theology of Luke nor Paul's but the first Christian community); M. Miguéns (-> 1962: a historical perspective: insists on the authority of Peter; James is on Peter's side); E. Ravarotto (-> 1962: state of the question; a fundamentalistic analysis of the texts; resolves four questions: a) a council concerning a fundamental point of doctrine and not of praxis; b) the Church of Jerusalem is considered as the guardian of the doctrine and truth, led by Peter and not James; c) if John is present, Mary is also: the council unfolds thus in the "shadow" of the Virgin! d) the decree is the first Christian text. Conclusion: the passage from particularism to universalism); C. H. Talbert (-> 1967); M. Philonenko (-> 1967); Y. Tissot (-> 1970: on the Western text of the decree); J. Mánek (-> 1972). We

did not have access to F. Mussner (-> 1962), nor T. Fahy (-> 1963). In 1969 a novel by M. Leturmy concerning Act 15 was published in Paris. The title was **Le concile de Jérusalem**. It figures in a few serious bibliographies!

46. Concerning the position of D. Gewalt in his dissertation manuscript, cf. the brief presentation by the author himself in TLZ 94 (1969) 628f.: "In Lk 5, 1ff. ist Petrus Paradigma des reuigen Sünders. Lk 22,31f. (ohne *ἐπιστρέψας* erinnert an Lk 13,34f. par und ist ein als Gerichtswort getarntes Heilswort für Simon in einer nachösterlichen Katastrophe. Im Werk des Lk tritt Petrus am Anfang (Lk 5,1ff.) und Ende (Lk 22,31ff.; 24, 34) programmatisch hervor. In Apg 1,15ff. übernimmt er die Führung der Urgemeinde, die er bis zur Rechtfertigung der Heidenmission durch Jerusalem (Apg 9, 1-15, 35) nicht angibt. An diesem heilsgeschichtlichen Höhepunkt löst ihn Paulus ab." Cf. the critique of W. Dietrich (-> 1972), p. 11, note 15. Let us mention here the interesting article of J. Crehan (-> 1957) which analyzes the figure of Peter according to the Western text of the Acts: the Western text reinforces the importance of Peter (so in Act 2:14 where Peter speaks first and in 15:7 where he is inspired. In our opinion, all the cases analyzed do not carry the weight the author gives them. Two conclusions seem a bit adventurous: a) this pro-Petrine tendency is based on exact historical knowledge; b) the revision of the Western text might be the work of John.

47. Several works have considered Act 10:11-18 and contain remarks concerning the Lucan role of Peter: R. Barthes (-> 1970); F. Bovon (-> 1967, first title; -> 1970); E. Haulotte (->1970, first title); L. Marin (-> 1970); J. Courtès (-> 1971); K. Löning (-> 1974). Recently a collective and ecumenical book concerning the person of Peter in the NT (cf. Peter...-> 1973). Two chapters interest us. One concerns Peter in the Acts and the other, in the Gospel of Luke (why are there two chapters instead of one?). If the chapter concerning the Acts attempts to extract the well analyzed Lucan redaction from the historical elements, the second presents in an interesting manner the Petrine figure in the third gospel. It nicely underlines the appearance of the pair Peter-John, already present in the Gospel (Lk 22:8).

48. According to C. F. D. Moule (-> 1950, summarized above in note 23 of this chapter), Stephen's opinion relative to the sanctuary and the cult was not exceptional in early Christianity. From the same author (->1958-1959), an article dealing with the Hellentists: it is an interpretation based on the language. The Hellenists spoke only Greek; the Hebrews, Greek and a semitic language.

49. Lastly, O. Cullmann (-> 1975). On the ties between the Hellentists and the Essenes, cf. P. Geoltrain (-> 1959): the Hellenistic tendency must have developed in the Essene tertiaries and the Essene centers in Egypt. The Hellenists of the Acts appear to be the heirs to this Hellenizing wing of Essenism. J. Delorme (-> 1961) proposes not to identify the Hellenists with the Essenes and not to underestimate the Christian character of the Stephen's ideas. O. Soffritti (-> 1962) insists on Stephen as a witness inspired by the Spirit.

50. Let us mention here J. D. McCaughey (-> 1959) concerning the same episode (Act 6:1-6). The evangelist wants to bring close the institution of the Seven and that of the seventy (Num 11:1-25). In the two cases, it was following the "murmurs" of the people. Luke may also evoke the choice, the qualities and ordination of Joshua (Num 27:16-23). He eventually also makes allusion to the Levite ordination (Num 8:10). Thus there is a "wealth of O.T. background" (p. 32). In the OT, like here, there is the problem of succession and problem of the unity of the people. The solution comes then by the creation of the Levites and now by that of the Seven, new Levites. To the Gentil Christian reader, Luke presents the installation of the leaders with a Greek name, and to the Jewish Christian reader, the institution of the authorites according to the Biblical customs. The author again notes that the turning takes place at this moment in the history of the Church and Luke's insistance on the attentive role of the Spirit in this operation. Moreover, he sees a parallel between the Twelve and the Seventy in the Gospel and the Twelve and the Seven in the Acts. We were unable to consult the article of H. Zimmermann (-> 1960) on the same subject. Cf. recently, J. T. Lienhard (->1975).

51. The dissertation manuscript of D. C. Arichea (-> 1965) which we know only through the summary in **Diss Abstr**, A, 26, (1966), p. 4838, comes to the conclusions close to those of J. Bihler: "Through this inquiry, it is made clear that the Stephen speech is similar in nature and function to the other speeches: it is a composition of Luke, and it aids in the furtherance of the Lukan motif which are found not only in the book of Acts, but also in the Gospel of Luke, e.g., the universality of the Gospel, the polemic against the Jews as a result of their rejection of the Gospel, and the relation of the Church to the Roman Empire." In his article concerning the Speech of Stephen, T. Holtz (-> 1965) makes a subtle distinction between the traditional elements (the major part of vss. 2-50) and the redactional elements (the prophetic quotations of vss. 42f. and 48f.; vss. 35 and 37; vss. 36 and 38 have been touched up by Luke). From being positive in the tradition, the history of Israel becomes negative in Luke. T. Holtz refuses to distinguish between a legitimate Tabernacle and an illegitimate Temple (against M. Simon -> 1951 and -> 1958). O. Glombitza (-> 1962, second title) would like to correct Haenchen's commentary (-> 1956) concerning a point of detail. "Wisdom", "faith" and the "Spirit" which dwell in Stephen (Act 6:3, 5 and 10) are not a practical intelligence not a thaumaturgical faith not even a spiritual activity, but rather the wisdom which is expressed in the Torah, the faith in the Messiah and the Holy Spirit received at baptism. For us, this interpretation seems not to be rooted in the world vision of Luke. Other contributions concerning Stephen, G. Duterme (-> 1950), W. Foerster (-> 1953), A. F. J. Klijn (-> 1957), H. Zimmer - mann (-> 1960), W. Schmithals (-> 1963), pp. 9-29, J. Kilgallen (-> 1976) and G. Stemberger (-> 1976).

52. Certain works either compare Peter and Paul or study their relationship: H. M. Féret (-> 1955); J. N. Sanders (-> 1955); J. Dupont (-> 1957, first title: a critique of Sanders' article); J. Dupont (-> 1957, second title: critique of Féret's work); J. Fenton (-> 1966: thinks that there is a "pattern in the order in which Peter's miracles and Paul's are recorded." (p. 381)); L. Peretto (-> 1967); concerning this parallelism, like the one which concerns Jesus and

Paul, cf. C. H. Talbert (ch 1, -> 1974); W. Radl (-> 1975) and A. J. Mattill (ch 1, -> 1975).

53. D. T. Rowlingson (-> 1950); S. Giet (-> 1951, first title); **Saint Paul's Mission to Greece** (-> 1953); S. Giet (-> 1953); Th. H. Campbell (-> 1955); J. Dupont (-> 1955, third title); E. Fascher (-> 1955: the baptism of Paul must be historical. Interesting remarks concerning the title Nazorene, attributed to Paul in particular), A. Kragerud (-> 1955: Luke uses a missionary rapport for Act 13:4 and 21:16); O. Bauernfeind (-> 1956); J. Dupont (-> 1956, first title: an excellent study of Act 12:25; he retains the phrase "toward Jerusalem", but hesitates to attach these words to the verb "to return" or to the participle "having fulfilled their service"); A. P. Davies (-> 1957); S. Giet (-> 1957); W. Prokulski (-> 1957: the conversion of Paul was a mystical experience; a dialogue with the Christ within the soul of the apostle; Paul was not tormented by his errors, but in love with God); J. Schwartz (-> 1957); B. Schwank (-> 1960: interesting geographical remarks concerning Paul's journey from Malta to Rome); J. Creten (-> 1963); F. F. Bruce (-> 1963-1964); E. Dabrowski (-> 1963) B. Schwank (-> 1963: concerning Samothracia, Neopolis, Philippi, Saloniki and Berea); R. E. Osborne (-> 1965); J. T. Sanders (-> 1966); S. Giet (-> 1967); and we could lengthen the list with no problem.

54. Cf. above 1, I, a.

55. G. Schulze (-> 1960).

56. On this point, we share the view of O. Betz (-> 1970). In this penetrating article, Betz seeks the function of this vision in the framework of the entire Lucan work. It is not an event which competes with the appearance on the road to Damascus. Luke wants to explicitly announce the mission to the Gentiles in what is the heart of Judaism, the Temple. It was necessary that Paul, like Peter, have a vision of hte Resurrected One in Jerusalem. With this text, Luke visualizes the conception which the historical Paul gives us of his vocation, a vocation nourished by the Scriptures, especially Isa 6 (the vocation of the prophet in the Temple).

57. The reader will find a critique of C. Burchard's book in an appendix of the mongraph by K. Löning (-> 1973), pp. 211-216. We could not consider the last work of C. Burchard (-> 1975).

58. J. Beutler (-> 1968): a good redactional analysis of Act 14, a chapter which Act 15 often leaves in the shadow. The contribution of the editing is more than has been normally said. In Act 14, Luke prepares the capital decision of the Jerusalem conference (the author hesitates to see a redactional intention in the usage of the title "apostles" confered on Barnabas and Paul (Act 14:4 and14). There is a crescendo of interest for the Gentiles and a descendo of that for the Jews. Paul's speech to the Gentiles takes place in a conciliatory tone. The parallelism between the miracle in Act 14 and the one in Act 3 permits us to establish a link between Paul and Peter. Luke wants to show how the passage from a mission within the Synagogue to a mission outside of the Synagogue took place. The Church (Act 15) will confirm this passage effected by God by means of Paul.

59. F. Bovon (-> 1976), p. 176f.

60. On Act 20, cf. J. Munck (-> 1950) and C. Exum and C. Talbert (-> 1967).

61. Cf. above 7, III, 1, j.

62. Cf. our pages on Israel and the Church in Luke according to J. Jervell, above 7, II, g.

63. The exegetes are relatively little interested in the other figures in the Acts: the most we can mention is an article concerning James, the son of Zebedee (J. Blinzler -> 1962) and a few works on James, the brother of the Lord: a) from a historical point of view, H. von Campenhausen (-> 1950-1951); G. Jasper (-> 1963); W. Schmithals (-> 1963); G. Rinaldi (-> 1966); b) from a redaktionsgeschichtlich point of view: J. Jervell (-> 1972): James must be known by the readers, for he is not presented. He is a personage whose authority is not contested. Luke confers on him an important role in two central texts, where the attention is on Paul and the respect of the Law (Act 15 and 21). Because of the prestige he has with the Jewish Christians, James, according to Luke, can take less rigorous and more liberal attitudes than Paul himself: he flies to the aid of Paul who is menaced in the eyes of the readers.

64. The articles of K. H. Rengstorf (-> 1933) and H. Mosbech (-> 1948) are precious, but they do not seek to discern the specifically Lucan apostolate.

65. L. Cerfaux (-> 1954) distinguishes two elaborations concerning the apostles. One, attested by Paul and the Acts, starts with the resurrection of Jesus and the mission of the apostles. The other, in the Gospels, flows from certain words of the earthly Jesus, meditated in the light of the Scripture, particularly Dan 7:23: the corporative unity of the Twelve comes close to the Saints of the Most High. The Twelve represent the new people and the unity of the Church, understood as a flock and as the representation of the Kingdom in small, passes by the union of the apostles. In a second article (-> 1960), Cerfaux notes two contrary movements, attested in the Acts: a limitation of the apostolate to the Twelve and a ministerial enlarging beyond the Twelve.

66. In his state of the question (ch 1, -> 1950), pp. 83-85 of the colection of essays, J. Dupont presents several studies of this pericope. Since then, cf. A. Lemaire (-> 1971); R. H. Fuller (-> 1973); Annie Jaubert (-> 1973); A. George (->1974); G. Lohfink (-> 1975, first title) and E. Nellessen (-> 1975).

67. E. Stauffer (-> 1949) affirms that the Jewish influence on eclesiastic law goes back to the origins of the Church and not only, as some think, to the 2nd or 3rd centuries. Act 1:12-26, which reports notions, rules and Jewish practices, is an indicationeven more in favor of this idea as the procedure at Luke's time no longer corresponds to that of the apostolic era applied in the case of Matthias.

68. As we will see, P. H. Menoud rebuked his colleague for having under - estimated the redactional work of Luke. In a collection of his articles, C. Masson

accepts this criticism. He corrects his article in this direction. He nonetheless persists in believing in the traditions he has discerned.

69. In eight pages, W. A. Beardslee (-> 1960) deals with a question neglected by K. Rengstorf (-> 1961) and others: the drawing of lots as a mode of decision-making. He analyzes this manner of proceeding in the Jewish (where it becomes metaphorical with time) and Greek (where it will be really used with time) religions (the support for this thesis seems meager). He then concludes that in the tradition before Luke, the drawing of lots was understood metaphorically: "Luke has recast the story to make explicit the mechanism by which the divine will was revealed. If so. this procedure would be quite in keeping with Luke-Acts throughout, for the author frequently makes more explicit and visible the process by which God acts." (p. 250). In the redaction, it is God who elects. In the tradition, it should be Christ (why?). Certain articles mentioned above in note 66 deal with the drawing of lots as well. See the complementary bibliography and summaries in E. Grässer, "Acta-Forschung seit 1960", **TRu** 41 (1976) 173f.

70. G. Klein thinks that Luke knew the Pauline corpus, but discarded it to sustitute it with a literature less suspect, his double work. Cf. G. Klein (ch 1, ->1964, summarized above in 1, I, g).

71. Let us mention a critical and precise article byJ. Dupont (-> 1956): Jesus did not give his disciples the title apostles, which is thus post-Easter. The appearance of the term in the Gospels, even in Lk 11:49, must be ascribed to the ecclesiastical tradition or the redaction. When he speaks of the apostles in the Gospel, Luke designates the group known to his readers. He does not mean to suggest with this that the Twelve were instituted apostles at the time of their vocation. This use of the term in the Gospel goes hand in hand with the one, typical of Luke, of Lord to designate Jesus. Concerning the ministers in the Acts, cf. J. Dupont (-> 1973, second title), article which we have just received.

72. On the notion of witness since the book of N. Brox, cf. C. Burchard (-> 1970), pp. 131-135; G. Schneider (-> 1970), which has remained inaccessible to us; K. Löning (-> 1973), pp. 137-154 and J. A. Jauregui (->1973), which presents numerous studies. On the collegiality of the Twelve (under the personal authority of Peter!), cf. T. Ballarini (-> 1964). We are waiting all the more for an important article from D. van Damme on the subject. Cf. now especially E. Nellessen (-> 1976).

73. This is E. Trocmé's opinion (-> 1969).

74. H. Greeven (-> 1952-1953: mainly concerning the prophets); P. Bonnard (-> 1957: the relation Christ-Church determines the ties Spirit-Church. The ministries as a gift from the Lord. Ministry as service. The importance of the kerygma to evaluate the institution and the event); E. Schlink (-> 1964: on the succession. The role of the entire community as the successor of the apostles. The mission with a view to service. Not to oppose charism and ministry. The NT does not know a dogmatic definition of ministry); W. Rordorf (-> 1964: on the origin and development of the main ministries in the primitive Church). Cf. **Amt und Eucharistie**, ed. by P. Bläser (-> 1973).

75. S. E. Johnson (-> 1954: thinks that the Church in Jerusalem, as it appears in the Acts, recalls the sect of Qumran in many ways. It was founded, like the latter, on an experience of the Spirit. The believers become members of the community after repentance and baptism. Here and there, the communal life is very developed: sharing of goods (of course, not obligatory in the Church), poverty, leadership by a college where the number twelve plays a role are other signs of relationship. Are there ties between the Christian Eucharist and the Essene sacred meals? Between the Christian and the Essene interpretation of the Scripture? In any case, in some places the Temple of Jerusalem is criticized (this remark must be nuanced, since it is not the Jerusalem community as a whole, but the Hellenists alone who, in Acts, attack the Jewish sanctuary). While mentioning several significant differences, J. Daniélou (-> 1955) makes a comparison of the same type which opens up to the early Church and its rites. The local hierarchy in two degrees is a Judeo-Christian institution which was created first in Jerusalem. This is an adaptation of the primitive system of apostles (universal) - elders (local) in relation to the Essene organization. J. Schmitt (-> 1955): the continuity between the OT priesthood and the Christian one is not assured by the conservative and Saduccean priesthood of Jerusalem, but the Messianic and reformist priesthood which we meet in Qumran. The principle indication is that the "overseer" of Qumran becomes the Christian "episcope". D. J. McCarthy (-> 1957) works in the same direction as the summaries above. The reader can read a more developed panorama in the more recent works of H. Braun (-> 1966), I, pp. 184-211.

76. Cf. above 7, III, 1, c-g.

77. C. Bridel (-> 1971), pp. 19-21.

78. Concerning the prophet, cf. A. George (-> 1974), p. 217f. and the bibliography he indicates.

79. J. Jeremias (-> 1957) has shown that the word *πρεσβυτέριον* was used by the Jews before the Christians.

80. A. Lemaire analyzes successively the election of Matthias, the signification of certain revealing proper names of ministries (but were they Christian?), the election of the Seven (Hellenist counterpart of the Ancient Arameans already established), Act 13:1ff. (rite of sending and not ordination), the role of the collaborators of the mission (the *ὑπηρέται*), Act 11:27-30 and 12:25; Act 15; the organization of the local churches (Act 14:22-24 and 20:17-38), Philip and his daughters, the prophet Agabus.

81. E. Käsemann sets the ecclesiastic organization of Luke over against the functional charisms as Paul represents them. The installation of the Elders according to Act 20:17ff. has an anti-enthusiastic character. As eyewitnesses, the twelve apostles are the protectors of the tradition. By the imposition of hands, they confer the succession on the Seven. "Denn nur die Kontinuität der apostolischen Kirche gewährt den Geist." (p. 131). We have presented in ch 7 Käsemann's interpretation concerning John's disciples in Ephesus, cf. 7, III, d.

82. "Die Idee der Kontinuität apostolischer Sukzession ist lückenlos durchgeführt." (p. 175). One should read § 30 of the book.

83. H. Schürmann shows that tradition and ministry are indispensible auxiliaries for the post-apostolic epoch. Even if the apostolic ministry cannot be repeated, the Elders nonetheless take over the guard. In Luke's view, this presbyter is not only a fact, but a jus divinum. Its mission: to shepherd the flock and watch. The Spirit is at the origin of the ministry and never ceases to animate it. "Nicht das Amt 'verfügt' hier also über das Wort, andererseits aber auch nicht das Wort über das Amt, sondern der Heilige Geist unterscheidet den Glauben vom Irrglauben." (p. 334). We think Schürmann is wrong to use the expression of ministerial power with reference to the ministries, according to Luke.

84. On pp. 91-97.

85. A. George embraces the subject in all its fullness: he analyzes the form of the Church of Jerusalem with the apostles, the Seven, the prophets and the Elders; the organization of the pre-Pauline churches, that of Antioch mainly, whose ministerial structure differs from that of Jerusalem; the Pauline missions (Paul and his collaborators; the Elders he installed). What follows is a theological analysis of the ministries: Luke, for him, "especially applies himself to describe the service of the apostles and of Paul... The other ministries are numerous and divers depending on the location, but Luke does not make a halt to describe them." (p. 229). Father George finally studies what the Gospel of Luke points to: it does not forestall the ministries of the Church in the time of Jesus, but presents Jesus as the model minister, the one who shows in his life the manner to understand ministry as service.

86. M. Black (-> 1951-1952) evokes th possibility of translating χειρ-οτονήσαντες δὲ αὐτοῖς (Act 14:23) by "having elected them with raised hands" (election by assembly) rather than by "having designated them" (designation by Saul and Barnabas alone). J. M. Ross (-> 1951-1952) excludes this possibility for philogical reasons. Concerning Act 13:1-3, cf. G. N. Sevenster (-> 1953), which we could not read for language reasons, and E. Best (-> 1960) who sees in the solemnity of the circumstance, the organization of the first mission confided to professionals. The rite practiced at this moment is not inspired from the ordination of rabbis, but rather from the setting apart of the Levites (Num 8). It is not a blessing (in this case the hands would be lifted and not laid on). The text of Act 19:1-6 plays also a role in the question of the ministries. We have mentioned this in our chapter on the Holy Spirit, above 4, III, d. Y. Tissot (-> 1970) renewed the study of the apostolic decree. In its primitive Western version, this text must be understood in a ritual manner, like in the Eastern version. This Western version is the work of a reviser hostile to Jewish Christianity and its 'presbyters'. Other specific western variants attest to this (Act 15:5a, 12a and 41). "Everything indicates that in the mind of the reviser, the Judaizers also went down to Antioch, sent by the presbyters." (p. 334).

87. In the work of G. Forkmann (-> 1972) we can find a study concerning excommunication in the OT and primitive Christianity. The author presents a

suggestive state of the question concerning the studies relative to the ecclesiastic discipline of early Christianity. He gives a few pages to Act 5:1-11 and Act 8:18-24: the rupture of the communion constituted an attack on the Holy Spirit. There is a possible link with the sin against the Holy Spirit (Lk 12:1-11).

88. We are using the term sacrament for the sake of convenience without prejudice to the true sacramental value of baptism, the Eucharist and the laying on of hands in Acts.

89. A. J. and Mary Mattill, **A Classified Bibliography of Literature on the Acts of the Apostles** (Leiden, 1966), pp. 290-293.

90. Cf. the book of G. Delling (-> 1961) which interprets on the contrary the formula in the sense of a transmission of salvation to the baptized, and the book review of W. Michealis TLZ 87 (1962) col. 600-602. Since then H. von Campenhausen (-> 1971).

91. Cf. above 4, III, a-f.

92. On the relations between baptism, confirmation and the Spirit, cf. G. W. H. Lampe (-> 1951).

93. Here we must mention that the polemic around the books of M. Barth (->1951) and K. Barth (-> 1967) was nourished partly from the Lucan sources. With a play on the punctuation (a comma instead of a full stop between vss. 4 and 5 of Act 19), M. Barth refuses the <u>re</u>baptism of the disciples of John the Baptist in Ephesus. The global result is the abandon of baptism as a sacrament. Cf. C. Masson (-> 1953). With regard to K. Barth's first position, cf. H. W. Bartsch (-> 1948-1949): the cross and the resurrection are <u>Heilsgeschehen</u>. Baptism is the <u>Heilsgeschehen pro me</u>. From the beginning, Christian baptism was regeneration and not only purification. The real character of baptism. On two points he is agreed with K. Barth: 1) the cross and baptism are not two distinct salvific acts; 2) baptism as <u>cognitio</u> of salvation. In his work concerning adoption, M. Dujarier (-> 1962) thinks he is able to deduce that Acts 10 is a primitive ecclesiastic discipline of admission to baptism: 1) request for admission; 2) catechetical formation; 3) admission to baptism. On J. A. T. Robinson's article, cf. above ch 5, note 23.

94. A. Benoit, **Le Baptême chrétien au second siècle** (Paris, 1953).

95. H. Lietzmann, **Messe und Herrenmahl** (Bonn, 1926).

96. Cf. recently Sister Jeanne d'Arc (-> 1977). On the Lucan account of the institution of the Supper, cf. A. Vööbus (-> 1970).

97. P. H. Menoud (-> 1952, first title), pp. 35-43.

98. Cf. J. Prado (-> 1954: relations, from Act 13:1-4, between the Eucharistic liturgy and mission. We esteem it is nice to speak, as the author does, of the Eucharist as a center of missionary irradiation, but does it concern

the Eucharist in Act 13? Furthermore the author correctly notes the contrast that Luke establishes between the end of Herod, typical of the fate which awaits earthly kings, greedy for apotheosis, and the liturgical beginning of the triumphant mission of the Church, of the pacific Lord. He signals that the missionaries were legitimately designated and received their mission from God); R. D. Richardson (-> 1959) and A. Vööbus (-> 1970).

99. Cf. J. L. Houlden (-> 1973).

100. Cf. the chapter "Die Gegenwart des Heils in der Gemeinde", pp. 122-145.

101. To speak of ethics in Acts is clearly to speak of the summaries. We can find a precise survey of the divers hypotheses concerning the reports between tradition and redaction in Act 2:42-47; 4:32-35 and 5:12-16, in J. Dupont (-> 1969, p. 898f., notes 2-4), in particular the studies of P. Benoit (-> 1950), H. Zimmermann (-> 1961), C. Ghidelli (-> 1968) and E. Rasco (-> 1968).

102. That indeed is the question.

103. We can read the analysis of the parable of the sower in Luke which J. Dupont published (-> 1964).

104. In the final synthesis (pp. 168-178), P. Ortiz Valdivieso concludes that the *ὑπομονή* is a human virtue (the term is never applied to God). It is manifested in the most diverse circumstances. It is associated to faith, hope and charity.

105. The author mentions also, as a connotation, the fact that Luke uses here - the only time in the NT - the Greek category of *καλοκάγαθια*. He does not however understand it in the civic sense nor the philosophical sense of the Greeks. Plato (**Gorgias** 507d and 527cd) already brings *ὑπομονή* and *καλοκ-άγαθια* together.

106. According to the author, this interpretation is also valid for vs. 18.

107. Like J. Dupont has seen (-> 1971).

108. Cf. already E. Haenchen (-> 1956), p. 112 of the third edition.

109. Why does the author (p. 166) refuse to admit that the poverty of the disciples of Jesus on the roads of Galilee might have served as a model at the time of the Church?

110. This is a new point in relation to the summarized articles above: "Under the antithesis between the Christians, poor and persecuted, and the people who are rich and honored, we believed we could recognized on several occasions a discreet echo of the conflict, opposing the Church and the Syna - gogue, at the same time as an echo of the problem posed by the unbelief of Israel, strongly felt by Luke." (p. 97). Concerning poverty in Luke, cf. cf. Bammel (-> 1959), pp. 904-907, who thinks that the Evangelist did not succeed in harmonizing the two different attitudes concerning goods, one

which tolerates a certain possession, and the other which is radically hostile. With the help of Jewish law, J. D. M. Derrett (-> 1971) proposes what follows: 1) in Act 5, Sapphira is at the origin of the sin of the couple. She accepts that Ananias dispose even of her ketubah (the part of the woman in the case of divorce) with the condition that the couple conserve a sum of money in precaution (it is necessary to make plans for the failure of the Church!); 2) the first Christians had to administer the common property like the Jewish priests managed the property of the Temple. As no sanction was provided by the Law for abuse in this area, the Jews threw themselves on divine chastisement ("excision" or "death at the hands of Heaven"). It is this last punishment which Ananias and Sapphira received (thus the absence of a religious ceremony, like in a similar case in Judaism); 3) losing their lives, Ananias and Sapphira were not excluded for all this from the world to come, if we follow the Jewish parallels and I Co 5:4-5. We must ask, why should the initial fault be laid on the woman?

111. Particularly the work of J. Y. Campbell (1932), H. Seesemann (1933), F. Hauck (1938) and S. D. Currie (1962, an unpublished dissertation which C. Bori can be thanked for presenting). The article of E. Dumont (-> 1962) is not directed only to specialists. He defends the traditional theses concerning the communion of those who, in matters of faith in the exalted Lord, orient and direct the minds; concerning the communion in the cult (the author understands Act 2:42 in a liturgical sense): presence of the Spirit; concerning charity as consequence of the communion of faith and prayers. With not true Greek or Jewish parallels, the *κοινωνία* of the Acts is religious not economical. It is marked by human liberty different from Qumran) and by the call of God (different from the modern communal efforts). It is a movement of unity marked by the relationship to God before being by on the horizontal contact. It is a continuous movement where we receive and give in the Spirit.

112. For S. Lyonnet, the community in Act 2:42 implies the sharing of goods. The perspective of Acts is not juridical but practical. For Luke, the Christians put their possessions at the disposal of the commmunity but they did not sell them except in case of need. The Eucharist supposed, fulfilled and expressed their *κοινωνία*. it follows the demand of peace (the theme of the Eucharistic congress for which this study was written).

113. G. Rinaldi's article is a paraphrase of the first chapters of the Acts. The author insists on the communitarian aspect of the life and mission of the primitive Church. He thus balances the numerous studies which underline the role of the apostles, precursors of the ecclesiastic heirarchy.

114. Cf. above ch 7, note 18.

115. J. Coppens (-> 1970) presented his reactions to the reading of the article of J. Dupont. He follows it in text critical questions, but attaches - like B. Gerhardsson - the "a soul" to the OT rather than to Greece; to the LXX, he specifies. concerning the sharing of goods, as free disposition of one's fortune rather than as a vow of poverty, the author joyfully gives his adherence to the monk of Ottignies. He then indicates differing opinions on the origin of this sharing of goods: influence of the Greek tradition, influence of Qumran, impact of preaching, interaction of these different contributions, etc. He turns

toward this last solution while recalling the creative audacity of of the primitive faith.

116. On this first prayer, cf. J. Dupont (-> 1955, first title). As the title of the note indicates, the author thinks that "their compagnons" joined by the released Peter and John are the apostles alone. The object of the prayers answered in vs 31 is the freedom of language. If miracles give courage to the apostles in their mission, it is especially the Holy Spirit who is the source of their *παρρησία*. The couple *δεσπότης - δοῦλοι* is found with regard to Simeon (Lk 2:29) and is applied to the servants of God, here to the apostles. Cf. A. Hamann (-> 1956).

117. S. Cipriani's article on prayer in the Acta (-> 1971) ignores the contribution of W. Ott and brings little new. Prayer in the Acts is communal (cf. Act 1:14 and 2:42) perseverant (Act 2:42 and 6:4)l, liturgical and yet open to the problems of the world (Act 13:1-3). The texts of prayer of the Acts are analyzed (Act 1:24; 4:24-31: 7:59f.). The article also presents interesting opinions concerning prayer, but we have a hard time finding their roots in the Lucan texts; communion with the absent in prayer; prayer as an actualization of the presence of God; without being exclusively the expression of the community, prayer favorizes its building up; our life and death become prayers. Cf. recently, L. Monloubou (-> 1976).

118. Let us mention several articles which consider other aspects of Lucan ethics. On hositality, related to mission, cf. Helga Rusche (-> 1957). On Luke's interest in Roman justice and its application (Act 25:16), J. Dupont (-> 1961: "This spontaneous movement of Christian charity accords marvelously on this point with the preoccupation of Roman law protecting an accused against his accusers and against the arbitrariness of his judges." (p. 552 of the collectionof essays). On the public confession of the name of Jesus and the suffering with accompanies it , G. Lohfink (-> 1966: in Act 9:15, we should understand *βαστάζειν* in the sense of to confess and not to carry (because of the parallels of Hermas, **Sim**. VIII, 10, 3 and IX, 28, 5). In writing Act 9:15ff., Luke had Lk 21:12-19 in mind: he historicized in this manner the prophecy of persecution. Luke thus established a link between the mission and suffering. Lohfink believes he see a gradual process concerning the sending of Paul on mission to the pagans of Act 9 to 26 passing by way of Act 22. This last point seems hardly convincing). On the daily bearing of the cross (Lk 9:23), A. Schulz (-> 1969: addressed to "all" this injunction situates every day life in the perspective of the cross). On the imitation of Christ, R. Pesch (-> 1969: Luke uses an old martyrdom account for Stephen 1) to mark the official rupture between the Church and Judaism and 2) to show that the true disciples of Jesus so hide behind their mission that they can suffer a fate similar to their master's. Stephen is the imitator of Christ). On the joy in the theology of Luke, P. J. Bernadicou (-> 1973). Author of a thesis partially published, on the subject (Greg. Pont. Uni., 1970) the Jesuit recalls Luke's well known insistance on joy. He does it in quite a complete manner but like a school teacher at the same time. After an inventory of the vocabulary, he defines Lucan joy as the fulfillment of the person in the integration into the Christian community by the word of salvation and thanks to the Spirit. Thus it is a communal joy with eschatological, soteriological and Christological implications. To attain this joy one must experience a movement, a "journey", a dynamic ascesis. In relation

to the Synoptics, Lucan joy is more communal. With regard to Paul, it is more associated with the historical Jesus. With respect to John, it has more social implications. Let us finally mention an article of J. A. Sanders (-> 1974): according to Luke, Jesus contests the abusive interpretation which some of his contemporaries give of election according to Deuteronomy. For him, poverty and suffering are not the signs of the disfavor of God. This criticism explains Luke's reticence to use the vocabulary of election.

APPENDIX

1. This article first appeared as "Chroniques du côté de chez Luc" in **RThPh** 115 (1983) 175-189. Reproduced with permission.

2. This survey follows, in a slightly different form, my article "Orientations actuelles des études lucaniennes" which appeared in **RThPh**, 3rd series, 26 (1976) 161-190, adapted in English in **ThD** 25 (1977) 217-224 and my book **Luc le Théologien** (chapters 1-7 of this book), (cf. note 12 below for French reference).

The abbreviations used in this article are in accord with the lists of S. Schwertner, **Internationales Abkürzungsverzeichnis für Theologie und Grenzgebiete** (Berlin, de Gruyter, 1974).

3. The reader will find the bibliographical references to the works of these authors in W. Gasque's book (cf. note 10 below).

In 1969, the publishing house, Kraus Reprint Co. in New York reprinted in one volume H. J. Cadbury's book, **The Style and Literary Method of Luke** (HThS, 6) (Cambridge, Mass., Harvard University Press, 1919-1920) which had appeared in two fascicules.

4. C. H. Talbert, "Shifting Sands: The Recent Study of the Gospel of Luke", **Interp** 30 (1976), 381-195.

5. A. del Agua Pérez, "Boletín de literatura Lucana", **EstB** 38 (1979-1980) 166-174.

6. M. Cambe, "Bulletin de Nouveau Testament: Etudes lucaniennes", **ETR** 56 (1981) 159-167.

7. J. Guillet, "Exégèse lucanienne", **RSR** 69 (1981) 425-442.

8. M. Rese, "Neuere Lukas-Arbeiten", **ThLZ** 106 (1981) 225-236.

9. E. Rasco, "Estudios Lucanos", **Bib** 63 (1982) 266-280.

10. E. Grässer, "Acta-Forschung seit 1960", **ThR** N.F., 41 (1976) 141-194 and 259-290; 42 (1977) 1-68.

11. W. Gasque, **A History of the Criticism of the Acts of the Apostles** (BGBE, 17), (Tübingen, Mohr, 1975).

12. E. Rasco **La Teologia de Lucas: origen, desarrollo, orienta - ciones** (AnGr, 201, SFT, Sectio A, n. 21) (Rome, Università Gregoriana Editrice, 1976).

13. [This note mentions pp. 79-81 in **Luc le Théologien** which corresonds to 1, III, u above. The translator]

14. E. Delebecque, **Evangile de Luc, texte traduit et annoté** (CEA) (Paris, les Belles Lettres, 1976) and from the same author, **Etudes grecques sur l'Evangile de Luc** (CEA) (Paris, les Belles Lettres, 1976).

15. J. Jeremias, **Die Sprache des Lukasevangeliums. Redaktion und Tradition im Nicht-Markusstoff des dritten Evangeliums** (KEK, Sonderband) (Göttingen, Vandenhoeck & Ruprecht, 1980).

16. J. Reiling and J. L. Swellengrebel, **A Translator's Handbook on the Gospel of Luke** (HeTr, 10) (Leiden, Brill, 1971; French adaptation: Ch. Dieterlé J. Reiling and J. L. Swellengrebel, **Manuel du traducteur pour l'Evangile de Luc** (Stuttgart, Alliance Biblique Universelle, 1977).

17. H. Schürmann, **Das Lukasevangelium, Erster Teil. Kommentar zu Kap. 1, 1-9, 50** (HThK 3, 1) (Freiburg, Herder, 1969).

18. J. Ernst, **Das Evangelium nach Lukas**, (RNT) (Regensburg, Pustet, 1977).

19. W. Schmithals, **Das Evangelium nach Lukas** (ZBK 3, 1) (Zurich, Theologischer Verlag, 1980).

20. G. Schneider, **Das Evangelium nach Lukas** (Ökumenischer Taschenbuchkommentar zum Neuen Testament, 3, 1 and 3, 2), 2 vols. (Gerd Mohn, Gütersloher Verlagshaus and Würzburg, Echter Verlag, 1977).

21. E. Schweizer, **Das Evangelium nach Lukas** (NTD, 3) (Göttingen, Vandenhoeck & Ruprecht, 1982); ET: **The Good News According to Luke** (Atlanta, John Knox Press, 1984). In the same collection, he published a commentary on Mark in 1967 (ET, 1970) and Matthew in 1973 (ET, 1975).

22. E. Schweizer, **Luke. A Challenge to Present Theology** (Atlanta, John Knox Press, 1982).

23. I. H. Marshall, **The Gospel of Luke. A Commentary on the Greek Text** (The New International Greek New Testament Commentary) (Exeter, The Paternoster Press, 1978). The first volume of J. A. Fitzmyer's commentary has just arrived, **The Gospel According to Luke (I-IX). Introduction, Translation, and Notes** (The Anchor Bible, 28) (New York, Doubleday, 1981). [The second and last volume is now available, **The Gospel According to Luke (X-XXIV). Introduction, Translation, and Notes** (The Anchor Bible, 28A) (New York, Doubleday, 1985): The Translator].

24. Here are three popular commentaries in English: F. W. Danker, **Luke** (Proclamation Commentaries) (Philadelphia, Fortress Press, 1976); R. J. Karris, **Invitation to Luke. A Commentary on the Gospel of Luke with Complete Text from The Jerusalem Bible**, (New York, Doubleday, Image Books, 1977); M. Wilcock, **The Savior of the Word. The Message of Luke's Gospel** (The Bible Speaks Today) (Leicester, Inter-Varsity Press, 1979); let us mention also the second edition of the good commentary by E. E. Ellis, **The Gospel of Luke** (Century Bible), (London, Oliphants, 1975[2]) and a reprint of E. Klostermann's commentary, **Das Lukasevangelium** (HNT, 5) (Tübingen, Mohr, 1975[3]). There is a political reading in Italian: G. Girardet, **Il Vangelo della liberazione. Lettura politica di Luca** (Piccola collana moderna, serie biblica, 27) (Turin, Claudiana, 1975). There is a FT: **Lecture politique de l'évangile de Luc** (Eglise, pouvoir et contre-pouvoir), (Brussels, Editions ouvrières, 1978). Note the considerable success of the popular interpretation of the Nicaraguan farmers collected by E. Cardenal, **El Evangelio en Solentiname**, (Pueblo de Nicaragua, Departamento Ecuménico de Investigaciones, 1979). The work has been translated into German, **Das Evangelium der Bauern von Solentiname.** Gespräche über das Leben Jesu in Lateinamerika, 2 vols. (Wuppertal, Jugenddienst-Verlag, 1979[4] and 1978; there is also a partial FT, **Chrétiens du Nicaragua. L'évangile en révolution** (Paris, Karthala, 1980); concerning the Acts, there is a precious reprint of O. Bauernfeind, **Kommentar und Studien zur Apostelgeschichte mit einer**

Einleitung von M. Hengel, herausgegeben von V. Metelmann (WUNT, 22) (Tübingen, Mohr, 1980); the commentary appeared in 1939, it is accompanied by an unfinished update by the author, who died in 1972, including five articles which already appeared and one unpublished contribution ("Vorfragen zur Theologie des Lukas"); an original and intelligent commentary from E. Haulotte **Acts des apôtres. Un guide de lecture** (Suppléments à Vie Chrétienne, 212) (Paris, 1977) (he underlines three particular things at stake: the relation between the Christian communities; the faith confronted by new cultures; the life of the Churches, a rejoinder to the life of Jesus); a commentary by an Italian specialist of Luke, C. Ghidelli **Atti degli Apostoli** (SB (T)) (Turin, Marietti, 1978) (on the left, the Italian translation, on the right, the Greek text; and on the bottom of the pages the notes and commentary; at the end of the commentary, there is a worthy theological lexicon). Several commentaries on the Acts in German have just appeared: G. Schneider, **Die Apostelgeschichte** (HThK, 5, 1-2) (Freiburg, Herder, 1980-1981); J. Roloff, **Die Apostelgeschichte übersetzt und erklärt** (NTD, 5) (Göttingen, Vandenhoeck & Ruprecht, 1981); W. Schmithals, **Die Apostelgeschichte des Lukas** (ZBK, 3, 2) (Zurich, Theologischer Verlag, 1982); A. Weiser, **Die Apostelgeschichte, Kapitel 1-12** (Ökumenischer Taschenbuchkommentar zum Neuen Testament, 5, 1) (Gerd Mohn, Gütersloher Verlagshaus and Würzburg, Echter Verlag, 1981).

25. PH. Bossuyt and J. Radermakers, **Jésus, Parole de la Grâce selon saint Luc**, 2 vols. (Brussels, Institut d'Etudes Théologiques, 1981).

26. R. Meynet, **Quelle est donc cette Parole? Lecture "rhétorique"de l'évangile de Luc (1-9, 22-24)** (LeDiv 99 A-B), 2 vols. (Paris, Le Cerf, 1979).

27. Without counting the thematic issues of journals: **Interpretation** 30 (1976) 339-421 (this fascicule 4 of the year deals with the Gospel of Luke) and **Lumière et Vie** 30 (1981) No. 153/154, which bears the title **Au commencement étaient les Actes des apôtres.**

28. F. Neirynck (ed), **L'Evangile de Luc. Problèmes littéraires et théologiques, Mémorial L. Cerfaux** (BEThL, 32) (Gembloux, Duculot, 1973); J. Kremer, (ed), **Les Acts des apôtres, Traditions, rédaction, théologie** (BEThL, 48) (Gembloux, Duculot and Leuven, University Press, 1979).

29. L. E. Keck and J. L. Martyn (eds), **Studies in Luke-Acts. Melanges P. Schubert** (Philadelphia, Fortress Press, 1980[2]).

30. G. Braumann (ed), **Das Lukasevangelium. Die redaktions- und kompositionsgeschichtliche Forschung** (WdF, 280) (Darmstadt, Wissenschaftliche Buchgesellschaft, 1974).

31. Ch. H. Talbert (ed), **Perspectives on Luke-Acts** (Perspectives in Religious Studies 1978, Special Studies Series, 5) (Danville, Va., Association of Baptist Professors of Religion., 1978).

32. He is the author of a book which I did not see: R. J. Karris, **What Are They Saying about Luke and Acts? A Theology of the Faithful God** (New York, Paulist Press, 1979).

33. Cf. note 13 above and 7, IV, 2which corresponds to pp. 410-415.

34. L. Schottroff and W. Stegemann, **Jesus von Nazareth - Hoffnung der Armen** (Urban-Taschenbücher) (Stuttgart, Kohlhammer, 1978), pp. 89-153.

35. G. W. E. Nickelsburg, "Riches, the Rich, and God's Judgment in 1 Enoch 92-105 and the Gospel according to Luke", **NTS** 25 (1978-1979) 324-344.

36. J. Delorme and J. Duplacy (eds), **La Parole de Grâce. Etudes lucaniennes à la mémoire d'A. George** (Paris, Recherches de Science Religieuse, 1981) (= RSR 69 (1981) 1-324).

37. A. George, **Etudes sur l'oeuvre de Luc** (Sources Bibliques) (Paris, Gabalda, 1978).

38. E. Plümacher, art. "Apostelgeschichte", **TRE** 3, Berlin, 1978, pp. 483-528.

39. M. Hengel, **Zur urchristlichen Geschichtsschreibung** (Stuttgart, Calwer, 1979).

40. P. Vielhauer, **Geschichte der urchristlichen Literatur...**(de Gruyter Lehrbuch) (Berlin, de Gruyter, 1975), pp. 366-406; H. Köster, **Einführung in das Neue Testament...**(de Gruyter Lehrbuch) (Berlin, de Gruyter, 1980), pp. 747-762. For a wide audience, cf. the pages I wrote in the book J. Auneau, F. Bovon, E. Charpentier, M. Gourgues and J. Radermakers, **Evangiles synoptiques et Actes des Apôtres** (Petite Bibliothéque des Sciences bibliques, Nouveau Testament, 4) (Paris, Desclée, 1981)pp. 195-283. I did not read J. Drury's **Tradition and Design in Luke's Gospel** (Darton, Longmann and Todd, 1976) who conceives of the Gospel of Luke as a developed midrash from Mark, and maybe Matthew, in the light of the OT, especially Deuteronomy, without the contribution of any other source (cf. E. Schweizer, op. cit. note 21 (p. 103, note 62).

41. R. Cassidy, **Jesus, Politics and Society. A Study of Luke's Gospel** (New York, Maryknoll, Orbis, 1978) (second impression 1979). In this book which promises more than it offers, and whose long appendices do not nourish the corpus of the book enough, the author analyzes the social and political declaration of the third Gospel, which corresponds essentially to the preoccupations of Jesus. Non-violent, Jesus was not less dangerous for the empire which was not sacrosanct in his eyes.

42. D. L. Tiede, **Prophecy and History in Luke-Acts** (Philadelphia, Fortress Press, 1980). The author inserts Luke into the framework of Judaism. Like the Jewish theologians, Luke is up against the problem of theodicy. The theme of the rejection of the messengers of God is conceived of in the line of the prophets of the OT. The punishment of the people of God does not exclude the outcome of repentence.

43. M. del Verme, **Comunione e condivisione dei beni. Chiesa primitiva e giudaismo esseno qumranico a confronto. Introduzione de F. Montagnini** (Brescia, Morcelliana, 1977). Cf. L. T. Johnson, **The Literary Function of Possessions in Luke-Acts** (Society of Biblical Literature, Dissertation Series, 39) (Missoula, Scholars Press, 1977).

44. M. Dumais, **Le langage de l'évangelisation. L'annonce missionaire en milieu juif (Actes 13, 16-41)** (Recherches, Théologie, 16) (Tournai, Desclée, 1976).

45. L. Monloubou, **La prière selon saint Luc. Recherche d'une structure** (LeDiv, 89) (Paris, Le Cerf, 1976); J. Caba, **La Oración de petición. Estudio exegético sobre los evangelios sinópticos y los escritos joaneos** (AnBib, 62) (Rome, Biblical Institute Press, 1974).

46. L. Legrand, **L'annonce à Marie (Lc 1, 26-38), une apocalypse aux origines de l'Evangile** (LeDiv, 106) (Paris, Le Cerf, 1981).

47. R. E. Brown , **The Birth of the Messiah. A Commentary of the Infancy Narratives in Matthew and Luke** (Garden City, Doubleday, 1977); C. E. Freire, **Devolver el evangelio a los pobres. A propósito de Lc 1-2** (Biblioteca de estudios bíblicos, 19) (Salamanca, Ediciones Sígueme, 1978).

48. U. Busse, **Das Nazareth-Manifest Jesu. Eine Einführung in das lukanische Jesusbild nach Lk 4, 16-30** (SBS, d91) (Stuttgart, Katholisches Bibelwerk, 1978).

49. U. Busse, **Die Wunder des Propheten Jesus. Die Rezeption, Komposition und Interpretation der Wundertradition im Evangelium des Lukas** (Forschung zur Bibel, 24) (Stuttgart, Katholisches Bibelwerk, 1979²).

50. On the account of the journey, there are two important books: M. Miyoshi, **Der Anfang des Reiseberichts, Lk 9, 51-10, 24. Eine redaktionsgeschichtliche Untersuchung** (AnBib, 60) (Rome, Biblical Institute Press, 1974); R. Maddox, **The Purpose of Luke-Acts** (FRLANT, 126) Göttingen, Vandenhoeck & Ruprecht, 1982); I did not read W. Bruners' **Die Reinigung der zehn Aussätzigen und die Heilung des Samariters - Lk 17, 11-19...** (Forschung zur Bibel, 23) (Stuttgart, Katho - lisches Biblelwerk, 1977); nor F. Keck's **Die öffentliche Abschiedsrede Jesu in Lk 20, 45-21, 36...** (Forschung zur Bibel, 25) (Stuttgart, Katholisches Biblewerk, 1976).

51. F. G. Untergassmair, **Kreuzweg und Kreuzigung Jesu. Ein Beitrag zur lukanischen Redaktionsgeschichte und zur Frage nach der lukanischen "Kreuzestheologie"** (Paderborner Theologische Studien, 10) (Paderborn, Schöningh, 1980). Before him, there is A. Büchele's **Der Tod Jesu im Lukasevangelium. Eine redaktionsgeschichtliche Untersuchung zu Lk 23** (FTS, 26) (Frankfurt, Knecht, 1978).

52. J.-M. Guillaume, **Luc interprète des anciennes traditions sur la résurrection de Jésus** (EtB), (Paris, Gabalda, 1979).

53. H. Weder, **Die Gleichnisse Jesu als Metaphern. Traditions- und redaktionsgeschichtliche Analysen und Interpretationen** (FRLANT, 120) (Göttingen, Vandenhoeck & Ruprecht, 1978).

54. H.-J. Klauck, **Allegorie und Allegorese in synoptischen Gleichnistexten** (NTA, NF, 13) (Münster, Aschendorff, 1978).

55. J. D. Crossan, **In Parables. The Challenge of the Historical Jesus** (New York, Harper & Row, 1973).

56. Cf. Sallie McFague, **Speaking in Parables. A Study in Metaphor and Theology** (Philadelphia, Fortress Press, 1975).

57. P. Ricoeur and E. Jüngel, **Metapher. Zur Hermeneutik religiöser Sprache. Mit einer Einführung von P. Gisel, EvTh**, Sonderheft, 1974. This infatuation for the metaphor seems to go back to an article by M. Black entitled "Metaphor" in Black's **Models and Metaphors: Studies in Language and Philosophy** (Ithaca, Cornell University Press, 1962), pp. 24-47; but P. Ricoeur in **La métaphore vive** (l'ordre philosophique) (Paris, Seuil, 1975) reminds us of the role of the pioneer, I. A. Richards, **The Philosophy of Rhetoric** (Oxford, Oxford University Press, 1936). Against the abuses of the metaphor, cf. G. Genette, "La rhétorique

restreinte" in G. Genette, **Figures III** (Poétique) (Paris, Le Seuil, 1972), pp. 21-40, especially pp. 25, 28 and 33: "Thus in virtue of a centrocentrism apparently universal and irrepressible, that which tends to install itself at the heart of rhetoric - or of what remains - is no longer the polar opposition metaphor/metonymy, where a little air could still filter in and circulate some debris of a grand game, but the metaphor alone, fixed in its useless royalty." (p.33).

58. G. Sellin, "Lukas als Gleichniserzähler: die Erzählung vom barmherzigen Samariter (Lk 10, 25-37)", **ZNW** 65 (1974) 166- 189 and 66 (1975) 19-60.

59. K. E. Bailey, **Poet and Peasant, A Literary Cultural Approach to the Parables in Luke** (Grand Rapids, Eerdmans, 1976). And since then from the same author, **Through Peasant Eyes: More Lucan Parables...** (Grand Rapids, Eerdmans, 1980) has appeared. [The two works can now be found in a combined edition, **Poet & Peasant and Through Peasant Eyes** (Grand Rapids, Eerdmans, 1983), the translator]

60. I could just summarize G. Schneider's book **Parusiegleichnisse im Lukas-Evangelium** (SBS, 74) (Stuttgart, Katholisches Bibelwerk, 1975) cf. above in 1, III, o. On the temptations of Jesus (Lk 4:1-13), cf. the nice thesis by H. Mahnke, **Die Versuchungsgeschichte im Rahmen der synoptischen Evangelien. Ein Beitrag zur frühen Christologie** (Beiträge zur biblischen Exegese und Theologie, 9) (Frankfurt am Main, Lang, 1978). By manifesting himself as a faithful Israelite, Jesus refuses the triple seduction of Satan: he rejects false images of the prophet, the king and the priest.

61. R. Geiger, **Die lukanische Endzeitreden. Studien zur Eschatologie des Lukas-Evangeliums** (EHS. T, 16) (Bern, Lang, 1973. Cf. 1, I, k.

62. A. J. Mattill, **Luke and the Last Things. A Perspective for the Understanding of Lukan Thought** (Dillsboro, NC, Western North Carolina Press, 1979).

63. E. Franklin, **Christ the Lord. A Study in the Purpose and Theology of Luke-Acts** (London, SPCK, 1975); J. Ernst, **Herr der Geschichte. Perspektiven der lukanischen Eschatologie** (SBS, 88) (Stuttgart, Katholisches Bibelwerk, 1978).

64. R. Glöckner. **Die Verkündigung des Heils beim Evangelisten Lukas** (WSAMA.T, 9) (Mainz, Matthias-Grünewald-Verlag, n.d. (1975?).

65. M. Dömer, **Das Heil Gottes. Studien zur Theologie des lukanischen Doppelwerkes** (BBB, 51) (Köln, Hanstein, 1978).

66. J. M. Nützel, **Jesus als Offenbarer Gottes nach den lukanischen Schriften** (Forschung zur Bibel, 39) (Würzburg, Echter Verlag, 1980).

67. I. Bosold, **Pazifismus und prophetische Provokation. Das Grussverbot Lk 10, 4b und sein historischer Kontext** (SBS, 97) (Stuttgart, Katholisches Bibelwerk, 1978).

68. G. Perrino, **La Chiesa secondo Luca. Riflessioni sugli Atti degli Apostoli** (Turin, Elle Di Ci, 1978).

69. W. Bösen, **Jesusmahl, Eucharistisches Mahl, Endzeitmahl. Ein Beitrag zur Theologie des Lukas** (SBS, 97) (Stuttgart, Katholisches Bibelwerk, 1980).

70. B. Guilliéron, **Le Saint-Esprit. Actualité du Christ** (Essais Bibliques, 1) (Geneva, Labor et Fides, 1978), pp. 43-78 and 119-127.

71. M.-A. Chevallier, **Souffle de Dieu. Le Saint-Esprit dans le Nouveau Testament**, I (Le Point Théologique, 26) (Paris, Beauchesne, 1978), pp. 160-225.

72. Cf. since then, M.-A. Chevallier, "Luc et l'Esprit Saint. A la mémoire du P. A. George (1915-1977)", **RevSR** 56 (1982) 1-16. Let us mention also an unpublished dissertation from Strasbourg: J.-D. Dubois, **De Jean-Baptiste à Jésus. Essai sur la conception lucanienne de l'Esprit à partir des premiers chapitres de l'Evangile** (Thèse de 3e cycle) (Strasbourg, Faculté de Théologie protestante, 1977).

73. J.-W. Taeger, **Der Mensch und sein Heil. Studien zum Bild des Menschen und zur Sicht der Bekehrung bei Lukas** (StNTm 14) (Gerd Mohn, Gütersloher Verlagshaus, 1982).

74. Cf. J. Dupont, **Les tentations de Jésus au désert** (Studia Neotestamentica, Studia 14) (Bruges, Desclée de Brouwer, 1968) p. 57: "It is thus permitted to think that he [Luke] is the one who accentuates the promise of the devil by specifying that it concerns a power exerted over the entire inhabited earth."

75. I reviewed the stimulating book by P. S. Minear, **To Heal and to Reveal. The Prophetic Vocation According to Luke** (New York, The Seabury Press, 1976) in **The Ecumenical Review** 31 (1979) 207f. Other mongraphs exist, especially concerning the Acts: O'Toole's merits attention: R. F. O'Toole, **Acts 26: the Christological Climax of Paul's Defense: Act 22, 1-26, 32** (AnBib, 78) (Rome, Biblical Institute Press, 1978). The references can be found in the bulletins mentioned in notes 5-10, in the works mentioned above, e.g. D. L. Tiede's (note 42), L. Legrand's (note 46) and J.-W. Taeger's (note 73), as well as in the review of C. Burchard, **ThLZ** 106 (1981) 38 and in the usual bibliographical instruments: EBB, NTA and IZBG.

76. I would add three recent titles: C. Paliard, **Lire l'Ecriture, écouter la Parole. La parabole de l'économe infidèle** (Lire la Bible, 53) (Paris, Cerf, 1980); Agnès Gueuret, **L'engendrement d'un récit. L'évangile de l'enfance selon saint Luc** (Lectio Divina, 113) (Paris, Cerf, 1983); F. W. Horn, **Glaube und Handeln in der Theologie des Lukas** (Göttinger Theologische Arbeiten, 26) (Göttingen, Vandenhoeck & Ruprecht, 1983).

INDEX OF THE AUTHORS CITED